THE IRWIN SERIES IN ECONOMICS

CONSULTING EDITOR

LLOYD G. REYNOLDS

YALE UNIVERSITY

BOOKS IN THE IRWIN SERIES IN ECONOMICS

MODERN PUBLIC FINANCE

MODERN PUBLIC FINANCE

BY

BERNARD P. HERBER
ASSOCIATE PROFESSOR OF ECONOMICS
THE UNIVERSITY OF ARIZONA

1967
RICHARD D. IRWIN, INC.
HOMEWOOD, ILLINOIS

Library of Congress Catalog Card No. 67–17041

PRINTED IN THE UNITED STATES OF AMERICA

TO JEAN

PREFACE

The study of public finance in Western society traditionally has been conducted in an asymmetrical manner. In other words, undue emphasis has been placed upon certain aspects of the budgetary process while the adequate consideration of certain other significant fiscal elements has been sacrificed. More specifically, for several generations throughout the nineteenth century and during the first several decades of the twentieth century, orthodox Western public finance stressed the "ability-to-pay" principle of equity in the distribution of tax burdens. Importantly, this emphasis on equity in *taxation* led to a critical theoretical neglect of the equally significant "other side" of the budget, namely, governmental *expenditures*. Unquestionably, exhaustive and transfer expenditures by the public sector also exert an influence on distributive equity. Moreover, both governmental taxes and expenditures have a critical bearing on the allocation, stabilization, and economic growth goals of a society. Yet, the unrealistic traditional emphasis placed upon tax equity has resulted in an incomplete consideration of the total economic activities of the public sector. Not only has the expenditure side of the budget been under-emphasized in theoretical analysis, but the overstress on taxation and its related equity concept has until recently led to a relative underemphasis of the allocation, stabilization, and economic growth branches of public finance.

The preceding statement, of course, does not deny the renaissance of interest in macroeconomic problems which occurred during the Keynesian and Neo-Keynesian eras. It does suggest, however, that for a critically-long period of time theoretical analysis in public finance lacked the symmetry necessary for a comprehensive and adequate guidance of policy decisions. Furthermore, the overall economic significance of the public sector in a market-oriented economy has not been appreciated until recent times. This omission has been partially due to the failure of economics in general, and of public finance in particular, to provide a comprehensive analytical framework whereby the public sector could be viewed in its proper perspective alongside the private sector in the "mixed" type of industrial economy which characterizes the Western world. In addition, studies of the American public sector frequently fail to consider the total economic impact resulting from its decentralized nature. Each of the three levels and 90,000 units of government, of course, exert an economic influence—either positive or negative—on the allocation, distribution, stabilization, and economic growth goals of the society when budgetary actions take place. Hence, an "aggregate" or "composite" consideration of the American public sector is at times required if rational policy decisions are to be made.

Furthermore, orthodox economics has been characterized by a very narrow interpretation of the term "neutrality." The usual application of "neutrality" in public finance suggests that *any* public sector decision which distorts (changes) the individual market decisions of satisfaction-motivated consumers and profit-motivated businesses is "nonneutral"—thus creating an "undesirable" excess burden or distortion. Such a conclusion, however, ignores the nature of collective consumption and assumes that a pure market economy—primarily through the forces of competitive general equilibrium conditions—inherently reaches optimal resource allocation. Yet, the indivisible (in price terms) nature of some economic goods, the presence of significant externalities, and decreasing production costs over a wide range of output scales (among other things) help to establish an economic case for substantial resource allocation through the public sector in a market-oriented society. Thus, a distortion of private economic activity, as introduced by governmental fiscal policy, may either "improve" or "worsen" the society's actual resource allocation in reference to its optimal social balance point depending upon the previous allocation position. Indeed, the orthodox, theoretical public finance position on neutrality must be termed "asymmetrical" or "incomplete" in its consideration of the economic interaction between the public and private sectors of the economy.

Moreover, a symmetrical approach to public sector economics must not only consider the question of *intersector* neutrality mentioned above, it must also consider the inevitable interaction between the various goals (branches) of economic behavior. The latter emphasis, as applied to public finance, may be termed *intergoal* neutrality. A tax or expenditure policy directed toward the improvement of allocation efficiency, for example, may worsen the rationality of the distribution, stabilization, and economic growth objectives of the society. On the other hand, the influence upon these other goals might be favorable. The nonneutral effect of a policy directed toward the attainment of one goal thus may be either positive (desirable) or negative (undesirable) in its influence upon one or more of the other objectives.

The author attempts in this book to provide a symmetrical approach which comprehensively includes both governmental taxes and expenditures as well as the concepts of both intersector and intergoal neutrality. In addition, governmental fiscal activities will be considered in the light of the "composite" or "aggregate" public sector. Part I of the book, though requiring a distribution value judgment as a prerequisite to "optimal" resource allocation, essentially considers the allocation branch. Overall principles of fiscal efficiency, in addition, are developed in this section of the book. Parts II and III, which primarily represent the distribution branch of public finance, emphasize governmental spending and taxation both separately and as interacting variables. Part IV applies public finance principles to a macroeconomic base in its analysis of the stabilization and economic growth branches of public finance. The ability of deliberate fiscal policy to help attain better aggregate performance is emphasized at this point. The final section of the book, Part V, discusses specific public finance problems in the areas of education, poverty, urban living, and national security. These issues primarily involve allocative and distributive considerations.

Finally, any success which this textbook might be fortunate enough to realize is due in an important way to the efforts of many people who have assisted me on the project. In the early stages of planning the book, Charles Schotta provided valuable organizational assistance in developing the approach to public finance used in this textbook. Moreover, his constructive comments regarding the manuscript are very much appreciated. Thanks also go to Donald R. Fraser for his extremely competent assistance on the project. In addition, I wish to acknowledge the helpful suggestions of Yung-Ping Chen and Sherman Shapiro. The research assistance of Kenneth Peyton, W. R. Graham, and Page Gray also deserves recognition as does the general encouragement on the project provided by Jefferson Hooper and William T. Foster. Furthermore, the qualitative secretarial work of Rachel Maynard and Lorelle Huebner should be noted. Moreover, I shall be forever indebted to the late James K. Hall of the University of Washington for his pedagogical stimulation to my interest in public finance. Finally, sincere appreciation is expressed to my wife, Jean, for her patience during the extended period of writing and revising the manuscript and for her proofreading and clerical assistance. To these people, and to others whose assistance is not formally acknowledged here though it is very much appreciated, I extend a sincere "thank you."

Tucson, Arizona
March, 1967

BERNARD P. HERBER

TABLE OF CONTENTS

PART I. THE PUBLIC SECTOR AND ECONOMIC WELFARE

PART II. PUBLIC SECTOR INSTITUTIONAL ARRANGEMENTS AND EXPENDITURE TRENDS

PART III. FINANCING THE PUBLIC SECTOR

PART IV. ECONOMIC STABILIZATION, ECONOMIC GROWTH, AND THE PUBLIC SECTOR

PART I

The Public Sector and Economic Welfare

The fundamental problem of the social science of economics revolves around the issue of resource scarcity. In other words, unlimited aggregate wants are constrained by the quantitative and qualitative limitations imposed by the scarce productive resources which must be used to provide want-satisfying economic goods. In an economy "mixed" between market and governmental resource allocation decisions, not only must a decision be made concerning what goods are to be produced, but also the relevant allocation decisions concerning the "institutional sector" (market or government) which allocates the "right" goods and the "unit" of business or government within each sector which actually produces the goods are very important considerations.

The critical decision as to the "proper" proportion of resource allocation between the public and private sectors constitutes the issue of social balance. Moreover, in a society historically oriented toward market resource allocation, an economic case for public sector allocation of some resources by government besides the basic provision of minimal law and order demands special proof. Since a mature market economy, given present levels of technology and the inevitable existence of indivisible economic goods and significant externalities, cannot perfectly allocate scarce economic resources, it is observed that a logical economic case can be established for substantial resource allocation through the public sector.

Yet, even though rational economic justification can be provided for governmental influence upon resource allocation, this justification does not specify the actual "allocation technique" to be used. Thus, depending upon the value judgments of the society pertaining to such interdisciplinary considerations as political structure and "freedom," a variety of allocation procedures—some direct and comprehensive and others indirect and specific—may be employed. Finally, certain other fiscal efficiency techniques are developed which help provide symmetrical rationality guidelines to public finance. They include a broadening of the traditional economic "neutrality" concept as well as an effort to relate the revenue and expenditure sides of the budget to each other in a comprehensive manner.

Chapter 1

SCARCE RESOURCES AND THE ISSUE OF SOCIAL BALANCE

SCARCITY AND THE PROBLEM OF ALLOCATION

The basic economic problem of scarcity provides a logical point of departure for a study in public finance. The productive resources of any society[1] are characterized by both quantitative and qualitative limitations.[2] *Land*, which may be defined generally as natural resources, is limited physically by the geographical area of the society and by the quantity of raw material deposits within this land area. Land resources are also limited qualitatively, including the overall limitation imposed by the existing state of technology used to exploit the natural resources. *Labor* is limited in quantity by population size and age distribution and in quality by such forces as the prevailing ethical, health, and educational standards of the community. *Capital* is limited in quantity by the society's past practices of capital formation and qualitatively by the extent of its obsolescence as determined by the level of scientific technology prevailing in the community.

The basic limitation of productive resources leads to the allocation function of economics. The *unlimited* scope of aggregate human wants, alongside the *limited* productive resources which produce the economic goods capable of satisfying these wants, necessitates the allocation of scarce resources among alternative ends or uses. An infinite quantity of economic goods cannot be produced.[3] Thus, when some goods are produced with scarce resources, the opportunities to produce other goods are foregone. Yet, the allocation function has important dimensions besides

---

[1] The terms "society" and "community" are used synonymously in this book.

[2] Although the traditional classification of resources into land, labor, and capital components will be used in this book, it should be acknowledged that an alternative classification system is preferred by some economists. This alternative viewpoint classifies all productive resources under capital, and further distinguishes "material" capital from "human" capital. It is represented in such works as: Frank H. Knight, "Capital and Interest," *Encyclopaedia Brittanica*, Volume IV, 1946, and Milton Friedman, *Price Theory* (Chicago: Aldine, 1962), pp. 199–202, 245. Since resource scarcity exists under either classification system, however, the particular classification system which is selected will not affect the present discussion.

[3] In this textbook, the author will use the term "economic good" to include both tangible and intangible products. An automobile, for example, is a tangible product and the services of a doctor are intangible.

3

the determination of what economic goods shall be produced. Allocation also must be concerned with the *institutional means* through which the allocation decisions are processed. Herein, the link between the basic economic problem of scarcity and public finance is provided.

Modern society offers two primary institutions for channeling allocation decisions, namely, the market and the government means of allocation.[4] The forces of supply and demand and the price mechanism, based upon consumer sovereignty and choice, characterize the market means of allocating scarce resources among alternative uses. The government means of allocation is accomplished through the budgetary practices of taxing and spending. In reality, no economic society allocates all of its resources through a single allocating institution. Instead, all world economies are mixed to one degree or another between market-determined and government-determined resource allocation. In this book, the market allocation institution will be designated the "private sector" and the governmental allocation institution will be designated the "public sector."

OTHER PUBLIC FINANCE GOALS

In addition to the allocation function, public finance is also concerned with the three other major areas of economic activity—distribution, stabilization, and economic growth.[5] Government budgets, through the related processes of taxing and spending, will inevitably affect these ends whether such influence is accomplished through rational policy or without design. Thus, public sector economic decision making, just as private sector decision making, necessarily influences allocation, distribution, stabilization, and economic growth when budgetary action takes place. While *allocation* is concerned with the division of scarce productive resources between alternative uses and between the two economic sectors, *distribution* deals primarily with the division of the society's income and wealth among the people of the society, *stabilization*

---

[4] Admittedly, a *third* allocation institution exists in the form of the "nonprofit sector" which is exemplified by many organizations engaged in religious and philanthropic work. The nonprofit institution, however, is much less important an allocator of resources, in both absolute and relative terms, than are the market and government institutions. In addition, the economic operations of nonprofit organizations, though operating from a basis which is somewhat analogous to private property, do not pursue the profit motive. Instead, they frequently pursue social goals. Thus, because of their relative unimportance as well as their "hybrid" motivations, nonprofit organizations will not be considered as constituting a primary allocation institution in this book. Rather, the choice between market and governmental resource allocation will be emphasized.

[5] An excellent work in which the economic areas of public finance are divided into allocation, distribution, and stabilization branches is Richard A. Musgrave, *The Theory of Public Finance* (New York: McGraw-Hill Book Co., Inc., 1959). In the present textbook, the stabilization branch will be treated independently from the problem of economic growth. The latter will thus be considered as a separate, though related, public finance goal.

concentrates upon the macroeconomic aggregates of full-employment output and stable prices, and *economic growth* relates to a "satisfactory" rate of increase in a society's resource base and the subsequent growth in output on both a per capita basis and in constant dollar terms over a period of time.

Allocation, distribution, stabilization, and economic growth will be considered as "branches" of public finance in this book, though it should be remembered that they are also divisions of private sector economic activity since the two sectors together constitute aggregate economic decision making in a mixed economy. Public finance theory and policy cannot always separate these goals (branches) in a precise manner. A given budgetary act often influences more than one goal and the resulting complexities with which public finance may become involved will be evident throughout this book.

THE SOCIAL BALANCE CONCEPT

Part I of the book emphasizes the allocation goal of public finance. A highly relevant question arises concerning the "optimal" allocation mix between the public and private sectors of an economy.[6] The term *social balance* has been used by Galbraith to describe a satisfactory relationship between the supply of privately produced goods and those of the public sector.[7] The determination of a precise social balance point involves significant theoretical and operational obstacles. In Chapter 4, these impediments will be noted in detail as the welfare criteria for optimal allocation are evaluated. However, the difficulties which confront any attempt to define a social balance point in no way detract from the basic reality and importance of the social balance concept. Galbraith observes that the inability to find the precise point of balance "will be of comfort only to those who believe that any failure of definition can be made to score decisively against a larger idea."[8]

In Figure 1–1 let point *A* indicate the optimal point of aggregate output division between the public and private sectors. Conceptually, this social balance point reflects true community preferences for resource allocation between the two sectors.[9] Since the percentage of total private sector output is measured on the horizontal axis and that of the public

---

[6] This question is intrinsically related to the problem of the proper role of government which occupied so much of the thought of the great classical economists Adam Smith and John Stuart Mill.

[7] John Kenneth Galbraith, *The Affluent Society* (Boston: Houghton-Mifflin Co., 1958), pp. 254–55.

[8] *Ibid.*, p. 321.

[9] In effect, an optimal allocation point as derived from community preferences will be subject to the existing state of "distribution"—in both a market voting and political voting sense. This important point will be analyzed later in this chapter and in Chapters 4 and 5.

sector on the vertical axis, point A represents an allocation mix where 75 percent of society's economic resources result in private sector output and 25 percent contribute to public sector output.

If point A is the social balance point, and the society is actually allocating at point A, then *social balance* and *actual allocation* are synonymous and no social imbalance exists. Given the present preference patterns of the individuals of the community, no welfare improvement would result from any reallocation toward greater or lesser public sector output. On the other hand, if A is social balance, but the society's actual allocation is at point B, or at point C, then social imbalance exists and

FIGURE 1–1

VARIOUS DIVISIONS OF AGGREGATE OUTPUT
BETWEEN THE PUBLIC AND PRIVATE
SECTORS OF THE ECONOMY

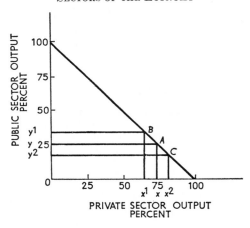

some resource reallocation between sectors is required if community preferences are to be optimally met. The imbalance gap between points A and B represents an underallocation of resources to the private sector and an overallocation of resources to the public sector by the amounts xx^1 and yy^1 respectively. The imbalance gap between points A and C represents an overallocation of resources to the private sector and an underallocation of resources to the public sector by the amounts xx^2 and yy^2 respectively. Over a period of time such imbalances may be widened, reduced, eliminated, or even reversed in the direction of imbalance. In addition to changes in actual allocation, the social balance point itself may change over time as the preference patterns of members of the society change.

An indifference graph presentation of the social balance concept adds further insight to the previous discussion. In Figure 1–2 community or social indifference curves S^1, S^2, S^3, and S^4 represent the marginal rates of substitution between different combinations of public and private sector goods which would yield the same total amount of satisfaction along each curve.[10] The higher the indifference curve on the graph, the greater the total amount of satisfaction to the community. Curve R is a resource-possibility (production-possibility) curve which represents the marginal rates of transformation in the production of public and private goods along the curve. In other words, it represents the various combina-

FIGURE 1–2

SOCIAL BALANCE BETWEEN PUBLIC SECTOR AND
PRIVATE SECTOR OUTPUT
(In Absolute Terms)

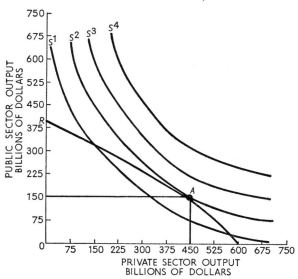

tions of public and private goods that can be produced with a given set of resources. The higher the resource-possibility line, moreover, the greater the productive capacity of the society because of greater quantities and/or qualities of the productive resources available to the society. It is assumed that the resource-possibility curve, in its indication of the aggregate output potential of the society, reflects conditions of technically most efficient production with least-cost combinations of resource inputs.

The social indifference curves are convex to the origin. This convexity shows the lack of perfect substitution between public and private sector goods in providing a given level of community satisfaction. Two reasons for imperfect substitutability may be considered. *First*, due to

[10] The position and slope of the social indifference curves will be dependent upon the existing state of distribution. See footnote 9 in this regard.

natural characteristics inherent within the economic goods themselves, some goods are provided best by the government and others are provided best by the market.[11] For example, there would likely be too much defense and too few automobiles if the public sector were producing most of the economic output. Hence, the society would be willing to give up a more than proportionate number of defense units to obtain a few more automobiles. A *second* reason why social indifference curves are convex is that costs of freedom (both economic and political) are incurred as government allocation approaches 100 percent toward the upper end of the indifference curves. Thus, a society would likely choose to sacrifice more than a proportionate amount of public goods in order to attain a smaller amount of private goods and, as a result, retain greater amounts of economic and political freedom. Toward the lower (private sector) end of the curve, the convexity may be explained by the fact that most or all allocation by the market would tend to create an undesirable anarchistic state devoid of basic law and order.

The resource-possibility curve is concave to the origin. This means that resources cannot be substituted with equal efficiency between the production of public and private goods. For example, a dollar's worth of resources taken from one sector—when it could be used more efficiently in the other—would add more than a dollar in value when allocated to the second sector. There are two reasons for this concavity. *First,* some economic goods are produced more efficiently (with less real input costs per unit of output) by one sector of the economy than by the other. If the national defense function were transferred from central government to the market, for example, production efficiency in defense would doubtless decline and there would be a greater dollar loss in the public sector than added in the market. *Second,* increasing costs tend to occur when too many goods are produced by one sector since the principles of diminishing returns and decreasing returns to scale come into operation.[12] These laws of increasing costs are ordinarily applied to private economic activity, but they also may be applied in a meaningful way to public sector production.

Optimal resource allocation (social balance) is determined by the point of tangency between the prevailing resource-possibility curve and a social indifference curve. Thus, if *R* in Figure 1–2 represents the present

---

[11] The nature of "pure public goods" and their distinction from "pure private goods" will be considered in Chapter 2.

[12] The short-run principle of *diminishing returns* states that as successive units of a variable productive resource (like labor) are added in production to a resource constant in quantity used (like capital), real input costs per unit of output will eventually increase. The long-run principle of *decreasing returns to scale* states that as the quantities of all resources are increased by equal proportions in a production situation, real input costs per unit of output will eventually increase. Both principles may be classified as "laws of increasing costs."

productive capacity of the community, optimal allocation is indicated by the tangency of R to social indifference curve S^2 at point A. It should be observed that the resource-possibility curve and the social indifference curve have the same slope at this point. Social balance thus exists when the marginal rate of transformation in the production of public and private goods is equal to the marginal rate of substitution by the community in the consumption of these goods. The social balance point in Figure 1–2 reflects a private sector output of $450 billion and a public sector output of $150 billion—a quite realistic percentage for market-oriented Western nations. The percentage division, of course, could be elsewhere on the graph depending upon the positions of the relevant resource-possibility and social indifference curves.

The point of tangency reflects not only optimal "allocation" efficiency between the two sectors but also the optimal "technical" efficiency which has been assumed to be present along the various resource-possibility curves. To distinguish, *allocation* efficiency implies selection of those goods which the society prefers to consume as provided by the appropriate sector in keeping with community preferences. *Technical* efficiency implies the least-cost combinations of productive resources in providing these goods.

ELASTICITY AND INTERTEMPORAL ALLOCATION PATTERNS

The concept of elasticity may be used to demonstrate trends in intersectoral resource allocation by relating changes in the real per capita output of an allocating sector to changes in real per capita income over time. Since the nonprofit institution of allocation is not considered to be a primary allocation institution in this book, total economic production in the society is assumed to be the summation of public sector and private sector output. Hence, the elasticity coefficient derived for one sector's behavior will be interdependent with that of the other sector.

The major elasticity categories of elastic, unitary, and inelastic are used in the application of the concept. If the real per capita output of public goods increases more rapidly than the increase in real per capita income over a period of time, the growth in public goods output is said to be *elastic*. Conversely, if the real per capita production of public goods increases less than proportionately with increases in real per capita income, the elasticity coefficient for public sector output growth is *inelastic*. Hence, the elasticity coefficient for public goods would be *unitary* if the real per capita output of public goods grows by the same proportion as real per capita income. In the latter case, of course, the demand for private goods would also be unitary since the summation of changes in the outputs of both public and private goods is equal to the total increase in output during the period.

Relatedly, if the elasticity coefficient for the growth in the real per capita production of public goods is elastic, the coefficient for private goods would necessarily be inelastic. In other words, if the real per capita output of public goods increases by a greater proportion than real per capita income increases, then the real per capita output of private goods production must increase less than proportionately because the total output growth over time is equal to the sum of the output growth of each sector. Following the same reasoning, an inelastic elasticity coefficient for public goods would necessarily mean an elastic coefficient for private goods.

The elasticity concept thus helps to demonstrate the second dimension of the economic issue of allocation, namely, the competition for scarce resources between the public and private sectors of the economy. This is closely related, of course, to the long-term controversy over the proper role of government. Given a constant amount of resources, an *absolute* increase in output by one sector will cause an *absolute* decrease in output by the other. Correspondingly, the former sector would experience a *relative* increase in the percentage of the total resource usage which it commands and the latter would experience a *relative* decline. Resources, of course, may expand in quantity and/or quality over time. When this occurs, both sectors may experience absolute growth in output, but relative percentages could either change or constant proportions could be maintained over time. The latter situation would provide a unitary elasticity coefficient over time even though both the market and government sectors increase the absolute volume of their economic outputs.

THE SOCIAL BALANCE CONTROVERSY

The contemporary social balance controversy may be traced from books written by Hansen and Galbraith.[13] The subject, of course, was not new at this time. Yet, the keynoting of social balance in recent times may be traced to the interest created by these books. Hansen asserts that the public sector should be used to promote the educational and cultural development of Americans. This is related, in turn, to the necessity of raising the living standard of the bottom decile (10) percent of America's population, called the "submerged tenth" by Hansen. He believes that economics in a mature society must not concentrate upon maximum production and full employment, but instead should emphasize "social priorities" and the efficient allocation of resources. In other words, the primary goal of economic policy should be to obtain the products most needed by the people and *not* maximum production. A related issue is

[13] See Alvin H. Hansen, *The American Economy* (New York: McGraw-Hill Book Co., Inc., 1957); and John K. Galbraith, *The Affluent Society* (Boston: Houghton Mifflin Co., 1958).

the selection of the "best" sector for the allocation of the needed goods. According to Hansen, social imbalance should be corrected by making the public sector relatively more important than it historically has been in the allocation of resources in the United States.

At the time of his book (1957), Hansen observed that America had 8 million families and individual household units with money incomes below $1,000 annually. An additional 6.5 million families and individual household units had incomes between $1,000 and $2,000 per year. Conditions have not changed appreciably since Hansen's book was written. In 1960, some 20 percent of America's families and individual household units earned an average mean income of $1,576. Many of these people live in depressed communities or regions incapable of providing adequate educational and other public services for all their citizens, thus causing a vicious circle whereby poverty begets poverty.[14] According to Hansen, it is up to the public sector to break the circle if the living standards of the submerged tenth are to be improved. He believes it to be indefensible that a society with such pockets of poverty should allocate twice as much of its aggregate expenditure to automobiles, *excluding* money spent on roads, than is allocated to schools, *including* school construction and other capital outlays. He asserts that "the problem of social priorities is hard upon us. It is not enough to achieve maximum employment and production. It is not enough to have quantitative goals. We cannot allow full employment to become merely a device to make our economy an efficient treadmill."[15]

Galbraith, like Hansen, believes that a social imbalance exists in the form of an underallocation of resources through the public sector. He relates the origin of this imbalance to a so-called dependence effect whereby consumer wants are dependent upon emulation and advertising, the latter deriving from the forces of production. He contrasts human wants of high urgency with those of low urgency. Galbraith observes that until the industrial revolution allowed nations to achieve economic maturity, mankind was oppressed by scarce resources to the extent that all his wants were basic to survival—food, clothing, shelter, and an orderly environment in which the first three might be enjoyed. The private sector had historically provided the first three of these high-urgency wants. In the meantime, government, which provided the fourth (environmental) want, was largely unstable and unreliable in preindustrial revolution and early industrial revolution days. Thus, according to Galbraith, an irrational bias was built up in favor of private sector goods and against those of the government. "Alcohol, comic books, and mouth

---

[14] Admittedly, some poverty can be found in the midst of affluent communities and regions. Nevertheless, the degree of poverty incidence seems to be greater in economically underdeveloped or stagnated communities and regions.

[15] Hansen, *op. cit.*, p. 147.

wash all bask under the superior reputation of the market. Schools, judges, and municipal swimming pools lie under the evil reputation of bad kings."[16]

Galbraith contends that the above imbalance is widened through the efforts of modern advertising in behalf of market-provided goods. He suggests that wants are of low urgency if they must be contrived for man by the process of production which creates the wants through advertising. A man need not be told through advertising that he is hungry. In a world of independently determined consumer wants, the consumer as a voter can make fairly rational independent choices between public and private goods. However, given the dependence effect—that consumer wants are created by the process by which they are satisfied—the consumer does not make such rational choices. Thus, according to Galbraith, the consumer is subject to the advertising and emulation by which production creates its own demand.

Galbraith admits that a point of social balance cannot be precisely determined.[17] Yet, he considers this unimportant as long as the *direction* of imbalance is evident (as he believes it to be in America today). Galbraith would thus increase the relative size of the public sector by reducing the biases which work against governmental resource allocation. The expanded public sector activities would be enacted at all levels of government—federal, state, and local. Like Hansen, Galbraith views America's present problem not to be one of maximizing output in an aggregate sense but one of *disaggregation*, that is, one of improving the allocation of resources by allocating the right or most needed economic goods.

Hayek opposes the viewpoints of Galbraith and Hansen.[18] He particularly objects to Galbraith's dependence-effect concept. Hayek argues that all wants except the innate wants—which he defines as food, shelter, and sex—arise because we see others enjoying them. "To say that a desire is not important because it is not innate is to say that the whole cultural achievement of man is not important."[19] Hayek asserts that very few needs are "absolute" in the sense that they are independent of social environment and indispensable for survival.

He believes that the *non sequitur* (illogic) of Galbraith's argument is best indicated when the dependence effect is applied to the arts, such as music, painting, or literature. "Surely an individual's want for literature is not original with himself in the sense that he would experience it if

[16] Galbraith, *op. cit.*, p. 135.

[17] *Ibid.*, p. 321.

[18] Hayek is a noted European economist who probably is best known for his book *Road to Serfdom.*

[19] F. A. Hayek, "The *Non Sequitur* of the 'Dependence Effect,'" *Southern Economic Journal* (April, 1961), p. 346.

literature were not produced. Does this mean that the production of literature cannot be defended as satisfying a want because it is only the production which provokes the demand?"[20] Furthermore, he argues that public education instills a taste for literature in the young and it employs producers of literature (teachers) for that purpose. Hayek points out that the similarity of this procedure to advertising and salesmanship does not suggest that the utility or urgency of cultural wants is zero simply because they do not arise spontaneously through innate human needs.

It would seem that an essential point of contention between the Galbraith and Hayek viewpoints involves the necessity of distinguishing between goods with "zero" marginal utility as opposed to those with "low" marginal utility. Galbraith's general argument suggests that the public sector, due to present social imbalance, can allocate goods with higher marginal utility than can the private sector. The Galbraith argument does *not* require that private goods have zero marginal utility, only that some of them provide lower marginal utility than alternately produced public goods could provide.

Wallich, in his book *The Cost of Freedom*, agrees in substance with the Hansen-Galbraith conclusion that we are satisfying too many of the "wrong wants."[21] He argues, however, that such misallocation of resources does not imply that improved allocation can result only from the allocation of a higher proportion of total resources through the public sector. He comments that one should not conclude "that the only alternative to foolish private spending is public spending. Better private spending is just as much of a possibility."[22] According to Wallich, the choice between public and private financing (resource allocation) is a choice between *means* while those dissatisfied with present market allocation should concentrate upon changing the *ends* or *objectives* of private sector allocation.

Wallich observes that the bulk of both undersatisfied needs and new needs are in a competitive area that might be provided with reasonable efficiency by either the market or government sectors. These include such items as services for the aged, health services, college education, housing, and natural resource development. He contends that where the needs can be provided with comparable efficiency by either sector, the private sector should be allowed to meet them because of costs in the form of reduced freedom and lost incentives which accompany the displacement of private resource allocation by public sector allocation. It should be observed, however, that the question still remains whether the private sector will have the inducement to allocate these desirable goods

[20] *Ibid.*, p. 347.
[21] Henry C. Wallich, *The Cost of Freedom* (New York: Harper and Row, 1960).
[22] *Ibid.*

in optimal quantities. This important issue will be examined more thoroughly in Chapter 2 when the nature of public goods, private goods, and quasi-public (private) goods is discussed.

The viewpoint of Friedman on social balance is somewhat similar to that of Wallich.[23] Friedman believes that both economic welfare and freedom may be enhanced by fuller utilization of the price (market) mechanism with minimal government intervention. The Swedish economist Myrdal takes an alternate position, asserting that a properly implemented government welfare state enhances rather than restricts freedom.[24] He comments that "as the material and social limitations upon the individual's freedom to act and move are broken down, and replaced by rules laid down by legislation and collective agreements, they pass under democratic control, and can be changed by a process where nobody is without a voice."[25] Thus, according to Myrdal, a mature welfare state is able to reduce the degree of direct legislation and regulate via an infrastructure[26] of organized society through the collective decisions of societal subunits. He believes that America has not reached, as yet, this mature welfare state status.

Petit holds a viewpoint partially similar to that of Myrdal, in which he argues that economic freedom can exist in a complex industrial society only within an orderly political environment imposed by government.[27] He comments:

We have come to realize that economic freedom and economic order have a reciprocal relationship. We cannot have one without the other, and each is as much the cause of the other as it is its effect. If the capitalistic system cannot provide its own economic order through the force of competition, it must be provided in some other way if economic freedom is not to suffer. So far nobody has found any other way than government guidance of the economy to accomplish this objective.[28]

POLITICAL FREEDOM AND ECONOMIC FREEDOM

The subject of public finance, which is necessarily one involving the related disciplines of political science and economics, must distinguish between so-called political and economic freedoms. *Political freedom*

[23] Milton Friedman, *Capitalism and Freedom* (Chicago: University of Chicago Press, 1962).

[24] Gunnar Myrdal, *Beyond the Welfare State* (New Haven, Conn.: Yale University Press, 1960).

[25] *Ibid.*, p. 86.

[26] "Infrastructure" refers, in this context, to an internal operating procedure by which collective decisions are made in a quasi-democratic fashion without strict government guidance.

[27] Thomas A. Petit, *Freedom in the American Economy* (Homewood, Ill.: Richard D. Irwin, Inc., 1964).

[28] *Ibid.*, p. 33.

incorporates such traits as representative government, free speech, and the free practice of religion. *Economic freedom* includes the right to own and use the property factors of production, land and capital, without undue restraint as well as the right to use one's labor factor without undue governmental restriction.

Political and economic freedom, though related, are not synonymous. The social balance controversy can be appraised more comprehensively and more objectively when this fact is understood. There exists a wide range of institutional allocation arrangements between the extremes of complete resource allocation to either the public sector or to the private sector. By comparing the real world examples of Russian socialism, the Western European welfare states, fascistic Germany under Hitler, and the contemporary mixed political economy of the United States, it is obvious that political and economic freedoms do not change in identical manner as a society possesses a greater or lesser degree of public sector resource allocation.

Assume that economic freedom is the bench mark to which changes in political freedom will be compared. As resource allocation to the private sector decreases to less than 100 percent, the relative importance of resource allocation to the public sector increases. Economic freedom will be lessened, of course, as the public sector receives more resources. However, will political freedom he reduced in *equal proportions* to the reduction in economic freedom? The answer is no and the inevitable conclusion must be that political freedom and economic freedom are *not* identical concepts. The political democracies of Western Europe and the United States, for example, retain substantial political freedoms in the form of such democratic tenets as free speech, free practice of religion, and representative government. Yet, they are mixed economies with approximately one third of their resources (on the average) being allocated to the public sector. In England, for example, government spending accounts for nearly 40 percent of the British gross national product, though considerable political freedom is retained. Thus, economic freedom can be reduced rather substantially without political freedom being reduced proportionally.

As a further example, fascistic Germany under Hitler retained important elements of economic freedom since most property factors of production remained under private ownership. However, the loss of political freedom in the form of free speech, free practice of religion, representative government, and the like was very great. Again, economic and political freedom did not change proportionally. In the case of Russian socialism, both economic freedom and political freedom have been reduced very substantially. Nevertheless, the degree of political freedom in the post-Stalin era has expanded more than has the degree of economic freedom.

In comparing fascistic Germany and socialist Russia, it is obvious that political freedom may be reduced substantially under either a capitalistic economic system, where considerable economic freedom is retained, or under a socialistic economic system, where economic freedom is slight. The corollary of this is that economic freedom can be substantially reduced (say that 50 percent of society's resources are allocated to the public sector), but political freedom and the basic tenets of democracy need not be seriously impaired. Hence, the social balance arguments of Wallich and Friedman, which concentrate upon the loss of freedom, require a distinction between political and economic freedom before a relevant consideration of social balance may be undertaken.

Chapter 2

THE CONCEPT OF PUBLIC GOODS AND COLLECTIVE CONSUMPTION

The previous chapter considered the issue of social balance—an optimal division of resources between the public and private sectors of a mixed economy. A more basic approach to this concept requires the establishment of an economic case for the existence of a public sector. Conceivably, all production could be by the market except for the governmental function of maintaining minimal law and order in a society. The market approximates more closely the political designs of democratic government which are so popular in the Western world. Why, then, do substantial public sectors exist in all democratic societies of the West? Can an economic case be established to justify substantial public sector economic activity in societies bent historically toward the market means of allocation and toward democratic political structures? The nature of public goods becomes a relevant point as the above question is considered in Chapter 2.

HISTORICAL EVOLUTION OF PUBLIC SECTOR ARGUMENTS

In *The Wealth of Nations* (1776), Adam Smith enumerated four justifiable categories of governmental activity.[1] These were: (1) the duty of protecting the society from violence and invasion by other independent societies which, of course, is the function of national defense; (2) the duty of protecting every member of a society from the injustice or oppression of every other member of the society. This is the duty of establishing an "administration of justice" which will provide law and order in the society; (3) the duty of establishing and maintaining those highly beneficial public institutions and public works which are of such a nature that the profit could never repay the expense to any individual or small number of individuals, and which it therefore cannot be expected that any individual or small number of individuals should erect or maintain; and (4) the duty of meeting expenses necessary for support of the sovereign, an expense which varies depending upon the form of political structure.

[1] Adam Smith, *The Wealth of Nations* (London: Routledge, 1913), Book V, pp. 541–644.

17

Though Smith often has been described as a bold advocate of minimal governmental activity, his writings fail to indicate significant fear of the public sector. To the contrary, his four functions of government require a level of public sector economic activity somewhat greater than a laissez-faire economic system would permit.[2] Undoubtedly, the modest restraint which Smith does reveal concerning the economic role of government, and particularly of central government, results from the understandable reaction of his era against the restrictions of mercantilism. The widespread historical misinterpretation of Smith's viewpoint on governmental economic activity seems to derive partially from the fact that the rising capitalists of the industrial revolution in England found in Smith's acute analysis of the inner workings of a market economy a contemporary theoretical framework from which they could oppose factory legislation. "Thus by a strange injustice the man who warned that the grasping eighteenth-century industrialists 'generally have an interest to deceive and even to oppress the public' came to be regarded as their economic patron saint. Even today—in blithe disregard of his actual philosophy—Smith is generally regarded as a *conservative* economist, whereas in fact, he was more avowedly hostile to the *motives* of businessmen than most New Deal economists."[3]

The most controversial of Smith's four functions of government are the first and the third, namely, the national defense and public works functions. The second function, that of preserving law and order and protecting property, and the fourth, that of maintaining the sovereign or executive level of government, could be logically opposed only by an avowed anarchist. Even primitive societies provide a semblance, if not more, of the "law and order" and the "sovereign-support" functions. Since these are *not* controversial functions of government, they do not require lengthy analysis in the effort to construct an economic case for the existence of a public sector in a market-oriented economy.

The national defense function, however, is less intrinsic to governmental provision than the justice and sovereign-support functions. For example, defense need not be a collective undertaking in a primitive society. Smith observed, quite accurately, that government becomes involved increasingly in the defense function as a society "advances in civilization."[4] In a primitive society, the warrior "maintains himself by his own labor, in the same manner as when he lives at home. His

---

[2] Laissez-faire, in this context, refers to private sector resource determination in all areas of economic activity except for the use of resources by government to provide minimal law and order in the society.

[3] Robert L. Heilbroner, *The Worldly Philosophers*, Revised Edition (New York: Simon and Schuster, 1961), p. 54. In the quotation, the term "New Deal economists" refers to those economists associated with the Presidential administration of Franklin D. Roosevelt between 1932–45.

[4] Smith, *op. cit.*, p. 555.

society . . . is at no sort of expense, either to prepare him for the field or to maintain him while he is in it."[5] By contrast, in civilized societies government undertakes a more distinctive and a more extensive defense function on a collective basis. Smith recognized the change introduced into the art of war by the invention of firearms as a significant cost-increasing factor. Indeed, history since the time of Smith has experienced an enormous growth in the complexity of weaponry and, consequently, in the absolute resource cost and relative importance of the national defense function of government. Thus, little controversy exists in modern indus-trial nations regarding government's role in the allocation of national defense.

The most controversial of Smith's four governmental functions is that which relates to "public works." Jeremy Bentham, a contemporary of Smith, held a viewpoint similar to Smith's regarding the requirement that government, under certain conditions, influence the output of public works. Smith realized that certain social capital items like roads, bridges, canals, and harbors would not be allocated without the influence of government because they could not be provided by private enterprise on a profitable basis.[6] Public works are subdivided further into (1) those facilitating commerce and (2) those promoting instruction or education. A further subdivision of "educational" public works classifies them into (*a*) the "education of youth" and (*b*) the "instruction of people of all ages." Smith intended the latter to perform the role of religion in society. He advocated the use of tolls or fees (user pricing), wherever possible, in the financing of works of commerce.

As mercantilism faded further into the shadows of history, general opposition to government declined in the Western world. John Stuart Mill, in his *Principles of Political Economy* (1848), accepted government on an even more comprehensive basis than did Smith.[7] Mill argued that in the particular conditions of a given age or nation "there is scarcely anything really important to the general interest, which it may not be desirable, or even necessary, that the government should take upon itself, not because private individuals cannot effectually perform it, but *because they will not*." (Italics provided.)[8] Mill thus believed that at cer-tain times and places the public sector would be required to provide roads, docks, harbors, canals, irrigation works, hospitals, schools, col-leges, printing presses, and other public works. He thought that gov-ernment should enhance the happiness of its subjects "by doing the things which are made incumbent on it by the helplessness of the public,

---

[5] *Ibid.*, p. 541.

[6] *Ibid.*, p. 567.

[7] John Stuart Mill, *Principles of Political Economy* (London: Longmans, Green, 1926).

[8] *Ibid.*, p. 978.

in such a manner as shall tend not to increase and perpetuate, but to correct that helplessness."[9] Mill favored, as far as possible, the attainment of these publicly provided services through means requiring "individual energy and voluntary cooperation."[10]

Many years later, John Maynard Keynes reiterated the viewpoints of Smith, Bentham, Mill, and others on the importance of public works by commenting that "government is not to do things which individuals are doing already, and to do them a little better or a little worse; but to do those things which at present are not done at all."[11] The Smith-Bentham-Mill-Keynes position on public works will be developed later in this chapter as part of the "decreasing costs" characteristic of public goods.

The economic case for substantial public sector resource allocation underwent a substantial evolution following the theoretical development of marginal concepts during the 1870's and 1880's. William Stanley Jevons (England), Leon Walras (France), and Eugen von Bohm-Bawerk (Austria) were the men most responsible for applying marginal utility analysis to demand, while Alfred Marshall (England) was most responsible for applying marginal analysis to supply as well as reconciling both sides of the market mechanism.[12] Marginal analysis was incorporated expertly into public finance theory by A. C. Pigou in his *A Study in Public Finance* (1928).[13] Pigou observed that "just as an individual will get more satisfaction out of his income by maintaining a certain balance between different sorts of expenditure, so also will a community through its government."[14]

In the situation of both the individual and of the community, the common Pigovian postulate is that resources should be allocated among different uses in such a manner that the marginal return of satisfaction is the same for all of them. Pigou applies marginalism both to *exhaustive* governmental expenditures, which absorb resources, and to *transfer* expenditures, which redistribute income and wealth. Furthermore, Pigou applied marginalism to the intrapublic sector problem of deciding which public goods shall be provided. He observed that "expenditure should be distributed between battleships and Poor Relief in such wise that the last shilling devoted to each of them yields the same real return."[15]

[9] *Ibid.*

[10] *Ibid.*

[11] John Maynard Keynes, *"The End of Laissez-Faire"* in *Laissez-Faire and Communism* (New York: New Republic, Inc., 1926), p. 67.

[12] See Alfred Marshall, *Principles of Economics* (8th ed.; London: Macmillan & Co., 1930).

[13] A. C. Pigou, *A Study in Public Finance* (London: Macmillan & Co., 1928).

[14] *Ibid.*, p. 50.

[15] *Ibid.*

The Pigovian approach may be applied in the effort to define a precise social balance point. Pigou observed that if the community were a unitary being, "expenditure should be pushed in all directions up to the point at which the satisfaction obtained from the last shilling expended is equal to the satisfaction lost in respect of the last shilling called up on government service."[16] Thus, in defining the theoretical point of optimal resource allocation between the public and private sectors, Pigou implicitly recognized the need for a public sector.

Pigou recognized, moreover, that the public sector necessarily will grow larger along with a growing economy. He reasoned that the optimum amount of public expenditure will be larger, the larger is the aggregate income of a society (the population remaining constant) because the marginal sacrifice involved in raising shillings from the public "will be smaller, the larger is the number of shillings constituting the public income."[17] In addition, using marginal utility theory, Pigou argued that the more uneven the distribution of income within a society, the larger will be the expenditure of the public sector because the marginal disutility involved in acquiring additional revenue will be less (if the tax structure is progressive). These arguments are based, of course, upon the assumption of a "diminishing marginal utility of income." Hence, the public sector of an economy may be expected to be greater, in both absolute and relative terms, the higher the national income and the greater the inequality of income distribution in a society. The implication of a functional relationship between economic growth and the size of a nation's public sector is not novel to Pigou. Others, including the late 19th-century German economist, Adolph Wagner, have held similar hypotheses.[18]

CONDITIONS FOR OPTIMAL PRIVATE SECTOR PRODUCTION OF ALL ECONOMIC GOODS

What conditions are required for all output to be directed in an optimal manner by consumer sovereignty? If the market can allocate in a perfect manner, of course, no economic case for the existence of a public sector can be established. The conditions of optimal market output derive, for the most part, from what is known in economics as "general equilibrium theory." This theory was formulated primarily by Leon Walras, the 19th-century French economist mentioned above in connection with marginalism and utility theory, and in the early 20th century it was mathematically implemented by the Italian economist Vilfredo

---

[16] *Ibid.*

[17] *Ibid.*, p. 51.

[18] The Wagner hypothesis will be examined in Chapter 8.

Pareto. In general equilibrium theory, all prices are interdependent and all markets are presumed to be perfectly competitive.

The basic *conditions* necessary for the attainment of optimal allocation through the market are enumerated below. The first four conditions listed below derive directly from general equilibrium requirements while the last two do not.

1. Many sellers and many buyers in *every* industry—whether in the product or factor markets. A *single* perfectly competitive industry in a world of imperfect markets likely would not achieve optimal allocation because of intermarket distortions imposed by the imperfect markets on the perfect market.

2. Perfect knowledge by all sellers and buyers in both product and factor markets.

3. Perfect mobility of productive resources.

4. "Profit-maximization" motives by all firms and "utility-maximization" motives by all consumers. The former is an implicit requirement subject to the existence of the other general equilibrium conditions. If the other general equilibrium conditions are satisfied, only long-run normal (economic) profits would exist and all firms would have to maximize profits in order to survive.

5. Complete divisibility of all economic goods, that is, all goods may be priced to individuals. If the individual does not offer monetary payments for the good, he will be excluded from consuming it. In other words, the *exclusion principle* applies.

6. No consumption interdependencies between consumers, no production interdependencies between firms, and no "mixed" interdependencies between consumers and firms. In other words, no *externalities* can exist.

Given these six conditions, the following consequences would result from competitive markets and maximizing behavior.

1. All units of a productive resource would be paid the same price. This is attained through the forces of competition.

2. Prices of the various productive resources would be in proportion to their marginal products. This is attained by the process of substituting one factor for another whenever their prices become disproportional to their marginal products. This determines the proportions to which the various productive resources are used.

3. At equilibrium, the prices of each of the productive resources would be equal to their marginal products. This determines the quantity in which the productive resources are used.

4. All units of each productive resource whose supply price is equal to or lower than the price of the factor would be employed.

5. All consumers would allocate their individual incomes in such a manner that the marginal utilities of the last dollar of expenditure are equal in all directions of expenditure.

The remainder of the chapter will examine the six conditions necessary for optimal market allocation to observe whether these conditions are met in contemporary American society. In accomplishing this task, a distinction will be drawn between pure public wants and pure private wants and between pure public goods and pure private goods. In addition to these extremes on the wants-goods continuum, a wide area of quasi-public (quasi-private) wants and goods will be designated. Figure 2–1 expresses these distinctions. An attempt will be made to demonstrate the logical interrelationship between the nature of *wants*, the nature of the economic *goods* meeting these wants, and the nature of the allocation

FIGURE 2–1

CONTINUUM OF PUBLIC GOODS AND PRIVATE GOODS

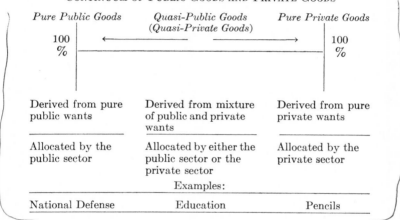

Pure Public Goods	*Quasi-Public Goods* *(Quasi-Private Goods)*	*Pure Private Goods*
100%	← —— —— →	100%
Derived from pure public wants	Derived from mixture of public and private wants	Derived from pure private wants
Allocated by the public sector	Allocated by either the public sector or the private sector	Allocated by the private sector
	Examples:	
National Defense	Education	Pencils

institutions—market or government—which provide the goods. It will be observed that because of the breakdown of several criteria required for optimal market allocation, an economic case may be established for the allocation of all pure public goods and some quasi-public goods by the public sector.

THE CASE FOR A PUBLIC SECTOR

The breakdown of the conditions for optimal private sector output may be approached through an analysis of the following characteristics of economic wants and of the economic goods which serve them: (1) product indivisibility, (2) external effects of consumption and of production (externalities), (3) decreasing costs of production and imperfect markets, and (4) various supply characteristics such as risk and the extreme scarcity or uniqueness of certain productive resources. Depending upon the extent to which these criteria are present, an economic good may be purely public in nature, purely private in nature, or mixed, in the sense that it incorporates significant characteristics of each extreme. This is analogous to the determination of a good's price elasticity of demand, which may be influenced by the composite relationships of several criteria.

Product Indivisibility

One manner of describing an indivisible good is to observe that such a good cannot be priced in the market. Looking further into this phenomenon, it becomes evident that such a good cannot be priced because of an inability to apply the *exclusion principle* to it, that is, an individual cannot be prevented from consuming the good simply because he does not pay for it. Where the exclusion principle can be applied, an individual will not receive the good unless he pays for it. Indivisible goods are "consumed equally" by all in the market.

The following example may clarify the applicability and inapplicability of the exclusion principle: If an individual is allowed to make his own consumer-sovereign decision about the expenditure of $500, he might decide to spend it for new clothes, knowing that he cannot acquire these clothes unless he pays for them. He can be excluded from consuming them by not paying for them. On the other hand, he would not volunteer a $500 contribution to national defense since he can consume just as much defense as others while allowing others to pay for it. He cannot be excluded from enjoying its benefits because of a failure voluntarily to pay for it. Thus, he will not volunteer payments for defense and will pay only by *compulsion*—something quite inconsistent with consumer sovereignty and market-directed output. Pure public goods will not be provided unless government exists and compels the financing of such goods. This is a breakdown of condition Number 5 for optimal allocation, namely, that all economic goods must be completely divisible.

Musgrave refers to wants which cannot be satisfied through the market because their enjoyment cannot be priced as "social wants."[19] These are comparable to the indivisible wants and goods described above, which will be designated *pure public wants* and *pure public goods* in this book. In addition, Musgrave defines "merit wants," which are wants so "meritorious" that their satisfaction is provided for through fiscal means over and above what is provided for through market means and purchased voluntarily by buyers.[20] Education and postal operations would be included in the merit wants category. These contain both divisible and indivisible benefits and will be designated in this book as either *quasi-public* or *quasi-private* wants and goods, depending upon whether the government sector or market sector produces them.

We have observed that pure public goods contain complete indivisi-

[19] Richard A. Musgrave, *The Theory of Public Finance* (New York: McGraw-Hill Book Co., Inc., 1959), p. 9.

[20] *Ibid.*, p. 13.

bility, that is, none of their benefits can be priced. At the other extreme, pure private goods possess benefits which are completely divisible in the sense that buyers' offer prices reveal the utility values or preferences which they assign to the goods, thus telling producers the types and quantities of goods to provide with society's scarce resources. Pure public goods are most efficiently produced by government and pure private goods by the market, though in many instances the opposite sector could produce the good—but only with a waste of resources for the society. National defense, a pure public good, could be provided by the private sector, for example, but not with efficiency comparable to its provision by the public sector. Likewise, pencils and electric toothbrushes could be produced by government enterprise, but likely with less efficiency than in the divisible manner of the market. A logical interrelationship thus appears to exist between the nature of a want such as the pure public or social want, national defense, the nature of the economic good which meets this want (defense services), and the institutional sector which produces the good (the public sector). In other words, national defense is a pure public (social) want and a pure public good provided by the public sector. A similar line of argument may be presented for the logical interrelationship between pure private wants, pure private goods, and private sector production of the good in the market. An important thing to remember from this discussion is that when a good contains a significant public good characteristic such as indivisibility, its production by the public sector, and hence *the existence of a public sector,* is economically rational.

External Effects

The identification of external effects with economic goods is a second means of differentiating pure public goods from pure private goods. External effects are known synonymously by such other general terms as "externalities," "neighborhood effects," "third-party effects," and "spillover effects" as well as by specific references to external economies and diseconomies of consumption and production. At this point, economic effects must be defined and a distinction between external and internal economic effects must be established.

An "economic effect" may be viewed as an economic gain or loss to one or more economic units resulting from an economic action initiated by a single economic unit (consumer or producer). The gain may be in the form of additional utility or satisfaction to the consumer or greater production efficiency to a firm. Losses imply disutility to the consumer or reduced production efficiency by the firm. Gains and losses may thus appear on either the demand or supply side of the market mechanism. Internal effects are those gains or losses which are retained within the economic unit which initiates the economic action. External effects are those gains or losses which emanate from the economic unit initiating the economic action and which affect other economic units. Obviously, the collective interest is more at stake in the consideration of external economic effects to households and firms than in the case of internal effects.

Several combinations of internal and external effects are possible. For example: (1) an internal consumption effect may yield external production effects; (2) an internal production effect may yield external consumption effects; (3) an internal consumption effect may yield external consumption effects; and (4) an internal production effect may yield external production effects. The possible combinations increase in number and complexity when the classifications of economies (gains) and diseconomies (losses) are added. Realistic examples of the four combinations listed above may be enlightening regarding the overall concept of external effects and their relevance to the nature of public goods and to the existence of a public sector.

Example 1: Suppose that the utility or satisfaction of consumers living in a residential neighborhood may be increased if unsightly telephone and electric wires are placed underground. Suppose also that the residents are able to exert enough influence on the regulatory commission to compel the telephone and electric companies to follow this policy. In this event, internal economies of consumption accrue to the residents of the neighborhood. The effect of this policy on the businesses, however, would be one of added costs with no offsetting gain in production efficiency from the wires being buried instead of overhead. External diseconomies of production are thus incurred by businesses as a result of a policy which provided internal economies of consumption to the residents.

Example 2: Suppose that the internal production function of a firm which manufactures steel is made more efficient by the acquisition of new, technologically improved blast furnaces. Suppose also that the new blast furnaces filter air pollutants less effectively than the older blast furnaces. In this event, the internal economies of production accruing to the steel firm from the new blast furnaces would yield external diseconomies of consumption to residents of the surrounding area, who are forced to breathe the additional air pollutants.

Example 3: Suppose that an individual who loves jungle animals decides to convert his residential backyard into a home zoo. His individual utility or satisfaction increases as he purchases the animals and enjoys their presence. Yet, the internal economies of consumption to the owner of the menagerie of jungle animals render external diseconomies of consumption to his neighbors in the form of noise, unpleasant odors, and lowered property values.

Example 4: Suppose that a telephone communications firm introduces new equipment which lowers the cost of providing telephone service and also improves the quality of the service. Suppose also that part of the monetary gain and all the quality gain are passed on to business customers who now purchase the higher quality communications services at lower prices. The improved "communications package" to the business customers may be viewed as allowing management to combine productive resources more efficiently than in the past. In this event, the internal economies of production of the telephone firm yield external economies of production to the business customers.

In the above examples, the existence of external effects, whether of a gain or loss nature and whether of a consumptive or productive nature, implies "public" interest in the economic actions involved. This is true particularly when the external effects defy pricing as a means of inclusion in demand and supply functions. Those external economies and diseconomies that cannot be priced are designated *nonmarket external effects.* Those external economies and diseconomies which may be priced in demand and supply functions are designated *market external effects.* Nonmarket external effects are elusive, though real, and the public interest may be significantly involved, as in the cases of the air pollution from the steel mill and the backyard zoo. There is no self-correcting market mechanism at work when the external effects are not measurable in price values. Such economic effects thus cannot be controlled through the market.

A prevalence of external effects over internal effects, whether they be market or nonmarket external effects, suggests "publicness" in the nature of a want and the good which satisfies the want. When the external effects are considerable in magnitude, the good involved may even be considered to be a pure public good. When external effects are scarce or nonexistent, internal effects predominate and the good may more properly be considered a pure private good. Again, as with indivisibilities, a large in-between area of wants and goods with moderate mixtures of external and internal effects exists. These may be considered as quasi-public (quasi-private) wants and goods. The presence of external effects violates condition six of the requirements for optimal market allocation. Thus, another tenet of the economic case for public goods is established, as the market process breaks down when external effects become prominent, and especially when the external effects are of the nonmarket variety. Just as with indivisibilities, a logical thread of relationship seems to exist between the nature of a pure public want, a pure public good (denoted here by the external effects trait), and the producing institution (the public sector).

In the latter part of the 19th century, Alfred Marshall discussed external economies and diseconomies.[21] A. C. Pigou refined the discussion

---

[21] Marshall, *op. cit.*

in his *Economics of Welfare,* first published in 1920.[22] Pigou distinguishes between *social* benefits and costs and *private* benefits and costs. Social benefits refer to total benefits inclusive of both internal and external benefits. Social costs refer to total costs inclusive of both internal and external costs. On the other hand, private benefits and costs are synonymous with internal effects. External economies exist when social benefits exceed private benefits. External diseconomies exist when social costs exceed private costs. Where external economies exist, a private firm is likely to produce less than an optimum amount of the economic good because the firm is adding benefits greater than the amount for which it is being compensated. On the other hand, when external diseconomies are present, a private firm is likely to overallocate the economic good because part of the total cost is being absorbed by individuals other than the initiating economic agent. Thus, it should be observed that government must play a role if the goal of optimal allocation is to be achieved. The case for a public sector receives another foundation stone in its structure.

Finally, clarification of the relationship between the two characteristics of public goods which have been established so far—indivisibilities and external effects—is advisable. An attempt to say that indivisibilities and external effects are identical concepts may be answered by pointing out that when external effects involve measurable market effects, they may be priced and, hence, they are *not indivisible* since the exclusion principle may be applied to them. Thus, an external effect is not necessarily indivisible.

A further example of the difference between the indivisibility and external effects concepts follows: Suppose that 90 percent of the economic gains resulting from improved technology in the production function of a private electric utility are passed on to business users of electricity in the form of lower electricity prices and that the remaining 10 percent of the gains are retained internally as incremental profits within the electric utility. In this event, *all* of the total gains may be measured or priced. Indivisibilities are thus equal to zero, but external economies constitute 90 percent of the total economies or gains. It is again obvious that the indivisibility and externality concepts differ.

Decreasing Costs and Imperfect Markets

Another point of weakness in the case for optimal market allocation stems from the related conditions of decreasing production costs and market imperfection. In turn, these same characteristics serve as additional characteristics of pure public goods. This concept has been developed over the years, with significant contributions being made by Smith, Mill, Walras, Marshall, Pigou, Bergson, Hotelling, Samuelson, and Bator,

[22] A. C. Pigou, *The Economics of Welfare* (London: Macmillan & Co., 1920).

among others.[23] Earlier in this chapter it was observed that Smith, Bentham, Mill, and Keynes specified the obligation of government to provide those desirable goods which private enterprise cannot provide profitably. These are essentially goods of a decreasing cost nature.

Private sector production optimality relies heavily upon the existence of perfect markets throughout the society. Optimality conditions 1, 2, 3, and 4, all of which are general equilibrium conditions, reflect a world of perfect competition. These are: (1) many sellers and many buyers in *every* industry, (2) perfect knowledge by all sellers and buyers, (3) perfect mobility of productive resources, and (4) profit-maximization motives by all firms and utility-maximization motives by all consumers. The failure of the first of these conditions supports the arguments now to be developed in support of a public sector.

In the United States, high levels of *technology* working through factor specialization and divisibility yield *economies* of large-scale production in many industries. These economies, in turn, represent *decreasing unit costs* of production over a wide range of output scales. The relevant demand in most American markets is sufficiently limited that many firms could not exist in each industry and still operate at or near optimal technical efficiency (the bottom of the long-run average unit cost curve). Thus, *market concentration* occurs with a few firms dominating most national industries as well as many regional and local markets. Thus, a chain reaction series of effects takes place. High-level technology causes economies of scale which cause decreasing production costs which, in turn, cause market concentration because of limited relevant demand. Imperfect markets with *few sellers* are thus created and the first condition of optimal market allocation through general equilibrium conditions is violated.

The above phenomenon is displayed in Figure 2–2. Scale 3 is the most efficient scale in technical factor-combination terms, but would allow the fewest firms to produce the relevant demand. Scale 1 is the technically least efficient scale, but would allow the largest number of firms to meet the relevant demand. Thus, as firms follow the understandable motivation of minimizing production costs, many industries are left with only a few sellers in them. Such markets do *not* have a coincidence of the best-profit point of production for the firm with optimal allocation for the society. A comparison of Figures 2–3 and 2–4, discussed below, reveals this fact.

Business firms maximizing profits produce the output and charge the price consistent with the equality of marginal cost and marginal revenue. However, in imperfect markets (monopolistic competition, oligopoly, and monopoly) the firm, in fixing its output where marginal

[23] A good presentation of this concept may be found in Francis M. Bator, *The Question of Government Spending* (New York: Harper & Row, 1960).

FIGURE 2–2

ECONOMIES OF SCALE OFTEN LEAD TO MARKET
CONCENTRATION

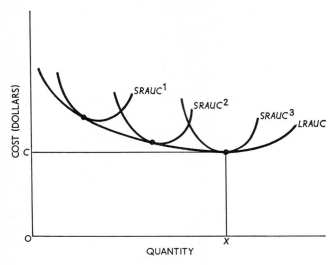

cost and marginal revenue are equal, necessarily selects a price-quantity
combination where marginal cost is *less than* price (average revenue)
because of individual firm monopoly power (control over price). Thus,
efficient allocation in conformance with consumer sovereignty is not
attained since output is not carried up to the point where the additional
cost of the marginal unit just equals the price that people are willing to

FIGURE 2–3

PRICING AND OUTPUT FOR FIRM IN PURE
COMPETITION

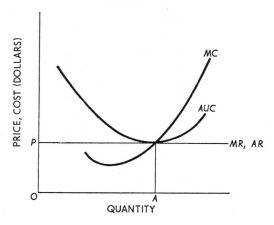

pay for it. In Figure 2–3, the perfectly competitive firm producing at the best-profit point where marginal cost equals marginal revenue is also producing where marginal cost equals price. At output *OA,* marginal cost equals marginal revenue for the best-profit position and marginal cost equals price (average revenue) for optimal allocation.

In Figure 2–4, however, the imperfectly competitive firm producing at the best profit point *OA,* where marginal cost equals marginal revenue, does *not* produce also at the optimal allocation point *OB,* where marginal

FIGURE 2–4

PRICING AND OUTPUT FOR PURE MONOP-
OLY FIRM AS COMPARED TO PURELY
COMPETITIVE FIRM

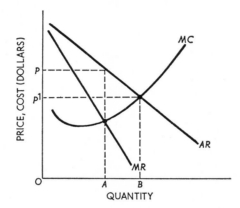

cost equals price. At profit maximization point *OA,* marginal cost is less than price and misallocation occurs by the reduced output *AB.* In other words, *OA* is the best-profit output, *OB* is the optimal allocation output, and *AB* is the amount of misallocated (reduced) output. In particular, if the economic good in question is necessary or desirable, a case is established for public sector influence on the allocation of the good in quantities closer to, if not at, the social optimum point *OB.*

An important complication arises if marginal cost equals price when average unit costs of production are decreasing. Under these conditions, the point of optimal allocation *cannot* yield a profit. Figure 2–5 displays this phenomenon. In Figure 2–5, *OA* is the best-profit point of production and *OB* is the optimal social allocation point. At output *OA,* the firm is earning monopoly profits by the amount *abcd.* Misallocation would exist at output *OA* by the amount of reduced output *AB.* Significantly, the firm could *not* produce the optimal output *OB* profitably because, under decreasing average unit costs, marginal cost must be below average unit cost and the intersection between marginal cost and price must thus be where price is less than average unit cost. Consequently, total losses are *wxyz* when optimal output *OB* is produced. Loss per unit is the vertical amount *wx*, *yz*, or *CP*. Since losses cannot be sustained in the long run, public sector influence (like outright production or subsidization) is necessary for optimal allocation of this good.

While a good produced under these conditions might be divisible in a pricing sort of way, and not be a pure public good from that standpoint, it may be a necessary or highly desirable good. If so, a case for public sector influence on its allocation in optimal amounts can be established.

FIGURE 2–5

LOSS AT POINT OF OPTIMAL ALLOCA-
TION UNDER DECREASING COST
CONDITIONS OF PRODUCTION

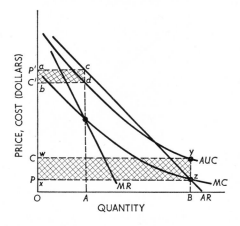

Such divisible and desirable goods would be the same as those which are classified by Musgrave as satisfying merit wants. They fit into the quasi-public (quasi-private) goods terminology of this book. It may well be that such obvious losing ventures as the New York Transit Authority and the New Haven Railroad, and subsequent governmental intervention, would involve the decreasing average unit cost–low marginal cost phenomenon. Government action, however, would require adequate consideration of the distribution effects of financing the subsidies.

A polar case of the above phenomenon exists for those economic goods whose marginal costs are zero. This is displayed in Figure 2–6. Since all costs are fixed, the marginal cost curve (*MC*) coincides with the horizontal axis. Since optimal allocation is at output *OB*, where marginal cost equals price, the price must be zero because the marginal cost is zero at this point. The traditional bridge example is a case in point: Suppose that the marginal cost of an additional vehicle crossing a bridge is zero and that the output of bridge crossings may be increased up to capacity without decreasing the output of anything else by drawing scarce resources away from their production. Any price for bridge crossings, whether a uniform price or a price charged according to discrimination, would misallocate resources because bridge crossings would be reduced in number below the number that would exist where price equals the marginal cost of the last crossing, which, of course, is a price of zero. Admittedly, if the demand for bridge crossings exceeds the capacity of

FIGURE 2–6

OPTIMAL ALLOCATION OF A PURE PUBLIC GOOD

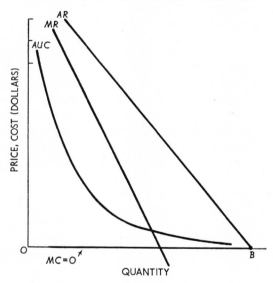

the bridge, a price per crossing may be desirable in order to ration use of the scarce resource. This constitutes a separate argument for public sector allocation, however, and is discussed under "additional supply characteristics" later in the chapter.

Bator refers to this polar case of decreasing costs as involving public goods, that is, a good whose consumption by X would lead to no subtraction from what is left over for consumption by Y and Z, such as tuning in a radio program or enjoying protection through national defense.[24] The similarity of this to indivisible goods, and the inability to apply the exclusion principle as discussed earlier in this chapter, is apparent. The inadequacy of the market in allocating pure public goods, however, is not totally dependent on the inability to price them in a divisible manner. Even with complete divisibility, there would remain the dominating fact that *any price* above zero would be restricting output away from the

[24] *Ibid.,* p. 94.

optimal allocation point where marginal cost equals price when the marginal cost of an additional unit is at zero. Bator observes that "the proposition that government has a significant allocating function turns out to be a corollary of the doctrine of consumer sovereignty."[25] Indeed, the case for a public sector is strengthened by decreasing cost conditions when they lead to a marginal cost of zero. An extreme degree of "publicness" exists in the polar case of decreasing costs. The logical interrelationship between pure public wants, pure public goods, and public sector allocation of the goods continues to apply in a consistent manner.

The American economy fits well into the model developed above. Economies of scale lead to decreasing production costs over a wide range of output in many industries. Market concentration, especially of an oligopoly variety, is prevalent. Optimal allocation of many desirable economic goods is not forthcoming at the optimal allocation point, marginal cost equal to price, without public sector production, regulation, or subsidization. In some instances, no output of the good would take place at all without governmental influence. This bears a close resemblance to the traditional arguments of Smith, Bentham, Mill, Keynes, and others that the public sector must influence the provision of those desirable goods which the private sector does not provide in adequate quantities, if at all, because of the inability to produce them profitably.

Bator observes, based upon U.S. Department of Commerce data, that some 97 percent of governmental purchases of goods and services in the United States relate to goods with strong "decreasing-cost public-good qualities."[26] National defense, general government, international affairs and finance, public health and sanitation, education, police, fire protection, highways, and postal services are among the publicly provided goods which contain important decreasing-cost public-good qualities. Major exceptions to the above type of governmental expenditures are agricultural subsidies and welfare payments which involve the distribution objective rather than the allocation objective of public finance. Bator comments:

Agriculture aside, then, free markets would not do well by most of the major functions now served by government. . . . The rule that allocation by markets cannot be improved upon, that shifting of resources from government to private use will necessarily improve allocation, is—or ought to be—dead.[27]

Various Supply Characteristics of Public Goods

Economic goods may take on the trait of publicness through characteristics other than those of indivisibilities, external effects, and decreas-

---

[25] *Ibid.*, p. 98.
[26] *Ibid.*, p. 100.
[27] *Ibid.*, pp. 102, 108.

ing costs discussed above. Some additional characteristics of a supply nature are: (1) the lack of perfect knowledge by all sellers and buyers and the related problem of risk; (2) the lack of perfect mobility of resources; (3) the failure of many firms to maximize profits; and (4) the unique scarcity or other unique characteristics of certain productive resources, particularly natural resources. These characteristics essentially violate conditions 2, 3, and 4 as required for optimal production of all economic goods by the private sector.

The lack of adequate market knowledge by a firm is more severe in some cases than in others. Sometimes this lack of knowledge will prevent sufficient output of an important economic good by the market. Several examples may be provided. First, risk probabilities were assessed incorrectly by the market regarding the supply costs and the demand for electricity in rural areas of the United States prior to 1936. In that year, a system of federal government loans and subsidies were initiated through the Rural Electrification Administration. This program demonstrated that rural electrification was feasible on a private basis in many parts of the United States. Presently, almost 100 percent of American farmers use electricity, which is provided by both the public and private sectors. Regarding this, Philip E. Taylor comments:

> The point here is that the feasibility of handling this problem through the market principle has had to be demonstrated by an agency capable of taking the risk of experimentation. Lack of knowledge of the facts with respect to demand and cost had obstructed progress; the provision of knowledge has essentially solved the problem.[28]

Other examples of a long-run payoff from "collective risk taking" may be drawn from such occurrences as the development of atomic energy by the Atomic Energy Commission, the development of communications satellites under the substantial (but not complete) public sector influence of the National Aeronautics and Space Administration, and the development of public power through the Tennessee Valley Authority. The extensive development of public power during the 1930's proved to privately owned electric utilities that the demand for electricity is not as inelastic as they had believed it to be. Hence, improvements in market knowledge as attained through collective risk taking may enhance the long-run profit positions of private firms.

The immobility of productive resources will also help to prevent the attainment of long-run general equilibrium conditions. The nature of plant and equipment, in many instances, makes the geographical mobility of capital very difficult, if not impossible. Moreover, labor resources may be immobile due to such forces as the nature of pension plans, seniority

[28] Reprinted with permission of The Macmillan Company from *The Economics of Public Finance* by Philip E. Taylor. 3d ed. Copyright 1961, The Macmillan Company.

provisions, and entry restrictions into new job markets. In any case, when resources are not free to move to their most efficient points of usage, as indicated by market forces, the conditions of long-run general equilibrium are not attained and a subsequent retardation of the ability of the private sector to allocate resources efficiently results.

Not all firms in the American economy maximize, or even seek to maximize, profits. This would prevent, of course, the attainment of optimal resource allocation under the general equilibrium conditions of the market.[29] Some firms prefer not to maximize short-run profits for fear of encouraging federal or state antitrust action against their imperfect market positions. Others may not desire short-run profit maximization because of fear of damaging their "public image," an important consideration apart from the fear of external imposition by government of antitrust action upon them. In addition, public utility firms are not allowed by regulatory commissions to maximize profits. Many firms which seek maximum profits, moreover, fail to achieve their goal because of inadequate market knowledge. Thus, condition 4 of the requirements for optimal market allocation is not met because many firms, for a variety of reasons, do not maximize profits.

The conservation of certain productive resources is sometimes necessary when the resources are uniquely scarce and/or uniquely important. While society considers the full employment (as reasonably defined) of most labor and capital resources to be desirable, it cannot consider the short-run full employment of natural resources (the land factor of production) to be desirable. Thus, when short-run profit considerations would lead to overutilization of uniquely scarce or important natural resources such as the radio-wave spectrum or the cutting of 2,000-year-old redwood trees, long-run societal welfare may require the practice of resource conservation. Among the techniques which can be employed for the conservation of natural resources are government ownership, public utility regulation, severance (depletion) taxes, and nonutilization subsidies. In summary, the risk which accompanies imperfect market knowledge, inadequate resource mobility, the failure of many firms to maximize profits, and the unique characteristics of certain resources each may add publicness to an economic good.

The analysis of this chapter demonstrates that many of the conditions required for optimal resource allocation through the market-directed production of *all* economic goods are not present in the American economy. Relatedly, it is also shown that an economic case *does exist* for the production of economic goods by government other than the provision of minimal law and order. Yet economic analysis alone cannot provide the

[29] Yet, as observed above, if *all other requirements* for perfect competition exist, this point is irrelevant because all firms would be forced to seek maximum profits, in this case "normal profits," in order to survive in the long run.

exact social balance point of optimal intersectoral resource allocation since this must depend, in part, upon the noneconomic value judgments of the society regarding such important matters as political freedom and the proper state of income and wealth distribution. Clearly, a study in public finance is a study in "political economy." Economic principles and political institutions interact in the determination of economic behavior in an economy mixed between private and public sector decision making. Indeed, the public finance economist cannot ignore the analytical tools of the political scientist.

Chapter *3*	# PUBLIC SECTOR ATTRACTION OF ECONOMIC RESOURCES

Having established the need for a public sector through recognition of the characteristics of pure public and quasi-public goods, the discussion now turns to consideration of the alternate techniques or means whereby the public sector may influence the allocation of resources in production. Where allocation influence by the public sector is deemed necessary, government may produce the economic good, it may regulate the private production of the good, or it may follow a variety of "in-between" techniques.

ECONOMIC GOODS AND ALLOCATION TECHNIQUES

Economic goods which are purely public in nature and characterized by such dimensions as indivisibilities and external effects are ordinarily provided in a direct and complete manner by the public sector. On the other hand, purely private goods require no public interest in their allocation except, of course, in the indirect sense that they compete with public goods for the allocation of scarce resources. Quasi-public (quasi-private) goods may be influenced in their allocation by a variety of governmental techniques. This controversial area essentially is the "battleground" of the current social balance controversy. Musgrave observes that two allocation decisions are required: "In the context of an efficiently operated Allocation Branch, the necessary degree of adjustment in resource allocation is one thing to be decided upon, and the choice of techniques to secure the adjustment is another."[1]

The selection of a particular public sector technique for influencing the allocation of quasi-public (quasi-private) goods is often decided on noneconomic grounds. Considerations of freedom, both political and economic, along with other related social and cultural criteria are highly relevant in this case to the selection of allocation techniques. Prevailing American culture and tastes prefer minimal public sector influence on resource allocation. American society continually weighs through the political process the relative economic efficiencies of direct or indirect,

[1] Richard A. Musgrave, *The Theory of Public Finance* (New York: McGraw-Hill Book Co., Inc., 1959), p. 45.

complete or partial public sector allocation influence against the existing social, cultural, and political values. Walter Heller comments that "one would be naive to think that efficiency alone dictates the choice," and further, "the role of both economic and noneconomic constraints must be given full weight" in policy decisions as to the method of allocation.[2] As observed in Chapter 1, Henry Wallich argues that unless the public sector has a decided edge in the technical efficiency of combining productive resources to produce the optimal output, the community may prefer indirect and partial allocation influence—and this *only* when circumstances require any influence at all.[3]

A typical example of the argument in behalf of partial and indirect public sector allocation influence is found in Milton Friedman's suggestion that subsidies in the form of transfer payments be paid to individuals to be used to purchase educational services from schools.[4] Specifically, Friedman suggests a system of both public and private schools, at least for primary and secondary education, whereby parents who choose to send their children to private schools would be paid a sum equal to the estimated cost of educating a child in a public school, provided that at least this amount will be spent on education in an approved school.[5] Through this technique, a quasi-public good (education) would be acquired in adequate quantities through public sector influence, but the good would be produced to substantial proportions in the market. Thus, it is argued that economic gains accrue from the increased education and from the competition between the schools, while both economic and noneconomic gains accrue from the greater freedom of choice regarding the selection of a school.

TECHNIQUES VERSUS ISMS

Most resource allocation decisions do not involve a sharp distinction between socialistic planning and market decentralization. The majority of allocation decisions, to the contrary, are concerned with selection between a variety of mixed techniques which contain elements of both market and government allocation. Dahl and Lindblom comment:

. . . techniques and not "isms" are the kernel of rational social action in the Western world. Both socialism and capitalism are dead. The politico-economic

---

[2] Walter W. Heller, "Economics and the Applied Theory of Public Expenditures," *Federal Expenditure Policy for Economic Growth and Stability* (Joint Economic Committee, 85th Cong., 1st sess.) (Washington, D.C.: U.S. Government Printing Office, 1957), pp. 106–7.

[3] Henry C. Wallich, *The Cost of Freedom* (New York: Harper and Row, 1960).

[4] Milton Friedman, *Capitalism and Freedom* (Chicago: University of Chicago Press, 1962), chap. 6.

[5] *Ibid.*

systems of the United States and of Britain differ in important respects, to be sure; yet both major parties in both countries are attacking their economic problems with fundamentally the same kinds of techniques. Ideological differences between the parties in each country and between the countries themselves are significant in affecting the choice of techniques; but policy in any case is technique-minded, and it is becoming increasingly difficult in both countries to argue policy in terms of the mythical grand alternatives.[6]

Economic planning, for example, occurs under *governmental* influence both in socialist Russia and in (largely) capitalistic France. Furthermore, the management of large private American firms such as the American Telephone and Telegraph Company and General Motors involves extensive planning operations. Planning per se is neither socialistic nor capitalistic, though the ends of planning may be "social welfare" in the one case and "profits" in the other. Nonetheless, planning is a technique for improving administrative efficiency in either a governmental or a market situation.

Dahl and Lindblom also observed that the number of alternative techniques is continually increasing through discovery, invention, and innovation.[7] Invention and innovation, moreover, are not confined to technology and the physical sciences. The social structure may also benefit from innovations in social techniques. Lend-lease, scientific management, slum clearance, old age and survivors insurance, workmen's compensation, collective bargaining, and the Peace Corps are a few of many available testimonies to this fact. Thus, many of the techniques through which the public sector may influence resource allocation need not be confined to a static either-or choice between socialism and capitalism. Instead, they may be efficient and dynamic compromises between the two "isms." Similarly, the social balance controversy (discussed in Chapter 1) need not be an either-or choice between pure public sector and pure private sector resource allocation. Since this controversy centers upon the quasi-goods category, techniques may be selected which will commit the society to neither extreme socialism nor to laissez-faire capitalism.

CONTINUUM OF ALTERNATIVE TECHNIQUES

Table 3–1 presents a continuum showing some of the major alternative techniques which the public sector may use to affect resource allocation. These techniques range from those which are applied directly and completely by government to those where the public sector's influence is very indirect and incomplete. In the former case, government power and

---

[6] Robert A. Dahl and Charles E. Lindblom, *Politics, Economics and Welfare* (New York: Harper, 1953), p. 16.

[7] *Ibid.*, pp. 6–7.

compulsion prevail. In the latter case, the techniques more closely resemble market power and individualism. At point 1 on the continuum, governmental allocation influence is direct and complete. The public sector produces the economic good (like defense); it produces the component parts of the good (like missiles, ships, planes), and it conscripts all labor used in the production of the components and the final good.

TABLE 3–1

CONTINUUM OF SOME ALTERNATIVE TECHNIQUES OF PUBLIC SECTOR RESOURCE ATTRACTION

100%	PUBLIC SECTOR ALLOCATION (direct and complete)	Percentages refer to the "directness" and "completeness" of public sector resource allocation			*NO PUBLIC SECTOR ALLOCATION INFLUENCE*	0
	2	4	50%	6	9	11
	3	5		7	10	
1				8		

1. The public sector produces the final good; it produces all intermediate components of the good, and it controls directly all resources used in producing the components and/or the final good.
2. The public sector produces the final good, but purchases the intermediate components and/or labor in the market.
3. Monetary system owned or basically controlled by the public sector.
4. Substantial subsidy plus direct (public utility) regulation of an economic good produced by private enterprise in the market.
5. Combined public-private ownership of a firm, or publicly and privately owned firms coexisting in the same market.
6. Substantial subsidy of a market-produced good.
7. Direct regulation of a market-produced good.
8. Tax penalty or fee to ration consumption of a good.
9. Public sector licensing of private enterprise in the form of charters, franchises, and licenses.
10. Transfer-type operations and other fiscal acts which redistribute income and wealth and political voting power.
11. General antitrust regulation.

Even national defense is not a pure public good to this extreme degree in the United States. Most intermediate components of the final good, national defense, are produced in the market and purchased by the federal government. Furthermore, many members of the armed forces (the labor element of national defense) serve in peacetime on a voluntary rather than on a compulsory basis. Though provision of national defense in the United States cannot be located at the polar extreme of pure public goods, the federal government, of course, does possess considerable power to divert resources toward defense production. Thus, point 2 on the continuum represents the approximate directness and completeness of public sector defense influence in the United States. At this position on the continuum, the public sector produces the final good but buys most intermediate components and labor from the market and, in the case of national defense, possesses great legal authority to allocate optimal quantities of the good through budgetary means.

In the United States, the federal government influences the performance of the money and banking system in a significant manner. The monetary tools of the Federal Reserve System control the money supply (including demand deposits) through the behavior of a fractional reserve banking system. The Federal Reserve System and the Treasury Department, moreover, issue all circulating currency and coins. The Federal Reserve is, in a sense, a quasi-government body. The 12 regional banks are owned by the commercial banks of their respective areas and, in addition, are partially managed by business and banking representatives of the regions which they serve. Thus, point 3 on the continuum is used to denote the approximate influence of the federal government on the allocation of money and banking services in the economy. Indeed, it is a substantial influence. Yet, it is not a direct and complete one in the polar sense.

The public sector may influence resource allocation by combining the techniques of subsidy and direct regulation. Each of these means, of course, may also be used separately. The combined subsidy-direct regulation technique of allocation may be located approximately at point 4 on the continuum diagram if the subsidies and regulation are substantial.

Subsidies may take a variety of forms. A subsidy, for example, can be derived from the spending side of a government budget in the form of an outright payment to a private economic unit or as a productive resource or economic good provided to the private unit. The above market price purchases of farm products by the Commodity Credit Corporation is representative of the expenditure type of subsidy. Partial expenditure subsidies occur when government provides a productive resource or an economic good to a private economic unit at a price beneath the cost of providing the resource or good. Long-term, low-interest loans and commercial mailing privileges are examples of this type of subsidy. On the revenue side of the government budget, subsidies may take the subtle and disguised form of tax advantages (loopholes). Regardless of its obscurity, such a subsidy may nonetheless be of significant monetary importance to the recipient. Basically, the subsidy alternatives reduce to the broad categories of private gains resulting from either (1) the receipt of public expenditures or (2) reduced tax obligations on the revenue side of the budget.

Direct regulation is best exemplified by public utility regulation in the United States. The first comprehensive and effective application of this technique in the United States was on the railroads during the 1870's and 1880's through the state granger laws and the federal Act to Regulate

Commerce (Interstate Commerce Act). All states presently possess public utility commissions. In addition, many municipalities have regulatory bureaus, while the federal government sponsors such powerful regulatory agencies as the Interstate Commerce Commission, Civil Aeronautics Board, Federal Power Commission, Federal Communications Commission, and the Securities and Exchange Commission. Public utility regulation provides direct control of private business firms in such economic facets as (1) the conditions of entry into the industry, (2) prices, (3) quantity of service, and (4) quality of service.

A historic example of combined subsidies and direct regulation is provided by the development of the Western railroads in the United States. These railroads received substantial land grant subsidies constituting 242,000 square miles of land—much of which was wealthy in terms of soil, minerals, and timber. These subsidies helped to promote the rapid development of a highly effective transcontinental railroad network during the last half of the 19th century. Substantial services were provided and the various external effects emanating from improved transportation benefited the entire economy. Furthermore, during this era the state governments of Iowa, Illinois, Minnesota, and Wisconsin introduced the granger laws, which directly regulated railroads. The era witnessed, moreover, the beginning of direct federal regulation of interstate railroad services through the creation of the Interstate Commerce Commission in 1887. The railroads thus received substantial subsidies, but they also faced substantial regulation. Though combined subsidization and public utility regulation of privately owned enterprises does not constitute the polar extreme of direct and complete public sector allocation, it can constitute a substantial influence by the public sector on the allocation of scarce resources.

An allocation technique which may be located on the continuum at approximately the same point as the combined subsidy–direct regulation technique is the combined public-private ownership means of allocation. It may be applied either to a firm or to an industry. Examples of this technique being applied to firms include public corporations with tripartite control such as those employed in the French electricity and railroad industries. In the United States, the Satellite Communications Corporation, as endorsed by Congress, contains many features of joint government-market ownership and control of a firm. Furthermore, the development of nuclear energy under the leadership of the Atomic Energy Commission, and its cooperation with private enterprise, constitutes another example of the partnership means. In addition, the research-oriented Sandia Corporation is owned by the Atomic Energy Commission and operated by the American Telephone and Telegraph Company. An industrywide application of this technique is found in Canada's transcontinental railroad service where two companies, one government owned and the other private, provide virtually parallel routes. Similarly, the Tennessee Valley Authority provides a "yardstick" of competition to privately owned utilities in the Tennessee Valley region. The partnership technique serves as a compromise between the extremes of direct and complete public sector influence and no public sector allocation influence at all.

It was observed above that combined subsidies and public utility regulation provide substantial allocation influence. It should be remembered, however, that subsidies and direct regulation often exist on a separate basis in the American economy. When this occurs, the directness and completeness of the public sector's influence on allocation is necessarily less than when the two techniques are used jointly. It is estimated roughly, for purposes of the continuum displayed in Table 3–1, that separate usage of either the subsidy technique or of the direct regulation technique would fall at points 6 and 7, respectively, along the continuum. The subsidies and direct regulation would need to be substantial, of course, in order to provide this degree of allocation influence. Slight or unimportant subsidies and weak regulation would fall much further to the right along the continuum.

Point 8 on the continuum represents an estimate of the relative importance of tax penalties or fees as an instrument of allocation influence by the public sector. Sometimes the most rational governmental allocation technique, given the nature of community preferences, requires "discouragement" instead of "encouragement" of consumption. Prevailing community feelings regarding the consumption of liquor and tobacco products, for example, may result in the classification of these economic goods as "vices" which need to be discouraged. Given such community preferences, the public sector may impose substantial excise taxes on the consumption of liquor and tobacco products, or it may control their marketing as in the case of government-operated liquor stores. In other instances, government may charge a price (fee, toll) for the use of some economic good or resource in order to ration its use within available supply or capacity. Heavy bridge or road traffic, for example, may necessitate the charging of a substantial toll in order to regulate traffic usage within the capacity of the bridge or road. A further usage of tax penalties or prices to discourage consumption occurs on an aggregate basis during the inflationary pressure conditions of a wartime economy. The desire, in this case, is to restrain aggregate demand by imposing new taxes, or by raising present tax rates, in order to reduce the allocation of private goods relative to war goods.

The public sector can restrict entry to professions and industries via the issuance of charters, franchises, or licenses. More often than not, franchise policies worsen allocation rather than improve it because they increase monopoly power and thus cause a greater deviation between the profit-maximization point of output and the optimal allocation point where marginal cost equals price. At times, however, they may improve allocation by conserving uniquely scarce or important productive resources. The issuance of charters, franchises, or licenses are located at point 9 on the continuum. Charters, franchises, and licenses do not directly involve the expenditure and tax sides of the budget in an important manner. Instead, they are an incomplete and indirect means of public sector influence over resource allocation.

A subtle and incomplete technique whereby government may influence resource usage is by redistributing monetary income and wealth and political voting power so that a different pattern of community allocation decisions, and thus a different "real" income and wealth distribution, occurs. Examples of this include: (1) transfer operations such as compulsory social security in the United States and (2) the manner in which an asymmetrical (unequally distributed) public debt is maintained in terms of taxes collected and interest payments made on the debt. Of course, many other fiscal actions of a tax or expenditure nature can be employed to change a given structure of income-wealth distribution and, in so doing, change the allocation preferences of the society. In any event, since this technique often works "indirectly" on allocation, while working "directly" on the important distribution objective of public finance, it is classified as an indirect and incomplete method of governmental *allocation* influence. The redistribution technique is located at point 10 on the continuum.

General antitrust regulation is the final allocation alternative to be considered. In the United States it is a very indirect and incomplete technique, in terms of its allocation influence, and is classified far to the right on the continuum at point 11 in Table 3–1. Just as with the policy of issuing franchises, this technique may worsen allocation if it is used improperly, that is, to enhance a monopoly position. For considerations of this book, general antitrust regulation and public licensing will not be considered as important public sector allocation techniques. Transfer-type operations will be considered important only because of their interrelationship to the distribution objective of public finance. In addition, because of the specialized and separate importance of money to a mature economic system, this technique of allocation will be excluded from the basic fiscal consideration of the book except as it relates to the stabilization, growth, and debt policies of the public sector.

INTERRELATIONSHIP BETWEEN WANTS, GOODS, TECHNIQUES, AND SECTORS

Table 3–2 provides a composite of major points established in Chapters 2 and 3 regarding the nature of public goods and collective

TABLE 3–2

INTERRELATIONSHIP BETWEEN ECONOMIC WANTS, GOODS,
ALLOCATION TECHNIQUES, AND ALLOCATING SECTORS

Government		*Market*
Pure public wants	Quasi-public (Quasi-private) wants	Pure private wants
Pure public goods	Quasi-public (Quasi-private) goods	Pure private goods
Tendency toward "direct" and "complete" public sector allocation techniques	Mixed allocation techniques containing traits of both sectors	Tendency toward private production of good. No appreciable public sector influence
Pure public goods are characterized by at least one of the following: 1. Indivisibility 2. Predominant external effects 3. Decreasing costs at optimal allocation point ($MC = AR$) 4. Marginal cost approaches zero at optimal allocation point 5. High risk due to very imperfect market knowledge 6. Unique resource scarcity or conditions	Quasi-public (Quasi-private) goods contain mixed characteristics of both pure public goods and pure private goods.	Pure private goods are characterized by at least one of the following: 1. Divisibility 2. Few, if any, external effects 3. Constant or increasing costs at optimal allocation point ($MC = AR$) 4. Marginal cost is above zero at optimal allocation point 5. Moderate or little risk due to reasonably good market knowledge 6. No unique resource scarcity or conditions
Economic criteria of allocation and technical efficiency prevail in determining allocating sector and allocation techniques.	Noneconomic criteria assume considerable importance in determining allocating sector(s) and allocation techniques	Economic criteria of allocation and technical efficiency prevail in determining allocating sector and allocation techniques

consumption and how this differs from private goods and private consumption. A logical interrelationship exists between the nature of pure public wants, the nature of the pure public goods which satisfy these wants, and the provision of these goods by the public sector using substantially direct and complete allocation techniques. While a pure public good need not contain all six characteristics shown in Table 3–2, at least one of the characteristics would need to be present for the good to be a pure public good. Just as there exists a logical interrelationship between public wants, goods, sector, and techniques, there also exists a logical interrelationship between pure private wants, pure private goods, and the provision of these goods by the private sector with minimal, if any, governmental influence on their allocation.

Finally, Table 3–2 demonstrates the extensive area of quasi-public (quasi-private) goods which contain significant characteristics of both pure public goods and pure private goods. Both economic considerations of efficiency (technical and allocation efficiency) and noneconomic considerations of a social, political, and cultural variety are weighed by society through the political process in determining the allocating sector or sectors, and the allocation techniques employed, to provide quasi-public (quasi-private) goods. A variety of allocation techniques containing traits of both governmental and market allocation are available for the provision of these "quasi-goods."

CONSUMPTION OF THE VARIOUS TYPES OF ECONOMIC GOODS IN THE AMERICAN ECONOMY

Though precise measurement of the consumption of pure public, pure private, quasi-public, and quasi-private goods in the American economy is impossible from existing data, useful approximations of the consumption of each type of economic good can still be provided. Table 3–3 presents estimates of such consumption for the years 1952 and 1963.[8] In order to be consistent with the available data, *pure public* goods are classified as those goods provided by government to which the "exclusion principle" cannot be applied and *quasi-public* goods are considered as governmental expenditures for other than pure public goods. Further-

TABLE 3–3

ECONOMIC GOODS BY TYPE OF GOOD, IN BOTH DOLLAR
AND PERCENTAGE TERMS, FOR 1952 AND 1963

Type of Good	Dollar Terms (Billions)		Percentage Terms		
	1952	1963	1952	1963	
Pure Private........	186.5	306.0	62.0	61.3	} Total
Quasi-Private........	33.2	69.8	11.0	14.0	} Private = 75.3% Sector
Pure Public..........	53.1	69.6	17.7	13.9	} Total
Quasi-Public.........	28.0	53.8	9.3	10.8	} Public = 24.7% Sector

SOURCE: An unpublished manuscript by Harold M. Stults, University of Arizona, entitled "Economic Wants: A Quantitative Classification."

[8] The present discussion is based upon an unpublished manuscript by Harold M. Stults, University of Arizona, entitled "Economic Wants: A Quantitative Classification." Department of Commerce data are used in this study. In particular, "government expenditures by type of function" and "personal consumption expenditures by type of product" are employed. Government transfer payments are excluded from the governmental expenditure data in order to emphasize exhaustive expenditures. Since consumption is the direct purpose of the study, business acquisition of capital goods is also excluded.

more, *quasi-private* goods are defined as those goods provided by the market which are judged to possess significant externalities while the remaining category, *pure private* goods, consists of those consumption items acquired from the private sector which do not have important external effects.

In 1963, some 75 percent of the economic goods consumed were produced by the private sector. Most of these market goods were pure private goods, though quasi-private goods such as utilities, communications, transportation, and medical care constituted more than one fifth of the private sector total. Total public sector output constituted nearly 25 percent of total economic goods. More than one half of the public sector total was in the form of pure public goods inclusive of such items as national defense, international affairs and finance, and general government.

The production of economic goods by the private sector constituted a higher percentage of total economic goods in 1963 than in 1952. This difference, however, may be explained by the abnormal impact of the Korean War on the pure public goods category of the public sector in 1952. The most pronounced trend indicated by the data is the relative expansion in the importance of quasi-goods, both quasi-private and quasi-public, during the period.

Chapter 4

WELFARE CRITERIA FOR
OPTIMAL ALLOCATION OF
SOCIETY'S RESOURCES

The social balance discussion of Chapter 1 considered the problem of optimal resource allocation between the public and private sectors of a mixed economy. This earlier discussion, however, dealt with the issue in a general manner. The present chapter, on the other hand, will be able to develop the concept of optimal intersectoral allocation in a much more comprehensive fashion now that an economic case has been established for the existence of a public sector (Chapter 2) and the nature of public and private wants and goods have been analyzed (Chapter 3). The analysis to follow will be complex since it derives from the complex area of knowledge known as "welfare economics."[1] The chapter will be concerned, in an overall sense, with both the allocation and distribution branches of public finance. Particular emphasis, however, will be placed on the former. Distribution will be discussed only when the interrelationship between allocation and distribution becomes relevant.

As discussed in Chapter 1, a society must decide the basic economic questions of resource allocation: What economic goods shall be produced? Which economic sector, public or private, shall produce the goods? Which levels and units of government within the public sector and which firms within the private sector shall produce the goods? The social balance issue is primarily concerned with the second of these questions, which can be rephrased to ask: What is a "satisfactory" overall division of output between the public and private sectors? A highly significant consideration arises regarding the ability to detect and to implement the society's preferences concerning resource allocation.

Two important approaches to the allocation efficiency goal derive from established public finance concepts of distribution. These normative distribution concepts are the *benefits-received* and *ability-to-pay* principles of fiscal decision making and taxation. The benefit norm has been refined into the "voluntary-exchange" theory of allocation by economists

[1] Welfare economics considers the performance of the economy in terms of its ability to achieve certain "desirable" goals. "Positive economics," on the other hand, studies the performance of the economy without interest in the "desirability" of the results in terms of goals.

such as Howard Bowen and Eric Lindahl. The ability-to-pay approach to allocation is presented in its most comprehensive form by the late British economist, A. C. Pigou. Both the benefit and ability-to-pay approaches may be traced back to Adam Smith, who provided earlier, less polished, formulations. Yet, certain theoretical and operational weaknesses appear even in the better developed approaches to allocation efficiency through the distribution norms. The issue of allocation is isolated more clearly, however, in the modern social welfare analysis of such economists as Paul Samuelson.

This chapter will examine the benefit and ability-to-pay approaches and will indicate their strengths and weaknesses. It will then present the Samuelson analysis. The impediments, both theoretical and operational, to the derivation of a "social welfare function" and to optimal intersectoral allocation will be assessed.[2] Subsequently, a discussion of the various methods of revealing community preferences for public goods, and the advantages and the drawbacks of these methods, will be presented.

THE BENEFIT (VOLUNTARY-EXCHANGE) APPROACH TO OPTIMAL ALLOCATION

The Bowen model of the voluntary-exchange theory will be used to demonstrate efficient allocation through the benefits-received method.[3] Figure 4–1 presents the Bowen model in graphical form. Essentially, the voluntary-exchange theory suggests that resources be allocated to the public sector in a manner analogous to that of the market and its pricing system. According to this theory, an individual should buy public goods through taxes as he elects to purchase private goods through market prices, with the standard consumer equilibrium principles of utility maximization by the individual applying. The individual pays taxes for public goods in accordance with the benefits received from them—thus equating the ratios of the marginal utilities to the tax prices of the public goods as well as equating the ratios between public goods and private goods. The consumer buys fire protection and national defense from the public sector through his own choice and according to the benefits received just as he buys automobiles, clothes, and food from the private sector. In other words, the doctrine of consumer sovereignty is applied to the provision of public sector goods.

The following assumptions apply at least implicitly to the Bowen model as illustrated in Figure 4–1:

[2] The social welfare function concept is essentially the same as the discussion of "social indifference curves" in Chapter 1. The analysis of the concept, however, is considerably more intense in this chapter.

[3] Howard R. Bowen, *Toward Social Economy* (New York: Rinehart, 1948), pp. 176–78.

1. The economic goods are produced under constant costs, as indicated by the supply curve SS. The cost conditions of production, however, need not be constant in order for the argument below to be valid. They are assumed constant only to simplify the presentation of the model.
2. The community consists of three consumers (taxpayers). This, again, is a simplifying assumption for the purpose of convenient presentation. The principles developed here would apply in a community of more than three consumers.
3. The three taxpayers are consuming only one type of public good, but the concept could be widened to include allocation decisions between different public goods as well as between public and private goods.
4. The public good is a pure public good, as defined in Chapter 2, and not a "quasi-public good."
5. It is assumed that true preferences will be revealed by the three consumer-taxpayers. They will not engage in interpersonal strategy whereby one may pay less than he would be willing to pay knowing his consumption of the indivisible pure public good will remain the same.

FIGURE 4-1

OPTIMAL ALLOCATION OF RESOURCES, BENEFITS-RECEIVED
(VOLUNTARY-EXCHANGE) APPROACH: BOWEN MODEL

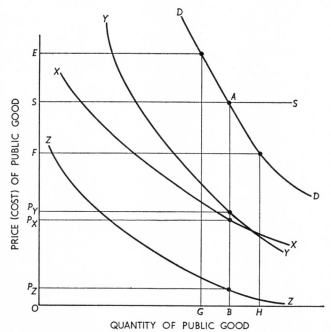

QUANTITY OF PUBLIC GOOD

SOURCE: Adapted from Howard R. Bowen, *Toward Social Economy,*
(New York: Rinehart, 1948) Figure 2, p. 177.

The consumers are designated X, Y, and Z. Together X, Y, and Z must be willing to pay a price which will cover the total cost of supplying the public good. All three consume the public good equally and there is no opportunity to exclude any of the three taxpayers from the benefits of the good on the basis of not paying for it as may be done with a private good. Thus, if one consumer pays more of the total cost of supplying the good, the other consumers may pay less.

In Figure 4–1, the quantity demanded and supplied of the public good is measured on the horizontal axis. On the vertical axis, the demand prices and supply costs of the public good are presented. Line XX shows the demand by Consumer X for the public good; line YY shows the demand by Consumer Y, and line ZZ demonstrates the demand by Consumer Z. These lines indicate the prices that X, Y, and Z would be willing to pay for various quantities of the pure public good. Line DD represents the *vertical* summation of lines XX, YY, and ZZ which constitutes the total demand for the public good by the three consumers of the community. The summation is vertical because the pure public good must be "consumed equally" by all three consumers. In other words, the exclusion principle cannot be applied to the good since it is a pure public good. This contrasts with private goods where individuals may acquire more or less of a good depending upon their total monetary outlay for it. Line SS represents the supply cost of providing additional units of the good.

The equilibrium output of the public good is quantity OB which is determined at point A by the intersection of the aggregate demand line DD and the aggregate supply line SS. Output is thus carried to the point where the demand price per unit equals the supply cost per unit of the public good. At a quantity greater than OB, for example at quantity OH, supply cost per unit exceeds demand price per unit by the amount SF and output would be reduced toward OB. At a quantity less than OB, for example at quantity OG, demand price per unit exceeds supply cost per unit by the amount ES, and total output would be increased toward the optimal allocation point OB. At output OB, taxpayer X will pay a price per unit OP_x, taxpayer Y will pay a price per unit OP_y, and taxpayer Z will pay OP_z. Their combined price payments will equal cost per unit OS.

One weakness in the voluntary-exchange theory is found in the assumption (number five above) that true preferences will be revealed. Such revelation is impossible when the goods are purely public (see Chapter 2). The exclusion principle cannot be applied. Consumer X will consume amounts of a purely public good equal to the amounts consumed by Consumers Y and Z regardless of his individual payments for the good. Unless *compulsion* exists to require Consumer X to pay, he will benefit by use of strategy to avoid or minimize payment. The pure public good is incapable of division to particular individuals and will not be paid for voluntarily by individual consumers.

Another weakness in the voluntary-exchange theory is its conflict with democratic ideals. For example, if public goods are to be allocated in a manner perfectly analogous to the market allocation of private goods, then individuals with greater income and wealth, and consequently greater purchasing power, should have greater voting influence in the political process than those of lesser means. This is true, of course, in the market where demand is made "effective" by the amount of purchasing power available to the consumer for expenditure. Prevailing democratic ideals, however, suggest an equal vote for all in the political process, regardless of income and wealth. Indeed, the determination of a pattern of income, wealth, and voting distribution is a highly relevant consideration for optimal and actual intersectoral resource allocation. Yet, as observed in Chapter 2, positive economics cannot determine an optimal state of distribution. Instead, noneconomic value judgments must render this important decision.

A third weakness of the voluntary-exchange theory is that it is stated in terms of partial rather than general equilibrium conditions. Only public goods are directly discussed, thus underemphasizing the important social balance division *between* public and private goods. Later in this chapter, the general equilibrium approach to allocation efficiency, inclusive of both public and private goods, will be represented in the models of Pigou and Samuelson.

THE ABILITY-TO-PAY APPROACH TO OPTIMAL ALLOCATION

The ability-to-pay principle is a second distribution concept which sheds light upon society's problem of efficient intersectoral resource allocation. Unfortunately, this principle has often been applied in an asymmetrical rather than in a symmetrical (balanced) manner. The asymmetrical or disproportionate application of the ability-to-pay approach emphasizes only the tax side of the budgetary process. Justice or equity in the distribution of tax burdens, and the related welfare approach of minimizing both total community sacrifice (disutility) and individual taxpayer sacrifice in the payment of taxes, have dominated the ability-to-pay approach to distribution and allocation. Since the major goals of public finance (allocation, distribution, stabilization, and economic growth) may be affected as much by the expenditure side of the budgetary process as by the tax side, an approach which considers only the latter is necessarily incomplete.

The lifesaver of the ability-to-pay approach was A. C. Pigou, who provided a comprehensive ability-to-pay concept encompassing both the tax and spending sides of the government budget. Pigou applied the principles of marginalism to public finance theory. He included the *tax side* of the fiscal process by means of the disutility or sacrifice incurred in paying taxes. This represents, of course, an opportunity cost in the form of the private sector goods which might have been purchased with the money had the taxes not been paid. The *expenditure side* of the budget is considered by means of the utility or benefits received from the consumption of public sector goods. Hence, the Pigovian version of the ability-to-pay approach is symmetrical, as is the benefit (voluntary-exchange) approach, in that both the tax and expenditure sides of the budget are considered and are related to each other. Pigou's version of ability to pay is superior, however, to the voluntary-exchange version of the benefit principle since it works under general equilibrium conditions by including both public and private goods. The voluntary-exchange theory, by contrast, suffers from the incompleteness of partial equilibrium analysis since it directly considers only the demand and supply of a single public good and excludes the private sector from direct reference.

Figures 4–2a and 4–2b represent one method of displaying Pigou's comprehensive ability-to-pay approach, while Figure 4–3 represents a second method of displaying the same concept. Pigou's approach, which is sometimes denoted as the "marginal utility principle of social balance," may be stated alternately as (1) or (2) below:

1. An optimal intersectoral allocation equilibrium is attained when the last unit of resource expenditure (usage) would yield equal marginal utility if used in either the public sector or the private sector. At this point, total societal utility is maximized.
2. An optimal intersectoral allocation equilibrium is attained when public sector expenditures are made up to the point at which the utility to the people resulting from the last unit of public sector expenditure equals the utility which the people forego in giving the tax revenue to the government instead of spending it in the market.

Each of the above statements requires that the marginal utilities of the various goods *within* the public sector and the marginal utilities of the various goods *within* the private sector be equal. They require, moreover, the equality of marginal utilities *between* the two sectors. Optimality thus requires the right goods to be allocated by the right sectors, in accordance with consumer preferences. Furthermore, it is significant to observe that the Pigovian ability-to-pay concept equates only *aggregate* community utilities and disutilities while the voluntary-exchange theory attempts a complete approximation of market conditions by equating the *individual* benefits and tax expenditures for public goods on a *quid pro quo* basis.

In Figure 4–2a, the marginal utility of private goods is measured on the vertical axis. On the horizontal axis, quantity may be interpreted to mean *either* product output by the private sector *or* the resource usage required to provide this product output. In Figure 4–2b, the marginal utility of public goods is measured on the vertical axis and quantity, as interpreted in Figure 4–2, is measured for the public sector on the horizontal axis.

Comparing Figures 4–2a and 4–2b, assume that resource allocation in the private sector is at output OX, providing marginal utility OA, and resource allocation in the public sector is at output OX^1, providing marginal utility OA^1. Since marginal utility OA in the private sector exceeds marginal utility OA^1 in the public sector, *net* additions may be made to total utility in the society by means of reallocation toward more private sector goods and fewer public sector goods. As private sector output increases, quantity or output increases from OX toward OZ while marginal utility, due to the law of diminishing marginal utility, declines

FIGURE 4–2

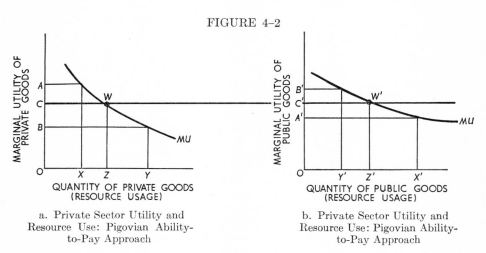

a. Private Sector Utility and
Resource Use: Pigovian Ability-
to-Pay Approach

b. Private Sector Utility and
Resource Use: Pigovian Ability-
to-Pay Approach

from OA toward OC. In the meantime, with fewer resources being allocated to government, output of public sector goods declines from OX^1 toward OZ^1 and marginal utility increases from OA^1 toward OC^1. Total utility (satisfaction) in the community thus increases as resources are reallocated toward greater private sector activity.

Again comparing Figures 4–2a and 4–2b, assume resource allocation in the private sector is at output OY, providing marginal utility OB, and resource allocation in the public sector is at output OY^1, providing marginal utility OB^1. Since marginal utility OB in the private sector is less than marginal utility OB^1 in the public sector, *net* additions may be made to total utility in the society by means of reallocation toward more public sector goods and fewer private sector goods. As public sector output increases, quantity expands from OY^1 toward OZ^1 while marginal utility, due to the law of diminishing marginal utility, declines from OB^1 toward OC^1. Meanwhile, with fewer resources being allocated to the private sector, output of private sector products declines from OY toward OZ

and marginal utility increases from *OB* toward *OC*. Total utility in the community thus increases as reallocation occurs toward more public sector goods.

As demonstrated in the above discussion, optimal allocation is at output *OZ* for the private sector, and at output OZ^1 for the public sector. At this point, total utility for the community is maximized because the intersectoral marginal utilities *OC* and OC^1 are equal. Any reallocation away from this point where marginal private utility (*MPU*) equals marginal social utility (*MSU*) will diminish total societal utility.

FIGURE 4–3

PIGOVIAN ABILITY-TO-PAY APPROACH TO RESOURCE ALLOCATION

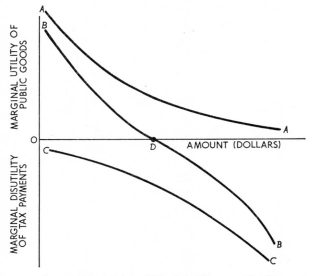

SOURCE: Adapted from Richard A. Musgrave, *The Theory of Public Finance* (New York: McGraw-Hill, 1959), Figure 5-4, p. 114.

An alternate graphical demonstration of Pigou's approach to optimal allocation through ability to pay is provided in Figure 4–3. The conceptual framework is identical to that provided in Figures 4–2a and 4–2b, only the graphical style is different.[4] Once again, resources are (1) to be allocated among different public sector goods and among different private sector goods so as to equate the marginal utilities of each type of good within each sector, and (2) resources should be allocated to the public sector up to the point of equality of the marginal utilities of both the private and public sectors (*MPU* = *MSU*).

[4] The graphical approach used in Figure 4–3 was developed by Richard A. Musgrave. See Musgrave's *The Theory of Public Finance* (New York: McGraw-Hill Book Co., Inc., 1959), p. 114.

In Figure 4–3, the marginal utility and disutility derived from resource allocation to the public sector is measured vertically while budget size in dollars is measured on the horizontal axis. The marginal utility of public sector output, allocated optimally between different public goods, is displayed by line *AA*. The disutility of tax payments, arranged according to ability to pay and progressive taxation so as to minimize total sacrifice, is displayed by line *CC*. Line *BB* shows net marginal utility and disutility at different budget sizes. As long as the marginal utility of resources allocated to the public sector exceeds the marginal disutility of the tax payments, total societal utility is increased through governmental production. This is true of the range of allocation on the horizontal axis indicated by *OD*. To the right of *OD*, net benefits become negative (losses) as marginal disutility exceeds marginal utility. To the left of point *OD*, net benefits are positive as marginal utility exceeds marginal disutility. At point *OD*, net benefits are zero as marginal utility equals marginal disutility. Here total societal utility is maximized as marginal private utility equals marginal social utility.

The ability-to-pay approach, in a strict sense, requires full employment of resources in order to be valid. The disutility of a tax dollar, as caused by the opportunity costs of private goods foregone, may not exist in an aggregate sense, for example, when there are unemployed resources which can be used to maintain societal production of private goods at the same level while the incremental public goods are provided from previously unemployed resources. In other words, if the supply of unused resources is sufficient, total utility to the society may be increased by the incremental public goods, without a reduction in the utility derived from private goods, because no cutback need occur in the society's private goods production. In addition, with less than full employment the output of the private sector can also be increased, with a consequent increase in total societal utility.

Certain strengths and weaknesses may be enumerated regarding the ability-to-pay approach to optimal resource allocation. The discussion will be based upon this approach in its most refined and comprehensive fashion, namely, the approach provided by Pigou and analyzed above. The asymmetrical ability-to-pay approach, of course, was previously rejected because it emphasizes only the tax side of the budget. The Pigovian approach, as noted earlier, possesses the advantage of being symmetrical in that it encompasses both the taxation and expenditure sides of the budgetary process. In addition to this advantage, it also possesses the quality of being a general equilibrium approach instead of concentrating only upon the allocation of resources to the public sector, which would cause it to ignore the important social balance issue of an optimal allocation of resources *between* the public and private sectors.

Despite its merits, several weaknesses reduce the overall quality of the approach. For example, no effective means exists whereby utility and disutility can be quantified (measured). Hence, an optimal point of allocation cannot be precisely detected. Though *cardinal* measurements are impossible, an *ordinal* approach can shed some light upon the ability to reveal community preferences and their implied utilities.[5] This will be discussed further below.

A related objection arises in the form of the inability to make interpersonal comparisons of utility. The ability-to-pay concept, for example, implies that the ability to make tax payments increases more than proportionately with increases in income because the marginal utility of income declines as income becomes greater. Hence, the last (marginal) dollar of income to a man with a $40,000 yearly income, it is suggested, provides lower marginal utility than the last dollar of income to the $5,000 yearly income individual, other considerations, such as family size, being equal between the two individuals. Many economists, especially those associated with the new welfare economics, refuse to accept interpersonal comparisons of utility and attack Pigou's implicit assumption that all individuals are equal.

Are all individuals equal? Might not the wealthy man enjoy the prestige of the marginal dollar spent toward another Rolls Royce as much as the poor man might enjoy the marginal dollar spent for food? The new welfare economics would answer yes to the question and in so doing would reject the ability-to-pay approach and its assumption that all individuals react equally to the same economic stimuli. The answer, unfortunately, cannot be tested by cardinal measurement because of the inability to quantify utility. It does seem, however, that interpersonal comparisons of utility should *not* be totally rejected. In reality, there must be such a thing as pleasure or utility from the receipt and use of income. Interdisciplinary observations in psychology and sociology indicate that the individuals of a given community tend to possess certain similarities of behavior. These behavioral similarities may well include diminishing "income utility" as income increases.

The problem of interpersonal comparisons of utility requires a value judgment regarding the proper distribution of utilities and disutilities among individual consumers. The equating of marginal disutility to marginal utility for the society as a whole, rather than on an individual *quid pro quo* basis, means that some individuals may derive either more or less marginal utility than the marginal disutility which they incur. In other words, the question becomes: How should the marginal utilities and disutilities be distributed among the population? The distribution of income, wealth, and political voting power will bear upon this answer.

---

[5] Cardinal measurement refers to absolute counting, while ordinal measurement deals with the order or ranking in which items appear.

Value judgments rather than positive economic criteria must be called upon to solve the distribution issue. This will be discussed below.

SAMUELSON'S MODEL OF OPTIMAL ALLOCATION

Samuelson provides a more refined and comprehensive approach to allocation efficiency than either the voluntary-exchange theory or the Pigovian ability-to-pay approach.[6] Samuelson's model, among its other advantages, is designed to reflect the weaknesses in the other two approaches involving the inability to apply the exclusion principle in the case of pure public goods. In addition, it helps to emphasize the importance of the distribution value judgment which is prerequisite to optimal allocation.

Samuelson presents an extreme or polar case in his argument for public sector resource allocation. This extreme position offsets the extreme case for private goods represented by the Walrasian general equilibrium case of perfect competition. Thus, it constitutes the other terminal point of the public goods–private goods range or spectrum (see Chapter 2). The polar case for public goods may be cloaked in either an authoritarian or a democratic political environment. The former "group mind" approach is virtually devoid of economic implications and involves political value judgments about an authoritarian role for government which cannot be challenged in economic terms. The latter approach is consistent with "individualism," which is, of course, the keynote of democratic political economies such as those existing in Western Europe and North America.

The individualistic approach may be further divided into (1) those who refuse to accept interpersonal comparisons of utility and (2) those who accept such comparisons. If interpersonal comparisons cannot be made, then the social welfare of the community is merely a heterogeneous collection of individual welfares. This analysis leads to the conditions of *Pareto optimality* whereby community welfare is said to increase only if one person gains without another person losing from an allocation readjustment. This is a restrictive approach since no judgment about community welfare can be made when one person loses as another gains. Thus, Pareto optimum conditions per se emphasize the fundamental problem of scarcity in economics and the consequent need to divide output in some manner among the consumers of the society. The second individualism group accepts interpersonal comparisons of utility in the

---

[6] See Paul A. Samuelson, "The Pure Theory of Public Expenditure," *Review of Economics and Statistics* (November, 1954), pp. 387–89; "Diagrammatic Exposition of a Theory of Public Expenditure," *Review of Economics and Statistics* (November, 1955), pp. 350–56, and "Aspects of Public Expenditure Theories," *Review of Economics and Statistics* (November, 1958), pp. 332–38.

sense that it accepts the use of ethical or value judgments regarding the aggregation of individual welfares to acquire community welfare. The Samuelson model essentially follows the individualistic approach in the latter form, that is, the acceptance of interpersonal comparisons of utility based on *value judgments*, though it applies these ethical judgments to a Pareto optimum norm.

A pure private good like food is divisible among consumers. Thus, if W equals the total amount of a private good, and the community has two consumers A and B, and if W_a and W_b are the quantities of the private good consumed by A and B respectively, then W must equal the summation of W_a and W_b ($W = W_a + W_b$). If Consumer A uses more of W, Consumer B must use less under conditions of full resource employment.

To the contrary, a pure public good like national defense is not divisible among consumers. Instead, it is consumed equally by all. Thus, let Z reflect the total quantity of the public good and let Z_a and Z_b refer to Consumer A's and Consumer B's consumption of the good. Since the consumption of the total cannot be divided between A and B, the relevant equations are: ($Z = Z_a$) and ($Z = Z_b$), respectively. There is no way whereby Consumer A can cause Consumer B to consume less, if he consumes more, as is the case for the pure private good above. The exclusion principle does *not* apply and A and B each individually consume the total quantity of the pure public good.

In Figures 4–4a, 4–4b, and 4–4c, private goods are measured on the vertical axis and public goods are measured on the horizontal axis. The quantity of public goods on each graph is OZ. In Figure 4–4a, the relative preference pattern of Consumer A between private and public goods is shown along the indifference curves Ia^1, Ia^2, and Ia^3. In Figure 4–4b, the relative preference pattern of Consumer B between private and public goods is indicated by indifference curves Ib^1, Ib^2, and Ib^3. Figure 4–4c demonstrates resource-possibility curve RS (see Chapter 1), which may be called variously a transformation curve or a production-possibility curve. In other words, it shows the various combinations of private and public goods that can be produced with the society's limited productive resources. The curve is concave to the origin (convex from above) in order to reflect the diminishing returns principle of increasing production costs.

In Figures 4–4a, 4–4b, and 4–4c, public goods must possess the same horizontal scale value on each graph because an increase in the total quantity of public goods (like a move to the right of Z on Figure 4–4c) would increase the quantities available to Consumers A and B (Figures 4–4a and 4–4b) by amounts equal to the total increase. However, since this is not true for private goods, which are not consumed equally, the vertical axis in Figure 4–4c must be extended to include the summation of private good consumption by Consumers A and B.

The preceding discussion has indicated the resource constraint imposed on optimal allocation by the resource-possibility curve (Figure 4–4c). The discussion, in addition, has indicated the individual preferences between private and public goods for the two consumers in the society (Figures 4–4a and 4–4b). What then is the optimal allocation point between public and private goods for the society? In other words, what is the allocation division which will maximize satisfaction according to the preferences of the two individuals of this community?

Assuming a social welfare norm (through a value judgment) whereby social welfare is increased if one individual moves to a higher indifference curve without another man's satisfaction level being moved to a lower indifference curve (Pareto optimum), allocation efficiency points can be determined in Figures 4–4a, 4–4b, and 4–4c.[7] In order to

FIGURE 4–4

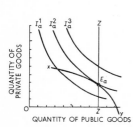 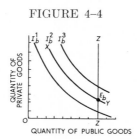 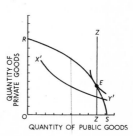

a. Consumer A's indifference schedule between private and public goods.

b. Consumer B's indifference schedule between private and public goods.

c. Resource-possibility (transformation) schedule for the society.

SOURCE: Adapted from Paul A. Samuelson, "Diagrammatic Exposition of a Theory of Public Expenditure," *Review of Economics and Statistics* (November, 1955), Charts 1, 2, and 3, p. 351.

apply this norm, assume that one consumer is at a *specified* level of indifference so that his satisfaction level will not be changed. The problem, then, of optimal allocation becomes one of moving the second consumer of this two-consumer community to his highest possible indifference curve (satisfaction level).

In Figure 4–4b, set Consumer B on the *specified* indifference curve I_b^2, which will now be designated XY. Noting the constraint of the resource-possibility line RS in Figure 4–4c, what is the highest level of satisfaction (the highest indifference curve) that Consumer A can attain? The answer is shown by tangency point E_a in Figure 4–4a. The corresponding equilibrium points on the other graphs are E_b in Figure 4–4b and E in Figure 4–4c.

This equilibrium is derived by placing indifference curve XY from Figure 4–4b on Figure 4–4c and designating it X^1Y^1. Then, subtract X^1Y^1

---

[7] As indicated above, the Pareto optimum criterion of welfare holds that any change which makes some people better off (in their own estimation) while making no one else worse off is an *improvement*.

vertically from resource-possibility line RS, the residual being the quantities of public goods and private goods which are available to Consumer A. This amount may be placed on Figure 4–4a and designated *xy*. Consumer A thus reaches his highest satisfaction level at tangency point E_a where *xy* touches the highest attainable indifference curve I_a^2, *xy* providing the constraint of resource scarcity and I_a^2 reflecting the relative preferences of the consumer between public and private goods. This Pareto optimum point means that there is no movement away from this point, in terms of a reallocation of resources, that would not make one of the consumers worse off than before in terms of satisfaction.

FIGURE 4–5

OPTIMAL SOCIETAL ALLOCATION AS DETERMINED BY TANGENCY OF THE SOCIAL WELFARE FUNCTION AND THE UTILITY FUNCTION

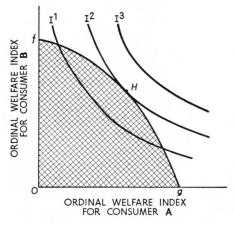

SOURCE: Adapted from Paul A. Samuelson, "Diagrammatic Exposition of a Theory of Public Expenditure," *Review of Economics and Statistics* (November, 1955), Chart 4, p. 352.

Because an optimal state of distribution must be dependent upon a societal value judgment, an infinite number of such Pareto optimum points exists. That is, for every infinite specified indifference curve where Consumer B might rest, a different optimal tangency point of satisfaction would occur for Consumer A. In other words, E_a in Figure 4–4a would not be the optimal allocation point if Consumer B were consuming along an indifference curve other than XY (I_b^2) in Figure 4–4b. These infinite Pareto optimum points cannot be compared without a normative social welfare function, arrived at through ethical judgments, which can render interpersonal comparisons of utility and thus establish a proper state of distribution.

Figure 4–5, in ordinal measurement terms, reflects the utility possibilities for Consumers A and B who comprise the total consumption demand of the society. The utility frontier of Pareto optimum points is indicated by line *fg.* Any point within (to the southwest) of this line, as designated by the shaded area, represents a less than Pareto optimum point. The Pareto optimum line slopes to the southeast to reflect the conflicting consumption interests between Consumers A and B. This inverse relationship means, of course, that a reorganization of budget policy would improve one consumer's position by making the other consumer's position worse. Since society cannot be maximizing its satisfaction from any of the non-Pareto optimum points within the frontier, it is obvious that any movement from within the frontier to the frontier line *fg* will be a welfare improvement for the community.

However, a critical question arises: Where along the utility frontier in Figure 4–5 is the point of optimal allocation for the society? The answer: At point *H* where the utility frontier *fg* is tangent to the highest attainable social indifference curve I^2. Lines I^1, I^2, and I^3 reflect the various combinations of preferences for the members of the society, A and B. This entire schedule may be designated as the social welfare function. It is composed of various possible social indifference curves. The social welfare function, however, cannot reveal a true ordering of preferences *through economic analysis.*

The true ordering of social preferences becomes a *reality* only when the state of ex ante distribution is established, causing one social indifference curve to become the effective demand of the society for private and public goods.[8] Importantly, it is the voting power of income and wealth distribution which determines effective demand in the market sector, and political voting power which determines the effective demand for public goods. The actual resource allocation which follows from this effective demand for public and private goods leads to the ultimate state of real income and consumption distribution, in a welfare or living standard sense, among the consumers of the society. This latter distribution concept may be referred to as ex post distribution. Thus, in summary, ex ante distribution determines the relevant social indifference curve which becomes tangent to the utility frontier with the resulting *actual* allocation of economic output between public and private goods and ex post distribution of these goods among the consumers of the society. In a real sense, *actual* allocation and ex post distribution thus become synonymous concepts.

Bergson and others have stressed the role of such value judgments in the determination of the social welfare function and the prevailing

---

[8] The student may wish to refer to the social balance discussion of Chapter 1 at this point, especially the description of Figure 1–2.

social indifference curve.[9] These ethical judgments may be those of an economist, legislature, or some other person or group in the society. Yet, some composite societal value judgment is effective at any one time. The distinction between *positive* and *welfare* economics is relevant to the present discussion. Positive economics concentrates upon the microeconomic and macroeconomic principles which operate toward the attainment of goals in an economy. It is *not* concerned with the desirability of the goals. On the other hand, welfare economics is normative in the sense that it establishes *goals*—and judges their desirability—mostly from noneconomic value judgments. The Bergson social welfare function represents an appreciation of the distinction between positive and welfare economics, and the fact that a social welfare function must be specified through normative decisions of welfare economics before the attainment of these goals can be evaluated through the established principles of positive economics.

The inability to apply the exclusion principle to *pure public goods* complicates the revelation of the true preferences which have been made effective by the ex ante state of distribution. This is to be contrasted with conditions as they would exist in a society of competitive markets (Walrasian general equilibrium) in which the market would accurately reveal the demands for *divisible private goods* and "strategy" between buyers would be insignificant. In other words, consumers would not be motivated to outmaneuver each other in financing an economic good because pure private goods are *not* consumed equally by all. In the case of public goods, the introduction of large numbers of consumers complicates allocation efficiency by increasing the potential use of strategy. The greater the number of consumers of a public good, the easier it is to consume the good equally with others and avoid or reduce one's payments for it. *Compulsion* thus becomes a necessary condition in the financing of pure public goods.

In addition to the problems involved in revealing true preferences for pure public goods (Musgrave's "social wants"), public finance theory also faces the problem of finding a rational procedure whereby the optimal allocation of quasi-public goods (Musgrave's "merit wants") may be determined. Quasi-public (quasi-private) goods are often allocated by the market, but at times not in sufficient quantities, considering their highly desirable nature, their often present conditions of decreasing production costs, or their possession of other traits of publicness. In this case, government production of the good, or governmental subsidization of private production, may be required. Moreover, in the case of overallocation of undesirable goods, or in the case of a uniquely scarce good or

---

[9] A. Bergson, "A Reformulation of Certain Aspects of Welfare Economics," *Quarterly Journal of Economics* (February, 1938), pp. 310–34.

resource, a tax penalty or price may be required to reduce quantities and thus improve allocation.

WICKSELL'S APPROACH TO REVEALING SOCIAL PREFERENCES—"QUALIFIED MAJORITY" VOTING

The political process and voting is extremely important to the attainment of an optimal societal allocation of resources. If the ex ante distribution value judgment of the society states a preference for political voting influence of the *democratic* variety, the institutional problem involved in revealing true preferences in this manner may be considerable. In other words, true preferences based on an "equal vote for all" individualistic democratic ideal are *not* revealed and implemented by simple majority voting. The Swedish economist Knut Wicksell was alert to the importance of this fact.[10] The distribution of voting power will help determine the social welfare function which, in turn, allows the selection among the infinite Pareto optimum points along the utility frontier. There are two dimensions to the importance of voting: (1) the distribution of voting power in the political process helps to determine the effective social indifference curve which becomes tangent to the production possibility curve and (2) good voting techniques help to reveal these true (effective) preferences. Wicksell's qualified majority voting approach refers primarily to the latter dimension of voting.

Wicksell favored the benefit approach to allocation efficiency. This approach is consistent with his preference for a democratic political system and its basic premise of individualism. He believed that preferences could be revealed best through qualified majority voting, which is known also as "relative unanimity." Wicksell argued that fiscal decisions on taxing and spending should be acceptable only if approved by *more than* a "simple majority" of 51 percent of the democratically elected representatives of the people. Wicksell did *not* provide a specific qualified majority percentage to be applicable at all times. Instead, he generally advocated that the percentage should be as close to 100 percent as is practically possible. Thus, Wicksell ideally favored complete unanimity whereby no fiscal decision of a tax or expenditure nature could be implemented into the budget unless there was unanimous assent from the members of the legislature. The inability to apply this in practice, and the fact that it would lead to an essentially inactive budgetary policy, led Wicksell reluctantly to endorse qualified majority voting. It was reasoned that a majority percentage greater than 51 percent—for example, two-thirds, three-fourths, or seven-eighths—approximates market deci-

[10] Carl G. Uhr, *Economic Doctrines of Knut Wicksell* (Berkeley: University of California Press, 1960), pp. 164–90.

sion making more closely and protects individualism to a greater extent than does the simple 51 percent majority.

Wicksell believed, moreover, that expenditure and tax decisions should be made *simultaneously* by the legislature. This means, of course, a symmetrical tie-in between spending and tax decisions. Marginal benefit should be related to marginal cost and qualified majority voting then applied to the decision. This is similar in principle to the development of cost-benefit analysis as applied to business and government decision making through the scientific approach of "operations research" in modern society.[11]

An argument against the Wicksellian approach is that making a budgetary decision so difficult to approve works against the will of the majority and in favor of the minority. Thus, although the simple majority rule is far from a perfect approximation of market decision making, it is still a rule whereby considerable fiscal activity does take place and whereby more people are satisfied than dissatisfied with any one fiscal decision. Perhaps, then, the replacement of simple majority voting by qualified majority voting would be undesirable because of the essentially "inactive" fiscal system which it would tend to create.

REVEALING SOCIAL PREFERENCES THROUGH VOTING— ARROW'S "IMPOSSIBILITY THEOREM"

Kenneth Arrow has provided a lucid analysis of the problems involved in making community or social decisions consistent with individual preferences when a majority voting technique is used.[12] Arrow asserts that the following conditions must be met if collective decisions are to be rational in revealing the true individual preferences which constitute the effective social welfare function:

1. Social choices must be transitive (consistent), that is, if Choice X is preferred to Choice Y, and if Choice Y is preferred to Choice Z, then Choice Z cannot be preferred to Choice X in the social welfare function. A unique social ordering must exist regardless of the manner in which individuals in the community order their alternative choices.

[11] See Charles J. Hitch and Roland N. McKean, *The Economics of Defense in the Nuclear Age* (Cambridge, Mass.: Harvard University Press, 1960); J. V. Krutilla and Otto Eckstein, *Multiple Purpose River Development* (Baltimore: Johns Hopkins Press, 1958); Roland N. McKean, *Efficiency in Government Through Systems Analysis* (New York: Wiley, 1958); and other sources for consideration of operations research and cost-benefit analysis.

[12] Kenneth Arrow, *Social Choice and Individual Values* (New York: Wiley, 1951). Critical evaluations of the Arrow thesis include: Clifford Hildreth, "Alternative Conditions for Social Orderings," *Econometrica* (January, 1953), pp. 81–94 and Leo A. Goodman and Harry Markowitz, "Social Welfare Functions Based on Individual Rankings," *American Journal of Sociology* (November, 1952), pp. 257–62.

2. The social welfare function must be nonperverse in the sense that an alternative which would have been chosen otherwise by the community must not be rejected because some individuals have changed the relative rankings of the other alternatives.

3. The rankings of the choices in the social welfare function between two alternatives must not be dependent on the ranking by individuals of other alternatives which are irrelevant to the choice between the two alternatives.

4. Social choices must not be dictatorial, that is, they must not be based solely on the preferences of one individual imposed either from within or without the community. The individuals of the community must be able to vote freely among all alternatives.

Table 4–1 displays a situation where majority voting violates Arrow's set of minimum conditions necessary for consumer sovereignty to be maintained in collective democratic decision making. Specifically, condition number one is violated in the table since a majority prefer Policy X to Y, Y to Z, and Z to X. The result is intransitive (inconsistent).

TABLE 4–1

INTRANSITIVITY IN MAJORITY VOTING
ALTERNATIVE INDIVIDUAL POLICIES
X, Y, AND Z

	Alternative	Alternative	Alternative
Individual A prefers..............X to	Y to	Z
Individual B prefers..............Y to	Z to	X
Individual C prefers..............Z to	X to	Y

Summary: Individuals A and C prefer Policy X to Y.
Individuals A and B prefer Policy Y to Z.
Individuals B and C prefer Policy Z to X.

A majority (2 of 3 individuals in this case) prefer Policy X to Y, Y to Z, and Z to X. The result is intransitive (inconsistent).

Arrow thus maintains that it is often impossible to make community or social decisions consistent with individual preferences when a majority voting technique is used to select between three or more alternatives.

Though Arrow's requirements for rational collective decision making through majority voting may be somewhat rigorous, his analysis still points out some basic problems present in collective decision making of the democratic-individualistic type. One requirement which seems highly rigorous is the condition that society, in selecting between two choices, must consider all other choices as irrelevant. (Requirement number three above.) For example, half of the community might prefer improved highways and streets to solve an urban area's traffic congestion while the other half may prefer a government-subsidized or -operated mass transportation system to solve the problem. Assume the cost to be equal for both traffic congestion solutions. If those who prefer the highway solution rank traffic congestion as a much lower priority program among the various program alternatives than those who prefer the mass transportation system, the program selected obviously should be the mass transportation system. Requirement three above, however, stipulates that a consideration of these other alternatives or priorities is irrelevant.

The Arrow approach thus ignores the ranking and intensity of desires among alternative choices by requiring that only the rankings of the alternatives be considered. It is difficult for a system of social choice which ignores these other considerations to reveal true community preferences. In addition, the order in which votes are taken may influence the nature of the social welfare function. This would happen, for example, if the ordering of decisions between alternative choices allowed an interplay of strategy so that various voters could understate their true preferences for public goods.

REVEALING SOCIAL PREFERENCES THROUGH "PLURALITY VOTING"

Qualified majority voting, as an improvement over simple majority voting in revealing community preferences, was discussed above in relationship to the concepts of Knut Wicksell. Another alternative to simple majority voting in the derivation of the social welfare function is plurality voting. This allows each voter to rank all relevant alternative choices by aggregating for each alternative the rankings assigned to it by each voter in the community. The alternative selected would be that with the

TABLE 4–2

PLURALITY VOTING AND THE REVELATION
OF COMMUNITY PREFERENCES

	Policy A points	Policy B points	Policy C points
Voter Number One ranks...............3	2	1
Voter Number Two ranks...............2	3	1
Voter Number Three ranks.............2	1	3
Total Score..........................7 points	6 points	5 points

Rank 1 = 3 points
Rank 2 = 2 points
Rank 3 = 1 point

highest total score based on the rankings, provided we assume that each voter gains an equal increment of utility by moving up one rank between any two ranks in his rating scale, and that the utility increments are equal between the voters. This approach would help offset the rigorous requirements of the third Arrow assumption and improve the revelation of true community preferences.

Suppose in Table 4–2, for example, that the voters of a community are selecting between choices A, B, and C. Assume further that the community has only three voters. If Voter Number One ranks his preferences as A, B, and C in order, let A be scored as three points, B as two points, and C as one point, with the points being scored on the basis of ranking. Similarly, if Voter Number Two ranks his preferences as B, A, and C in order, B receives three points, A two points and C, once again, one point. If Voter Number Three ranks the alternatives as C, A, and B, in order, C receives three points, A two points, and B one point. Aggregating the results, alternative A receives the highest total points and, consequently, is the alternative policy which should be selected. The total points are: A = seven points; B = six points and C = five points, as displayed in Table 4–2. This improved technique, which stresses the rankings of all alternatives, however, still does not preclude possible intransitive results (condition number one above).

REVEALING SOCIAL PREFERENCES THROUGH "POINT VOTING"

Another means of detecting community preferences is the adoption of a point method of voting. This method emphasizes the intensity of desires as contrasted with the emphasis on rankings in plurality voting. Both techniques, however, appear to improve the revelation of true preferences as compared to simple majority voting. Assume in Table 4–3 that Voters One, Two, and Three of the community are each given 50

TABLE 4–3

POINT VOTING AND THE REVELATION OF COMMUNITY PREFERENCES

Division of 50 points by	for	Policy A	Policy B	Policy C
Voter Number One........................		40	5	5
Voter Number Two......................		5	25	20
Voter Number Three.....................		20	20	10
Total Score............................		65	50	35

points whereby they can specify their relative intensities of desire among three alternative policies on any divisional basis they prefer. Moreover, suppose the following: Voter Number One gives 40 points to alternative A and 5 points each to alternatives B and C; Voter Number Two gives 25 points to alternative B, 20 points to alternative C, and 5 points to alternative A; Voter Number Three gives 20 points to alternative A, 20 points to alternative B, and 10 points to alternative C. Alternative A is thus selected and the margin of preference for it is obvious. The total points, as provided in Table 4–3, are A = 65 points; B = 50 points; and C = 35 points. Yet, even here intransitivity, in the sense of Arrow's first rationality requirement, could result.

Consumer sovereignty is approximated more closely in point voting than it is in plurality voting and, of course, much more closely than in majority voting. Why, then, should not the political process be structured so as to increase the use of point voting, or at least plurality voting, and to decrease the use of majority voting? Aside from the institutional and administrative problems of change, the significant problem of *strategy* must be considered. Though it would appear that point and plurality voting should reveal community preferences better than majority voting, this may not be true in practice if the increased knowledge diffused throughout the community through the more accurate revealing of true individual preferences allows strategy to become pronounced. Thus, a paradox seems to exist. If strategy is neutral, then point voting is the best method because it best records the intensity of desires. If point voting allows many new opportunities for strategy, however, majority voting may be the best voting technique for revealing true community preferences. In any event, voting is an imperfect method of revealing the true social welfare function in the political process. Interdisciplinary research, however, may improve the means of revealing a social welfare function which is more consistent with individual preferences and less dependent upon ethical judgments. In an institutional sense, the recent (1962) reapportionment decision by the United States Supreme Court may also contribute improvement in the revealing of true preferences according to the "equal vote for all" political distribution mandate.

COMPENSATION PRINCIPLE AS A WELFARE NORM

A decisive element in the determination of optimal allocation is the selection of a social norm toward which social welfare decisions can be directed. As observed above, the Pareto optimum norm considers societal welfare to be improved if one person gains from an economic reorganization while other persons are unaffected by the change. Essentially, however, this principle merely states the economic problem of scarcity. In an attempt to improve on this norm, to reduce value judgments, and to widen the area of welfare application, J. R. Hicks, Nicholas Kaldor, and Tibor Scitovsky introduced the "compensation principle."[13] This principle considers the welfare of society to be increased if the gainers from a resource reallocation evaluate their gains at a higher monetary figure than

[13] J. R. Hicks, "The Foundations of Welfare Economics," *Economic Journal* (December, 1939), pp. 696–712; Nicholas Kaldor, "A Note on Tariffs and the Terms of Trade," *Economica* (November, 1940), pp. 377–80, and Tibor Scitovsky, "A Note on Welfare Propositions in Economics," *Review of Economic Studies* (November, 1941), pp. 77–88.

the losers evaluate their losses. The implication is that the former could reimburse the latter for their losses, still experience a net gain in utility, and thus increase community welfare. The principle does not require *actual* compensation for the welfare improvement to occur, but only that the gainer be able *potentially* to pay the compensation from his gains.

Scitovsky considers the Kaldor version of the compensation principle to be inconsistent since a given resource reorganization may provide a higher gain for the gainers than for the losers, while a reversal of this reorganization may provide a higher gain for the previous losers than for the previous gainers.[14] In this instance, there is no criterion for saying which circumstance represents the preferred improvement. Continuous "best positions," not a discrete best position, would exist. Scitovsky then includes a "double criterion" in the compensation principle which asserts that an improvement would have to pass the test of both the initial resource reallocation and its reverse reallocation.

Although the Scitovsky refinement of the compensation principle represents an improvement over the Hicks-Kaldor versions, the principle still faces rather serious theoretical and operational difficulties. The compensation principle becomes logically inconsistent in the sense that monetary values are not good indicators of interpersonal differences in utility values. Consumer A might suffer much more disutility from a $50 loss than Consumer B enjoys in additional utiltiy from a gain which he values at $500. Differences in income and wealth distribution cause monetary values to be inadequate indicators of true utility values.

Operationally, the compensation principle faces the void of no market mechanism being available through which the gains and losses may be evaluated. The principle can be applied only if there is knowledge as to how much compensation should be paid. Unless true preferences are revealed, a political process must exist and it must make ethical judgments as to the amounts and distribution of the compensation payments. Furthermore, if true preferences are revealed, there is less need for the compensation principle because the exclusion principle then may be applied more effectively and the price system will help solve the problem.

ROTHENBERG'S INTERDISCIPLINARY APPROACH TO THE SOCIAL WELFARE FUNCTION

Jerome Rothenberg argues that a social welfare function may be determined substantially by the interacting and interdisciplinary characteristics of group behavior in a society.[15] He points out that social

---

[14] Scitovsky, *op. cit.*

[15] Jerome Rothenberg, *The Measurement of Social Welfare* (Englewood Cliffs, N.J.: Prentice-Hall, Inc., 1961), chap. 13.

psychologists, anthropologists, and sociologists are developing a concept of social choice which stresses the high degree of culturally implemented "value consensus" which exists in any going society. This consensus integrates the several institutional networks in the society in order to avoid conflict. Thus, values are not imposed externally upon a system of social institutions, but instead "values and institutions are mutually engendering, mutually reinforcing, mutually sustaining."[16] Rothenberg thus suggests that welfare economics should be interrelated with intellectual advancements in cultural anthropology, learning theory, psychoanalysis, individual and group field theory, political theory, and sociological theory in order to better reveal the social welfare function.

[16] *Ibid.*, p. 315.

Chapter 5

PRINCIPLES OF FISCAL EFFICIENCY

THE CRITERIA FOR "FISCAL RATIONALITY"

This chapter will develop principles of fiscal efficiency in addition to those which have already been developed for the efficient allocation of resources. Anglo-American public finance has traditionally placed considerable emphasis on the *distribution* branch of public finance. This emphasis, moreover, has often been asymmetrical in nature in that the major concern has been with "equity" in the distribution of tax burdens among taxpayers. Yet, the determination of tax equity rests outside the framework of economic analysis and relies upon noneconomic value judgments. In fact, distribution—as a branch of public finance—is more directly dependent upon value judgments than are any of the other branches. Economics, for example, cannot provide "substantive," but only "methodological," bench marks for the determination of an ideal or proper state of distribution. Noneconomic value judgments must determine the substantive nature of income, wealth, and political voting distribution in the society. The previous chapter, as well as Chapter 1, indicated the necessity of this distribution determination before actual and/or optimal allocation can be ascertained.

The asymmetry of the orthodox emphasis upon tax equity, and thus upon the revenue side of the budget, is in sharp contrast to the comprehensive nature of the fiscal process and the symmetrical analytical approach which it requires. Indeed, fiscal rationality must consider (1) both the revenue and expenditure sides of the budget, (2) the economic effects which derive from the budgetary activities of *all* levels and units of government, and (3) *all* the branches of public finance which can be influenced by fiscal activity. None of these facets of the subject should be treated in isolation. Instead, their various interdependencies must be considered. In addition, the importance of value judgments must be recognized, not only for distribution as observed above, but also within the allocation, stabilization, and economic growth branches of public finance, as well as between the four branches.

Figure 5-1 demonstrates some of the critical areas of value judgment which are involved both in theoretical and in applied public finance. It may be observed that society must first select a pattern of relative emphasis between the interrelated allocation, distribution, stabilization, and economic growth objectives (goals). For example, the determination of a state of distribution is prerequisite to allocation, as previously observed, and an important involvement exists between short-term performance (the stabilization branch) and long-term economic growth. Value judgments are relevant, moreover, in selecting the "desired" stabilization goal if two stabilization goals conflict, say full employment and price stability, as well as in selecting the desired "rate of economic growth" objective. Thus, any set of fiscal rationality principles must not only be symmetrical in a combined revenue-expenditure sense and in an aggregate public sector sense, but they must also be able to

FIGURE 5–1

SOME CRITICAL VALUE JUDGMENT AREAS OF
PUBLIC FINANCE

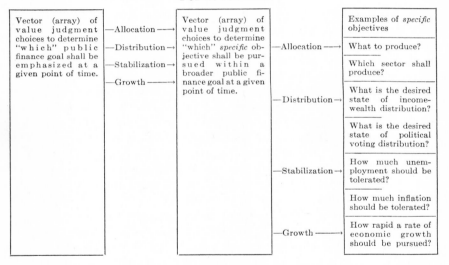

Vector (array) of value judgment choices to determine "which" public finance goal shall be emphasized at a given point of time.	—Allocation —→ —Distribution—→ —Stabilization—→ —Growth ———→	Vector (array) of value judgment choices to determine "which" *specific* objective shall be pursued within a broader public finance goal at a given point of time.	—Allocation ——→ —Distribution—→ —Stabilization—→ —Growth ———→	Examples of *specific* objectives
			—Allocation	What to produce?
				Which sector shall produce?
			—Distribution	What is the desired state of income-wealth distribution?
				What is the desired state of political voting distribution?
			—Stabilization	How much unemployment should be tolerated?
				How much inflation should be tolerated?
			—Growth	How rapid a rate of economic growth should be pursued?

distinguish the critical determinations which economic analysis can render from those which are dependent upon noneconomic value judgments.

The concept of "fiscal neutrality" is basic to the determination of fiscal rationality. The neutrality principle is often used in reference to the desirability in taxation of achieving the objective of a tax, for example—income redistribution—without distorting the functioning of the market sector of the economy. Neutrality, in this context, is deemed desirable while its converse, nonneutrality, is considered undesirable. Similarly, the literature of public finance refers to nonneutrality as constituting an "excess burden" resulting from a tax, that is, a result which interferes with market decision making of a consumptive or productive nature, thus reducing efficient decision making and possibly reducing real income. A reduction in real income can be considered as the measure of excess burden.

Fiscal neutrality, in order to serve as an efficiency or rationality bench mark for public finance, must also be treated in a symmetrical and comprehensive fashion. In other words, the expenditure as well as the tax side of the budget must be considered as a possible source of market distortion. The disaggregation of the aggregate public sector budget, moreover, must be considered in the sense of tax-expenditure policy by one level or unit of government creating fiscal effects on other levels or units of government. In addition, an excess burden may be created when the accomplishment of one public finance goal, such as redistribution, influences the society's goals in other branches of public finance, such as allocation or stabilization. Importantly, in a society already operating at nonoptimal points in terms of the four public finance goals, a nonneutral effect or distortion could either *improve* or *worsen* fiscal rationality. Nonneutrality may thus lead to either rational or irrational results. This significant point will be developed later in the chapter.

A rational fiscal system requires certain criteria which can guide fiscal decision making along the lines of efficiency. The remainder of this chapter will develop three relevant fiscal rationality criteria. Unfortunately, two of these are asymmetrical (partial) in their approach since they emphasize *tax* rationality alone. These are the *tax equity* and *revenue productivity* criteria. The considerable attention given historically to these two criteria, however, and the resultant effects upon the institutional arrangement of fiscal structure in Anglo-American society, suggest that such bench marks be considered. Moreover, valuable insight for general fiscal rationality may be derived from these criteria. The only point upon which they may be criticized is that "by themselves" they are incomplete. Consequently, another criterion—one which is both symmetrical and comprehensive in its inclusion of both revenues and expenditures, all levels and units of government, and all public finance goals—will be presented. This bench mark, which is discussed below, may be termed the *general fiscal rationality* criterion.

THE GENERAL FISCAL RATIONALITY CRITERION

Intersector Fiscal Neutrality

A discussion of the general fiscal rationality criterion requires further elaboration of the term "neutrality." Economic literature normally considers a government fiscal action to be neutral if it does not interfere with consumer or business decisions in the market sector of the economy. This orthodox interpretation may be referred to as *intersector neutrality* in the sense that public sector budgetary action does not alter consumer want-satisfaction and business profit-seeking behavior in the private sector. If such economic effects do occur in the private sector, "intersector nonneutrality" is said to exist. The intersectoral interpretation of neutrality is essentially concerned with the *allocation* branch of public finance since it deals with consumer, business, and societal decisions which affect the use of productive resources. Of course, the distribution prerequisite is involved in the allocation decision. This rather restricted interpretation of neutrality is based upon the assumption that the allocation of resources through the market is optimal and that any alteration of private sector decision making introduces inefficiency.

However, the conditions required for optimal market allocation of *all* resources, as observed in Chapter 2, are not entirely fulfilled within the institutional environment of the American economy.[1] Optimal allocation thus requires the provision of some economic goods by the public sector. Yet, the goal of market approximation in public sector decision making remains a desirable one since it underscores the traditional societal preference in Western culture for individual economic and political freedom. Thus, a "second-best" approach may be deemed desirable. The second-best solution would stipulate that governmental budgetary action, in a situation where some government production is called for, should concentrate upon the selection of the tax or expenditure technique which least interferes with market choices.[2] The rule of "least allocation distortion," however, cannot be applied in a blanket manner to *all* those public sector nonneutral actions which influence private allocative behavior, since the governmental action may at times introduce additional consumption and production efficiencies.

Negative and Positive Nonneutrality

A further neutrality distinction is thus required, namely, the distinction between those intersector nonneutral effects or distortions which introduce economic inefficiencies and which thus interfere with the market process of allocation and those intersector effects (distortions) which provide economies to the private sector. The former (undesirable) intersector distortions may be termed "negative nonneutral effects" and the latter (desirable) intersector distortions may be referred to as "positive nonneutral effects." Thus, when optimal conditions do not exist in the market, governmental budgetary action may improve private sector allo-

---

[1] The conditions for optimal private sector allocation, as developed in Chapter 2, are: (1) many sellers and many buyers in *every* industry, (2) perfect knowledge by all sellers and buyers, (3) perfect mobility of productive resources, (4) profit-maximization motives by all firms, (5) the complete divisibility of all economic goods, and (6) no external effects (interdependencies) between different economic units.

[2] See Chapter 4 for a discussion of "second-best conditions," including Wicksell's "relative unanimity" approach.

cation as well as provide those public and quasi-public goods demanded by community preferences.

Intergoal Fiscal Neutrality

The meaning of neutrality, in order to serve as a guide to general fiscal rationality, needs to be broadened beyond the narrow scope of intersector neutrality within the allocation branch. Since budgetary behavior of government is inherently concerned with all four goals of public finance, not allocation alone, a concept of intergoal neutrality is required. Fiscal policy directed toward a goal of income-wealth redistribution, for example, may either restrict or promote the achievement of the allocation, stabilization, and economic growth goals. In the event of restriction in a second goal, a *tradeoff* would be established between the two goals. The existence of multilevels and multiunits of government within the United States public sector further complicates the intergoal issue. The policy of one level or unit of government, directed toward the attainment of a particular goal, may be either impeded or reinforced by the budgetary actions of the other levels or units of government. Since intergoal effects may be either efficient or inefficient in nature, the terms "negative nonneutral effects" and "positive nonneutral effects" may be applied here just as they are applied to intersector nonneutrality.

Nonneutrality Is Not Bad per se

It must be concluded that nonneutrality is not undesirable per se. Indeed, negative nonneutrality, whether of an intersectoral nature or of an intergoal nature, should be *minimized* in the best manner that second-best policies will permit. Positive nonneutrality, however, is desirable if the public sector budgetary actions: (1) introduce economies to the private sector without unduly restricting individual freedoms, (2) provide public and quasi-public goods in conformance with consumer preferences, or (3) promote more than one public finance goal through a given fiscal action.

Distribution and Fiscal Efficiency

Though intersector neutrality emphasizes the allocation branch, the discussion of general fiscal rationality is concerned also with the other branches of public finance. The state of real income distribution may be influenced via budgetary policy. The direct transfer of funds between individuals through taxes and transfer payments, for example, may be employed to influence the distribution of income. The tax-transfer technique, however, ignores the important allocative influence of the expenditure side of public sector budgeting, which contributes real income in the current period through the production of public and quasi-public goods for consumption.

Figure 5–2, using a Lorenz curve, demonstrates how public sector budgetary behavior, including tax, transfer, and exhaustive expenditure flows, can influence both real income flows and long-term wealth accumu-

FIGURE 5–2

EFFECT OF PUBLIC SECTOR TAX AND EXPENDITURE POLICY
ON THE DISTRIBUTION OF REAL INCOME*

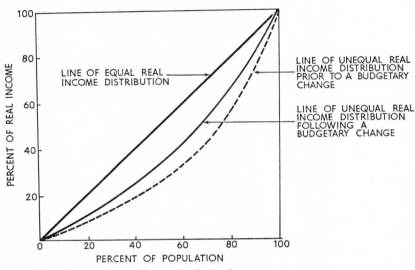

* See Table 21–1 for actual income distribution data.

lations. In this particular example, the budget is used to make the distribution of real income (and wealth) more equal, though clearly fiscal behavior could redistribute in the direction of a greater degree of inequality.

Stabilization, Economic Growth, and Fiscal Efficiency

Public sector revenue collecting and spending also can promote or retard the *stabilization* and *economic growth* objectives. The stabilization goal includes the full employment of labor (up to some value judgment-determined acceptable percentage), high utilization of capital or plant capacity, high levels of production and national income, and a relatively stable price level. The economic growth goal seeks to maintain, over a period of years, a value judgment-determined rate of increase in real per capita output and income, assuming at least a constant quality in the economic goods constituting this output. The budgetary effects on stabilization and growth may remain "isolated" to a particular goal or they may involve "intergoal nonneutrality." Changes in governmental tax rates and expenditures, or changes in the level of a government budget, will tend to provide a variety of multiplier effects capable of influencing aggregate economic performance during both short-run and long-run time periods.[3] Generally, expenditure increases and tax rate reductions exert an expansionary influence on aggregate demand through a positive multiplier effect, while expenditure reductions and tax rate increases are contractionary in their multiplier performance. Moreover, an increase in budget size tends to be expansionary and a decrease tends to be contractionary.[4]

In addition, government budgeting may affect aggregate short-run performance and long-run economic growth through the particular *composition* of the revenue and expenditure flows. An investment-credit tax subsidy for certain strategic growth industries, for example, may encourage investment of the sort that will increase the rate of long-run economic growth as well as short-run aggregate demand in the society. Furthermore, federal expenditures for research may improve the efficiency of production functions in certain private industries and thus increase aggregate output as well as promote economic growth.

Another possible governmental budgetary influence upon stabilization and growth goals concerns the ability of tax-expenditure procedures to influence the economic incentives of both businesses and consumers in the private sector. This caused particular concern during the 1930's when deliberate federal fiscal policy programs to relieve depression conditions were initiated by the New Deal administration of Franklin D. Roosevelt. Today, the widespread acceptance of federal fiscal policy directed toward stabilization and economic growth goals tends to reduce disincentive effects. Thus, most incentive effects from federal fiscal policy at the present time appear to be of the positive variety which encourage consumption and investment.

Fiscal Efficiency within the Aggregate Public Sector

The existence of three levels and some 90,000 units of government in the United States creates a situation of substantial economic interdependence between the various levels and units of government. Importantly, the four economic goals of public finance will be affected, for better or for worse, by the nature of this interdependence. Aggregate community preferences may be either better achieved or thwarted depending upon whether the various levels and units of government reinforce or neutralize each other's efforts to meet the demands of the public.

---

[3] See Part IV of the book for a detailed discussion of the ability of government budgets to influence short-run aggregate performance and long-run economic growth.

[4] See the discussion of the "balanced budget multiplier" in Chapter 18.

Intergovernmental fiscal relationships assume two dimensions. First, intergovernmental budgetary relationships exist between levels of government. This may be referred to as *vertical intergovernmental fiscal relations.* The fiscal interaction between the federal and state or between the state and local levels of government exemplify this dimension of the concept. Second, the interrelationship between different segments of government can take the form of fiscal interaction between different units of government at the same level of government. This may be termed *horizontal intergovernmental fiscal relations,* which can occur, of course, only at the state and local levels of government since only one unit of government exists at the federal level. Thus, the influence of the budgetary actions of one state on other states or of the actions of one municipality on other municipalities exemplify this dimension of intergovernmental fiscal behavior. Rational intergovernmental fiscal behavior should thus take into account whether the budgetary actions of taxation and expenditure will promote or retard society's collective goals.

The remainder of this chapter will concentrate upon the two "tax rationality" criteria, namely, the *tax equity* and *revenue productivity* bench marks. As observed above, these criteria are asymmetrical in that they consider only the revenue side of the budget. Nonetheless, their historical importance as well as their high sophistication in analysis requires that they be considered in a comprehensive discussion of fiscal efficiency bench marks. The particular application of the tax rationality norms will appear in Part III, which analyzes the various types of taxes, though the theoretical development of the criteria will be undertaken in Part I so that all relevant fiscal efficiency norms can be considered in one locus.

TAX EQUITY AS A FISCAL RATIONALITY CRITERION

History of Tax Equity Analysis

Several hundred years of attention in public finance economics have been devoted to the importance of distributing tax burdens equitably among taxpayers. The impressive list of "interested economists" includes such names as Smith, Locke, Petty, Ricardo, Mill, Seligman, Wagner, Edgeworth, and Pigou. In fact, equity in taxation was the "obsession" of public finance during much of the period. Many variables, both economic and noneconomic, have been considered relevant to the topic. For example, that which appears to be the locus of the tax burden—the point of original payment of the tax to the government—may be far removed from the ultimate locus of the tax burden which is subject to influence by market adjustments subsequent to the imposition of the tax. Thus, "tax shifting" (the subject of Chapter 10) will influence the ultimate location of the tax burden with which the criterion of tax equity is concerned.

Purposes of Taxes

As observed earlier in the book, taxes may exist for a variety of purposes. Most taxes, moreover, serve more than one purpose, though a single purpose usually is dominant. All taxes, of course, provide *revenues* for the unit of government which imposes the tax. In most instances, this is the primary motive for the existence of a tax. In some instances, however, a tax may exist primarily, or at least importantly, for regulatory purposes. Taxes may be *regulatory* in either a microeconomic or in a macroeconomic sense. In the former case, for example, they can influence the consumption of a particular good or the utilization of a particular productive resource. In this context, liquor excise and natural resource severance taxes are typical.[5] On the other hand, an important purpose of the federal personal income tax is its adaptability to macroeconomic fiscal policy directed toward stabilization and economic growth goals. The revenue motive for taxation, as opposed to the regulatory or control motive, fits closely with the asymmetric "revenue productivity" and "tax equity" criteria. The microeconomic and macroeconomic regulation motives, however, adapt better to the general efficiency criterion of total budgetary behavior since they are more symmetrical and comprehensive in scope.

Value Judgment Determination of Equity

In dealing with the concept of tax equity, it should be kept in mind that the terms "equity" or "justice" are noneconomic terms. There is no way that positive economic methodology can define an exact meaning of equity or justice. Economics can merely recognize an individual or community value judgment as to the meaning of equity and then methodologically indicate how the objective can be attained through economic policy. The noneconomic interpretation of tax equity provided by a society, of course, is part of the overall collective value judgment which selects a particular income-wealth and political voting distribution complex for the society.

Alternate Tax Equity Principles

The Principle of Absolute Equity.   A very strict interpretation of equity in the distribution of tax burdens would entail general application of the principle of *absolute equality*. The statistical computation of individual tax burdens would be very simple in this case since the total spending of the government unit is merely divided by the number of taxpaying units, the resulting quotient being the tax liability of each taxpaying unit. Under this approach, each taxpaying unit pays an equal absolute amount of tax. For example, suppose that federal government

---

[5] These taxes are described further in Chapters 13 and 15.

spending is defined for purposes of the absolute equality approach as that amount which appears in the administrative budget for a particular fiscal year. Then, suppose that taxpaying units are defined in terms of family (or unmarried adult individual) spending units. If the expenditures in the administrative budget total $100 billion, and the number of spending (taxpaying) units equals 100 million, the resulting quotient of $1,000 constitutes the tax liability per spending (taxpaying) unit. In no way does this approach take into account the differential taxpaying abilities, based on such considerations as income and property, which exist among these spending units. It is conceivable that the income of the spending unit might not equal the amount of tax liability. Needless to say, community preferences, in determining the proper state of distribution, have traditionally rejected the tax principle of absolute equity.

A specific application of the principle of absolute equality in taxation would exist in the hypothetical case where *all* tax revenues would be collected in the form of per capita (poll) taxes. In other words, a flat tax per person is perfectly neutral in terms of distribution equity if, of course, equity is defined in terms of "absolute equality" among taxpayers. While every person is a comparable unit in the poll tax, every unit is not comparable if the income of individuals or the property of individuals is the basis for the tax. In other words, individual circumstances differ as to income and wealth, but they are identical in the sense that each is a single unitary human being. The specific policy application of the principle of absolute equality in terms of a universal poll tax is rejected along with the general absolute equality approach described above.

Modified Equity Principles. Since the absolute equality version of tax equity is viewed as too extreme by society, the search begins for *modified approaches* to tax equity. Generally, this search has provided the following categorical guidelines regarding modified equity:

(1) Equals should be treated equally; (2) unequals should be treated unequally. The first of these statements is referred to in the literature of public finance as the concept of *horizontal equity*. In other words, persons with the same level or amount of taxpaying "ability" should bear equal tax burdens. The definition of taxpaying ability, of course, is highly strategic to the basic concept. The second of the above statements is referred to as *vertical equity*, which means that persons of differential taxpaying circumstance or ability should ·pay different amounts of tax. Once again, the meaning of ability is important. Yet, positive economics cannot provide a definition of taxpaying ability. Instead, noneconomic value judgments, collectively undertaken by the community, must be relied upon to provide a bench mark for the ability to pay taxes. Anglo-American society has generally selected *income differences* between taxpayers as the primary indicator of ability

to pay, though, to a lesser extent, the *value of property* also serves as an important bench mark.

The Ability-to-Pay Principle. Two "specific" modified equity principles have been theoretically developed and institutionally applied in the public sectors of Western nations. One of these—the *ability-to-pay principle*—rests largely upon the general modified equity premise discussed above while the other specific principle—the *benefit principle*—approaches tax equity from a substantially different standpoint.[6]

Ability to pay should not be construed specifically to mean the direct "monetary" funds (purchasing power) necessary to meet a particular tax obligation. To the contrary, ability is given the connotation of "sacrifice" when used as a tax equity principle since the taxpayer is deprived of alternative uses of the tax payment money. This consists primarily of sacrificing disposable income which would have been available for the purchase of economic goods from the private sector, though admittedly some of the tax funds might have been used for the voluntary purchase of quasi-public goods sold commercially by the public sector. In any event, the subjective *sacrifice* of utility (satisfaction) in the payment of taxes, through the loss of alternative uses for the tax funds, comprises the basic tenet of the ability-to-pay principle of tax equity.

Ability to Pay and the Three Sacrifice Theories. Three sacrifice theories may be discussed in connection with the ability-to-pay principle. These are the equal, proportional, and minimum-aggregate sacrifice theories. Each theory defines sacrifice in terms of "consumption disutility." The *equal sacrifice* approach suggests that all taxpayers should bear the same tax burdens. This would require that a tax be levied on an individual with lower income which would cause him sacrifice (disutility) equal to that which would be borne by a higher income individual from a tax imposed on him. Yet, this approach does not provide the rate structure relative to income which would provide such equal sacrifice results. Would it require a progressive, regressive, or proportionate rate structure?[7] If progressive or regressive, what degree of progression or regression in rates should be used? The *proportional sacrifice* theory at least makes a suggestion regarding rate structure. It proposes that sacrifices by individuals in the payment of taxes be proportionate to their income. In other words, a higher income person should bear greater disutility than a lower income person in the payment of taxes. This would be accomplished

---

[6] The ability-to-pay and benefit approaches were developed in the previous chapter, but with *primary emphasis* on their relationship to allocation efficiency, not distribution.

[7] Progressive, regressive, and proportionate tax rate structures are described later in this chapter. However, it is necessary to stipulate now that if the tax rate increases as the income increases, the tax is *progressive;* if the tax rate decreases, it is *regressive;* if the tax rate does not change as income increases, it is *proportionate.*

through progressive rates applied to the income tax base, the latter serving as the indicator of ability to pay.

The *minimum-aggregate sacrifice* theory states that government revenues should be collected first from the highest income individuals and then from successively lower income groups as additional revenues are required. This would ultimately result, of course, in after-tax disposable incomes being equalized between all taxpayers as long as government revenue requirements were large enough that all but the lowest income group was taxed. This theory, unlike the equal and proportional theories, is "aggregate" rather than "individual" in scope since it seeks to minimize the sacrifice of *all* individuals within a political jurisdiction.[8] The minimum-aggregate sacrifice theory suggests a highly progressive rate structure. In fact, it could result in the elimination of all high incomes through taxation. In effect, it applies marginal tax rates of 100 percent to the highest income group for that differential of income which separates the highest from the next highest group, and so on.

The Diminishing Marginal Utility of Income Concept and the Problem of Quantitative Utility Measurement. Both the proportional sacrifice and minimum-aggregate sacrifice theories assume the controversial concept of "diminishing marginal utility of income." In other words, taxpaying ability is said to increase as income increases because the marginal utility of income declines as income becomes greater. The attempt is made to draw an analogy between additional income, which may be used for a variety of purposes including saving, and the additional consumption of a particular economic good such as Coca-Cola. Admittedly, the successive consumption of additional units of Coca-Cola within a reasonably defined time period is likely to provide decreasing incremental amounts of pleasure, and eventually disutility may result. When an individual's income as a whole is viewed, however, the analogy is weakened because the person may switch his consumption patterns to other goods with higher marginal amounts of pleasure, or he may derive considerable pleasure from saving the incremental income, or from investing it, or from the prestige which American culture places upon high income and large accumulations of wealth. These are merely a few of the many alternative uses of incremental higher income which may provide high marginal amounts of utility to the high-income taxpayer.

The above behavior is analogous to the insatiability of aggregate human wants which is basic to the economic problem of scarcity. This is much different, however, from the law of diminishing marginal utility as applied to the continuing consumption of a *single* economic good. Nonetheless, since lower income individuals tend to allocate most or all

[8] Though dealing with some of the same concepts, this theory essentially is distinct from the Pigovian marginal utility approach to social balance which was discussed in Chapter 4.

of their incomes for the purchase of *necessity* goods while higher income individuals spend a greater proportion of their incomes on *nonessential* goods, a reasonably logical case can still be established for the adoption of the diminishing marginal utility of income concept. It is difficult, however, to use this concept as the basis for the prescription of specific fiscal policy measures.

All individuals are subjectively different in their preference patterns. To compare the specific circumstances which contribute to the satisfaction of one person with those which contribute to the pleasure of another person, without cardinal measurement, is impossible. The ability-to-pay approach to equity and progressive tax rates, moreover, implies quantitative measurement for the purpose of interpersonal utility comparisons. Hence, the sacrifice theories fall under significant criticism. Most of this criticism, however, is "specific" and "technical." It still remains rational for an individual and for society collectively to make the general value judgment that progressive income taxes are the most desirable of available tax structure alternatives for minimizing sacrifice.

The Benefit Principle. This tax equity principle is the primary alternative to the ability-to-pay approach. The benefit approach has the advantage of relating the revenue and expenditure sides of the budget to each other.[9] It basically involves an approximation of market behavior in the allocative procedures of the public sector. An individual or business voluntarily exchanges purchasing power for the acquisition of government economic goods—a *quid pro quo* arrangement whereby the individual consumers and businesses pay directly for the products of the public sector from which they derive benefit. Equity is suggested by the dual facts that: (1) the exchange of purchasing power for the economic good is "voluntary" and (2) the payments are made in accordance with the benefits that are received. The benefits may be priced either according to the governmental *cost* of providing the service or according to the *value* of the service to the purchaser. In either case, the benefits should be viewed in a marginal rather than in a total sense in order to avoid the various allocation efficiency pitfalls which occur when marginal analysis is ignored.

In theory, the benefit principle of tax equity is quite attractive. Its institutional application, however, is greatly restricted by the inherent nature of pure public and quasi-public goods. The indivisible nature of all pure public goods and the partial indivisibility of many quasi-public goods thus make it impossible to apply the benefit principle comprehensively to public sector resource allocation. This does not suggest, however, that extended use of the benefit principle could not improve fiscal efficiency.

---

[9] See Chapter 4 for a discussion of the benefit approach to social balance, a discussion containing much relevant material for this chapter.

Tax Base—Tax Rate Relationships and the Modified Equity Principles

The *base* of a tax is that object to which the tax rate is applied. This may be income, property value, the value of an economic good, or the value of a productive resource, among other possibilities. The *tax rate* is the amount of tax applied per unit of tax base. The tax base times the tax rate equals the *tax yield* to the government. The yield to the government is essentially the same as the *burden* to the taxpayer, except for certain differentials resulting from collection costs to government or compliance costs to the taxpayer.[10] The relationship between the size of the tax base and the tax rate of any particular tax, in technical terms, falls within one of three possible classifications. If the tax rate increases as the tax base grows

FIGURE 5–3

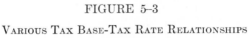

Various Tax Base-Tax Rate Relationships

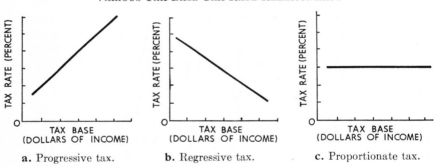

a. Progressive tax.	**b.** Regressive tax.	**c.** Proportionate tax.

larger, the tax is said to be progressive. To the contrary, a tax rate which decreases as the size of the tax base increases is regressive in its technical structure. The third category, that of proportionate taxes, represents a tax structure whereby the rate remains constant as the tax base increases in size. Since income is generally accepted as the best indicator of taxpaying ability, however, it is customary to regard income size as the tax base to which various tax rates are applied in order to determine the progressive, regressive, or proportionate nature of a tax. Hence, a tax rate which increases as income increases will be considered *progressive,* one which decreases as income increases will be *regressive,* while a *proportionate* tax will reflect a constant tax rate as income expands. Figure 5–3abc represents these relationships in graphical fashion.

The federal personal income tax serves as an excellent example of a progressive tax while general sales, excise, and property taxes are usually regressive in their tax rate–income relationships. Tax rates which are

[10] The burden, of course, may be shifted (transferred) by the initial taxpayer. See Chapter 10 on "Tax Shifting."

progressive or regressive with respect to income need not change in any particular pattern as the tax bases increase in size. The tax rate, for example, may increase in only one step (bracket) as the income expands, as is true for the federal corporation income tax, and still have a progressive rate structure because the general direction of relationship is positive; that is, the tax rate tends to increase (at least at one point) as income grows larger. Furthermore, the tax rate may increase through a series of steps at either an increasing rate, a constant rate, or a decreasing rate with increasing income, and still properly be classified within the progressive category. Similarly, a regressive tax might have the tax rate decreasing in only one step, or decreasing through several brackets at different rates of decline as the income increases in size, and properly be classified within the regressive category.

Regressivity of the General Sales Tax

The following example will serve to exemplify the regressive nature of the general sales tax used as a primary revenue source by 42 states (in 1966) and a substantial number of local governments: Suppose that Consumer A earns an income of $50,000 annually, from which he spends $25,000 or 50 percent for consumption, the remainder being saved. (Consumer A's *Average Propensity to Consume* equals 50 percent). On the other hand, suppose that Consumer B earns an annual income of $5,000, from which he spends $4,800 or 96 percent for consumption goods. (Consumer B's *Average Propensity to Consume* equals 96 percent). Moreover, assume equal family size for both consumers and the existence of a broad-based retail sales tax of 4 percent to the consumption purchases of each consumer. In this instance, Consumer B pays $192 in sales taxes from his $5,000 annual income and Consumer A pays $1,000 in sales taxes from his $50,000 annual income. Significantly, the sales taxes paid by the lower income taxpayer, Consumer B, constitute 3.84 percent of his income while the higher income taxpayer, Consumer A, pays only 2 percent of his income in the form of the general sales tax. The sales tax thus tends to be regressive due to the fact that the average propensities to consume of lower income taxpayers tend to be higher than those of the higher income groups. The progressivity of the federal tax structure is thus neutralized by the regressivity of the state-local structure. The overall conclusion from such reasoning is that the aggregate public sector tax structure in the United States is neither highly progressive nor highly regressive, but instead approximates proportionality.

REVENUE PRODUCTIVITY AS A FISCAL RATIONALITY CRITERION

Tax Equity in the Enforcement Sense

The basic purpose of most taxes, and at least a secondary purpose of all taxes, is the ability of taxes to provide needed government revenues.

Hence, the efficiency with which the revenue function is accomplished can be extremely important to the continued use of a tax. Revenue productivity is thus treated as a separate fiscal rationality criterion. It is similar to the tax equity criterion discussed above in that it is asymmetrical in approach because it likewise does not always directly consider the expenditure side of the budget. The revenue productivity criterion, moreover, is also concerned with tax equity, though not in the theoretical sacrifice sense discussed above. Instead, the revenue productivity bench mark concerns itself with equity in the "enforcement" sense.

Certainly, the term tax equity is as important a consideration in the enforcement sense as it is in the "distribution of burden" sense. Tax equity must mean more than a theoretically rational tax system. It must consider also the equitable enforcement of the tax structure upon all taxable subjects, seeing to it that no one illegally transfers his tax burden to others through evasion practices. Tax equity, in this connotation, requires the consistent and unbiased imposition of taxes upon all those prescribed by the law as taxpayers. Though a good enforcement system cannot improve the rationality of an irrational tax structure, a poor system of enforcement can undo the advantages of a rational tax system. The importance of equitable enforcement cannot be doubted.

Tax Evasion, Tax Avoidance, and Tax Delinquency

At this point in the discussion, it is desirable to distinguish three significant terms in relationship to tax enforcement, namely, tax evasion, tax avoidance, and tax delinquency. *Tax evasion* involves a fraudulent or deceitful effort by a taxpayer to escape his legal tax obligations. This is a direct violation of both the "spirit" or "intent" and the "letter" of tax law. On the other hand, *tax avoidance* may involve a violation of the spirit of tax law, but it does not violate the letter of the law. Tax avoidance occurs when a taxpayer manipulates his economic behavior in such a manner as to maximize his tax position—which means to minimize his tax obligations. This may be done in the short run by cleverly taking advantage of loopholes in the tax laws and in the long run by actually influencing tax legislation through the support of pressure groups and lobbies which represent the special interests of the taxpayer. Tax avoidance is lawful, while tax evasion is unlawful. *Tax delinquency* refers to the failure to pay a tax obligation on the date when it is due. Usually tax delinquency is associated with the inability to pay a tax because of inadequate funds. However, the term does cover the possibility of nonpayment even though adequate funds are available. In the former case, tax delinquency would not be illegal, but in the latter case it would violate tax law. In any event, tax delinquency ordinarily is only a temporary escape from tax payment since the government unit which is owed the tax can place liens on property and future earnings as well as use other devices to secure the tax money.

Techniques of Tax Enforcement

Various techniques of tax enforcement are used within the United States public sector.[11] One of the most commonly employed devices is that of *voluntary taxpayer compliance*. This technique is especially important for the collection of income taxes. The federal personal income tax also uses the *withholding* technique of tax administration whereby tax funds are withheld at the income source of the taxpayer. This device was first used by the federal government during World War II when extremely critical requirements for federal funds existed to finance the war, and inflationary pressures were severe. Secretary of the Treasury Henry Morgenthau and Beardsley Ruml pioneered the withholding technique at that time.

Auditing, whether electronic or clerical, is basic to any tax enforcement program. The federal government presently is expanding its use of electronic computers to assist tax administrators in their enforcement efforts. Taxpayer account numbers are now required by law as part of this administrative program. Tax auditing by government requires adequate information. Information of tax evasion—the illegal escape from legitimate tax burdens—may be gathered in a variety of ways. Among the most important techniques are: (1) the routine check of tax returns by a tax administrative agency; (2) the check of large or unusual business transactions; (3) the appraisal of relevant newspaper reports, court proceedings, and legal filings; (4) the routine check of the business activities of gangsters and racketeers (here the revenue motive of taxation is well supplemented by a "regulatory" motive); (5) the exchange of information with other agencies of the same unit of government and between levels of government; (6) information obtained from businesses, as required by law, to report various information items such as wages, dividends, and interest paid to taxpayers; and (7) the use of tax informers.

Tax Enforcement Agencies

The primary tax enforcement agency of the federal government is the Internal Revenue Service, formerly called the Bureau of Internal Revenue, which was established as part of the Treasury Department during the Civil War. Since most Treasury tax revenues are domestic in origin, the Internal Revenue Service (IRS) is of primary importance to federal tax enforcement. The other tax collection agency of the federal government, the Customs Bureau, enforces taxes of an external nature such as tariffs based on international economic transactions. It also operates under the Treasury Department. At the state level of government,

---

[11] These techniques will also be discussed later in Part 3 of the book when the particular types of taxes are discussed.

tax commissions serve as tax collection agencies for various state taxes such as general sales taxes, specific sales (excise) taxes, and state income taxes. The various units of local government use somewhat diverse tax collection techniques, though the collection of property taxes through county assessors is a uniform practice throughout the nation.

"Secondary Effects" from Tax Enforcement

Various secondary effects may result from tax enforcement efforts. The creation of consumption and investment "disincentives" through irritating and irrational tax enforcement efforts is undesirable. On the other hand, tax evasion—the target of enforcement efforts—is equally undesirable. Thus, tax enforcement efforts, though justified, should be efficient and rational so as to avoid unnecessary disincentives. Another secondary result of tax enforcement activities may be the evasion efforts which "never occur" because taxpayers know that an adequate tax enforcement system is in effect. Although the additional revenues collected *directly* as a result of the detection of tax evasion can be estimated, the additional revenues which *indirectly* accrue because potential tax evasion is discouraged cannot be determined. Yet, this latter amount may be much greater than the direct incremental revenue collections resulting from adequate tax enforcement.

Enforcement Costs and Revenue Stability

A rational tax requires that its direct monetary costs of enforcement not be an exceedingly high percentage of the revenues collected from the tax. This is particularly true when reasonable tax source alternatives are available to the unit of government in question. In the present context, the term "enforcement costs" should be construed to include both the direct administrative costs of the public sector and the voluntary compliance costs of the private sector.

When several alternative tax sources are available to a unit of government, it becomes increasingly important to define the *capacity* of a given tax. A rational government would first use the tax with the lowest marginal social costs.[12] When this tax reaches a certain level of revenue, however, further utilization of the tax may cause it to have marginal social costs greater than those for another tax. At this point it would be said that the first tax has "reached its capacity."[13] Additional revenues will then be raised by the second tax until its marginal social costs become greater than those for a third tax, and so on, as alternative taxes are used in an efficient manner at the margin in the provision of tax

[12] Amotz Morag, *On Taxes and Inflation* (New York: Random House, 1965), p. 8.

[13] *Ibid.*

revenues to government. Policymakers can learn an important lesson from such analysis:[14]

Thus an income tax may seem to be much better than, say, an excise on sugar, but an increase in an income tax is not necessarily "better" than the imposition of that excise.

In other words, the addition of a new tax to the tax system will at times be preferable to an increase in the rates or base of a present tax.

A rational tax should also provide an adequate degree of revenue stability over the expansion and contraction phases of the business cycle. Conflicting public finance objectives may exist in this case, however, since those taxes which serve as automatic anticyclical stabilizers, such as the federal income taxes, fluctuate as a facet of their stabilization objective. Yet, the extent of revenue deviation is generally moderate in the case of the federal income taxes, thus serving both the stabilization and revenue goals in a satisfactory manner.[15]

[14] *Ibid.,* pp. 8–9.
[15] This important point will be developed further in Part 4 of the book, particularly in Chapter 19.

PART II

Public Sector Institutional Arrangements

and Expenditure Trends

The federalistic political structure of American society provides a very decentralized public sector arrangement. Three levels and some 90,000 units of government, for example, comprise the American public sector. Each unit of government inevitably influences the allocation, distribution, stabilization, and economic growth goals of the society when it makes taxation, debt, and expenditure decisions. Policy decisions directed toward the attainment of these goals, of course, are sometimes difficult to coordinate because of the multitude of governmental units. Yet, an effort must be made to "rationalize" intergovernmental fiscal relationships so as better to achieve the economic goals of the society.

Expenditure trends, as well as revenue behavior, indicate a growth of the American public sector relative to aggregate economic activity during this century. Furthermore, the federal and state levels of government have undergone relative expansion *within* the public sector while the proportion of local government economic activity has declined. Budgets at all levels of government, of course, have increased enormously in absolute terms. Certain theoretical hypotheses attempt to explain these phenomena for the United States and for Western industrial societies. However, these hypotheses, though helpful, are not comprehensive enough to explain adequately the complex interdisciplinary variables involved with the phenomena.

Chapter 6

FISCAL INSTITUTIONS AND
BUDGET CONCEPTS

CONSTITUTIONAL DIVISION OF FISCAL POWERS

The federal Constitution is the basic document which legally allocates the fiscal powers of taxing and spending between the federal and state levels of government in the United States. The structure of the public sector in the United States is that of a "federal system" with a division of sovereign governmental power between the central government and its immediate components—the states. This may be contrasted with a "unitary" or "parliamentary" system of government, such as that in England, where only the central government is sovereign.[1] In the United States, local governments are entities created by state government authority. They are not sovereign and their existence is not directly provided for by the Constitution.

Two powers inherent in sovereign government give the public sector the "right" to institute tax laws. These are the taxing and police powers of government. The former includes the basic right of government to collect *revenues* for the support of public sector functions. The latter gives authority to sovereign government to control persons and property for the purpose of promoting the *general welfare*. The general welfare or regulatory goal is exemplified in such fiscal devices as the automobile license and liquor license taxes. Though significant revenues are provided by these taxes, an important element of their reason for existence rests in the regulatory area. Admittedly, few taxes exist for the sole purpose either of raising revenue or of regulation. Instead, most taxes exist for both revenue and welfare purposes, though one purpose or the other will usually be dominant. For example, the American public sector uses the license taxes described above, which have regulation as a dominant motive, and the (federal) personal income tax which, though it exists primarily for revenue-raising purposes, still performs many important regulatory functions such as assisting in the detection and conviction of noted gangsters, racketeers, and other "undesirable" members of the community.

---

[1] The central government in England, however, grants significant operational powers to municipalities.

95

The Constitution, by denying certain rights and powers to the federal and state governments, reserves them to the American people. Furthermore, it defines certain "enumerated" powers for the federal government, which are supplemented by other "implied" powers which have their origins in court interpretation. State governments, in turn, have certain powers "reserved" to them by the Constitution. Regarding these reserved powers, Amendment Ten to the Constitution states that "the powers not delegated to the United States by the Constitution, nor prohibited by it to the states, are reserved to the states respectively, or to the people."

The boundary line between federal and state authority is difficult to define in a precise manner. While a unitary system of government can primarily rely upon unwritten traditions for its political-economic direction, a federal system requires a written constitution and subsequent judicial interpretation of the laws which are legislated under the constitution. The gradual trend in the United States during the 20th century has been toward a more liberal interpretation of the Constitution in behalf of greater central government authority in setting the political-economic direction of the society. A perennial conflict exists, however, between the federal government's obligation to "promote general welfare" and its constitutional incapacity to compel coordination and uniformity among the tax and expenditure policies of the various states.

An extremely important public finance clause of the Constitution is that which gives Congress "power to lay taxes and imposts, pay the public debt, provide for the common defense, and promote the general welfare."[2] This represents a very extensive grant of power from the Constitution to the federal government. The Constitutional Convention had been called in 1787 primarily for the purpose of solving the post–Revolutionary War financial crisis of the new nation. Prior to the adoption of the Constitution, the Continental Congress, which directed the country, possessed no taxing powers, as states alone had the authority to levy taxes. A major financial crisis resulted. The extensive fiscal clause quoted above was the product of intense discussion at the Continental Congress. The interpretation of "general welfare" in this clause has become more liberal over the years, partially from a more liberal interpretation of what is included in the concept of "interstate commerce."

Several important fiscal limitations are placed on the activities of the federal government by the Constitution. First, the federal government is prohibited from taxing exports of goods to other countries. It is not prohibited, however, from levying taxes (duties) on goods imported from other nations. The export clause was placed in the Constitution primarily at the insistence of the southern states which wanted their farm staples to stay competitive in world markets, that is, not made higher in

[2] *U.S. Constitution*, Art. I, Sec. 8.

price by export duties. The export tax prohibition includes specific domestic excise taxes, such as the manufacturer's excise tax on automobiles, on goods that subsequently are exported. If a new car is exported, the manufacturer's excise tax does not apply.

Another limitation placed on federal fiscal authority is the constitutional provision that "all duties, imposts and excises shall be uniform throughout the United States."[3] This clause refers to geographical uniformity, that is, legal residence in one state rather than in another cannot be the basis of differential tax rates and taxes. The federal gasoline excise, in other words, cannot be 10 cents per gallon in New York and 4 cents per gallon in California. Furthermore, the federal government cannot impose a gasoline tax in one state without imposing it in all other states. However, it can legally tax an object which is relevant to only part of the states in the sense that it is found in some states and not in others. The manufacturer's excise tax is imposed on automobiles, for example, even though automobiles are manufactured in only a few states.

A third important fiscal limitation in the Constitution is the clause which holds that "no capitation or other direct tax shall be laid, unless in proportion to the census."[4] This limitation has been more important historically than it is at the present time because of the adoption of the 16th Amendment to the Constitution in 1913. The Constitution does not define clearly what it means by a "direct" tax, though probably the founding fathers had property taxes and poll taxes in mind. The clause was used to question the constitutionality of a federal personal income tax, however, which led supporters of the income tax to seek a constitutional amendment. An income tax, of course, would be unacceptable if it had to be apportioned among the various states according to population. For example, two states might each have a population of 20 million people. However, one state might have taxable income of $30 billion and the other (poorer) state have a taxable income of $15 billion. If the income tax is considered a direct tax, each state would have to contribute the same absolute amount of tax even though one state possesses much greater taxpaying ability than the other. Obviously, the tax would be inequitable according to the ability-to-pay principle of distribution. Consequently, the 16th Amendment excludes the income tax from the direct tax apportionment limitation. It states: "Congress shall have power to lay and collect taxes on incomes, from whatever source derived, without apportionment among the several States, and without regard to any census or enumeration." The constitutionality of the federal personal income tax is made abundantly clear by this amendment.

The Fifth Amendment to the Constitution is applicable as a public finance clause. This amendment states that "no person shall be deprived

[3] *U.S. Constitution,* Art. I, Sec. 9.
[4] *U.S. Constitution,* Art. I, Sec. 9.

of life, liberty, or property, without due process of law." The implication is that taxes and other fiscal acts cannot be so arbitrary or discriminatory as to result in the confiscation of property. Actually, the federal courts have not employed this clause to any great extent as a limitation on federal fiscal powers. A similar limitation is placed against state governments by the 14th Amendment to the Constitution. As applied to taxation, this prohibits the imposition of taxes by state and local governments beyond their legal territories of jurisdiction and also prohibits unduly arbitrary or confiscatory taxation.

There are several additional constitutional limitations on the taxing power of states and on local government units. Some of these pertain directly to fiscal matters while others affect fiscal activity within a broader range of influence. States are directly prohibited from levying export taxes, as is the federal government, but they are also forbidden to levy import duties without the consent of Congress. Furthermore, state governments are directly prohibited from the levying of tonnage taxes, based on size or capacity of water carrier, without the permission of Congress. Since state governments are explicitly forbidden to levy export, import, and tonnage taxes, it is implied—and verified by judicial interpretation—that they cannot tax interstate and foreign commerce. The Constitution relegates this authority to the federal government when it gives Congress the right "to regulate Commerce with foreign Nations, and among the several States, and with the Indian Tribes."[5] Another indirect limitation on state fiscal authority results from the fact that the Constitution gives the federal government exclusive authority to make treaties with other nations. When such treaties relate to fiscal matters, state governments are bound to set their tax and spending actions in accordance with the terms of the treaties.

An important area of indirect constitutional limitation on both federal and state governments involves the taxation of "instrumentalities." This is not explicitly stated in the Constitution, but has been developed through judicial interpretation. According to this limitation (which is replete with exceptions to the rule), state governments cannot tax federal instrumentalities and the federal government cannot tax state instrumentalities. Such a concept could occur only in a federal system of government, where sovereign states exist alongside a sovereign central government. Instrumentalities of government are difficult to define. Harold M. Groves notes that, in its broadest scope, the term would include "all corporations (they get their charters from governments), all land (underlying title lies with state governments), banks, copyrights and patents, voting, college football games, sales to or by the government, government property, government bonds, and government enterprises."[6]

[5] *U.S. Constitution*, Art. I, Sec. 8.

[6] Harold M. Groves, *Financing Government* (New York: Holt, Rinehart and Winston, 1964), p. 434.

Because of this limitation, the federal government was not allowed to apply the federal income tax to most state and local government salaries until the Supreme Court reversed this position in 1938. The taxation of interest earned on state and local government securities under the federal income tax remains a constitutional question mark. There is no opportunity at the present time to test the constitutionality of such taxation because the federal income tax law excludes this type of interest income from the tax base. However, the similarity between interest income (which is earned on the use of money capital as a factor of production) and wage-salary income (which is earned on the use of labor as a factor of production) suggests that taxation of interest income earned on state and local securities might be constitutional. In addition, the 16th Amendment states clearly that the income tax can be levied on "income from any source whatsoever."

State government constitutions impose fiscal limitations, though considerable variation exists between the states as to the nature and extent of these limitations. The most common limitation found in state constitutions is that which stipulates that taxes must be uniform and/or equal. For example, property tax rates and assessments should be uniform for the same class of property in the same jurisdiction. Among the wide variety of other limitations are the following:

1. Rate limitations on taxes, especially on property taxes, though sometimes on income and specific excise taxes.
2. Earmarked taxes, such as highway user taxes (typified by the state gasoline taxes which all 50 states use).
3. Exemptions on property and income taxes.
4. Origination of revenue bills in the lower house of the state legislature.
5. Specification that taxes must be for public purposes, not for particular business, religious, or other special interest groups.
6. Prohibition of particular types of taxes such as income taxes and poll taxes.

Thus, we have observed that the federal Constitution and the various state government constitutions place many limitations on the fiscal activities of the public sector in the United States. None of the constitutions (federal or state), however, places any significant limitations upon the "purpose" for which taxes may be imposed. As observed earlier in this chapter, taxes may be imposed for revenue purposes, for regulatory (nonrevenue) purposes, or (as is usually the case) for a combination of both purposes.

THE AGGREGATE PUBLIC SECTOR BUDGET

The federal system of government which exists in the United States introduces complexities into the aggregate public sector budget concept and its application. This is in contrast to the relative simplicity of the concept for unitary systems of government. Where two sovereign government levels exist, a proliferation of the total number of government units is not surprising. Furthermore, the volume of governmental units is greatly expanded in the United States by the ability of state governments to create additional units of local government. In addition to one sovereign federal government and 50 sovereign state governments, there are more than 90,000 units of local government in the United States. These include counties, municipalities, towns, school districts, and special districts. Yet, each of these is a part of the public sector and each is endowed with the fiscal powers of taxation and expenditure. Consequently, each exerts an economic impact on the allocation, distribution, stabilization, and economic growth goals of public finance.

The issue of fiscal coordination between the various levels and units of government thus becomes highly significant when the number of governmental units is large and when the sovereign authority is possessed by two levels of government. Indeed, there *is* such a reality as an aggregate public sector in the United States through which the budgetary process allocates scarce productive resources. Yet, this important resource-allocating institution is not unified and its components frequently work at cross-purposes to each other. Since it is inevitable that the public sector, regardless of its decentralization, exerts significant economic effects through the spending and taxing policies of government, it is desirable, in terms of economic welfare, that such influence be exerted in a coordinated manner.[7]

Thus, while the European Common Market nations (West Germany, Italy, Belgium, France, Netherlands, Luxembourg) seek fiscal coordination on an *international* basis, the United States is beset with the problems of an uncoordinated *domestic* fiscal effort on important economic issues such as education and poverty. The expansionary effects of the federal personal and corporation income tax rate reductions in 1964, moreover, were partially offset by increased state and local government taxes.[8] The public finance goals of federal fiscal activity may thus be frustrated in part by state and local government fiscal action (and vice versa). Indeed, such a lack of fiscal coordination between the levels and units of government on major goals can be economically harmful to the entire society.

A relevant problem caused by government decentralization is the

---

[7] This point can be logically defended in the "ideal world" of general welfare analysis where community preferences would be accurately revealed. It might be argued that in the absence of such ideal conditions, however, decentralized government provides a system of checks and balances which approximates a consumer-sovereignty optimum. This issue will be analyzed further in Chapters 8 and 9.

[8] This offset, however, has not proven to be as substantial as was expected by certain experts.

determination of which level of government shall perform particular allocation functions and provide particular economic goods. Another dimension is thus added to the already complicated allocation branch of public finance. Not only must society decide which economic goods to produce and which sector, public or private, shall produce these goods, but it must determine also which level of government shall provide the goods *within the public sector* if the goods are to be produced by government. Comparative economic efficiencies between the different levels of government exert some influence upon this community decision. However, noneconomic value judgments involving concepts such as freedom also play an important role in determining the division of allocation functions between federal, state, and local units of government.[9] Hence, the economic costs resulting from decentralized government may be partially offset by significant noneconomic goals.

HISTORY OF PUBLIC SECTOR BUDGETING IN THE UNITED STATES

Formal public sector budgets at the executive level were developed in the United States at a later date than in most other advanced nations of the world.[10] In addition, the pattern of governmental budgetary development in the United States differs from that of most other nations in that it was initiated first at the local government level, later utilized by state governments, and then finally by the federal government. England had developed a comprehensive executive budget at the central government level by the early 19th century and vestiges of budgeting in England may be traced back several centuries earlier. In France, an evolutionary budgetary transition which was initiated during the 18th-century French Revolution culminated in a comprehensive executive budget by the third decade of the 19th century.

The lag in federal government budgetary usage in the United States may be explained by two causes: *First,* until the beginning of the present century, federal revenues exceeded expenditures during most fiscal years. These revenues were mostly derived from tariffs and from specific domestic excise taxes such as those on tobacco and liquor. There was little popular effort to increase "efficiency" and "responsibility" in the federal government through budgetary control. A related factor working against the development of a formal federal budget was the fact that combined state-local fiscal activity typically exceeded federal government taxing and spending until the wartime periods of the 20th century and the "cold war" which followed World War II. Hence, the tendency of the federal govern-

---

[9] This issue will be considered in detail in Chapter 8.

[10] Under this arrangement, the executive branch of government follows an established, legally approved procedure in planning its expenditures and receipts.

ment to have surplus budgets throughout most of its history, and the related fact that the federal government was a relatively less important component of the public sector than combined state-local fiscal activity, created an environment in which no significant pressure existed for the adoption of a formal federal executive budget.

The relative importance of the federal component of the public sector, however, gradually increased following the Civil War as the federal government became involved in policies to regulate business and growing wealth concentration. This cause, supplemented by the considerable expenditures by the federal government during World War I and the growing confusion surrounding the financial operation of a major nation without an executive budget, combined to accelerate the transition to formal federal budgeting in the third decade of the 20th century (1921).

A *second* basic explanation for the slowness in acquiring a federal executive budget rests in the historical desire for a separation of powers between the executive, legislative, and judicial branches of government. Considerable alteration had to occur in the conceptual and practical relationships between the executive and legislative branches of government before a federal executive budget was possible. There was fear in the minds of the founding fathers at the Constitutional Convention regarding excessive power at the executive level of government. Consequently, Congress was given the power of budgeting as well as that of legislating, though it was not well qualified to perform the former function. The President's only important control over the composition of the budget would come through the right to veto, and this was to be restricted in practice by institutional behavior in the form of "riders" on appropriation bills, "pork-barreling," and "logrolling."[11] The primary budgetary function of the executive was to execute the budget passed by Congress, not to help formulate the budget.

Alexander Hamilton, the first Secretary of the Treasury, and the first Congress did not seek a formal executive budget. Hamilton, however, in accordance with his "federalist" philosophy, formulated plans for both revenues and expenditures in an aggressive fashion and then submitted them to Congress. Under Hamilton, and Wolcott, who succeeded him in 1795, the executive branch played a prominent role in fiscal decisions. Opposition to Hamilton's position gradually became stronger, however, and in 1801 the leader of the opposition, Albert Gallatin, became Secretary of the Treasury. He soon recommended that the House Committee on Ways and Means be made a permanent standing committee and this

---

[11] A rider is an extraneous provision attached to a general appropriation bill with the belief that the executive will not veto the entire bill because of the extraneous provision. Pork-barreling refers to legislation favorable to a certain local district, and logrolling refers to the exchange of support among legislators for such pork-barrel legislation.

was accomplished in 1802. This represented the termination of continuous executive control over the federal government's finances. A fragmented budgetary operation began which was to last until the third decade of the 20th century. Arthur Smithies comments that "the defeat of the Federalists, which might at the time have appeared to have settled the balance of financial power, actually began a period of financial confusion from which we have by no means fully recovered."[12]

Both revenue and appropriation control was centered in the House Committee on Ways and Means between 1802 and the end of the Civil War in 1865. The role of the Secretary of the Treasury was primarily a clerical rather than a functional decision-making role. In 1865, a House Appropriations Committee was formed, and further decentralization of budgetary decisions within the legislative branch resulted. The Appropriations Committee became so overloaded with work, however, that it did not have time to make specific appropriations. Thus, appropriation authority gradually became dispersed among the various standing legislative committees of the Congress. By 1885, there were eight committees of the House of Representatives possessing authority to recommend appropriations. Later, the total increased to ten committees in the House and eight in the Senate possessing appropriation authority.[13] Pork-barreling and logrolling flourished as the various standing committees, each interested in a particular type of activity, influenced appropriation recommendations and legislation in behalf of their respective areas of interest.[14]

Perhaps it was only the wealth of America's productive resources which allowed her to progress under such an inefficient fiscal operation. Apparently, the momentum of economic growth stemming from the application of increasing quantities of labor and capital to America's natural resource base more than offset the inefficient federal fiscal arrangement. Beginning in 1890, a number of attempts took place to improve the federal fiscal operation. These efforts were not very successful until the growing debate led to the establishment of the Taft Commission in 1911 and its subsequent report in 1912.[15]

The transition to federal executive budgeting during the 20th century was assisted in an important way by the movement toward municipal budgeting in the United States. The municipal budget movement preceded the federal budget movement by at least one decade. The fact that the municipal budget transition came first is explained in part by

[12] Arthur Smithies, *The Budgetary Process in the United States* (New York McGraw-Hill Book Co., Inc., 1955), p. 53.

[13] Vincent J. Browne, *The Control of the Public Budget* (Washington, D.C.: Public Affairs Press, 1949), pp. 50–73.

[14] Admittedly, logrolling "tradeoffs," at times, may be partially efficient as an allocation mechanism to achieve second-best welfare goals.

[15] Taft Commission on Economy and Efficiency, 62d Cong., 2d sess., House Doc. 854.

the historic fear by many Americans of a strong central government. This philosophy provided an "environment of reluctance" to improve the efficiency of federal fiscal activities. In the meantime, a strange marriage was occurring between two opposing groups which was to result in the strong movement toward municipal budgeting, as well as toward public sector budgeting in general, during the early 20th century. One group was composed of "social reformers" who wanted to strengthen the ability of the aggregate public sector to provide efficient social welfare programs. The other group was composed of "businessmen" who were seeking retrenchment in aggregate public spending and greater governmental fiscal efficiency in order to reduce their tax burdens. These two contrasting groups combined to guide the municipal budget movement to a successful conclusion. "It is difficult to assign a precise date, but it is appropriate to say that by the mid-1920's most major American cities had undergone a more or less thorough reform in municipal financial practices and had established some sort of a budget system."[16] The municipal budget movement helped pioneer the way for improvements in federal budgeting procedure.

The states followed the municipalities, and slightly preceded the federal government, in sponsoring a transition to executive budgeting. Like the federal government, the states had not been forced to adopt efficient budgeting practices because of the long-run tendency for receipts to exceed, or at least to match, expenditures and because of America's resource wealth. Also, the stability of the property tax for revenue yield was partially responsible for the formal budget void among the state governments because it provided adequate revenues even with its somewhat inefficient administration. The same conditions that were encouraging the growth of municipal and federal budgeting in the early 20th century, however, were also affecting the state governments. The first state law authorizing the semblance of an executive budget was passed in Ohio in 1910. This was followed by considerable legislation in other states during the ensuing decade and by 1920 budgetary improvement action had been taken by 44 states, about one half of which had authorized formal executive budgets.

The federal government's *Commission on Economy and Efficiency,* known as the Taft Commission, reported in 1912. This report became the direct source of the nine-year transition to the establishment of a federal executive budget in 1921. The Commission's proposals for fiscal reorganization covered five areas:[17]

1. The adoption of a comprehensive executive budget, inclusive of both revenues and expenditures, and based not only on existing statutes

[16] Jesse Burkhead, *Government Budgeting* (New York: Wiley, 1956), p. 14.

[17] Smithies, *op. cit.,* pp. 68–71.

but also to include the budgetary consequences of any new tax and expenditure legislation which may be proposed by the President. This was a departure from the assumption that budget policy can be determined *only* by Congress.

2. The adoption of a functional or program classification of expenditures in the budget. In relation to this, it was also proposed that a classification between capital and current expenditures be provided.

3. A distinction between the program aspect of the budget and the issue of economy and efficiency. For example, the President's budget message was to treat separately the financial program of the government, the economy and efficiency with which fiscal matters are transacted, the work program of the government, and changes in law deemed necessary to improve the economy and efficiency with which the public business is transacted.

4. The execution of the budget should depend upon vertical arrangements permitting discretionary actions at the various levels of fiscal responsibility.

5. Systematic review of the budget through a comprehensive accounting system under control of the Treasury, but reflecting the interests of Congress.

Proposals one and five represent the areas stressed in the legislation of 1921. The five proposals constitute the basis for both the budgetary reforms that gradually followed the Taft Commission report as well as the major areas where improvement is still needed. The areas of improvement were further enunciated by the Hoover Commission report in 1949. This report will be discussed later in the chapter.

The Taft Commission report led to the Budget and Accounting Act of 1921. This act created the Bureau of the Budget to assist the President in the preparation and execution of the budget. For the first time in American history, it became the obligation of the President to prepare a formal federal budget. The budgetary procedure established by the legislation of 1921 remains in effect today. Estimates of revenues and expenditures are to be made for the current fiscal year and data are also to be provided for the preceding fiscal year by the executive branch of government. The act created a Director of the Budget, to be appointed by and responsible to the President, and to be the chief official of the Bureau of the Budget. The Bureau was placed under the administration of the Treasury Department. This has become a highly influential policy-making office of the federal government. Only the President is in a position to observe the full scope of federal fiscal activity to the extent that the Director of the Budget can observe it. Furthermore, the Director of the Budget is in a unique position to affect the technical and allocative efficiency of federal government fiscal operations.

The act also established the office of Comptroller General which is responsible to Congress in the auditing and authorization of expenses. The Comptroller General, as chief official of the General Accounting Office, is appointed for a 15-year term of office. The General Accounting Office might be termed "a giant auditing firm." It also performs the quasi-judicial function of interpreting the intent of many statutes.

The Budget and Accounting Act of 1921 established that there should be only two fiscal committees in each house of Congress, one on revenues and the other on expenditures. The revenue committees are the House Committee on Ways and Means and the Senate Finance Committee and the expenditure committees are the House and Senate Appropriations Committees, respectively. This reduced the extreme decentralization of fiscal decision making which had existed in Congress. The revenue and expenditure sides of the budget, however, are still considered by different committees in each house of Congress despite the fact that ultimately the budget must be a single document.

While the General Accounting Office was interpreting its responsibilities broadly and aggressively in the early years under the legislation of 1921, the Bureau of the Budget was content to define its sphere of influence narrowly. Hence, the *legislative* control over budget planning remained essentially effective until Franklin D. Roosevelt took office in 1933. Before Roosevelt, the Bureau of the Budget had primarily sought efficiency in the expenditure of appropriated funds, not assistance in the planning and formulation of the budget from a policy standpoint.

In the Reorganization Act of 1939, the Bureau of the Budget was transferred into the new Executive Office of the President which, in turn, had developed from the work of the President's *Committee on Administrative Management* appointed during 1937. The Reorganization Act stipulated that the Bureau should analyze the administrative and financial implications of proposed legislation, control statistics, act as an administrative-management agency for the President, and plan fiscal policy. The last authority, however, was subsequently deleted by a statute passed in 1952. Nevertheless, the institutional groundwork had been laid for the Bureau of the Budget and its Director to become a significant component of the federal government fiscal operation.

In 1949, the *Commission on Organization of the Executive Branch of the Government,* which was known as the Hoover Commission because it was directed by the late President Herbert Hoover, made many significant recommendations for improvement in the federal fiscal process. The Commission recommended, for example, that "the whole budgetary concept of the Federal Government should be refashioned by the adoption of a budget based upon functions, activities, and projects."[18] This

[18] Commission on the Organization of the Executive Branch of the Government, "Budgeting and Accounting" (February, 1949), p. 8. This is commonly known as the Hoover Commission Report.

referred to what have become known as "performance" and "program" budgets.[19] Legislation passed by Congress during 1949 and 1950, following the Hoover Commission's suggestion, made such budget presentation mandatory as a supplement, but not as a replacement, for other budget classifications. Many other suggestions made by the Commission for improvement in the federal fiscal process have *not* been put into practice but, like the Taft Commission report of 1912, we may expect that some of these additional recommendations will be gradually integrated into federal fiscal procedure.

The federal government began its sovereign history on the basis of a fiscal year corresponding to the calendar year. In 1842, however, Congress abandoned the calendar year for the present July 1–June 30 fiscal year arrangement.[20] The change was undertaken because of difficulty that Congress had experienced in completing its action on annual appropriations prior to January 1. In these early decades of American history, Congress would convene for the purpose of appropriations in October or November which, indeed, did not provide much time for budgetary decisions before the January 1 deadline. By moving the beginning of the fiscal year back to July 1, more time was provided for the enactment of a budget. However, conditions have changed greatly since 1842 and, in many ways, the operation of the federal government fiscal year on a basis other than the calendar year is now irrational.[21]

FEDERAL BUDGETARY PROCEDURE

As noted above, the present federal budgetary process was designed by *The Budgeting and Accounting Act of 1921.* This budgetary procedure may be divided into four phases: (1) executive preparation and submission, (2) legislative review and enactment, (3) executive implementation, and (4) auditing by the General Accounting Office. These four steps in federal budgeting will be discussed in the sequence with which they are practiced.

1. *Executive Preparation and Submission of the Budget.* The proposed budget is formulated in the executive branch of the federal government. Preliminary planning begins some 14 months before a budget goes into effect. Federal agencies prepare estimates of their desired expenditures for the fiscal year which will begin 14 months later. For example, Fiscal Year 1969 begins on July 1, 1968, and ends on June

[19] A performance budget is based upon activities, functions, and projects. The performance units (the activities, functions, and projects) are parts of a broader, more comprehensive program. These budget types are discussed in greater detail later in the chapter.

[20] S. Stanley Katz, "The Federal Fiscal Year: Its Origin and Prospects," *National Tax Journal* (December, 1959), pp. 346–62.

[21] *Ibid.*

30, 1969.[22] Federal agencies thus prepare estimates in April of 1967 for the 1969 fiscal year. In May of 1967, these estimates are submitted to the Bureau of the Budget for preliminary review. By this time, the executive branch will have formulated its overall fiscal philosophy for the fiscal year in question. This will be done by the Bureau of the Budget and the President, who will be assisted by revenue estimates from the Treasury Department and economic forecasts from the Council of Economic Advisers and other sources.

The Bureau of the Budget then returns the budget requests to the agencies, accompanied by both (1) a statement of the administration's overall fiscal philosophy for the fiscal year and (2) suggested budgetary policies for the agencies. In the summer of 1967, the agencies recast their budget requests in accordance with the administration's philosophy and requests. The revised estimates are then resubmitted to the Bureau of the Budget, which reviews and discusses them with the respective agencies. The agencies may be asked to defend or change their requests. The President possesses considerable authority to reduce budget requests. By late November or December of 1967, the Bureau of the Budget under the leadership of the Director of the Budget, following the desires of the President, assembles the various estimates into a unified budget document inclusive of estimated receipts from taxes. The President submits the proposed budget for Fiscal 1969 to Congress in his budget message during the third week of January, 1968.

2. *Legislative Review and Enactment of the Budget.* Unlike a unitary or parliamentary system of government where the legislature usually adopts the executive budget in the form in which it is presented, the executive budget in our system is likely to be altered considerably by Congress. The budget is referred first to the Appropriations Committee of the House. In our example, this would occur in late January, 1968. Then, various subcommittees of the House Appropriations Committee conduct hearings at which the government agencies are asked to explain and defend their budget requests. The separate appropriations bills are subsequently returned to the House Appropriations Committee which submits them to the floor of the House for ultimate debate and passage. The Senate Appropriations Committee follows a procedure similar to that in the House but concentrates upon the relationship between the monetary magnitude of the President's appropriations requests and that authorized in the House Appropriations bill.

When an appropriations bill is passed by both Houses of Congress, which usually is after differences have been ironed out, it goes to the President for signature. The Chief Executive does *not* have the power of selective (item) veto. He must accept the bill totally, or not at all. This

---

[22] The fiscal year of the federal government takes the name of the calendar year in which the fiscal period terminates.

encourages, of course, the attachment of riders and the practices of pork-barreling and logrolling. The selective (item) veto is used by most states. However, Congress traditionally fears that the selective veto represents a dangerous extension of Presidential power.[23] Smithies observes that the problem appears to be in the definition of "item" in such a manner that it relates exclusively to an item which does not affect the operation of the remainder of the appropriations bill.[24] Otherwise, the President could alter the effect of the entire bill by vetoing a single item. The need for a selective Presidential veto would be intensified if Congress used an omnibus (all-inclusive, single) appropriations bill, as it attempted during the 1951 fiscal year. In our example, appropriations bills should be passed by July 1, 1968, for Fiscal Year 1969. Sometimes, the deadline is barely made; frequently, it is missed—and by a wide mark.

Tax bills as well as appropriations bills, according to constitutional provision, must originate in the House of Representatives. Revenue bills thus work their way from the House Committee on Ways and Means to the floor of the House and, when passed, to the Senate Finance Committee. Subsequently, Senate revenue bills are considered in the Senate Finance Committee, go to the Senate floor, and eventually are voted upon. When voted upon, the Senate bills reflect the compromise results of the Conference Committee composed of members of both houses. When passed, they go to the President for signature.

There is no formal consideration by Congress of the budget as a whole. Tax bills and appropriations bills are considered separately in both the House and in the Senate by different committees. Furthermore, the bills are passed as separate statutes by Congress and are signed into law as separate statutes by the President. This decentralization of procedure differs vastly from budgetary procedure in most other mature Western nations. In particular, there is a sharp contrast to the consideration and passage of a unified budget under the parliamentary system of government such as that in England. It is particularly difficult under the American system to relate program benefits and costs to each other and to generally apply efficiency criteria. It is also difficult to formulate fiscal policy for stabilization and economic growth objectives.

3. *Presidential Implementation of the Budget.* The President has the obligation to implement (execute) the budget. The Bureau of the Budget authorizes the various agencies to spend the appropriated funds on a quarterly basis. This is to prevent an agency from spending too much of its yearly appropriation early in the fiscal year. Once the budget authorizations are received, the agencies may purchase economic goods

---

[23] For a discussion favoring the selective veto, see: Hearings before the House Expenditures Committee, July 8 and 18, 1950, on H. R. 8054, 81st Cong., 2d sess.

[24] Smithies, *op. cit.*, p. 100.

and productive resources, as needed, to perform their various functions. The Treasury Department releases funds in accordance with vouchers that have been prepared by the spending agencies. The funds are to be spent within the legislative intent of the appropriations bills, but a reasonable amount of discretion is left to the agencies.

4. *Auditing of the Budget by the General Accounting Office.* Congress has created the General Accounting Office, headed by the Comptroller General, to assure that appropriated funds are spent in accordance with the provisions of the appropriations bill and to discourage fraud. This office reports directly to Congress. Several thousand accountants are employed by the GAO to help it perform its huge task. As noted earlier, it is a quasi-judicial agency in the sense that it must interpret the intent which Congress had at the time the legislation was enacted. The broad powers of the GAO include: (1) the authority to decide most questions involving payments made by government agencies, (2) the auditing and settling of all public accounts, (3) settling, adjudicating, and adjusting all claims for and against the government, (4) prescribing systems and procedures for administrative appropriation and fund accounting, and (5) the investigation of all matters relating to receipts and disbursements of public funds, including the right to examine pertinent books, documents, papers, and records of government contractors and subcontractors. In addition, the Office of Comptroller General makes specific studies and analyses of the administration of expenditures by particular governmental agencies for the benefit of Congress.

TYPES OF BUDGETS

Public sector budgets exist for two substantially different purposes. One purpose of a government budget centers around the function of accounting. An orderly arrangement for control of expenditures and for their relationship to governmental receipts is necessary for every large financial operation. Government is no exception. This purpose of public sector budgeting, however, is not directly connected to the four goals or objectives of public finance. It is merely a bookkeeping function. On the other hand, the purpose of governmental budgeting relevant to public finance centers upon the economic problem of resource scarcity and the related issues that derive from it. Hence, the budget is viewed, in this context, as an economic means whereby resource allocation, income and wealth distribution, economic stabilization, and economic growth can be affected for the society as a whole through governmental budgetary activities. The discussion that follows will emphasize the latter interpretation of the budget as it applies, primarily, to federal government budgeting.

The federal government does not possess a single budget type which meets all requirements for rationality in affecting the allocation, distribution, stabilization, and economic growth goals. Instead, a variety of budget types exist, or have been proposed. These include the administrative, consolidated-cash, national-income-accounts, full-employment, capital, performance and program budgets. They are described below:

1. *The Administrative Budget.* The budget submitted by the President to Congress in January is the "administrative budget" which is sometimes referred to as the "conventional budget." Essentially, it is this budget which reflects the *general* tax and expenditure flows to and from the federal Treasury. It excludes special earmarked taxes and expenditures. The administrative budget, among the various budget concepts, receives the most attention from Congress and from the nation's press. This budget forms the basis for congressional supervision of federal taxing and spending activities. The administrative budget is essentially an accounting budget incorporating statistics derived directly from the accounting records of federal agencies. It does not serve especially well as a guide to economic policy because of inherent problems of "incompleteness" and "timing."

The administrative budget is incomplete in that it excludes two major types of fiscal flows, namely, trust funds and certain transactions of government corporations and credit agencies. Since federal trust funds comprise a volume of activities now exceeding $30 billion, their exclusion renders the administrative budget incomplete as a representation of the impact of the federal government on the allocation, distribution, stabilization, and economic growth goals of public finance. The excluded special account activities include the Old-age and Survivors Insurance Trust Fund, federal employees retirement funds, railroad retirement account, veterans' life insurance funds, and some 150 other miscellaneous trust and deposit funds. The treatment in the administrative budget of government corporations such as the Post Office Department and of government credit agencies such as the federal land banks is also incomplete. This is shown by the fact that only the *net* earnings or losses of such enterprises are included in the administrative budget, not the gross revenues and expenditures.

The economic effects of federal fiscal activity may be difficult to ascertain, from a policymaking standpoint, because of certain timing problems in the administrative budget. The pattern of corporate behavior, for example, may well be influenced by corporation income taxes at the time when they accrue instead of when the payments are actually made. Yet, the administrative budget only records taxes when they are actually collected. Moreover, a time lag frequently exists between the "authorization" of expenditures and the "actual" expenditures for productive resources and economic goods. Some current fiscal year expenditures have been authorized during the preceding fiscal year and some of the next fiscal year's expenditures will be authorized during the present fiscal year.

The receipts included in the administrative budget are primarily tax revenues such as those from personal income taxes, corporation income taxes, excise taxes, estate and gift taxes, and customs duties. Receipts from borrowing are not included in the administrative budget. All expenditures are classified as current, recurring-type expenditures. Thus, no distinction is made between current and capital investment expenditures.

2. *The Consolidated-Cash Budget.* The consolidated-cash budget is in official use by the federal government, but historically it has not been publicized as much or used as extensively by Congress as the administrative budget. Yet, its popularity seems to be increasing. Generally, this budget attempts to measure all cash flowing into and out of the Treasury *including* special trust and deposit fund activities. Like the administrative budget, it does not distinguish between current and capital expenditures. Moreover, it likewise does not indicate tax receipts on an accrual basis, but only on a collection basis. Furthermore, it also lists the receipts and expenditures of government corporations on a net basis. For example, it lists the postal deficit instead of the gross receipts and gross expenditures of the Post Office Department.

Although several differences exist between the administrative and consolidated-cash budgets, by far the most important difference is the inclusion of trust fund activities in the consolidated-cash budget. This inclusion makes the latter budget more effective for economic policy decisions than the less comprehensive administrative budget. Some minor differences between the two budgets are (1) the adjustment (deduction from cash expenditures) in the consolidated-cash budget of certain noncash transactions like interest accrued, but not yet paid, on Treasury securities and (2) the elimination in the consolidated-cash budget of intragovernmental transactions such as interest paid by the Treasury to the Old-Age and Survivors Insurance Trust Fund.

3. *The National-Income-Accounts Budget.* Increased attention has been given in recent years to the national-income-accounts budget as a budget well suited for policymaking decisions. The data for the national-income-accounts budget are derived from the system of national income and product accounts provided by the Department of Commerce. These accounts present aggregate "resource-absorbing" production and "income creation" by the public and private sectors of the economy on a quarterly basis. They disaggregate private sector activities into consumption and investment and public sector activities into federal and state-local components. The federal component of these public sector receipts and expenditures comprises the national-income-accounts budget.

Similar to the administrative and consolidated-cash budgets, the national-income-accounts budget does not distinguish current from capital expenditures. Also, like the consolidated-cash budget, but unlike the administrative budget, it does include trust fund activities. It thus avoids one of the serious errors of incompleteness, for policymaking purposes, of the administrative budget. Several essential differences exist, however, between the consolidated-cash and the national-income-accounts budgets, though both are similarly comprehensive in their important inclusion of trust fund activities.

The national-income-accounts budget, for example, concentrates upon income-creating and resource-absorbing activities instead of on cash flows. It thus seems more closely associated with basic economic activity—the use of productive resources to produce economic goods in the current period. Moreover, after-tax individual and business income, the single most important determinant of the private sector purchasing power which leads to the creation of a major segment of gross national product, is considered.

In its concentration upon income-creating activities in the current period, the national-income-accounts budget excludes capital transactions such as the sale by government of used plant and equipment and the purchase or sale by government of land. Furthermore, certain loan transactions which are included in the consolidated-cash budget are excluded. An important advantage of the national-income-accounts budget over the administrative and consolidated-cash budgets, however, is that it treats many expenditures on the accrual basis, which is when the resources are absorbed and not when the payments are made. Moreover, it records some major revenues such as corporation income taxes on an accrual basis. This recording of many expenditures and some major receipts on an accrual basis is advantageous for policymaking purposes. Also, the better timing provided by the quarterly measurements of economic flows must be considered an advantage. The exclusion of loans to other governmental units, to industry, and to individuals, however, must be considered a drawback to the policymaking quality of the national-income-accounts budget because such credit extensions are certain to affect economic activity and the four public finance goals. Table 6–1 reflects the similarities and differences of the federal government's three most important budget types—the administrative, consolidated-cash, and national-income-accounts budgets—which have been discussed above.

4. *The Full-Employment Budget.* This is the newest of the budgetary concepts. The full-employment budget essentially consists of the national-income-accounts budget as projected to conditions of full employment, given current federal tax rates and expenditure patterns. This budget concept was instrumental in the "historic" federal personal

TABLE 6–1

RELATION OF FEDERAL GOVERNMENT RECEIPTS AND EXPENDITURES
IN THE NATIONAL INCOME ACCOUNTS TO THE ADMINISTRATIVE
AND CASH BUDGETS, FISCAL YEARS 1965, 1966,* 1967*
(Billions of Dollars)

		1965	1966	1967
Receipts:				
	Administrative budget receipts	93.1	100.0	111.0
Less:	Intragovernmental transactions	4.3	4.5	5.5
	Receipts from exercise of monetary authority	.1	.9	1.6
Plus:	Trust fund receipts	31.0	33.5	41.6
Equals:	Federal receipts from the public (cash receipts)	119.7	128.2	145.5
Less:	Adjustment for agency coverage: District of			
	Columbia revenues	.3	.3	.3
	Other	.1	.1	.1
	Financial transactions	.4	.1	.2
	Miscellaneous	.2	.1	.1
Plus:	Netting differences:			
	Contributions to government employees' retirement			
	funds	2.2	2.2	2.2
	Other	−1.5	−2.1	−2.3
Plus:	Timing differences	.2	1.0	−2.6
	Miscellaneous	.1†	.1	.1
Equals:	Receipts in national income and product accounts	119.6	128.8	142.2
Expenditures:				
	Administrative budget expenditures	96.5	106.4	112.8
Plus:	Trust fund expenditures (includes government-			
	sponsored enterprises (net)	29.6	33.8	37.9
Less:	Intragovernmental transactions	4.3	4.5	5.5
	Debt insurance in lieu of checks and other adjust-			
	ments	− .6	.7	.2
Equals:	Federal payments to the public (cash expenditures)	122.4	135.0	145.0
Less:	Coverage differences:			
	District of Columbia	.4	.4	.5
	Federal Home Loan Banks and Federal Land Banks	1.2	.4	.5
	Other	.2	.3	.3
Less:	Financial transactions:			
	Net lending	2.4	1.5	−1.4
	Net purchases of foreign currency	.9	1.0	1.0
Less:	Timing differences:			
	Checks outstanding and certain other accounts	.9	−.1	.1
	Miscellaneous	.7	.4	.7
Plus:	Netting differences:			
	Contributions to government employee retirement			
	funds	2.2	2.2	2.2
	Other	−1.5	−2.1	−2.3
	Timing differences	1.5	− .6	− .8
	Miscellaneous	.4	.4	.3
Equals:	Federal expenditures in national income and			
	product accounts	118.3	131.0	142.7

* 1966 and 1967 figures are estimates.
† Less than $50 million.

SOURCE: U.S. Department of Commerce, *Survey of Current Business*, Vol. 46, No. 2 (February, 1966),
p. 7.

and corporation income tax reductions of March, 1964.[25] The full-employment budget concept was suggested first by the Committee for Economic Development which, in 1947, recommended that tax rates and expenditures be set so that a "slight" (not overly restrictive) surplus would exist at full employment. In recent times, it has been suggested that this budget usually would have shown a "considerable" surplus at full employment. Hence, it has been concluded that the persistent short-run unemployment and the lagging rates of long-run economic growth which the United States experienced from the end of the Korean War until the 1960's are to be explained by the overly restrictive federal budgetary policies then in effect. This served as a background argument for the substantial income tax reduction bill passed by Congress during 1964.

Specifically, the full-employment budget "surplus" may be defined as "the federal budget surplus, on a national-income-accounts basis, that would be generated by a given budget program if the economy were operating at full employment with stable prices throughout the entire fiscal year."[26] Full employment is usually defined as a situation where 4 percent or less of the seasonally adjusted labor force is involuntarily unemployed. When the full-employment budget shows a surplus, the surplus represents the quantity of federal government "saving," as measured through the national-income accounts, that will exist under conditions of full employment (so defined). In many ways, the full-employment budget possesses considerable potential for successful usage as a policymaking tool. It will be discussed in fiscal policy terms in Part IV of this book.

5. *The Capital Budget.*   A capital budget separates total governmental expenditure into current and capital items. This type of budget was suggested for the federal government as long ago as the Budget and Accounting Act of 1921. None of the four budget concepts previously discussed makes such a distinction. The "current" part of the budget reflects expenditure on recurring items such as salaries for government workers and office supplies. The "capital" component of the budget reflects nonrecurring expenditure on capital assets of a durable nature. According to the capital budget concept, the budget is "balanced" if current tax collections (or other receipts except those from borrowing) equal current expenditures, including depreciation allowances for existing durable goods. It is thus implied that long-term capital items should be financed through borrowing (debt-creation) activities.

The capital budget concept for central government was popular in

---

[25] These reductions are termed historic by many people who assert that the tax cuts represent for the first time a rational consensus in favor of reducing taxes to promote employment and growth objectives.

[26] Michael E. Levy, *Fiscal Policy, Cycles and Growth* (New York: National Industrial Conference Board, 1963), p. 22.

Scandinavia, especially in Sweden, during the 1930's and is now used in other nations such as the Netherlands, England, Canada, India, Union of South Africa, and Ecuador. Moreover, states such as Connecticut, Maryland, Michigan, Minnesota, North Carolina, and Oregon employ the technique. In addition, it is used by many American municipalities, which obviously cannot expect to pay for acquisitions of new durable capital out of current receipts, given the restricted nature of their taxing authority.

The capital budget may be defended on the grounds that it shows that government spending often results in the acquisition of durable, productive capital and is not "money poured down a rathole" as too many unthinking people prefer to believe. The capital budget, moreover, has the advantage of pointing up the often overlooked fact that the failure of current receipts to cover all expenditures, both current and capital, is not indicative per se of "fiscal irresponsibility."[27] On the other hand, the capital budget could provide a disservice to society if it led to excessive investment in durable capital goods at the expense of current services and also at the expense of worthy investment in human resources by causing reduced expenditures for health, education, and safety. These items would not necessarily be treated as capital items under the capital budget concept. Indeed, the whole issue of classifying expenditures as current or capital is a complex one. Furthermore, though the failure of current receipts to cover all expenditure is not indicative per se of fiscal irresponsibility, a complete divorcement from the orthodox idea of budget balance could lead to irrational fiscal action. Moreover, the reader should be reminded that fiscal efficiency requires that the *social rate of return* from public investment, including indirect and nonmeasurable benefits, must equal the rate of return which the employed resources could earn in the private sector. A recent study by Comiez recommends against the adoption of capital budgeting for the federal government.[28]

6. *The Performance and Program Budgets.* Because of the close relationship between the performance and program budget concepts, they will be discussed together in this chapter. Though the two budget concepts are similar, they are not synonymous.[29] The performance budget concentrates upon the efficiency of input-output relationships directed toward a particular budgetary goal. The particular performance goal is a *component* of a broader, more comprehensive program. Performance and program budgets may follow either a "maximization" or "minimization" approach, that is, they can either achieve the greatest output results from

[27] Fortunately, this version of fiscal responsibility is much less common than it was a generation ago.

[28] Maynard S. Comiez, *A Capital Budget Statement for the U.S. Government* (Washington, D.C.: Brookings Institution, 1966).

[29] Burkhead, *op. cit.*, p. 139.

a given resource input, or can minimize resource costs for the attainment of a given output or goal. Actually, a program budget ordinarily includes several performance units.[30] A government agency may participate in several different programs, but performing units within the agency are responsible for the efficiency of serving any particular program. Program and performance budgeting also may be distinguished according to a time dimension. Budgetary programs are forward looking or ex ante plans and projections, while performance budgeting looks backward, ex post, at the efficiency of action already undertaken.[31] Program budgets which relate to broad programs can assist policymaking decisions at the top levels of Congress and the Executive Office of the President. Performance budgets are more useful for efficiency control within a particular government agency. The Hoover Commission (1949) is responsible for encouraging the use of program and performance budgeting by the federal government.

The idea behind performance and program budgeting is to increase efficiency in decision making. It relates closely to the established idea of operations research which now is used so prominently in business decision making in the private sector of the economy. Choices need to be known concerning both the alternative programs of objectives and also concerning the alternative means of achieving a particular objective. Social benefits and costs need to be related. In general, these budgeting techniques involve the application of scientific methodology to public sector decision making. At the federal level, they have been used particularly in Defense Department and in water resource development decisions, though recently they have been extended by executive order to *all* federal government agencies.[32]

Other Sources of Government Fiscal Information. Several additional budgetary concepts and sources of fiscal information exist which may be put to policymaking use at the federal level of government. In the 1930's, President Franklin D. Roosevelt introduced the *emergency budget* concept. All depression-relieving expenditures were classified as part of an emergency component of the budget and it was not expected that current tax receipts should cover these expenditures. This was intended to reveal that the government was being operated in a fiscally responsible

---

[30] *Ibid.*

[31] *Ibid.*

[32] See Charles J. Hitch and Roland N. McKean, *The Economics of Defense in the Nuclear Age* (Cambridge, Mass.: Harvard University Press, 1960); J. V. Krutilla and Otto Eckstein, *Multiple Purpose River Development* (Baltimore: Johns Hopkins Press, 1958); Roland N. McKean, *Efficiency in Government Through Systems Analysis* (New York: Wiley, 1958); Alain C. Enthoven, "Economic Analysis in the Department of Defense," American Economic Association Proceedings (May, 1963), p. 413; and other sources for consideration of operations research and cost-benefit analysis.

manner since the ordinary, nonemergency functions of government were being financed on a pay-as-you-go basis through taxes. It was thus suggested that the budget was balanced in the ordinary sense and unbalanced with a deficit only because of the depression emergency. This concept of budgeting did not catch on with the American public and was subsequently eliminated.

A good source of information on federal fiscal activity is found in the various data and information services reported by the Federal Reserve System. Most of these figures are provided on a net basis. The Federal Reserve data include such items as individual and corporate income taxes, excise taxes, customs receipts, estate tax receipts, gift tax receipts, fines, payments to the Treasury on federal reserve notes outstanding and social insurance program data. The Federal Reserve System shows net purchases of goods and services in a manner similar to the national income accounts.

The Bureau of the Census also provides valuable federal fiscal information. In general, the census data include all federal budget receipts and expenditures except those for unemployment compensation and for the District of Columbia. Intragovernmental fiscal transactions are treated similarly to their presentation in the national-income accounts except for the inclusion of interest payments on Treasury securities to trust funds in both the receipts and expenditure accounts. Government loans are excluded from the census data. Most data are presented on a cash rather than on an accrual basis. One distinct advantage of the census data is that government corporations are treated on a gross basis for both receipts and expenditures. In addition, the *Census of Governments* provided by the Bureau of the Census is a valuable source of aggregate public sector fiscal information.

Other sources of federal fiscal information include the various *Congressional Hearings* on tax and appropriation matters. In addition, the works of the special research components of the government created by the Employment Act of 1946, namely, the *Council of Economic Advisers* at the executive level and the *Joint Economic Committee* at the congressional level, are extremely valuable for policymaking purposes. Finally, the various Treasury Department statistics and publications add to the stock of economic information available concerning the impact of the federal component of the public sector on the public finance objectives of allocation, distribution, stabilization, and growth. These include the *Treasury Bulletin* and the *Annual Report of the Secretary of the Treasury.*

No single one of the various budget concepts discussed in this chapter can be selected as the ideal federal government budget from a policymaking standpoint. Each contains some features helpful to the policymaker. Yet, some types of budgets serve policymaking purposes better than do others. Indeed, the consolidated-cash and national-income-accounts budgets are far more comprehensive, and the latter represents much better timing, than does the administrative budget. In addition, the full-employment budget has been particularly applicable during the recent era of underfull-employment equilibrium and slow economic growth rates (1954–64). And so on—each budget type has certain advantages. The inevitable conclusion is that the budget information available to the federal government policymaker must be an "eclectic," but organized, array of the best components of *all* the budget types and information sources discussed above. It is to our advantage that we have several "looking glasses." Much work remains to be done in providing an orderly and integrated array of fiscal knowledge, but interest and progress can presently be detected in this direction.

Chapter 7 : PUBLIC SECTOR GROWTH IN THE UNITED STATES

Although the symmetrical character of the budgetary process is stressed throughout the book as a whole, the present chapter will approach public sector growth trends and changes in a somewhat asymmetrical manner. Of course, the tax or revenue side of the budget will be used to help demonstrate government fiscal trends in the United States. However, the primary emphasis herein will be upon changes in public sector *expenditure* patterns, which serve as ideal "indicators" of governmental fiscal trends, since they show the functional reasons for which governmental economic activity occurs. Meanwhile, the tax, or revenue, side of the budget receives due stress in Part III of the book while the residual of certain tax-expenditure arrangements, government debt, is considered in Part IV.

EXPENDITURE PATTERNS

Prior to 1900

Federal expenditures display a secular growth trend throughout American history. The growth, however, has been cyclical rather than continuous. Moreover, even when adjusted for both intertemporal price level differences and for population growth, federal expenditures in real per capita terms also display an interrupted pattern of growth. Real per capita federal expenditures, for example, were either stationary or declining between 1794–1811, 1817–46, 1866–84, and 1899–1916.[1] Thus, real per capita federal expenditures did not increase for a total of 81 years of American history prior to World War I.

Federal expenditures at the present time may be compared to the very small federal expenditure base at the beginning of the sovereign history of the United States. During the first full year of its existence, 1789–90, the federal government spent less than $1 million. Federal expenditures did not reach $10 million until 1800, more than a decade after national sovereignty had begun. Federal spending first reached the $20–$30 million range during the War of 1812, but waited many addi-

[1] M. Slade Kendrick, *A Century and a Half of Federal Expenditures*, Occasional Paper 48, National Bureau of Economic Research, 1955.

tional years before shooting past the $40 million dollar mark to $57 million in 1847, a figure more than double the spending in the previous year, 1846. The first year in which federal expenditures exceeded the billion-dollar mark was the last year of the Civil War, 1865, when they totaled nearly $1.3 billion. Following the war, they dropped sharply and stayed under $1 billion until the nation's entry into World War I in 1917. American history thus clearly demonstrates the pronounced impact of wars upon federal expenditure patterns. During both the War of 1812 and the Civil War, the ratio of federal expenditures to gross national product increased, though generally this ratio was considerably lower during the 19th century than it is today. In fact, the ratio of federal spending to gross national product was as low as one half of 1 percent during extended periods of America's early history.

The fiscal activities of *state* governments, after a relatively slow beginning, increased significantly during the second quarter of the 19th century.[2] At this time, the states assumed the responsibility for many internal improvements of a social capital nature from the federal government as well as considerable responsibilities in the fields of charity and corrections from local government.[3] In addition, the states initiated aid to schools, with most of the funds coming from the sale of public lands, though later federal surpluses distributed to the states provided an additional revenue source. Some states furnished financial assistance to private colleges and several states in the South and West established state universities prior to the Civil War. Still others, particularly New York, founded free teachers colleges. State expenditures, which were correlated closely with the business cycle during this period, increased sharply during prosperities and declined during depressions.

During the latter half of the 19th century, conservative politico-economic philosophies were influential in restraining state government participation in the provision of internal improvements and in furnishing credit to private enterprise. Nevertheless, the states indirectly provided for such functional expenditure activities by making it legally possible for local units of government to undertake them. The states, in addition, gave local government the powers to organize basic educational activities.

During the 1860's and 1870's, most state expenditures were dominated by the Civil War and its consequences. Compensation was paid to volunteers during the war and to veterans and their survivors after the war. Considerable state revenues were allocated during the 1870's to the

[2] For an excellent coverage of the expenditure activities of state and local governments prior to 1900, see Paul Studenski and Herman E. Krooss, *Financial History of the United States* (New York: McGraw-Hill Book Co., Inc., 1963), chaps. 12 and 17.

[3] A classic example of state internal investment in social capital is the Erie Canal Project sponsored by New York State between 1817–25. This project initiated the vast state investments in internal improvements.

repayment of debts accumulated during the Civil War era. A significant increase in state expenditures subsequently occurred between 1880 and 1900 as the states extended their regulatory, educational, and social service functions.

Local government fiscal activity prior to 1900 followed a pattern similar to that of state governments during the early part of the period. Like the state governments, local governments were beginning by the second quarter of the 19th century to meet the increased demand of the population for internal social capital improvements and for various social services—objectives which both levels of government had met quite modestly prior to 1825.

These activities intensified as the incipient American industrial revolution and heavy population immigration led to a rapid growth of American cities during the second quarter of the century. Thus, municipal governments increasingly provided such social capital items as water systems, sewer systems, and all-weather streets and such social services as fire protection, police protection, and free public education.[4]

During the latter part of the century, local government further increased its internal improvement and assistance to private enterprise activities. The continuing growth of sheer numbers in urban area population justified this action. In the 40 years between 1860 and 1900, urban population increased from 20 percent to 40 percent of the growing total population. The expansion in local government expenditures occurred mostly during prosperities, with subsequent slowing down of expenditure growth, or even retrenchment, during business cycle downturns.

20th-Century Expenditure Trends

Public sector expenditures have increased significantly as a percentage of gross national product during the 20th century. This is, of course, a direct indication that the point of "actual" resource allocation in the American economy is increasing in the direction of greater relative resource allocation by the public sector.[5]

Table 7–1 shows that public expenditures have nearly quadrupled as a percentage of GNP during the century. Moreover, a significant threefold increase may be detected between 1929, the end of the prosperous 1920's, and 1966. During the height of World War II (1944), the expenditures of government were nearly 50 percent of GNP, while in 1966 they stood at a ratio of less than 30 percent.

Total public sector expenditures, in current prices, have increased

[4] Some municipalities, with at least implicit state government approval, provided for the organization of *independent school districts* to administer the public education needs of the community. Significantly, such school districts possess the important symmetrical budgetary functions of both tax collecting and spending.

[5] See Chapters 1 and 4 for the discussion of social balance and actual allocation.

TABLE 7–1

TOTAL PUBLIC SECTOR EXPENDITURES AS A
PERCENTAGE OF GNP, SELECTED
CALENDAR YEARS, 1902–66

Year	Total Public Expenditures* as a Percentage of GNP
1902	8.0
1913	8.5
1929	9.8
1940	18.4
1944	48.8
1947	18.7
1950	21.5
1955	24.8
1960	27.2
1965	26.0
1966†	29.4

* Expenditures are from the U.S. Department of Commerce's National Income and Product Accounts. These are presented on an accrual basis and include government trust fund transactions, but exclude those capital transactions not representing current production.

† 1966 figures are first quarter estimates based upon Department of Commerce data.

SOURCE: U.S. Department of Commerce, Office of Business Economics, *Survey of Current Business* (May, 1966), p. 5; U.S. Department of Commerce data since 1929; author's estimates for data prior to 1929, with reference given to national product data from Simon Kuznets, *National Product Since 1869*, National Bureau of Economic Research, 1946.

from $1.6 billion in 1902 to nearly $206 billion in 1964–65 (see Table 7–2). The federal government accounted for $130 billion, or 63 percent of the total, in 1964–65 while state governments accounted for over 17 percent and local government nearly 20 percent. Significantly, federal government expenditures have increased from approximately one third to approximately two thirds of total public sector spending during the 20th century. At the same time, state government expenditures have increased from nearly 11 percent to more than 17 percent while local government spending has decreased sharply from more than one half to less than one fifth of the total. The relative decline of the combined state-local component of the public sector, and particularly of the local government component, occurred despite sharp absolute increases in both state and local government spending.

A disaggregation of these aggregate expenditures into four components—direct, intergovernmental, utility and liquor store operations, and trust fund-financed expenditures—reveals a number of significant trends:[6] (1) intergovernmental expenditures of the federal government

[6] The information in the next two paragraphs is primarily based upon Department of Commerce data.

have increased from a negligible amount in 1913 to approximately 9 percent of total federal expenditures in 1965; (2) trust fund expenditures have grown to a position of substantial importance (in 1913, these expenditures were insignificant at all levels of government, but now they are extensively used by the federal government and used prominently, though to a lesser extent, by state government); and (3) expenditures for the operation of utilities and liquor stores by state and local governments have doubled in relative importance since 1913.

TABLE 7–2

FEDERAL, STATE, AND LOCAL GOVERNMENT EXPENDITURES,* IN ABSOLUTE TERMS
AND IN PERCENTAGE DISTRIBUTION, BY LEVEL OF GOVERNMENT,
SELECTED FISCAL YEARS, 1902–65

	Absolute Dollar Terms (Millions)				Percentage Distribution				
Year	Total	Federal	State	Local	Total	Federal	State	Local	Combined State-Local
1902......$	1,660	$ 572	$ 179	$ 909	100.0	34.4	10.8	54.8	65.6
1913......	3,215	970	372	1,873	100.0	30.2	11.6	58.3	69.9
1927......	11,220	3,533	1,882	5,805	100.0	31.5	16.8	51.7	68.5
1932......	12,437	4,266	2,562	5,609	100.0	34.3	20.6	45.1	65.7
1936......	16,758	9,165	3,144	4,449	100.0	54.7	18.8	26.5	45.3
1940......	20,417	10,061	4,545	5,811	100.0	49.3	22.2	28.5	50.7
1944......	109,947	100,520	4,062	5,365	100.0	91.4	3.7	4.9	8.6
1950......	70,334	44,800	12,774	12,761	100.0	63.7	18.2	18.1	36.3
1955......	110,717	73,441	17,400	19,875	100.0	66.3	15.7	18.0	33.7
1960......	151,288	97,284	25,035	28,970	100.0	64.3	16.5	19.2	35.7
1964–65†..	205,958	130,059	35,594	40,305	100.0	63.1	17.3	19.6	36.9

* Expenditures are treated in terms of the financing rather than the final spending level of government; i.e., by treating amounts represented by intergovernmental transactions as expenditures of the originating rather than the recipient government.

† The financial statistics presented here for 1964–65 relate to governmental fiscal years which ended June 30, 1965, or at some date within the 12 previous months.

SOURCE: Data from U.S. Department of Commerce, Bureau of the Census. 1964–65 data from Department of Commerce, Bureau of the Census, *Governmental Finances in 1964–65* (Washington, D.C.: U.S. Government Printing Office, 1966), pp. 5–6.

If total public sector spending is disaggregated into the functions undertaken by the different levels of government, the following observations may be made: The federal government provides the highest percentage of such functional expenditures as national defense, health, natural resources, air transportation, interest on debt, and insurance trust fund activities. State governments, meanwhile, lead the way with the highest percentage expended on such items as highways and hospitals. Local governments, in turn, spend the most for such functions as education, utility operations, and general control. Importantly, the substantial growth in both defense-related activities and in transfer payments, the latter inclusive of trust fund operations of a social insurance nature, are provided by the federal component of the public sector, while the "other governmental purchases of goods and services" category is essentially state-local in origin.

A functional distribution of *federal* expenditures for the 1967 fiscal year demonstrates the considerable importance of national defense to the federal budget. Nearly 54 percent of administrative budget expenditures go for direct defense spending, with no other functional expenditure category constituting more than 11.3 percent of the total, as demonstrated in Table 7–3. Moreover, approximately 74 percent of federal administra-

TABLE 7–3

FEDERAL EXPENDITURES BY FUNCTION AND BY PERCENTAGE
DISTRIBUTION, FISCAL 1967, IN ADMINISTRATIVE
BUDGET TERMS

Function	Total Dollar Expenditure (Millions)	Percent of Total Expenditure
Total expenditures..........................	$112,847	100%
National defense.........................	60,541	53.6
International affairs and finance............	4,177	3.7
Space research and technology.............	5,300	4.7
Veterans benefits and services.............	5,721	5.0
Health, labor and welfare.................	9,962	8.8
Education..............................	2,834	2.5
Agriculture and agricultural resources......	3,372	2.1
Natural resources.......................	3,062	2.7
Commerce and transportation.............	2,672	2.3
Housing and community development.......	123	.1
General government......................	2,591	2.3
Interest................................	12,854	11.3
Allowance for contingencies...............	350	.3
Interfund transactions (deduct)............	717	.6

SOURCE: *Budget in Brief, Fiscal Year 1967* (Washington, D.C.: U.S. Government Printing Office), pp. 66–67.

tive budget expenditures may be classified as "defense spending" if the concept is broadened to encompass such "indirect" defense items as: (1) international affairs and finance (including foreign aid), (2) veterans benefits and services, and (3) interest on the federal debt, most of which was accumulated during periods of war or high defense spending (see Table 7–4).

Surprisingly, defense spending (broadly defined) accounted for more than two thirds of total federal spending (in administrative budget terms) prior to World War I, as the data in Column 8 of Table 7–4 indicate for the years 1900 and 1910. Moreover, the impact of World Wars I and II increased the defense spending/administrative budget ratio to over 90 percent in 1920 and again in 1945. Despite the absolute increase in defense spending (broadly defined) between 1960 and 1967, however, the ratio has declined during the period. This behavior reflects, in part, the effective cost-saving devices implemented by the Department

TABLE 7–4

FEDERAL "WAR-RELATED EXPENDITURES,"* BY FUNCTIONAL CATEGORY AND AS PERCENTAGES OF TOTAL FEDERAL EXPENDITURES,† SELECTED FISCAL YEARS, 1900–67

(1)	(2)	(3)	(4)	(5)	(6)	(7)	(8)
							War-Related Expenditures (columns 3, 4, 5 & 6) as a Percentage of Total Expenditures
Year	Total Federal Expenditures	National Defense	International Affairs & Finance*	Veterans Benefits & Services	Interest*	All Other	
1900....$	521	$ 191	$ —‡	$ 141	$ 40	$ 149	71.4%
1910....	694	284	—‡	161	21	228	67.1
1920....	6,357	3,997	435	332	1,024	569	91.0
1930....	3,320	734	14	821	697	1,054	68.3
1940....	9,055	1,498	51	552	1,056	5,898	34.9
1941....	13,255	6,036	145	566	1,123	5,385	59.4
1945....	98,303	81,216	3,312	2,095	3,662	8,018	91.8
1948....	32,955	11,771	4,566	6,653	5,248	4,717	85.7
1955....	64,389	40,695	2,181	4,522	6,438	10,553	83.6
1960....	76,539	45,691	1,832	5,266	9,266	14,484	81.1
1965....	96,507	50,163	4,304	5,495	11,435	25,110	74.0
1966....	106,428§	56,560	3,932	5,122	12,104	28,710	73.0
1967....	112,841§	60,541	4,177	5,721	12,854	29,548	73.8

* Since "international affairs & finance" usually have at least an indirect defense connotation, and since most federal debt upon which "interest" is paid is war debt, these two items are included in a *broad definition* of "war-related expenditures."
† The expenditure totals exclude trust fund operations and constitute the administrative budget concept.
‡ Included in "all other" category.
§ Estimated figures.

SOURCE: Historical Data from U.S. Treasury Department; Current Data from Bureau of the Budget: *Budget of the United States, Fiscal Year 1967* (Washington, D.C.: U.S. Government Printing Office 1966), p. 69.

of Defense in recent years, but also reflects the relatively higher percentage of aggregate resource utilization during the latter year.[7]

In addition, it should be observed in Table 7–4 that such transfer-type expenditures as "veterans benefits and services" and "interest" on the federal debt comprise a combined total of more than $18 billion in federal spending during Fiscal 1967. When this amount is added on to such substantial federal spending items as "trust fund expenditures," which are included in the consolidated-cash budget, the importance of

[7] These cost-saving devices will be further discussed in Chapter 23, "Defense Economics."

federal transfer-type activities is further evident. During Fiscal 1967, for example, federal trust fund expenditures totaled nearly $38 billion.

Changes in the functional distribution of direct *state* government expenditures during the 20th century may be observed in Table 7–5. Several significant trends or patterns are evident from the data. These trends or patterns (summarized below) occurred within an environment of rapid growth in the magnitude of state spending during the century. State direct expenditures in 1902, for example, amounted to only $136 million and they totaled only $297 million in 1913. However, some 50 years later (in 1965) direct spending by state governments exceeded $31 billion. The following patterns of direct state expenditure may be summarized from the data for the 52-year period, 1913–65, except for point (7) which represents a somewhat shorter period:

1. State expenditures for highways tripled in terms of relative importance.
2. Public welfare expenditures by states nearly doubled in relative importance.
3. State spending on health and hospitals was reduced by approximately one half of its earlier relative importance.
4. Natural resource expenditures by the states were reduced by about one sixth in relative importance.
5. General control expenditures were about one twelfth as important in 1965 as they were in 1913.
6. "Other" expenditures, mostly for police, correction, bond interest, and social insurance administration, decreased from about one third to about one sixth of total direct spending by the states.
7. The importance of insurance trust and liquor store activities, both virtually nonexistent in 1913, increased during the period.
8. State expenditures for education remained at approximately the same relative position.

Expenditures for education and highways presently constitute nearly 46 percent of the total direct spending of state governments, with highways being the single largest functional item at approximately 26 percent of the total.

Total direct spending by *local* governments has also increased enormously during the 20th century. Table 7–6, for example, reveals an increase in direct spending from $959 million in 1902 to nearly $56 billion during 1964–65. The following patterns of direct local government expenditure may be summarized from the data for the period 1902–65, though points (9) and (10) represent a somewhat shorter period:

1. Local expenditures for education increased from approximately 25 percent to more than 40 percent of total local government spending.
2. The relative importance of highway expenditures by local government decreased in 1964–65 to less than one half of what they were in 1902.

TABLE 7-5

Total State Direct Expenditures* for Own Functions, and Percentage
Distribution by Function, Selected Calendar Years, 1902–65.

| | Total Direct Expenditures (Millions of Dollars) | Percentage Distribution by Function | | | | | | | | |
Year		Education	Highways	Public Welfare	Health & Hospitals	Natural Resources	General Control	Other†	Insurance Trust	Liquor Stores
1902	$ 136	—	—	5.4	—	—	—	—	—	—
1913	297	18.5	8.8	5.4	17.8	4.7	12.8	32.0	—	—
1927	1,451	15.0	35.4	2.8	11.7	6.5	6.6	17.1	4.9	—
1932	2,028	13.7	41.6	3.6	10.6	5.9	5.6	15.9	3.1	—
1936	2,445	12.2	30.8	17.3	9.0	3.8	5.3	12.5	3.2	5.9
1940	3,555	10.6	22.3	14.8	8.4	4.1	4.2	12.4	16.9	6.3
1944	3,319	14.7	16.3	17.4	10.0	4.9	4.9	12.2	6.8	12.8
1948	7,897	13.7	19.1	12.2	8.4	4.4	3.4	17.2	12.9	8.7
1952	10,790	13.8	23.7	13.1	10.5	5.0	3.3	10.8	13.1	6.7
1956	15,148	14.1	28.8	10.6	9.7	4.4	3.2	10.5	13.1	5.6
1960	22,152	15.3	27.4	10.1	8.6	3.8	3.0	12.2	15.6	4.1
1963	27,698	17.9	26.8	9.8	8.4	4.0	3.0	11.3	15.6	3.2
1965	31,334	19.7	26.2	9.6	8.6	3.9	1.1	14.3	13.3	3.3

* Direct expenditures include all expenditures except intergovernmental expenditures.
† Primarily police, correction, interest, and social insurance administration.

Source: U.S. Department of Commerce, Bureau of the Census. 1965 data from *Compendium of State Government Finances 1965* (Washington, D.C.: U.S. Government Printing Office, 1966).

TABLE 7-6

TOTAL LOCAL DIRECT EXPENDITURES* FOR OWN FUNCTIONS, AND PERCENTAGE DISTRIBUTION BY FUNCTION, SELECTED CALENDAR YEARS, 1902–65

Percent Distribution of Total Direct Expenditures

Year	Total Direct Expenditures (Millions of Dollars)	General Expenditure							Utility	Liquor Stores	Insurance Trust
		Education	Highways	Public Welfare	Health & Hospitals	Police & Fire	General Control	Other†			
1902	$ 959	24.8	17.8	2.8	2.9	9.4	12.3	21.6	8.4	—	—
1913	1,960	26.6	20.1	1.8	2.8	8.4	8.8	21.6	9.5	—	0.4
1927	6,359	31.7	20.4	1.8	2.9	7.3	5.0	22.6	7.7	—	0.6
1932	6,375	31.9	14.1	5.8	3.8	8.0	5.6	21.8	8.1	—	.09
1936	6,056	31.0	11.1	6.7	4.1	8.2	6.1	22.3	9.1	0.1	1.3
1940	7,685	29.4	10.2	8.2	4.0	7.4	5.3	20.1	14.2	0.1	1.1
1944	7,180	32.1	9.2	7.7	4.5	8.7	6.1	18.0	11.4	0.5	1.8
1948	13,363	32.2	11.4	8.5	4.2	7.4	4.6	17.7	12.1	0.6	1.3
1952	20,073	34.0	10.4	6.9	5.2	7.1	4.1	19.2	11.2	0.5	1.4
1956	28,004	39.6	9.2	5.5	4.6	6.8	3.9	17.5	11.1	0.4	1.4
1963	48,062	39.6	7.7	5.8	4.9	6.6	3.4	20.0	10.2	0.3	1.5
1964–65‡	55,629	41.0	7.2	5.9	4.8	6.3	2.1	20.5	10.5	0.3	1.4

* Direct expenditures include all expenditures except intergovernmental expenditures.
† Includes natural resources, sanitation, recreation, interest on general debt, housing and community redevelopment, nonhighway transportation, correction, local libraries, general public buildings, and other general government.
‡ The financial statistics presented here for 1964–65 relate to governmental fiscal years which ended June 30, 1965, or at some date within the 12 previous months.

SOURCE: U.S. Department of Commerce, Bureau of the Census. 1964–65 data from *Governmental Finances in 1964–65*, U.S. Department of Commerce, Bureau of the Census (Washington, D.C.: U.S. Government Printing Office, 1966), pp. 21–23.

3. Public welfare expenditures more than doubled in relative importance during the period.
4. The relative importance of health and hospital spending by local government increased by approximately two thirds.
5. Police and fire expenditure declined by about one third in relative importance.
6. In 1964–65, general control expenditures were only about one sixth of their relative position in 1902.
7. "Other" expenditures—including those for natural resources, sanitation, debt interest, correction, and the like—maintained the same approximate relative importance during the century.
8. Utility spending increased by 26 percent in importance.
9. Between 1936 and 1964–65, liquor store expenditures by local government more than tripled in importance.
10. Between 1913 and 1964–65, insurance trust fund activities more than tripled in importance.

Expenditures for education presently constitute the single largest functional item of local government expenditure (41 percent of total direct expenditures).

The considerable absolute growth in public sector spending is shared by all levels of government and is sizable even when converted to a per capita basis (see Table 7–7). While total public sector spending (in current dollars) was only $21 per capita in 1902, it reached more than $1,000 per capita in 1964. The federal component was the largest single contributor of per capita government spending in 1964, though local

TABLE 7–7

FEDERAL, STATE, AND LOCAL EXPENDITURES*
PER CAPITA, SELECTED CALENDAR YEARS,
1902–64
(Current Dollars)

Year	Total	Federal	State	Local
1902............$	21	$ 7	$ 2	$ 12
1913............	33	10	4	19
1927............	95	30	16	49
1936............	132	72	25	35
1940............	156	77	35	44
1944............	821	751	30	40
1950............	467	297	85	85
1955............	676	449	106	121
1960............	846	544	140	162
1964............	1,032	660	178	194
(estimate)				

* Total expenditures include spending for liquor stores, utilities, and insurance trust funds. Grants-in-aid are counted as expenditures of the level of government which first disburses the funds.
SOURCE: Basic Data—U.S. Department of Commerce.

government had been in the first position in 1902. The state level of government ranks third among the three levels of government in per capita spending both early in the century as well as at the present time. Finally, it is interesting to note that in terms of aggregate public sector "employment data," as provided by the Department of Commerce, the division of public sector resource allocation between the federal and combined state-local segments of governmental economic activity has not changed significantly during the last 25 years if *defense spending* is excluded and *only* federal civilian employment is counted.

Analysis of 20th-Century Expenditure Trends

Although a theoretical and empirical analysis of public sector growth will be the principal topic of the next chapter, a cursory treatment of the subject will be presented at this time. The reasons for the relative expansion of the public sector within aggregate economic activity in the United States may be classified into two broad categories: (1) the more *intensive* application of governmental economic activity within areas of allocation already provided by the public sector and (2) the lateral or *extensive* movement of government into new areas of economic activity. The latter movement may involve, for example, the allocation either of economic goods previously allocated by the private sector or of newly developed goods resulting from technological innovation and previously allocated by neither sector.

The primary causes of the relative growth of the public sector in the United States may be found within the first category which refers to the more intensive performance of established governmental functions. War or defense, education, and highways are long-established public sector goods in the American economy. Tables 7–3 and 7–4 (discussed above), for example, reveal the astounding expansion of direct national defense expenditures by the federal government from $191 million in 1900 to more than $60 billion in 1967. Thus, direct military spending by the federal government increased from 37 percent of a much lower federal expenditure base in 1900 to nearly 54 percent of the much larger federal spending base in 1967. The significance of defense to governmental growth, of course, is indicated even more sharply if indirect defense spending is included in the defense total.

The influence of war upon public sector spending may be dramatized further by the following facts:[8] The federal government spent more money financing the Civil War between 1861 and 1865 than it had spent from its beginning in 1789, under George Washington's first administration, until Abraham Lincoln's first administration. The federal

---

[8] See Troy J. Cauley, *Public Finance and the General Welfare* (Columbus, Ohio: Merrill, 1960), pp. 39–41.

government, moreover, spent in its next major war, World War I, whose primary influence covered the years 1917–20, more than it had spent for all other purposes, including all previous wars, from the first administration of George Washington until Woodrow Wilson's second administration. The spending during World War I included loans to other Allied nations, most of which were never repaid.

Yet the story has not ended! The federal government undertook more expenditures to conduct World War II between 1941 and 1945 than it had spent throughout its entire history for all purposes combined, other wars included, between the first administration of George Washington and the third administration of Franklin D. Roosevelt. This cumulative spending total includes those measures employed to alleviate the depression of the 1930's, a fact which exposes the prevalent mythology that New Deal domestic economic policy primarily caused the relative growth of the federal component of the public sector as well as that of the entire public sector as a proportion of aggregate economic activity during the last 30 years.[9] Furthermore, the current data which show that more than one half of federal administrative budget expenditures are for direct defense purposes and that approximately 75 percent are for defense in a "broadly defined" sense suggest that no significant change in the importance of the defense function is presently taking place.

While war and defense were causing the federal government to perform more intensively its time-honored function of national protection, state and local governments were expanding their expenditures to meet the growing demands of an urban-industrial population for education, highways, police and fire protection, public health, and other services. Ever-improving technology, and related cultural adjustments connected with an urban-oriented society, help to explain the growing demands for these governmental economic products. As demonstrated previously, state governments have assumed the primary responsibility for highway services and local governments for educational services.

It has been observed that the lateral expansion of government into new areas of allocation has been a less significant cause of absolute and relative public sector growth than has the more intensive performance of established functions. Three areas of lateral expansion, however, deserve comment, namely, social security measures, macroeconomic anticyclical and growth policies, and microeconomic regulatory policies. During the 20th century, government in the United States has accepted a mandate from the population to increase the allocation of social welfare services. These services include old age plans for retirement, survivors insurance,

---

[9] Admittedly, the above comparisons are presented in terms of current dollars and thus do not adjust for secular inflationary trends. Inflation, however, does very little in an overall sense to explain the impressive influence of war and defense expenditures upon relative federal government and public sector growth trends in the United States.

unemployment compensation, medical care for the aged, and industrial accident benefits. Though the historical evolution of public sector allocation of these services was initiated in other Western nations (such as Germany and England), the public sector in the United States has moved to a present position where these have become prominent areas of economic influence. Importantly, the provision of such services by the public sector may be essentially viewed as a new function of government in the United States as compared to long-established functions such as the provision of defense and roads.

Government also has moved during the 20th century into the rational and deliberate influencing of aggregate economic activity in terms of production, employment, income, price levels, and economic growth goals. This may be considered alternately as anticylical policy or as "regulation" in a macroeconomic sense. The development of Keynesian economics has led to widespread acceptance in the Western world of aggregate *fiscal policy*. The United States was among the last of the Western industrial nations to accept the deliberate fiscal policy technique. The federal tax reductions of 1964 and 1965, however, are good evidence of the culmination of an evolutionary profiscal policy movement which had been historically initiated in the United States in the form of the New Deal "public works" measures of the 1930's and supported in principle by the Employment Act of 1946. Aggregate fiscal policy of both the tax and expenditure variety undoubtedly represents an important movement by American government into a new functional area of responsibility.[10]

The public sector in the United States also has moved laterally during the last 100 years into new areas of microeconomic regulation. This expansion takes the form of such allocative techniques as general antitrust laws and public utility regulation. This is not to suggest, however, that American government ever completely avoided microeconomic regulatory influence. Nonetheless, the preindustrial American economy of the pre–Civil War era did not require allocative regulation to the extent that it is required today. Big business and big labor require governmental guidance and restraint in a manner unknown to agricultural societies. Growing population and urbanization, moreover, both of which are related to America's industrial revolution, place additional demands on governmental allocative influence. Regulation of this type may thus be considered a lateral expansion of government into a new area of economic activity.

[10] There is, of course, a strategic interrelationship between the fiscal policy goals of stabilization and economic growth and such functionally important areas of expenditure as the long-established defense function. During the last 25 years, for example, much of the contribution to stabilization and growth made by the federal government has been achieved through increases in aggregate demand caused by war and defense expenditures.

In summary, the public sector in the United States has grown both in relative and absolute terms during this century. The primary explanations of this growth are found in the category of more intensive performance of traditional governmental functions. The lateral movement of government into new areas such as social welfare, macroeconomic regulation, and microeconomic regulation, however, has been significant. Nevertheless, these have been far overshadowed by the impact on the public sector of the long-established governmental functions of defense, highways, and education—especially defense.

REVENUE PATTERNS

Prior to 1900

Federal revenues exceeded expenditures during 74 of the first 110 years of federal budgetary history. The minute nature of early federal budgetary behavior is exemplified by the fact that the federal government's budget displayed a surplus during its first fiscal year despite revenues of only $4.4 million. In fact, federal revenues did not reach $10 million until the year 1800. Moreover, it was not until a Civil War year, 1863, that federal receipts first surpassed $100 million. Furthermore, federal receipts stayed under $1 billion until America's entry into World War I in 1917.

Table 7–8 displays characteristics of the federal revenue structure between 1790–1916 as arranged by time-period groupings. Expectedly, a high percentage of total federal revenue consisted of "tax revenue" during each time period. Nevertheless, "nontax revenues" such as land sales provided substantial receipts, in relative terms, during several of the time periods. Land sales, for example, averaged $7 million annually between 1891–1916. Significantly, the primary source of tax revenue as late as the first part of the 20th century consisted of external taxes (tariffs or customs) rather than internal (domestic) taxes.

State revenue sources required expansion when the considerable growth in state expenditures took place during the 19th century.[11] Investment revenues (such as dividends on bank stock), land sales, and lotteries were insufficient to meet the growing state revenue requirements. State revenue needs were thus met during the first half of the 19th century by bank taxes, particularly on capital stock, and by the general property tax. The bank taxes were used regularly following the War of 1812, and property taxes were used steadily for the first time during the 1840's. State governments, however, were forced at times during the century to borrow to meet their functional expenditure requirements, especially those of a social capital (internal improvement) nature. State

[11] See Studenski and Krooss, *op. cit.*, chaps. 12 and 17, for an excellent discussion of state and local government revenue patterns prior to 1900.

government debts totaled $175 million during the late 1830's at which time no federal government debt existed. Another state government "borrowing spree" took place during the 1850's.

Continued pressure for state government revenues during the latter half of the 19th century caused the states to seek additional tax sources. Thus, taxes on insurance companies, franchise taxes on railroads and public utilities, general corporation franchise taxes, inheritance taxes, and liquor license taxes became important supplementary sources of state

TABLE 7–8

CHARACTERISTICS OF THE FEDERAL REVENUE STRUCTURE,
BY TIME-PERIOD GROUPINGS, 1790–1916
(Millions of Dollars)

Time Period	Number of Years	Average Annual Tax Revenues				Nontax Revenues		Total Revenues
		Customs	Income & Profits	Other	Total	Land Sales	Other	
1790–1811....22		9.3	*	0.4†	9.7	0.3	0.1	10.1
1812–15...... 4		9.5	‡	2.9§	12.4	1.1	0.4	13.9
1816–36......21		22.8	‡	0.8§	23.6	4.1	0.2	27.9
1837–61......25		35.8	—	—	35.8	3.5	1.4	40.7
1862–65...... 4		121.0	22‖	71.0	213.0	1.0	9.0	223.0
1866–90......25		200.0	12#	136.0	348.0	6.0	4.0	358.0
1891–1916....26		235.0	15#	245.0	495.0	7.0	15.0	517.0

* Tax on bank dividends, 1796–1802—no separate data.
† Levied 1791–1802 only.
‡ Tax on bank dividends yielded about $0.1 million annually, 1815–18.
§ Levied 1814–17 only.
‖ Levied 1863–72 only.
Beginning 1910 on corporate profits.

SOURCE: Selected from table compiled by Paul B. Trescott and appearing in "Some Historical Aspects of Federal Fiscal Policy, 1790–1956," *Federal Expenditure Policy for Economic Growth and Stability* (Joint Economic Committee, 85th Cong., 1st sess., November 5, 1957), p. 68.

revenue. State debts, meanwhile, reached a post–Civil War high of $450 million during the 1870's, but then declined throughout the remainder of the century.

Local government relied heavily upon the property tax to support its expanding functional expenditures during the 19th century. The increased utilization of the property tax, however, was still inadequate and many large capital outlays by local government had to be financed through debt creation. Municipal debt, for example, was approximately equal to state debt, and exceeded the federal debt by a ratio of three to one, in 1860. The depression of 1873 caused severe problems for municipal finance, which led to more restrained and more competent financial behavior by city government during the remainder of the century. The property tax continued to be the single most important revenue source for municipalities and for other forms of local government. Property tax rates eventually were further increased and assessed valuation rose sharply, particularly for "real" as opposed to "personal" property, as the century progressed.

20th-Century Revenue Trends

During the 36-year period between 1929 and 1965, public sector tax collections in the United States increased from approximately 10 percent to more than 23 percent of net national product (see Table 7–9).[12] This represents a direct growth in allocation influence by the public sector during the period to the extent that governmental "exhaustive" (as opposed to "transfer") expenditures are involved. The relative growth in public sector tax receipts is shared by both the federal and state-local categories of government. The primary growth, however, is that of the

TABLE 7–9

PUBLIC SECTOR TAX REVENUES, TOTAL AND BY
LEVELS OF GOVERNMENT, AS PERCENTAGES OF
NET NATIONAL PRODUCT, SELECTED
CALENDAR YEARS, 1929–65

Year	*Tax Receipts* as a Percentage of Net National Product†		
	Total Public Sector	Federal	State-Local
1929	10.8%	3.9%	6.9%
1930	11.8	3.6	8.2
1935	16.3	6.0	10.3
1940	18.3	9.3	9.0
1944	25.1	20.4	4.7
1948	23.6	17.7	5.9
1952	27.3	20.8	6.5
1956	27.6	20.0	7.6
1960	29.5	20.8	8.7
1963	30.5	21.2	9.3
1965	23.5	15.1	8.3

* Tax receipts as they appear in the National Income and Product Accounts. Business taxes are treated on an accrual basis. Contributions for social insurance are included.

† Net national product, which consists of gross national product minus capital consumption allowances, is used since it is assumed that the tax burden does not fall on national product allocated to replace consumed capital.

SOURCE: U.S. Department of Commerce, Bureau of the Census. 1965 data from *Government Finances, 1964–65*, Department of Commerce, Bureau of the Census (Washington, D.C.: U.S. Government Printing Office, 1966), p. 16.

[12] The relative decline between 1963–65 in (1) governmental tax receipts as a percentage of net national product and in (2) the intragovernmental importance of federal tax receipts reflect, in part, the federal income tax reductions of 1964 and the federal excise tax reductions of 1965.

federal government, which at the present time collects approximately two thirds of total public sector taxes. Between 1929 and 1965, federal tax receipts as a percentage of net national product more than quadrupled while combined state-local tax collections increased by a much smaller ratio.

Thus, while there has been astounding growth in federal revenues since 1929, it is important to consider that between 1949 and 1965 the relative importance of the different types of federal tax revenue remained about the same.[13] For example, the federal income taxes (personal and corporation) comprised 63 percent of total federal receipts in 1949 and 62 percent in 1965. All other sources of tax receipts—including excise taxes, employment taxes, estate and gift taxes, customs and trust fund receipts—indicate comparable stability during the period.[14] It is possible, however, that the second half of the 1960's *may* experience significant shifting in the relative importance of the various federal revenue sources due to: (1) the reduction of federal income tax rates in 1964, (2) the elimination or reduction in rates of many federal excise taxes during the 1965 session of Congress, and (3) *medicare* (Medical Care for the Aged) which was added to the federal social security program in 1965 (effective in 1966) to accompany other already scheduled increments in federal payroll taxes.

It is conceivable, however, that federal income taxes may maintain or increase their relative importance within the federal tax system, despite rate reductions, because the expansionary multiplier effects resulting from the tax cuts are capable over time of stimulating national production and real national income in a less than full-employment economy. Since income is the tax base of the income tax, if income expands by a greater proportion than rates are lowered, the yield of the income tax will increase. Accordingly, its relative importance as a source of revenue could increase despite the tax rate reductions. In fact, a higher income tax yield resulting from lower income tax rates seemed evident in 1965 as the aggregate results of the 1964 federal income tax reductions were compiled.

Meanwhile, it is likely that the relative importance to the federal revenue system of excise taxes will decline following the elimination of some excise taxes along with the reduction in rates of certain others by Congress during 1965. This is true beyond the fact that the extent of the excise tax cutbacks was greater than that of the federal personal and corporation income tax reductions. However, the relative importance of

[13] The present discussion of federal tax types is in "consolidated-cash" budget terms.

[14] Interestingly, customs duties (tariffs) have accounted for only a little more than 1 percent of total federal receipts in recent decades though they were the primary federal revenue source throughout American history prior to World War I.

federal excises would tend to decline while that of federal income taxes would tend to increase—even with tax reductions of similar severity—because of the different characteristics of the bases of the two taxes. Hence, although lower prices of the specific commodities subject to the federal excise tax may be expected to increase the quantity purchased of these items, many of these items possess inelastic demand characteristics and increased sales cannot be expected to be proportionate to the price reductions made possible by the excise tax cutbacks. The additional purchasing power in the hands of consumers, moreover, is likely to be spent only in small additional amounts for goods subject to (or previously subject to) the excise taxes because the excise tax bases are "narrow" and many alternative expenditure possibilities exist. Hence, the excise tax bases will likely expand in smaller proportions than the rate reductions. On the other hand, the expanded general purchasing power made available by the income tax reductions will increase aggregate money income and thus will increase the "broad" taxable income bases of the federal personal and corporation income taxes in a direct and significant manner.

The income tax base, moreover, could grow at an increasing rate with incremental money income, given the assumption of a progressive tax rate structure. The unequal distribution of tax avoidance loopholes among various income brackets with the majority of loopholes being conducive to the higher income levels, however, tends to offset these results. The income tax base does nevertheless tend to expand following a rate reduction, though it does not necessarily do so at an increasing rate.

Regarding the incremental *medicare* component of the federal Old Age and Survivors Insurance (Social Security) program, along with the scheduled future increases in the federal payroll tax which had been legislated prior to *medicare,* it is likely that these two forces will cause a relative increase to take place in the importance of trust funds within the federal revenue system during the remainder of the decade. Consequently, the nearly complete status quo in specific federal revenue sources, which was evident between 1949 and 1965, may not continue for the reasons cited above.

Many changes have occurred in the relative importance of *state* government tax revenue sources during the 20th century. Several taxes used in an important manner by the states today were nonexistent, or virtually so, at the beginning of the century. During 1965, for example, 25.7 percent of state tax revenue came from the general sales tax category (including use and gross receipts taxes). This category was nonexistent in 1902. Furthermore, individual and corporation income taxes, which contributed more than 21 percent of state tax revenue in 1965, contributed no revenue at all in 1902. In addition, the motor vehicle fuels tax, which provided 16.5 percent of state tax revenue in 1965, was nonexistent in 1902. To a lesser extent, similar trends may be observed for the tobacco tax, motor vehicle and operator's license fees, and the severance taxes collected by state governments. On the other hand, the relative importance of certain other taxes declined during the century. This is particularly true of the property tax, which decreased from a 52.6 to a 2.9 percent ratio of total state tax revenue between 1902 and 1965, an intentional result of state government efforts to improve the "revenue picture" of local government. Also experiencing downward relative trends, but to a lesser extent, during the period were sales and license taxes on the sale of alcoholic beverages, death and gift taxes.

The pattern of *local* government revenue sources also demonstrates significant changes during the 20th century. The property tax has declined in relative importance for local government, as it has for state government, from 88 to 87 percent of *tax* revenues from own sources and from 72 to 57 percent of *total* revenues from own sources. The degree of decline, however, is much less severe for local government than for state government. The property tax still provides over one half of total local government revenues and most of its tax revenues, but less than 3 percent of state government tax revenues.

Several local government revenue sources increased their relative importance between 1902 and 1963, namely, sales taxes, income taxes, charges and miscellaneous receipts, utility revenues, liquor store revenues, insurance trust fund taxes, and intergovernmental revenues. Importantly, there has been a considerable increase in local government revenues derived from intergovernmental sources. Between 1902 and 1963, the proportion of total local government revenues received from state governments increased from 5.7 percent to 25.4 percent of total revenues and that received from the federal government grew from 0.4 percent to 1.9 percent of total local government revenues.

When public sector tax revenues are converted to constant dollars and computed on a per capita basis, the growing reliance on certain types of taxes by each level of government during the 20th century becomes obvious (see Table 7–10). The personal and corporation income taxes, for example, bear the brunt of federal tax revenue requirements, as do the sales and gross receipts taxes for state government and the property tax for local government. Interestingly, income taxes for federal government and sales–gross receipts taxes for state government were *not* primary revenue sources at the beginning of the 20th century. However, property taxes were the primary revenue source for local government both in 1902 and in 1965 (see Table 7–10).

FUTURE FISCAL PATTERNS AND REQUIREMENTS

In 1965, the ratio of federal government expenditures, in consolidated-cash budget terms, to gross national product was approximately 20

TABLE 7-10

General Tax Revenues, Per Capita, by Level of Government and by Type of Tax, 1961 Dollars, Selected Calendar Years, 1902–65

Year	Federal Taxes				State Taxes					Local Taxes			
	Personal Income	Corporate Income	Sales & Gross Receipts	Other	Personal Income	Corporate Income	Sales & Gross Receipts	Property	Other	Personal Income	Sales	Property	Other
1902	$ 0	$ 0	$25	$ 1	$ 0	$ 0	$ 1	$4	$ 2	$0	$ 0	$ 30	$4
1913	0	1	20	0	0	0	2	5	4	0	0	40	4
1927	15	21	18	2	1	2	8	6	11	0	0	74	2
1932	8	12	15	2	1	2	15	7	14	0	2	85	2
1936	13	14	36	11	3	2	26	4	14	0	2	73	2
1940	16	19	37	6	4	3	32	4	14	0	2	72	3
1944	256	191	61	15	4	6	28	3	12	0	4	57	3
1948	170	85	67	11	4	5	36	2	12	0	4	52	3
1952	210	160	70	10	7	6	43	3	15	1	5	62	3
1956	211	137	69	11	9	6	51	3	19	1	6	74	4
1960	228	120	70	12	12	7	59	3	20	1	7	88	4
1962	242	109	71	14	14	7	64	3	21	2	8	98	3
1964–65*	252	131	81	19	19	10	78	4	24	2	10	114	4

* The financial statistics presented here for 1964–65 relate to governmental fiscal years which ended June 30, 1965, or at some date within the 12 previous months.

Source: U.S. Department of Commerce, Bureau of the Census. 1964–65 data from *Governmental Finances in 1964–65* (Washington, D.C.: U.S. Government Printing Office, 1966), pp. 18, 22.

percent. Table 7–11 provides data from three separate research projects which provide projected ratios of future federal spending to GNP. The Eckstein and Bureau of the Budget studies are stated in consolidated-cash budget terms while the National Planning Association study is stated in terms of the national-income-accounts budget. The Eckstein estimate for 1968 places federal expenditures in a range from a low estimate of 17.3 percent to a high estimate of 21.7 percent of GNP. The median of this range would be lower than the present 20 percent ratio. The same is true for the Bureau of the Budget's projected federal spend-

TABLE 7–11

SELECTED TEN-YEAR PROJECTIONS OF TOTAL
FEDERAL SPENDING, TO 1968, 1970, AND 1971

Projector	*Federal Expenditure Concept Used*	*Year Projected*	*Range from "Low" to "High" Projection as Percent of GNP*
Otto Eckstein*	Consolidated-Cash	1968	17.3–21.7
Bureau of the Budget†	Consolidated-Cash	1970	15.2–22.0
National Planning Association‡	National Income and Product	1971	13.7–18.4

* Otto Eckstein, *Trends in Public Expenditures in the Next Decade,* Committee for Economic Development, 1959.

† *Ten-Year Projection of Federal Budget Expenditures,* Bureau of the Budget, 1961. (Disarmament alternative disregarded in computing range shown above.)

‡ National Planning Association, 1961 Projection Series. Upper end of range taken from the "high government, low growth" alternative; lower end from the "high consumption, fast growth" alternative.

SOURCE: Wilfred Lewis, Jr., "The Federal Sector in National Income Models," in *Models of Income Determination, Studies in Income and Wealth,* Vol. 28, by the Conference on Research in Income and Wealth (Princeton: Princeton University Press, 1964), Table 8, p. 248. Reprinted by permission of Princeton University Press. Copyright, 1964.

ing/GNP ratio range of 15.2 to 22 percent for 1970. Thus, if these projections hold true, federal spending will increase less rapidly than GNP during the latter half of the 1960's, causing the ratio of federal spending to GNP to decline. According to the National Planning Association, the federal fiscal program will constitute spending within a low to high range from 13.7 percent to 18.4 percent of GNP, in national-income-accounts budget terms, by 1971.

Table 7–12 presents total public sector expenditure projections for 1970, in terms of functional categories of expenditure, by Colm and Helzner. Expenditures for education, health and hospitals, housing and urban renewal, and "other" nondefense programs are expected to increase as percentages of GNP, while national defense, highways, and the transfers-interest payments categories are predicted to be declining percentages. Once again, however, the war in Vietnam may void the national defense prediction. A projected relative decline in government spending as a percentage of GNP is also shown in this table.

The primary reasons for a projected absolute growth of public sector spending include the following. First, the population of the United States in 1985 is expected to be in excess of 275 million people, a total nearly 100 million higher than the American population in 1960. Thus, even without a relative expansion in resource allocation by the public sector, an enormous absolute growth in government spending would be

TABLE 7–12

GOVERNMENT EXPENDITURES 1958–70
(Dollars in 1958 Prices)

	1958 Actual			1970 Judgment Model		
	Billions	Per Capita	Per-centage of GNP	Billions	Per Capita	Per-centage of GNP
Goods and Services:						
National defense........	$ 44.0	$253	10.1%	$ 53.5	$250	6.8%
Education.............	15.6	90	3.6	30.7	144	3.9
Highways.............	8.4	48	1.9	13.1	61	1.7
Health and hospitals.....	3.3	19	0.8	9.8	46	1.2
Housing and urban renewal	.6	3	0.1	7.9	37	1.0
Other nondefense programs............	19.3	111	4.4	39.8	186	5.0
Total goods and services....	$ 91.2	$524	20.9%	$154.8	$724	19.6%
Transfer, interest, etc.......	33.3	191	7.6	49.9	233	6.3
Total government expenditures................	$124.5	$715	28.5%	$204.7	$957	25.9%

SOURCE: Gerhard Colm and Manuel Helzner, "Financial Needs and Resources Over the Next Decade: At All Levels of Government," in *Public Finances: Needs, Sources, and Utilization*, National Bureau of Economic Research Study (Princeton, N.J.: Princeton University Press, 1961), Table 10, p. 18. Reprinted by permission of Princeton University Press. Copyright, 1961.

anticipated. Second, the growth in population will place a tremendous burden upon the "education industry" in the United States, a burden made greater by the fact that American culture in an expanding technological age places greater quantitative and qualitative stress on education. College-age population is predicted to expand from the 15.3 million people in 1957–58 to 27.2 million in 1975–76. The number of people enrolled in institutions of higher education, moreover, is expected to increase at a much faster rate than the increase in college-age population during the same time period. Thus, college enrollment, which was 19.6 percent of college-age population in 1957–58, is projected to move to a ratio of 31.6 percent by 1975–76. Furthermore, the predictions suggest that public education will bear an increasing share of college educational responsibility in the years ahead. In addition, considerable growth is also predicted in secondary and elementary school enrollments. The totals are expected to increase from 42.2 million in 1960 to 55.3 million in 1975. Surprisingly, private schools are counted on to enroll a higher percentage in 1975 (14.3 percent) than in 1960 (14.0 percent), a prediction in sharp contrast to that for college education.[15]

A study by Wilfred Lewis predicts that gross national product will reach $841 billion by 1970 (see Table 7–13). He further suggests that

TABLE 7–13

"Illustrative" Ten-Year Projection of Gross National Product and Federal Receipts,* 1960 and 1970
(National Income Account Basis, Billions of Dollars)

	Calendar 1960 (Actual)	Calendar 1970 (Projected)
Gross National Product	$504.4	$841.4
Federal receipts		
Corporation Income Taxes	21.2	33.6†
Personal Taxes	43.2	81.5‡
Indirect Business Taxes	14.0	21.7§
Contributions for Social Insurance		
OASDI	12.0	31.0‖
Other	5.6	9.4#
Total Receipts	96.0	177.2
Total Receipts as Percent of GNP	19.0%	21.1%

* Assuming 3.5 percent per year real growth in GNP, a 1.75 percent increase per year in the GNP deflator, and unit GNP elasticity of corporate profits, personal income, and wages and salaries.
† Profits elasticity of tax of 0.92.
‡ Personal income elasticity of tax of 1.25.
§ GNP elasticity of tax of 0.85.
‖ Wages and salaries elasticity of tax of 1.0, plus increases scheduled in present law in combined rate on employers and employees, from 6 percent in 1960 to 9.25 percent by 1970.
Wages and salaries elasticity of tax of 1.0.
Source: Wilfred Lewis, Jr., "The Federal Sector in National Income Models," in *Models of Income Determination, Studies in Income and Wealth*, Vol. 28, by the Conference on Research in Income and Wealth (Princeton: Princeton University Press, 1964), Table 5, p. 242. Reprinted by permission of Princeton University Press. Copyright, 1964.

total federal receipts, which stood at $96 billion in 1960 (in consolidated-cash budget terms), will skyrocket to over $177 billion by 1970. As discussed earlier, recent reductions in the rates of the federal income taxes and recent reductions in some federal excise tax rates, plus the outright elimination of certain other excise taxes, do not necessarily suggest that total revenues collected from these taxes and/or their relative importance will decline. Such results depend upon the elasticity ratios between tax rate reductions and the resulting effect on the tax bases of the respective taxes. According to the estimates by Lewis, the

[15] U.S. Department of Health, Education, and Welfare and U.S. Department of Commerce data.

greatest relative growth in federal revenues between 1960 and 1970 will come from the expanding importance of the social security taxes. Lewis predicts that *federal revenues* will become an increasing proportion of GNP in the next few years. Moreover, important trends and changes may be under way, not only in the federal component of public sector budgetary activity, but also in the state and local government components of the aggregate public sector budget.

Chapter 8

THEORETICAL ANALYSIS OF
PUBLIC SECTOR GROWTH

The experience of the Western world during the last half of the 19th and the 20th centuries has been one of growth in the public sectors of most industrial nations. This growth was evident not only in an *absolute* sense—which would be expected in an environment of growing population, output, and complexity in economic activity—but also on a *relative* basis. In other words, the resource allocation division between the public and private sectors has moved toward a higher proportion of total resources being allocated through government.

WAGNER'S HYPOTHESIS OF INCREASING GOVERNMENTAL ACTIVITY

Statement of the Hypothesis

Adolph Wagner, the famous German political economist (1835–1917), believed that a functional relationship exists between the growth of an economy and the relative growth of its public sector. According to Wagner, relative growth of the government sector is an inherent characteristic of industrializing economies. He referred not only to Britain, which essentially had completed its industrial revolution before Wagner's time, but to nations such as the United States, France, and Germany (in the West) and Japan (in the East) whose industrial revolutions were contemporary to Wagner's life. Hence, the *Wagner Hypothesis of Increasing Governmental Activity* holds that as per capita income and output increase in industrializing nations, the public sectors of these nations necessarily grow in proportion to total economic activity.[1] Yet, the political, economic, and cultural structures of the industrializing nations studied by Wagner were so diverse that it is difficult to establish a functional (cause and effect) relationship between industrialization and the relative growth of government.

Wagner believed that social progress was the basic cause of the relative growth of government in the industrializing economies of his time. The "chain-reaction" circumstances described by Wagner are that

---

[1] Adolph Wagner, *Finanzwissenschaft* (3rd ed.; Leipzig: 1890).

(1) social progress leads to a growth in government functions which, in turn, (2) leads to the absolute and percentage growth of governmental economic activity. The hypothesis is clearly secular (long term) in nature.

In his attempt to test the hypothesis, Wagner distinguished certain types of governmental activities or functions. One function is that of providing law and order. This includes both internal and external law and order and pertains essentially to the provision of the "environmental conditions" necessary for market functioning. Next, Wagner described governmental participation in the material production of economic goods, including the provision of certain "social products" like communications, education, and monetary-banking arrangements.

It is argued that the first type of public sector activity, law and order, increases along with increasing per capita output because an inevitable growth in centralized administration results in the impersonalization and automation of many social and economic institutions. Economic growth and centralization of administration thus increase labor specialization and cause greater complexities and interdependencies in economic and social life. Efficient performance of the economy, given the existence of these interdependencies and the desirability of maintaining qualitative governmental services, suggests the need for additional public sector economic influence.

Wagner believed that government corporations must produce certain economic goods requiring large fixed investment because private corporations could not undertake such investment on a profitable basis. The similarity of this viewpoint to those of Smith, Mill, Bentham, and others (as discussed in Chapter 2) is obvious. Closely related to the requirement for increased public sector activity is the observation by Wagner that social services like communications, education, and banking need to be provided by government. These industries tend to be characterized by natural monopoly conditions of production, which usually involve heavy fixed costs, and important external effects (externalities). These goods take on important characteristics of publicness and thus possess a legitimate social (collective) interest in their allocation.

Graphical Presentation of the Wagner Hypothesis

The Wagner hypothesis of increasing governmental activity is demonstrated in Figure 8–1. In this graph, the real per capita output of public goods is measured on the vertical axis and real per capita income on the horizontal axis. Time is an important third dimension implicit to the graph because the growth both in the real per capita output of public goods and in real per capita income is realistically assumed to take place on a historical basis over an extended period of time. The 45-degree angle line, labeled PG^1, represents a situation where the public sector maintains a constant proportion of the total economic production of the society over time. In other words, as real per capita income increases due to economic growth in the society, the real per capita output of public goods increases at the same rate.

The constant proportions line may now be used as a reference point to the graphical presentation of the Wagner hypothesis as depicted by line PG^2. Along line PG^2, the proportion of resources devoted to the output of public goods is expanding over time. This means that the real

FIGURE 8–1

WAGNER HYPOTHESIS: THE RELATIVE EXPANSION
OF PUBLIC SECTOR ECONOMIC ACTIVITY
OVER TIME

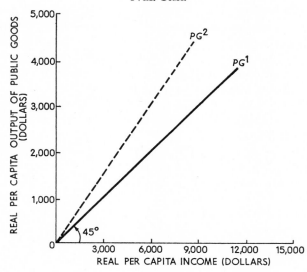

per capita output of public goods is increasing at a more rapid rate than is real per capita income as industrialization and economic growth take place. Such is the essence of the Wagner hypothesis. Real per capita public sector production possesses an "elastic" relationship ($\epsilon > 1$) to the growth in real per capita income over an extended period of time. Of course, along the 45-degree line—PG^1—the Wagner hypothesis does not hold and the elasticity of the real per capita output of public goods to the growth in real per capita income is unity ($\epsilon = 1$).

The Wagner Hypothesis, Preindustrial and Postindustrial Maturity Stages of a Society's Economic Development

Since Wagner's analysis was directed toward industrializing nations, a discussion of the hypothesis should delimit the industrialization era in a nation's history from a possible earlier preindustrial stage and from a possible later period of postindustrial maturity at which time living standards are affluent not only on an *average* basis, but on a *distributive* basis as well.[2] Figure 8–2 provides in line PG^2 an example of how the elasticity relationship between the growing real per capita output of public goods and the growth in real per capita income may

FIGURE 8–2

RELATIVE CHANGES IN PUBLIC SECTOR ECONOMIC ACTIVITY DURING
PREINDUSTRIALIZATION, INDUSTRIALIZATION, AND
POSTINDUSTRIALIZATION PERIODS
OF ECONOMIC DEVELOPMENT

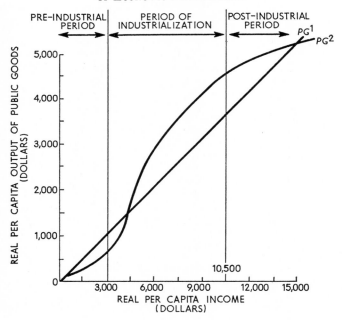

change depending upon the particular stage of development in a nation's economy. It seems likely that the elasticity is less than one in the preindustrialization and postindustrialization stages of a society's economic evolution. The reasons for this are described below.

Most subsistence wants and goods have traditionally been provided by the private sector through market-type arrangements since food, clothing, and shelter are divisible goods to which the exclusion principle can be applied. Consequently, economic expansion in a preindustrial society

[2] For a discussion of the postindustrial maturity stage of a society's economic development, see Walt Whitman Rostow, *Economic Growth* (New York: Cambridge University Press, 1960).

would likely cause the real per capita output of private goods to increase by a more than proportionate amount than real per capita income which would mean that the real per capita output of public goods would increase by a less than proportionate amount ($\epsilon < 1$).

As real per capita income grows still more, however, the relative elasticity may be expected to change. For example, investment in social capital items such as communications, transportation, and educational capital goods must take place as part of the economic growth process. Since these goods contain many collective characteristics, they are often provided more efficiently by the government sector of the economy than by the market. Thus, let us say that as real per capita income rises above $3,000 in Figure 8–2, the economy enters an industrialization stage and the real per capita output of public goods now increases more rapidly ($\epsilon > 1$) than the growth in real per capita income over an extended period of time. This stage, which represents the Wagner hypothesis, is largely explained by the fact that important social capital items provided by the public sector have now become part of aggregate demand. Ultimately, these social overhead items will be provided in sufficient quantities and the society will attain postindustrial maturity at a real per capita income level of (say) $10,500. *All* spending units now possess a good standard of living. It seems plausible to conclude that at this stage of development government will have already provided those economic goods which it can provide with an efficiency advantage. Thus, a relative increase in the real per capita output of private goods can be expected as real per capita income continues to increase. This means, of course, that the elasticity relationship between the growth of real per capita public goods output and the growth of real per capita income would become inelastic ($\epsilon < 1$) in the postindustrial maturity stage.

Critique of the Wagner Hypothesis

Though Wagner's hypothesis contains certain attributes, it also contains several rather serious defects. Primarily, it should be observed that the hypothesis deals with "interdisciplinary" phenomena though it is not interdisciplinary in its analytical framework. Political science, economics, and sociology are among the several disciplines which must be involved in any theory of public sector expenditure. Such theories must consider the cultural characteristics of a society. As the Wagner hypothesis suggests, empirical studies of industrial nations reveal that most such nations have experienced an extended period of time during which the public sector grew in proportion to aggregate economic activity. This was accomplished, however, in societies with diverse social, economic, political, and cultural backgrounds. It thus seems unlikely that the causal conditions described by Wagner, which essentially are of an economic nature, constitute *all* the primary determinants of a relatively expanding public sector during industrialization. Although the Wagner hypothesis possesses the attributes of accumulating and partially explaining important historical facts, its lack of a comprehensive analytical framework causes it to fall short in these explanations.

It is observed by Peacock and Wiseman that the Wagner argument contains two serious defects:[3] (1) the fact that it is based upon an organic self-determining theory of the state, which is not the prevailing theory of state in most Western nations and (2) the fact that Wagner stresses a long-term trend of public economic activity which tends to overlook the significant "time pattern" or "process" of public expenditure growth.

THE DISPLACEMENT, INSPECTION, AND CONCENTRATION EFFECTS

Peacock and Wiseman stress the time pattern of public expenditure trends.[4] Their general approach is inclusive of three separate though related concepts, namely, the *displacement, inspection,* and *concentration* effects. Using empirical data for the British economy after 1890, they observe that the relative growth of the British public sector has occurred on a "step-like" rather than on a "continuous growth" basis. Government fiscal activities, in other words, have risen step by step to successive new plateaus during the 20th century. Most of the absolute and relative increases (steps upward) in taxing and spending by British government have taken place during periods of major social disturbance such as war and depression. These disturbances create a "displacement effect" when the previous (lower) tax and expenditure levels are displaced by new and higher budgetary levels. After the social disturbance has ended, the new levels of "tax tolerance" which have emerged support the higher plateau of public expenditure since the society realizes that it is capable of carrying a heavier tax burden than it previously had thought possible. Thus, when the major social disturbance ends, no strong motivation exists for a return to the lower predisturbance level of taxation. The greater revenue magnitudes are used instead to support a higher level of public sector economic activity. Meanwhile, the private sector's proportion of society's total resource allocation is partially displaced by additional public sector allocation. Over the secular period 1890–1960, this displacement procedure occurred several times in Great Britain.

Figure 8–3 demonstrates the displacement effect. Time (in years) is measured along the horizontal axis while public sector revenues (mostly taxes) and public expenditures are measured as a percentage of gross

---

[3] Alan T. Peacock and Jack Wiseman, *The Growth of Public Expenditure in the United Kingdom* (Princeton, N.J.: Princeton University Press, 1961), p. xxiii.

[4] *Ibid.,* chap. 2.

national product along the vertical axis. Peacock and Wiseman suggest that as social disturbances cause a relative expansion in public sector growth, a displacement effect occurs which helps to explain the time pattern by which the governmental growth took place. This displacement effect does *not* require that the new higher plateau of expenditure continue the same expenditure pattern that was created by the social disturbance. Although some of the increased expenditures, such as veterans benefits and debt interest, are direct results of a social disturbance, other expenditure items frequently involve the expansion of government into new areas of economic activity. Some of these new areas may have been provided formerly by the private sector while others may be the result of technological advancement which allows new goods to exist

FIGURE 8–3

THE "DISPLACEMENT EFFECT"

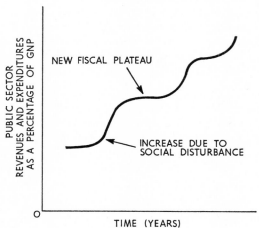

which have no previous allocation history. Moreover, war or other social disturbances frequently force people and their governments to seek solutions to important problems which previously had been neglected. This is referred to as an "inspection effect."

In addition to the displacement and inspection effects, Peacock and Wiseman also describe a "concentration effect." This concept refers to the apparent tendency for central government economic activity to become an increasing proportion of total public sector economic activity when a society is experiencing economic growth. This means, of course, that lower levels of government necessarily will grow less rapidly than the public sector as a whole. Empirical data for the British economy are consistent with this hypothesis during the 20th century. Data for the United States are less definitive in this regard and since 1946 the federal government of the United States has been a declining proportion of total public sector economic activity.[5] The American economists, Colm and Helzner, suggest that the concentration effect works in the United States only during wartime or serious depression because the traditional American resistance to central government control breaks down only under such dire circumstances.[6] Peacock and Wiseman describe the concentration effect hypothesis as follows:

In many societies, the functions of government are shared between a central authority and other (state and local) authorities whose powers may be protected by statute (as in legal federations) or shared by the central government. In such countries, local autonomy usually has many defenders and its preservation is frequently a matter of political importance. At the same time, economic development produces changes in the technically efficient level of government and also produces demands for equality of treatment (e.g., in services such as education) over wider geographical areas. These opposing pressures are reflected in the relative evolution of the expenditures undertaken at different levels of government. Purely, this evolution is distinct from the displacement effect, since the forces just described operate in normal as well as in disturbed times. Nonetheless, given the political importance of local autonomy and the barrier it may create to change, periods of displacement are also going to be periods of interest from the viewpoint of the concentration process.[7]

In summary, Peacock and Wiseman conclude that in Great Britain (1) public sector growth tends to occur on a steplike basis and at a faster rate than the growth in aggregate economic activity, (2) an inspection process occurs whereby existing problems are more clearly defined with potential solutions more carefully studied during a major disturbance, and (3) a concentration process exists whereby central government becomes an increasing proportion of the entire public sector. The Peacock and Wiseman approach to governmental spending trends is much more modest in what it purports to explain than is the Wagner hypothesis. It does not claim to be an immutable economic principle or law; it merely attempts to point out some characteristics of the growth pattern, not to isolate *all* the important causal variables involved in public sector growth. Both the Wagner and Peacock-Wiseman arguments, however, contribute to the understanding of the process of public sector growth in industrial nations. Yet neither should be placed in the high status of an economic law.

The Peacock-Wiseman hypothesis would appear to apply less neatly

[5] See Chapter 7 for a detailed presentation of public sector expenditure trends in the United States.

[6] Gerhard Colm and Manuel Helzner, "The Structure of Government Revenue and Expenditure in Relation to the Economic Development of the United States," *L'Importance et la Structure des Recettes et des Dépenses Publiques* (Brussels: International Institute of Public Finance, 1960).

[7] Peacock and Wiseman, *op. cit.*, pp. xxiv–xxv.

to the pattern of public sector growth in the United States than it does to that of Great Britain. Nevertheless, the growth of governmental economic activity in the United States has been rather closely related to major social disturbances such as war (World Wars I and II) and depression (the 1930's). In this sense, some approximation of the steplike process of the displacement effect may be noted. Moreover, the 20th century has experienced a significant relative expansion in the importance of the federal government component of the public sector while a significant decline in the local government component has occurred. This would seemingly resemble the concentration effect segment of the Peacock-Wiseman hypothesis. The relationship of public sector economic activity to aggregate economic activity experienced a relative decline, however, after World Wars I and II which is inconsistent with the Peacock-Wiseman prediction that the new "disturbance-created" tolerance level of taxation would find additional expenditure outlets in other areas of economic activity in order to maintain the new tax collection level. Moreover, defense (national security) has played a unique role in any resemblance of American public sector behavior to the displacement and concentration effects so that perhaps it, and not the tolerance level of taxation and scale effects, should receive priority consideration in any cause-and-effect analysis of the phenomena. Hence, the hypothesis of Peacock and Wiseman appears to be only partially useful for application to the growth of the public sector in the United States.

THE CRITICAL-LIMIT HYPOTHESIS

Another hypothesis concerned with the tolerance level of taxation is the critical-limit hypothesis. This analysis was developed by the British economist, Colin Clark, immediately following World War II.[8] The critical-limit hypothesis concludes from the empirical data of several Western nations for the period between World War I and World War II that inflation necessarily occurs when the government sector, as measured in terms of taxes and other receipts, exceeds 25 percent of aggregate economic activity. This is alleged to be true even under circumstances when the budget remains in balance.

The critical-limit hypothesis is based upon institutional factors. Clark suggests that: (1) when taxes collected by government reach the critical 25 percent ratio, community behavior patterns change and people become less productive since incentives are harmed by the fact that increasing proportions of additional income must be paid in taxes under a progressive tax system and (2) people become less resistant to various inflationary means of financing government expenditures. The loss of

---

[8] Colin Clark, "Public Finance and Changes in the Value of Money," *Economic Journal* (December, 1945), pp. 371–89.

incentive thus tends to reduce aggregate supply while the increased purchasing power resulting from inflationary financing techniques tends to expand aggregate demand. According to Clark, inflation results from this new aggregate supply–aggregate demand equilibrium.[9]

The critical-limit hypothesis resembles the displacement effect in the sense that it concentrates upon institutional factors such as the tolerance level of taxation. Except for this similarity, however, the two hypotheses and their conclusions are quite distinct. The hypothesis has received very limited support from academic circles, but has been more popularly received in the business community. Empirical evidence, however, demonstrates that a number of nations have violated the 25 percent limit during recent decades *without* significant inflationary results.

CENTRALIZED VERSUS DECENTRALIZED PUBLIC SECTOR ECONOMIC ACTIVITY

An age-old controversy has existed in the United States, and to a considerable degree in the Western world as a whole, regarding the proper or best relative size and role of central government within the public sector. As observed in Part I, one dimension of a society's allocation decision is to determine which level and unit of government within the public sector shall allocate public goods. Historically, American culture has exhibited an attitude giving priority to state and local government in providing public goods. In fact, national defense aside, state and local government expenditures always have exceeded the nonwar (civil) expenditures of the federal government in the United States. There is not one year which serves as an exception to this fact from 1789 to the present time. Yet, despite this cultural preference for decentralization within the American public sector, there remain many situations whereby public goods may be provided with advantageous economies of scale by central government. Arguments will be presented below both in favor of a larger relative role by state-local government within the public sector and in behalf of a larger relative role by the federal government.

Arguments for Decentralized Government

First, the arguments favoring state-local as opposed to federal fiscal activity will be considered.[10] Stigler observes that the preservation of a

[9] Under this argument, full employment of resources would ordinarily (but not necessarily) exist for inflation to take place. Moreover, the Clark hypothesis pertains to "monetary" as opposed to "monopoly" inflation.

[10] For a good summary of the arguments favoring both decentralized and centralized governmental fiscal activity, see Otto Eckstein, *Public Finance* (Englewood Cliffs, N.J.: Prentice-Hall, Inc., 1964), pp. 34–37.

large role for local government in public sector fiscal activity is a widely accepted social goal in American society.[11] The strongest case for local government economic activity centers upon the argument that fiscal decisions in local government approximate those of the market more closely than do the economic decisions of central government. This argument focuses upon the relationship in the market between the benefits received from the consumption of an economic good and the monetary outlay for the good. In market transactions, a person voluntarily foregoes purchasing power in order to acquire a particular economic good.[12] This correlation between payments and goods received is partially approximated in local government, though tax payments (as opposed to fees) still retain their "compulsory" feature. By contrast, members of Congress at the federal level of government do not usually relate the taxes collected from their particular regions or states to the benefits received in their districts because so many revenues are collected from so many states and regions that a "diffusion effect" exists which makes it easy to say: "Why not give my state or my region a larger portion of the tax pie since the same total amount will be collected from it in any case?" Expenditure thus tends to be justified, *not* by a particular tax collection, but by an attempt to obtain more of the "diffused aggregate" of tax revenues. Moreover, since local government decisions are closer to the individual (in terms of political jurisdiction) than are federal government decisions, it is asserted that a representative of the people in local government will be under greater pressure to establish a meaningful relationship between the benefits received and the cost of a project. In addition, the local government representative will be in a better position to interpret the preferences of the community.

A further argument in behalf of local government claims that the existence of many local government units allows an individual to select the particular community in which he wishes to reside. The selection approximates consumer sovereignty in the market since extensive variations exist among the some 90,000 units of local government in the United States. As a result, individuals through *spatial mobility* are able to select the community which best fits their particular fiscal tastes in terms of tax structure and expenditure patterns. Obviously, there exists no similar choice at the central government level—the only remote comparison being the right of an individual to move from one nation to another national jurisdiction. *Inter*national mobility, however, involves considera-

---

[11] George J. Stigler, "The Tenable Range of Functions of Local Government," *Federal Expenditure Policy for Economic Growth and Stability* (Joint Economic Committee, 85th Cong., 1st sess.) (Washington, D.C.: U.S. Government Printing Office, 1957), p. 213.

[12] See Chapter 4 for a relevant discussion of the voluntary-exchange theory.

bly greater complications than does *intra*national mobility. Tiebout provides the following observation regarding the approximation of market conditions by local government through spatial mobility:

Policies that promote residential mobility and increase the knowledge of the consumer-voter will improve the allocation of government expenditures in the same sense that mobility among jobs and knowledge relevant to the location of industry and labor improve the allocation of private resources.[13]

Another argument favoring local government asserts that individuals attain greater "freedom and responsibility" when public goods are allocated by local government. In this regard, Stigler comments:

If we give each governmental activity to the smallest governmental unit which can efficiently perform it, there will be a vast resurgence and revitalization of local government in America. A vast reservoir of ability and imagination can be found in the increasing leisure time of the population, and both public functions and private citizens would benefit from the increased participation of citizens in political life. An eminent and powerful structure of local government is a basic ingredient of a society which seeks to give to the individual the fullest possible freedom and responsibility.[14]

Though Stigler desires a maximum of fiscal decision making by local government, he acknowledges that certain fiscal areas require central decision making. Furthermore, he believes that the great revenue-gathering capabilities of the federal government should be used more than they are at the present time to finance state and local government fiscal operations. Heller holds a similar viewpoint.[15] It is thus argued that the federal government should transfer sizable tax funds to state and local government which funds could be spent at the discretion of state and local government without strings attached by the federal government. It is argued that the adoption of this proposal would allow the federal government to contribute according to its most efficient fiscal advantage, namely, its great tax collecting potential, while state-local government would be following its comparative advantage of more closely reflecting consumer preferences.[16]

An additional argument which favors decentralized government is

[13] Charles M. Tiebout, "A Pure Theory of Local Expenditures," *Journal of Political Economy* (October, 1956), p. 423.

[14] Stigler, *op. cit.*, p. 219.

[15] In late 1964, the so-called Heller Plan was suggested to President Johnson by the (then) Chairman of the President's Council of Economic Advisers, Walter W. Heller. At this writing, however, no action has been taken for the extensive turnover of federal funds to state-local government. See Chapter 9 for a detailed discussion of the Heller Plan.

[16] For pro and con arguments regarding the Heller Plan see Edwin L. Dale, Jr., "Subsidizing the States," *New Republic* (November 28, 1964), pp. 11–12; Christopher Jencks, "Why Bail Out the States?", *New Republic* (December 12, 1964), pp. 8–10.

that it allows the meeting of regional and local values rather than an across-the-boards application of *uniform* standards on a national basis. Regional and local fiscal operations will differ as the cultural habits and attitudes of the people vary between regions and communities. On the other hand, a national government policy usually contains considerable uniformity. This uniformity could be partially offset, however, if the federal government would use its tax collecting power to a greater extent by transferring additional funds to the state-local levels of government without specifying the uses to which these funds are put as discussed above.

Finally, it is asserted that local government holds an advantage since logrolling and pork-barreling practices are less common to it than to federal government budgetary decision making. Supposedly, the *scope* of local budgetary decision making is sufficiently smaller than that of the central government to allow this difference. In other words, there is greater political pressure for a correlation between (tax) costs and benefits within the more "concentrated" local political jurisdictions than in the more "extensive" federal jurisdiction.

Arguments for Centralized Government

The fact that certain economic goods are collective in nature to regions or to the entire nation suggests that many important pure public and quasi-public goods should be allocated under central government influence. Pure public goods are *not* divisible while the benefits of quasi-public goods tend to be only partly allocable under the exclusion principle. National defense, for example, involves a common interest among all individuals in the nation. Because of the nature of national defense, it is not surprising that the central government possesses an efficiency advantage in providing this economic good. Part of the benefits or costs of quasi-public goods, on the other hand, are identifiable with the individual firm or consumer and part affect the community as a whole. When such goods are socially important, however, and many of them such as communications, education, and health are important to society, the public interest becomes involved to the extent that the goods should be provided in adequate quantities. The entire nation as well as the individual benefits from such quasi-public goods. Thus, a strong case for *central* government allocation may be established when important economic goods are collective or quasi-collective in nature and consumed, at least in part, by the entire nation.

Relatedly, an argument for central government economic activity results from the fact that only a geographically comprehensive central government can work toward the "leveling out" of significant differences in the consumption of various important public and quasi-public goods, incomes, and the like between the communities and regions of the nation.

Such leveling out, of course, may be desirable from the standpoint of both distribution and allocation objectives. The society, for example, may desire greater equality in incomes and complete equality in educational opportunities on a nationwide basis. It would seem that central government would be in the best position to help attain these goals.

It is observed above in the discussion of local government that one of the greatest advantages of central government is its ability to collect a large volume of tax revenues in an efficient manner. Even more importantly, the federal government can collect taxes without considering "tax cutting competition" such as presently exists between many states and localities in efforts to attract industry. Some states and communities reduce or eliminate property taxes or otherwise use the budget to subsidize business in an effort to attract industry to their political jurisdictions. A subsidization type of competition is frequently built up between such jurisdictions which frequently results in negative market distortions. The comprehensive nature of federal budgeting avoids this intergovernmental competition for industry by which taxes may be escaped or reduced, or expenditure subsidies received, as a reward for the spatial mobility of productive resources from one state or locality to another.

It is claimed, moreover, that federal fiscal activity holds an advantage over local activity because it is easier to enact rational fiscal legislation at the national level since communications are so efficient in America that issues can be presented to a complete cross section of the public. On the other hand, local decisions are more susceptible to influence by a biased segment of the community. Some property owners, for example, may be opposed to higher property tax rates to help finance education because they have no children despite a severe need for better educational facilities in the society. In other words, a larger sample providing a statistically more reliable cross section of opinion for decision making is provided by central government as opposed to state-local government budgetary action. It is thus concluded from the argument that federal fiscal legislation operates in closer proximity to community preferences.

In analyzing the reasons for the relative growth of central government within a relatively growing public sector, reference may be made to the concentration effect (discussed above). Social disturbances such as war, which involve obvious central government fiscal obligations, lead to an emergency increase in central government budgetary operations. Immediately, there is a relative decline of total tax collections by lower levels of government. When the disturbance ends, the inroad made by the central government within the public sector is maintained in a manner similar to the displacement effect whereby the public sector grows as a proportion of total economic activity. Thus, central government makes a relative advance within the public sector, in terms of tax collections and expenditures, at the expense of lower levels of government.

In addition, Peacock and Wiseman explain the relative growth of central government by (1) the fact that living standards are rising, (2) the increased efficiency of transportation, and (3) the associated growth in the efficient size of economic and social organizations.[17] They believe these phenomena have made central government relatively more efficient than local government as compared to periods of time before these improvements occurred. Meanwhile, they point out that many of the major problems of urban life such as the provision of sewage and of public health services, which have been borne traditionally by local government, are now largely completed. Hence, the new economic requirements which are arising are conducive, for the most part, to provision by central government while the traditional functions of local government which now have been completed merely require maintenance operations.[18] This appears to be more true for Britain, however, than it is for the United States.

In addition, changes in social ideas and the accompanying changes in economic environment have supported central government growth.[19] Local government has shared in the growing acceptance of government intervention, which has encouraged the development of total government activity. This growing governmental activity, according to Peacock and Wiseman, involves a shift from emphasis on the relief of outright distress, such as poor relief, to emphasis upon providing public services on the basis of positive desirability, such as education and improved transportation. The economic and social changes mentioned above may tend to carry with them a reduction of interest in the safeguarding of local fiscal autonomy and responsibility.

In conclusion, it may be observed that intergovernmental fiscal relationships are among the most important economic issues of our times. Not only are we concerned with the social balance controversy as to the proper role of government, we are concerned also with the relative importance of central government within the public sector. The next chapter will consider various intergovernmental tax and expenditure relationships. In addition, it will discuss the future revenue requirements of the public sector as a background for the need to improve intergovernmental fiscal relationships.

[17] Peacock and Wiseman, *op. cit.*, pp. 118–20.
[18] *Ibid.*, p. 119.
[19] *Ibid.*

THE AGGREGATE PUBLIC

Chapter

SECTOR BUDGET—

9

INTERGOVERNMENTAL

FISCAL RELATIONS

IMPORTANCE OF THE AGGREGATE PUBLIC SECTOR BUDGET CONCEPT

The United States public sector is composed of some 90,000 separate units of government, each capable of performing the basic fiscal functions of taxing and spending.[1] Aggregate allocation, distribution, stabilization, and economic growth effects of public sector budgetary behavior will inevitably result from the collective actions of these many separate governmental units. Though no single unit of government determines the entire aggregate effects, some units obviously exert greater influence than do others. The effects of *federal* budgetary behavior, for example, are of much greater significance than the budgetary actions of a local school district.

The federalistic basis of public sector structure in the United States complicates the aggregate operations of government in this nation as compared to nations with unitary political structures. Tax and expenditure policies often lack coordination in reference to national economic goals. A tax reduction at the federal level for stabilization-growth purposes, for example, may be neutralized by tax increases at the state-local level.[2] The multiplicity of state and local units of government, moreover, tends to cause many conflicting policies *within the same level of government* (state and local) regarding the four public finance goals.

The nature of intergovernmental fiscal relations thus constitutes an extremely relevant consideration for the achievement of fiscal rationality within a decentralized political structure. The aggregate public sector

---

[1] In 1962, the Bureau of the Census reported the existence of 91,158 government units in the United States, inclusive of 91,107 units of local government in addition to the 50 state governments and the federal government.

[2] The federal personal and corporation income tax reductions of March, 1964, were not followed immediately by state-local tax increases of any significant nature. The reasons for this relative status quo apparently were: (1) the federal tax reduction came too late in the legislative year to influence the actions of most state legislatures and (2) 1964 was an election year, at which time tax increases are politically unpopular. The latter point is supported by the fact that state-local tax increases were considerable during 1965, a nonelection year. Hence, the initial inaction of state-local government may only have been temporary.

budget concept, indeed, is an important one. As observed in Chapter 5, these significant fiscal relations assume two dimensions: (1) intergovernmental budgetary influence between levels of government which is referred to as *vertical* intergovernmental fiscal relations and (2) intergovernmental budgetary influence between different government units within the same level of government which is termed *horizontal* intergovernmental fiscal relations. The latter type of interrelationship is possible, of course, only at the state and local levels of government in the United States.

INTERGOVERNMENTAL BUDGETARY PROBLEMS

Divergence of Revenue Sources and Expenditures

As observed above, *federalism*—whereby two or more sovereign units of government coexist within the same political environment—provides the primary basis for the intergovernmental fiscal problems of the United States public sector. This is particularly true in the area of *vertical* intergovernmental fiscal relations where it must be decided which level of government will perform the specific functions which community preferences require. In addition, the revenue sources necessary to finance these expenditure functions must be allocated in some manner among the various levels of government. This does not mean, of course, that each governmental level should possess exclusive rights to a particular type of revenue, but it does mean that overall consideration should be given to the combined effects of the revenue-gathering activities of *all* components of the public sector.

A considerable divergence exists at the present time between the sources of tax revenue and the functional items of governmental expenditure within the United States public sector. This lack of coordination is found along the lines of both vertical and horizonal intergovernmental budgetary activity. Unfortunately, the comprehensive symmetrical relationship between the revenue and expenditure sides of the aggregate public sector budget, which is required for complete governmental fiscal rationality, is difficult to approximate under a decentralized governmental structure. Some levels and units of government possess comparative efficiency advantages in meeting particular economic functions. These same levels and units of government, however, often possess inadequate revenue sources to meet their functional expenditures. Meanwhile, certain other levels and units of government may possess revenues in excess of their functional expenditure requirements. Though such noncorrelation between revenues and expenditures could probably be reduced by a more unitary political structure, important noneconomic reasons favoring decentralized government exist in the United States. Many Americans have historically feared a large central government believing that it unduly reduces the freedom of the individual to determine his economic and political destiny.[3]

Generally, central government can collect taxes more efficiently than lower levels of government. A lower level of government, however, may be in a preferred position to detect community preferences for public and quasi-public goods. Yet, the budget in essence is a single unified document relating both revenue sources and expenditure patterns to each other. The goal of fiscal rationality within the United States public sector requires improvement in the means of relating public sector revenues and expenditures in a more symmetrical manner between levels and units of government.

The comparative advantage which higher levels of government possess in gathering tax revenues stems from several factors. First, a level of government with broad political jurisdiction is in a preferred position to discover items relevant to the tax base and to enforce the tax rates which are imposed upon that base. Broad jurisdictional authority, moreover, discourages migration of the tax base to lower tax locations. If a municipality, for example, levies a comprehensive personal income tax on all types of income and does not receive any enforcement assistance from the state or federal government, it would be at a comparative efficiency disadvantage with the higher levels of government. Some income would be earned outside of the political limits of the city and would be difficult to discover. Moreover, in the long run economic activity could migrate to other municipalities with lower income tax burdens. Obviously, the discovery of a personal income tax base is easier, and the opportunities to transfer economic activities to lower tax jurisdictions are fewer, the broader the scope of the political jurisdiction levying the tax. Generally, *only* the property tax among the major types of taxes is conducive to local government administration without considerable assistance from higher levels of government. Information regarding the property tax base is readily available to local government and the migration of taxable property to lower tax areas is fairly difficult. Yet, despite its limited revenue sources, local government can provide many economic goods in an efficient manner. Again, the critical divergence between revenue sources and expenditure functions among the levels of government is observed.

Significant fiscal problems may also exist horizontally within the same level of government. For example, considerable differences in the distribution of income and wealth exist between the several economic regions of the nation. Since several states (or parts of states) comprise each economic region, these regional differences in income-wealth

---

[3] See the pro and con discussion of centralized versus decentralized government in the previous chapter.

endowment cross state boundaries and involve interstate fiscal relationships within the same (state) level of government. Furthermore, significant variation in the distribution of income and wealth exist among local units of government even within the same state. The considerable differences in the resource endowments of localities, and the consequent differences in their income-earning abilities, cause the range of tax bases between communities to vary sharply. Admittedly, one advantage of decentralized fiscal decision making is the fact that a particular local tax structure may be adapted to the unique resource characteristics of that community. Since income and wealth are the ultimate sources of all taxpaying ability, however, a community enjoying considerable resource wealth and income-producing ability is capable of providing a greater volume of public and quasi-public goods than is a resource-poor community. This is the *crux* of the problem at hand.[4] The question may then be asked: Should deliberate budgetary policy be undertaken to equalize the consumption of public and quasi-public goods between regions and between localities?

The answer to the above question involves the concept of external effects (externalities) as well as certain other economic and noneconomic considerations. In an advanced industrial society replete with highly efficient transportation and communications, the significance of external effects is certain to be greater than in a society involving less specialization and interdependence.[5] In an interdependent specialized society, a poor community or region cannot help but influence the consumption, production, and government service patterns of the wealthier communities or regions. Isolation, with purely internal effects, may have been possible during the Middle Ages, given the existence of a society divided into many self-sufficient manorial units. This is not possible, however, in a specialized, highly interdependent industrial society. The allocation patterns within the private and public sectors of one region or one locality are interdependent with the budgetary patterns of other regions or communities.

Furthermore, if the society has "fiscal equity" as a distribution goal, significant per capita inequality in the distribution of public and quasi-public goods between regions and localities must be removed if this goal

---

[4] It is possible, of course, that a poorer community can provide a level of public and quasi-public goods equal to that of a wealthier community. This would tend to be at a relative sacrifice of private consumption, however, since tax burdens would tend to constitute a higher proportion of the income-wealth base of the poorer community.

[5] Pure public goods of a national variety such as defense, which are consumed equally by each individual, are somewhat more likely to exert significant external effects than quasi-public goods whose benefits and costs may be partly assignable to individual economic units and to economic regions.

is to be attained. In this instance, rational fiscal policy of a redistributive nature is required.

The quality of productive resources in a poor community, moreover, is likely to be lower than in a community capable of providing a higher level of public consumption. Labor, for example, is likely to be less educated and health standards lower in a poor as opposed to a wealthy community. The aggregate stabilization-growth implications of this suggest that lower volumes of short-run production and slower rates of long-run economic growth will occur for the economy as a whole. Thus, horizontal intralevel fiscal problems add a further dimension to the overall problem of achieving an efficient aggregate public sector budgetary operation.

Intergovernmental Economic Competition

State and local units of government frequently engage in horizontal intergovernmental fiscal competition in an effort to attract business firms to their respective political jurisdictions. Tax concessions, the provision of economic resources such as land, and the financing of manufacturing plants are among the most important fiscal subsidies used in this regard. Unfortunately, such *supply* subsidies tend to distort the allocation of business operations among various geographical areas since the market mechanism is not allowed to allocate resources among alternative locations on the basis of most efficient resource combinations. It may be argued, however, that community differences in revenue and expenditure patterns will increase the efficiency of *consumer demand* for government-provided goods since an individual may select his residential location from among various communities, each with differential budgetary bases, in a manner similar to the free selection of private economic goods in the market.[6] In any event, the greater the diversity of governmental levels and units, as under a federal system, the greater is the motivation for fiscal competition for industry on the supply side and for the spatial mobility of consumers between political jurisdictions on the demand side.

Multiple Taxation

Various situations arise whereby the same tax base is taxed more than once. This multiple or overlapping taxation may be imposed by (1) different levels of government, (2) different units of government at the same level, or (3) the same unit of government.[7] Examples of multiple taxation by different levels of government include federal, state, and

---

[6] As discussed in Chapter 8, see the argument of Charles M. Tiebout, "A Pure Theory of Local Expenditures," *Journal of Political Economy*, Vol. LXIV (October, 1956), pp. 416–24.

[7] This often is referred to as "double taxation," though clearly "multiple taxation" is a better term because the same tax base may be taxed more than twice.

(sometimes) local government imposition of a personal income tax.[8] Another prime example of multiple taxation by different levels of government occurs when both state and local government apply property tax rates on the same property base.

Multiple taxation by different government units at the same level of government is less prominent than overlapping taxation by different levels of government. Some important examples of the former variety exist, however, especially in situations involving state inheritance, business, and personal income taxation. For example, two states may apply inheritance taxes to the same intangible property transferred at death or an individual's income may be taxed both where it is earned and at the location of the recipient's domicile.

The third variety of multiple taxation, the same base being taxed more than once by the same unit of government, exists to a moderate extent within the American public sector. The best example occurs in the dual imposition of federal income taxes—both corporation and personal —on corporate dividend income with only slight offsets provided by law. As will be observed in Chapter 10, however, the volume of this type of double taxation may be significantly reduced through the process of tax shifting.

The fact that multiple taxation is not undesirable per se must be emphasized. Multiple taxation becomes irrational only when it is practiced by one unit or level of government without concern for its aggregate effects within the public sector and between the public and private sectors. This includes the interacting effects of multiple taxation upon allocation, distribution, stabilization, and growth efficiency. The cumulative tax burden created by multiple taxation, for example, may distort the society's concept of equitable distribution. It may lead, moreover, to a waste of economic resources and thus reduce technical efficiency to the extent that duplicate government enforcement and taxpayer compliance efforts are undertaken.

Regarding the extent of the multiple taxation (referred to as "tax overlapping") in the United States, the Advisory Commission on Intergovernmental Relations observes:

While tax overlapping is widespread in the sense that often a tax category providing the major part of the tax revenues at one level—Federal, State, or local—is used also, if only to a minor degree, at another level, the system is characterized by a substantial degree of revenue separation. Most of the tax overlapping is minimal and could be largely eliminated by foregoing about 20 percent of collections. If by some magic, for example, all three levels of government could turn back the clock just three years (in terms of their latest tax collections), and each could rearrange its tax take of three years ago, they

---

[8] Residents of St. Louis, Missouri, for example, are subject to federal, state, and muncipal personal income taxes.

could utilize such a 20 percent reduction in their tax take, in terms of averages, to eliminate tax overlapping. They would accomplish this by leaving the Federal Government with only income taxes, local governments with only property taxes, and the States largely with consumer taxes.[9]

Some reduction in multiple taxation by different levels of government has occurred during recent decades. Most states, for example, are reducing emphasis on the property tax which is now used almost exclusively by local government. In addition, the federal government has abandoned the tax on electrical energy and most of its admissions taxes thus leaving these taxes to lower levels of government.

TECHNIQUES FOR SOLVING INTERGOVERNMENTAL FISCAL PROBLEMS

Separation of Revenue Sources

Several alternate approaches may be directed toward the solution of vertical and horizontal intergovernmental budgetary problems. The most comprehensive of these alternatives involves the separation of revenue sources between the various levels of government. To an extent, the Constitution provides a basis for separation of revenues. Customs duties (tariffs), for example, may be collected *only* by the federal government. Furthermore, the Constitution in effect prohibits the imposition of a federal property tax since it would have to be apportioned in accordance with the population of each state.

In practice, the revenue structure of the United States public sector bears considerable resemblance to a separated revenue system. The vast majority of revenues which are collected from individual and corporation income taxes, from selective sales taxes, and from inheritance, estate, and gift taxes are collected by the federal government. The vast majority of general sales tax receipts and motor vehicle and operator license revenues are collected by state governments. Meanwhile, local government absorbs an extremely high proportion of property tax receipts.

Complete separation of revenue sources between the federal, state, and local components of the public sector may appear on the surface to be a utopian arrangement. Closer analysis, however, demonstrates that such is not the case. Admittedly, the complete separation technique would eliminate multiple taxation on an interlevel basis with its attendant problems. In addition, it would preserve state-local autonomy as compared to the conditional tax sharing, tax supplement, tax credit, and tax deduction techniques (to be discussed later in this chapter). Nevertheless,

[9] The Advisory Commission on Intergovernmental Relations, *Tax Overlapping in the United States—1964* (Washington, D.C.: U.S. Government Printing Office, July, 1964), p. 18.

several important qualifications offer opposition to the technique of completely separating tax revenues.

First, there are not enough potentially good tax sources to adequately serve the three levels and some 90,000 government units which comprise the American public sector. An overriding constraint of revenue scarcity is thus imposed. This constraint cannot be alleviated merely by separating tax revenue sources between the three levels of government. In addition, considerable economic differentiation exists within the state and local levels of government. Consequently, a rational tax structure for one state or local governmental unit will probably be significantly different from that of another. For example, the resource base of one state or locality, which largely generates its income base (from which ultimately all taxpaying ability derives), may differ greatly from the resource combinations of another state or locality. Fiscal irrationality surely would result if two highly differentiated states or communities had identical tax structures.

Another defect in the separations approach concerns its lack of symmetry in considering only the tax side of the aggregate public sector budget. The spending side of the budget, which can influence allocation, distribution, stabilization, and growth with force equal to that of the revenue side, is ignored by the separations approach. In addition, the separations technique does not provide the complete intergovernmental uniformity in tax rates, exemptions, and so forth which would be necessary to eliminate intergovernmental competition for industrial location—a practice with significant connotation regarding efficient resource usage. A related consideration involving the asymmetry of the separations approach concerns the fact that it may frustrate the collective value judgments of the society regarding minimal living standards of the population. Such value judgments ordinarily suggest that a minimum (ex post) real income distribution be attainable for the residents of all states and communities. Federal grants-in-aid to states and their subdivisions for such things as highways, public assistance, and unemployment compensation programs exemplify this attitude. Yet, the asymmetrical nature of the separations approach prevents it from working toward the equalization of minimal consumption of certain basic economic goods between states and localities.

Furthermore, the separations technique would likely distort any distribution objective based upon the desirability of a progressive tax rate system for the public sector as a whole. For example, "complete tax separation" in the United States would undoubtedly consist of the exclusive use of income taxes by the federal government, the general sales tax by state governments, and the property tax by local governments. Complete revenue separation along these lines would thus result in a public sector revenue structure containing significant "regressive" elements in the form of general sales and property taxes.[10] Under such conditions, the distribution goal in question would not be attained.

A final qualification regarding use of the tax separation device concerns the stabilization and growth branches of public finance. Considerable budgetary rigidity would necessarily accompany complete tax separation. Yet, changing conditions of the business cycle and changing growth rates will affect the revenue yields of the "separated taxes" as well as the functional spending needs of the various levels and units of government. The inflexibility of a revenue separation system, however, would restrict the appropriate budgetary adjustments required for anticyclical and growth policies as well as for the maintenance of allocation and distribution goals.

Tax Sharing

This solution to intergovernmental fiscal problems has received much discussion in the United States and is in moderate use at the present time. Certain phases of this approach, moreover, are now being considered for significant future expansion.[11] *Tax sharing*, broadly defined, involves a government unit at a higher level collecting tax revenues prior to the disbursement of some part of these revenues to government units at a lower level or levels, the disbursements falling into conditional (strings attached) and unconditional (bloc) categories.[12] There is strong evidence that the most efficient governmental scale for revenue collection tends to be at a higher level of government than is the most efficient scale for expenditure decisions.[13] Thus, comparative efficiency advantages are followed for both the revenue and expenditure sides of the budget when the tax sharing technique is employed. However, the lack of a symmetrical *quid pro quo* correlation at each level of government between the two flow sides of the budget remains a problem.

In the United States, conditional tax sharing plans are used more extensively than are unconditional plans.[14] The federal government is involved in many conditional grant-in-aid programs to state and local governments. State governments, in addition, conduct certain conditional

---

[10] This result would assume the exclusion of grants-in-aid.

[11] See the discussion of the Heller Plan later in this chapter.

[12] The author uses a "comprehensive" definition of tax sharing due to the fact that even such intergovernmental assistance as conditional grants-in-aid still must derive ultimately from the revenue collections of the higher level of government. Thus, why should they not be considered as tax sharing?

[13] See the relevant discussion in Chapter 8 and, to a lesser extent, the discussion earlier in this chapter.

[14] "Trust fund" grants-in-aid such as the federal interstate highway program will be discussed in detail in Chapter 16. Hence, the total discussion of grants-in-aid in this chapter will be reduced accordingly.

grant-in-aid programs for which local units of government are the recipients. Regarding unconditional grants-in-aid, virtually no use is made of this bloc-grant, no-strings attached, device between the federal government and lower levels of government in the United States. Moderate usage of unconditional bloc grants is undertaken by state governments, however, in their fiscal relationships with local governments.

Table 9–1 displays the functional programs through which the

TABLE 9–1

FEDERAL AID TO STATE AND LOCAL GOVERNMENTS BY FORM OF AID
AND FUNCTION, 1965 FISCAL YEAR, AND 1966, 1967 ESTIMATES
(Millions of Dollars)

	1965	*1966 (est.)*	*1967 (est.)*
Total Aid to State and Local Governments	$11,127.4	$13,299.8	$14,646.7
Grants-in-aid, budget accounts	6,346.4	8,520.3	10,020.1
Veterans services and benefits	8.1	9.4	8.7
Health, labor, and welfare	4,084.2	5,729.6	6,114.3
Public assistance	2,787.2	3,240.8	3,306.2
Health services and research	448.1	544.1	733.1
Labor, manpower, and vocational rehabilitation	124.0	253.4	318.3
Other welfare activities	272.2	364.1	288.8
Education and general research	610.3	1,024.2	2,031.0
Agriculture and agricultural resources	517.6	541.3	428.1
Natural resources	107.1	163.5	193.1
Commerce and transportation (except highways)	406.5	289.4	280.2
Housing and community development	559.2	688.4	877.6
General government	15.8	36.6	43.0
National defense	33.3	33.2	38.8
International affairs and finance	4.4	4.8	5.2
Grants-in-aid, trust funds	4,372.8	4,374.6	4,530.4
Highway trust fund	3,979.5	3,923.2	4,027.8
Unemployment trust fund	393.3	450.4	500.6
Other revenues	408.1	404.8	96.3

SOURCE: *Special Analyses, Budget of the United States, Fiscal Year, 1967* (Washington, D.C.: U.S. Government Printing Office), pp. 138–43.

federal government provided aid to state and local governments in Fiscal Years 1965, 1966, and 1967. Two types of grants-in-aid appear, namely, grants-in-aid paid from general treasury funds and those used for programs which operate under separate trust funds. In each type of program, however, the grants-in-aid are conditional in nature. The federal government during Fiscal 1967 distributed more than $10 billion in grants-in-aid through the general treasury budget and over $4.5 billion through the trust fund accounts.

More than one half ($6.1 billion) of the general treasury grants went for the health, labor, and welfare expenditure category. By far the largest proportion of this amount was used for public assistance grants, including aid for dependent children, the needy aged, and the blind. The remainder of health, labor, and welfare expenditures were for such functional activities as health services and research, labor, manpower, and vocational rehabilitation. Other sizable expenditure areas within the general treasury category—aside from those for health, labor, and welfare—include the education, the housing and community development, and the agricultural categories. Meanwhile, the grants-in-aid channeled through trust fund financing primarily consisted of the highway and unemployment insurance trust funds.

The grant-in-aid approach for federal government revenue support of state and local government activities dates back many years. Most of the growth in this approach, however, has occurred during the last 30 years. Some significant early examples of federal aid to lower levels of government include: (1) the disposal of the federal Treasury surplus by President Andrew Jackson in 1836–37 and (2) the Morrill Act of 1862 which led to the establishment of state land-grant universities.

Projections for the future suggest that significant absolute and relative growth in the use of federal grants-in-aid will occur in such functional areas as health, labor, and welfare, education, and in housing and community development. This is predicted to be part of a continuing post–World War II growth in the absolute and relative importance of federal grants-in-aid to state and local governments. Such growth is evident in the data which show that federal spending for grants-in-aid to state and local governments amounted to less than $1 billion in 1946, but increased to $3.1 billion in 1955 and to $14.6 billion in 1967.

Conditional grants-in-aid of the federal government ordinarily follow formulas for allocation which have been provided by the controlling statutes. Specifically, the formulas are based on such criteria as income per capita, geographical area, and population. In addition, the sharing formulas are usually guided by either the actual amount of revenue collected in each state, or for the purpose of returning relatively greater amounts of revenue to the poorer states. The latter approach recognizes "need" and the desirability of supplementing revenue-gathering ability at the state and local levels of government. Obviously, the recognition-of-need approach can yield substantial effects on the distribution of income and wealth in the society.

State governments often provide shared taxes to local units of government. Some of these are provided on a strings-attached basis and others on an unconditional basis. The general sales, gasoline, and excise taxes are the most commonly shared state taxes, though in a few states income and death taxes are shared with local governments. Such sharing contributes to administrative efficiency by avoiding duplicate enforcement efforts and by placing the enforcement responsibility in the higher level of government which has a comparative advantage in such matters.[15] Another advantage of state-local shared taxes is the discouragement of economically irrational local government budgetary competition for the attraction of industry.

Though conditionally shared revenues are more prominently used within the United States public sector than are unconditional (bloc) grants, recent developments suggest a possible bright future for the latter tax sharing approach. In 1964, a special economic task force suggested to President Johnson that an elaborate expansion of the unconditional grant-in-aid approach be undertaken by the federal government. The task force was headed by Joseph Pechman. The proposal was consistent with earlier studies by Walter Heller, who was Chairman of the Council of Economic Advisers at the time of the Pechman report. This proposal has subsequently been termed the Heller Plan.[16] Moreover, bipartisan political interest in this form of tax sharing was indicated in April, 1966, when the Republican National Committee recommended a similar plan.

The Heller-Pechman proposal contains several significant features. First, a fixed percentage of federal personal income tax collections would be set aside for distribution to the states (with the possible distribution of some of these amounts by the states to local units of government). This amount would constitute a separate trust fund equal to 1 percent of all personal income subject to tax. During the 1965 calendar year, this would have amounted to approximately $2.5 billion, which is 1 percent of the approximate federal income tax base of $250 billion for the year. The money would then be distributed to the states, generally in proportion to their population, but with some adjustments made for the needs of each state. The funds could be used for whatever purposes desired except for possible restriction on road expenditures which are covered by the separate highway grant-in-aid program. The alternate Republican plan would turn over to the states 2 percent of federal personal and corporation income tax revenues at the present time with the percentage increasing to 10 percent in eight years.

The two basic premises of the Heller Plan are (1) the recognized *need* of state and local government for additional revenues to meet expanding functional expenditure requirements in such areas as education, health, and welfare and (2) the probable existence of a *federal budgetary surplus* at full employment under the present federal tax

---

[15] In some instances, however, shared state-local death and automotive license taxes are administered by local government.

[16] Among the excellent discussions of the Heller Plan are: Alan L. Otten and Charles B. Seib, "No-Strings Aid for the States?" *Reporter* (January 28, 1965), pp. 33–35; "No-Strings Federal Aid Finds Backers at Forum," *Business Week* (April 3, 1965), pp. 28–29; Edwin L. Dale, Jr., "Subsidizing the States," *New Republic* (November 28, 1964), pp. 11–12; Christopher Jencks, "Why Bail Out the States?," *New Republic* (December 12, 1964), pp. 8–10; and Harvey E. Brazer, "Our Hard-Pressed State and Local Governments," *Challenge* (January–February, 1966), pp. 6–9, 41.

structure.[17] The proposal does not suggest a reduction in the absolute amount of conditional grants-in-aid nor in their relative dominance in the overall federal aid programs. During 1965, for example, the $2.5 billion of unconditional grants would have been less than 25 percent of the value of conditional federal grants-in-aid to state and local governments.

The reasoning behind the Heller Plan, which derives from the basic premises cited above, may now be considered. It is estimated that the national economy would provide a $6 billion surplus at full employment during 1965 under the present federal tax structure. In order to avoid a "drag" or depressive effect upon the economy, federal budgetary revision would be required. Among the alternative policies of revision are: (1) reduce "progressive" federal income tax rates and return the surplus to the private sector; (2) reduce regressive federal excise taxes and return the surplus to the private sector; (3) retain the surplus within the federal component of the public sector and use it to meet expanded federal spending; (4) adopt the *Heller Plan* and distribute the surplus to state and local governments with no strings attached; (5) adopt some combination of the above alternatives.[18]

Alternative (1), the reduction of federal income taxes, represents the extreme conservative position while alternative (3), the increase in federal spending, represents the extreme liberal position.[19] Alternative (2) represents an approach leaning toward the conservative position while the Heller Plan itself, and alternative (5), represent compromise positions. The Heller Plan avoids antagonism of the extreme liberals by maintaining the same relative importance for the public sector. Furthermore, it avoids antagonism of the extreme conservatives by opposing expansion of federal spending. In fact, what appears to be a likely course of legislative action, if the Heller Plan is eventually accepted by Congress, is to combine it with alternative (2)—thus effectively making alternative (5) the prevailing course of action. In a sense, this was partly accomplished through the federal excise tax reductions of 1965.

In 1965, Congress reduced federal excise tax rates on some

---

[17] This potential surplus refers to the federal revenue structure as it existed *after* the income tax reductions of 1964. During 1966, however, the full-employment economy of the nation was not providing a budget surplus. This fact is apparently explained by (1) the federal excise tax reductions which were subsequent to the Pechman report and (2) intensified Vietnamese war spending since the report was submitted in 1964.

[18] In these proposals, the surplus referred to is potential, not actual. It exists only in the sense that full employment (with its surplus) cannot be attained unless the federal budgetary structure is *first altered* to make the budget more expansionary in nature. See also the discussion of the full-employment budget concept in Chapter 19.

[19] The author admits that use of the terms "conservative" and "liberal" involves semantical problems. It is hoped, however, that the general discussion below will be clear without the time-consuming efforts required for a precise distinction.

economic goods and eliminated the tax on many others. The total revenue reduction amounted to approximately $4.8 billion, an amount equal to about 80 percent of the potential full-employment surplus for the year. This will quite possibly be followed in later years by an adoption of the unconditional grant concept of the Heller Plan to absorb the remaining potential surplus as well as any additional surplus which could be expected to come about due to the growing productive base of the economy.

Proponents of the Heller Plan say that it is a "pleasant compromise" in that (1) the federal government does not expand within the public sector (thus satisfying conservatives), (2) that the public sector still continues to operate at the same absolute level (thus satisfying liberals), while (3) severe functional expenditure needs such as education, health, and welfare can be met by state and local governments under the plan. *Opponents* argue that (1) state-local government is not "forward-looking," (2) that it is full of graft, and (3) that it is unduly subject to influence by pressure groups. They doubt that the functional needs mentioned above would receive appropriate amounts of the money distributed, with no strings attached, from the federal government to the lower levels of government. The groups opposing the Heller Plan include not only those who lack confidence in the fiscal efficiency of state and local government but also some extreme liberals and conservatives who refuse to accept a compromise position.

In terms of fiscal rationality, the Heller Plan provides mixed results. The plan appears to be neutral, for the most part, within the stabilization and growth objectives of public finance. Admittedly, if state governments used the distributed revenues to reduce debt instead of to increase spending, some deflationary results might occur. The bulk of economic effects which would derive from the Heller Plan, however, appear to fall within the allocation and distribution branches of public finance. Unconditional grants-in-aid, for example, enlarge the ability of lower levels of government to make expenditure decisions. To the extent that lower levels of government may approximate *quid pro quo* type market decisions better than central government, allocation efficiency would thus be enhanced by the unconditional grant-in-aid approach. Moreover, community preferences in the United States, from an individual freedom standpoint, have traditionally been sympathetic to fiscal decision making by lower levels of government.

The allocation dimension which is most influenced by unconditional tax sharing is that which divides allocation among the various levels of the public sector (vertical intergovernmental fiscal relations). Any reallocation of revenue-expenditure patterns among levels of government which may result from adoption of an extensive federal unconditional grant-in-aid program could either increase or decrease fiscal rationality.

No single determinate result applicable to all cases can be predicted. It is important to recognize, however, that such an important allocation dimension would be affected by the adoption of the Heller Plan which would significantly extend such grants.

Distribution, of course, is closely intertwined with allocation. Shifts in allocation necessarily redistribute income and wealth in a "living standard" or "real income" sense. A given (ex ante) state of distribution, moreover, is prerequisite to the actual allocation and real income distribution which takes place. These important facts were emphasized in Chapters 4 and 5. In conclusion, it should be observed that interrelated allocation and distribution effects would inevitably result from the adoption of the Heller Plan. The exact nature of these effects is not determinate because of the influence of secondary variables. Each potential allocative and distributive effect would have to be analyzed on the basis of its individual characteristics.

Tax Supplements

The *tax supplement* technique of intergovernmental fiscal coordination involves the application of separate tax rates to the same tax base by different levels of government. The higher level of government usually imposes the basic tax. This technique is used moderately between the federal and state levels of government but is used rather extensively between the state and local levels of government. The best example of its present use between federal and state government is the income tax of the state of Alaska. This tax adopts the federal income tax base and merely collects a fixed percentage of an individual's federal income tax payment. State and local governments using a combined tax supplement approach ordinarily add the local tax rate to the state tax rate. The general sales tax provides an excellent example of the tax supplement device being used by the state and local levels of government. The receipts of both the state and local sales taxes are collected by the state government. They are then allocated to local government on the basis of the geographical origin of the tax revenues. Local governments traditionally collect property tax revenues, however, when both state and local governments impose taxes on the same property tax base.

The tax supplement device appears to have little direct influence upon the distribution, stabilization, and economic growth branches of public finance. In terms of technical allocation efficiency, however, enforcement savings in the form of reduced tax collection costs accrue to both the public sector and to the taxpayer who prepares tax returns. Allocative irrationality could be reduced, moreover, if all states used the same tax supplement arrangement for a federal tax because interstate budgetary competition for industrial and residential location would be reduced. Such uniformity, however, should not be obtained for *all* types of taxes since the characteristics of state resource bases differ so greatly between states. Thus, an allocative disadvantage would result from the tax supplement device if the lower level of government is compelled to accept the revenue structure of the higher level of government imposing the tax even though its "resource base" (which determines its taxpaying base) differs greatly from that of the higher level of government. This circumstance would cause irrational allocation of resources among the various levels of government.

Tax Credits

Under the *tax credit* technique of intergovernmental revenue coordination, one level or unit of government allows an offset for taxes paid to another governmental jurisdiction. Credits for taxes paid to other jurisdictions differ from deductions in that the latter *reduce tax liabilities* to the individual while tax credits usually do not alter liabilities. For example, the crediting device merely allows a taxpayer to pay federal taxes with state tax receipts. Deductions, moreover, do not provide the same strong motive for tax uniformity among various units of government at the lower level of government that tax credits provide. This uniformity is more adaptable to the fiscal structure of a unitary political system than that of a federal system since the latter involves dual autonomy which discourages the imposition of decisions by one level of government upon another. It is possible, however, to use tax credits on an intralevel basis without violating the philosophy of a federal system of government, but this is not the usual nor the most efficient use of the credit device.

In the United States, the federal government used the tax credit device as early as 1918 to minimize the multiple international taxation of incomes. In 1924, the federal estate tax was introduced for the purpose of discouraging the interstate competition for wealth location based on competitive state death tax rates. The federal government extended its usage of the tax credit device in 1936 through the introduction of the unemployment insurance program payroll tax credit. In this instance, the states were placed under virtual economic compulsion to adopt payroll taxes which would be part of the planned federal-state program. The federal unemployment insurance tax of 3.1 percent on wages (as appropriately defined) allows a 2.7 percent credit (nearly 90 percent) if paid under a state unemployment insurance tax. Thus, any state not imposing such a tax would lose substantial revenues from its boundaries which otherwise could be retained. All states subsequently passed such a tax. It has been recently suggested that an approach similar to that for the unemployment insurance credit be adopted for the personal income tax in order to encourage all states to use this revenue source and, in addition, to encourage more uniform personal income taxes among the various states, that is, uniform up to the value of the proposed federal income tax credit.

The tax credit device has been used in a limited manner between local units of government and between the state and local levels of government. One example of the former use is found where county and city sales taxes are imposed in such a manner that the county must allow credit for sales taxes paid to the cities. This places an aggregate limit on the combined county and city sales taxes. California and Utah apply this technique. In addition, a rationality case might be established at the state-local level for limiting local sales tax rates to the amount of the credit allowed by a state in order to discourage intercommunity tax rate competition.

Tax credits have little *direct* influence upon the distribution, stabilization, and economic growth branches of public finance, but the application of this intergovernmental coordination device could have significant indirect influence on stabilization and growth. This would result if the federal government used the tax credit device to encourage the states to adopt revenue structures, primarily based upon income taxes, which would be contracyclical in nature and thus serve as automatic stabilizers. Tax credits can directly influence allocation by affecting the intrapublic sector division of allocative efforts between levels of government. To a lesser extent, they may also influence the division of allocation between governmental units at the same level. Moreover, tax credits can affect (improve) technical allocation efficiency by discouraging intergovernmental fiscal competition. They do *not*, however, eliminate duplicate enforcement efforts. Furthermore, tax credits would harm fiscal rationality if the argument is valid which says that lower levels of government approximate the efficiency of market decision making better than do higher levels. This would be true because the tax credit approach transfers revenue decision making to the higher level of government.[20]

During 1966 the Advisory Commission on Intergovernmental Relations, a special commission created by Congress in 1959, recommended extensive federal government use of the tax credit device to encourage state government usage of the personal income tax. Fourteen states, for example, do not use the personal income tax though *all* states are under considerable pressure to find adequate revenue sources. Moreover, a majority of the states which do impose the tax apply it at "low" to "moderate" rates. The Commission suggests the adoption of a high federal income tax credit (such as 40 percent) for state income taxes paid, which amount would then be subtracted from the total federal income tax liability of the taxpayer. It is argued that a state would thus be able to collect additional personal income tax revenues to the amount of the tax credit without increasing the tax liabilities of its taxpayers.

A 40 percent credit would be worth more than the present deduc-

---

[20] The argument of efficient market decision making requires an assumption of long-run general equilibrium and other unrealistic assumptions in a society of purely competitive industries. See Chapter 2 in this regard.

tion for state income taxes paid to taxpayers with taxable incomes up to $50,000. Under the plan, however, those taxpayers with incomes above $50,000 would be allowed the option of continuing to deduct their state income tax payments. It is estimated that the revenue loss to the federal government from the plan would not be very large—approximately $700 million annually at the present rate levels of state personal income taxes—and would not exceed $2 billion even if all 50 states imposed a moderately high personal income tax. Pechman does not agree that the tax credit approach is superior to the Heller Plan (discussed earlier in the chapter).[21] He points out, for example, that the tax credit device would assist the wealthier states the most, in absolute terms, and the poorest states the least.[22] Furthermore, it may be politically difficult to obtain state personal income taxes in those states where they are forbidden by the state constitution.

Tax Deductions

The *tax deduction* approach to intergovernmental fiscal coordination is used between all levels of the public sector. The most significant use of tax deductions involves the various deductions from the federal personal income tax for such taxes as income, general sales, use, personal property, and gasoline taxes paid to other jurisdictions. These deductions are subtracted from adjusted gross income. Many state income tax structures, moreover, allow deductions for the federal income tax. In addition, some states also allow deductions for certain excise taxes.

The tax deduction approach exerts no direct influence upon the stabilization and growth branches of public finance, though it may exert indirect effects through its influence upon consumption, work, and investment incentives. Certain direct effects, however, flow from the tax deduction technique to the allocation and distribution branches. For example, consumption patterns would be distorted if excise taxes on some economic goods are deductible while other specific excise taxes are not deductible. In addition, allocation will be influenced as the revenue source pattern between units and levels of government is altered. The higher level of government is able to influence the tax structure adopted by the lower level through this device. Yet, the influence is much less severe than it is with the tax credit approach. Finally, it appears that tax deductibility may serve the distribution objective of fiscal equity in a positive manner by reducing multiple taxation.

Federal-State Tax Immunities

Intergovernmental *tax immunities* are not spelled out clearly in the Constitution. Instead, they have developed over the years through the

---

[21] Pechman, *op. cit.*, p. 41.

[22] *Ibid.*

judiciary process. At times they have constituted a significant point of controversy between the federal and state levels of government. The practice of both federal and state governments' exempting certain of each other's instrumentalities from taxation was initiated by the famous *McCulloch* v. *Maryland* case in 1819. The practice expanded throughout the remainder of the 19th century, but some narrowing of immunities has occurred during the 20th century.

The principal immunities at the present time are: (1) the "mutual" income tax exemption of interest on federal and state government debt obligations and (2) the exemption of properties of the federal government from certain state and local government property taxes. Some minor exceptions exist regarding the latter, namely, (1) a certain small amount of federal property is subject to taxation in the manner of private property, (2) in some cases, payments are made in lieu of property tax payments to state and local government, and (3) the federal government, on occasion, shares the revenue derived from its property with state and local government.

Regarding rationality, it appears that immunities on state and local government securities by the federal government, and vice versa, can distort allocation efficiency in a rather severe manner by diverting investment funds away from the corporate security market. The growing use of industrial development bonds, moreover, suggests rather serious questions regarding fiscal rationality. Such bonds are typically issued by local governmental units to finance projects aimed at the encouragement of business firms to locate within their political jurisdictions. Such arrangements, of course, are subsidies to the business firms involved. In some cases, a local government issues bonds to finance plant construction, the bonds being sold to the same firm which subsequently purchases or leases the plant. Meanwhile, the firm receives tax-exempt interest income. Conventional financing and plant location economics are indeed threatened with distortion by these practices.

Administrative Cooperation between Levels and Units of Government

Congressional and executive endorsement by the federal government of administrative cooperation between federal and state tax administrations has existed for more than a generation. Such cooperation has been rather limited in practice, however, and has consisted mostly of the exchange of income tax information. In some cases, it has amounted to a one-way flow of federal information to the states, though the trend is toward improvement and the Internal Revenue Service now has formal agreements with 41 states for the exchange of tax information.

Among the important considerations in developing a higher degree of administrative cooperation on a vertical basis between levels of government on fiscal matters is the significant fact that the basic tax collection technique used within the public sector of the United States is that of *voluntary compliance* on the part of taxpayers. Administrative efficiency through intergovernmental cooperation is thus desirable for the encouragement of accuracy in compliance and for subsequent enforcement equity. The Internal Revenue Service reports that $10.6 million in additional federal revenue could be directly attributed in Fiscal 1960 to information provided by state governments.[23] Undoubtedly, the gain to the states from the federal government was also of considerable magnitude. Furthermore, the indirect revenue benefits which derive from the taxpayer's knowledge that more efficient enforcement efforts are being undertaken will help both levels of government. Meanwhile, certain nations such as Australia, Canada, Norway, and West Germany have attained a high degree of cooperation in tax administration between their central governments and lower levels of government. On a horizontal intralevel basis, some state governments exchange information on the income of corporations which operate in more than one state. This is for the purpose of more effectively enforcing state corporation income taxes.

[23] Advisory Commission on Intergovernmental Relations, *Intergovernmental Cooperation in Tax Administration* (Washington, D.C.: June, 1961), p. 7.

PART III

Financing the Public Sector

Taxes comprise the traditional basic source of revenues for the financing of governmental economic activity. Various types of taxes are used throughout the American public sector. Income taxes—personal and corporation—constitute the major source of tax revenue to the federal government, for example, while the states rely primarily upon sales taxes and local governments upon property taxes. Different types of taxes, of course, exert differential nonneutrality effects. Hence, the selection of a particular type of tax for use by a unit of government should involve adequate consideration of its potential impact on the private sector as well as upon other levels and units of government. Moreover, the consideration of its intergoal effects on those public finance objectives not primarily involved in the selection of the tax is relevant.

Taxes, of course, are not the only source of public sector revenues. Borrowing is discussed in the next section of the book, however, because of the peculiar relationship of debt creation to macroeconomic fiscal policy. An important (though not dominant) segment of governmental revenues, moreover, comes from user prices and administrative fees. The former are primarily used in relationship to the financing of quasi-public goods which are subject, at least in part, to the application of the exclusion principle.

Finally, the discussion of governmental revenue sources—just as the discussion of the pattern of public sector spending in the previous section of the book—cannot ignore the potential income and wealth distribution effects resulting from the particular public sector tax structure in effect. A relevant consideration at this point is the concept of tax shifting since the initial bearer of a tax burden may differ from the one who bears the final burden. The outward appearance of a tax system as to its economic effects thus may differ greatly from its ultimate economic results if substantial tax shifting takes place.

Chapter

10

THE THEORY OF
TAX SHIFTING

The public finance goal of distribution may be significantly affected by the budgetary process of taxing and spending. The
ability of taxes to influence the pattern of income-wealth distribution in
the society, moreover, is importantly related to the economic phenomenon of *tax shifting*. The shifting or transferring of tax burdens is an
extremely complex procedure involving the functional interdependence
of many variables. While theoretical *ceteris paribus* assumptions allow
economic analysis to isolate certain predictable tax shifting results from
the operation of a single tax shifting determinant (variable), it cannot as
easily predict the composite results deriving from the interaction of
multiple tax shifting determinants. This interrelationship of tax shifting to
the economic environment demonstrates the general equilibrium nature
of tax shifting. In this regard, the multiple criteria which determine tax
shifting results are analogous to the multiple variables which determine
the price elasticity of demand of a good or resource.

Thus, it should be observed that theoretical tax shifting analysis, as
well as the empirical measurements of tax shifting, involve complicated
and difficult procedures. In this chapter, several significant tax shifting
criteria will *each* be analyzed separately, with *ceteris paribus* assumptions applied to the remaining criteria. This will allow isolation of the
pure effects deriving from the influence of each criterion. Yet, the reader
should be aware of the fact that real world conditions usually involve the
interacting influences of several criteria with resulting complexity in the
analysis and in the measurement of tax shifting results.

TAX IMPACT, TAX INCIDENCE, AND TAX SHIFTING

In order to understand the nature of tax shifting, it is necessary to
distinguish between the terms tax impact and tax incidence. *Tax impact*
may be designated as the point which receives the initial burden of a tax.
Since individuals are the fundamental claimants of all factor incomes, the
point of impact, in the ultimate sense, must be upon an individual or

individuals.[1] One way of looking upon tax impact is to ask the question: "Who pays the tax to the government?" This is *not* meant to suggest the technical or administrative handover of tax funds, but instead, the person who bears the initial financial burden of paying the tax. For example, the employer by means of payroll deductions may actually hand over personal income tax funds to the federal government. Yet, the worker from whose income the tax is withheld certainly bears the immediate impact. *Tax incidence*, as distinguished from tax impact, is the point where the ultimate or final burden of the tax rests. Once, again, the true burden—whether initial or ultimate—may fall *only* upon an individual or individuals, not upon a legal business entity.

Tax shifting can be demonstrated by a comparison of the impact and incidence points of a tax. If the point of incidence is identical with the initial point of impact, the burden rests ultimately where it initially fell and tax shifting, that is, transference of the tax burden among individuals *does not* occur. On the other hand, if part or all of the financial burden of the tax rests at a point or points other than the point of impact, tax shifting, at least to some extent, *does* occur. Tax shifting may be partial; it may be complete; in some instances, due to the taxpayer's taking advantage of "unrealized gains" it may (in a sense) be greater than 100 percent.[2] Thus, a range exists from zero, or no tax shifting, at the one limit to greater than 100 percent tax shifting, given sufficient unrealized gains, at the other limit.

Tax shifting must occur through the market mechanism of supply and demand. This means that tax shifting will usually occur through a change in the market price of an economic good or productive resource. Two possibilities are important in this respect: On the one hand, if the price of the economic good is *increased*, as the result of a new or higher tax, and this allows part or all of the tax burden to be transferred to someone else, it is said that the burden has been "shifted forward." On the other hand, if the result of the tax is a decrease in the price of a factor (resource) of production, and this allows transference of part or all of the tax burden, the tax burden has been "shifted backward." Thus, *forward tax shifting* ordinarily results from a rise in the price of an economic good in a product market and *backward tax shifting* ordinarily results from a reduction in the price of a productive resource in a factor market. In the first instance, the burden of the tax has been shifted forward to the consumer while in the latter case the burden has been passed backward to the factor of production.

---

[1] Businesses, including corporate businesses, are correctly viewed as earning income for their individual owners. Thus, only these owners may receive the impact (initial burden) of a tax.

[2] Unrealized gains as a tax shifting criterion will be discussed later in the chapter.

A related technique by which a tax may be shifted is that of "tax capitalization." Again, the shifting takes place through a change in price, but in the tax capitalization case the price is the capitalized value of the expected future earnings of the asset subject to the tax. This technique is particularly important in the case of a property tax involving commercial property. The following example will illustrate the possibility of transferring a property tax burden through tax capitalization.

Suppose that the average annual net income of a motel investment is $10,000. Suppose also that 10 percent is the normal rate of return needed in the community to attract capital into the motel business. In this instance, since $10,000 is 10 percent of $100,000, the capital value of the motel may be estimated at $100,000 (excluding depreciation considerations). Now, suppose that property taxes imposed on the motel are increased by $1,000 per year. This tax increment lowers the after-tax income of the motel to $9,000 from $10,000. Since $9,000 is 10 percent of $90,000, the capital value of the motel in terms of its earning potential is decreased by $10,000 to $90,000 as the property tax rates are increased.

If the owner of the motel decides to sell the asset, and is able to sell it at the pretax increment capitalized value of $100,000, he has shifted the burden of the tax increment by selling the property. If the owner sells the property at the posttax increment value of $90,000, he absorbs the incremental property tax. If the owner sells at any price over $90,000, but less than $100,000, part of the tax burden is transferred through the process of tax capitalization. Tax shifting in this example is dependent, of course, upon imperfect market knowledge by the purchaser of the property after its capital value has declined. Moreover, long-run considerations may allow an adjustment which would increase the room prices charged by motels as some reduction of motel capacity takes place in the community because of reduced after-tax earnings. Nevertheless, the tax capitalization example does demonstrate a peculiar market method whereby, under favorable conditions—primarily based upon imperfect knowledge by the purchaser of an asset—tax shifting can occur.

Tax shifting is sometimes disguised by an implicit rather than an outward (external) price change. This would occur, for example, when the quality or size of an economic good or productive resource is lowered while price is held constant in order to shift a tax. Thus, a special excise tax levy on candy bars could be shifted by lowering the quality or size of the candy bar while its price remains stable at five cents. Implicitly, and effectively, the price is raised when a reduced quality or size is attained at the same per unit price. Thus, in an indirect and disguised manner, the burden of the tax may be transferred (at least partially) through a market adjustment involving a quality or size change rather than a direct price change.

Tax shifting should not be confused with the terms tax evasion, tax avoidance, and tax delinquency as defined in Chapter 5. While tax shifting refers to the transference of part or all of a tax burden which has *already been paid* at the point of impact, the other terms refer to situations where the tax is *not paid* to the government in the first place. Moreover, the term "tax effects" should be distinguished from tax shifting. Tax effects include all economic and noneconomic results which may derive from a tax cause. A very high tax on alcoholic beverages, for example, might cause some individuals not to drink who otherwise would consume alcoholic beverages. Yet, not only is there an economic change in the consumption pattern of the individuals involved but there may be noneconomic effects in terms of changes in their social or cultural traits. Further examples of tax effects include the fairly recent occurrence in Great Britain, after a tightening in the deductibility of business limousine expenses from the corporation income tax, of a 75 percent reduction in domestic orders for Rolls Royce limousines within three weeks after the deductibility rules were changed. Indeed, tax effects include a multitude of economic and noneconomic possibilities. In fact, tax burdens sometimes become diffused with tax effects in the long run to the extent that the two concepts become partly indistinguishable from each other.

TAX SHIFTING CRITERIA (DETERMINANTS)

This section will analyze six tax shifting criteria, or determinants. These are the market structure, price elasticity, cost conditions of production, type of tax, political jurisdiction, and unrealized earnings (gains) criteria. There is no intention, however, to imply that *only* six determinants exist. Again, as with price elasticity of demand, a multiple of variables influence the final result. The criteria analyzed in this chapter are among the most important determinants of tax shifting. They are not discussed in any intended order of relative importance. All six are considered to be significant.

Market Structure

The extent to which a tax may be shifted, either forward or backward, is importantly affected by the nature of the market structure within which the firm functions. In order to explain the effect of different market structures, let us look at the possibilities of tax shifting, in both the short and long run, and under pure competition, monopolistic competition, pure monopoly, and oligopoly conditions. In these cases, it will be initially assumed that firms attempt to maximize profits.

Pure Competition. This market structure is characterized by many sellers and buyers of homogeneous goods. Figures 10–1a and 10–1b show the initial equilibrium position for both the firm and industry before the imposition of an excise tax in a purely competitive market. The firm

FIGURE 10–1

PURE COMPETITION, SHORT-RUN TAX SHIFTING CONSIDERATIONS

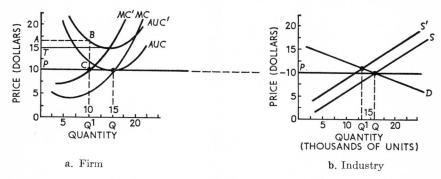

a. Firm   b. Industry

is producing output at *OQ* and selling at price *OP*. If a specific excise tax of $5 is now imposed, the result is as follows: In the short run, the firm will be forced to absorb all of the tax. However, since the specific excise tax increases the costs to the representative firm, it will force an upward adjustment in the marginal cost and average unit (average total) cost curves, *MC* and *AUC*, to MC^1 and AUC^1, respectively. The amount of the tax is equal to *PT* ($5) in Figure 10–1a. The firm now moves to an after-tax position at output OQ^1 as opposed to the pretax output *OQ*. The purely competitive firm, of course, cannot manipulate price in the short run because of its complete lack of monopoly power. This position results in a loss (*PABC*), instead of the normal profit which had previously existed. Therefore, over the long run, the least efficient firms will be forced to leave the industry and the supply schedule will shift upward and to the left until market price has risen sufficiently so

FIGURE 10–2

PURE COMPETITION, LONG-RUN TAX SHIFTING CONSIDERATIONS

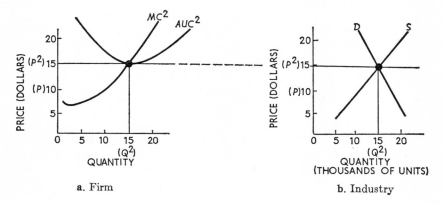

a. Firm   b. Industry

that the representative firm again earns a normal rate of return. The burden of the tax has thus been shifted forward though, significantly, this has not occurred through monopoly power by the individual firm, but instead through the operation of long-run competitive market forces. Such forward shifting, of course, assumes constant factor prices and hence the impossibility of backward shifting. Figures 10–2a and 10–2b depict these long-run results. The final equilibrium price OP^2 is higher than OP by the amount of the tax ($5).

Monopolistic Competition. This type of market structure, which is characterized by a substantial number of sellers of differentiated goods, provides tax shifting results similar to those found in purely competitive markets. The firm tends to absorb the tax in the short run, for example, though product differentiation may at times allow a modest amount of shifting which could not occur with the homogenous product conditions of the purely competitive market. In the long run, the exit of some firms from the industry because of the higher costs resulting from the tax tends to shift the tax to consumers as the industry approaches a normal rate of return position.

Pure Monopoly. As depicted in Figure 10–3 the pure monopoly firm, which is identical to the industry since no competitors exist, is in equilibrium producing output OQ, charging price OP and obtaining monopoly profit $PABC$. After the excise tax is imposed, the marginal and average costs shift upward to MC^1 and AUC^1, respectively. The new

FIGURE 10–3

PURE MONOPOLY
TAX SHIFTING CONSIDERATIONS

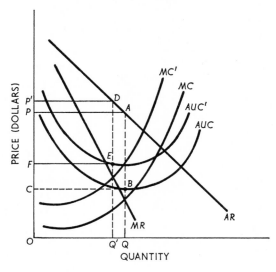

equilibrium rests at points OQ^1 and OP^1. The new monopoly profit is equal to P^1DEF, which is less than $PABC$. Since the marginal and average cost curves represent both short- and long-run positions due to the impossibility of entry to and exit from the industry if the monopoly is to be maintained, the firm is forced to bear part of the tax burden in both the short-run and long-run time periods. This burden borne by the firm is equal, on a total basis, to the difference between the initial and new equilibrium profit rectangles. Again, the ultimate change in price would measure the amount of the tax that is shifted forward while the difference between the original AUC and the ultimate AUC, if any difference exists, would illustrate the amount of the tax which has been shifted backward in the form of lower prices paid to the factors of production as made possible by "monopsony power" in factor markets. In Figure 10–3, however, it is assumed for simplicity in presentation that no change in AUC takes place except for the tax and, therefore, that any tax shifting which occurs is forward to the consumer.

Oligopoly. Significant interdependence between a few dominant sellers, and thus uncertainty, characterize oligopoly market structure. In the case of a new excise tax or an increase in the rate of a present excise tax, however, the degree of uncertainty is reduced since each firm recognizes that every other firm also has its costs increased by the amount of the tax. Thus, unless industry demand is elastic, or in the case of considerable product differentiation, it is likely that *each* firm will add the total amount of the tax to its selling price. If each firm has not previously been maximizing its profits, the increase in price may bring the firm to a profit position closer to a point of profit maximization than its previous operating position. Once more, many firms likely would not be maximizing profits due to such reasons as fear of antitrust, protection of public image, or imperfect knowledge. Thus, partial or total shifting of the excise tax burden may well occur. However, if the firm was previously maximizing profits, such shifting would be much less likely. This point will be expanded below under the discussion of unrealized gains as a tax shifting criterion.

Conclusions Regarding the Market Structure Criterion. The following conclusions emerge from market structure analysis regarding the shifting of a specific excise tax. First, if one accepts the theoretical assumption of profit-maximizing behavior by a firm, the greater the degree of competition, the greater is the probability of long-run tax shifting because the absence of monopoly profits forces shifting of the tax in order that firms survive in the industry. Thus, although it would seem on the surface that the existence of individual firm control over price (monopoly power) would enhance tax shifting as opposed to purely competitive conditions, this is not always the case, particularly in the long run. Instead, oligopolistic and pure monopoly firms approach full shifting of tax burdens in the long run (according to the market structure criterion) *only* under the condition of less-than-profit-maximizing behavior at the time the excise tax is imposed. In the short run, however, non-profit-maximizing behavior, combined with the control over price possessed by firms in imperfect markets, makes tax shifting easier than it would be in a perfect market.

Price Elasticity

A second significant determinant of tax shifting concerns the elasticity of demand of the economic good or the elasticity of supply of the productive resource in question. The elasticity concept relates the response of a quantity (demanded or supplied) change to a change in price. Such variables as product or factor substitutability, and the price of the good or resource in relation to the buyer's total income or outlay, help determine the elasticity value for a good or resource. By affecting the price-output result, demand and supply elasticity help to determine the net income level at the posttax equilibrium. The relationship of the posttax income level to the pretax income level will indicate, of course, the extent to which shifting may have occurred.

FIGURE 10-4

PRICE ELASTICITY OF DEMAND AND TAX SHIFTING
(Industry Graphs)

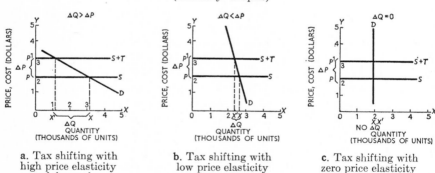

a. Tax shifting with high price elasticity of demand.

b. Tax shifting with low price elasticity of demand.

c. Tax shifting with zero price elasticity of demand.

Generally the more sensitive (elastic) the quantity demanded is to a change in price, the more difficult it is to shift a tax burden forward through a higher selling price. Conversely, the more inelastic or insensitive the quantity reaction to a price change, the greater the possibility of shifting the tax. Suppose that an excise tax is levied upon a particular economic good. In Figures 10–4a, b, c, let curve S represent the industry supply and curve *D* represent the industry demand for the good. The supply curve in each graph is that existing under constant cost conditions of production so as to neutralize the effects, at this point of discussion, of alternative production cost conditions which are treated below as a separate tax shifting criterion. Hence, the analysis can concentrate upon price elasticity as a separate tax shifting determinant at this time.

In Figure 10–4a, demand is *elastic* throughout the relevant portion of the demand curve while in Figure 10–4b demand is *inelastic* throughout the relevant portion. In Figure 10–4c, the demand for the good is *completely inelastic* throughout the entire curve. When the excise tax is imposed, under the assumed constant cost conditions of production, the price of the good is initially increased by the amount of the tax as the firms in the industry seek to shift the tax through the higher selling price. Whether the tax is successfully shifted or not will depend upon the nature of the demand elasticity for the product. The supply curve S will shift upward and become the new supply curve S + T in each graph as the tax is added on to the original selling price. Thus, the new selling price is P^1 in each graph as opposed to the pretax selling price P.

The greatest quantity reduction to the higher price occurs in the relatively elastic demand case (Figure 10–4a). In this instance, tax shifting is difficult because gross income to a firm in the industry (price x quantity) would decline. In Figure 10–4b, where the demand is relatively inelastic, as the price increases from P to P^1 by the amount of the tax, the quantity decrease from X to X^1 is less than proportionate to the price increase. As a result, gross income to the firm does *not* decline and tax shifting is more likely to take place. The best case for tax shifting occurs in Figure 10–4c where there is no quantity reaction to the price increase from P to P^1. The initial quantity X and the posttax quantity X^1 are the same. The student must continue to bear in mind, of course, that other criteria are at work in any single tax shifting situation. However, considering the price elasticity of demand criterion alone, it is an accurate generalization to say that the greater the price elasticity of demand, the lesser the opportunity for transferring a tax burden forward. Conversely, the greater the price inelasticity of demand, the more likely forward tax shifting is to occur.

While forward shifting is concerned with getting a higher selling price through a reduction in the *supply* of an economic good, backward shifting relates to a downward (leftward) shift in the *demand* for a productive resource in order to obtain a lower buying price. The following generalizations may be made concerning backward tax shifting as it would be influenced by the elasticity of supply: (1) the more elastic the resource supply, the less the amount of the tax that will be shifted back to the factor of production since the quantity supplied of the resource decreases sharply as the offer price for the resource declines, and (2) the more inelastic the resource supply, the greater the amount of the tax that will be shifted backward to the factor of production since the lower offer price induces little supply reduction. A comparison of Figures 10–5a and

10–5b demonstrates this result. In the limiting cases, if the resource supply is completely inelastic, the total tax burden will be borne by the

FIGURE 10–5

PRICE ELASTICITY OF SUPPLY AND TAX SHIFTING
(Industry Graphs)

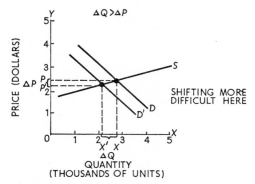

a. Tax shifting with high price elasticity of supply.

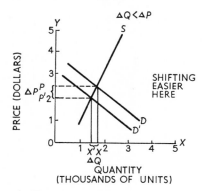

b. Tax shifting with low price elasticity of supply.

resource owner while a completely elastic resource supply would totally prevent the backward shifting of the tax to the resource owner.

Cost Conditions of the Industry

A third criterion of tax shifting derives from the cost conditions present in the industry where the attempt to shift the tax takes place. The three primary categories of industry cost behavior are those where (1) average unit cost (average total cost) remains constant as output expands, (2) where average unit cost decreases with expanding output, and (3) where average unit cost increases as output expands. These industry cost conditions are considered to be a long-run phenomenon involving the concept of scale economies and diseconomies as applied to resource markets. They influence tax shifting through their ability to affect the nature of the posttax price-output equilibrium. The latter will indicate by means of its comparison with the pretax equilibrium whether shifting has taken place.

In the constant cost industry (Figure 10–6a), price increases by the amount of the tax. The initial before-tax equilibrium is at the intersection of supply curve S and demand curve D, giving price P. After the imposition of the excise tax, price increases from P to P^1. This is also the amount of the tax as measured by the vertical distance between the two supply curves, that is, between the S curve before the tax and the S + T curve after the tax. In the constant cost case, the price elasticity of demand of the economic good will be the exclusive determinant of the ability to transfer the tax burden. In other words, constant costs are neutral or irrelevant to tax shifting in this example. In the cases of increasing and decreasing production costs, however, cost conditions of production emerge as a significant separate criterion of tax shifting.

FIGURE 10–6

COST CONDITIONS OF THE INDUSTRY AND TAX SHIFTING
(Industry Graphs)

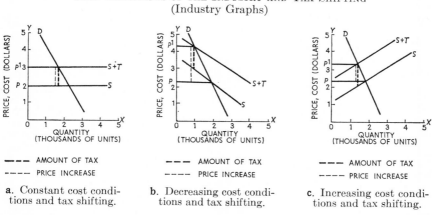

a. Constant cost conditions and tax shifting.

b. Decreasing cost conditions and tax shifting.

c. Increasing cost conditions and tax shifting.

In *all* three industry cost graphs (Figures 10–6a, 10–6b, and 10–6c), the price elasticities of demand are identical. This allows the student to concentrate on the tax shifting effects of industry cost conditions. Emphasis is to be placed on Figures 10–6b and 10–6c, however, as stipulated in the previous paragraph.

In Figure 10–6b, as price increases by the amount of the tax, production is reduced and, quite significantly, enters a higher cost range of output. This is true because the industry is a decreasing cost industry with costs declining as output expands, but increasing as output contracts. Hence, the new equilibrium price is higher than the original price plus the tax. Price has increased by more than the full amount of the tax and the resulting cutback in sales is larger than it would have been if price had increased by only the full amount of the tax or less. In this case, tax shifting is difficult.

To the contrary, as observed in Figure 10–6c, if the production cost conditions are those of an increasing cost industry, the reduced output enters a lower cost-output range. The output is thus reduced by a smaller amount because the new equilibrium price is higher than the original price by less than the full amount of the tax. In this instance, tax shifting is more likely to occur than it is under decreasing cost conditions because the smaller price increase will cause the quantity response to the price change to be less. In summary, increasing cost conditions of production are more conducive to tax shifting than are decreasing production costs.

Type of Tax

The nature of the tax as determined by such characteristics as whether it is (1) direct or indirect and (2) broad-based or narrow-based will help to determine its shiftability. Generally, the more *direct* the tax, the more difficult shifting becomes and the more *indirect* the tax, the greater the possibility of transferring its burden from the point of impact to another point of incidence. This is explained by the fact that a direct tax usually is applied to a tax base close to the individual such as a person's income and wealth. The most direct tax, in this sense, would be a per capita (poll) tax on the individual himself. Direct tax bases, in most instances, are further removed from subsequent market transactions after the taxes are imposed than are the bases of indirect taxes. Thus, direct taxes such as the personal income tax are not especially conducive to the further market transactions which are necessary for the shifting of a tax. On the other hand, indirect taxes such as retail sales and excise taxes are more closely associated with further market transactions. Hence, they are more conducive to tax shifting, generally speaking, than are direct taxes.

The more broad-based (general) a tax, the easier it is to shift the tax.[3] Oppositely, the more narrow-based (specific) the tax, the more difficult tax shifting becomes. When the tax base is narrow, demand distortion in both the product market for consumer decisions and in the factor market for business decisions is more likely to occur through the operation of a substitution effect. Hence, there may be a movement of quantity demanded away from the tax base involved and purchases may be transferred to other untaxed or lower taxed goods or resources. When

---

[3] The reference to broad-based and narrow-based taxes under this criterion is concerned with the nature of the tax, not with the geographical size of the political jurisdiction imposing the tax. The latter is treated below as a separate tax shifting determinant.

such movement is possible due to the availability of substitutes, it will be very difficult for the seller to raise the product or resource price in order to shift the tax. Under such circumstances, shifting is difficult.

A tax on movie theatre tickets in a community where other forms of recreation are not taxed, for example, would likely cause consumption patterns to change somewhat away from movie theater consumption to substitute forms of recreation such as bowling, baseball games, or miniature golf. On the other hand, if the sales tax in question were broad-based and applied equally to all substitute recreational items in the community, the consumer would have no price incentive to move between the alternative forms of recreation and the sellers of recreation would be in a better position to raise prices in order to shift the tax.[4] Similarly, a tax on *one* mineral resource (say a severance tax on iron ore), while other mineral resources (say bauxite—for aluminum—and copper) go untaxed, will tend to distort the sales of the taxed ore.

Political Jurisdiction Imposing Tax

The geographical nature of the political unit which levies the tax also helps to determine its shiftability. In this context, a political unit may be a local, state, national, or even international government. Generally, the *narrower* the geographical limits of a political unit, the more difficult it is for sellers to shift the tax. For example, a new (or increased) retail sales tax in a city may lead to consumption readjustments toward increased purchases outside the city (in other cities or counties). Retail merchants would find it difficult not to absorb part of the tax by holding the line on prices if similar taxes were not applied in nearby cities and counties. Efficient communications and transportation increase the possibility of buying outside a limited geographical (political) area.

Taxes levied at the state level, since they involve a wider geographical area of political jurisdiction than those imposed at local levels of government, improve the possibility of tax shifting by sellers in the form of higher prices. There are reduced opportunities for buyers to purchase in "no-tax" or "lower tax" areas. Furthermore, states frequently attempt to reduce tax escape by imposing *use taxes* whereby the residents of a state may be made subject to a tax applied in lieu of the state sales tax which they have failed to pay because they have purchased retail items elsewhere. Use taxes are very difficult to administer, however, because of the considerable difficulty in gathering adequate information about purchases.

---

[4] If a tax is *direct* instead of *indirect*, then it will be difficult to shift the tax burden even though the tax may be broad-based. For example, a personal income tax, even if applied equally to *all types* of income, would not be conducive to tax shifting because the direct nature of the tax would tend to exclude it from a further market transaction.

Since taxes levied at the national level comprehend a wider geographical area than do those of individual state governments, the chance of tax shifting is enhanced by national taxes. The opportunities for consumption and resource purchases to move to no-tax or lower tax political jurisdictions are very limited for national taxes. In fact, this can be accomplished only by purchasing outside of the national political jurisdiction, that is, by purchasing within the political boundaries of another nation. A tax which was imposed and administered *uniformly* throughout the world—a true international tax—would provide the strongest potential for shifting according to the political jurisdiction criterion. In this case, no political jurisdiction would remain in which taxes might be lower or nonexistent.

In summary, the narrower the geographical limit of political jurisdiction imposing a tax, the more difficult it is to shift a tax because there are more alternative geographical areas available where the good or resource might be purchased. Hence, the seller will be hesitant to raise the price by the amount of the tax. The following example is relevant:

A five cent tax per package of cigarettes imposed by a city government may lead to increased consumption purchases outside the city in other cities or counties. Thus, tax shifting by the seller is difficult.

A five cent tax per package of cigarettes imposed by a state government may lead to increased consumption purchases outside the state in other states. However, the geographical availability of such purchases is reduced as compared to the city government example above. Hence, tax shifting by sellers becomes increasingly possible.

A five cent tax per package of cigarettes imposed by a national government may lead to increased consumption purchases outside the nation in other nations. This is difficult, however, to accomplish and not an avoidance technique available to most smokers. Thus, tax shifting by sellers is considerably enhanced and is the most likely of the three examples so far cited.

A five cent tax per package of cigarettes imposed by an international agreement among all nations would leave no geographical (political) area to which consumption could transfer in order to escape the tax. In this instance, tax shifting is the most likely of the four political jurisdiction situations presented here.

Unrealized Gains

An often overlooked, though highly significant, criterion of tax shifting involves the existence in many production situations of unrealized gains.[5] An unrealized gain may be defined as the amount of incremental profits (or of reduced losses) which could be attained if the firm

[5] In this chapter, unrealized gains will be spoken of in terms of business profits, though the principle involved applies equally to all productive resources and their earnings such as an individual's maximum compensation for labor input.

were operating at an optimal (marginal cost = marginal revenue) equilibrium of price and output instead of at a price-output position other than at this optimal point. Public finance theory, following strict classical economic principles, has frequently obscured the existence of unrealized gains and their relationship to tax shifting. Traditionally, classical economic theory has operated upon the premise that *all* business firms maximize profits at the marginal cost equals marginal revenue point. This being assumed, it is then concluded that a business profits (income) tax cannot be shifted. The reasoning is logical, given the premise that all businesses maximize profits, since a firm already operating at its best price and output would move away from this point and select a worse price-output position if it attempted to transfer an incremental tax burden by adjusting its price and output in the market.

The premise of profit maximization operation at $MC = MR$ is unrealistic, however, for most business firms in our society. Such considerations as imperfect market and production knowledge, the fear of antitrust action, the fear of an unfavorable public image, the fear of attracting new entrants to the industry, and public utility regulation prevent many firms from achieving, or even attempting to achieve, optimal profit positions, especially in the short run. Instead, these firms follow such rules or bench marks as: the maximization of gross receipts (sales); achievement of a target rate of return on investment; maintenance of price stability; and the improvement of competitive position within the market as a whole. When such rules or bench marks are followed, the firm usually does not attain an optimal price-output position. Consequently, in this gray area of unrealized gains, a margin is created from which tax shifting becomes possible (assuming that the other criteria permit the shifting). In other words, there is no possibility of shifting a profits tax when a firm is operating at the $MC = MR$ point, but it becomes possible to shift the tax through unrealized gains when this optimal point is not maintained.

Figure 10–7 displays the above phenomenon where rectangle *PCAB* at the profit-maximization point of $MC = MR$ exceeds rectangle *P¹CDE* at the nonprofit-maximization point shown on the graph. In this situation, imperfect knowledge, fear of antiturst action, and/or one of the other reasons mentioned above causes the firm to allow the unrealized gains margin of *PCAB* over *P¹CDE* to exist by charging a lower than profit-maximizing price. The firm would like to restrict output and utilize its monopoly power to increase price from P^1 to P at profit-maximizing output X. Yet, for one or more of the above reasons it is *not* doing this. Unrealized gains thus exist and the subsequent possibility of shifting a business profits tax becomes a reality. Then, given a new business income tax or a rate increase in a present tax, the firm may choose to push aside antitrust or other considerations which impede tax shifting and change price toward the "pretax change" profit-maximization position. In so doing, part or all of the tax burden may be shifted.

A recent study by Richard Musgrave and Marian Krzyzaniak on the shifting of the corporation income tax concludes that substantial short-run shifting does take place.[6] The existence of unrealized gains

FIGURE 10–7

UNREALIZED GAINS AS A CONDITION OF TAX SHIFTING FOR FIRM
IN IMPERFECT COMPETITION

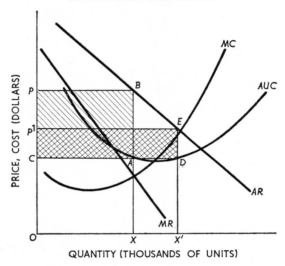

Explanation:
Rectangle $PCAB$ = Maximum Profits where $MC = MR$ at Output X.
Rectangle P^1CDE = Profits at Output X^1 which is beyond the profit-maximizing output.
The "Excess" of $PCAB$ over P^1CDE = Unrealized Gains, thus allowing the possibility of shifting the tax burden as price is increased toward P and output is decreased toward the profit-maximization output X.

would be an implicit requirement to this result. Moreover, public utilities appear to be in a unique institutional position to shift taxes. Public utility firms are ordinarily allowed to earn a particular rate of return on invested capital but, because of the nature of their market and production conditions, they are not allowed to charge profit-maximizing prices nor to produce profit-maximizing outputs. Thus, unrealized gains, operating through the institutional arrangement of public utility regulation, are built into the price-output policies of public utility firms. When additional tax burdens are imposed, the earnings on investment of utility

---

[6] Marian Krzyzaniak and Richard A. Musgrave, *The Shifting of the Corporation Income Tax* (Baltimore: Johns Hopkins Press, 1963).

companies tend to decline and a case is created for the firms to request higher prices (rates) from the regulatory commissions. Usually such requests are granted. The quantity demanded of the economic good, moreover, does not ordinarily decline very greatly as price increases, due to the typical inelastic demand for public utility goods. Farris contends that public utility firms tend to pass along increased taxes through regulatory approval, but at the same time are reluctant and are not pressed strongly by the regulatory commissions to lower prices on the occasion of tax reductions.[7]

Harberger concludes that the greater portion of the corporation income tax is shifted backward and is ultimately borne by capital.[8] This says, in other words, that the shareholders of the corporation bear most of the corporation income tax burden and that the tax, for the most part, is not shifted forward to consumers. It must be pointed out, however, that Harberger is concerned with the long-run incidence of the tax under conditions of perfect competition. Given these conditions of perfect competition, he observes:

It is hard to avoid the conclusion that plausible alternative assumptions about the relevant elasticities all yield results in which capital bears very close to 100% of the tax burden. The most plausible assumptions imply that capital bears more than the full burden of the tax.[9]

In an appendix to that article, the author also concludes that even with the existence of monopoly elements in the market, the results are not substantially modified from those described above.

GENERAL EQUILIBRIUM NATURE OF TAX SHIFTING—AN EXAMPLE

As suggested throughout the analysis of this chapter, tax shifting is a complicated phenomenon involving the interaction of multiple causal variables. In a sense, it may be said that the transference of tax burdens involves general equilibrium conditions. For example, if each of the six criteria analyzed above were weighted heavily toward shifting, then substantial tax shifting would likely occur. On the other hand, if each of the criteria were weighted heavily against shifting, then it is unlikely that much tax shifting would take place. Admittedly, the above analysis and the example below may seem to be oversimplifications of a complex phenomenon. The analysis does, however, possess the merit of isolating the separate effects of each tax shifting determinant while still revealing

[7] Martin T. Farris, "Tax Reductions and Utility Rates," *Public Utilities Fortnightly* (August 27, 1964), pp. 30–36.

[8] Arnold Harberger, "The Incidence of the Corporate Income Tax," *Journal of Political Economy* (June, 1962), pp. 215–40.

[9] *Ibid.*, p. 234.

the existence of substantial interdependencies between the determinants.

The following table (Table 10–1) demonstrates the above conclusions:

TABLE 10–1

THE GENERAL EQUILIBRIUM NATURE OF TAX SHIFTING

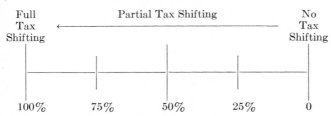

Full Tax Shifting		Partial Tax Shifting		No Tax Shifting
100%	75%	50%	25%	0

Case 1—Full Tax Shifting	*Case 2—No Tax Shifting*
1. Pure competition market structure in the long run. Pure monopoly market structure in the short run.	1. Pure monopoly market structure in the long run. Pure competition market structure in the short run.
2. Highly inelastic product demand. Highly inelastic resource supply.	2. Highly elastic product demand. Highly elastic resource supply.
3. Increasing production costs.	3. Decreasing production costs.
4. Indirect and broad-based tax.	4. Direct and narrow-based tax.
5. Broad political jurisdiction.	5. Narrow political jurisdiction.
6. Unrealized gains.	6. No unrealized gains.

Specific revenue sources are discussed in the remaining chapters of Part III. The burdens and overall effects of these taxes can be importantly influenced, of course, by the ability or inability of the initial taxpayers to transfer their tax burdens through the market mechanism. The student should thus keep the significant tax shifting determinants (criteria) in mind while reading Chapters 11 through 16.

Chapter 11

PERSONAL INCOME TAX

ALTERNATE CONCEPTS OF INCOME

The definition of income for the purpose of establishing an income tax base involves both theoretical and institutional complexities. Economists disagree somewhat concerning the theoretical ideal of what should be taxed. Moreover, accounting concepts of income, stressing the "internal control" of a business, differ from those used in economics. Government policymakers (legislators and tax administrators), meanwhile, institutionalize the concept of income by using a hybrid concept which is not totally consistent with either the economic or the accounting concepts. Yet, if income is to be accepted as the indicator of ability to pay, and if the income tax is to be used prominently within the United States public sector, a rational economic definition of income for tax base purposes is essential to the attainment of fiscal rationality.

Some economists adhere to a definition of income which concentrates upon the monetary value of the *goods* and *services* consumed by an individual during a specified tax period. For example, under this approach an individual's actual expenditures for consumption plus the estimated monetary value of nonexchange (nonmarket) consumption items—such as the services of an owner-occupied home or the "psychic" income derived from taking a more pleasurable job at a sacrifice of higher monetary compensation—comprise taxable income.

The majority of economists, however, accept the *economic accretion* concept of taxable income. This concept defines taxable income as the algebraic sum of an individual's expenditures for consumption goods and services *plus* any change in the individual's net worth during a specified period of time.[1] Under this concept, both consumption expenditures and net worth changes are measured in monetary terms. All accretions or diminutions to wealth are included in the definition of income regardless of: (1) their source, (2) the conditions under which they are received, or (3) the manner in which they are used. Factor earnings such as wages, interest, rents, or profits are thus included in taxable income as "accre-

[1] See Henry C. Simons, *Personal Income Taxation* (Chicago: University of Chicago Press, 1938), for a representation of this concept.

tions" alongside inheritances, gifts, and gambling profits. On the other hand, depreciation, obsolescence, decline in the market value of assets, and gambling losses constitute "diminutions" to wealth. The accretion definition of income, however, consists of more than just the *net* flow of wealth (including factor earnings, realized capital gains, and consumption items) over and above the costs incurred in attaining this flow. It also includes the value of that consumption activity which does not involve economic transactions as well as any increase in wealth which has accrued, but has not been realized.

In practice, the concept of taxable income used within the public sector of the United States does not follow completely, though it resembles in part, the economic accretion bench mark. In the United States, taxable income is generally looked upon as a current flow of wealth to an individual (or family) spending unit in the form of money receipts and economic goods, but it includes only part of the value of consumption activity outside the exchange mechanism and of unrealized gains in the value of capital assets. Hence, the theoretically rational economic accretion definition of taxable income is only approximated in practice. This deviation is primarily due to administrative expediency since the cost of collecting accurate information and of making monetary estimates of nonmonetary economic activities (those outside the direct exchange mechanism) is considerable. A second-best approximation to the theoretical ideal, however, may be considered to be a worthy policy objective. The second-best objective may be pursued toward the attainment of a higher degree of second-best efficiency than exists at the present time.

In summary, the public sector in the United States may be said to follow a concept of taxable income which stresses monetary, not psychic income; monetary "flows," not "stocks" or "assets," and a "family" taxpaying unit. Thus, monetary income flows taxed to a family spending unit constitute the essence of the income tax base as used in the United States. Though certain statutory concessions are made to changes in the net worth of a taxpaying unit, these are not basic to the concept of income as defined in the United States and must be considered secondary in nature. The arbitrary selection of a family taxpaying unit is based upon equity considerations and is discussed at various points later in the chapter.

THE FEDERAL PERSONAL INCOME TAX

Historical Development

The first federal personal income tax was enacted by Congress on August 5, 1861, during the Presidential administration of Abraham Lincoln. Before the beginning of the Civil War in 1861, the federal government had relied heavily upon revenues derived from tariffs and from the sale of public lands. Under the stress of wartime spending, however, increased reliance was placed upon excise, inheritance, and income taxes. Though the federal government had not enacted a personal income tax at any previous date, several states had experimented with them and some still had them in force at the beginning of the Civil War.

Congress deliberated in 1861 between the adoption of a direct tax on real property and a personal income tax, but adopted the latter because it seemed less likely that an income tax would require apportionment among the states according to population.[2] Of course, there was no doubt whatsoever that a tax on real property was a direct tax requiring such apportionment. It was feared, moreover, that a real property tax would place undue tax burdens upon the agricultural areas along the frontier, primarily in the Midwest and West.

Before the collection machinery for the 1861 income tax law was arranged, Congress enacted the income tax law of July 1, 1862, which superseded the earlier legislation. The first federal income tax revenues were thus collected under the 1862 legislation. The 1862 act provided a slightly progressive rate structure with a minimum rate of 3 percent and a maximum rate of 5 percent on incomes above $10,000. A personal exemption of $600 was allowed. The basic characteristics of the 1862 law prevailed, with some modification in rates, until repeal of the first federal personal income tax in 1872. The law was amended six times during its 11-year life. In 1865, the highest rate was reached—a maximum of 10 percent on incomes over $5,000.

The Civil War income tax provided adequate revenues despite many enforcement problems. During the period 1863–73, a total of $376 million was collected.[3] The largest amount collected in a single year was $73 million in 1866, which equaled about 15 percent of total federal tax collections during that year.[4] The Civil War income tax, which was in many ways unpopular to taxpayers, underwent rate reductions in 1867, prior to its repeal in 1872. America's first federal personal income tax was challenged in the courts and found to be constitutional despite its close identification with the economic characteristics of a direct tax. The Supreme Court of the United States held in *Springer* v. *United States* that direct taxes, within the meaning of the Constitution, referred only to capitation taxes and to taxes on real estate, and that the federal personal income tax was "within the category of an excise or duty."[5]

The next use of a personal income tax by the federal government was motivated by reform movements rather than by an emergency

[2] The Constitution requires in Article I, Section 9, that direct taxes must be apportioned among the several states according to the census.

[3] Joint Economic Committee, Congress of the United States, *The Federal Tax System: Facts and Problems* (Washington, D.C.: U.S. Government Printing Office, 1964), p. 14.

[4] *Ibid.*

[5] *Springer* v. *United States,* 102 U.S. 586 (1880).

demand for revenues. President Grover Cleveland was elected in 1892 on a platform which promised to reduce the importance of tariffs within the federal revenue system and to fill the gap by reintroducing the income tax. Populist farmers in the West and South, who vigorously opposed tariffs which they viewed as interrelated with the growing industrial and wealth concentrations of the nation, strongly supported Cleveland's election to office. As a result, a second federal personal income tax became law in 1894, though it was so altered from its proposed form by the Senate that President Cleveland allowed it to become law without signing the bill.[6] Basically, however, the 1894 personal income tax resembled its Civil War predecessor.

Soon after its enactment, a test case was introduced in the courts challenging the constitutionality of the new law. The case pivoted upon the interpretation of direct tax as intended by the founding fathers of the Constitution. Are *only* land and capitation taxes direct, or should the income tax also be considered a direct tax? The Supreme Court, in the case of *Pollock* v. *Farmers' Loan and Trust Co.,* reversed the earlier opinion handed down in the *Springer* decision and declared the 1894 income tax to be unconstitutional on the grounds that it taxed income earned from real estate, from personal property, and from state and local government bonds.[7] Hence, the 1894 income tax died an early death and only $77,000 in revenue was collected from it.[8]

The social reformers, however, refused to accept defeat. A more powerful reform campaign concerned itself with the need for an amendment to the Constitution which would clearly exempt the personal income tax from the requirement that direct taxes be apportioned among the states according to population.[9] In 1909, the income tax goal approached fruition in the form of the corporation excise tax legislation of that year. This legislation provided for a corporation income tax of 1 percent on income in excess of $5,000. The tax, though an income tax in essence, was described in the legislation as an excise tax on the privilege of doing business as a corporation. The privilege was to be indicated or measured by the *net income* of the corporation. The Supreme Court split

[6] E. R. A. Seligman, *The Income Tax* (2d Ed.; New York: Macmillan, 1914), pp. 499–505.

[7] *Pollock* v. *Farmers' Loan and Trust Co.,* 157 U.S. 429 (1894); rehearing: 158 U.S. 601 (1895).

[8] *The Federal Tax System, op. cit.,* p. 14.

[9] Obviously, a personal income tax would be unworkable, on traditional equity grounds, if it had to be apportioned among the states according to population. For example, two states may have equal population, but one state may be twice as wealthy in productive resources and produce twice the income of the other state. Yet, each state would be required to pay the same "absolute amount" of income tax under the constitutional requirement that direct taxes be apportioned even though one state had much greater taxpaying ability than the other.

hairs to uphold the constitutionality of this law.[10] Yet, the basic position of a federal income tax remained tenuous. Finally, in 1913, the reform drive achieved success when Wyoming became the 36th state to ratify the 16th Amendment to the Constitution. This amendment makes abundantly clear the right of Congress to impose personal and corporation income taxes without apportionment among the states according to population. The 16th Amendment states:

The Congress shall have power to lay and collect taxes on incomes, from whatever source derived, without apportionment among the several States, and without regard to any census or enumeration.

The path having been opened by the ratification of the 16th Amendment, Congress enacted income taxes applying to both individuals and corporations as part of the Tariff Act of 1913. The 1913 legislation, which superseded the Corporate Excise Tax Act of 1909, provided for a progressively rated personal income tax and for a flat-rated tax on corporation income. The combined normal and surtaxes of the new personal income tax constituted a rate structure ranging from 1 to 7 percent, the latter figure applying to taxable incomes in excess of $500,000. The new corporation income tax was levied at a rate of 1 percent on corporate incomes above $5,000.

The income taxes gained considerable revenue importance during the period of World War I. The maximum rate of the personal income tax, which was 7 percent from the enactment of the 1913 bill until 1915, was increased to 77 percent by 1918. The corporation levy, moreover, was increased from its 1913–15 flat rate of 1 percent to 12 percent by 1918. By 1917, income tax revenues had surpassed customs revenues and by 1920 approximately two thirds of total federal revenues were derived from the two income taxes.

Personal income tax rates were reduced during the 1920's through a series of tax cuts which resulted in a range of rates between three eights of 1 percent and 24 percent by 1929. Meanwhile, the corporation income tax rate was increased slightly, though overall corporate tax burdens were reduced as a result of an increased surtax exemption and repeal of wartime excess profits and capital stock taxes during the decade. The depression of the 1930's caused income tax collections by the federal government to decrease. This is exemplified by the drop in income tax revenues from a level of $2.4 billion in 1930 to less than $750 million in 1933. Income tax receipts, however, rose to $2.1 billion by 1940, which was still less than their total in 1930. Income tax collections, moreover, represented only 40 percent of the total federal tax revenues collected in

[10] The corporation excise tax was upheld in *Flint* v. *Stone Tracy Co.*, 220 U.S. 107 (1911).

1940 while they had amounted to approximately 67 percent of federal tax revenues 10 years earlier.

The decline in the absolute and relative importance of the income tax during the depression decade of the 1930's occurred despite the legislation of 1936 and 1937, which not only increased the maximum personal income tax rate to 79 percent but also reduced personal exemptions. The minimum rate remained low at 4 percent on the first $4,000 of taxable income as rates in the higher brackets were increased. The growth in total federal tax receipts which took place during the last half of the decade may be explained by the increased significance of excise taxes, particularly taxes on alcoholic beverages, which now could be collected because of the repeal of Prohibition.

The advent of World War II turned the federal personal income tax into a tax on the "masses" and established the overriding importance of the federal personal and corporation income taxes to the federal revenue

TABLE 11–1

FEDERAL PERSONAL INCOME TAX RATE RANGES*
AND PERSONAL EXEMPTIONS, SELECTED YEARS,
1861–1966

Year	Minimum Rate (Percent)	Maximum Rate (Percent)	Personal Exemption (Single Individual)
1861	3	3	$ 800
1862	3	5	600
1865	5	10	600
1894	2	2	4,000
1913	1	7	3,000
1918	6	77	1,000
1929	⅜	24	1,500
1939	4	79	1,000
1945	23	94	500
1954	20	91	600
1966	14	70	600

* Only the maximum and minimum rates are shown. The taxable incomes at which the rates apply are not shown in the table.

structure. In terms of enforcement, the mass personal income tax was made possible by the adoption of "withholding at the source," as proposed by Beardsley Ruml and supported by Secretary of the Treasury Henry Morgenthau. In addition to providing an enormous increase in the revenues needed to finance the war, the income taxes also helped to restrain inflationary pressures. By 1945, the personal income tax had reached an all-time high in rates with a range between 23 and 94 percent. In 1945, some 50 million taxpayers filed personal income tax returns, a substantial increase over the 6 million who filed returns during 1937.

Personal income tax rates were reduced in 1945 and, in addition, the excess profits tax was eliminated. In 1948, further personal income tax rate reductions were enacted by Congress. The Korean War emergency during the early 1950's, however, motivated Congress to increase personal and corporate income tax rates and to reimpose an excess profits tax. After the Korean War ended, the personal income tax rates were lowered in 1954 to their pre–Korean War levels and the excess profits tax was allowed to expire. The Revenue Act of 1964 established the present personal income tax rate structure which will be discussed below.[11] Table 11–1 summarizes the historical pattern of federal personal income tax rates from the Civil War until today.

Federal Personal Income Tax Base

The base to which federal personal income tax rates are applied is complex due to the existence of numerous exclusions, deductions, and personal exemptions.[12] These adjustments represent the source of considerable deviation between gross income and taxable income. In the sequence of their administrative application, (1) exclusions from gross income, (2) deductions from gross income, (3) deductions from adjusted gross income, and (4) personal exemptions will be discussed in that order.

A wide variety of personal receipts may be treated as *exclusions from gross income, that is, they need not even be reported on an individual's income tax return.*[13] Moreover, "income in kind," though not

---

[11] The 1964 legislation also established the present federal corporation income tax rate structure which will be discussed in the following chapter.

[12] An excellent coverage of the federal personal income tax is contained in *The Federal Tax System, op. cit.,* chap. 2.

[13] The primary exclusions from gross income include:
1. Social Security Act (OASDI) benefits.
2. Unemployment compensation.
3. Relief payments.
4. Payments under the Railroad Retirement Act.
5. Veterans' pensions, except retirement pay based on age or length of service.
6. Life insurance payments made upon reason of death.
7. Death benefits, up to $5,000, paid to the beneficiary of an employee by an employer upon the death of the employee.
8. Workmen's compensation, damages for illness or injury, accident and health insurance payments.
9. Payments in lieu of wages during periods of sickness or injury financed by employers (subject to limitations).
10. Contributions by employers to qualified employee pension, annuity, accident, or health plans.
11. Employer payments for employees on group term life insurance coverage up to $50,000.
12. Meals or lodging furnished on premises by and for convenience of employer.
13. Reimbursed moving expenses of existing employees. (*continued on p. 208*)

excluded explicitly from gross income, has not in practice been included in the gross income concept under the *Internal Revenue Code*. This includes such things as food and fuel produced and consumed on farms and the rental value of owner-occupied homes. During 1962, the Department of Commerce estimated the net rental income from owner-occupied residences to be $6.9 billion and the value of food and fuel produced and consumed on farms to be $1.1 billion.[14] Yet, some of the other exclusions bear even greater monetary significance. For example, federal transfer payments—including social security benefits, veterans benefits, and military pensions—amounted to $26.7 billion.[15] Moreover, tax-exempt interest amounted to approximately $900 million.[16]

Once the exclusions from gross income have been considered, the next step in finding the taxable income base of the federal personal income tax is to apply various *deductions from gross income*.[17] It should be pointed out that most deductions from gross income constitute ordinary and necessary "business and trade expenses." The income concept remaining at this point of tax accounting—after exclusions and deduction

---

14. Subsistence allowance, rental allowance, combat pay, and mustering-out pay for members of the Armed Forces.
15. Clergyman's rental value of dwelling or rental allowance.
16. Gifts and inheritances.
17. Interest paid on state and local government securities.
18. Fellowship and scholarship grants (subject to limitations).
19. Income from discharge of indebtedness incurred in connection with property used in trade or business.
20. Dividends received from domestic corporations, up to $100 annually per taxpayer.
21. Income earned abroad, up to $20,000, for a taxpayer living abroad for 17 out of 18 months, and $25,000 for a bona fide resident abroad for 3 or more years.

[14] *The Federal Tax System, op. cit.*, pp. 18–19.

[15] *Ibid.*, p. 19.

[16] *Ibid.*

[17] Deductions from gross income include:
  1. All ordinary and necessary expenses paid or incurred during the taxable year in carrying on any trade or business, except in the performance of services as an employee. Allowable deductions include wages and salaries, depletion, depreciation, interest, and taxes.
  2. Certain employee expenses incurred in behalf of an employer, including those as an outside salesman and for travel while away from home.
  3. One half of the excess of net long-term capital gains over net short-term capital losses.
  4. Expenses which may be attributed to the production of rent and royalty income.
  5. Net losses incurred from the sale or exchange of capital assets used in the production of income, up to $1,000 in a single taxable year. Net losses in excess of $1,000 may be carried over to future years until exhausted.
  6. Certain deductions of self-employed individuals for pension, annuity, profit-sharing, and bond purchase plans.
  7. The expenses of moving because of a change in job locations by new or continuing employees (subject to various limitations).

from gross income adjustments have been made—is that of "adjusted gross income."

The next step in determining the taxable income base of the federal personal income tax is to apply various *deductions from adjusted gross income*.[18] It may be observed that deductions from adjusted gross income tend to be of a nonbusiness or personal nature. The above deductions must be itemized on the taxpayer's return unless he prefers to use the standard deduction. For single persons and married couples filing joint returns, the standard deduction amounts to the greater of *either* 10 percent of adjusted gross income *or* an amount equal to $200 plus $100 times the number of claimed exemptions, including exemptions for age and blindness. The standard deduction may not exceed $1,000 for single persons or for married couples filing jointly. In the case of married persons filing separate returns, the standard deduction is equal to the greater of 10 percent of adjusted gross income or an amount equal to $100 plus $100 times the number of claimed exemptions. The standard deduction may not exceed $500 for married persons filing separate returns. During 1961, deductions were itemized on 41 percent of the personal income tax returns filed for the year. The gross value of the itemized deductions amounted to $38.4 billion.[19] Of this total, $11.8 billion was for

---

[18] Deductions from adjusted gross income include:

    1. Various taxes such as *state and local* personal property, real property, income, general sales, and gasoline taxes and *foreign* real property and income taxes. (A change in 1964 eliminated the deduction of such *state and local* taxes as the excises on tobacco products, alcoholic beverages, admissions and occupancy, as well as auto license taxes, driver registration fees, and poll taxes).

    2. Interest on indebtedness (subject to various limitations).

    3. Contributions to certain nonprofit institutions, such as religious, educational, scientific, and charitable organizations (subject to various limitations).

    4. Various expenses associated with the occupation of the taxpayer, such as union dues, membership fees in professional associations, subscriptions to professional journals, uniforms, other types of special work apparel, and educational expenses incurred to maintain or improve skills required in the taxpayers employment, trade, or business, or to meet the requirements of the taxpayer's employer.

    5. Medical expenses incurred on behalf of the taxpayer, his wife, and dependents, if not reimbursed by insurance (subject to various limitations). Limitations do not apply if the taxpayer or his spouse, or both, are age 65 or over, or to medical expenses for a dependent parent of the taxpayer who is 65 or over.

    6. An amount equal to the excess over $100 of each loss due to fire, theft, or other casualty to the extent that the loss is not compensated by insurance.

    7. Alimony and separate maintenance payments to the extent that these amounts are includable in the recipient's gross income.

    8. Expenses incurred by a widow, a widower, a divorced or legally separated person, or the husband of an incapacitated wife for the care of certain dependents to enable the taxpayer to be gainfully employed (subject to various limitations).

[19] *The Federal Tax System, op. cit.,* p. 21.

taxes paid, $9.3 billion for interest, $7.1 billion for contributions, and $5.6 billion for medical expenses.[20] The standard deduction, which was used on the remaining 59 percent of the returns filed, amounted to $12.9 billion.[21]

The final step in computing taxable income under the federal personal income tax is to deduct *personal exemptions.* The taxpayer may deduct an exemption of $600 for himself and additional exemptions of $600 for his spouse and for each dependent. Also, additional $600 exemptions are allowed for a taxpayer who is age 65 or over, for his spouse if 65 years of age or over, for a blind taxpayer, and for a blind spouse. In 1961, personal exemptions totaled $106.5 billion, $82.5 billion on taxable returns, and $24 billion on nontaxable returns.[22]

Federal Personal Income Tax Rate Structure

A discussion of the federal personal income tax rate structure requires the distinction between "average" and "marginal" rates of tax. The average tax rate is computed by dividing the *total* tax liability by the *total* tax base.[23] The marginal tax rate is computed by dividing the

TABLE 11–2

THE RELATIONSHIP BETWEEN MARGINAL AND AVERAGE TAX RATES
AND PROPORTIONATE, PROGRESSIVE, AND REGRESSIVE
TAX RATE STRUCTURES

Rate Structure	Tax Liability	Tax Base	Average Tax Rate	Marginal Tax Rate
Proportionate	$1,000	$ 50,000	2 %	
	2,000	100,000	2	2%
Progressive	1,000	50,000	2	
	4,000	100,000	4	6
Regressive	1,000	50,000	2	
	1,500	100,000	1.5	1

change in total tax liability by the *change* in total tax base. If the tax rate structure is proportionate, the marginal rate must be equal to the average rate as the tax base increases in size. If the tax rate structure is progressive, the marginal rate must be higher than the average rate as the tax base increases. If the tax rate structure is regressive, the marginal rate must be less than the average rate as the tax base increases. Table 11–2 demonstrates these relationships.

[20] *Ibid.*

[21] *Ibid.*

[22] *Ibid.*, p. 22.

[23] The federal personal income tax base consists of taxable income as computed above.

The present rate structure of the federal personal income tax is progressive in technical structure. The degree of progressivity was reduced, however, by the Revenue Act of 1964. Table 11–3 demonstrates

TABLE 11–3

PRESENT (1966) FEDERAL PERSONAL INCOME TAX
RATE STRUCTURE, MARGINAL AND AVERAGE
RATES OF TAX, FOR MARRIED PERSONS
FILING JOINT RETURN

Taxable Income Bracket	Marginal Tax Rate	Average Tax Rate*
$ 0– 1,000	14%	14 %
1,000– 2,000	15	14.5
2,000– 3,000	16	15
3,000– 4,000	17	15.5
4,000– 8,000	19	17.2
8,000– 12,000	22	18.8
12,000– 16,000	25	20.4
16,000– 20,000	28	21.9
20,000– 24,000	32	23.6
24,000– 28,000	36	25.4
28,000– 32,000	39	27.1
32,000– 36,000	42	28.7
36,000– 40,000	45	30.3
40,000– 44,000	48	32.0
44,000– 52,000	50	34.7
52,000– 64,000	53	38.2
64,000– 76,000	55	40.8
76,000– 88,000	58	43.2
88,000–100,000	60	45.2
100,000–120,000	62	48.0
120,000–140,000	64	50.3
140,000–160,000	66	52.2
160,000–180,000	68	54.0
180,000–200,000	69	55.5
over 200,000	70	55.5–

* Based on maximum figure in each taxable income bracket rather than on minimum figure or mean figure of the bracket.

the marginal and average rates of tax now in effect for the federal personal income tax. Obviously, the average rates represent a lower range than the marginal rates because they encompass the effects of the lower marginal rates on all previous marginal brackets as well as the higher marginal rates on the highest bracket reached by the taxpayer. For example, on $2,000 of taxable income the marginal rate of 14 percent would apply on $1,000 of the total amount and the marginal rate of 15 percent on the remaining $1,000. The average rate is only 14.5 percent on the total $2,000, however, because one half of the total amount was taxed at a 14 percent instead of at a 15 percent rate.

Income splitting provides an important rate modification under the federal personal income tax rate structure. Married couples filing a joint return compute their joint liability by applying the statutory tax rates on one half of their combined taxable income and multiplying the result by two. With a progressive tax rate structure, married couples enjoy tax savings from this device as long as either spouse has a taxable income in excess of the maximum taxable income in the first rate bracket. A single person who qualifies as head of a household, however, may experience tax saving by filing under a separate rate schedule which provides approximately one half of the tax savings provided by the income-splitting technique.

Various *tax credits* also may influence federal personal income tax liabilities.[24] In addition, tax liabilities in a given year may be influenced significantly by the existence of *averaging* devices. Fluctuating income over a period of years, as opposed to more stable earnings, may penalize a taxpayer under a progressive tax rate structure (in the absence of an averaging device). An individual earning $10,000 of taxable income during *each* of the next five years, for example, would incur a total tax liability for the five-year period of $10,950 on the $50,000 total taxable income (under present federal personal income tax rates). However, an individual earning an equivalent total of $50,000 during the five-year period—with all of the earnings being made in a single year—would pay a much larger tax of $22,590. Hence, the need for an averaging device is clear.

Prior to the Revenue Act of 1964, only partial consideration was provided for fluctuating incomes. Some occupations were covered by averaging devices or other special rules while others were not covered. The 1964 legislation replaced these scattered provisions with a general averaging device. This new comprehensive provision, which avoids the recomputation of taxes paid in previous years, generally applies as follows: The amount of taxable income in the computation year which exceeds four thirds of the average taxable income of the preceding four years, if it amounts to at least $3,000, is taxed at five times the rate otherwise applied to one fifth of the averageable income.[25] The general

---

[24] Tax credits include:
1. A credit for foreign income taxes paid (subject to various limitations). This is applicable *only* if a deduction is not applied for this amount.
2. A credit for tax withheld at the source of income.
3. A credit for partially tax-exempt interest on certain federal government securities. This credit may not exceed 3 percent of taxable income.
4. A retirement income credit for persons 65 or over, and for those under 65 who are retired under a public retirement system (subject to various limitations).
5. A credit equal to 7 percent of qualified investment in depreciable personal property placed in service during the tax year in connection generally with a trade or business (subject to various limitations).

[25] This provision does not apply to net long-term capital gains, income from previous gifts, and gains from wagering.

averaging device, however, cannot be used by individuals who were nonresident aliens at any time during the five-year period, or who were not members of the labor force throughout the period.

Federal tax law provides for the differential tax treatment of business or trade profits depending upon the legal form of organization under which the business functions. Businesses which are legally organized as *corporations* are taxed as separate entities and have a particular scale of tax rates applied to them. This specific base-rate structure constitutes the federal corporation income tax (see Chapter 12). Generally, holders of corporate stocks report on their federal personal income tax returns *only* that part of net corporation profits which have been distributed to them as cash dividends. On the other hand, businesses organized as *sole proprietorships* or *partnerships* are not taxed as separate entities and all taxable profits are reported on the individual returns of the owners.[26]

Fiscal Rationality Criteria Applied to the Federal Personal Income Tax

The "General Fiscal Rationality" Criterion. The personal income tax will be evaluated in terms of the tax rationality criteria developed in Chapter 5. Although the analysis will relate primarily to the *federal* personal income tax, it will also apply in a general sense to the personal income tax per se regardless of the government level imposing the tax. For convenience of presentation, the analysis below will merge the tax equity criterion into the general fiscal efficiency criterion. Thus, *two* fiscal rationality bench marks will be used for the evaluation of the personal income tax, namely, the general fiscal rationality and revenue productivity criteria.

The general fiscal rationality criterion is based largely upon the economic concept of *neutrality.* The orthodox version of this concept suggests that governmental budgetary behavior should not influence private sector economic behavior, particularly that of an allocative variety. Neutrality, in this sense, may be classified as *intersector neutrality.*[27] In this context, any public sector fiscal action which distorts private economic activity is undesirable. It is thus suggested that governmental budgetary behavior, if deemed necessary, should utilize those fiscal techniques which *least distort* market decisions.

It is very important to remember, however, that very stringent conditions are required for the validity of the conclusion that all public sector distortions of market behavior are economically irrational. These conditions are: (1) an economy operating under long-run, perfectly

---

[26] Under certain conditions, unincorporated businesses may elect to be subject to the corporation income tax instead of to the personal income tax.

[27] See Chapter 5 for a relevant discussion.

competitive equilibrium, (2) the absence of externalities, and (3) the ability to apply the exclusion principle to all economic goods.[28] Under such circumstances, the economic role of government in a market-oriented economy would be insignificant.

The conditions required for optimal market allocation of *all* resources, however, are not present in the American economy. Hence, the public sector must allocate some resources if economic efficiency—both allocative and technical—is to be attained. Consequently, the private sector nonneutrality which government may create is not necessarily irrational. In fact, nonneutral effects should be classified as "positive" or "negative" depending upon whether they move an individual consumer, business, or the entire national community closer to or further away from their optimal positions regarding the goals of public finance. Figure 11–1

FIGURE 11–1

OPTIMAL ALLOCATION BETWEEN PUBLIC AND PRIVATE
GOODS (SOCIAL BALANCE) FOR SOCIETY—AND TWO DIS-
EQUILIBRIUM POINTS

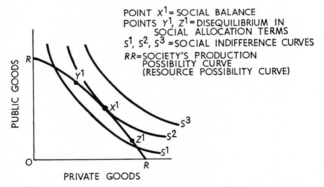

demonstrates these relationships, in terms of allocation efficiency, for the society as a whole.

Public sector fiscal action which moves the society away from the optimal allocation point would be undesirable or irrational and should be termed negative nonneutrality. However, any budgetary action of government which moves the consumer or society closer to the optimal tangency point X^1, as from points Y^1, or Z^1 toward X^1, may be classified as positive allocative nonneutrality. Though not demonstrated graphically, the utility-maximization position of a consumer and the profit-maximization position of a business firm also may be improved or worsened by governmental budgetary action under conditions where the consumer or firm is not previously operating at an optimum position.

[28] In other words, all the conditions required for optimal market allocation of resources, as developed in Chapter 2, are required.

The discussion below will present several viewpoints regarding the neutrality of personal income taxes. Since the originators of these viewpoints ordinarily define neutrality in the orthodox intersector sense (which assumes long-run, perfectly competitive equilibrium, and so forth), the arguments will be presented in the form used by their authors. The reader should keep in mind, however, the important distinctions cited above regarding positive and negative nonneutrality. Consequently, it should *not* be concluded that all nonneutral effects imposed upon the market by governmental fiscal activity are undesirable or irrational.

1. *Is the income tax or excise tax more neutral?* The traditional economic viewpoint holds that income taxes are more neutral toward private behavior than are excise taxes.[29] The argument, as presented by Joseph, that an income tax is more neutral than an excise tax yielding the same revenue, is demonstrated in Figure 11–2.[30] Point P^1 represents the

FIGURE 11–2

INCOME TAX AND EXCISE TAX NEUTRALITY—
THE JOSEPH ARGUMENT

SOURCE: M. F. W. Joseph, "The Excess Burden of Indirect Taxation," *Review of Economic Studies* (June, 1939), Figure II, p. 227.

initial equilibrium for the representative consumer. He consumes goods X and Y in the quantities determined at point P^1, at which point the marginal rate of substitution between the two goods is equal to the "effective" demand for these goods as determined by the budget line AB (based on the consumer's income and the prices of the goods). An excise

[29] This approach is represented in M. F. W. Joseph, "The Excess Burden of Indirect Taxation," *Review of Economic Studies* (June, 1939), pp. 226–31, and in several other sources.

[30] *Ibid.*

tax is then placed on good X, with no change in money income and product prices, and the result is a new equilibrium at point P^2 which is the tangency point between the new budget line AC and a lower consumer indifference curve I^1. The same revenue could be raised by an income tax, as shown by budget line DE, which passes through point P^2 providing an equilibrium under the income tax at point P^3. This point is on a higher indifference curve I^2 than is point P^2. Hence, the income tax is alleged to be more neutral and thus superior to the excise tax because it results in less distortion—the reduction from indifference curve I^3 to I^2 under the income tax being less than the reduction from I^3 to I^1 under the excise tax.

This approach was subsequently challenged by other economists and the issue further clarified.[31] Friedman attacked the traditional approach on the grounds that it uses a partial equilibrium methodology which ignores technical production possibilities and that it disregards the uses to which tax revenues are put.[32] Friedman agrees that the conclusions of Joseph and others could be true for an isolated individual, but asserts that such partial equilibrium analysis cannot be generalized for the entire community. Such generalization is deemed incorrect because it supposes that an excise tax reduces the range of alternatives to an individual in a way which is calculable by simply taking the differences in alternatives available between budget lines AB and AC in Figure 11–2 and multiplying them by the number of individuals. Yet, this supposition is invalid, according to Friedman, because the imposition of an excise tax does not change the location of the production possibility frontier. It may reduce the flow of productive resources to goods X and Y, but only because it increases the production of a third economic good, Z. Hence, Figure 11–2 is inapplicable and the traditional analysis falters since, being a partial equilibrium approach, it ignores production possibilities for other goods. Friedman observes, moreover, that the traditional approach is inadequate because it does not consider alternative uses of the excise tax receipts. The conclusion of traditional analysis remains the same whether the tax proceeds are impounded, used to subsidize the production of good X or good Y, or used for general consumer subsidies. Undoubtedly, this critical analysis by Friedman adds further dimensions of understanding to the complex issue of income v. excise tax neutrality.

Friedman offers an alternative approach to the above neutrality issue (See Figures 11–3a and 11–3b).[33] Figure 11–3a integrates produc-

---

[31] See Milton Friedman, "The Welfare Effects of an Income Tax and an Excise Tax," *Journal of Political Economy* (February, 1952), pp. 25–33; I. M. D. Little, "Direct vs. Indirect Taxes," *Economic Journal* (September, 1951), pp. 577–84; and Richard A. Musgrave, *The Theory of Public Finance* (New York: McGraw-Hill Book Co., Inc., 1959), pp. 140–48.

[32] Friedman, *op. cit.*, pp. 27–29.

[33] *Ibid.*, pp. 29–33.

tion possibilities into the analysis and serves as a general equilibrium approach. In Figure 11–3a, let *GH* represent a transformation (production possibility) function for the production of *X* and *Y* and *II* the relevant consumption indifference curve for *X* and *Y*. The constant receipts line of the consumer is represented by *AB*. Point P^1 serves as the equilibrium consumption point between goods *X* and *Y* because at this point the marginal rates of substitution in both consumption and production are identical. In other words, each individual in the society is consuming at point P^1 (assuming perfectly competitive equilibrium). If

FIGURE 11–3

INCOME VERSUS EXCISE TAX NEUTRALITY:
FRIEDMAN ARGUMENT

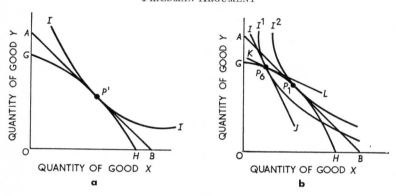

SOURCE: Milton Friedman, "The Welfare Effects of an Income Tax and an Excise Tax," *Journal of Political Economy* (February, 1952), Figure 3, p. 30, and Figure 4, p. 31.

the desired amount of revenue is raised through an income tax (Friedman assumes a "proportionate" income tax), the neutrality effect will depend upon the use of the revenue. If the revenue is used to grant a per capita subsidy, for example, there would be no change in the equilibrium position on the graph because an income tax and subsidy change neither the relative prices of *X* and *Y*, the transformation curve, nor the consumer indifference curve. If the revenue is used to produce good *Z*, however, a new transformation curve between *X* and *Y* would be required as determined by the quantity of *Z* produced, since resources are drawn away from the production of *X* and/or *Y*. Importantly, the change in the transformation curve would depend *only* on the quantity of *Z* produced and *not* on the type of tax used to raise the revenues. If the amount of *Z* is assumed to be fixed, the new transformation curve will be the same whether an income tax or an excise tax is imposed to raise the revenues in which case *GP¹H* can be considered as the transformation curve after the subtraction of resources to produce *Z*. Figure 11–3a thus can be used to represent the situation both before and after a proportional income tax is imposed.

In Figure 11–3a, the equilibrium point under a personal income tax is at point P^1. However, where is the equilibrium point for the excise tax? A highly relevant consideration in this regard is that the excise tax results in a divergence between the prices paid by the consumer and the prices received by the firm. Hence, the rate at which individuals can substitute the goods in consumption is different from the rate at which producers can substitute the goods in sale. Yet, the optimal consumer equilibrium requires that the consumption indifference curve be tangent to the budget line, that is, the rate at which individuals can substitute goods in purchase must be equal to the rate at which they are willing to substitute in consumption. Moreover, the optimal producer equilibrium requires that the production possibility curve be tangent to the constant receipts line AB, that is, the rate at which producers can substitute in sale be equal to the rate at which they can substitute in production.

In Figure 11–3b, point P^6 is the optimal equilibrium point for both consumers and producers under the excise tax as described in the preceding paragraph. Line IJ is the budget line as it appears to the consumer and line KL is the constant receipts line as it appears to the producer. Point P^3 is on a lower indifference curve than point P^1 and thus provides less total satisfaction. If P^1 is a point of perfectly competitive equilibrium, it may be said that an excise tax providing consumption at point P^6 is socially less desirable in terms of allocation neutrality than the income tax which allows greater total consumption at point P^1. If the initial position had been less than optimal either because of other taxes or because of imperfect competition, however, an excise tax on good Y could move the consumption point toward P^1 and thus increase consumer satisfaction.

The obvious conclusion is that it is impossible to state categorically whether an income or an excise tax is superior in terms of neutrality. The answer depends upon such considerations as the initial equilibrium position which prevails before the tax is imposed. The most that can be inferred is that the broader the tax base, and the more equal its incidence in terms of slight rate progressivity and fewness of exemptions, the less likely it is that the marginal rate of substitution between consumption goods (and thus allocation neutrality) will be affected. Such important considerations as the rate of substitution between income and leisure, between market and nonmarket (public sector) activities, and between consumption and savings are outside the direct scope of the above analysis. Several of these additional tax neutrality phenomena and their relevance to the personal income tax will now be considered.

2. *Labor Nonneutrality and the Personal Income Tax.* (*a*) Effect of Personal Income Tax on Work Effort: A personal income tax can distort the substitution between work effort and leisure and thus create nonneu-

tral effects.[34] Such nonneutrality, however, may be either positive or negative in its allocative effects depending upon whether the previous work-leisure allocation was optimal. The degree of noneutrality will increase, of course, as the income tax rates become progressive instead of proportional because it is the marginal tax rate which influences the work-leisure choice and the marginal rate exceeds the average rate under a progressive tax.

The work-leisure distortion tends to be rather insignificant, in general terms, because of two offsetting effects which result from income taxation. On the one hand, income taxation impairs work incentives by reducing the net monetary reward from work effort, thus causing leisure to be substituted for work effort at the margin. On the other hand, income taxation lowers the disposable income of the taxpayer and places pressure upon him to earn more in order to maintain desired living standards. The latter "income effect" which stimulates work effort thus tends to neutralize the "substitution effect" which tends to retard work effort.

(*b*) Effect of Personal Income Tax on the Choice of a Profession: Apparently, the personal income tax exerts only a modest influence on the choice of professions. To the extent that such effects occur, however, the patterns of production, money wages, and prices will be influenced thus affecting both the allocation of resources and income-wealth distribution. A recent study provided a survey of randomly selected graduating seniors at a major American university to ascertain whether the progressive personal income tax influenced their choice of occupation.[35] Not one student mentioned on his own accord that taxation had influenced his decision.

There are nevertheless several ways by which a personal income tax could influence the selection of a profession.[36] Progressive income taxes, for example, may be expected to discourage the kinds of work which entail the largest amount of nondeductible costs. Also, a progressive income tax may encourage nonmarket work effort as opposed to market work effort since labor which escapes an explicit monetary transaction is difficult to assess and thus difficult to tax. Self-employed professions are favored in this regard. In addition, self-employment offers greater opportunity for tax evasion due to the fact that business earnings are not

[34] See Musgrave, *op. cit.*, pp. 232–49. Also, for pertinent discussions of the topic, see Richard Goode, "The Income Tax and the Supply of Labor," *Journal of Political Economy* (October, 1949), pp. 428–37; and George F. Break, "Income Taxes and Incentives to Work: an Empirical Study," *American Economic Review* (September, 1957), pp. 529–49.

[35] Herbert G. Grubel and David R. Edwards, "Personal Income Taxation and the Choice of Professions," *Quarterly Journal of Economics* (February, 1964), pp. 158–63.

[36] See Goode, *op. cit.*

subject to withholding as are wages and salaries. On balance, however, these effects on occupational choice tend to be insignificant.

(c) Effect of Personal Income Tax on Labor Mobility: It has been asserted that the federal personal income tax retards labor mobility between professions through its encouragement of deferred compensation programs, particularly when the pension rights are not vested.[37] Thus, if an employee were to lose most or all of his pension accumulation through changing jobs, it would appear unlikely that he would be motivated to change. Older workers, in particular, would be affected.

As plausible as these assertions appear to be, they have been rejected in several empirical studies. For example, Ross tests the proposition that the American labor force is being immobilized by the attractions of seniority and negotiated fringe benefits.[38] He charts the secular trend of the "quit rate" in manufacturing industries and, after adjusting these data for business cycle variations, concludes that the weight of evidence stands against the hypothesis. Though a long-term decline in the quit rate is detected, it does not appear to be due to seniority and to deferred compensation programs. This is evident when the data are disaggregated and related to years of service. When this is done, no decline is demonstrated where it would need to take place to support the hypothesis, namely, among workers who have been with a firm a considerable number of years. Instead, the quit rate for older workers has remained relatively constant. The decline in the overall quit rate is the result of a substantial decline in the rate for younger workers which Ross attributes to unionization and to prosperity.

A related study on the effect of nonvested pensions on labor mobility within the higher education industry was conducted by Lurie.[39] He attempts, as does Ross, to test empirically the hypothesis that the effect of nonvested pensions is to reduce the mobility of the labor supply. Lurie follows a methodology which relates faculty separation rates with pension programs, both vested and nonvested. The conclusion is reached that the mobility of labor in the higher education industry is as large from institutions with nonvested pension programs as with vested programs. Consequently, the hypothesis is rejected. The effects of the federal personal income tax on labor mobility through the encouragement of

[37] Many firms develop deferred compensation programs for their executives in order to spread their incomes over retirement years and thus to increase their long-term after-tax earnings. Deferred compensation, in addition, may take the form of various fringe benefits negotiated by labor unions with management for the benefit of nonmanagement employees.

[38] Arthur M. Ross, "Do We Have A New Industrial Feudalism?" *American Economic Review* (December, 1958), pp. 903–20.

[39] Melvin Lurie, "The Effect of Non-Vested Pensions on Mobility: A Study of the Higher Education Industry," *Industrial and Labor Relations Review* (January, 1965), pp. 225–37.

deferred compensation programs may thus not be as restrictive as originally suspected.

(*d*) Effect of Personal Income Tax on Residential Location: It does appear, however, that the personal income tax at the state level can distort residential living patterns between states, particularly in metropolitan areas which overlap state boundaries. In this context, a person will prefer to live in a state without a state personal income tax rather than in a state with a personal income tax assuming that other taxes are equal in scope between the states. Many states have attempted to remedy this problem by taxing income at its point of origin, but this has not proved to be a satisfactory solution. On the one hand, this attempted solution may involve multiple taxation and, on the other hand, it may encourage the usage of avoidance and evasion devices. The existence of a state personal income tax, moreover, may distort the *aggregate supply of labor* between two states, increasing the supply in the state without the tax and decreasing the supply in the state with the tax. To the extent that the interstate labor supply is distorted, the patterns of resource allocation, technical production efficiency, labor and product prices, and the distribution of income and wealth may be altered. These distortions, however, may be positive as well as negative if the previous "preincome tax equilibrium" was not optimal.

3. *Saving-Investment Nonneutrality and the Personal Income Tax.* (*a*) Effect of Personal Income Tax on Saving: The ability of the personal income tax to influence saving is demonstrated in the following example:[40] Assume the existence of a single economic good. Thus, the only possible allocation distortion is between the present and future consumption of the single good. In the preincome tax equilibrium, the consumer's marginal rate of substitution between present and future consumption equals the producer's marginal rate of transformation between present and future goods. The application of a proportionate personal income tax will distort the equality of these two rates because it reduces the rate at which future consumption may be substituted for present consumption. The income tax thus reduces the *net* rate of interest if interest income is taxable. In other words, the *net* rate of interest upon which the marginal rate of substitution by the consumer depends is reduced while the rate of transformation by the producer depends upon the *gross* rate of interest. The condition of optimal allocation is distorted when the two rates are made unequal. The distortion would be accentuated under a progressive income tax because the degree of inequality between the marginal rates of substitution and transformation depend upon the marginal rate of tax.

Smith studied the effect of changes in the degree of personal income

---

[40] See Musgrave, *op. cit.*, pp. 152–53.

tax progression on the saving behavior of individuals.[41] The results of this empirical analysis indicate that increases in the degree of income tax rate progression tend to reduce individual saving in both an absolute sense and in terms of the saving/income ratio. Attention should also be paid to the various effects on personal saving which may result from the encouragement of deferred compensation programs by the personal income tax.[42] When personal saving is institutionalized, saving may be increased beyond the desires of an individual. This is particularly true in the case of group retirement plans where the individual has little choice in the matter. In addition to this allocation nonneutrality, another allocation distortion occurs to the extent that pension trusts make funds available which must necessarily go into low-risk, relatively high-priced issues, thus driving their prices up and reducing the amount of funds available to speculative, high-risk firms. Regarding intergoal nonneutrality, pension fund activity may serve as an automatic stabilization device since contributions to the fund, and thus saving, increase during periods of prosperity and decline during periods of recession. However, pension funds may at times become destabilizers through their influence on stock and bond markets. The above analysis strongly suggests that saving can be significantly affected by a personal income tax, especially one which is progressive.

(*b*) Effect of Personal Income Tax on Risk Taking and Investment Incentives: A study by Domar and Musgrave concentrates upon two aspects of risk and investment, namely, how proportional income taxation affects the yield and risk of an investment and, secondly, how the investor will react to the risk and investment changes.[43] Three cases of *yield-risk relationship* emerge: *First,* if losses cannot be offset through the income tax structure, the investor will bear the entire burden of the loss since the tax reduces the yield but leaves the degree of risk unchanged. Hence, the compensation per unit of risk taking is reduced by the amount of the tax rate. The *second* case considers what would happen if a complete offset of losses is allowed under the income tax law. In this situation, both the yield and the risk of the investment are reduced by the rate of the tax. Hence, the compensation per unit of risk taking remains the same. In the *third* case, where partial offset to losses is allowed, the yield is reduced by a greater percentage than the degree of risk. Hence, the results are intermediate between cases one and two above, and the compensation per unit of risk taking is only partially reduced.

[41] Paul E. Smith, "Individual Income Tax Rate Progression and the Savings Function," *Quarterly Journal of Economics* (May, 1964), pp. 299–306.

[42] See the discussion in *The Federal Tax System, op. cit.,* pp. 125–28.

[43] Evsey D. Domar and Richard A. Musgrave, "Proportional Income Taxation and Risk Taking," *Quarterly Journal of Economics* (May, 1944), pp. 388–422.

It is suggested that *investors will react* to these changes in yield and risk as follows:[44] In the *first* case, since the yield is cut while the risk is unchanged when loss offsets are not allowed, the substitution effect would result in the investor's taking less risk. The income effect, however, would induce him to accept more risk. Hence, the result is uncertain though practical evidence would indicate that the investor is likely to move in the direction of less risk. In the *second* case, if loss offsets are allowed, risk taking has not become less attractive through a substitution effect but the income reduction may induce an income effect in the direction of greater risk taking. In the *third* case, conditions of partial loss deduction reduce the yield by a greater percentage than they reduce the risk with the effect on the investor being uncertain. There is little doubt, however, that the higher the rate of loss offset, the higher will be the degree of risk taking after the tax.

A corollary result of the above analysis is that a large investor has an advantage over a small investor in risk taking since he will tend to have more income against which to offset a loss. Hence, a possible policy objective with both allocation efficiency and distributive equity in mind would be the creation of equally favorable loss offsets for *all* types of investors and income classes.

A book by Butters, Thompson, and Bollinger concentrates upon the effect of taxes, particularly income taxes, on the *supply of capital* required to finance the formation of new enterprises and the growth of existing enterprises.[45] This study places particular stress on the effect of taxes on the amount of external equity capital supplied by private investors. Three sets of empirical data are used to support the survey (published in 1953) which offered the following conclusions: (1) the upper income classes are the source of most equity capital since more than 50 percent of the total marketable securities are held by a very small percentage of the population whether classified by size of income or wealth, (2) changes in the tax structure since the mid-to-late 1930's have substantially reduced the capacity of upper-bracket individuals to accumulate new investment funds though their capacity is still very large, (3) the income tax has decreased the willingness of many investors to make equity-type investments though appreciation-minded investors may be stimulated by the tax structure to seek investments offering large capital gains potential which would increase the flow of capital to new ventures. The general conclusion is that a large amount of equity capital remains, though the amount would have been still larger in the absence of income taxation.

Finally, the personal income tax, in conjunction with the lower

---

[44] *Ibid.*

[45] J. Keith Butters, Lawrence E. Thompson, and Lynn L. Bollinger, *Effects of Taxation: Investment by Individuals* (Boston: Harvard University Press, 1953).

rate capital gains tax, may be observed to result in a bias in favor of corporations retaining earnings rather than paying profits out in the form of cash dividends. This is true because stockholders in high tax brackets tend to prefer compensation in the form of the price appreciation of their securities, which are taxed as capital gains (when realized), rather than in the form of cash dividends, which are taxed at higher rates as ordinary personal income. This not only results in an allocation distortion, in the sense that investments financed from retained earnings may be undertaken which otherwise would not have been warranted, but it also encourages the market concentration of large enterprises and the resulting increase in market imperfection. Undoubtedly, a personal income tax will tend to affect risk taking and the supply of capital—the *specific* effects depending upon such factors as the allowance of "loss offsets" and the special treatment of capital gains.

(c) Effect of Personal Income Tax on the Use of Tax-Exempt Securities: One of the notable exclusions from the federal personal income tax base is the interest paid on state and local government securities.[46] This policy has exerted an allocative effect through encouragement of the use of these debt instruments for financing by state and local government and a distributive effect through providing a prime source for tax avoidance by wealthy individuals. It is alleged by opponents of the exclusion that investors' decisions on the allocation of capital to both the private and public sectors are distorted. It is contended, moreover, that there is a net revenue loss to the public sector as a whole since tax savings to bondholders exceed the reduced cost of borrowing by state and local government.

Advocates of the exclusion claim that repeal of the exemption would greatly increase the cost of borrowing for state and local government and thereby interfere with the provision of essential governmental services. It is asserted, moreover, that such increased costs would entail the greater use of other taxes, such as property and sales taxes, which would tend to be regressive to lower income groups. In addition, the advocates of tax-exempt government securities dispute the claim that repeal of the exclusion would provide a net revenue gain to government. Thus, although it is clear that the exclusion under the federal personal income tax of interest income earned on state and local government securities can exert significant allocative and distributive effects, the exact nature of these effects is not always clear.

The nonneutral effects discussed to this point, regarding the general fiscal rationality bench mark for tax rationality, fall generally under the intersector nonneutrality classification with particular stress upon the

[46] See George L. Lent, "The Origin and Survival of Tax-Exempt Securities," *National Tax Journal* (December, 1959), pp. 301–16, for a comprehensive discussion of the subject.

allocation branch of public finance. In the broader sense, however, nonneutrality refers also to the interdependence between budgetary policies directed toward a particular fiscal goal and the effects of such policy on other fiscal goals. The "progressively rated" federal personal income tax, for example, serves the society's income-wealth redistribution objective, but also serves the stabilization objective through its performance as an automatic stabilizer; that is, income tax collections increase at a faster rate than national income as (potentially inflationary) prosperity approaches and decrease at a slower rate than national income during recessionary periods. Moreover, though the progressive income tax serves the distribution goal better than would a proportional income tax, given a community goal of greater equity in distribution of income, it results in greater allocative nonneutralities (though some distortions may be favorable) than would the proportional tax. Furthermore, it is possible that the progressive income tax will discourage both long-run saving and investment and thus deter economic growth. The above examples of intergoal nonneutrality, as influenced by the federal personal income tax, are a few of many that might have been selected. They demonstrate nonetheless the *considerable nonneutrality*, both positive and negative, which can exist between the various goals of public finance as well as the ability of the personal income tax to affect these goals.

The Revenue Productivity Criterion. A theoretically rational tax remains rational only if it is efficiently implemented in practice. Thus, tax rationality in the "enforcement sense" is a critical consideration for a totally efficient tax structure. The federal personal income tax appears to pass the enforcement efficiency test, though further significant improvements are possible. In addition to the somewhat measurable direct revenue results of income tax enforcement efforts, an untold additional amount of income taxes are collected due to the indirect persuasion which an effective tax enforcement system provides. In any case, the aggregate revenue collected, both directly and indirectly, from the federal personal income tax far outmeasures the monetary costs of enforcement incurred by the federal government. Furthermore, the federal personal income tax avoids the creation of severe disincentives to consumption, saving, and investment behavior in the market. Thus, the tax may be considered to adequately serve the revenue productivity bench mark for tax rationality. A detailed discussion of the tax enforcement characteristics of the federal personal income tax follows below.

The enforcement structure of the federal personal income tax may be described as one of voluntary taxpayer compliance. The taxpayer assesses his own tax liabilities and reports them to the federal government on the appropriate tax return. The federal government provides an administrative structure which assists the taxpayer in his efforts of voluntary compliance, coordinates the overall collection program, collects the taxes, and audits the returns for accuracy. The administrative unit of the federal government exercising this authority is the Internal Revenue Service (IRS), a division of the Treasury Department.

The IRS assists the taxpayer in his self-assessment and voluntary compliance efforts through the following programs: (1) direct personal taxpayer assistance by district and local offices in answering questions and filing returns, (2) publication of tax guides covering specific tax situations, (3) dissemination of information to taxpayers by a broad public information program through various news media, and (4) the preparation and distribution of regulations, rulings, tax forms, and instructions. The actual collection of the federal personal income tax by the Internal Revenue Service involves such varied enforcement techniques as (1) withholding, (2) payments of estimated tax, (3) information at the source of income, (4) auditing, (5) rewards to informers, and (6) the assessment of penalties.

While the final tax return for a calendar year need not be filed before the following April 15, "provisional payments" are normally required during the course of the tax year. Primarily, this involves the *withholding* of wage and salary income at the source of the income, as supplemented by declarations and quarterly *payments of estimated tax.* Later, when the final return is submitted, the taxpayer credits amounts withheld from wages and estimated tax payments against his tax liability. If there is remaining tax due, it must be paid when the final return is submitted. If the provisional payments exceed the final liability, the excess may at the discretion of the taxpayer be either refunded, applied toward the purchase of federal savings bonds, or applied as a credit against the following year's tax liability.

Most employers are obligated to withhold provisional income tax payments before wages and salaries are paid to employees. At various times since 1943, the withholding tax rate has ranged betweeen 14 percent (as in 1965) and a high of 22.5 percent, the difference essentially reflecting changes in the statutory personal income tax rates. In early 1966, however, President Johnson asked Congress to increase the withholding rate on personal incomes as an anti-inflationary measure and Congress complied with his request by applying a graduated range of withholding rates between 14 and 30 percent depending upon earnings.

Single persons who can reasonably expect their gross income to exceed $5,000, and married couples or heads of households who can reasonably expect their gross income to exceed $10,000, must file a declaration of estimated tax not later than April 15 of the current tax year. A declaration also must be filed by any person whose gross income reasonably can be expected to include more than $200 of income not subject to withholding. However, no declaration is required if, after the deduction of anticipated withholding and other credits against tax, the estimated tax is less than $40. Payments of estimated tax are made in equal quarterly installments which are due on or before April 15, July 15, September 15, and January 15 for calendar year taxpayers.

During 1964, more than 330 million *information returns* were filed with the Internal Revenue Service.[47] About two thirds of these were statements of wages and salaries paid and taxes withheld by employers, including both the copies attached by employees to their income tax returns and the copies filed by employers. In addition, 114 million information returns regarding payments of dividends and interest were filed during the year.[48] Such wage, salary, dividend, and interest information is extremely important in the efforts to provide rational tax enforcement. Information returns, moreover, can be used with increasing effectiveness as the advanced data processing system of income tax *auditing* is developed further by the IRS. Until recent years the techniques of income tax auditing were primarily clerical, not mechanical. However, the IRS is developing a computer system which will result in the existence of a comprehensive nationwide electronic auditing program for the personal income tax. Present plans call for machine processing of *all* income tax returns filed by April 15, 1967, on 1966 incomes.

A less known though long-established technique of personal income tax enforcement by the federal government is the payment of *rewards to tax informers.* This device was used with the first federal personal income tax during the Civil War and is still in use with the income tax today. During the 1965 fiscal year, awards totaling more than $597,000 were paid by the Internal Revenue Service to tax informers, mostly for income tax enforcement.[49]

Personal income tax collections by the Internal Revenue Service during 1965 totaled nearly $49 billion—an amount which exceeds overall collection costs by a considerable ratio. In conclusion, the federal personal income tax appears to be effectively administered by the Internal Revenue Service in conjunction with the voluntary compliance efforts of the taxpayers. The federal personal income tax clearly passes the revenue productivity test of tax rationality.

Some Special Federal Personal Income Tax Characteristics and Issues[50]

The Size of the Federal Personal Income Tax Base Relative to Personal Income. The concept of personal income, as defined and

[47] *Commissioner of Internal Revenue Annual Report for 1964* (Washington, D.C.: U.S. Government Printing Office, 1964), p. 11.

[48] *Ibid.*

[49] *Ibid.*

[50] Many of these special characteristics and issues apply also to the federal corporation income tax which is discussed in the following chapter. An excellent reference for the discussion which follows is *The Federal Tax System, op. cit.*

measured by the Department of Commerce, displays a sharp divergence in monetary magnitude from the taxable income base of the personal income tax, as measured by the tax collections of the Internal Revenue Service. In recent years, taxable income has constituted less than one half of personal income. In 1961, for example, the Department of Commerce estimated personal income to be $417.4 billion. At the same time, the taxable income reported on tax returns submitted to the IRS by individual taxpayers for that year amounted to $181.6 billion—only 43.5 percent of the personal income total.

Table 11–4 demonstrates those excluded items which constitute the divergence between the two income magnitudes. Conceptual differences in the legal and economic definitions of income (net) amounted to $54.5 billion (in 1961), which is approximately 13 percent of personal income. Another $51.6 billion, or approximately 12 percent of personal income, consisted of income not reported on tax returns (income of persons not required to file returns, income disclosed by audit, income of tax evaders, and so forth) and of adjusted gross income of nontaxable returns (adjusted gross income less deficit, individual returns). The remaining (and the largest) difference between personal and taxable income during 1961 consisted of the deductions and exemptions claimed on the taxable returns of individuals. This amounted to $129.7 billion, part of which were personal exemptions totaling $82.5 billion, itemized deductions of $35.6 billion, and the standard deduction totaling $11.6 billion.

Interestingly, the effective average tax rate on the taxable income of individuals, computed by dividing the total tax liability by the taxable income of individuals (after tax credits), was only 23.2 percent during 1961 at a time when the marginal rate structure of the federal personal income tax was 20–91 percent. In fact, not one American paid the 91 percent marginal rate prevailing in 1963. Obviously, the various items which differentiate personal income from taxable income erode the tax base to a considerable extent. Whether they do so from a rationality standpoint, of course, is another question. The determination of rationality in this regard is an extremely elusive proposition primarily because the definition of taxable income impinges upon the "sacred" value judgment (noneconomic) territory of determining distributive equity.

Though the erosion of the income tax base in the relative terms of the ratio between taxable income and personal income has not recently grown, the erosion has substantially increased in absolute terms as the aggregate economy has grown. The absolute difference between personal income and taxable income was approximately $118.9 billion in 1945 as compared to the $236 billion in 1961. It is argued by opponents of the various conceptual differences that elimination or modification of these *loopholes* to the taxable income base would greatly increase the revenue potential of the income tax. Income tax rates could thus be lowered while

TABLE 11–4

RECONCILIATION OF PERSONAL INCOME WITH TAXABLE INCOME
UNDER THE FEDERAL PERSONAL INCOME TAX, 1961

Item	Amount (Dollars)		
Personal Income	$417.4		
Deduct:			
Transfer payments (except fees and military retirement pay)	32.9		
Other labor income (except pay of military reservists)	10.7		
Imputed interest	11.6		
Imputed rent	7.0		
Nontaxable military pay	2.0		
Income-in-kind[1]	3.2		
All other deductions[2]	7.6		
Total deductions	$ 75.0		
Add:			
Employee contributions for social insurance	9.5		
Net gains from sale of assets[3]	8.3		
All other additions[4]	2.7		
Total additions	$ 20.5	$417.4	
		−54.5	
Personal income adjusted	$362.9	$362.9	
Income not reported on tax returns[5]	33.0		
Adjusted gross income reported on tax returns[6]	$329.9	$362.9	
Adjusted gross income, nontaxable returns[6]	18.6	−51.6	
Adjusted gross income, taxable returns	$311.3	$311.3	
Deduct:			
Standard deduction	11.6		
Itemized deductions	35.6	$311.3	
Personal exemptions	82.5	−129.7	
Taxable income of individuals	$181.6	$181.6	
Taxable income of fiduciaries[7]	1.1		
Total taxable income	$182.7		
	Percent		
Effective tax rate[8]	23.2		

[1] Including food and fuel consumed on farms.

[2] Tax-exempt interest and savings bond accruals, inventory items, excludable dividends and sick pay, undistributed fiduciary income, and income of pension funds and tax-exempt organizations, and so forth.

[3] Net gains and losses on capital and other assets reported on individual and fiduciary returns.

[4] Pensions and annuities, and some miscellaneous reported income.

[5] Income of persons not required to file, income disclosed by audit, income of tax evaders, income of fiduciaries, estimating errors in personal income, sampling errors in Statistics of Income, and so on.

[6] Adjusted gross income less deficit, individual returns.

[7] Estimate based on recent years.

[8] Effective rate on taxable income of individuals, after tax credits.

SOURCE: U.S. Treasury Department, Office of Tax Analysis.

the same revenue could be collected from a broadened tax base. It is estimated that an elimination of about 10 percent of the tax base difference between personal and taxable income in 1962 would allow average personal income tax rates to be reduced by approximately 12 percent.[51]

Pechman suggests a tax simplification plan whereby the prevailing (1966) federal personal income tax rate range of 14–70 percent could be reduced to a range of 7–35 percent.[52] The proposed plan would involve the taxation of income from *all* sources which, of course, would mean the elimination of special treatment for certain types of income such as capital gains, state and local bond interest, and dividends. Meanwhile, deductions would be limited under the plan to such strategic items as large medical expenses, casualty losses, and charitable contributions above 2 percent of income. Other less important deductions, including the standard 10 percent optional deduction, would be removed. The $600 personal exemption, however, would be retained under the proposal.

Proponents of an eroded federal personal income tax base argue that the difference between personal and taxable income is accounted for by items which either cannot be included in taxable income on the basis of practical administration and compliance problems, or which conflict with other basic objectives of public policy. The following paragraph should serve to stimulate thought on the subject.

Others voice the opinion that the progression in the (income) tax rate structure is more apparent than real. They point out that in 1959, among the 1,002 returns listing adjusted gross incomes of $500,000 or more, there were 20 returns on which there was no tax liability and 73 returns with effective tax rates of under 30 percent. Furthermore, adjusted gross income excludes one-half of capital gains. Measuring tax against adjusted gross income augmented by the excluded portion of capital gains, the median effective tax rate on these returns was only 28 percent. Moreover, since these returns were selected on the basis of adjusted gross income, they do not include the returns of some persons with large incomes from tax-exempt interest or with income from mineral production that was offset by depletion deductions. On the basis of these considerations, it is argued, the degree of actual progression in the tax system should be strengthened, not reduced.[53]

In 1962, moreover, only 1,146 individual income tax returns were filed which reported gross incomes of $500,000 or more.[54] Indeed, an eroded personal income tax base can help offset a progressive rate structure.

Family Status and Taxable Income. The family size of the tax-paying unit carries an important impact upon the effective rate of tax

[51] *Ibid.*, p. 33.

[52] "What's Wrong With Our Tax System?" a discussion by Frank Fernbach, Joseph Pechman, and Martin Gainsburgh, *Challenge* (July–August, 1966), p. 17.

[53] *The Federal Tax System, op. cit.*, p. 40.

[54] Treasury Department, Internal Revenue Service, *Individual Income Tax Returns, 1962* (Washington, D.C.: U.S. Government Printing Office, 1965).

progression under the federal personal income tax. The right of married couples to file a joint return along with the ability to add an additional $600 exemption for each child in a family greatly reduces the marginal tax rate bracket of taxable income for the family as opposed to that of the single unmarried individual. Arguments in support of preferential treatment for family status include the assertion that the ability to pay taxes is an inverse function of family size since families with children have increasingly expanded requirements for space, food, health services, and educational services. On the other hand, it can be argued that deductions for family size may encourage the growth of large families and thus create a long-run population problem.

Capital Gains Taxation. Gains accruing on capital assets are taxed under the federal personal income tax only at the time when they are realized through the sale or exchange of the property.[55] Capital gains realized on the sale or exchange of capital assets held less than six months are fully taxable as ordinary income. Special tax treatment is given, however, to gains realized on capital assets held longer than six months. For individuals, the tax liability on the long-term gains is determined by including in adjusted gross income only 50 percent of the excess of net long-term capital gains over net short-term capital losses. The tax is then computed at regular rates on the taxpayer's adjusted gross income. The result of this procedure is that the capital gain is taxed at one half the marginal rate applied to ordinary income. If the alternative tax computation technique would result in a lower tax liability, however, a tax at regular rates may be computed on all income excluding capital gains and this amount increased by 50 percent of those gains taken into account which are 25 percent of the excess of net long-term gains over net short-term losses. In effect, the maximum rate at which long-term capital gains are taxed under these computation techniques is 25 percent.[56] Table 11–5 compares long-term capital gains rates to ordinary rates under the federal personal income tax. The effective 25 percent maximum rate is evident from this table. In addition, the advantage of preferential capital gains treatment to high-income taxpayers is also obvious.

A controversy exists over the rationality of treating capital gains in a differential manner from the treatment of ordinary income. Those who

---

[55] Capital assets are defined by the Internal Revenue Code to include all property held by the taxpayer except certain specified categories such as: (1) stock in trade; (2) property held primarily for sale to customers in the ordinary course of the taxpayer's trade or business; (3) property used in trade or business which is subject to an allowance for depreciation; (4) real property used in trade or business; (5) a copyright, literary, artistic, or musical composition which is the product of the personal efforts of the taxpayer; (6) accounts or notes receivable acquired in the ordinary course of trade or business; and (7) certain government obligations which are sold at a discount.

[56] The corporation income tax also limits, in effect, the tax on net long-term capital gains to 25 percent.

favor preferential treatment for capital gains, even to the point of imposing no tax at all on such gains, use a variety of arguments. Among these
are: (1) an investor may feel "locked in" if his asset or investment has
increased significantly in value. Thus, he may hesitate to sell because of
the existence of a capital gains tax, with a resulting distortion of business
and investment decisions. On the other hand, if capital values fall, many
taxpayers are induced to sell in order to deduct the capital losses. Thus,
distortion occurs in investment decisions concerning the retention of

TABLE 11-5

COMPARISON OF EFFECTIVE RATES OF TAX ON ORDINARY
INCOME AND NET LONG-TERM CAPITAL GAINS,
JOINT RETURN, 1965 TAX RATES

| Taxable Income (Joint Return) | Tax on 1 Additional Dollar of— | | Capital Gains Rate as a Percent of Regular Rate |
	Ordinary Income	Net Long-Term Capital Gains	
	Percent	Percent	
$ 1,000	14.0	7.0	50.0
5,000	19.0	9.5	50.0
10,000	22.0	11.0	50.0
25,000	36.0	18.0	50.0
45,000	50.0	25.0	50.0
101,000	62.0	25.0	40.3
401,000	70.0	25.0	35.7

SOURCE: Joint Economic Committee, Congress of the United States, *The
Federal Tax System: Facts and Problems, 1964* (Washington, D.C.: U.S. Government
Printing Office, 1964).

capital; (2) if the long-term capital gain is taxed in the particular year in
which the gain is realized, a severe burden on the taxpayer may result.
This problem would be avoided if capital gains were not taxed at all, and
it would be reduced if capital gains were taxed yearly on an accrual basis
instead of in one lump sum when they are realized; and (3) a capital
gains tax at lower than ordinary income tax rates encourages the "plow-
ing back" of profits into a corporation with resulting distortion of the
capital market structure in the economy.

Proponents of taxing capital gains income, some of whom advocate
full taxation of such income, offer arguments such as the following: (1)
capital gains at times represent an unearned increment of income in the
sense that such things as an increase in the site value of land, a discovery
of oil, or a rise in bond prices due to changes in the market rate of interest
are gains for which the asset holder is not directly responsible. Hence,
these gains should be taxed at least on an *equal basis* with ordinary wage
and salary income, if not more heavily; (2) the taxation of capital gains

income as ordinary income would close a major tax avoidance loophole, a loophole available primarily to higher bracket taxpayers; and (3) the revenue productivity of the income tax would be increased if capital gains could be fully taxed, thus reducing the stress on certain other federal revenue sources.

Taxation of Income from Natural Resources. Various special provisions for the taxation of income derived from natural resources are provided by the Internal Revenue Code. *Depletion allowances* may be applied to capital sums invested in the development of natural resource properties. For mineral properties, depletion allowances are computed by either a "cost depletion" or a "percentage depletion" method. Under the cost method, which must be used for timber resources, the adjusted basis of the property is divided by the total number of units estimated to remain in the deposit or property (for example, barrels of oil, tons of ore, and board feet of lumber), and the result is multiplied by the number of units sold during the year. When the adjusted basis of the property is lowered to zero, the cost depletion allowance ceases.

Under the percentage depletion method, depletion is computed as a specific percentage of the annual gross income from the property. It cannot, however, exceed 50 percent of the net income from the property. The percentage depletion rates for various minerals are as follows:

1. 27.5 percent for oil and gas.
2. 23 percent for sulfur and uranium and, if mined in the United States, for asbestos, bauxite, cobalt, lead, manganese, mercury, nickel, platinum, thorium, tin, titanium, tungsten, zinc, and 23 other minerals.
3. 15 percent for certain clays, asphalt, vermiculite, and certain metals not covered by (2) above.
4. 10 percent for asbestos (if not covered by [2] above), coal, lignite, salt, and certain other minerals.
5. 5 percent for brick and tile clay, gravel, sand, clam and oyster shells, peat, pumice, sand, scoria, shale, rough stone, and certain brine well products.
6. 15 percent for all other minerals except soil, sod, dirt, turf, water, or mosses or minerals from sea water, the air, or similar inexhaustible resources.[57]

In a recent court decision in the Fifth Court of Appeals, water was allowed as a depletion allowance for a farmer in a regional area of declining water tables, despite vigorous opposition from the Internal Revenue Service.[58]

---

[57] Certain exceptions apply to group 6 above. For example, some of these minerals may be listed in (2) if they are produced in the United States. All of these minerals, moreover, are subject to a "use test," that is, they are restricted to a 5 percent rate, whether produced domestically or not, when they are used for purposes comparable to common sand, gravel, or rough stone.

[58] *United States* v. *Shurbet,* 347 F 2d 103.

The Internal Revenue Code provides special treatment, other than depletion allowances, for certain capital expenditures incurred in bringing mineral properties into production. A taxpayer is allowed, for example, to write off as incurred the costs of *exploring* for mineral deposits (except oil and gas wells which are treated separately) or to set these costs up as deferred expenses to be deducted ratably as the deposit is exhausted. These expenses include expenditures to determine the existence, location, extent, and quality of mineral resources. Deductions for exploration expenditures are limited to $100,000 per year and to a total of $400,000. Another special provision permits a taxpayer either to write off as incurred the costs of *developing* a mineral deposit (except oil and gas wells which are treated separately) or to set these up as deferred expenses to be deducted ratably as the mineral deposit is exhausted. Expenditures for development include the costs of mine shafts, tunnels, and strip mine activities. No dollar limitation is placed upon deductions for development costs.

The statutes also grant a special provision to oil and gas operators by providing an option of either capitalizing or charging as current expenses so-called intangible drilling and development costs of oil and gas wells. These deductible expenses include costs of fuel and power, labor, materials, tool rental, repairs of drilling equipment, and the like. No dollar limit is placed upon these deductions.

Among the other special provisions for taxpayers in the extractive industries is the one which pertains to the recipients of grants from the United States for the encouragement of exploration, development, and mining of minerals or metals which are strategic for national defense. Such grants may be excluded from taxable income. Moreover, special treatment is provided to income arising from certain types of timber-cutting and iron and coal mine operations. A taxpayer owning timber, or the contract right to cut timber for a six-month period prior to the beginning of the taxable year, may elect to treat the proceeds received from cutting the timber as a long-term capital gain. Also, a taxpayer owning timber, coal, or iron ore for a period of six months before its disposal and who retains an economic interest following such a disposal may treat the royalties received as a long-term capital gain.

Taxation of Income from Foreign Sources. A critical problem of equity arises when the same income is subject to tax by more than one nation. In the absence of special provisions, American individuals and corporations could be fully taxed on foreign income by both the federal government and by the government of the foreign nation in which the income is earned. The Internal Revenue Code, however, in conjunction with some 21 tax treaties or conventions between the United States and foreign nations does provide special tax treatment for income earned from foreign sources. The Code directly determines, for the taxpayer's return filed with the Internal Revenue Service, what income is to be taxed, when it is to be taxed, and what credits or deductions are to be given for foreign taxes paid. Tax treaties or conventions also influence the manner in which the foreign nations tax residents of the United States as well as the manner in which the United States taxes foreign residents who derive income from economic activity in the United States.

At present (1966), the federal government is expanding and revising its network of income tax treaties with foreign nations. The primary motivation behind this effort is to improve the flow of international investment and trade. One specific goal is to obtain standard tax treatment for American investors overseas and for foreign investors in the United States. Moreover, an additional goal of the treaties in underdeveloped nations is to encourage additional American investment by allowing the same 7 percent investment credit for overseas investment that was available until recently for domestic investment in capital equipment.

STATE AND LOCAL PERSONAL INCOME TAXES IN THE UNITED STATES[59]

History of State and Local Personal Income Taxes

At the beginning of the 20th century, some states still carried statutes providing for personal income taxes which had been enacted during and after the Civil War. These flat-rate (proportional) taxes, which were administered by local property tax officials, were quite ineffective as revenue producers and can scarcely be considered the legitimate forerunners of the present state personal income taxes. The "new era" of personal income taxation at the state and local levels was initiated in 1911 when Wisconsin adopted a well-planned state personal income tax which was centrally administered by a State Tax Commission. The Wisconsin tax, moreover, provided progressive rates and personal exemptions.

The success of the Wisconsin tax led to the early adoption of similar personal income taxes by several other states. By 1920, nine states (plus the Territory of Hawaii) levied such taxes. During the 1920's five additional states adopted personal income taxes. The depression of the 1930's provided strong impetus for additional state adoptions of personal income tax laws and 16 states established such taxes between 1931 and 1937. Since 1937, the only states to adopt the tax were Alaska (then a

[59] For an excellent description of municipal income taxes in the United States, see The Advisory Commission on Intergovernmental Relations, *Tax Overlapping in the United States—1964* (Washington, D.C.: U.S. Government Printing Office, 1964).

Territory), West Virginia, New Jersey (on a very specialized basis), and Indiana. In addition, the District of Columbia adopted a personal income tax in 1939. Table 11–6 summarizes the pattern of adoptions of personal income taxes by the states during the 20th century.

Present Status of State and Local Personal Income Taxes

Personal income taxes are imposed by 36 states and the District of Columbia at the present time. This total includes the New Hampshire and Tennessee taxes which apply only to dividend and interest income, the New Jersey tax which applies in effect only to New York residents

TABLE 11–6

YEARS OF ADOPTIONS OF STATE PERSONAL INCOME TAXES

Before 1911	1911–20	1921–30	1931–40	Since 1940
Hawaii, 1901	Wisconsin 1911	North Carolina, 1921	Idaho, 1931	Alaska, 1949
Total, 1	Mississippi, 1912	South Carolina, 1922	Tennessee, 1931*	New Jersey, 1961†
	Oklahoma, 1915	New Hampshire, 1923*	Utah, 1931	West Virginia, 1961
	Massachusetts, 1916	Arkansas, 1929	Vermont, 1931	Indiana, 1963
	Virginia, 1916	Georgia, 1929	Alabama, 1933	Total, 4
	Delaware, 1917	Oregon, 1930	Arizona, 1933	
	Missouri, 1917	Total, 6	Kansas, 1933	
	New York, 1919		Minnesota, 1933	
	North Dakota, 1919		Montana, 1933	
	Total, 9		New Mexico, 1933	
			Iowa, 1934	
			Louisiana, 1934	
			California, 1935	
			Kentucky, 1936	
			Colorado, 1937	
			Maryland, 1937	
			Total, 16	GRAND TOTAL, 36

* Income from stocks and bonds only, namely, dividend and interest income.
† In effect, applies only to New York residents who derive income from New Jersey sources.

SOURCE: The Advisory Commission on Intergovernmental Relations, *Tax Overlapping in the United States—1964* (Washington, D.C.: U.S. Government Printing Office, 1964), p. 22.

earning incomes in New Jersey, and the Indiana flat-rate net income tax. Meanwhile, the personal income tax is used by cities and other local units of government in seven states. For the most part, the local income tax is a post–World War II phenomenon, though the city of Philadelphia had initiated the trend in 1939. Despite the increasing use of the personal income tax by state and local governments in the United States, the tax remains primarily a source of federal government revenue. Almost 94 percent of the $48.6 billion collected from personal income taxes in Fiscal 1962 accrued to the federal government.[60] State governments collected $2.7 billion, or 5.6 percent, and local governments collected $308 million, about one half of 1 percent, of the remaining personal income tax revenues in that year.[61] More than one third of the total U.S. population is not subject to a state income tax. Such heavily populated industrial states as

[60] *Ibid.*, p. 113.
[61] *Ibid.*

Connecticut, Illinois, Michigan, New Jersey, Ohio, and Pennsylvania do not impose the tax.

In recent decades, state personal income taxes have increased in revenue importance more rapidly than any other major state tax source. Several reasons for this growth in relative importance may be noted. First, aggregate personal income doubled between 1951 and 1963, thus greatly expanding the potential income tax base. Closely related to the growth of aggregate personal income is the significant upward shift of lower income population on the income scale. In addition, rates have been increased and exemptions lowered by a number of states. Moreover, the enforcement of state personal income taxes has been enhanced both by the introduction of withholding at the source and by the exchange of tax records with the federal government.

The present rate structures of the state personal income taxes generally provide for a moderate degree of progression. For the hypothetical median state, the effective rate at a taxable income level of $25,000 is nearly six times as great as the effective rate at the $5,000 taxable income level, though at higher income levels the state taxes tend to become regressive due to the deductibility of the federal personal income tax. At the $5,000 taxable income level, effective rates range from zero in two states to 1.9 percent in one state, and at the $25,000 taxable income level the effective rate range is between 0.8 percent and 5.5 percent. In addition to rate structures, the patterns of deductions and exemptions also determine the "effective" degree of progressivity. States using the personal income tax rely upon it for revenue to varying degrees. In 1963, when 13.4 percent of all state tax revenues were derived from personal income taxes, five states received less than 5 percent of their tax revenues from this source while eleven states received more than 25 percent of their tax revenues from the tax.

Most state personal income taxes resemble the federal personal income tax, but differ in structural details, particularly those involving rate levels and exemptions. Similar to the federal tax, all state taxes except the Tennessee tax on dividends and interest allow personal exemptions. The exemptions are ordinarily allowed as a deduction from income, though five states provide the exemptions as a tax credit. The state of New York supplements its personal exemption with a tax credit.

There is a trend toward the adoption of the federal personal income tax base for the state personal income taxes. This is advantageous from the standpoint of assisting voluntary taxpayer compliance in paying the tax. It also facilitates federal-state administrative cooperation for enforcement purposes. Fourteen states now utilize the federal tax base.[62]

---

[62] These states are: Alaska, Hawaii, Idaho, Indiana, Iowa, Kentucky, Minnesota, Montana, New Jersey, New Mexico, New York, North Dakota, Vermont, and West Virginia.

Moreover, those states which do not define adjusted gross income in the same manner as the federal tax often provide specific provisions which are identical or similar to the federal tax. These provisions include those for capital gains and losses, depreciation, depletion, deductions for charitable contributions, deductions for medical expenses, and deductions for interest. Alaska assesses the state personal income tax liabilities of its residents as stipulated percentages of their federal tax liabilities.

The federal personal income tax allows the payment of state income taxes as a deduction against the federal personal income tax liability. About one half of the states using the personal income tax, moreover, allow personal income taxes paid to the federal government to be deducted in computing state tax liabilities. It should be noted that deduction of the federal personal income tax from state personal income tax liabilities tends to reduce the effective rate progressivity of the state taxes. Such influence may be offset, however, by an appropriate structure of rates and exemptions.

A significant problem in the administration of state and local income taxes involves the inherent conflict between taxation of income on the basis of the residence or domicile of the taxpayer versus taxation on the basis of the site or place where the income is earned. No completely satisfactory solution to this issue has been developed and, in fact, the problem worsens as the mobility of individuals becomes greater through improved transportation. This problem tends to be particularly acute in large metropolitan areas where the majority of income may be earned in the central city, but the majority of middle to higher income taxpayers may live in the suburbs.[63]

Local government personal income taxes, as noted above, are used in seven states and recent legislation has paved the way for use of the tax at the local level in an eighth state—Maryland. The states where local income taxes are now used are Alabama, Kentucky, Michigan, Missouri, Ohio, Pennsylvania, and New York. In addition, Washington, D.C., levies a personal income tax. They are used extensively in only two states— Ohio and Pennsylvania. Eleven of the 43 largest cities in the nation with populations above 300,000 use personal income taxes.[64] Moreover, 29 additional cities with populations in excess of 50,000 levy personal income taxes. Eleven of these cities are in Ohio and nine are in Pennsylvania. Michigan, Ohio, and Pennsylvania, though allowing local personal income taxes, do not apply overlapping state income taxes. The local taxes in Kentucky, in Gadsden, Alabama, and in St. Louis and Kansas

---

[63] This issue will be discussed in Chapter 22 on "Urban and Regional Economic Problems."

[64] These cities are: Cincinnati, Columbus, Detroit, Kansas City, Louisville, New York, Philadelphia, Pittsburgh, St. Louis, Toledo, and Washington, D.C. Source: *Tax Overlapping . . . op. cit.*, p. 134.

City, Missouri, however, all result in the payment of *three* personal income taxes at these locations, namely, federal, state, and local personal income taxes.

Local personal income taxes tend to be imposed at low, flat (proportionate) rates. The highest rate, 2 percent, is imposed by Gadsden, Alabama, Newport, Kentucky, and New York City. The local personal income taxes are usually levied on the gross earnings of individuals and the net profits of professions and unincorporated businesses. Corporation net profits are also taxed by Ohio cities, some Kentucky cities, Kansas City and St. Louis, Missouri, and Detroit, Flint, and Hamtramck, Michigan. Income from wages and salaries is generally taxed on a gross basis, without exemptions or deductions, and with the full amount of the tax withheld by the employer. Dividends, interest, rents, and capital gains received by individuals are usually exempt from the tax. Five states—Maryland, New Hampshire, South Carolina, Tennessee, and Wisconsin—share their personal income tax collections directly with local governments. The increased usage of local personal income taxes represents a distinct trend. While in 1955 only 370 local units of government used the tax, the number imposing it in 1965 had grown sharply to 1,909 localities.

CORPORATION INCOME

TAX

HISTORY OF THE FEDERAL CORPORATION INCOME TAX

A federal corporation "excise tax" was levied on the net income of corporations in 1909. However, this was in essence an "income tax" since net income was used as the indicator of the tax base. Finally, legislation in 1913 recognized the tax as an income tax by passing a new corporation income tax law which eliminated the hypocrisy of calling the tax an excise. The 1913 legislation also eliminated the $5,000 exemption which had previously existed but maintained the 1 percent proportionate rate. The rate was increased to 12 percent in 1918, however, and varied between 10 and 13.5 percent during the 1920's. Progressive rates were introduced in 1936, ranging from 8 to 15 percent, and a supplemental surtax ranging from 7 to 27 percent was placed on undistributed profits. The undistributed profits surtax was repealed two years later (in 1938).

Effective federal corporation income tax rates ranged from 25 to 40 percent throughout most of World War II. These were supplemented by an excess profits tax between 1943–45, which brought the maximum combined tax rate on corporate income to 80 percent. Effective tax rates ranged from 21 to 38 percent during the years 1946–49. In 1950, the system of progressive rates for corporations with taxable incomes under $25,000 was replaced by both a single normal tax rate, which was applicable to the full amount of taxable income, and a surtax which was applicable to taxable income in excess of a specific $25,000 surtax exemption. The Korean War caused both the normal and surtax rates to be increased and an excess profits tax to be levied. Hence, the combined corporation income tax rate reached a ceiling of 70 percent during the Korean War. The excess profits tax was allowed to expire at the end of the war. Between 1952 and 1963, the normal tax rate was 30 percent and the surtax rate was 22 percent, for a combined rate of 52 percent on taxable corporation income in excess of $25,000. The present rate structure, described later in the chapter, resulted from the Revenue Act of 1964 which reduced the maximum combined rate to 48 (47.99) percent.

PRESENT STATUS OF THE FEDERAL CORPORATION INCOME TAX

The Federal Corporation Income Tax Base

Taxable corporation income is computed by deducting from gross income the expenses which are incurred in creating that income.[1] Such expenses must be "ordinary and necessary" to the operation of a trade or business. Among the deductible expenses are wages and salaries, remuneration of executives, rents, royalties, material costs, bad debts, casualty losses, taxes, advertising expenses, interest payments, and the depreciated cost of fixed capital for the year in question. Dividends paid to stockholders are *not* deductible as expenses, except in certain cases involving the preferred stock dividends of public utility companies. Thus, in effect, the tax base of the federal corporation income tax consists of the return to equity capital.

In addition to these deductible expenses, certain other expenses are deductible, though subject to rather stringent qualifications. Among these are contributions to charity, contributions to profit-sharing plans and pension funds, and entertainment expenses. The federal corporation income tax base is influenced, moreover, by several special provisions which are applicable to certain types of corporations and to certain types of income and expenditures. In most instances, the special provisions for certain types of income and expenditures apply under the federal income tax structure to both corporate and noncorporate businesses.

Certain corporations are exempt from the corporation income tax on the basis of qualification as nonprofit companies.[2] These include such companies as those organized for charitable, religious, scientific, literary, and educational purposes. No part of the net profits of these corporations may be applied, however, to the benefit of any individual, nor can the organization substantially engage in propaganda or participate in political activity. Additional exemptions are provided for labor and agricultural organizations, business leagues and chambers of commerce, credit unions, recreational clubs, fraternal organizations and, under certain circumstances, small mutual life insurance companies and farmers' producer cooperatives.

Insurance companies have historically received preferential treatment under the federal corporation income tax structure, though recent

[1] For a good discussion of the structure of the federal corporation income tax, see Joint Economic Committee, Congress of the United States, *The Federal Tax System: Facts and Problems—1964* (Washington, D.C.: U.S. Government Printing Office, 1964).

[2] Within recent years partial taxation of the profit-making business operations of otherwise tax-exempt organizations has been provided—when the profit-making operations do not relate substantially to the basic purpose of the organization.

years have witnessed a significant reduction in these advantages. The first of these important modifications occurred under the Life Insurance Company Income Tax Act of 1959. Prior to this act, life insurance companies were taxed on only a portion of their net investment income. The 1959 legislation, however, provided for taxing one half of underwriting income when earned and the other half when distributed, and also provided for the taxation of investment income under a new formula which measures the taxable margin of investment earnings on an individual company basis. Furthermore, capital gains of these companies are now taxed.

Additional modifications in the taxation of insurance companies under the corporation income tax were provided by the Revenue Act of 1962. The changes at this time concentrated upon mutual fire and casualty insurance companies. These companies were required by the legislation to be taxed at regular corporation income tax rates on their underwriting income as well as on their investment income, with provision for deducting certain additions to a "protection against losses" account. Smaller mutual fire and casualty insurance companies with total annual receipts under $150,000, however, are tax exempt while those with receipts between $150,000 and $500,000 are taxed only on their investment income. Insurance companies other than life or mutual companies are taxed at regular corporation income tax rates, but their taxable income is computed under special rules.

Other special considerations include those of mutual and cooperative savings banks, mutual building and loan associations, cooperatives, and regulated investment companies. Mutual and cooperative savings banks and mutual building and loan associations are allowed to deduct amounts paid or credited to the accounts of their depositors. Prior to 1962, these institutions virtually escaped the federal corporation income tax because they also were allowed to deduct additions to bad-debt reserves as long as the total of these reserves did not exceed 12 percent of the amount of total reserves plus surplus and undivided profits. Legislation in 1962, however, restricted such deductions for additions to bad-debt reserves. Cooperatives are provided special treatment since they may deduct dividends allocated to patrons if at least 20 percent of the face value of the dividends is paid in cash. Patrons are taxed on these distributed dividends and the cooperatives are taxed on the undistributed income. Regulated investment companies, under certain conditions, are taxed only on their undistributed profits.

Among the exclusions and special deductions allowed on the federal corporation income tax base is the right to deduct from the gross income of the corporation 85 percent of the dividends received from a domestic corporation if the total deduction does not exceed 85 percent of the taxable income computed without regard to the deduction. Moreover, under certain conditions complete exemption is allowed for dividends received from another member of an affiliated group of corporations and for dividends received by a small business investment company. Other special treatments include those which apply to the income derived by a corporation from foreign sources, the interest received on debt issues of state and local governments, and the capital costs of extractive industries.

Federal Corporation Income Tax Rate Structure

At the present time (1967), the basic rate structure of the federal corporation income tax consists of a normal tax on the full amount of taxable income and a surtax on the amount of taxable income above a $25,000 surtax exemption. The normal rate on the first $25,000 of taxable corporate income is 22 percent and the surtax rate is 25.99 percent. Hence, the rate range of the federal corporation income tax, combining both the normal and surtax rates, is 22 percent to 47.99 percent. The Revenue Act of 1964 provided this rate structure, which is somewhat lower than the rate range of 30 percent to 52 percent in effect from 1954–63. The present rate structure was reached by means of a two-step transition, the 1964 rates being lower than the 1954–63 rates, but higher than the present rates.

Long-term capital gains realized by corporations on property not considered part of normal operations are taxed at the rate of 25 percent. These gains arise from the sale or exchange of capital assets held for more than six months. Capital gains tax treatment is extended also to special types of income, not otherwise defined as gains, arising from the sale of capital assets. Included here (subject to limitations) are profits from the sale of depreciable and real property, profits from the sale of certain draft, breeding, or dairy livestock, coal and iron ore royalties, income from timber cutting operations, and profits from the sale of unharvested crops on land sold or exchanged. Net losses realized from these sources of income may be deducted in full against other sources of taxable income.

The effective rate structure of the federal corporation income tax is also affected by tax credits. As noted in the previous chapter, the Revenue Act of 1962 provides a credit against income tax liability for expenditures on depreciable machinery and equipment used in a trade or business within the United States. [Recent legislation (late 1966) substantially reduced the magnitude of the "investment credit."] The credit is equal to 7 percent of qualified investment, except for public utilities, for which, with certain limitations it is 3 percent.[3] Differential treatment is also available to small corporations, which may elect *not* to pay a corporation income tax if all stockholders consent to the taxation of the income of the corporation at the stockholder level under the personal income tax. The

---

[3] This subject will be discussed in greater detail in connection with the fiscal policy analysis of Chapter 18.

qualifications for such tax treatment are rigorous, however, and many small corporations are excluded from the option.[4]

The Internal Revenue Code provides special provisions to inhibit the use of the federal corporation income tax by high-bracket taxpayers to avoid the higher marginal rates of the federal personal income tax. A corporation which accumulates earnings in excess of the "reasonably anticipated" needs of the business, for example, may legally be required to pay a penalty tax on the excess in addition to the regular corporation income tax. The burden of proof regarding "improper accumulations" generally falls upon the Internal Revenue Service. Another special provision provides a tax at the rate of 70 percent on the undistributed income of companies defined by the law as personal holding companies.[5]

FISCAL RATIONALITY CRITERIA APPLIED TO THE FEDERAL CORPORATION INCOME TAX

The General Fiscal Rationality Criterion

The federal corporation income tax will now be analyzed with reference to the general fiscal rationality and revenue productivity criteria which were applied to the federal personal income tax in the preceding chapter. The general efficiency effects will be approached from the dual standpoints of both *aggregative* and *disaggregative* analysis. The former approach will consider the influence of the federal corporation income tax upon overall investment incentives and upon capital availability in the national economy while the latter will consider the impact upon such allocative decisions as internal versus external financing and equity versus debt financing.

The Corporation Income Tax and Aggregate Nonneutral Effects.
1. *Effect of the Corporation Income Tax on Investment Incentives.* It is often asserted that the corporation income tax has a negative or retarding effect on *aggregate* investment expenditures in the economy. Indeed, an unshifted corporation income tax does reduce net after-tax

---

[4] To qualify for this choice, a corporation must be a domestic corporation with no more than 10 shareholders, each of whom must be an individual or an estate, and no one of whom may be a nonresident alien. In addition, the corporation must have only one class of stock and it may not be a member of an affiliated group of companies eligible to file a consolidated tax return. Furthermore, the corporation must not receive more than 80 percent of its gross receipts from sources outside the United States nor may it receive more than 20 percent of its gross receipts from rents, royalties, dividends, interest, annuities, and gains from the sale or exchange of stocks and securities.

[5] In general, a corporation is considered to be a personal holding company if it is controlled by not more than 5 individuals, and if its personal holding company income (such as dividends, interest, royalties reduced for depletion deductions, rents reduced by depreciation, taxes, and interest) constitutes up to 60 percent or more of its gross income reduced by the amount of deductions for depreciation, depletion, interest, and taxes.

profits on new investments, which would tend to reduce investment incentives. Moreover, such profit reduction would occur whether the investments were for the expansion of present capacity or for the replacement of existing facilities. Yet, there exist certain important forces which tend to reduce or neutralize the retardation effect of the corporation income tax on business investment.[6] The corporation income tax, for example, is *not* the only tax which corporations must pay. Since other taxes thus require consideration when investment decisions are made, the relative impact of the corporation income tax on investment decisions is lessened. Furthermore, the assumption that the corporation income tax is not shifted is a dubious one, especially if one assumes "nonshiftability" in the sense that not even partial shifting of the tax occurs.[7]

Still other forces may help to neutralize the retarding effect on aggregate investment resulting from the corporation income tax.[8] These forces are (1) the inelasticity, in many instances, of investment demand, (2) the fact that many businesses use a rate of return "before taxes" as an earnings goal, (3) the fact that many businesses look to the loss potential as well as to the rate of return from an investment—and a high tax reduces the risk of loss through income offsets, (4) the fact that businesses, particularly modern corporations, may have other goals in addition to the earnings goal, and (5) the fact that the volume of investment is determined, in many instances, by bottleneck factors such as management size and the availability of internal funds.

No definitive conclusions can be reached regarding the retardation of aggregate investment incentives by the corporation income tax. The variables mentioned above, and many others, will help to determine the result in any one case. Yet, the weighting or importance of the various parameters is difficult to measure. In addition, the parameters may be expected to change over time. Thus, only generalizations and not specific conclusions can be rendered. Among these generalizations are the observation that a shiftable corporation income tax is less likely to reduce aggregate investment incentives than is one which cannot be shifted. In addition, investment incentives are less likely to be harmed by a corpora-

[6] Gerhard Colm, "The Corporation and the Corporate Income Tax," *American Economic Review* (May, 1954), pp. 486–503.

[7] See Chapter 10 for a detailed discussion of tax shifting criteria as they may apply to the corporation income tax. Economic literature provides a variety of analyses on this controversial subject. Among recent studies, Krzyzaniak and Musgrave (Marian Krzyzaniak and Richard A. Musgrave, *The Shifting of the Corporation Income Tax* [Baltimore: Johns Hopkins Press, 1963]) conclude that substantial shifting of the corporation income tax does take place while Harberger (Arnold C. Harberger, "The Incidence of the Corporation Income Tax," *Journal of Political Economy* [June, 1962], pp. 215–40) concludes that very little shifting occurs.

[8] John Lintner, "Effect of Corporate Taxation on Real Investment," *American Economic Review* (May, 1954), pp. 520–34.

tion income tax when the economy is prosperous and earnings potentials are high than in a depressed economy. When the demands for their products are high, stronger motivation exists for businesses to modernize equipment and to expand output. This is supplemented, in turn, by the fact that high personal income tax rates, combined with a low rate on capital gains, encourages the retention and subsequent reinvestment of earnings by corporations.

2. *Accelerated Depreciation and the Encouragement of Investment.* In recent decades, *accelerated depreciation* allowances have been used as a fiscal device, in part to offset the general investment retardation effects of the corporation income tax discussed above, and in part to encourage business investment in a direct manner.[9] An accelerated depreciation allowance refers to a tax write-off for the wearing out of a capital asset over a shorter period of time than the actual physical wearing out of the asset. To the extent that normal depreciation allowances delay and sometimes prevent the full recovery of capital from the earnings of a new asset, accelerated depreciation will be effective in reducing the discouragement of investment.[10] The more rapid recovery of capital, made possible by accelerated depreciation, offers an interest (time-discount) gain to investors and permits growing firms to finance more of their capital requirements from retained earnings. Moreover, it reduces risk and uncertainty.

Goode argues that the introduction of accelerated depreciation stimulates investment primarily by lowering a tax obstacle rather than by creating new incentives.[11] Hence, the potential significance of accelerated depreciation would depend upon the severity of the obstacles presented by the income tax under normal depreciation methods. At this point the attitude of the investor is an important variable. Accelerated depreciation will significantly influence those investors who apply a fairly heavy, though not excessive, discount for interest and risk and who adopt a payoff period considerably shorter than the normal useful life of the asset, but still long enough to permit recovery of a substantial fraction of the investment outlay during the payoff period by means of accelerated depreciation.[12]

The stabilization effects of accelerated depreciation may not be as satisfactory as the allocation and economic growth effects discussed above. It is argued, for example, that accelerated depreciation is very likely to intensify economic fluctuations, that is, widen the range of the

[9] See the discussion in Chapter 18 regarding the nature of accelerated depreciation as well as the use of this device as a fiscal policy tool.

[10] Richard Goode, "Accelerated Depreciation Allowances as a Stimulus to Investment," *Quarterly Journal of Economics,* Vol. LXIX, No. 2 (May, 1955), pp. 191–220.

[11] *Ibid.*

[12] *Ibid.*

business cycle between peak and trough.[13] Moreover, it is likely to extend it in duration.[14] These results will tend to follow because the allowance will encourage investment when profits are high and when tax relief is important while, in the absence of profits during depression, it will become ineffective or, even worse, it may make it worthwhile to postpone investment until profits reappear and advantage can be taken of larger allowances. Furthermore, the heavy amortization of investment during prosperity leaves little depreciation to charge during a depression. Taxable profits will thus be understated in the first instance (prosperity) and overstated in the second instance (depression), with parallel undesirable movements in the magnitude of tax liabilities.[15]

Accelerated depreciation may also be criticized in the sense of its "single tax" characteristic. Thus, it is argued that to be effective it must be introduced only once and tax rates must not be raised in the future.[16] If legislative behavior causes investors to expect that permissible rates of depreciation will increase in the future, for example, investors effectively receive an "announcement" that the capital values of assets acquired at the present time will decline in the future. Such knowledge would tend to discourage investment by distorting its "time dimension."[17]

The above analysis suggests that the accelerated depreciation technique provides "mixed" economic results, some providing *positive* and others *negative* nonneutrality. On balance, however, accelerated depreciation appears advantageous in terms of its allocation and economic growth effects, though somewhat negative in terms of stabilization. Thus, a distortion cost is paid in terms of intergoal nonneutrality in order to achieve positive results in the allocation and economic growth areas.

3. *Other Devices for the Encouragement of Investment.* Accelerated depreciation, of course, is only one of several alternative policies for the inducement of investment. Tax rate reduction, tax credit, and interest rate reduction are among the other alternatives. The comparative influence of accelerated depreciation, the tax credit, and an interest rate reduction upon the present value of a prospective investment is analyzed by Brown.[18] Each of these devices tends to increase the present value of an investment, but they involve substantially different secondary effects from one another.[19] The accelerated depreciation method appears

[13] Evsey D. Domar, "The Case for Accelerated Depreciation," *Quarterly Journal of Economics* (November, 1953), pp. 493–519.

[14] *Ibid.*

[15] *Ibid.*

[16] J. A. Stockfisch, "Investment Incentive, Taxation, and Accelerated Depreciation," *Southern Economic Journal* (July, 1957), pp. 28–40.

[17] *Ibid.*

[18] See E. Cary Brown, "Tax Incentives for Investment," *American Economic Review* (May, 1962), pp. 335–44.

[19] *Ibid.*

to have a substantial revenue disadvantage since the achievement of a given increase in present value requires a large reduction in government revenues—a reduction much greater than that under the tax credit. In addition, the accelerated depreciation method has the characteristic that, after large transitional revenue losses have been sustained, a particular firm will receive no extra reduction in income tax unless its current investment exceeds normal depreciation.[20] On the other hand, the investment credit draws no distinction between firms which are growing and those which are stable except to the extent that a larger tax reduction arises under conditions of growth than under stable conditions. If outlays were to fall below some kind of past average, a tax credit nevertheless would be given on these outlays.

The accelerated depreciation technique has the advantage of being more selective than the alternatives of tax rate reduction and lower interest rates, since the benefits are restricted to those who acquire new depreciable assets. In addition, it offers a greater stimulus to investment than does a general reduction in tax rates and is less likely to stimulate varieties of investment which the federal government does not wish to promote.[21]

The Corporation Income Tax and Disaggregate Nonneutral Effects. 1. *The Corporation Income Tax and Horizontal Equity.* Next, the *disaggregate* nonneutral effects of the corporation income tax will be considered. The first disaggregative consideration relates to the concept of horizontal equity.[22] This concept stipulates that "equals should be treated equally" in the payment of taxes. It is implied, of course, that only individuals, *not* legal corporate business entities, can bear tax burdens. Nevertheless, a tax on business income should be designed to treat different firms equally in the payment of taxes.[23] The "business case," however, is a matter of allocation efficiency rather than a matter of distributive equity in the sense of horizontal tax equity between individuals.[24] Since businesses are owned by individuals, business income should be taxed to the owners if horizontal distributive equity is to be achieved. Retained earnings, however, pose a problem and, if the corporation income tax were to be eliminated, a way would have to be found to tax such earnings as if they were distributed. In any event, the corporation income tax cannot be accepted as a rationale for horizontal equity in distribution, though the tax may be quite acceptable on other grounds.

2. *Effect of the Corporation Income Tax on Consumption.* The effects of income taxes on consumption differ, depending upon whether

---

[20] *Ibid.*

[21] Goode, *op. cit.*

[22] The horizontal equity concept was developed in Chapter 5.

[23] Richard A. Musgrave, *The Theory of Public Finance* (New York: McGraw-Hill Book Co., Inc., 1959), p. 173.

[24] *Ibid.*

the tax is a personal or a corporation income tax.[25] In the case of the unshifted corporation income tax, a change in the tax rate or base may be reflected in either a change in retained earnings or a change in dividends. If retained earnings are affected, personal income and personal consumption expenditures will be unchanged. Thus, *substitution* of a corporation income tax for a personal income tax would increase consumption while the reverse, substitution of a personal income tax for a corporation income tax, would decrease consumption. The distinction between a tax on personal income and a tax on business income is less severe if the business tax is on the profits of unincorporated firms, since there is a close relationship in unincorporated businesses between personal income and business income. Nevertheless, the same general principles apply whether the tax is a corporate or a noncorporate business income tax.

3. *Effect of the Corporation Income Tax on Alternative Investment Decisions.* The discussion in the preceding section refers to consumer demand effects, but the effects on investment demand are also relevant.[26] In the case of a general tax on investment income, the problem focuses *first* upon the manner in which the income tax affects the investor's choice between holding cash and investing and, relatedly, between investing at various degrees of risk; *second,* if the tax applies differentially to earnings in different types of industries, the problem involves further allocation distortion involving the transfer of capital from discriminated to favored industries. This twofold problem needs to be viewed both from the standpoint of the *financial investor* and from the standpoint of the *firm buying real capital.*

In the case of the financial investor, a proportional income tax with perfect loss offset will not reduce and may increase the total level of risk taking in the economy. The same tax, with less than perfect offset, will reduce the level of risk taking. Moreover, a progressive income tax, even with full offset, will reduce the amount of risk taking. Obviously, the lower the level of risk taking, the greater the holding of cash and the smaller the volume of financial investment.

Regarding a firm buying real capital, the avoidance of allocation distortion between "discriminated" and "favored" industries and the subsequent achievement of neutrality between investments requires a proper combination of the particular statutory tax rate and the particular depreciation period which will provide the same effective income tax rate for all investments. Assuming real investments with equal yields, short investments are discriminated against if there is no depreciation allowance. If straight-line depreciation is permitted, short investments are still discriminated against, but to a lesser degree. Discrimination against short investments is increased under the declining balance method and is increased, to an even greater extent, under the sum-of-the-years digit

25 *Ibid.,* pp. 173–74, and chap. 12.
26 *Ibid.,* chap. 14.

method. Yet, the degree of discrimination is slight under the annuity method of depreciation. Assuming real investments with different yields, low-yield investments are discriminated against if depreciation charges are not allowed. Moreover, discrimination is reduced by the straight-line method. As the length of the investment is reduced, however, the pattern is changed and low-yield investments enjoy the benefit of a smaller effective tax rate. In any case, the shorter the depreciation period, the greater the benefit to the owner of the depreciable asset.

4. *The Corporation Income Tax and Inefficiency in Corporate Management.* Another efficiency effect of the federal corporation income tax, definable in terms of both allocative and technical efficiency, is the influence of the tax upon inefficiency or waste in corporate management. Colm observes that there are certain facts which suggest that a corporation income tax with high marginal rates invites extravagance in business management.[27] This waste may occur in the form of compensation to executives which is charged as business expenses to the corporation but which are not taxed as the income of the executives. Moreover, liberal spending by business for advertising, for participation in good will campaigns, and for investment in the beautification of factories may be partially explained by the high marginal rates of the federal corporation income tax.

5. *The Corporation Income Tax and Industrial Location.* An additional allocative effect of the corporation income tax may be found on the state and local level in the sense of the redistribution of industrial location. Industries tend to move, for example, from areas which have high state and/or local corporation income taxes to areas which either do not have corporation income taxes or which impose them at low tax rate or narrow tax base levels. Admittedly, many other factors such as comparative labor costs and comparative property taxes also influence industrial location, but comparative differences in the corporation income tax between states and localities still must be included as a pertinent consideration.

6. *The Corporation Income Tax and the Preferential Treatment of Certain Types of Business and Sources of Income.* As suggested earlier in the chapter, one of the most critical areas of allocation distortion resulting from the federal corporation income tax exists in the preferential treatment given to certain types of businesses and to certain sources of income. A study by Guthman in 1951 demonstrates the ability of the corporation income tax, as it was then structured, to affect resource allocation in a significant manner.[28] In particular, this study concentrated upon exemption from the federal corporation income tax as a factor which gives certain kinds of businesses competitive advantage over other

---

[27] Colm, *op. cit.*, pp. 497–98.

[28] Harry G. Guthman, "Competition from Tax-Exempt Business," *Journal of Finance* (June, 1951), pp. 161–77.

business units subject to the tax. Two types of tax-exempt business are analyzed, namely, the cooperative and the government-owned utility.

It is concluded that the exemption of the net income of cooperatives encouraged the economically unwarranted growth of these institutions. For example, 1949 data indicate that an exempt cooperative in the retail grocery field could charge its customers 1.2 percent less than a competing business corporation and make the same profits for its stockholders because of exemption from the federal corporation income tax.[29] Furthermore, it was observed that prices in the farm implements field could be 8.6 percent less, in the oil business 3.3 percent less, and in the electric utility 6.3 percent less than for comparable businesses *not* exempt from the federal corporation income tax as it was then structured.[30] In addition, cooperatives, by escaping the corporation income tax, could reinvest the tax savings for growth.[31] Moreover, since patronage dividends were treated as refunds on sales and were taxed neither to the corporation nor to the received, a strong incentive was created to pay patronage dividends instead of regular stock dividends. While the disparity in tax rates has now been narrowed, the essence of the argument remains intact.

In the case of government-owned utility operations, a local government owning its own utility escapes the federal corporation income tax. In 1948, this resulted in the fact that consumers using private power from a company subject to the federal corporation income tax were paying an additional 7 percent which municipal power companies saved.[32] Also, many municipal utilities purchase power from federal hydroelectric sources which themselves enjoy a special tax position, including the sale of tax-exempt bonds for capital.

Thus, exemptions from the federal corporation income tax appear to have contributed to nonneutrality by encouraging the growth of farm cooperatives and government-owned utilities. The differential rates of taxation applied to various types of corporations, however, are equally important in their nonneutrality influence. Commercial banks, for example, have traditionally been taxed at a higher rate than either savings and loan or life insurance companies though some reduction of this differential has taken place in recent years. A professional investment survey stated recently (1965) that its studies indicate "the maximum federal income tax rate for these companies (savings and loan) is likely to be 19.2 percent, still far below the 48 percent levy on the profits of industrial corporations."[33] This income tax differential results not only in a direct stimulant to these lower taxed financial institutions, but it can also

---

[29] *Ibid.*, p. 163.

[30] *Ibid.*

[31] *Ibid.*, p. 166.

[32] *Ibid.*, p. 174.

[33] *The Value Line Investment Survey,* Vol. XX, No. 26, Arnold Bernhard and Co., April 16, 1965.

indirectly affect the allocation of resources throughout the entire economy because of the substantial importance of financial intermediaries on the economy.

The degree of taxation, in addition, is a critical element in determining the portfolio policies of financial institutions. Commercial banks, for example, maintain a large volume of tax-exempt securities because of the high tax rates which they must pay on their taxable income. A market is thus provided for tax-exempt securities, which constitutes a significant allocation nonneutrality. On the other hand, savings and loan associations and life insurance companies hold few tax-exempt securities because they pay lower federal corporation income tax rates.

Another allocation effect from the corporation income tax involves the "carry-over of losses" which are available as part of the averaging device. The loss carry-over device may encourage mergers and industrial concentration in the economy. Hence, although loss carry-over may ameliorate the incentive impact of the corporation income tax on investment, it could, on the other hand, encourage a firm with substantial profits to reduce its tax liability by merging with a company which has substantial losses. By this device, the profitable firm acquires a loss offset against its substantial profits and, in addition, may be adding diversification to its holdings. The result is an increased tendency, through mergers, toward the increased monopolization of markets. Thus, allocative nonneutrality exists, though it may be (at least partially) rational or beneficial. A benefit would result, for example, if the losing firm was made technically more efficient by the management of the profitable firm or if the losing firm eventually exits the market because of insufficient market demand for its product(s).

7. *Effect of the Corporation Income Tax on the Choice between External and Internal Financing.* Another area of possible distortion involves the business decision between internal and external financing. Federal income taxation can affect the choice between external and internal financing in three ways, namely, by *influencing* (1) the level of profits, (2) the decision by business management to retain or to distribute these profits, and (3) the terms on which external or outside capital can be acquired.[34] An unshifted corporation income tax will directly reduce corporate profits and will thus tend either to restrict expenditures on business investment or to stimulate an increased reliance on external financing.[35] For many small corporations, the expected rate of return on an investment financed by external capital needs to be higher than that for an investment using internal capital because of the importance of self-employed factors of production. Thus, higher income taxes which reduce the internal sources of funds will tend to curtail the investment

[34] See J. Keith Butters, "Federal Income Taxation and External vs. Internal Financing," *Journal of Finance* (September, 1949), pp. 197–205.

[35] *Ibid.*, p. 200.

expenditures of these small firms rather than stimulate external financing. Large firms, however, which can raise external capital more easily than small firms, will tend to react to the reduction in internal funds by diversion to external sources of capital rather than the curtailment of investment. This is true, particularly, when a large firm has considerable flexibility in dividend policy and thus can partially offset the reduction of internal funds by distributing a lower proportion of profits in the form of dividends.

In addition, a corporation income tax will tend to impair the terms on which equity capital can be obtained since it subtracts from the earnings potential of a company. Hence, whether the form of external financing selected is equity or debt may also be influenced by the corporation income tax. This nonneutrality effect on equity financing will tend to be more severe for rapidly growing companies than for mature firms. Furthermore, the federal corporation income tax encourages a corporation to increase its debt/equity ratio by allowing the deduction of bond interest in computing tax liability. Although the lower rated capital gains tax tends to reduce the distortion against equity financing, the incomplete deduction for losses reduces the ability of the capital gains tax to be an offsetting force.[36]

The Revenue Productivity Criterion

The federal corporation income tax adequately meets the revenue productivity criterion of fiscal rationality. The tax provides a large volume of tax revenue at a relatively low collection cost. In Fiscal 1964, federal corporation income tax collections totaled $24.3 billion, while expenditures by the Internal Revenue Service for the collection of *all* taxes during that year amounted to only $550 million (though admittedly certain additional expenses were incurred by businesses in complying with the taxes).[37] Business compliance costs, however, are small relative to the magnitude of federal corporation income tax collections, but these costs may be significant, at the margin, for a particular firm.

Similar to the federal personal income tax, the system of enforcement of the federal corporation income tax is essentially one of voluntary compliance. The importance of this enforcement technique is accentuated for the corporation income tax by the fact that the number of returns filed is fairly small. In Fiscal 1964, for example, only 1.4 million corporation income tax returns were filed, a figure much smaller than the more than 64 million personal income tax returns filed with the Internal Revenue Service.[38] Yet, voluntary compliance even works effectively in personal income tax collection. Moreover, a small percentage of the

---

[36] Paul L. Howell, "The Effects of Federal Income Taxation on the Form of External Financing by Business," *Journal of Finance* (September, 1949), pp. 208–22.

[37] *Annual Report of the Commissioner of Internal Revenue—1964*, pp. 7, 98.

[38] *Ibid.*, p. 87.

returns filed provide most of the taxable income. In 1961, for example, 4,238 corporations with incomes above $1 million, or 0.6 percent of all corporations reporting net income on their returns, accounted for 71 percent of total corporate income.[39] Thus, enforcement is made easier since a relatively small number of corporations contribute most of the revenue derived from the tax. It should be observed, however, that corporation income tax returns tend to be more complex than personal income tax returns which would somewhat reduce the corporate tax enforcement advantage discussed above.

The Revenue Act of 1964 provides for the payment of the corporation income tax on a basis similar to the "estimated tax technique" used for the personal income tax. After a seven-year period of transition is completed, that part of a corporation's estimated tax liability which exceeds $100,000 will be paid in equal quarterly installments during the tax year. This will tend to improve the enforcement of the tax.

SOME SPECIAL FEDERAL CORPORATION INCOME TAX CHARACTERISTICS AND ISSUES

The Multiple (Double) Taxation of Dividend Income

Corporate dividends are taxed by the federal personal income tax as taxable income to shareholders and by the federal corporation income tax as part of corporate profits. Technically, this is multiple (double) taxation, though such market adjustments as tax shifting may substantially alter the eventual effective results. Opponents of the imposition of dual income taxes upon dividend income contend that, in the absence of relief provisions, the burden of multiple taxation is particularly heavy on low-income taxpayers who receive dividends. For example, the combined corporation and individual income tax on a dollar of corporate income (at 1965 tax rates and disregarding the dividend exclusion) is approximately 84 cents for a taxpayer in the top bracket, which is approximately 14 cents above his individual liability alone. The tax is about 55 cents for a first-bracket taxpayer, however, which is approximately 41 cents above his personal income tax liability on wage income.[40]

Opponents of special relief for dividend income contend that the effective extent of multiple taxation is exaggerated. They argue that a substantial portion of the tax is shifted both backward to wage earners in the form of lower wages and forward to consumers in the form of higher prices. To the extent that the tax is not shifted, moreover, it is claimed that stockholders do not generally base their decisions with respect to stock purchases on pretax corporate earnings per share, but instead upon

[39] *The Federal Tax System, op. cit.,* p. 48.
[40] *Ibid.,* p. 58.

the after-tax earnings available for distribution. It is thus argued that stockholders take full account of the existence of the corporation income tax in determining the price which they will pay for corporate stock. Hence, the burden is limited to those who purchase stock before an increase in corporation income tax rates occurs.

Treatment of Depreciation

Business expenditures for capital assets such as plant and equipment cannot be fully deducted, under ordinary circumstances, in the year in which they are acquired. Instead, the deduction must be apportioned over the estimated useful life of the asset. The income of each year's operation is charged with a proportion of the cost of the capital asset until the full amount of the investment, less any salvage value, has been deducted. Allowances for depreciation may be taken only for that property used in trade or business, or otherwise held for the production of income. The depreciation allowance cannot exceed the original cost of the capital asset.

The Internal Revenue Code specifies several permissible methods for the computation of depreciation. Though the firm may use *any* estimated useful life for tax purposes which is consistent with retirement practices, depreciation guidelines are provided by the Internal Revenue Service. Moreover, the IRS provides an objective test which can be used to determine whether estimated lives of assets for tax purposes conform to the actual useful lives of the assets. In other words, the "tax lives" and the "service lives" of the assets are compared.

Prior to 1954, permissible methods of computing depreciation allowances for income tax purposes were not specified by the Internal Revenue Service. The straight-line method was the one used most frequently at this time, though other methods such as the unit-of-production method and the declining balance method were permitted. In 1946, the declining balance method's availability was liberalized, but it continued to be used rarely because its rate was limited to 150 percent of the corresponding straight-line rate. The Revenue Act of 1954 specifically authorized the use of the more liberal 200 percent or "double" declining balance and sum-of-the-years digit methods of depreciation. The Internal Revenue Code of 1954, however, did not authorize any changes in the determination of the useful life over which an asset could be written off. In 1962, following an extensive study of depreciation rules, methods, and existing practices, the Treasury Department issued an administrative ruling which (1) substantially reduced suggested tax lives, thus allowing accelerated depreciation, (2) provided explicitly for the computation of depreciation allowances on a "class" rather than an "item" basis, and (3) established an objective procedure for testing the acceptability of depreciation allowances. A special provision had existed prior to 1960 whereby the President could allow accelerated depreciation allowances for certain strategic defense industries. The Revenue Act of 1962 also provided a credit against income tax liability based on expenditure for depreciable machinery and equipment used in a trade or business located in the United States.[41]

STATE AND LOCAL CORPORATION INCOME TAXES

History of State and Local Corporation Income Taxes

States began to charge fees for incorporation and to levy capital stock taxes during the 19th century.[42] The modern period of state corporation income taxation, however, was not initiated until the enactment of the Wisconsin personal and corporation income taxes in 1911, though the Territory of Hawaii had enacted a corporation income tax in 1901. Between 1911 and 1920, 7 additional states passed corporation income tax laws. During the 1920's, 8 states passed such legislation while 15 additional states added the corporation income tax during the 1930's. Since 1947, 4 more states and Alaska as a territory adopted the tax, bringing the present total to 37 states plus the District of Columbia. Table 12–1 summarizes the pattern of adoptions of corporation income taxes by the states during the 20th century.

TABLE 12–1

YEARS OF ADOPTIONS OF STATE CORPORATION INCOME TAXES*

Before 1911	1911–20	1921–30	1931–40	Since 1940
Hawaii, 1901	Wisconsin, 1911	Mississippi. 1921	Idaho, 1931	Rhode Island, 1947
Total, 1.	Connecticut, 1915	North Carolina, 1921	Oklahoma, 1931	Alaska, 1949
	Virginia, 1915	South Carolina, 1922	Utah, 1931	Delaware, 1957
	Missouri, 1917	Tennessee, 1923	Vermont, 1931	New Jersey, 1958
	Montana, 1917	Arkansas, 1929	Alabama, 1933	Indiana, 1963
	New York, 1917	California, 1929	Arizona, 1933	Total, 5
	Massachusetts, 1919	Georgia, 1929	Kansas, 1933	
	North Dakota, 1919	Oregon, 1929	Minnesota, 1933	
	Total, 8	Total, 8	New Mexico, 1933	
			Iowa, 1934	
			Louisiana, 1934	
			Pennsylvania, 1935	
			Kentucky, 1936	
			Colorado, 1937	
			Maryland, 1937	
			Total, 15	
				GRAND TO-TAL, 37

* Exclusive of South Dakota's tax applicable to financial institutions only.
   SOURCE: The Advisory Commission on Intergovernmental Relations, *Tax Overlapping in the United States—1964* (Washington, D.C.: U.S. Government Printing Office, 1964), p. 22.

[41] The accelerated depreciation and investment credit techniques for promoting economic growth will be described in Chapter 18.

[42] See the Advisory Commission on Intergovernmental Relations, *Tax Overlapping in the United States—1964* (Washington, D.C.: U.S. Government Printing Office, 1964), for a discussion related to the material in this section.

Present Status of State and Local Corporation Income Taxes

Most states which impose personal income taxes also impose corporation income taxes. The only exceptions to this arrangement are New Hampshire and West Virginia. On the other hand, four states which do *not* impose personal income taxes do impose corporation income taxes. These states are Connecticut, New Jersey, Pennsylvania, and Rhode Island. While the corporation income tax accounts for about 25 percent of federal government revenues (1963 administrative budget), state corporation income tax revenues represent less than 7 percent of total state tax revenues, excluding levies for unemployment compensation. In 1963, federal corporation income tax collections totaled $23.1 billion as compared to state collections totaling $1.5 billion.

A number of cities impose corporation income taxes though concentration of these cities occurs within a small number of states. Approximately 80 cities in Ohio, 7 cities (and 1 county) in Kentucky, 3 cities in Michigan, and St. Louis and Kansas City in Missouri impose municipal corporation income taxes. These taxes are supplementary taxes to the low-rate personal income taxes and the taxes on the net profits of unincorporated businesses levied by these cities.

Most *state* corporation income taxes are applied with flat (proportionate) rates. Only 8 of the 37 states applying the tax use progressive tax rates. The rate structures of the state taxes are low as compared to the federal corporation income tax. The rates vary between 1.75 percent and 10.5 percent, with the most common rates being 5 percent and 4 percent, respectively. All corporation income taxes used by *local* governments are low, proportionally rated taxes. The highest rate is only 1.5 percent. The municipal corporation income taxes overlap state corporation income taxes in the cities of St. Louis and Kansas City in Missouri, and in several Kentucky cities. Increasingly, the state taxes are being made more similar to the federal corporation income tax base. Sixteen of the states which now levy corporation income taxes have substantially adopted the federal corporation income tax base, with certain modest deviations.

Chapter

13

SALES TAXES

DIFFERENT TYPES OF SALES TAXES

Levels of Sales Tax Placement

Sales taxes may be distinguished by the various levels of business activity at which they are imposed. Among the alternative points of placement are the manufacturing, wholesale, and retail levels of transactions. A sales tax may be placed at any one or combination of these levels of activity. In the latter case, the tax is referred to as *multiple* since it involves more than one point of placement.

A sales tax imposed upon an economic good at the time when it is sold by the manufacturer or producer may be referred to as a *manufacturer's* sales tax. A sales tax imposed upon a commodity when it is sold by a wholesaler to a retailer, in turn, may be called a *wholesale* sales tax, while a sales tax levied on the final sale of the commodity to its ultimate purchaser is known as a *retail* sales tax. Multiple sales taxes, imposed at more than one level of transactions, may take various forms. Among the most prominent types of multiple sales taxes are the "turnover" and the "value-added" taxes, which are discussed under broad-based sales taxes later in the chapter.

Narrow-Based Sales Taxes

In addition to being differentiated by means of the various levels of business activity at which the taxes are placed, sales taxes also may be classified as to whether their tax bases are narrow or broad in scope. In this regard, a sales tax applied to one or to a few commodities is considered *narrow-based* and a sales tax levied on a wide range of commodities is *broad-based*. In addition, a sales tax base may be further classified in terms of whether it measures the monetary value or the number of units purchased. If the tax base is defined in terms of the monetary value of the purchased item, the sales tax is *ad valorem* in nature. If the tax base is defined in terms of the number of units of the commodity purchased, the sales tax is *specific* in nature.

Narrow-based sales taxes often are referred to as excise taxes. An excise tax may be imposed either externally or internally. An *external* excise tax is applied to the movement of an economic good or productive resource across an international boundary. External excise taxes are commonly known as customs duties or tariffs. Such taxes may be imposed either by the nation exporting or by the nation importing the economic good or resource. Thus, an external excise tax may be either an export duty or an import duty. Though external excise taxes are taxes in every meaningful sense of the word, they will not be discussed at length in this book since the emphasis herein is intended to be upon internal or domestic public finance.

An *internal* excise tax may be applied to any one or any small number of items involving business transactions within the political boundaries of a sovereign nation. Many different commodities are, or have been, subject to excise taxes in the United States. These include the excise taxes on tobacco products, alcoholic beverages, motor fuels, jewelry, cosmetics, luggage, and transportation. Internal excise taxes may be imposed for a variety of reasons other than the primary reason (in most cases) of providing revenue. For example, some excises are applied on luxury items with a "redistribution" purpose in mind. Other excises, known as "sumptuary taxes," are intended to discourage the consumption of certain so-called undesirable commodities such as liquor and tobacco products. Another use of excise taxes involves the benefit principle of taxation, and an attempt is made to tie the payment of the excise tax to the consumption of a particular quasi-public good. The federal gasoline tax, for example, goes into a special trust fund whereby the tax funds are earmarked for the provision of an interstate highway system. It should thus be noted that the revenues from an excise tax may go either into a general treasury fund for nonearmarked purposes or they may enter a particular trust fund for specified purposes. A final purpose for excise taxes involves their usage to control or ration the consumption of certain commodities in times of extreme scarcity or general inflation. Such application of the excise tax technique is most often found under wartime conditions of scarcity and inflationary pressure in the economy.

Broad-Based Sales Taxes

Sales taxes which are applied to a wide variety of items may be referred to as broad-based sales taxes. These taxes take several forms such as the general sales tax, turnover tax, gross income tax, transactions tax, value-added tax, spendings tax, and the use tax. The turnover tax is very similar in nature to the gross income and transactions taxes while the general sales, value-added, spendings, and use taxes constitute wider degrees of differentiation. The tax base of a broad-based sales tax generally is ad valorem in nature due to the wide variety of economic goods included in the base.

A *general sales tax,* regardless of the placement level of the tax, is applied at only *one* rather than multiple levels of business activity. This is not true, however, of the turnover, gross income, transactions, and value-added taxes, which are imposed at multiple levels of economic activity. The "typical" general sales tax in the United States, for example, is imposed at the retail level and applies a rate of approximately 3 percent to a broad base of retail purchases (with certain exemptions) valued in monetary terms. Thus, in effect, a general sales tax of 3 cents is paid on every dollar of retail purchases in such instances. A *spendings tax* also is applied at only one level of transactions, but otherwise is significantly different from the general sales tax. This tax is imposed upon the money value of a taxpayer's consumption expenditures during a certain period of time under the assumption that such expenditures indicate the taxpayer's ability to pay taxes. Saving and investment are ordinarily exempt from the base of the spendings tax.

The *turnover tax* applies, on a gross basis, to all business transactions through which a tangible economic good passes. This tax differs from a *gross income tax* in the sense that the latter tax also includes intangible services as well as tangible economic goods. In addition, the *transactions tax* is differentiated from both the turnover and the gross income taxes in that it extends beyond those exchange transactions which are inclusive of both tangible and intangible economic goods and also includes such transactions as the depositing of money in banks.

The *value-added tax*, though applied at multiple stages of business activity, differs from the turnover and related taxes in the sense that it attempts to identify the tax base at each level only in the *net* sense of the value added at that stage of production. The value added is ascertained, in general terms, by subtracting the cost of taxable goods from their selling price at the various stages or levels of production. The value-added tax is used in several European nations and has been the subject of serious discussion recently in the United States.

The revenue productivity of a broad-based sales tax imposed by a state or local unit of government may be threatened by the possibility of purchasing the commodity in another political jurisdiction in which comparable sales taxes do not exist. In order to discourage such tax avoidance efforts, states levying broad-based sales taxes ordinarily impose a *use tax* which applies the state sales tax rate to economic goods purchased outside the state, but subsequently brought into the state. The use tax is difficult to enforce because of the problems involved in discovering out-of-state purchases.

HISTORY OF SALES TAXES IN THE UNITED STATES

Excise Tax History

The federal government has collected both internal and external excise taxes since the early days of the republic. Meanwhile, state and local governments are forbidden by the Constitution to levy external excise taxes (tariffs, customs duties) though during the latter part of the 20th century these levels of government have actively engaged in the imposition of internal excise taxes.

External excise taxes served as the primary source of federal revenue between 1790 and the beginning of World War I.[1] Internal excise taxes, nonetheless, were imposed during the period extending from 1791–1802 and again during the emergency surrounding the War of 1812. Then during the Civil War internal excises once again became prominent in the federal revenue picture. At this time, the taxes were imposed upon a long list of economic goods including tobacco products and alcoholic beverages. After the Civil War emergency, most of the excise taxes were repealed, though the ones on tobacco and alcoholic beverages were retained. As the century progressed, these internal excises increased in importance. Following the earlier wartime pattern, the Spanish-American War brought about the introduction of miscellaneous new excise taxes, most of which were repealed by 1902. Thereafter, important use was made of a wide variety of excise taxes during World War I. During the prosperous 1920's, most existing excises either were repealed or reduced sharply and by the end of the decade the only important federal excise tax remaining was that levied on tobacco products. The alcoholic beverage excise remained in effect but declined greatly in importance due to the existence of prohibition. The repeal of prohibition during the early 1930's, however, revived the importance of the tax. Meanwhile, a federal excise tax on gasoline, following the mass production of the automobile, was enacted into law during 1932 and has remained in continuous use since that time. Most of the manufacturer's excise taxes still in use as late as the 1960's had been revived during the early 1930's as a depression tax device in lieu of adopting a manufacturer's general sales tax. As a result, excise tax revenues increased substantially through the remainder of the 1930's. Federal excise tax rates were increased during World War II and retailer's excise taxes were introduced, as were transportation excise taxes. General excise tax reductions were enacted by Congress in 1954 and again in 1965 with other specific reductions in several intervening years. The legislation in 1965 was substantial and involved the outright repeal of many excise taxes, as well as reductions in the rates of others. In early 1966, however, several of the excise tax reductions were cancelled as a part of antiinflationary legislation.

The use of excise taxes at the state and local levels of government has largely been a 20th century phenomenon. The gasoline tax was initiated by five states, led by Oregon, in 1919. This excise spread rapidly and by the end of the decade of the 1920's all 48 states were using the tax. Meanwhile, 29 states adopted excises on alcoholic beverages during the

[1] See Chapters 7 and 8 for a discussion of the historical patterns and trends of public sector revenue in the United States.

decade of the 1930's and 3 additional states have adopted them since that time, bringing the present total to 32 states. The first state excise tax on cigarettes was adopted by Iowa in 1921. There were 7 additional enactments during the 1920's, 19 during the 1930's, and 22 since that time. Thus, 49 states now impose cigarette excise taxes.

Most state amusement taxes are also relatively recent in origin. Though a wide assortment of amusement taxes were in existence during the 1920's (and earlier), the taxes did not assume significant revenue importance until the 1930's. The first state admissions tax was enacted by Connecticut in 1921. Meanwhile, state public utility taxes on intrastate public utility gross receipts, gross earnings, or units of service sold date from the latter part of the 19th century. Presently, 38 states obtain revenue from such taxes imposed on telephone, telegraph, transportation, and other public utility companies. Local levels of government in the United States, to varying degrees, impose excise taxes on gasoline, alcoholic beverages, tobacco products, amusements, and public utility companies. The time origin of these local excise taxes is primarily a 20th-century phenomenon and, for the most part, followed the adoption of such taxes by state governments.

General Sales Tax History

The federal government has never employed a broad-based sales tax though Congress has considered the matter on a number of occasions. A majority of states use such taxes, however, with the general sales tax being the most prominent. The use by the states of broad-based sales taxes in general, and of the general sales tax in particular, is a 20th-century phenomenon. More specifically, the general sales tax movement grew largely out of the Great Depression of the 1930's. Though some states imposed taxes on gross business receipts during the 1920's, the first permanent general sales tax was enacted by Mississippi in 1932. The next few years witnessed an avalanche of adoptions of state general sales taxes. Counting only those states that presently use the general sales tax, 13 states adopted the tax in 1933, 2 in 1934, 5 in 1935 (including the Territory of Hawaii), and 3 additional states between 1936–38. At the close of the depression, approximately one half of the states were using general sales taxes though several states which had adopted the tax earlier in the depression had discontinued its use. A revival of state general sales tax adoptions occurred following World War II as eight states enacted general sales tax laws between 1947–51. Since the Korean War, 10 additional states have adopted the tax. At the present time, 42 of the 50 states impose general sales taxes. Table 13–1 summarizes the pattern of adoptions of state general sales taxes since 1932.

The adoption of general sales taxes by some local units of government has been primarily motivated by the desire to relieve the pressure

TABLE 13-1

YEARS OF ADOPTIONS OF STATE GENERAL SALES TAXES

1931–40	1941–50	Since 1951
Mississippi, 1932	Connecticut, 1947	Georgia, 1951
Arizona, 1933	Maryland, 1947	Maine, 1951
California, 1933	Rhode Island, 1947	South Carolina, 1951
Illinois, 1933	Tennessee, 1947	Pennsylvania, 1953
Indiana, 1933*	Florida, 1949	Nevada, 1955
Iowa, 1933	Total, 5	Kentucky, 1960
Michigan, 1933		Texas, 1961
New Mexico, 1933		Wisconsin, 1961
North Carolina, 1933		Idaho, 1965
Oklahoma, 1933		New York, 1965
South Dakota, 1933		Massachusetts, 1966
Utah, 1933		New Jersey, 1966
Washington, 1933		Virginia, 1966
West Virginia, 1933		Total, 13
Missouri, 1934		
Ohio, 1934		
Arkansas, 1935		
Colorado, 1935		
Hawaii, 1935		
North Dakota, 1935		
Wyoming, 1935		
Alabama, 1936		
Kansas, 1937		
Louisiana, 1938		
Total, 24		GRAND TOTAL, 42

* Gross income tax; in 1963 Indiana enacted a 2 percent retail sales and use tax.
SOURCE: The Advisory Commission on Intergovernmental Relations, *Tax Overlapping in the United States-1964* (Washington, D.C.: U.S. Government Printing Office, 1964), p. 23; The Council of State Governments, *Book of the States, 1966–67* (Chicago: The Council of State Governments, 1966), p. 201; and "Highlights of State Fiscal Action—1966," Tax Foundation's *Tax Review* (September, 1966), pp. 33–34.

on the property tax following World War II. Only two major cities, New York City and New Orleans, used the general sales tax prior to the war. New York City adopted its original general sales tax in 1934 and New Orleans adopted its tax in 1938. Following World War II, a local general sales tax movement was initiated in California and spread to localities in certain other states, especially in Illinois, Mississippi, and Utah. Presently, local governments in 13 states impose the general sales tax. The role of broad-based sales taxes in the local government revenue picture, however, remains insignificant as is indicated by the fact that in 1962 only 4.6 percent of total local government tax revenue came from such taxes.

PRESENT STATUS OF SALES TAXES IN THE UNITED STATES

Federal Excise Taxes

Significant legislation passed by Congress during 1965 substantially reduced the federal excise tax burden on American taxpayers. Many federal excise taxes were either repealed or substantially reduced by the legislation. Prior to this action, federal excise taxes had been applied to a wide variety of economic goods.[2] Depending upon the particular excise tax in question, these federal excises were applied at proportional rates on either an *ad valorem* or on a *specific* basis.[3]

The following are among the significant changes enacted by the federal excise tax legislation of 1965:

1. Effective June, 1965: Outright repeal of the 10 percent excise taxes on furs, jewelry, luggage, handbags, cosmetics, room air conditioners, business machines, cigarette lighters, cameras and film, musical instruments, pens, radio and television sets, phonographs and records, and sporting goods (except fishing equipment).

2. Effective June, 1965: Outright repeal of the 5 percent manufacturers' excise taxes on household appliances, refrigerators, freezers, and movie projectors.

3. Effective June, 1965: Outright repeal of miscellaneous excise taxes on playing cards, pipe tobacco, pinball machines, pool tables, bowling alleys and safe-deposit boxes.

[2] *Alcoholic beverages:* including distilled spirits, still wines, sparkling wines, liqueurs, and cordials.

Tobacco products: including cigarettes, cigars, chewing and smoking tobacco, and snuff.

Stamp taxes, documentary, etc.: including those on bond issues, bond transfers, stock issues, stock transfers, deeds, conveyances of realty, foreign insurance policies, and playing cards.

Manufacturer's excise taxes: including air conditioners; automobiles; business machines; cameras, lenses, and film; cigarette lighters; electric, gas and oil appliances of a household variety; electric light bulbs and tubes; firearms, shells, and cartridges; fountain pens, mechanical pencils, and ballpoint pens; gasoline and lubricating oil; matches; musical instruments, phonographs and records, radio and television sets, and components; pistols and revolvers; refrigerators, refrigerating apparatus, and quick-freeze units of a household variety; and sporting goods and equipment.

Retailer's excise taxes: including those on furs and fur articles; jewelry; luggage and handbags; and toilet preparations.

Miscellaneous excise taxes: including those on admissions; bowling alleys, billiard and pool tables; cabaret and roof garden bills; club dues and initiation fees; coin-operated amusement or gaming devices; diesel fuel for highway vehicles and special motor fuels; leases of safe-deposit boxes; telephone, telegraph, radio, and cable facilities; transportation of persons by air; truck-use tax on vehicles in excess of 26,000 pounds; and wagering.

[3] For example, excises imposed on an *ad valorem* basis included: *stamp taxes* and *documentary taxes; manufacturers' excise taxes* on air conditioners, automobiles, business machines, cameras, household appliances, electric light bulbs, firearms, fountain pens, musical instruments, pistols and revolvers, refrigerators, and sporting goods; *retailers' excise taxes* on furs, jewelry, luggage, handbags, and toilet preparations, and *miscellaneous excise taxes* on admissions, cabarets, club dues, leases of safe-deposit boxes; telephone, telegraph, radio, and cable facilities; air transportation of persons; and wagering. On the other hand, excise taxes of a *specific* variety included those on the following items: *alcoholic beverages, tobacco products,* and *playing cards; manufacturers' excise taxes* on automobile tires and tubes, gasoline, and lubricating oil; and *miscellaneous excise taxes* on bowling alleys, billiard and pool tables, coin-operated amusement and gaming devices, diesel fuel for highway vehicles, and the truck-use tax based upon weight.

4. Effective June, 1965: Reduction of the excise tax on automobiles from 10 percent to 7 percent.

5. Effective January 1, 1966: Outright repeal of the excise taxes on club dues, admissions, cabaret bills, telegraph service, private phone lines, auto parts and accessories, electric light bulbs, wire and equipment service, and documentary stamps.

6. Effective January 1, 1966: Further reduction of the excise tax on automobiles from 7 percent to 6 percent and reduction of the excise tax on local and long-distance telephone services from 10 percent to 3 percent. [This section was revised by subsequent anti-inflation legislation in March, 1966 so that the rate on automobiles was increased back to 7 percent and that on telephone service back to 10 percent.]

State and Local Excise Taxes[4]

Motor Fuel Taxes. The federal government, all 50 states, the District of Columbia, and some units of local government impose motor fuel taxes. The collections of motor fuel taxes by the combined public sector in 1963 totaled approximately $6.4 billion, of which $3.8 billion was collected by state governments, $2.4 billion by the federal government, and the relatively small remaining amount by local units of government.[5] State gasoline taxes range from 5 cents per gallon in five states to 8 cents per gallon in one state, Alaska. The Hawaii tax varies between 5 cents and 8 cents per gallon depending upon the county in which it is applied. Fifteen states and the District of Columbia impose a rate of 6 cents per gallon.

Diesel fuel and liquefied petroleum are taxed by the District of Columbia and by all states except Vermont. Vermont, however, levies additional highway registration fees on motor vehicles using fuels other than gasoline. The tax rate on diesel fuel is the same as the gasoline tax in all except nine states where diesel fuel is taxed at a higher rate. Various exemptions exist for the state motor fuel taxes. For example, interstate sales, export sales, and sales to governmental units are ordinarily exempt. In addition, tax refunds are generally allowed on motor fuels purchased for nonhighway uses such as those in agriculture, manufacturing, construction, and marine activities.

Local government gasoline taxes are levied by approximately 300 municipalities and by 36 counties in 7 states. These states are Alabama, Florida, Hawaii, Mississippi, Nevada, New Mexico, and Wyoming. The application of municipal gasoline taxes is extensive only in two states, Alabama and New Mexico, which account for more than two thirds of the municipalities levying such taxes. The most common local gasoline tax

---

[4] For a good discussion of the various state and local government excise taxes, see The Advisory Commission on Intergovernmental Relations, *Tax Overlapping in the United States—1964* (Washington, D.C.: U.S. Government Printing Office, 1964).

[5] *Ibid.,* p. 166.

rate is 1 cent per gallon. In Alabama, however, where several counties and some of the municipalities located within them both levy gasoline taxes, the combined local government rate (county plus city) may total 2 cents per gallon or more. In a few instances, counties and municipalities levy taxes on motor fuels other than gasoline.

Tobacco Taxes. The primary source of tobacco tax revenue is the excise tax levied on cigarettes. The federal government, 49 states (North Carolina is excluded), the District of Columbia, and approximately 500 municipalities in 8 states impose cigarette excise taxes. About two thirds of all tobacco tax revenue, however, accrues to the federal government. Most of the remaining one third is collected by the states. State cigarette tax rates vary between 2.5 cents and 11 cents per standard package and this has led to some "smuggling" of cigarettes from lower rate to higher rate states.[6] The most common rate is 8 cents per standard package.[7] Hawaii imposes an ad valorem tax on cigarettes. A total of 17 states impose an excise tax on cigars. In addition, excise taxes are placed on smoking tobacco by 15 states, on chewing tobacco by 14 states, and on snuff by 12 states. About three fourths of the 49 states which apply cigarette taxes also employ a general sales tax, and only 13 of these states exempt cigarette sales from the general sales tax.

The eight states which allow local units of government to impose tobacco taxes are Alabama, Colorado, Florida, Missouri, New Jersey, New York, Tennessee, and Virginia. Widespread use of local cigarette excises occurs in Alabama, Florida, Colorado, and Missouri. Most local cigarette tax rates range from 1 to 3 cents per standard package of cigarettes. As an alternative to specifically authorized local cigarette excises, nine states share their state cigarette excises directly with cities and counties.

Alcoholic Beverage Taxes. Excise taxes on alcoholic beverages such as distilled spirits, wine, and beer are levied by the federal government, the 50 states, and by some units of local government. In addition to these specific excise taxes, the group of alcoholic beverage taxes includes occupational license taxes imposed on the privilege of engaging in the alcoholic beverage business. Many states which have special excise taxes on alcoholic beverages, moreover, also impose general sales and use taxes on their purchase. State excise taxes on distilled spirits range from $1.15 per gallon to $4 per gallon. The median rate in 1964 was $1.68 per gallon.[7] Hawaii imposes an *ad valorem* instead of a *specific* excise tax on distilled spirits, while a few states apply both *ad valorem* and *specific* gallonage excises.

Sixteen states exercise monopoly power over the distribution of distilled spirits by operating state-owned liquor stores. All 50 states and

---

[6] A standard package of cigarettes equals 20 cigarettes.

[7] *Tax Overlapping in the United States, op. cit.,* p. 196.

the District of Columbia levy gallonage excise taxes on beer. Alcoholic beverages are subject to local government excise taxes in only a few states, but the application of local general sales taxes to the purchase of alcoholic beverages is more common.

Amusement Taxes. Excise taxes levied on general admissions are used by 31 states. These are levied on either the admission charge or the admission receipts of amusement operators. However, only 6 of these 31 states levy a special admissions or amusement tax as such. Eighteen of the states tax admissions under their general sales taxes, four tax admissions under their gross business receipts taxes, and the remaining three apply both a gross business receipts tax and a general sales tax on admissions. Special admissions taxes on boxing or wrestling exhibitions, or both, are imposed by 37 states and the District of Columbia while 10 states levy special admissions taxes on some or all forms of horse and dog racing. In many instances, these special admissions taxes are levied on top of the general admissions tax of the state. Pari-mutuel betting on thoroughbred and harness horse racing and on dog racing also is subject to excise taxes in 28 states. State tax collections relative to horse racing amounted to $370 million during 1965. Only a few states levy specific excise taxes on cabaret charges, club dues, and initiation fees, though in some instances the state general sales tax is applied to these items. Eleven states allow local units of government to impose admissions taxes. Local admissions taxes are used extensively, however, only in Ohio, Pennsylvania, and Washington.

Documentary Taxes. Taxes on the transfer of real estate and capital stock and on the issuance of corporate bonds and other evidences of indebtedness (such as mortgages) are known as documentary taxes. The District of Columbia and 18 states levy documentary taxes. Moreover, a considerable number of local government units in five states impose these taxes. Ordinarily, the taxes are ad valorem in nature and require that stamps be fixed to the pertinent documents. Though only four states, including New York, directly impose stock transfer taxes, almost all stock market transactions are subject to a state documentary tax because 90 percent of stock market transactions occur in New York City. During 1966, a proposed 50 percent increase in the state-administered tax on the transfer of stocks created threats of relocating the New York Stock Exchange.

Local Telephone Service Taxes. In 21 states, the general sales tax includes charges for local telephone service in the tax base. The general sales tax rate used most often by these states is 3 percent. Telephone companies, moreover, are subject to gross receipts taxes in 27 states and in the District of Columbia. The range of tax rates varies from three tenths of 1 percent to 7 percent applied to the gross receipts base. Only 10 states, however, levy a tax above 4 percent. The gross receipts taxes apply to other public utility companies as well as to telephone companies. One or more units of local government in some 23 states impose nonproperty taxes on local telephone service. Most of these taxes are also gross receipts taxes. In a few states, however, local units of government levy special excise taxes on local telephone service.

State and Local General Sales Taxes

Though the federal government never has imposed a general sales tax, 42 states, the District of Columbia, and more than 2,000 units of local government levied such taxes in 1966.[8] Most state general sales taxes are imposed at the retail level, though Hawaii and Mississippi levy "multiple stage" general sales taxes applied at more than one level of business activity. During the 12-month period ended June, 1963, state and local governments collected $6.5 billion in general sales taxes, of which $5.5 billion accrued to the states.[9] The general sales tax accounts for more than 25 percent of *all* state government tax collections despite the fact that 8 states do not levy such taxes. State general sales tax rates are proportionate in structure and range from 2 percent in eight states to 5 percent in one state, the most common rate being 3 percent. Despite the proportional structure of general sales (and excise) taxes, however, they are regressive in terms of an income base (see Chapter 5). Table 13–2 provides a summary of state sales tax rates.

The state general sales taxes ordinarily apply to sales of tangible personal property and to specified services at the retail level of business activity. The multiple-stage Mississippi levy, however, taxes wholesale sales in addition to the retail rate. The Hawaii multiple general sales tax, moreover, applies to manufacturers and to wholesalers in addition to the retail sales tax. Several states exempt certain "necessities" such as food, medicine, and clothing from the general sales tax base. Table 13–3 summarizes these exemptions.

General sales taxes are imposed by local governments in 13 states. Almost all municipalities in California and in Illinois impose such taxes. Six of the 15 largest cities in the nation—New York, Chicago, Los Angeles, Washington, D.C., San Francisco, and New Orleans—levy these taxes. The taxes are locally administered in seven states and are administered through cooperation between state and local or between county and municipal governments in the six remaining states. Eleven of the 13 states in which local general sales taxes are used also levy state general sales taxes. Under these conditions of dual general sales taxation, the local government rate tends to be quite low—usually either one half of 1 percent or 1 percent. New York City, however, imposes a 4 percent rate. Alaska and Virginia, which authorize local general sales taxes while not

---

[8] The term "general sales tax" excludes business licenses as well as occupation and privilege taxes based on gross receipts or gross income.

[9] *Tax Overlapping in the United States, op. cit.,* p. 96.

TABLE 13–2

State General Sales Tax Rates in 1966

State	Percentage Rate on Tangible Personal Property at Retail
Alabama	4%
Arizona	3
Arkansas	3
California	3
Colorado	3
Connecticut	3.5
District of Columbia	3
Florida	3
Georgia	3
Hawaii	4
Idaho	3
Illinois	3.5
Indiana	2
Iowa	2
Kansas	3
Kentucky	3
Louisiana	2
Maine	4
Maryland	3
Massachusetts	3
Michigan	4
Mississippi	3.5
Missouri	3
Nevada	2
New Jersey	3
New Mexico	3
New York	2
North Carolina	3
North Dakota	2.25
Ohio	3
Oklahoma	2
Pennsylvania	5
Rhode Island	4
South Carolina	3
South Dakota	3
Tennessee	3
Texas	2
Utah	3
Virginia	2
Washington	4.2
West Virginia	3
Wisconsin	3
Wyoming	2.5

Number of states with tax in 1966 (including District of Columbia) = 43

Source: The Council of State Governments, *The Book of the States, 1966–67* (Chicago: The Council of State Governments, 1966), Table 3, p. 205 (Table prepared by the Federation of Tax Administrators); and "Highlights of State Fiscal Action—1966," Tax Foundation's *Tax Review* (September, 1966), pp. 33–34.

TABLE 13–3

EXEMPTION OF FOOD AND MEDICINE IN
STATE GENERAL SALES TAXES, JANUARY 1, 1964

State	Tax Rate (Percent)	Food*	Medicine†
California	3	X	X
Connecticut	3.5	X	X
District of Columbia	3	X‡	X
Florida	3	X	X
Maine	4	X	X
Maryland	3	X	X
Michigan	4		X§
North Carolina	3		X
North Dakota	2.25		X
Ohio	3	X	X
Pennsylvania	5	X	X
Rhode Island	3.5	X	X
Texas	2	X	X
Wisconsin	3	X	X

* Food exemptions usually apply to "food for human consumption off the premises where sold." Restaurant meals are taxable in all states, although meals costing less than a specified amount are exempt in some states.

† The exemption is usually applicable to medicine sold on prescription or compounded by druggists, and often to medical and dental aids or devices such as artificial limbs, eyeglasses, and dentures. Some states exempt patent medicines and household remedies.

‡ Rate on food is 1 percent.

§ The exemption is applicable only to 50 percent of the amount charged for recorded drug prescriptions. Full exemption applies to artificial limbs and eyes.

SOURCE: The Advisory Commission on Intergovernmental Relations, *Tax Overlapping in the United States—1964* (Washington, D.C.: U.S. Government Printing Office, 1964), p. 105.

using state general sales taxes, allow local rates ranging between one half of 1 percent and 4 percent. Nine states share portions of their state general sales taxes directly with local units of government.

FISCAL RATIONALITY CRITERIA APPLIED TO SALES TAXES

The efficiency and rationality of sales taxes will be appraised, as with the previously discussed types of taxes, in accordance with the general fiscal rationality and revenue productivity criteria. The former criterion is concerned with the issue of neutrality while the latter is concerned with the enforcement efficiency and revenue importance of a tax. The discussion immediately below, which relates to general fiscal rationality, will attempt to isolate various important allocative, distributive, stabilization, and economic growth effects resulting from the imposition of sales taxes.

General Fiscal Rationality Criterion

1. *Sales Taxes and the Intertemporal Distortion of Consumption.* Buchanan and Forte provide an interesting analysis of indirect taxation, such as sales taxation, and its resulting distortions (nonneutral effects) on fiscal choice through time.[10] They stress the problem of individual choice and emphasize a long-run analysis inclusive of adjustments over time (intertemporal adjustments). In this setting, alternative tax instruments (types) are considered as "institutions" and not merely as analytical devices devoid of spatial or temporal dimension.

In a one-period analysis, as opposed to the long-run analysis, the following order of tax instruments would be preferred in a range from least to most distortion:[11] (1) a lump sum tax, (2) a proportionate income tax, (3) a progressive income tax, (4) a general spendings tax on total consumption by an individual, and (5) a specific (excise) tax on the consumption of one good. In other words, the lump sum tax results in the least market distortion and the specific excise tax in the most distortion.

However, long-run analysis, which is based upon the following assumptions, provides a different ordering of tax instruments regarding distortions from that of instantaneous analysis:[12] (1) the individual knows his future income, (2) his current decision-making process reflects consideration of expected fluctuations in wants and needs over time, (3) the individual saves only for the purposes of retiring debt or of accumulating funds for future consumption, and (4) the capital market is "imperfect" in the specific sense that differential interest rates exist between loans to consumers and loans for business acquisition of productive capital, the latter rates being lower because offsetting productive assets are provided which are absent in the case of human capital.

If the capital market is imperfect, for example, the individual will choose the tax which minimizes his need to go into the capital market. As a result, if needs are expected to be more stable than income over time, the individual will prefer the progressive tax on income earned in each period to either the lump sum tax, the proportionate income tax, the general spendings tax, or the specific consumption (excise) tax because of the intertemporal distortion factor which permits the *tax liability to be concentrated* in periods when the marginal utility of consumption of spending is expected to be low.[13]

The analysis leads to a different conclusion, however, if it is assumed that needs fluctuate more widely than income over time. In this instance, there will be considerable variation in the consumption of residual (luxury) commodities per period of time. Thus, a specific consumption tax levied on an item of residual consumption will likely involve less overall distortion than even the progressive income tax since

[10] James M. Buchanan and Francesco Forte, "Fiscal Choice Through Time: A Case for Indirect Taxation?" *National Tax Journal* (June, 1964), pp. 144–57.

[11] *Ibid.*, pp. 144–46.

[12] *Ibid.*

[13] *Ibid.*, p. 150.

it allows the possibility of reducing temporal distortion by considerable variation in per period consumption of luxuries (residual services) by *concentrating such spending* when the marginal utility derived from these services is low.[14] It is then concluded that when the various tax types (instruments) are arrayed in terms of the temporal distortions which they introduce, the general spendings tax becomes the least desirable of all tax instruments.[15] On the other hand, the specific sales tax (excise tax) on a luxury good allows tax liability to be concentrated into periods when the predicted marginal utility of spending is low. In addition, the income tax, whether proportionate or progressive, allows the tax liability to be spread equally over time. By contrast, the general spendings tax requires a higher total payment precisely in those years when the need for basic (nonluxury) consumption is greatest—a time when the marginal utility of spending is high.

2. *Sales Taxes and General Intersector Nonneutrality.* The nature of the burdens and benefits of excise taxes in an economy where imperfect markets dominate will first be analyzed.[16] Four basic patterns of excise tax effects, each of which is based upon the assumption of a fixed supply of labor, can be isolated. Assumed to exist are (1) an initial situation of full employment, (2) a given level of governmental expenditures, and (3) a tax structure consisting solely of a 10 percent tax on incomes. The income tax is then removed and replaced by a set of partial ad valorem excise taxes levied at rates sufficient to maintain government revenues. One effect will be to raise the prices of taxed commodities and to lower the prices of untaxed commodities. Some consumers will benefit and others will lose, thus providing a redistributive effect in terms of purchasing power. Nevertheless, the tax does not necessarily lead to an inferior allocation of resources. "The distinctive feature of pattern I . . . [under the above assumptions] is that the imposition of a set of partial excises moves the system from one full-employment resource allocation to a different full-employment resource allocation which may be either superior or inferior to the first one."[17] Thus, unless the pretax allocation of resources is ideal—and this seems unlikely in a world of imperfect markets—the excise tax may create positive nonneutral effects in terms of an "excess benefit" as well as negative nonneutral effects in the sense of an "excess burden," depending upon the circumstances of each individual case.

The conclusion changes if one drops the assumption of full employment.[18] Prices in the taxed industries will increase while there need be no

[14] *Ibid.*, pp. 149–51.

[15] *Ibid.*, p. 151.

[16] See George F. Break, "Excise Tax Burdens and Benefits," *American Economic Review* (September, 1954), pp. 577–94.

[17] *Ibid.*, p. 584.

[18] *Ibid.*

decrease in prices in the untaxed industries. Consumers are worse off since the overall price level has risen and money income has remained constant. Meanwhile, certain resource owners are burdened by involuntary unemployment. An excess burden is thus imposed upon consumers through inflation and upon resource owners through unemployment.

A third case assumes that the government combines the excise tax with induced monetary expansion.[19] In this instance, different conclusions once again occur, with the exact effect depending upon the type of government program that is initiated. Hence, the conclusion is reached that, since both prices and consumer incomes are higher, it is impossible to assert in a definitive manner that either an excess burden or excess benefit will result.

The final case considers what happens if the increase in monetary demand comes from the private sector.[20] In this instance, the result of the tax again will be higher prices and higher incomes. No significant burdens or benefits, however, need result.

Hence, the overall conclusion concerning excise taxes is that the classical indictment of these indirect taxes is upheld under certain conditions but not for the traditional reasons given. The excess burden argument is traditionally based upon the assumption that the reduction in output of the taxed commodity is not compensated by any increase in the output of other commodities.[21] Consumers are thus said to have had their real income reduced. Such an approach, however, implies that the reduced resources disappear from the economic scene. To answer the question whether a particular tax changes allocation and living standards, it is necessary to consider the gains in the output of nontaxed items occasioned by the reallocation of productive resources. When the problem is viewed in this manner, it is evident that excise taxes may improve as well as worsen allocation efficiency and living standards. In other words, if the initial point was not one of optimal resource allocation, the nonneutral effects of the excise tax may be positive; that is, these effects may improve the allocation of resources instead of worsening it.

Specific excise taxes on certain goods or certain industries will tend to influence the allocation of resources between these industries. A 5 percent tax on restaurant sales levied by a state, for example, will tend to transfer resources to other substitute products, the amount of reallocation depending upon the elasticity of demand for restaurant meals. State and local sales and excise taxes, moreover, will encourage the purchase of these items in other political jurisdictions which have either no sales tax or lower rates of sales tax. This is particularly true of large metropolitan areas which overlap state boundaries in the case of state taxation and of

---

[19] *Ibid.*, p. 585.

[20] *Ibid.*, p. 588.

[21] Earl R. Rolph and George F. Break, "The Welfare Aspects of Excise Taxes," *Journal of Political Economy* (February, 1949), pp. 46–54.

large metropolitan areas which are composed of numerous local units of government in the intrastate situation.

3. Sales Taxes and Intergoal Nonneutrality. The interrelated effects of a general sales tax on the goals of allocation and stabilization will now be considered.[22] One possibility is that resources would be shifted from the production of consumer goods into the production of capital goods. An immediate burden would thus be placed on consumers, but one that would be lessened gradually as the additional capital goods created by the reallocation of resources are brought into the production of consumer goods. Another effect of a general sales tax involves the reaction of consumers to the higher prices. If producers raise prices to cover the taxes, consumers either will have to increase their money expenditures and thereby accept the tax burden themselves or they will have to reduce their purchases, in which case producers may be forced to accept either unemployment or reduced money income. The probable result would be mixed, that is, there would be some lowering of employment and wage levels and some shifts within the economy away from luxury commodities. Ultimately, however, it is likely that consumer prices would gradually be reduced due to the lower business costs and the general sales tax burden would be shared between consumers and producers.

Sales taxes, like other taxes, may thus pose a problem of intergoal nonneutrality. This nonneutrality, however, may be either positive or negative if the pretax equilibrium is not optimal. If it is optimal, the distortion can only be negative. A further example of intergoal nonneutrality follows: Suppose that the nation places top priority on economic growth and thus relies heavily upon sales taxes which restrict present consumption and which make additional resources available for the accumulation of real capital. If aggregate demand is inadequate, however, the result may be additional unemployed resources instead of increased investment in real capital. The tax, in addition, may change the distribution of income. Finally, sales taxation, particularly excise taxation, may distort the allocation of resources. Thus, even though the sales tax policy might be successful in increasing investment, it may provide distorting side effects on income distribution and resource allocation.

Excise taxes appear tenuous in their ability to meet distributive equity goals. It is contended that if consumption is used as the measure of *horizontal equity* (equals should be treated equally), the tax base should be comprehensive rather than based upon specific excise taxes.[23]

[22] See the discussion by George F. Break, *Federal Excise Tax Structure* (Panel discussion before the Committee on Ways and Means, House of Representatives, 88th Cong., 2d sess.) (Washington, D.C.: U.S. Government Printing Office, June 15–16, 1964), Part II, pp. 33–35.

[23] See the discussion by Richard A. Musgrave, *Federal Excise Tax Structure, op. cit.*, p. 7.

However, the mixed bundle of selective federal excise taxes (prior to 1965, at least) did not meet this requirement and horizontal equity was violated. It is also contended that the then present federal excise tax structure violated the vertical equity benchmark.[24] This position may be qualified, however, relevant to automobile taxes which are justified on benefit grounds as far as distributive equity and efficient allocation are concerned and tobacco taxes which may be justified on sumptuary grounds.

Sales taxes, both general and specific, can thus exert a significant influence upon the distribution of income and wealth in the society. This is true because of their regressivity to income as a tax base (see Chapter 5). Since the marginal and average propensities to consume tend to be lower at higher income levels, the purchase of items subject to the sales taxes (except luxury excises) is ordinarily a smaller proportion of the higher incomes. Since sales taxes are the largest single source of state tax revenue, the potential effects on the nature of income and wealth distribution are significant. The progressivity of the federal tax system, however, may be viewed as a neutralizing offset to the regressive distribution effects of state and local sales taxes.

Regarding the implications of direct versus indirect taxes on economic stabilization and growth, a distinction between consumption and investment effects is required.[25] If indirect taxes are substituted for direct ones, the tendency would be for consumption to be reduced which, of course, is undesirable if the goal of the society is to increase consumer demand for expansionary purposes. The substitution is desirable, however, if the concern is to increase capital accumulation at a time when aggregate demand is sufficiently high. Regarding investment, the issue is not one of direct taxes in general but rather, when direct (income) taxes are used, one of high marginal rate brackets.[26] Investment will thus be increased if the high marginal tax brackets are lowered.

It may be argued that the total amount of investment over the years will be higher when the government relies more heavily upon consumption taxes and less heavily upon income and death taxes.[27] If the graduation of the personal income tax were lessened and the revenue made up by an increase in excise taxes, total personal savings would tend to rise. This is particularly true when the effect of personal income taxes on the amount of saving by unincorporated business is considered. Furthermore, though excise taxes do not serve as automatic stabilizers as well as do personal and corporation income taxes, they are more favorable to

[24] *Ibid.*, pp. 7–8.

[25] *Ibid.*, p. 8.

[26] *Ibid.*

[27] See the discussion by C. Lowell Harriss, *Federal Excise Tax Structure, op. cit.* pp. 9–18.

economic growth than income taxes, because they encourage investment.

Harberger analyzes the comparative welfare costs (excess burdens) of direct and indirect taxes.[28] The problem is approached by considering the effect of direct and indirect taxes on (1) the choice between work and leisure, (2) the choice between savings and consumption, and (3) the rate of economic growth. Regarding the effect on the work-leisure choice, it is concluded that an a priori case in favor of direct taxation cannot be established since both types of taxes affect the work-leisure choice. It may be demonstrated, however, that excise taxes—since they are not broad-based and are often imposed on goods with high elasticities of demand—involve greater distortion than an income tax of the same revenue yield. More specifically, the welfare cost of the income tax in the American environment is estimated to be approximately $1 billion per year while the excise tax need not, but because of its present structure does (as of 1964) involve a greater than $1 billion welfare loss.[29]

Regarding the savings-consumption choice, it is concluded that income taxation reduces the rate of saving more than does a consumption tax of equal revenue yield.[30] The effects of the present (1964) differential tax treatment of different kinds of capital income under the corporation income tax, however, are substantially greater than the welfare costs arising from the influence of the tax on the rate of savings. Thus, it is estimated that the misallocation of capital caused by the corporation income tax ranges between $.5 billion and $1.5 billion per year and that the misallocation caused by percentage depletion and related provisions totals between $.5 billion and $1.0 billion annually.[31] Finally, the study suggests that the effect of taxation on the labor-leisure choice will have little effect on the rate of economic growth; however, the effect of direct taxation on the savings-consumption choice may reduce the economic growth of the nation by up to two tenths of 1 percent and a shift to indirect taxation could increase the rate of growth by this amount.[32]

Considerable allocative and distributive effects may be expected to result from any shift in the use of a corporation income tax to the use of a value-added tax.[33] If the corporation income tax is not shifted, for exam-

---

[28] Arnold C. Harberger, "Taxation, Resource Allocation, and Welfare," in *The Role of Direct and Indirect Taxes in the Federal Revenue System* (A Conference Report of the National Bureau of Economic Research and the Brookings Institution) (Princeton, N.J.: Princeton University Press, 1964), pp. 25–81.

[29] *Ibid.*, pp. 42–58.

[30] *Ibid.*, pp. 58–62.

[31] *Ibid.*, p. 62.

[32] *Ibid.*, pp. 62–70.

[33] See the analysis by Richard A. Musgrave and Peggy Brewer Richman, "Allocation Aspects, Domestic and International," in *The Role of Direct and Indirect Taxes in the Federal Revenue System, op. cit.*, pp. 81–131.

ple, the substitution of a value-added tax of the income variety,[34] applicable to *all* production, will (1) redistribute tax burdens regressively away from profits and into wages, (2) raise investment incentives, and (3) reduce the excess burden (distortions) since the effects of the corporation income tax on the relative prices of commodities produced by corporate as opposed to noncorporate businesses will be eliminated. The effects on redistribution and on investment incentives, however, will tend to be insignificant. On the other hand, if a value-added tax of the consumption variety is substituted for an unshifted corporation income tax, the enhancement of investment incentives will be greater. Moreover, even in the case of a shifted corporation income tax, the substitution of a value-added tax of the consumption variety for the income tax will increase incentives to invest. Furthermore, in either case, the substitution of a value-added tax on consumption for the corporation income tax will favor savers as compared to the results of a value-added tax of the income variety.

Eckstein observes certain favorable allocative, distributive, and economic growth effects resulting from the adoption of a value-added tax.[35] The substitution of value-added taxation for the corporation income tax, for example, would tend to reduce the tax burden on high-profit corporations and raise the tax burden on low-profit corporations which, in turn, would tend to produce a more efficient allocation of capital by increasing the amount allocated to the more efficient (in most instances) high-profit producers.[36] Furthermore, such a change would lead to the substitution of capital for labor and, in addition, would bring certain tax-favored organizations like cooperatives into the tax base on a more complete basis. The value-added tax, moreover, would reduce tax-caused distortions in decision making. It may also be expected that an increased rate of business savings, reduced flexibility of the revenue system, and an expansion of exports would result from the adoption of a value-added tax.

---

[34] The distinction between value-added taxes of the income and consumption varieties is as follows: A value-added tax imposed on sales receipts minus materials and depreciation, with purchases of depreciable assets retained in the base, is said to be of the income variety. A tax imposed on sales receipts minus materials and purchases of depreciable assets, with depreciation retained in the base, is said to be of the consumption variety. In other words, the primary distinction is that *purchases of depreciable assets* are included in the tax base under the income variety of the value-added tax and excluded under the consumption variety while *depreciation* is excluded from the tax base under the income variety and included under the consumption variety.

[35] Otto Eckstein, "Comparison of European and United States Tax Structure and Growth Implications," in *The Role of Direct and Indirect Taxes in the Federal Revenue System, op. cit.*, pp. 217–85.

[36] *Ibid.*, pp. 247–48.

Revenue Productivity Criterion

The revenue productivity of sales taxes, both general and specific, is substantial. For example, general sales taxes, as the largest single tax source for the state level of government, provide approximately 25 percent of total state government tax revenues. Furthermore, the various specific excise taxes combined provide an additional 30 percent of total state tax collections. At the local government level, general sales taxes yield 7 percent and various excise taxes yield 2 percent of total tax revenues. The federal government, which does not levy a general sales tax, collected approximately 11 percent of its administrative budget receipts during 1964 from specific excise taxes. The revenue importance of excise taxes to the federal tax structure, however, may be expected to decline because of the excise tax modifications enacted by Congress in 1965.

The administrative cost of sales tax enforcement is generally modest, though considerable variability of enforcement costs exists depending upon the type of sales tax used and the political jurisdiction imposing the tax. Collection costs incurred by the states for the general sales tax average about 1.5 percent of the total revenues collected. The total costs of enforcement, however, are further increased by taxpayer compliance efforts which often entail additional bookkeepers and more expensive cash register equipment. To compensate for these business-incurred collection expenses, 22 states allow discounts to retailers on the total amount of general sales tax revenue paid to the state government. These discounts range from 1 percent to 5 percent of total tax receipts. Moreover, vendors often collect more than the tax liability calculated on the basis of their total sales through use of the "bracket system" of tax assessment whereby small sales bring in more than the established rate. In about one half of the states using general sales taxes, the vendors are allowed to retain these excess receipts which are known as "breakage." Most states not providing discounts to vendors allow the vendors to keep the breakage.

About one half of the states using general sales taxes administer the tax through an agency headed by a single director appointed by the governor of the state. Elected state comptrollers administer the tax in Maryland and in Texas. A number of other states use appointed or elected boards or tax commissions to enforce the tax. Normally, general sales taxes are collected by the state agency from the vendors of the taxable commodities, who collect the tax from the purchasers when the commodities are sold. All states require vendors to register with the state tax collection office. More than one half of the states require monthly returns and the remainder generally require returns on a quarterly basis. In order to discourage tax avoidance, all states levying general sales taxes apply use taxes on the purchase of goods outside the state for use within the state. Use taxes, however, are very difficult to administer.

Federal, state, and local excise taxes are collected with varying degrees of efficiency. The Alcohol and Tobacco Tax Unit of the Internal Revenue Service is responsible for collecting the important federal sumptuary excises on alcoholic beverages and tobacco products. Federal tobacco taxes are collected directly from the manufacturer while state tobacco taxes are collected from wholesale distributors of tobacco products. Obviously, the federal enforcement approach is more easily accomplished because there are relatively few manufacturers of tobacco products as compared to the number of wholesale distributors of tobacco products within a state. The federal government does not require that stamps be attached to the tobacco product packages, but most states attach stamps as evidence of payment of the tax. No discount for collection efforts is allowed to manufacturers for the federal tobacco excise tax, but most states allow discounts to distributors. These discounts cover a wide range among the various states extending from 1 percent to 10 percent of sales. In general, it is concluded that the revenue productivity of sales taxes is good, with a good ratio existing between collection costs and the total revenue collected. Considerable variation exists in the cost-revenue ratio, however, depending upon the type of sales tax employed and the particular political jurisdiction imposing the tax.

Chapter 14

PROPERTY TAX

HISTORY OF THE PROPERTY TAX

Use of the property tax dates from the colonial period in the United States and at least from the feudal period in Europe. Historically, the property tax has been used in one form or another by all levels of government in this nation. Primary usage of the property tax, however, has been reserved to state and local units of government with the former gradually relying less on property taxes as the 20th century has progressed. At various times during the 1800's, Congress levied direct taxes on real estate as apportioned among the states as required by the Constitution. These attempts to impose a federal property tax, however, were ineffective and the tax has continued under the control of state and local government. During the 20th century, states have turned increasingly to income, general sales, and excise taxes as sources of tax revenue and have reduced emphasis on the property tax. Although the states derived about 50 percent of their tax revenues from property taxes in 1902, this percentage has declined sharply to approximately 3 percent at the present time. On the other hand, local governments continue to rely heavily upon property taxes which presently supply approximately seven eighths of their tax revenues.

The nature of the property tax, as used in the United States, has changed considerably during its more than 200 years of usage.[1] Initially, it was a "selective" tax imposed on specified classes of wealth. Then, over a period of some 100 years the tax gradually evolved to the status of a "general" property tax which applied broadly to all classes of real and personal property. Since the Civil War, the trend has once again been reversed with a gradual narrowing of the tax base so that a "classified" property tax has replaced the general tax. The states have exempted some classes of property by constitutional amendment or statute. Moreover, personal property, both tangible and intangible, has been increasingly excluded from the tax base—if not by specific exemption, then by the implicit action of assessors, who have difficulty discovering this type of

---

[1] Jesse Burkhead, *State and Local Taxes for Public Education* (Syracuse, N.Y.: Syracuse University Press, 1963), p. 20.

property. In addition, differential rates have been applied among various types of property in some states.

In summary, the property tax today tends to have a fairly narrow classified base and continues as the mainstay of local government revenue. Its importance to the state level of government meanwhile has significantly declined. This is indicated by the fact that only three states derived more than 13 percent of their tax revenue from the property tax in 1962.[2]

PRESENT STATUS OF THE PROPERTY TAX IN THE UNITED STATES

Classes or Types of Property

General property may be classified into two major categories, namely, *realty* and *personalty*. Realty is also known as "real property" and personalty as "personal property." Realty may be further categorized into land and improvements while personalty may be further categorized into tangible and intangible. Table 14–1 summarizes these various classifications and supplements them with examples.

The Property Tax Base

As would be expected, considerable variability exists among the property tax bases of the many units of state and local government imposing this type of tax. There is general similarity, of course, in the sense that the property tax employed within the United States is a classified property tax. The techniques and degrees of classification, however, represent a considerable diversity.

A property tax may be classified or differentiated in the following ways: (1) classification by exemption of a certain type or types of property, (2) classification by "specific" exemptions, (3) classification by differential assessment ratios, and (4) classification by differential rates applied to various classes of property. The first three techniques of classification directly affect the property tax base. The last technique of differential property tax treatment, however, directly affects the rate structure of the tax. All four techniques nonetheless provide differential treatment among those who pay the tax.

Each of the above patterns is used in one or more states while some states employ a combination of two or more of the techniques. Fifteen states use a partial classification system which applies a low tax rate to intangible personal property. Five states use a comprehensive classification system which applies variable rates to several classes of property.

---

[2] The three states were Nebraska (28.6 percent), Wyoming (18 percent), and Arizona (13.3 percent). See The Advisory Commission on Intergovernmental Relations, *Tax Overlapping in the United States—1964* (Washington, D.C.: U.S. Government Printing Office, 1964), pp. 85–86.

TABLE 14–1

GENERAL PROPERTY CLASSIFICATIONS

Realty (Real Property)

A. Land
    1. Farm
    2. Residential
    3. Commercial
    4. Forest

B. Improvements
    1. Farm buildings
    2. Homes or residences
    3. Business buildings
    4. Fences, sidewalks, etc.

Personalty (Personal Property)

A. Tangible
    1. Livestock
    2. Farm machinery
    3. Furniture
    4. Jewelry
    5. Merchandise (inventories)
    6. Motor vehicles

B. Intangible
    1. Stocks
    2. Bonds
    3. Mortgages
    4. Money
    5. Bank deposits

Approximately 30 states differ in the manner by which certain classes of property are included in the tax base. Considerable differences exist among the states, moreover, in the practice of assessing utility and railroad properties.

Generally, the property tax base is predicated upon the ownership of property, regardless of any liens which may exist against it, and is measured in terms of monetary value.[3] In some instances, however, the property tax is levied upon leaseholds. In four states (Delaware, Hawaii, New York, and Pennsylvania), the tax is a *real estate tax* on land and improvements and ignores personal property. In the remaining 46 states and the District of Columbia, the property tax base includes varying combinations of tangible and intangible personal property such as household goods, livestock, motor vehicles, business inventories, machinery, money and credit, and stocks and bonds.[4] Even in these states, however, the primary part of the tax base consists of real estate, particularly

[3] See *Tax Overlapping in the United States, op. cit.*, for a good discussion of the property tax as it exists in the United States.

[4] *Ibid.*, p. 81.

improved realty. Considering the nation as a whole, more than three fourths of the $355.7 billion assessed value of property subject to local property taxes (1962) consisted of real estate.[5] The remainder consisted of personal property (16 percent) and state-assessed property, owned mainly by railroads and public utilities (8 percent).[6]

Most states either exempt household goods entirely or allow partial exemptions of some fixed amount. In addition, most states exempt intangible personal property such as money, stocks and bonds, accounts receivable, and so forth from the property tax, though a few apply the tax to selected intangibles on a very low-rate basis. The great difficulty involved in discovering personal property, particularly intangible personal property, is the primary reason for the tendency to exempt it. Hence, the differentiation of assessment by exempting certain types or classes of property is apparent, with the primary exemptions existing for personal property, especially that of an intangible variety.

Certain specific exemptions supplement those general exemptions distinguished by the property classes which are discussed above. For example, the property tax is classified in many states through partial exemptions for homesteads, veterans, aged people, and certain businesses for industrial location purposes. Such partial exemptions on real property amounted to $10.5 billion in 1961.[7] In addition, billions of dollars worth of educational, religious, and governmental real estate are exempted from the property tax base.

Another means of taxing certain types of property in a differential manner is to vary the ratios of assessed values to market values for the several property classes. A Census Bureau study (1961) indicates considerable variation of treatment among classes of property in this regard since the national average ratio of assessment for all locally assessed real estate was approximately 30 percent of market value while the average for nonfarm residential property was 32 percent and that on acreage and farm property was 19 percent.[8]

The Property Tax Rate Structure

The property tax is shared by two levels of government and by several types of local government units including state, county, municipal, school district, road district, and other special districts. Hence, the owner of property pays *several different property taxes* levied upon the same tax base. For each of the separate property taxes, the unit of government imposing the tax may classify the tax by applying differential

[5] *Ibid.*

[6] *Ibid.*

[7] *Ibid.*

[8] U.S. Bureau of the Census, *Taxable Property Values,* 1962 Census of Governments (Washington, D.C.: U.S. Government Printing Office), p. 7.

TABLE 14–2—Effective* Property Tax Rates for the
Fifty States and the District of Columbia, 1960

State	Effective Tax Rate
Alabama	0.5%
Alaska	1.1
Arizona	1.0
Arkansas	0.6
California	1.4
Colorado	1.4
Connecticut	1.6
Delaware	0.7
District of Columbia	1.3
Florida	1.1
Georgia	0.9
Hawaii	0.7
Idaho	1.0
Illinois	1.5
Indiana	1.2
Iowa	1.2
Kansas	1.4
Kentucky	0.8
Louisiana	0.8
Maine	2.4
Maryland	1.5
Massachusetts	2.4
Michigan	1.8
Minnesota	1.9
Mississippi	0.7
Missouri	1.1
Montana	1.1
Nebraska	1.4
Nevada	0.9
New Hampshire	1.9
New Jersey	2.3
New Mexico	0.6
New York	2.1
North Carolina	0.8
North Dakota	1.3
Ohio	1.4
Oklahoma	0.9
Oregon	1.6
Pennsylvania	1.3
Rhode Island	1.9
South Carolina	0.8
South Dakota	1.4
Tennessee	1.0
Texas	1.0
Utah	1.1
Vermont	2.1
Virginia	0.9
Washington	0.9
West Virginia	0.9
Wisconsin	1.9
Wyoming	1.0
UNITED STATES	1.4

* Effective property tax rates are computed by relating the tax liability
to the actual value of the taxed property.

Source: Advisory Commission on Intergovernmental Relations, *Tax
Overlapping in the United States–1964* (Washington, D.C.: U.S. Government
Printing Office, 1964), p. 89.

rates among the various classes of property. Thus, although the classified property tax is primarily structured by the techniques of exemption and differential assessment ratios which affect the tax base, differential treatment may also be accomplished by applying variable rates between different types of property.

In some instances, the property tax rate is limited explicitly by constitution or statute or implicitly by popular tax consciousness which attaches great importance to holding down the millage rate. Under such circumstances, pressure for additional revenue is likely to find an outlet in increased assessment levels. In all cases, the presence of other revenue sources such as federal or state grants to local government, or the use of nonproperty taxes such as general sales and income taxes by local government, will offset the amount of revenue that must be raised for local government through the property tax. With all nonproperty revenue factors taken into account, the decision then turns upon the expenditures required for desired services as weighed against the requirements that such expenditures place upon the property tax rate. As Burkhead comments, "this judgment reflects the socio-economic variables—income; attitudes toward government; elements of strategy, bargaining, and conflict—that characterize public sector decisions."[9]

Because of the significant interstate variations in assessment levels, the "nominal" rates, or "mill" rates, which are applied to assessed valuations cannot be compared between states in a meaningful manner. Valid comparisons can be achieved, however, by using statewide average effective property tax rates, which may be computed by relating the tax liability to the actual value of the taxed property. In 1960, such effective rates covered a wide range from an estimated low of 0.5 percent in Alabama to an estimated high rate of 2.4 percent in both Maine and Massachusetts, with an overall average for the United States of 1.4 percent.

Table 14–2 lists the estimated effective property tax rates for the 50 states and the District of Columbia in 1960.

Property Tax Administration

Assessment: Administration of the property tax involves the threefold tasks of *assessment, rate setting,* and *collection.* The first of these three functions, assessment, involves the discovery and evaluation of the property subject to tax. Discovery of realty such as land and buildings is relatively easy. The discovery of personal property, however, is much more difficult. In most states, the taxable value of railroad and public utility property is determined by the central tax agency of the state. Usually, this agency will arrive at a unit value on the entire operating property of the railroad or public utility company and then distribute the total valuation on some "equitable" basis among the taxing jurisdictions

[9] Burkhead, *op. cit.,* p. 23.

within which the properties of the company are located. The state agency in some states, in addition, appraises other types of specialized business property such as mines and business inventories.

Meanwhile, local assessors determine the vast majority of the assessed taxable value of property. Typically, local assessors are selected either by election or from appointment by popularly elected government officials. Considerable interstate variation exists in the local assessment organizations, ranging from 28 states in which the county is the primary assessing jurisdiction to 12 states in which hundreds of cities, villages, and townships use assessors to discover and evaluate the property subject to tax. In only one state, Hawaii, is property tax administration completely centralized at the state level. All of the remaining states, however, influence the administration of the tax by determining how the assessment and collection machinery is organized, including the division of responsibility between state and local government officials. Some states with efficient state tax agencies provide considerable direct assistance and guidance to local officials. In many other instances, however, the assessment of property remains subject to the arbitrary judgment of the assessor. In some areas the assessors are part-time workers and are poorly trained for the complexities of their assignment.

Ordinarily, property is assessed at a value less than its current market value. This policy, of course, cannot be defended on logical grounds. Lower assessment levels simply mean that tax rates must be higher in order to provide the same revenue yield. Clearly, the tax liability to the taxpayer would be unchanged if, for example, tax rates were doubled as the assessed value of the property was cut by one half. At times, the administrators of some local units of government such as counties deliberately evaluate property within their jurisdictions at lower ratios of market value than the ratios used by other counties in order to lower their shares of state property tax collections. This is referred to as "competitive underassessment" and it can be controlled only by an effective state tax agency which will coordinate and equalize the assessment ratios used by the local units of government.

Part and parcel with efficient enforcement procedure is the need for an adequate system of local review to equalize assessments of particular parcels of property, within a given category, in accordance with the applicable property tax law. Many of the abuses attributed to the property tax arise because of inadequate assessment procedures and part of this failure falls within the area of inadequate equalization procedures between different parcels of property of the same class or type. The state laws are clear—assessments must be uniform, at least within the same class of property. The Fourteenth Amendment to the Constitution stipulates, moreover, that fair treatment must be provided in the apportionment of the tax burden. Yet, the review and equalization procedures are ineffective in most states. Presently, the states are putting more emphasis on the improvement of assessment procedure than on the need for improved review and equalization. The state efforts for improved state supervision of assessment, improved training for assessors, and statewide revaluations, indeed, are desirable programs. Efforts for improved review and equalization procedures, however, also need to be expanded.

Rate Setting: The ultimate tax liability of the property owner is determined by the legislative body (bodies) of the jurisdiction (jurisdictions) in which the property is located. A tax rate (or rates) must be applied as a multiple to the property tax base. Each unit of government determines the amount of its expenditures. Its administrative officers then determine the amount of revenues available from nonproperty tax sources. The amount which remains to be financed by the property tax is divided by the total assessed valuation in order to arrive at the tentative rate, which is expressed usually either as a number of mills or as so many dollars of tax per $100 or per $1,000 of assessed valuation. If the amount to be financed is $4 million, for example, and the assessed valuation is $400 million, the tax rate is equal to 1 per cent or $1 per $100 of assessed valuation.

Collection: Once the tax rate is set, the assessment roll which contains the assessed valuation of each parcel of taxable property in the jurisdiction is provided to the tax collector. The collection officials then multiply the assessed valuation of the particular parcel of property by the tax rate in order to determine the tax liability which attaches to each parcel of property. In 20 states, property tax collection is exclusively a function of the county, and the county collector bills the taxes for all other jurisdictions within the county such as municipalities, school districts, and special assessment districts.[10] Eight other states provide for centralized county collection but allow cities to collect their own property taxes, with the option of contracting with the county for tax collecting services.

The property tax is usually collected in the year following the one in which the assessments are made. Until fairly recently, the entire annual tax was ordinarily paid in a single sum on or before a specified day. There is a current trend, however, toward the use of installment-type payments on a semiannual, quarterly, or monthly basis, the last of these being closely associated with monthly mortgage payments on residences.

Delinquent property taxes require the imposition of penalties. Normally, a penalty of 10 percent of the amount of the tax is imposed immediately after the tax payment becomes delinquent. In addition, interest charges at the legal rate are imposed upon unpaid taxes for as long as they remain unpaid. In most states, if the tax is unpaid for a

[10] *Tax Overlapping in the United States, op. cit.,* p. 92.

period of three years the government may foreclose on the lien and assume the property in essentially the same manner that a private mortgage holder can foreclose if the debtor fails to meet his payment obligations. The government later may sell the property at a "tax sale," though the purchaser usually gets a conditional title to the property. This "condition" is the right of the original owner of the property to redeem his property within a specified period of time by giving the purchaser at the tax sale the amount which he paid for the seized property.

Table 14–3 below depicts the various steps of property tax administration.[11]

TABLE 14-3

Determinants of Local Real Property Tax Revenue

1967	Assessment roll
+	New taxable construction
−	Demolition of taxable property
=	"Physical roll"
±	Revaluations induced by:
	Market Forces
	Public Policy
=	1968 Assessment roll
1968	Expenditure requirements
−	Nonproperty tax revenue plus federal and state aid
=	Property tax requirements for revenue
+	1968 Assessment roll
=	1968 tax rate (frequently subject to legal limitations)
+	Special district assessments
=	Tax rate for specific properties
1968	Assessment roll × 1968 tax rate = 1968 tax levy
	(potential property tax yield)
−	Delinquencies
=	1968 Property tax collections (actual property tax yield)

Source: Adapted from Jesse Burkhead, *State and Local Taxes for Public Education* (*The Economics and Politics of Public Education Series*, Vol. 7) (Syracuse: Syracuse University Press, 1963), Figure 1, p. 21.

The Single Tax on Land

David Ricardo espoused the doctrine that a tax on the nonreproducible properties of the soil is a tax on economic rent and thus cannot be shifted forward by higher prices. Henry George, in his famous book *Progress and Poverty* (written in 1879), applied the Ricardian analysis to urban land. He reasoned that a productive resource which is fixed in supply, such as urban land at a favorable location, earns an economic rent or site value which may be taxed with no resulting distortions of economic activity. Since the supply of "improved realty" is *not* fixed, however, reproducible improvements should not be taxed. It is reasoned that site value is a logical tax base because it provides a "socially created"

[11] This example is adapted from Burkhead, *op. cit.*, p. 21.

income rather than one derived from direct labor effort. The tax was called a single tax because it alone could have provided all the required revenue for the entire nation at the time when it was proposed.

"Economic rent" should not be confused with the net income from land. Idle land, for example, creates no net income, but it still may have a market value. In addition, land in use may be poorly managed and yield no net income, yet such land still has a site value or economic rent. Orthodox followers of the single tax theory would apply a rate of 100 percent to economic rent on an annual basis.

A practical disadvantage of the single tax involves the difficulty experienced in distinguishing the "land rent" from the "business rent." In other words, how much of net income is derived from the site or location value and how much from the reproducible assets and from the business entrepreneurial factor. In order to be equitable, moreover, the tax must be applied when land is first acquired. Otherwise, unearned wealth becomes diffused through the purchase and sale of property and also through inheritance. The price of land becomes a fixed parameter in the businessman's or investor's profit-motive decisions and, as a result, a single tax cannot effectively be applied unless it is imposed before land changes ownership. A concerted effort was made to introduce the single tax notion into the public sector of the United States during the latter years of the 19th century. The effort found only limited success, however, and the idea is essentially dead as far as application to the American public sector is concerned today.

FISCAL RATIONALITY CRITERIA APPLIED TO THE PROPERTY TAX

General Fiscal Rationality Criterion

As with the previous analyses of the various types of taxes, the general fiscal rationality and revenue productivity criteria will be used as bench marks for an analysis of the fiscal efficiency of the property tax. Judgment regarding the fiscal effects of property taxation should be comprehensive in nature. For example, an individual cannot judge the influence of the property tax upon his economic behavior solely by the rate of tax. Other critical variables, such as the ratio of assessed value to market value, the exemption of certain classes of property or other specific items from the tax base, and the distribution of the economic goods provided to taxpayers by the government unit imposing the property tax are all highly relevant.

1. *The Property Tax and the Political Structure of the Public Sector.* Many instances of both positive and negative allocative, distributive, stabilization, and economic growth distortions resulting from property taxes may be observed. The Advisory Commission on Intergovernmental Relations, for example, notes that several nonneutral effects result

from the use of constitutional or statutory property tax rate limitations.[12] The Commission concludes that while property tax restrictions initially may have had some influence in limiting tax rates, local governments have managed to increase their property tax revenues in the long run by other means. Meanwhile, the negative distortions placed on the structural and fiscal operations of local governments have been substantial. Property tax rate limitations, for example, have stimulated the creation of special assessment districts for the primary purpose of gaining additional taxing authority. This has caused a distortion by needlessly adding to the proliferation of local governments—some without rational economic and political justification. In addition, financial distortions have been introduced in the sense that rate limitations have made necessary the use of short-term financing in order to meet operating deficits. Such debt ultimately has to be funded. The rate limitations, furthermore, have encouraged long-term borrowing for activities which may have been financed more efficiently from current revenue.

2. *Influence of the Property Tax on Residential and Industrial Location.* The property tax, moreover, can influence allocation and technical efficiency through influencing residential and industrial location. Individuals in metropolitan areas may select one area of residence as opposed to another because of property tax differentials. This is sometimes decided on an irrational basis. For example, an individual may select a residential location on the basis of tax rate disparities rather than upon differences in exemptions, assessment ratios, and the quantity and quality of governmental services within the various political jurisdictions. The property tax, moreover, is increasingly becoming a tax upon improvements to real estate. As such, it tends to discourage investment in heavily taxed real estate improvements and to encourage the speculative purchase of lower taxed, unimproved land. Such distorted behavior may exert significant effects in rapidly growing communities where it can result in the existence of large tracts of unimproved land within the metropolitan community. This makes necessary, of course, the existence of additional miles of streets, gas, electric, and telephone lines, extensive areas of police and fire protection, and increased commuting costs and travel time. This is an outstanding case of a negative allocative distortion resulting from the structure of the property tax.

The use of property tax differentials by state and local government to attract industry is becoming increasingly prominent. Two approaches are used in this regard: *One* approach, which is quite direct, is simply to exempt the property of the invited industrial firm from state and/or local property taxes. The exemption may be either complete or partial. The

---

[12] See Advisory Commission on Intergovernmental Relations, *State Constitutional and Statutory Restrictions on Local Taxing Powers* (Washington, D.C.: U.S. Government Printing Office, 1962).

second approach involves the sale of industrial development bonds by a state or locality. These bonds provide funds for the acquisition of land and the construction of plant facilities which, in turn, are usually exempt from state and local property taxes since they are owned by units of government and are only leased to the private firms. Under both approaches negative distortions are introduced into the selection of business operating sites since patterns of allocative and technical efficiency are influenced by the subsidies. These distortions are increased by the fact that interest earned on the state and local bonds is exempt from the federal personal and corporation income taxes, and frequently from state income taxes as well. Hence, the financing is accomplished at a lower cost than the firm could have acquired itself. Furthermore, if the company buys a part of the new bond issue, it receives tax-free income from what amounts to an investment in its own business.

3. *General versus Classified Property Taxes and Nonneutral Effects.* A general property tax applied to *all* assets held by an individual or institution will reduce the expected income from each asset and thereby reduce the capitalized value of the asset. A general property tax, moreover, tends to discriminate against income from nonhuman sources, such as capital equipment, as opposed to income derived from the labor of human capital, because human capital is not included in the property tax base. Thus, investment in human capital (education) is favored relative to investment in nonhuman capital. This well may be a case, however, where the nonneutral effect (distortion) is positive or beneficial in nature.

A classified, or selective, property tax, on the other hand, will produce differential results depending upon the pattern of selectivity. The present *de facto* exemption of intangible personal property, for example, tends to encourage some individuals to hold their wealth in this form rather than to invest it in that property which is includable in the property tax base. In addition, the homestead exemption, combined with federal income tax deductions for interest payments, has encouraged owner-occupied housing, though admittedly the exemption of certain other types of property from the tax tends to increase the overall tax burden on buildings. Homeowners, moreover, often benefit from more favorable assessment practices than those afforded to many other types of property. The effective tax rates on owner-occupied residential property thus are usually below the average for all property. Mitchell observes that relatively unfavorable treatment is afforded to enterprises such as public utilities, commercial enterprises, department and food stores, service shops, residential rental housing, and residential rental offices which must be part and parcel of the city in order to exist.[13]

[13] George W. Mitchell, "Property Taxation in Relation to Investment in Urban Areas," *Journal of Finance* (June, 1951), pp. 200–208.

Another noteworthy selective exemption is the one traditionally granted to the property of nonprofit religious and charitable organizations. This exemption tends to encourage the holding of property by these institutions relative to the property held by profit-oriented institutions. This is particularly important in those instances where the property tax exemption may encourage a nonprofit organization to branch into new fields which differ from its primary function. A church, for example, may become a large-scale owner of urban real estate such as apartment buildings. While this distortion may be desirable and rational overall, it can take on negative rationality effects in terms of the basic function of the organization when it encourages the organization to operate outside of its primary domain.

Martin studies the results of the movements during the 1930's toward property tax rate limitations and toward the adoption of homestead exemptions.[14] The results, which are mostly of a mixed allocative and distributive nature, suggest the following economic effects as flowing from the introduction of property tax rate limitations:[15] (1) The decline in the relative importance of the property tax as a state and local government revenue source, (2) a shift of some of the weight of taxation away from real estate with a consequent increase in the prices of real estate, (3) transference of some of the tax burden from urban to rural areas because the tax rate limitation often did not apply to rural property, (4) the imposition of heavier tax burdens on low- and middle-income taxpayers and the reduction of tax burdens on high-income individuals and corporations, and (5) the encouragement of state government assumption of responsibilities formerly considered within the domain of local government.

It is then suggested that the following effects resulted from increased usage of the homestead exemption during the 1930's: (1) the decline of the relative importance of the property tax, (2) the transference of higher property tax burdens to those people not owning real estate, (3) increased tax delinquency brought about by the higher rates necessitated by the exemption, (4) substantial revenue losses for some units of local government, and (5) the encouragement of fictitious transfers of land ownership in order to secure the exemptions.[16]

4. *The Property Tax and Urban Economic Problems.* An interesting property tax issue involves the magnitude of property tax increases resulting from the annexation of suburbs by central cities. The following conclusions were reached in a study by Andrews and Dasso:[17] (1)

[14] James W. Martin, "Relationship Between the Property Taxes and the Economy," *Proceedings of the National Tax Association, 1952*, pp. 47–55.

[15] *Ibid.*

[16] *Ibid.*

[17] R. B. Andrews and Jerome J. Dasso, "The Influence of Annexation on Property Tax Burdens," *National Tax Journal* (March, 1961), pp. 88–98.

suburban residential areas which are undergoing rather intense development are likely to experience a sharp increase in school taxes. If areas
such as these were to annex to the central city, there is a strong possibility
that their school tax would stabilize or decline; (2) suburban districts
which are annexed to the central city are virtually certain to experience a
sharp increase in general taxes. Properties remaining outside the city
report, in the short run, very moderate general tax increases. These are
primarily due to inflation rather than to any change in governmental
services; (3) properties which remain outside the central city for a
prolonged period, and which are part of an area undergoing intense
suburbanization, will have general tax bills in the long run which are
comparable to those of the city, and school taxes which are even higher;
(4) a short-run pattern of tax bill change emerges whereby suburban
properties experience a general property tax increase when they are
annexed while their school tax tends to decline. On the other hand,
properties which do not annex will, in the short run, experience a stable
or mildly increasing general tax accompanied by a sharply increasing
school tax if they are located in an area experiencing intense development; (5) primarily as a result of the influence of the school tax, total
property taxes in two of the three areas studied by the authors were
higher for unannexed properties on the average. In the third area the
differential, though favoring the unannexed area, was quite narrow; and
(6) if suburban areas are annexed as they develop, the adjoining town-
ship taxes will stay at a much lower level for comparable properties.
Conversely, there is a tendency for comparatively heavier tax burdens, as
the price which must be paid for continuing independence from the city,
for suburban areas which are heavily developed and which rely on
property taxes as their main financial source. It thus may be observed
that a significant interplay exists between the political procedure of
suburban annexation and property tax patterns regarding the distribution
of tax burdens among political jurisdictions and the allocation of governmental services.

The question as to what is the true relationship between the
economic activities which occur within a city and the fiscal status of its
government is a worthy one. Margolis examines this question in a case
study of the metropolitan region surrounding the central cities of San
Francisco and Oakland.[18] The conclusions derived from the study are the
following: (1) the municipal property tax rate is higher for "business
cities" (central cities) which have a high rate of jobs for their residents
within their boundaries than for "dormitory cities" (suburban cities).
This higher rate is a function of their much higher public expenditures
per capita, their lower real property values, and the insufficient fiscal
advantage which they receive from nonproperty type revenues; (2) the

[18] Julius Margolis, "Municipal Fiscal Structure in a Metropolitan Region,"
Journal of Political Economy (June, 1957), pp. 225–36.

public expenditures of business cities are both higher and more inelastic relative to wealth than those of dormitory cities. Therefore, the lower the per capita wealth of business cities, the greater their tax burden; (3) the per capita value of taxable property of business cities is lower than that of dormitory cities; and (4) doubt is cast upon the rationality of a program which encourages industrial and commercial land use in the suburbs.[19]

The findings suggest that, accompanying the business use of suburban land, there will be a change in the nature of residential uses and an expansion of public services so that tax costs per dollar of property value will increase. The overall findings of the study are consistent with the hypothesis of suburban exploitation of central cities, but more intensive studies of this hypothesis should be undertaken especially, in the sense of an examination of the governmental services provided by the respective local governments.

5. *The Property Tax and Distribution Nonneutrality.* The distribution objective, in terms of the "equitable" distribution of tax burdens, is *not* met closely by the property tax. The amount of property owned does not closely approximate the receipt of benefits from governmental economic goods nor is it a good approximation of the ability-to-pay taxes in terms of income earned. Thus, neither the benefits-received nor the ability-to-pay principles of tax equity is served adequately by the property tax. Regarding the benefit principle, for example, the services of fire and police protection are not directly and precisely correlated with the assessed value of property and the subsequent property taxes paid on this property. The owner of a highly valuable, modern, fireproof, robbery-proof apartment building may receive less benefit from fire and police protection than the owner of a firetrap in the slums. Yet, he will pay much more in property taxes based upon the assessed value of the respective properties. The property tax also does not meet the principle of ability-to-pay in an adequate manner. Much property, such as vacant lots, has present value but will not yield income until some future date, if ever. Residential, owner-occupied dwellings, moreover, do not provide a direct relationship with the ability-to-pay taxes which ability must derive ultimately from either current income or from the long-term accumulation of wealth converted to cash. Thus, distributive equity in the bearing of tax burdens tends to be irrationally approached by the property tax.

Furthermore, distributive equity is difficult to achieve under the property tax because of severe administrative difficulties. Yet, even without the administrative distortion of distributive equity, the tax would be regressive from an income base standpoint since the classified property tax base, and thus effective tax rates, ordinarily do not increase in proportion to increases in income. Nevertheless, the regressive effects of

[19] *Ibid.*

the property tax still result primarily from poor assessment practices. This is particularly true in certain communities where, due to political influence, the higher priced property of the wealthy is assessed at a lower percentage of market value than lower priced property.

In addition, inflation combined with poor administration may introduce severe inequities into the distribution of property tax burdens as tax officials frequently fail to adjust the effective rate of property taxation in a manner consistent with the altered values of property. Assessors sometimes increase the tax roll by adding new construction while at the same time they fail to adjust the valuation of old property for inflation. The ratio of assessed value to market value thus may vary greatly between property of different ages. In addition to creating residential inequities, this can also be a major source of "unfair" competition between businesses. The overall allocation and distribution distortions found with property tax usage are not only extensive but also are negative (irrational) in many instances.

Revenue Productivity Criterion

The absolute revenue importance of the property tax cannot be challenged. Next to income and sales (including excise) taxes, no other tax source provides so much public sector revenue as does the property tax. Although the relative importance of the property tax for the state level of government has declined during this century, its absolute magnitude has increased for both state and local governments and its relative importance to local government has been maintained. As was observed earlier in this chapter, however, the property tax suffers from inadequate administration. A wide variability of efficiency, of course, exists among the many units of government using the tax. Many states are taking steps at the present time to improve property tax administration. Organizations such as the National Association of Tax Administrators, the International Association of Assessing Officers, and the federally sponsored Advisory Commission on Intergovernmental Relations are supporting these state government efforts.

The political-geographical organization for property assessment has been gradually moving toward centralization at the county level and the elimination of overlapping jurisdictions. More than 50 percent of the states now conduct assessment-ratio studies using techniques of sampling to reveal variations in the levels of assessment among political jurisdictions and among property classes within a particular jurisdiction. The knowledge derived from these studies indicates those areas which lack uniformity and provides a helpful tool for the correction of inequities and for the installation of a meaningful equalization procedure. It is likely that more states will tend to use assessment-ratio studies to improve property tax administration as the techniques of such studies are made more refined and as competent personnel become available to apply the studies. States are responsible for providing adequate revenue sources for local government since it is the states which provide the very existence of local government. It thus appears that the states must increasingly provide leadership for improving the administration of this important revenue source.

The Advisory Commission on Intergovernmental Relations suggests that the states:[20] (1) eliminate features from property tax laws which are impossible to administer and which subsequently encourage administrators to condone evasion and taxpayers to ignore the law; (2) remove details about property tax administration from state constitutions; (3) take a critical look at tax exemptions which eat away at the property tax base and repeal exemptions which would not be valid as a continuing state budget appropriation; (4) reimburse local governments for revenues lost when the state prescribes the tax exemption of property as an expression of its esteem for such groups as veterans or senior citizens; (5) consolidate small primary assessment districts into districts large enough to support an efficient assessment operation; (6) provide a strong state supervisory and coordinating agency for the property tax headed by a career administrator of recognized professional ability; (7) transfer to the state agency the responsibility for assessing property which customarily lies within more than one assessment district, or which requires appraisal specialists not available to most local districts; (8) require local assessors to be appointed to office on the basis of professional qualifications; (9) conduct continuing studies on the quality of local assessment practices and regularly publish the findings; and (10) simplify assessment review and appeal procedures for the protection of taxpayers.

Despite its present administrative weaknesses, the property tax remains an important revenue source which meets quite adequately the revenue productivity bench mark. It is reasonably dependable under various business cycle conditions and, in addition, is reasonably adjustable to the revenue needs of local government. This latter fact has been increasingly recognized in recent decades. The required revenue yield may be obtained from year to year with a convenient range of flexibility and with a satisfactory degree of precision. The collectibility of most classes of property taxes, moreover, is assured by the ability to apply enforceable liens on the property. The property tax does not, however, serve well as a compensatory tool for stabilization and growth purposes. It cannot be centrally administered to the point necessary for adequate stabilization and growth policies. Furthermore, it is not convenient to manipulate the property tax base and rate to meet stabilization and growth policy requirements.

[20] Advisory Commission on Intergovernmental Relations, *The Role of the States in Strengthening the Property Tax* (June, 1963), Vol. 1.

Cheng and Edwards, however, suggest that the property tax can be converted into a stabilization tool during periods of recession by allowing those who are unemployed to pay their property taxes with personal notes to the local or state government.[21] These notes could then be discounted to the federal government. When the prosperity phase of the business cycle returns, and the unemployed are back on the job, the federal government could ask the employers to withhold part of the pay of the employees so as to make the homeowner pay back the tax debt on an installment basis. It is thus argued that the results are the same as they would have been from rate and base changes, namely, the redistribution of the tax burden from recession to prosperity, without the problems of rate and base changes. The machinery needed to administer such a program, however, might prove to be very complex and expensive.

---

[21] Pao L. Cheng and Alfred L. Edwards, "Compensatory Property Taxation, an Alternative," *National Tax Journal* (September, 1959), pp. 270–75.

| Chapter | DEATH, GIFT, AND OTHER |
| 15 | TAXES |

DEATH AND GIFT TAXES

The Federal Estate and Gift Taxes

Death taxes consist of two main types—*estate taxes* and *inheritance taxes*. An estate tax uses the entire property which is transferred at death as its tax base. On the other hand, an inheritance tax uses a tax base consisting of only that portion of the property which is received by a particular beneficiary. The federal government has imposed death taxes on an intermittent basis since 1798.[1] However, the present federal estate tax dates from 1916. The first federal gift tax was levied for the two years, 1924 and 1925. In 1932, the present federal gift tax was introduced.

A sizable segment of Congress viewed the federal estate tax of 1916 as a temporary measure. Competition between states for wealthy residents during the early 1920's, however, provided important support for its continuance. Some states had begun to advertise in national publications regarding immunity from death taxation in their jurisdictions. Several states, moreover, had amended their constitutions to guarantee freedom from death taxes to those who established residence within their political boundaries. The Revenue Act of 1926 took an important step for continuance of the federal estate tax within the federal revenue structure by permitting an 80 percent credit offset of federal estate tax liability for death taxes paid to the states. This removed the interstate competition for wealthy residents since each state was left free to collect death taxes, not in excess of 80 percent of the federal tax liability, knowing that it would not increase the net death tax burden of its residents. Any state not levying a death tax would be sacrificing revenues to the federal treasury which it otherwise could possess.[2]

[1] For an excellent discussion of federal estate and gift tax history, see The Advisory Commission on Intergovernmental Relations, *Tax Overlapping in the United States—1964* (Washington, D.C.: U.S. Government Printing Office, 1964), chap. 10.

[2] The approach used here by the federal government to coordinate state activity resembles the approach used in the Social Security Act of 1935 to encourage states to adopt payroll taxes for unemployment compensation programs. See Chapter 16 in this regard.

Substantial revisions were made in 1932 in the federal estate tax structure along with the adoption of the federal gift tax. Gift tax rates were set at 75 percent of the estate tax rates, a ratio still in effect. The estate tax exemption was reduced from $100,000 to $50,000 and the maximum rate was increased from 20 to 45 percent. Subsequent legislation during the 1930's further reduced the exemption and further increased the rates. Another rate revision in 1941 established the schedule which is now in effect. In 1942, the exemption level was increased to its present $60,000 level. Though actual rates have remained unchanged since 1941, effective rates of the federal estate and gift taxes were lowered in 1948 through the introduction of marital deductions for the two taxes.

The federal tax credit for death taxes paid to the states achieved its primary goal of eliminating interstate competition for wealthy residents. It has not, however, been successful in achieving federal-state death and gift tax coordination. In fact, its capacity to achieve this result has been dwindling over the years. The nature of federal tax legislation subsequent to the legislation of 1926 has been a contributing factor to this declining influence. Federal estate tax rates have been increased and exemptions have been reduced. Accordingly, the importance of death and gift taxes to the states has declined. In addition, the federal gift tax, imposed at rates equal to 75 percent of the federal estate tax rates, and with a separate exemption, has contributed to the decline in the importance of state death and gift taxes by further usurping revenue sources. Obviously, the distribution of property through gifts during a person's lifetime, as encouraged by the lower rate federal gift tax, reduces the size of the estate subject to taxation at death. State death tax revenues are thus reduced. In 1935, the states received about 75 percent of total death and gift tax revenues. In 1965, they collected only 20 percent of the total.

The Federal Estate Tax Base and Rate Structure. The base of the federal estate tax consists of the gross estate transferred after adjustments are made for certain exemptions and deductions. The gross estate includes the total amount of property which, according to estate tax law, is deemed to have been transferred at death. The value of property may be determined for tax purposes either as of the date of death or as of one year after death. The executor may exercise this option.

Specific provisions govern the extent to which certain property interests of the decedent, such as those in trusts, joint tenancies, community properties transferred during the lifetime of the decedent, and insurance proceeds are included in the tax base. The base is influenced, of course, by the $60,000 exemption, which is large enough to eliminate most estates from liability under the tax. Furthermore, deductions from the base are allowed for such items as charitable bequests, administrative expenses, funeral expenses, and unpaid mortgages or other debt claims upon the estate properties. In addition, a marital deduction is allowed for property which passes to the decedent's wife or husband.

The federal estate tax is essentially an excise tax imposed on the transfer of property at death. The rate structure of the tax is progressive, ranging from 3 percent to 77 percent. Table 15–1 displays this rate structure. An estate tax return must be filed for any gross estate in excess

TABLE 15–1

FEDERAL ESTATE AND GIFT TAX RATES

Taxable Net Estate or Gift	Estate Tax Rates	Gift Tax Rates
$ 0 to $5,000	3%	2.25%
5,000 to 10,000	7	5.25
10,000 to 20,000	11	8.25
20,000 to 30,000	14	10.50
30,000 to 40,000	18	13.50
40,000 to 50,000	22	16.50
50,000 to 60,000	25	18.75
60,000 to 100,000	28	21.00
100,000 to 250,000	30	22.50
250,000 to 500,000	32	24.00
500,000 to 750,000	35	26.25
750,000 to 1,000,000	37	27.75
1,000,000 to 1,250,000	39	29.25
1,250,000 to 1,500,000	42	31.50
1,500,000 to 2,000,000	45	33.75
2,000,000 to 2,500,000	49	36.75
2,500,000 to 3,000,000	53	39.75
3,000,000 to 3,500,000	56	42.00
3,500,000 to 4,000,000	59	44.25
4,000,000 to 5,000,000	63	47.25
5,000,000 to 6,000,000	67	50.25
6,000,000 to 7,000,000	70	52.50
7,000,000 to 8,000,000	73	54.75
8,000,000 to 10,000,000	76	57.00
10,000,000 and over	77	57.75

of the specific $60,000 exemption. Generally, the return and tax payment are due within 15 months of the date of death. If the estate primarily consists of an interest in a "closely held business" such as a sole proprietorship, certain small partnerships, and certain small corporations, however, the tax may be paid in installments over a 10-year period.

Various tax credits are allowed against the estate tax liability. The most important of these is the already mentioned credit for the payment of state death taxes. The maximum allowable credit in this case is expressed as a percentage of the taxable estate in excess of $40,000. The law provides a graduated rate table for computing the credit. Credits against the estate tax also are allowed for gift taxes paid by the decedent on transfers made during his lifetime, but included in the gross estate, and for the payment of death taxes on the property to foreign governments.

The Federal Gift Tax Base and Rate Structure. The federal gift tax is levied upon a base comprised of the value of property transferred as gifts (see Table 15–1). The tax is the liability of the person who makes the gift. In computing the tax base in any one year, the first $3,000 of gifts to each recipient may be excluded. If a husband and wife agree to each contribute one half of a gift, each may claim a $3,000 annual exclusion, bringing the total exclusion for a married couple to $6,000 per recipient. Moreover, in addition to this annual exclusion, a specific exemption of $30,000 of total lifetime gifts to all donees is provided by the law. This exemption may be taken, at the discretion of the taxpayer, either in a single year or over a period of years until it is used up. If a married couple treats gifts as each contributing one half of the gifts, this specific exemption is doubled to $60,000.

In computing the gift tax base, certain important deductions are allowed. These include gifts made to charitable, civic, religious, and public organizations. In these instances, the gifts may be deducted in full. Moreover, one half of the value of gifts made between a husband and wife after April 2, 1948, may be deducted from the net aggregate gifts subject to the gift tax. This marital deduction is similar to that used for estate tax purposes.

The federal gift tax, like the federal estate tax, is an excise tax upon the transfer of property. The rate structure is progressive and, as noted above, the tax is levied at rates equal to 75 percent of those under the federal estate tax. The tax is cumulative in the sense that it applies each year to the aggregate sum of all taxable gifts made since enactment of the present tax in 1932. The tax liability in any one year consists of the difference between (1) the tax on the aggregate sum of all taxable gifts made since 1932 and (2) the amount of tax on the aggregate gifts made up to the beginning of the current taxable year. Gift tax rates in effect in the current taxable year are used to determine these two magnitudes.

State Death and Gift Taxes

The first state death tax was imposed by Pennsylvania in 1825. It consisted of an inheritance tax on collateral heirs. Subsequently, several other states enacted death taxes. Most of these fell into disuse following the Civil War, but a revival in their importance was initiated by New York State in 1885 with its adoption of a 5 percent tax on the transfer of property to collateral heirs. In 1903, Wisconsin adopted an inheritance tax imposed on transfers received by both direct and collateral heirs which set a pattern followed by many other states on such matters as progressive rates and central administration.

The various state death taxes are quite diversified in character.

These taxes, however, fall into several general classifications, as shown in Table 15–2. Five states use a "pickup tax," which is a tax originally patterned after the federal estate tax and designed originally to impose a tax liability equal to the maximum credit allowed against the federal tax. Some of these state taxes, however, have drifted away from the federal estate tax base so that their state liabilities exceed the federal credit. Four states impose estate taxes (not patterned initially after the federal estate

TABLE 15–2

TYPES OF STATE DEATH TAXES

Type of Tax	Number of States	State
Pickup tax only	5	Alabama, Arizona, Arkansas, Florida, Georgia
Estate tax only	2	North Dakota, Utah
Estate tax and pickup tax	4	Mississippi, New York, Oklahoma,* South Carolina
Inheritance tax only	2	South Dakota, West Virginia
Inheritance tax and pickup tax	35	Alaska, California,* Colorado,* Connecticut, Delaware, District of Columbia, Hawaii, Idaho, Illinois, Indiana, Iowa, Kansas, Kentucky, Louisiana,* Maine, Maryland, Massachusetts, Michigan, Minnesota,* Missouri, Montana, Nebraska, New Hampshire, New Jersey, New Mexico, North Carolina,* Ohio, Pennsylvania, Tennessee,* Texas, Vermont, Virginia,* Washington,* Wisconsin,* Wyoming.
Estate tax and inheritance tax	1	Oregon*
Inheritance, estate, and pickup taxes	1	Rhode Island*
No tax	1	Nevada

* Also has gift tax = 12 (total).
SOURCE: The Advisory Commission on Intergovernmental Relations, *Tax Overlapping in the United States—1964* (Washington, D.C.: U.S. Government Printing Office, 1964), p. 151.

tax), and 35 other states, including the District of Columbia, levy inheritance taxes. In both of these cases, pickup taxes supplement the regular death tax in order to absorb any unused federal credit. Two states, moreover, apply only estate taxes (not patterned initially after the federal estate tax), and two other states impose only inheritance taxes. A pickup tax is not used in either of these situations because the state inheritance and estate tax rates are considerably higher than the maximum federal credit. One state, Rhode Island, applies all three types of taxes—estate, inheritance, and pickup. Oregon imposes both an estate and an inheritance tax but no pickup tax. Nevada is the only state not to impose a death tax of any variety.

The considerable variation between state death tax structures includes differences in deductions, exemptions, and rates. Rates and exemptions even vary sharply among those states which impose the same type of death tax. Among the states with estate taxes, for example, maximum rates range from 6 to 23 percent and exemptions range from $10,000 to $100,000. Inheritance tax exemptions among the states, moreover, range from no exemptions for certain types of heirs to as high as $75,000. Furthermore, some states totally exempt the benefits received by certain heirs. State death tax rates tend to be progressive, though a few states impose proportionate rates within two or more categories of beneficiaries as differentiated by the relationship of the heir to the decedent.

Gift taxes are imposed by 12 states. These are generally patterned after the state death taxes. There is, consequently, considerable interstate variation in rates and exemptions. The Wisconsin gift tax is imposed each year without regard to the gifts of previous years, while other states follow a cumulative system.

Fiscal Rationality Criteria Applied to Death and Gift Taxes

The general fiscal rationality and revenue productivity criteria will be applied in this chapter as bench marks to test the economic behavior of death and gift taxes. The analysis which follows will primarily concentrate on the economic effects of the *federal* estate and gift taxes, though many implications also exist for the state taxes. The important efficiency effects of death and gift taxation are essentially of an allocative and distributive nature. The influence of death and gift taxation on the economic stabilization and growth goals tends to be modest, but the latter goal could be significantly influenced in a society where death taxes bear heavily upon the acquisition and accumulation of real capital.

1. *The Allocation Effects of Death and Gift Taxes.* Somers studies the effect of estate taxation on the business merger movement.[3] He suggests that two aspects of the estate tax exert an influence on business practice in closely held corporations. These are: (1) the uncertainty regarding the amount of the tax and (2) the fear of insufficient liquidity to pay the tax. The major areas of *uncertainty* reside in (*a*) the difficulty in evaluating closely held securities, (*b*) the application of the attribution rules which determine inheritance rights, and (*c*) the variety of court decisions which may exist on the same point of law. The *illiquidity* problem results from the fact that stock shares in closely held corporations are difficult to sell upon the death of one of the owners. Moreover,

---

[3] Harold M. Somers, "Estate Taxes and Business Mergers: the Effects of Estate Taxes on Business Structure and Practices in the United States," *Journal of Finance* (May, 1958), pp. 201–10.

even if a buyer is available, there is danger of bringing an individual into the business who may disrupt the operations of the firm to the detriment of the surviving owners or heirs.

Though several approaches may be undertaken to reduce the severity of the uncertainty and illiquidity problems, the best method of minimizing their effects is through the sale or merger of the property.[4] The owner in the case of merger may receive either cash or the listed securities of the larger corporation. Neither he nor his estate pays a capital gains tax if he receives securities. The brunt of the estate tax is lessened in such instances. Significant motivation thus exists for the merger of small business units with large corporations. As a result, an allocation distortion occurs and market structures are made more imperfect.

Rolph and Break also suggest that the liquidation problem occasioned by the transfer of property at death is significant.[5] They believe that the effects of estate taxes are more important in their influence upon the composition of the assets held in an estate than upon the size of the estate itself. The liquidity problem, that is, the need to liquidate part of the estate to raise money to pay the tax, discourages the acquisition or retention of assets with a "thin market."[6] A general bias is thus created by heavy death taxes toward the holding of highly marketable securities as opposed to real estate, works of art, libraries, and the securities of small corporations. Moreover, as discussed above, this bias against holding the securities of small corporations will encourage mergers. In any event, a significant allocation distortion will have occurred.

Other allocation distortions are discussed by Rolph and Break. One area of possible allocative nonneutrality is the impact of the estate tax upon the work-leisure choice. Rolph and Break conclude that a death tax may affect a person's decision to stay on the job, or to retire, in a manner similar to that of the income tax.[7] On the one hand, the price of leisure in terms of the after-tax net estate is reduced by the amount of the marginal rate of tax upon the estate. The individual may thus desire to purchase more leisure by working less since leisure is now a comparatively cheaper commodity than before. As a result, the substitution effect is adverse to work effort.

On the other hand, the income effect may be either adverse or advantageous to work effort. The individual is motivated to work more in order to leave the same amount of wealth to his survivors. He may work

---

[4] *Ibid.*, p. 208.

[5] Earl R. Rolph and George F. Break, *Public Finance* (New York: Ronald, 1961), pp. 261–64.

[6] The legislation in 1958 which allows for installment payments of federal estate tax liabilities in the case of closely held businesses tends to reduce the illiquidity problem.

[7] Rolph and Break, *op. cit.*, pp. 264–65.

less, however, since the amount of wealth he could bequeath with the same work effort is decreased by the amount of the tax. Nevertheless, since the income effect could expand work effort at a time when the substitution effect would retard it, neutralization could be the result. Thus, a determinate solution is not forthcoming.

While theoretically the conclusion is ambiguous, Rolph and Break conclude that (in practice) it is highly unlikely that the work habits of people are affected in a quantitatively significant way by estate taxes.[8] This conclusion is reached because the contemplation of death taxes will likely affect only the older segment of the population. A substantial fraction of this group, moreover, will not have a choice concerning the date of retirement. Furthermore, some of those who do have a choice are people who enjoy their work and do not wish to retire. Hence, the possibility of estate taxes affecting the work-leisure choice in a significant manner can be dismissed as being of little quantitative significance.

Musgrave also discusses the effect of death taxes upon work effort.[9] He observes that estate and inheritance taxes may be thought of as "delayed income taxes" payable at the time of death. They may be conceptually translated into a current income tax equal in amount to the premium payments required to purchase an annuity with which to pay the tax at the time of death. Though a discount factor can be applied to allow for the difference in the current value of present and future tax liabilities, the annuity approach, according to Musgrave, remains an oversimplification.[10] He observes that the distinction between taxes currently payable and taxes payable after death involves more than a time distinction. The opportunity to accumulate a fortune for oneself may well be a more important motivating force to work effort than the opportunity to bequeath a fortune to one's heirs. The taxpayer thus may disregard the burden of estate taxes more substantially than is suggested by the time factor alone. If a progressive income tax reduces work effort, an equivalent set of death taxes will reduce it to a lesser degree.

Another possible allocation effect of estate taxes, as cited by Rolph and Break, is their influence upon the consumption-savings decision.[11] Again, as with the work-leisure choice, the substitution effect and the income effect are relevant. By reducing the cost of a dollar of consumption in terms of its estate consequences, the tax will have a substitution effect favorable to consumption and unfavorable to saving. Since the income effect may go in either direction, however, as with the work-leisure choice, the theoretical conclusion is indeterminate. Rolph and

[8] *Ibid.*, p. 265.

[9] Richard A. Musgrave, *The Theory of Public Finance* (New York: McGraw-Hill Book Co., Inc., 1959), p. 248.

[10] *Ibid.*

[11] Rolph and Break, *op. cit.*, pp. 265–66.

Break feel, moreover, that the overall influence of the estate tax on the consumption-savings decision, whether determinate or not, is unimportant. They reason that by the time people have reached the age when estate considerations bear heavily on their thinking, they have reached the age when radical departures from previous modes of living are unlikely to occur.

The above discussion indicates the distinct ability of estate and gift taxation, particularly the former, to influence resource *allocation.* The most significant areas of influence include the effects of such taxation on the encouragement of business mergers and on the composition of the assets held in an estate. To a lesser extent, the estate and gift taxes may at times influence the choice between work and leisure as well as that between consumption expenditures and saving. The *distribution* effects of estate and gift taxation are also significant. These are discussed below.

2. *The Distribution Effects of Death and Gift Taxes.* Rhodes, in a British study, concludes that the range of income distribution within the higher income groups in England was narrowed by British estate taxes between 1920 and 1950.[12] In other words, the inequality among higher incomes declined during the period studied. The burden of estate taxes increased in Britain following 1920 and, according to Rhodes, the decrease in income variability as estate tax burdens increased does *not* represent a spurious correlation, but instead a genuine cause and effect relationship. This is true, he argues, because the estate tax reduces the incentive to accumulate additional funds.

Harriss points out the existence of a significant direct relationship between the level of stock prices and the size of the estate tax base.[13] This is true because a large percentage of the gross assets of individuals in taxable estates consists of corporate stock. Since widely varying stock prices cause widely varying estate tax liabilities, it is concluded that the estate tax does not perform well on equity grounds. With progressive estate tax rates in effect, two persons with identical estates in real terms (number of shares of the same stocks, and so forth) may bear different tax liabilities if the values at which the assets are appraised for tax purposes are not identical. Such values would not be identical due to fluctuating stock prices and different times of death. The accident of the date of death can thus make large differences in total estate tax liability. The result is that the tax does not adequately meet the bench mark of horizontal equity, that is, the principle that equals should be treated equally in the bearing of tax burdens.

Since the rate structures of the federal estate and gift taxes are

[12] E. C. Rhodes, "The Distribution of Incomes and the Burden of Estate Duties in the United Kingdom," *Economica,* New Series (August, 1951), pp. 270–77.

[13] C. Lowell Harriss, "Stock Prices, Death Tax Revenues, and Tax Equity," *Journal of Finance* (September, 1950), pp. 257–69.

progressive, some redistribution of income and wealth can be expected to occur. The $60,000 estate tax exemption and the various gift tax exemptions, moreover, help to intensify this redistribution effect. The estates of only a relatively small proportion of the adults who die each year are subject to federal estate tax liability. Less than 46,000 estate tax returns were filed in 1961, for example, though some 1.5 million adult deaths occurred that year.[14] Moreover, 30 percent of the estate tax returns filed during the year carried no tax liability. The redistribution effect of the estate tax is also exemplified by the fact that taxable returns listing gross estates valued at $150,000 or less accounted for 51 percent of all returns filed in 1961, but contributed only 4 percent of the total estate tax yield. On the other hand, taxable returns with gross estates valued at $1 million or more accounted for 50 percent of the total tax yield though constituting only 3 percent of the returns filed. In addition, tax liabilities as a percentage of gross estates, which constitute the effective estate tax rate, ranged from an average of less than 2 percent on returns with gross estates between $60,000 and $70,000 to an average of 21 percent on returns listing gross estates at $20 million or higher.

The redistributive effects of the gift tax appear to be similar. During 1961, for example, over 78,000 gift tax returns were filed with a total gift value of $2.3 billion. More than one half of the value of the gifts ($1.2 billion), however, was reported on less than 25 percent of the returns (less than 18,000). Yet, it seems to be a reasonable conclusion that such redistributive effects toward greater equality of income and wealth distribution, as caused by the federal estate and gift taxes, reflect a preference in the United States against vastly unequal distribution of income and wealth.

The federal estate and gift taxes also contribute to greater distributive equity by helping to close an implicit tax avoidance loophole. Specifically, the estate tax can include certain income in its tax base which escapes the federal personal income tax base. The interest on state and local government securities, for example, is exempt from the federal income tax base but the value of these securities is includable in the estate tax base. In addition, the existence of the gift tax serves to control tax avoidance by those who would escape both the income and estate taxes by giving property away. It may be argued, however, that the differential rates which exist between the federal estate and gift taxes create some inequity in themselves because they penalize those individuals who cannot easily transfer property during a lifetime as compared to those who can easily transfer it. The latter group, of course, will pay a 25

---

[14] Admittedly, the returns filed during 1961 pertained mostly to deaths which had occurred prior to 1961. The adult death totals between 1961 and earlier years, however, cannot be expected to vary significantly. Hence, the comparison of the 46,000 returns to 1.5 million adult deaths seems valid for discussion purposes.

percent lower rate under the gift tax as opposed to the estate tax. In summary, the overall influence of the federal estate and gift taxes on the control of tax avoidance is a favorable one.

A recently completed study (1966) by Shoup is highly critical of the present federal estate and gift tax structure, particularly in terms of distributive equity.[15] The effective tax rate on the transfer of property, for example, is too dependent on the time at which the transfer is made. Moreover, individuals who make gifts during their lifetime tend, on the average, to pay lower tax rates. In addition, trusts allow children to use the trust income without paying taxes on the trust capital. Furthermore, misallocation is encouraged by the provision of the incentive to give property away during one's lifetime even though such action may be irrational in economic terms.

The *revenue importance* of death and gift taxes to the American public sector is modest. Federal and state governments, for example, collected approximately $2.8 billion in death and gift tax revenues during the 1963 fiscal year. This amounted to around $2.2 billion for the federal government, or only 2.5 percent of its total administrative budget revenues, and to about $600 million for the states which constituted only 2.7 percent of state tax revenues. Eleven states derived less than 1 percent of their tax revenues from death and gift taxes. Only three states, namely, Connecticut, Delaware, and New Jersey, collected more than 5 percent of their tax revenues from these tax sources. The federal estate and gift taxes were most important (relatively) to the federal tax structure during the 1930's. They contributed more than 7 percent of administrative budget receipts in 1939, for example, as compared to only 2.5 percent during 1963. The federal and state death taxes are reasonably easy to enforce. On the other hand, the gift tax is more difficult to collect, particularly in the case of the state gift taxes which are used by 12 states.

OTHER TAXES

Severance Taxes

More than half the states (29) levy severance taxes. A severance tax may be defined as a special gross receipts or gross production tax levied upon the extraction of natural resources, including mineral ores, oil, gas, coal, and timber. Severance taxes imposed on timber-cutting operations are usually gross receipts taxes based on the stumpage *value* of the cut timber. The range of rates applied to the stumpage value base runs from approximately 2 percent to 12 percent depending upon the particular state levying the tax. Some of the state severance taxes on mineral ores, oil, gas, and coal are also gross receipts taxes. Most state severance taxes,

[15] Carl S. Shoup, *Federal Estate and Gift Taxes* (Washington, D.C.: Brookings Insitution, 1966).

however, impose *specific* rates such as 1 cent per ton of coal or 5 cents per barrel of oil. During 1965, severance taxes contributed approximately 1.9 percent of the total tax revenues collected by states.

In a sense, severance taxes are a "rationing" device which ideally would help establish an optimal societal "rate of use" of the resource in question. Instead of rationing the short-run use of a capital resource to avoid congestion and overuse, however, they are a long-run rationing device to discourage reckless exploitation of land (natural resources). They have been levied at times in lieu of property taxes, which have a built-in tendency to encourage natural resource usage. Though severance taxes as replacements for property taxes could involve a short-run revenue loss, they may well also cause a long-run revenue gain by helping to conserve natural resources for economically rational long-term usage. Under certain conditions, severance taxes, if unevenly applied among several states and among several types of substitutable resources, can cause undesirable allocation and distribution distortions. For example, a severance tax levied on copper ore, but not upon bauxite, which is the source of aluminum and a competitor of copper for many residential and industrial uses, would cause an allocation distortion. The owners of copper mines would thus bear an after-tax income distribution bias as compared to the owners of bauxite property. The revenue importance of severance taxes to the states is fairly modest. In 1964, the total collection of severance taxes by the states was under $500 million. However, in one state, Texas, severance taxes are a primary source of tax revenue.

Capital Stock Taxes

About two thirds of the states impose capital stock taxes, but with a wide variety of structures. A capital stock tax is a business tax uniquely applicable to only the corporate form of ownership. Essentially, the tax serves as a franchise or privilege tax for the right to do business as a corporation. It was originally intended, however, in many instances, to serve as a property tax on intangible personal property in the form of corporation stocks.

The tax may be imposed on a base consisting of either (1) the number of shares of authorized capital stock, (2) the number of shares of issued capital stock, or (3) the capital employed by the business firm within the state imposing the tax. There presently is a tendency for the replacement of taxes based on authorized capital with those applied to one of the other two bases. The par value of the stock is generally used to evaluate the base, but in the event of no-par stock the tax may be applied on the basis of the number of shares.

The tax seems to offend principles of distributive equity. Consideration of the par value of capital stock does little, for example, to indicate the genuine taxpaying ability of a corporation or of its stockholders. Par value of the stock may be vastly different from its market value. Bonds, moreover, may be an important part of the financial structure of a corporation. Yet, they are not ordinarily considered when the capital stock tax base is computed. In addition, capital stock taxes do not fit a precise *quid pro quo* relationship as required by the benefit principle of equity. The tax may be reasonably adequate, however, if it is levied at low rates and considered as an excise tax on the privilege of doing business as a corporation. The revenue productivity of capital stock taxes is quite modest—approximating $200 million annually.

The Poll Tax

Use of the poll tax dates back to ancient Greece and Rome and to medieval England. It was transplanted to the American colonies during the 17th century. The poll tax is a "head tax" imposed on a person "as a person." It may or may not be related to the privilege of voting within the political jurisdiction levying the tax. The 24th Amendment to the Constitution outlawed use of the tax as a prerequisite to voting in federal elections. During 1966, the U.S. Supreme Court declared the state poll taxes of Virginia, Mississippi, Alabama, and Texas unconstitutional as prerequisite to voting in *any* election—federal, state, or local. This action discourages the use of state poll taxes which were used by nine states during 1965. Poll taxes also have been used by some local governments in the United States. The poll tax, when used, is ordinarily limited to adults, but various exemptions from the tax apply for such disabilities as deafness, blindness, and insanity. Poll tax rates tend to be very low—generally ranging from $2 to $5 per person annually.

The poll tax is almost perfectly neutral in terms of allocation effects. No substitution effect, for example, is created when a poll tax is levied. Its payment does not directly influence market transactions. Thus, allocation distortion is virtually impossible. Admittedly, in the long run a poll tax with a high rate structure might induce some individuals to move to a political jurisdiction which does not impose the tax, thus creating an allocation effect. However, the tax has historically been applied at low rates in the United States so this kind of allocation distortion has not been significant (except where voting considerations apply).

Though the poll tax avoids allocation distortions, its record on distribution neutrality is extremely unfavorable. The poll tax, which is levied as a flat fee per person, is extremely regressive if income differences are used as the indicator of the ability-to-pay taxes. An individual with a $1 million annual income, for example, would pay the same amount of tax as the individual with a $1,000 annual income. There is no significant *quid pro quo* relationship of a cost-benefit nature, moreover, to justify the tax under the benefit principle of tax equity.

Chapter 16

THE PRICING OF

QUASI-PUBLIC GOODS:

USER PRICES AND TRUST

FUND OPERATIONS

PUBLIC SECTOR REVENUE SOURCES

The revenues necessary to support governmental functions are derived from a variety of sources. Most of these sources may be grouped into the following major classifications: (1) general tax revenues, (2) earmarked tax revenues, (3) commercial revenues, (4) administrative revenues, and (5) the creation of debt. Though taxes, both general and earmarked, are the traditional suppliers of public sector purchasing power, the other revenue sources are not unimportant.

General tax revenues go into the comprehensive general treasury fund of a governmental unit. Most tax revenues fall into this category. The federal personal and corporation income taxes, for example, which are the primary sources of federal tax revenue, accrue to the general treasury fund of the federal government. State general sales and income taxes, moreover, are commonly placed in the general treasury funds of the state governments. In addition, local government property taxes usually provide general (nonearmarked) revenues. Since the important taxes which provide general tax revenues are discussed in separate chapters (Chapters 11–15), they will not be emphasized in this chapter. Furthermore, intergovernmental grants-in-aid, which are discussed in Part II, will be excluded from the present chapter. Grants-in-aid, moreover, are not a "basic" revenue source, but are merely an intrapublic sector transfer. Hence, their exclusion is further justified. In addition, debt creation is treated as a separate revenue source in Chapter 20. The distinct characteristics of debt as a means of governmental financing will be discussed at that time.

Taxes are sometimes placed in separate budget accounts, apart from the general budget account of the governmental unit, and the funds reserved for specific expenditure purposes. When this procedure is followed, the taxes are called *earmarked taxes* and the special budget accounts are referred to as *trust funds*. The tax is ordinarily tied to a particular type of expenditure which, according to the benefit principle of taxation, correlates with the payment of the tax. The payment of a gasoline tax, which goes into a special road construction and maintenance fund, thus involves an approximate *quid pro quo* relationship between the nature of the tax and the ultimate use of the tax funds.[1]

Broad-based taxes are not conducive to the earmarking approach since they are difficult to tie in with any particular governmental expenditure function. The federal personal income tax, for example, is a general tax on income as derived from a wide variety of earning sources so that its revenues cannot be assigned to any specific logical beneficiary of federal expenditure. Similarly, the broad-based general sales and property taxes levied by state and local government are difficult to assign to particular governmental functions on a *quid pro quo* (benefits-received) basis. Thus, tax earmarking through the use of trust funds normally involves the correlation of narrow-based taxes with specific governmental expenditures. The actual use of earmarked taxes in the United States, for the most part, has been in the form of special excise taxes such as the federal payroll and gasoline taxes. Thus, a typical earmarked tax may be described as an excise tax whose revenues go into a single trust fund for specified expenditure purposes which are related to the nature of the tax.

The collection of *commercial revenues,* commonly known as *user prices,* represents another financial source available to government. This technique involves the production and/or sale of economic goods by a government unit for specified charges or prices.[2] User prices differ from earmarked taxes in that the former represent the outright purchase of the economic good from a unit of government while the latter merely represents the application of a special earmarked excise tax to the sale of an economic good by the market sector of the economy.

The exclusion principle may be applied to governmentally provided economic goods under the user price technique just as it may be applied to the acquisition of private goods from the market sector. In either case, the purchaser can be excluded from acquiring the economic good if he is unwilling or unable to pay for it. Examples of user prices include the payments made for postal service, highway and bridge tolls, tuition to public educational establishments, the purchase of water from a municipal water utility, and the purchase of liquor from a state-owned liquor store.

The goods to which user prices are applied under the commercial principle of government enterprise are usually characterized by both specific and obvious benefits to the purchasers and also by significant *external* benefits or costs. They are not by-products of a general governmental function. In most instances, those goods subject to user-prices

[1] Conceivably, an earmarked tax could be placed in a trust fund, the use of which is not correlated meaningfully with the nature of the tax. However, this is not the manner in which earmarked taxes have been traditionally used in the United States.

[2] For example, some state governments both *produce* and *sell* toll road services, but they only *sell* liquor which is produced by private enterprise.

could be produced by either the public or private sectors of the economy, though not necessarily with equal economic efficiency. In any event, their demand does not derive from a basic administrative function of government.

Those goods which are by-products of the general administrative functions of government are frequently paid for through *administrative revenues*. In a broad sense, the buyer has free choice concerning payment of the various types of administrative revenues to government. Hence, the exclusion principle generally applies to such fiscal behavior. Often, however, there is not a direct or close correlation between the payment of an administrative revenue and the receipt of a specific economic good by the purchaser. Indeed, government units collecting such revenues sometimes attempt to tie them to broad functional categories of expenditure. This relationship, however, is often loose. As a result, administrative revenues should not be confused with the much more precise *quid pro quo* relationships which ordinarily exist in the cases of both earmarked taxes and user prices. Administrative revenues include such revenue sources as licenses, permits, (some) fees, fines, forfeitures, escheats, special assessments, and lotteries.

A unit of government with *insufficient* revenue from one or more of the above sources may turn to *debt creation (borrowing)* as a revenue source. As observed above, however, this will not be emphasized here since it is the subject of another chapter. Moreover, taxes, user prices, and fees may be considered, in a sense, to be more basic revenue sources than debt since taxes are called upon at times to meet the specific interest payments and repayment of principal obligations of government debt. New debt, however, may also be sold to meet present debt repayment requirements and, particularly in the case of a sovereign central government with an internally held debt, the need for eventual retirement of the total debt of the governmental unit may be small or nonexistent.[3] Admittedly, taxes do not need to be relied upon as heavily under such circumstances to maintain and/or repay debt.

THE NATURE OF QUASI-PUBLIC GOODS[4]

A *pure private good*, which by nature carries little or no logical economic justification for governmental allocation, is completely divisible or priceable to its purchaser. In other words, the exclusion principle applies in a perfect manner. A potential purchaser may be excluded from acquiring the good if he does not forego the purchasing power necessary

---

[3] See Chapter 20.

[4] The discussion here will be in summary fashion since the characteristics of private goods, public goods, and quasi-public goods are discussed in detail in Chapters 2 and 3.

to acquire it. The buyer does *not* consume the good equally with other members of society. A pure private good, moreover, tends to have few, if any, external economies or diseconomies of either production or consumption. The benefits from the good reside totally, or nearly so, within the utility patterns of the consumer-buyer or within the production function of the business firm-buyer. In addition to these two primary characteristics of pure private goods—*divisibility* and the *lack of externalities*—one or more other characteristics may be present. These are: constant or increasing production costs at the optimal social welfare allocation point of marginal cost = price; marginal cost considerably above zero at this optimal allocation point; moderate to little investment risk due to reasonably good market knowledge; and the absence of unique resource scarcity and unique conditions of production.

Conversely, a *pure public good,* which by nature carries strong logical economic justification for governmental allocation, is consumed collectively and equally by all residents of the community. It is not divisible to the individual. A potential user cannot be excluded from consuming the good simply because he refuses to forego the necessary purchasing power. A pure public good, moreover, may possess important externalities. In addition to these two primary characteristics of pure public goods—*indivisibility* and the *presence of considerable externalities*—one or more other characteristics may be present. These are: decreasing production costs at the optimal social welfare allocation point of marginal cost = price; marginal cost at or approaching zero at this optimal allocation point; high investment risk due to very imperfect market knowledge; and the presence of unique resource scarcity or unique conditions of production.

Quasi-public goods, the type of economic goods most relevant to the present discussion, contain mixed characteristics of both pure private and pure public goods.[5] While the cases for private sector production of pure private goods and public sector production of pure public goods are strong, the question as to which sector will produce quasi-public goods involves the critical area of social balance controversy which can receive only partial guidance from economic analysis. The remaining part of the allocation decision as to which sector will produce a quasi-public good, and as to which technique of allocation will be employed, focuses upon community value judgments concerning the overall social balance question.

Quasi-public goods provide benefits, part of which are divisible to their users. A potential user can thus be excluded from acquiring the

---

[5] The term "quasi-private good" could be used instead of "quasi-public good" with equal validity. However, the adjective "public" will be used in this chapter due to the concern of the chapter with certain allocative and financial techniques used by the public sector.

good if the proper monetary compensation is not provided. Moreover, and very importantly, quasi-public goods frequently contain important external economies and/or diseconomies of consumption and/or production. These externalities, which permeate the community as a whole, may not be priceable or divisible. If the external benefits and/or costs are indivisible, the price mechanism which measures the private benefits and costs on a divisible basis to the economic agent (consumer or producer) initiating the economic action will *not* measure the social (external) benefits and costs which affect the community as a whole. Public interest thus becomes concerned with the adequacy to which these quasi-public goods are provided. The degree of this public interest will influence, in large part, the decision regarding the allocating sector.

Obviously, a wide range of possible economic good characteristics exists in the continuum between a pure private good and a pure public good and thus in the degree of public interest which may exist. In those cases, however, where the quasi-public goods are of considerable importance to the community, as is evident from the importance of their external effects, the case for public sector influence on their allocation is strong. In addition to the characteristics of partially divisible benefits and the presence of externalities, quasi-public goods may possess one or more of the following characteristics: production costs which are neither sharply decreasing nor sharply increasing at the optimal social welfare allocation point of marginal cost = price; marginal cost moderately above zero at this optimal allocation point; moderate investment risk due to somewhat imperfect market knowledge; and moderately unique resource scarcity or conditions of production.

ALTERNATIVE GOVERNMENTAL ALLOCATION AND FINANCING TECHNIQUES FOR QUASI-PUBLIC GOODS

Government can influence resource allocation in a variety of ways.[6] These techniques may be very direct and complete in their allocation influence, as in the situation where the public sector produces both the final good and all intermediate components of the good as well as all resources used in producing the components and/or the final good. On the other hand, a government allocation technique may be very indirect and incomplete as in the case of general antitrust laws. The various allocation techniques available to government are interrelated with the various techniques of revenue-gathering by the public sector. This chapter is particularly concerned with those revenue sources which are adaptable to governmental allocation of quasi-public goods.

Let us assume, based on the above discussion, that sufficient public interest exists to justify governmental production of a given quasi-public

[6] This is the primary subject of Chapter 3.

good. Justification for governmental production having been established, the primary governmental financial issue is then to select an appropriate revenue-gathering technique to pay for the good. It is at this point that the five classifications of governmental revenue sources developed earlier in the chapter become relevant. The governmental unit producing the good must determine whether general taxes, earmarked taxes, user prices, administrative revenues, or debt financing will pay for the quasi-public good. Since broad-based revenue sources such as general taxes (income, general sales, property, and so on) are most appropriate in the financing of indivisible *pure public goods,* to which the exclusion principle does not apply, they will not be considered as a relevant alternative in the present discussion. Debt, moreover, also will be excluded from this discussion.

Thus, earmarked taxes, user prices, and administrative revenues—all of which are capable, at least to some extent, of utilizing the exclusion principle when used as financing techniques—will be emphasized in this chapter. The exclusion principle, however, applies more rigorously to user charges than to excise taxes since the potential purchaser will not receive the economic good if he does not pay for it in the former case while in the latter instance he could, under certain conditions, pay for the good, receive it, and not pay the earmarked excise tax if the seller is forced by market conditions to absorb the tax. Regarding administrative revenues, the exclusion principle applies adequately in the sense that the potential purchaser of the governmental good (including service) can be excluded from receiving it if the administrative charge is not paid. The *quid pro quo* cost-benefit relationship, however, is generally more obscure than in the case of either user prices or trust fund activities.

The Use of Earmarked Taxes and Trust Funds

The federal social security program is the primary example of the trust fund allocation technique as presently used within the public sector of the United States. The Social Security Act, passed by Congress in the depression year 1935, went into effect in 1937. The initial legislation provided for an old-age and survivors insurance program and for unemployment compensation. Later provisions for disability benefits and for medical care for the aged were added, in 1957 and in 1965 respectively. These programs are financed through federal payroll excises, a technique also used to support a separate social security program for railroad employees. The various federally sponsored social security programs are discussed below.

Old-Age, Survivors, and Disability Insurance Program (*OASDI*). This program is financed by payroll taxes which provide the funds for the federal old-age and survivors insurance and the federal disability insurance trust funds. Amounts equivalent to collections of OASDI taxes are appropriated to these trust accounts and subsequently are invested in interest-bearing securities of the federal government. Both employers and employees pay the taxes, which are levied upon a tax base consisting of wage or salary earnings up to a certain maximum. In addition, self-employed persons are eligible to pay taxes under a different formula to obtain coverage by the program. The original legislation had exempted from coverage various categories of employment such as agricultural labor, domestic service in private homes, casual labor, services performed for religious, charitable, scientific, literary, and educational organizations, and services performed for the United States, a state, or its political subdivisions. Many of these exemptions, however, have been eliminated in the last 15 years and the program now applies to most people in paid employment. The only notable exceptions are federal civilian employees, self-employed persons whose income from self-employment is less than $400 annually, and domestic and farm workers when they earn less than a specified amount from a single employer.

OASDI is set up, broadly speaking, to resemble an ordinary insurance company. Compulsory premiums (payroll taxes) are calculated on a rough actuarial basis and reserves are accumulated to strengthen the fund and to assure payments when the claims of policyholders are due. A private insurance company being run on strict actuarially computed principles, however, would have to charge thousands of dollars annually for such benefits and privileges. The comparison between social and private insurance on an actuarial basis is thus somewhat loose. OASDI, however, is in closer accord with certain other private insurance principles. For example, only "insured" or "covered" workers (whose pay has been taxed) are eligible to receive benefits. The benefits, moreover, belong to the workers *by right*. No embarrassing proof of poverty or need is required. Furthermore, the programs are operated as separate financial operations with earmarked taxes (analagous here to premiums) going into special trust funds to help provide the benefits. It must be acknowledged, nevertheless, that the scale of benefit payments is not strictly proportional to the size of the tax payments.

Benefits are payable to individuals who have worked a sufficient number of quarters to be covered by the program and to their dependents and survivors. Monthly old-age insurance benefits are payable to a retired worker covered by the program, beginning at age 62. Benefits are also payable to the wife of a retired worker if she is either 62 or has a child in her care who is entitled to child's benefits. Child's benefits are payable to a retired worker's unmarried children under the age of 18 or, regardless of age, to any of his children who become permanently and totally disabled before the age of 18. Benefits, moreover, are payable to a dependent husband who has reached the age of 62.

Full survivor benefits are payable to the widow of an insured worker if she has reached the age of 62 (reduced benefits are payable at age 60), or has a child in her care who is entitled to benefits. In addition, survivor benefits are payable to unmarried children of such a worker under 18, unless the unmarried child is a student in a college or trade school, in which case benefits are payable until age 22 is reached. Moreover, unmarried children of such a worker, if over 18, may receive benefits if he or she becomes disabled before age 18. Benefits are payable also to a dependent parent aged 62 or more, and to a dependent widower aged 62 or more. In addition, a lump sum benefit equal to three times the worker's monthly benefit amount, but not to exceed $255, is payable on the death of an insured worker.

Disability insurance benefits are payable to a worker under age 65 who is unable to engage in any substantial gainful work because of a disability that can be expected to last for a long and indefinite period of time, or that can be expected to result in death. The dependents of a disabled worker may receive benefits under the same conditions that the dependents of retired workers receive them.

The amount of old-age insurance benefit is based on the monthly average earnings of the insured worker, the benefit for each amount of average monthly earnings being stated in the law. The average monthly earning is calculated by adding the worker's total covered earnings over the number of years specified in the law (generally, the years between 1951 and the age of 65, or 62 for women) and dividing by the number of months in those years. However, the five years in which earnings are lowest and periods of disability are excluded from the average monthly earnings calculation. Benefits for dependents and survivors are based on a percentage of the benefit payable to the insured worker.

Medical Care for the Aged Insurance Program (MEDICARE). Twenty years after President Truman had asked Congress to provide for medical insurance under the social security program (1945), President Johnson signed into law (1965), in the presence of the former President, a bill providing medical care for the aged as part of the federal social security system. A new *hospital insurance trust fund* was created, which brings the number of separate trust funds administered under the OASDI component of the federal social security program to three. The new trust fund is financed by a supplemental payroll tax. Some 20 million people aged 65 or over receive direct benefits under the program. Those who were not under social security at the time the program went into effect— about 2 million people—still are covered by the program with the federal government paying the amount necessary to bring them into the hospital insurance trust fund.

In addition to the mandatory hospital insurance program financed by a payroll tax, a voluntary supplementary insurance plan is available to all people aged 65 or over. For the small monthly premium payment of $3, each person is insured against doctor bills and other medical charges not covered by the mandatory program.

Most medical bills of those aged 65 or over will be paid, either entirely or in large part, by the combination of the two programs. Certification by a physician is required before benefits will be paid. Hospitals and doctors are free to select their own collection agencies. The program, moreover, remains individualistic in the sense that the doctor may charge more than the fee which the "reasonable customary charge" schedule provided by the government lists for the service. The doctor's fee is negotiated between the doctor and his patient, as previously was the case. In addition, the patient may go to any doctor he chooses. Table 16–1 summarizes the main points of the mandatory and voluntary medicare programs.

The employer and the employee pay identical payroll tax rates to finance the various old-age, survivors, disability, and medical care benefits. Beginning July 1, 1966, the employer and the employee will each pay 3.85 percent on the first $6,600 of taxed wages and salaries for the old-age, survivors, and disability insurance programs. Moreover, beginning the same date the employer and the employee will each pay 0.35 percent on the same wage-salary base for the mandatory component of medicare. The total tax rate for all benefits thus amounts to 4.2 percent *each* for both the employer and the employee, giving a combined tax rate for *both* the employer and the employee of 8.4 percent on the first $6,600 of taxable wages and salaries.

The total tax rate for self-employed persons covered by the old-age, survivors, disability, and medicare programs beginning January 1, 1966, is 6.15 percent on the first $6,600 of income, 0.35 percent of this amount being for medical care coverage. There is, of course, no matching contribution from an employer in the case of self-employed persons. Payroll tax rate increases are presently scheduled well into the future. Table 16–2 presents a summary of social security tax rates ranging from the 1965 actual rates to those scheduled for 1987 and beyond. During the latter half of the 1960's, social security taxes are expected to exceed trust fund outpayments by approximately $16 billion.

Federal-State Public Assistance Programs. The Social Security Act provides for grants-in-aid from the federal government to the states to support the needy aged, blind, widowed and orphaned, and the physically and mentally handicapped who are unable to contribute to their own support. This assistance is "direct relief." It is based upon need, not right. These programs are administered by the states, but the federal government contributes to the expenses incurred in the programs as long as certain minimum standards set by the Social Security Administration are met. At the present time, approximately 60 percent of the funds used

TABLE 16-1

MAIN FEATURES OF MANDATORY AND VOLUNTARY MEDICARE PROGRAMS

Mandatory Program	
Covered by Medicare	*Not Covered by Medicare*
Hospital Bills (beginning July 1, 1966) Up to 90 days for each sick spell, including mental illness. All hospital services normally furnished to in-patients. Drugs used in hospitals.	First $40 of hospital bill, plus $10 per day after first 60 days. Services of hospital-employed radiologists and pathologists. First three pints of blood.
Extended Care (beginning January 1, 1967) Up to 100 days in extended care facility, but only after hospitalization for 3 days. Drugs; physical therapy; speech therapy; care by interns and residents-in-training from hospital with which facility is associated.	After first 20 days, $5 per day up to 100-day limit.
Home Health Services (Beginning July 1, 1966) Following discharge from hospital or extended care facility, 100 home visits per year from health workers (visiting nurses, etc.) under plan established by physician. Hospital out-patient diagnostic tests.	Full-time nursing care. Drugs and biologicals. First $20 of cost and 20 percent of remainder of bill.

Voluntary Program	
Covered by Medicare	*Not Covered by Medicare*
Doctor Bills (beginning July 1, 1966) 80 percent of "reasonable charge" for physicians' services in or out of hospital; X-ray, radium treatments; diagnostic X-ray and other laboratory tests. Treatments for mental illness outside a hospital (50 percent of expense up to maximum benefit of $250 in any one year). Home health services up to 100 days without prior hospitalization.	$3 per month share of insurance premium. First $50 of bills for these services. Routine physical examinations; eye, hearing tests, eyeglasses, hearing aids; immunizations; cosmetic surgery.

for these joint federal-state programs are provided by the federal government. States with low per capita income receive relatively larger proportions of federal assistance than do high per capita income states. The public assistance component of the federal social security system has declined in relative importance as the OASDI coverage has been extended. Presently, OASDI beneficiaries exceed old-age assistance beneficiaries by a ratio of approximately 6 to 1.

The Social Security Act also provides for federal grants to state health and welfare agencies for the support of services rendered to mothers and children. These services include maternal and child health services, services for crippled children, and child welfare services. Such programs are state administered and require state funds to match the federal grants.

TABLE 16–2

SOCIAL SECURITY PAYROLL TAX RATES, MAXIMUM WAGES TAXED, AND MAXIMUM TAX PAYMENTS, FOR OLD-AGE, SURVIVORS, DISABILITY, AND MEDICARE COVERAGE, 1965–87

Year	Tax Rate for Cash Benefits	Tax Rate for Medicare	Total Tax Rate	Maximum Wages and Salaries Taxed	Maximum Tax Amount Paid
	Tax on Employer and Employee Each				
	(percent)	(percent)	(percent)		
1965	3.625	—	3.625	$4,800	$174.00
1966	3.85	0.35	4.2	6,600	277.20
1967–68	3.9	0.5	4.4	6,600	290.40
1969–72	4.4	0.5	4.9	6,600	323.40
1973–75	4.85	0.55	5.4	6,600	356.40
1976–79	4.85	0.6	5.45	6,600	359.70
1980–86	4.85	0.7	5.55	6,600	366.30
1987 on	4.85	0.8	5.65	6,600	372.90
	Tax on Self-Employed Person				
	(percent)	(percent)	(percent)		
1965	5.4	—	5.4	$4,800	$259.20
1966	5.8	0.35	6.15	6,600	405.90
1967–68	5.9	0.5	6.4	6,600	422.40
1969–72	6.6	0.5	7.1	6,600	468.60
1973–75	7.0	0.55	7.55	6,600	498.30
1976–79	7.0	0.6	7.6	6,600	501.60
1980–86	7.0	0.7	7.7	6,600	508.20
1987 on	7.0	0.8	7.8	6,600	514.80

In addition to the federal social security programs, various other social welfare services are provided by state and local governments independently of federal support. These include the state-sponsored workmen's compensation programs, used in all states, which provide medical services and cash benefits to a worker injured in connection with his job. More than three fourths of all nonagricultural employees are covered by such laws. The essence of most of the state workmen's compensation laws is that the employer is responsible for injuries resulting from any accident "arising out of or in the course of employment" and thus for insuring workers in the event that such injuries occur. The quality (coverage) of the programs varies greatly between the states. Many of the programs are inadequate in terms of their coverage, the length of the benefit period, and the amount of benefits. It would appear, however, that an indirect gain derived from the existence of such legislation is the encouragment of plant safety.

Unemployment Compensation Program. This program involves a combination of federal and state fiscal action. Both the federal government and the states levy payroll taxes on employers. The original Social Security Act (1935) established the unemployment compensation program. The legislation motivated state governments to cooperate in the program by placing a federal excise tax on certain employers, and by stipulating that if a state unemployment insurance law and administration meets certain requirements, the federal government will pay 100 percent of the administrative expenses and will permit employers to credit state excise taxes against the major portion (90 percent) of the federal taxes. Within a short time, all states passed unemployment compensation laws providing for state excise taxes on payrolls. Though all states participate in the program, considerable differentiation exists among the programs of the 50 states. States may determine such basic features of their programs as coverage, benefits, the rate of the state tax, eligibility, and disqualification provisions.

The Social Security Act of 1935 levied a federal excise tax of 1 percent on the payrolls of employers of eight or more workers in covered employment for the financing of the unemployment insurance program. Beginning in 1939, the tax was applied only to the first $3,000 of each covered employee's annual earnings. The federal tax rate was raised to 3 percent in 1938 and remained at that level until 1961. On January 1, 1961, the tax was increased to its present level of 3.1 percent. The additional .1 percent, which is earmarked for the federal share of the tax, is to assist in meeting the increasing administrative costs of the program and to provide additional money for the "loan fund." The latter supports advances made to states whose unemployment reserves become depleted. Credits for state taxes paid by employers continue to be computed on the basis of a 3 percent federal tax. Thus, 90 percent of the 3 percent federal rate—a rate of 2.7 percent—may be credited against state taxes paid by employers. Though no federal tax is levied on employees, three states impose unemployment compensation payroll taxes on employees. Under current legislation, the employer must have four or more employees on at least 1 day in each of 20 weeks in the calendar year in order to be liable for the tax.

Since 1954, states have been authorized to apply experience-rating tests to newly covered employers after one year of experience instead of the previously required three years. All states now use experience-rating systems to determine the degree of unemployment risk of particular employers. Some employers thus pay taxes of less than 2.7 percent of their federally covered payrolls to the states, though they still retain the full 2.7 percent credit against the federal tax.

Taxes collected by the states are deposited in a separate unemployment trust fund within the jurisdiction of the U.S. Treasury Department. The individual states have their own accounts in the fund against which they draw as required for the payment of unemployment benefits. The weekly system of benefit payments is geared to pay about 50 percent of gross wages up to a fixed maximum. This results in benefits which are usually higher than 50 percent of take-home pay, especially in the case of beneficiaries without dependents. Approximately 50 million wage earners are presently covered by the unemployment insurance program. Those not covered, totaling about 15 million, include employees of nonprofit organizations, state and local government employees, employees of small firms, domestic service workers, and farm and agricultural-processing workers. In addition to the long-established unemployment compensation programs, emergency legislation was passed by Congress in 1958 and again in 1961 to finance temporary unemployment compensation payments to individuals who had exhausted their benefit rights under regular state programs.

Interstate Highway and Other Trust Funds. Though the federal government has been continually assisting the states in highway development since 1916, a marked policy change occurred with the passage of the interstate highway legislation of 1956. This legislation not only provided for the long-term development of a 41,000 mile interstate highway system, but also changed the philosophy of federal highway financing. Previously, federal assistance to the states had been derived from general tax funds. Federal gasoline tax revenues went to the general treasury just as was true of any other nonearmarked tax. The legislation of 1956, however, changed this basic philosophy and earmarked various highway user-tax revenues, including those of the federal gasoline tax, for a special Highway Trust Fund which would be used to finance interstate highway construction. Specific excise taxes on gasoline, tires, trucks, and other economic goods closely connected to highway use thus became the revenue sources for the separate federal highway trust account.

The trust fund provides 90 percent of the costs of interstate highway construction, the remaining 10 percent being contributed by the states. The total long-term cost of the construction of the interstate highway network will be upward of $50 billion. As of March, 1966, 21,452 miles had been completed and 17,106 miles were under construction, leaving less than 2,500 miles not yet under construction.[7]

In all, the federal government has more than 100 special trust or deposit funds. Some of the more important ones, which will *not* be

[7] Bureau of Public Roads, U.S. Department of Commerce.

discussed specifically in this book, are the Railroad Retirement Trust Fund, the Federal Employees' Retirement Funds, the National Service Life Insurance and Government Life Insurance Fund, and the Federal Deposit Insurance Trust Fund. In addition, state and local governments also use the trust fund technique of allocating quasi-public goods. For example, the participation of state governments in the unemployment compensation program under federal social security has been discussed above. State and local governments, moreover, participate in various other earmarked financing programs such as those for workmen's compensation, retirement, and highway construction. The magnitude of those state-local government earmarked revenues of an insurance nature, including unemployment compensation, exceeds $7 billion at the present time. The state highway user-tax trust accounts would add significantly to this total.

Economic Analysis of Earmarked Taxes and Trust Funds. Economists disagree concerning the economic efficiency results of earmarked taxes. Margolis and Heller, in separate papers, suggest that earmarking tends to reduce the willingness of taxpayers to approve expenditures on specific public services.[8] On the other hand, Rolph and Break, Burkhead, and the Tax Foundation suggest earmarking as a device to generate taxpayer support for expansion of certain governmental services.[9]

Buchanan, in a study on the economics of earmarked taxes, reaches two conclusions.[10] *First,* he concludes that the condemnation of earmarked taxes cannot be supported on the basis of a distortion of (allocation) efficiency. To the contrary, earmarking may increase allocation efficiency by insuring more rational individual choice since with earmarking the individual can appraise more closely the relevant costs and benefits of a particular project. The individual is thus able to adjust the amount of each quasi-public good consumed in order to attain his most preferred consumption position. This is not true in general fund financing, which is similar to a "joint-product sale" in the sense that to get one commodity the consumer must also purchase another. The individual consumer of quasi-public goods, in the latter case, is subject to an allocation distortion since his independence of choice is reduced. *Second,* Buchanan concludes that general fund financing likely will attract a greater supply of public services and a supply in excess of consumer pref-

[8] Julius Margolis, "Metropolitan Finance Problems: Territories, Functions, and Growth," in *Public Finances: Needs, Sources, and Utilization* (National Bureau of Economic Research, 1961), pp. 261–66; Walter Heller, "CED's Stabilizing Budget Policy After Ten Years," *American Economic Review* (September, 1957), pp. 634–51.

[9] Earl Rolph and George Break, *Public Finance* (New York: Ronald, 1961), p. 62; Jesse Burkhead, *Government Budgeting* (New York: Wiley, 1956), p. 469; Tax Foundation, *Earmarked State Taxes* (New York: Tax Foundation, 1955).

[10] James M. Buchanan, "The Economics of Earmarked Taxes," *Journal of Political Economy* (October, 1963), pp. 457–69.

erences—as compared to earmarked financing. Moreover, general fund financing, as contrasted to earmarking, will probably increase the amount provided of a particular public service if the demand for the service is relatively elastic, and will likely reduce it as a percentage of total public services if the demand is relatively inelastic. A bachelor, for example, is likely to vote against funds which are earmarked only for education, but may vote for a bundle of additional services to be financed from a general fund which happens to include education. Thus, when general fund financing is used, the community receives a greater proportion of those public services with a highly elastic demand since they are tied in with the acquisition of other services and a smaller proportion of those public services which possess a less elastic demand.

Some economists argue that the federal social security program should be financed from general instead of earmarked tax funds since a significant negative allocation distortion can result from trust fund financing. It is claimed, for example, that payroll taxes, by increasing the cost of hiring new employees, encourage the substitution of capital for labor since capital is not subject to the payroll tax. Therefore, it is argued that labor will be forced into noncovered employment while capital is drawn to covered employment. It is thus concluded that severe allocation distortion takes place.

Opponents of earmarked payroll taxes also suggest that employment taxes are regressive in terms of their effect on income distribution. This is said to result because payroll taxes apply to only a limited amount of an employee's wages. Hence, such taxes work against the ability-to-pay principle of tax equity because the same benefits are received by two individuals even though one earns $6,600 and the other earns $100,000 annually. Furthermore, it is contended that the employer's share often is shifted either forward to consumers in the form of higher prices and/or backward in the form of lower wages to employees. Hence, distribution distortion is said to be increased by earmarked payroll taxes.

The above arguments against earmarked taxes, however, should be viewed also from a symmetrical fiscal standpoint. There is a *quid pro quo* relationship between that part of a payroll tax paid by the employee and his receipt of old-age, survivors, and medical care benefits. Hence, the asymmetrical ability-to-pay approach to equity, which concentrates only upon the tax side of the budget, cannot be used as the only bench mark for federal payroll tax rationality. Symmetry must also be provided to the rationality analysis of payroll taxes by including the expenditure side of the trust fund budgets in the analysis.

The unemployment compensation trust fund operates as an automatic fiscal stabilizer in reference to business cycle conditions.[11] Benefit

---

[11] This point will be discussed more thoroughly in Chapter 19.

payments tend to exceed payroll tax collections during recession. Tax payments tend to exceed benefit payments at times of full-employment prosperity. An expansionary multiplier effect is thus initiated by the unemployment compensation program during recession and a restrictive or negative multiplier is provided under inflationary gap conditions. This result occurs even without "on the spot" rate changes or changes in the benefits program. The magnitude of the stabilization effects resulting from the unemployment compensation program could be increased, of course, if deliberate rate or benefit changes were enacted. This has occurred, in part, on two occasions—when temporary supplementary benefit legislation was passed in 1958 and again in 1961.

The revenue productivity of federal trust fund taxes is considerable. The federal consolidated-cash budget for 1967 shows trust fund receipts of $41.6 billion. Moreover, the importance of trust fund activities of *state* and *local* government, as discussed above, should not be forgotten when the revenue importance of earmarked financing by the American public sector is being evaluated.

The Commercial Principle and User Prices

The Extent of Commercial Activity by American Government. Commercial revenues derive from the direct production and/or distribution and sale of economic goods by government to private purchasers. The government enterprises providing the goods charge *user prices* to the purchasers. All levels of government in the United States participate in this type of activity.

At the federal level, the examples of government commercial activity include the postal service, Panama Canal, Alaska Railroad, various power and reclamation projects such as the Tennessee Valley Authority and the Rural Electrification Administration, national forests and parks, various loan and insurance funds such as the Commodity Credit Corporation and the Federal Housing Administration, and the sale of surplus military goods. In 1965, outstanding direct loans by federal agencies exceeded $31 billion, while outstanding guaranteed and insured loans totaled an additional $91 billion. During the same year, the gross expenditures of federal enterprises amounted to more than $21.5 billion as compared to applicable receipts of nearly $20 billion generated from these activities.

In 1965, a program of user charges for national forest picnic and campground facilities was initiated. These fees are direct payments for the services received and are intended to support the construction and maintenance of the facilities. Hence, such fees are properly classified as user prices. Certain other fees, however, such as filing fees or operator's licenses, are administrative or regulatory in nature and will be discussed under administrative revenues later in the chapter.

The outstanding application of the commercial principle at the state level is found in the operation of state universities and colleges.[12] Tuition is the user price charged for the purchase of educational services, though typically the tuition amount only partially covers the costs of providing the education. This is particularly true for "in state" as compared to "out of state" students since the tuition charged to the nonresidents usually is considerably higher than the amount charged to residents of the state.

Another example of state commercial activity is found in the operation of toll roads. This type of public enterprise activity underwent a temporary slowdown period around 1960, after having experienced a period of rapid growth following World War II. Recent indications, however, are that toll road activity is reviving and plans are now being formulated to add more than 1,000 miles to the already existing 3,772 miles in operation. In addition, some *states* operate bridges and tunnels and charge user prices. Outstanding examples in this regard are the Golden Gate and San Francisco Bay bridges in California and the Lincoln Tunnel operated by the Port of New York Authority, the latter an interstate government compact between New York and New Jersey as approved by Congress through its jurisdiction over interstate commerce. The Port of New York Authority, which holds $1.8 billion in assets, was founded in 1921. Another state government usage of the commercial principle is found in the monopoly operation of liquor stores by 16 states. During 1963, these states derived more than $1.1 billion in revenues from the sale of liquor and associated products in state liquor stores. Moreover, "miscellaneous state charges," some of which are user prices and not administrative revenues, exceeded $3.5 billion during the year.

Significant operation of public enterprises exists also at the *local* level of government. The two most pronounced fields of local government commercial activity are found in the provision of water and in the generation and/or distribution of electricity. Other important local government enterprises include the operation of transit and gas supply systems. During 1962, local government derived more than $4 billion from utility and liquor store operations and an additional $6.5 billion from miscellaneous licenses and other charges, some of which were classifiable as user prices. In some instances, local governments operate toll bridges and tunnels.

It is evident from the above discussion that commercial fees are an important revenue source to the public sector. Yet, the critical question arises: what economic justification exists for the production and/or sale of divisible (at least in part) economic goods by government enterprises in a society orientated toward private sector economic activity? The next few pages shall consider this important question.

---

[12] The economics of education is a major point of discussion in Chapter 21.

Fiscal Rationality and Government Commercial Activity: The Choice between Private and Public Production of Quasi-Public Goods. A unit of government may undertake commercial activities for a variety of reasons. The most obvious reason is the need to obtain *revenue* for the support of governmental functions. In a society collectively preferring the market allocation of quasi-public (quasi-private) goods, however, this motivation cannot be considered the dominant reason for the engagement of the American public sector in commercial activities. Instead, the prevailing reasons for governmental participation in such activity focus upon the overall characteristics of quasi-public goods which, in certain cases,

FIGURE 16-1

VARIOUS PRICE-OUTPUT ALTERNATIVES FOR A FIRM
OPERATING UNDER DECREASING PRODUCTION COSTS
IN AN IMPERFECT MARKET

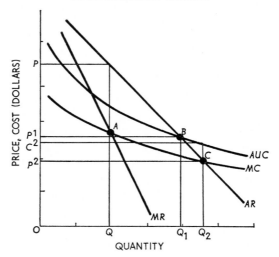

confer substantial degrees of publicness (public interest) upon particular economic goods. Within this context, publicness is conferred upon a particular economic good by the existence of certain inherent traits such as the presence of significant externalities, decreasing production costs over a wide range of output, and the other characteristics discussed earlier in the chapter. A sufficient combination and intensity of these public interest traits in a quasi-public good warrants consideration of public sector influence upon the supply of that good—if the goal of fiscal rationality is to be attained.

Figure 16-1 provides a framework for analysis of the relevant question of government versus market allocation of quasi-public goods. Since imperfect market structure, particularly that of an oligopolistic variety, characterizes American industry at the national level, the graph depicts monopolistic elements. Furthermore, since most instances of strong governmental allocation influence on the supply of quasi-public goods exist within decreasing cost industries, the graph also depicts economies of scale in production.[13] The price-output combination at point *A* is set under conditions of Profit-Maximization Pricing, that at point *B* under conditions of Average Cost Pricing, and that at point *C* under circumstances of Marginal Cost Pricing.

The major alternatives available for allocation of quasi-public goods are: (1) unregulated private sector provision of the good, (2) private provision of the good under direct governmental regulation, (3) private sector production of the good with governmental subsidy, or (4) public sector production of the good. If economies of scale exist over a wide range of output scales, the unregulated private industry likely will consist of either one pure monopoly firm or of a few oligopoly firms which dominate the industry. The pure monopoly firm, or the oligopoly firms if perfect or near-perfect collusion exists, prefer to produce at the profit-maximizing price and output determined by the intersection of marginal cost and marginal revenue at point *A* in Figure 16–1.[14] Thus, output *OQ* and price *OP* depict the profit-maximizing position. No direct governmental regulation exists in this case to compel lower prices and greater output. Distribution distortion will thus result from the "exploitative" monopoly price and allocation distortion will result because output is restricted below the optimal social welfare allocation point where marginal cost equals price. The conditions of high price and restricted output will be accentuated if the economic good is characterized by a highly inelastic price elasticity of demand.

If the economic good does not contain important externalities, and if its price elasticity of demand tends to be elastic, the best practical allocation approach (though not theoretically optimal) may be that of unregulated private production. This is especially true for a society whose community preferences favor market allocation. Thus, it may be concluded that governmental allocation of those quasi-public goods with elastic demand, and with insignificant external effects, is economically rational *only* if the revenue criterion receives top priority. Otherwise, market allocation is more appropriate.

---

[13] See Francis M. Bator, *The Question of Government Spending*, as cited in Chapter 2. Bator estimates that approximately 97 percent of federal administrative budget expenditures are for economic goods with significant decreasing cost–public good characteristics.

[14] The firm may choose *not* to maximize profits because of antitrust fear or public image considerations, or it may be unable to maximize them because of inadequate production and market knowledge. It seems reasonable to assume, however, that the firm will ordinarily come as close to point *A* as possible in its price-output combination.

A second alternative for allocating the quasi-public good in question is the application of the public utility concept. This approach, while continuing to allow private production of the good, provides for *direct regulation* of the private producer or producers of the good regarding such basic matters as price, quantity, and quality of output. In Figure 16-1, the firm subject to public utility regulation ordinarily would be allowed to produce at a price-output combination in the proximity of point B, at which point average revenue equates average unit cost, giving price OP^1 and quantity OQ^1. This is known as average cost or full cost pricing. The firm, in this instance, is earning a normal return on investment since alternative uses of the self-employed factors are compensated in a manner consistent with their opportunity cost values elsewhere. A public utility firm frequently is allowed to operate at a price-output combination slightly to the left of point B, thus earning modest monopoly profits.

By comparison with the unregulated case, it may be observed that public utility regulation provides a greater output at a lower price, OQ^1-OP^1, as opposed to the unregulated price-output, OQ-OP. Thus, if the good is a necessity to its purchasers, and if it possesses substantial external economies, the direct governmental regulation has reduced the amount of allocation distortion by increasing output from OQ to OQ^1, the latter output being closer to the social optimal output OQ^2. At output OQ^2, the price charged for the good is equal to the opportunity cost of the resources used in its production, as reflected in marginal cost. At any output to the left of OQ^2, the price which consumers are willing to pay for the good exceeds the marginal cost of supplying the good, thus distorting the ability of the market to meet consumer preferences.

In addition to its allocative effects, public utility regulation may reduce those distribution distortions which lead to greater income inequality because it does not allow the exploitative monopoly price to be charged. This result would be consistent with the American society's overall value judgment concerning an ideal state of distribution.

A third major alternative for the allocation of quasi-public goods is for the private sector to produce the good at optimal output OQ^2 and the nonmonopoly price OP^2 with government subsidizing the per unit loss (the vertical excess of OC^2 over OP^2). If the fourth alternative, government production of the good, is selected, production by the public sector ordinarily must be justified by some strong traits of publicness in the good itself. These characteristics, for example, may be of such a nature that the good is highly necessitous and possessive of highly significant external economies.

Following the marginal cost pricing technique, optimal allocation is achieved at point C in Figure 16-1 where marginal cost and price are equal. Yet, a private firm could not earn a profit producing optimal output OQ^2 and charging price OP^2 because average unit cost exceeds price at that output. This is *always* the case when increasing returns to scale (decreasing production costs) are being realized at the output where marginal cost equals price because marginal cost must be below average unit cost when average unit cost is declining. Government production of the good, or the subsidization of private production, is thus required if the good is to be allocated in optimal quantities.

At times, a quasi-public good with considerable external *diseconomies* will be supplied by government if, by the government's so doing, price can be kept high and the quantity purchased reduced. Optimal private allocation thus is purposefully avoided because of a higher priority social interest of a regulatory variety. To an extent, the monopoly operation of state-owned liquor stores in 16 states reflects this philosophy. In addition, a uniquely scarce good or resource with social importance may be allocated by government with a high price helping to ration use of the good. Of course, such rationing could also occur by direct mandate of the government without the charging of a user price. In any event, if strong traits of publicness are present in a quasi-public good, a case for government production, regulation, or subsidization of private production of the good can be established.

The Choice between General Tax and User Price Financing of Quasi-Public Goods. If government production of a quasi-public good is considered desirable, a variety of financing techniques are available to the unit of government supplying the good. Emphasis in the following pages will center upon the choice between general taxation and the user pricing commercial principle as alternative revenue means of paying for quasi-public goods. Other possible financing techniques such as earmarked excise taxes, administrative revenues, and debt financing are discussed elsewhere.

Pure public goods, which are not subject to the exclusion principle, cannot be allocated by the commercial principle. Quasi-public goods, however, whose benefits are divisible (at least in part), can be priced. Yet, quasi-public goods can also be allocated and financed through general taxation. The choice between general taxation and user prices as financial allocative techniques is thus relevant for quasi-public goods, but irrelevant for pure public goods.

The case for general taxation as the means of financing quasi-public goods rests upon several related points. First, general tax financing seems preferable to user pricing in those instances where the short-run marginal cost of an additional unit of output is very low or zero and the price elasticity of demand of the good is highly inelastic. The low or zero short-run marginal cost means that additional units of the good do not withdraw resources in any substantial way from alternative uses. For example, the marginal cost of additional usage of a park or playground up to capacity is negligible as is that of tuning in another television set to receive a program which is being transmitted anyway. There is, moreover, no purpose in charging a price for rationing the use of the good within its short-run capacity since the demand, being highly inelastic, is very insensitive to price.

Another argument in behalf of the general tax financing of quasi-public goods emphasizes the fact that pricing quasi-public goods with substantial external economies may cause a seriously short supply of these important goods. Thus, if the total cost of a university education were financed through tuition charges, with no general fund financing, there would be an undersupply of this important economic good.[15] This result would be assured by the economies of scale which seemingly exist in the provision of higher education. As a result, even though the user price may initially be set equal to marginal cost, providing a socially optimal output, the decreasing cost nature of the industry would not allow this price to cover unit costs of production. If costs are to be covered fully, and if general fund financing is not to be used, a higher tuition price would have to be charged. The higher price, of course, would tend to reduce the demand for and output of educational services below the optimum.

A further argument in favor of the tax financing of quasi-public goods concerns the cost of administering a user price system. If collection costs for user prices are substantial, general taxation would appear to be the preferred method of financing from this standpoint. Severe inconvenience to users from the collection system, moreover, may be looked upon as an important reduction in the utility derived from the consumption of quasi-public goods financed by user prices. If tolls were collected for the use of *all* streets, roads, and highways, for example, considerable disutility would be caused to their users, not to mention the added resource costs and time wasted.

The pursuit of certain distribution objectives provides another argument in defense of the general fund financing of quasi-public goods. The community may decide, for example, to make its real (ex post) income and wealth distribution more equal by means of either *direct* transfer payments or through the *indirect* method of concentrating first on the reallocation of resources. The use of transfer payments, however, is incompatible with the user pricing technique since they do not participate in resource-absorbing activities. *Direct* redistribution through transfer payments would thus have to depend upon some form of general financing (either tax or debt). Furthermore, the *indirect* redistribution of income, wealth, and living standards, as achieved by the reallocation of resources toward the provision of additional amounts of certain goods,

---

[15] Admittedly, student loans could reduce this undersupply of education, but it is very unlikely that their effects would be substantial.

would also require at least some dependence on general financing. For example, if the quasi-public goods are priced above the purchasing power means of lower income individuals, these people will be unable to acquire the goods in adequate quantities unless they are financed from general funds and not priced. Medical services or school lunches thus may not be available in adequate quantities to certain low-income people if they are available *only* on a direct pricing basis.[16] The argument again suggests a preference for the general tax financing of quasi-public goods as opposed to the user price alternative.

For the most part, the arguments in support of user pricing rest on the converse of the above points. If the marginal cost of a quasi-public good is substantially above zero, for example, the good should be priced in order to avoid wasteful oversupply in the long run. This is especially true when the demand for the good tends to be price-elastic. Hence, the free provision of goods without the involvement of a pricing mechanism loses sight of any long-term investment criterion or guide. User prices, on the other hand, provide at least a partial bench mark for long-run changes in capacity. The use of the commercial principle provides short-run prices which prevent overuse of short-run capacity and which, at the same time, constitute a bench mark for long-run investment decisions.

Another argument for use of the commercial principle is found in those quasi-public goods whose economic effects are mostly divisible. This is true of electricity consumption as compared to education. Furthermore, when the good does not possess significant external *economies*, the argument for tax financing loses strength and user pricing seems preferable. The presence of substantial external *diseconomies*, however, may call for user prices at high levels to discourage consumption of the good.

In addition, when the costs of collecting user prices are lower than the expenses of general tax administration for the same revenue yield, the former means of financing is to be preferred. Certain distribution goals, moreover, may be better met through user pricing than through tax financing. Since the consumption of electricity primarily benefits the purchaser, for example, the application of user prices conforms to the overall distribution philosophy accepted in American culture and demonstrated through the obvious community preference for market-type allocation and pricing.

User Pricing of Quasi-Public Goods: Pricing Alternatives. As noted earlier in the chapter, the commercial principle may be implemented by government through either profit-maximizing pricing, average cost pric-

[16] These goods, of course, could be provided through the technique of governmental *income subsidies* to low-income people but, even in this case, the goods are free in the sense that they are not obtained through private purchasing power.

ing, or marginal cost pricing. It was also observed that negative allocation and distribution distortions tend to be reduced as output is expanded toward the marginal cost = average revenue (price) equality (the social welfare optimal allocation point). The reader should be reminded, however, that isolated cases of marginal cost pricing in a society which has a majority of imperfectly competitive markets are not always the most rational solution available, though in most cases they constitute an improvement in allocation. The strongest case for marginal cost pricing under these circumstances would center around a good possessing considerable external economies. Nevertheless, an implicit danger remains that pursuit of the marginal cost pricing rule for public goods at a time when it is not being followed generally within the economy as a whole will irrationally expand the supply of public versus private goods. The point of actual allocation would thus be distorted and would rest at a position further away from the society's optimal social balance point of division between public and private goods.

Since the basis for governmental allocation of quasi-public goods rests primarily on the degree of publicness which the goods possess, however, an expanded supply of socially desirable goods may still be deemed rational despite the above social balance objection. Thus, use of the marginal cost pricing technique in the allocation of quasi-public goods may be considered at times as an acceptable "second-best solution" in a world inextricably associated with imperfect market structure and externalities. Use by government of the profit-maximizing price of $MC = MR$ in allocating a quasi-public good would best serve only the revenue goal unless the isolated case exists where the society is trying to reduce the consumption of an "undesirable" commodity. Average cost pricing, a third alternative, is generally preferable to profit-maximizing pricing since it helps to reduce negative allocation and distribution distortions. However, marginal cost pricing appears to be the most desirable of these three "less than optimal" alternatives for governmental pricing of quasi-public goods. Marginal cost pricing, nonetheless, faces several problems in addition to the one mentioned above concerning the absence of perfectly competitive conditions and the presence of externalities. Yet, these additional impediments to efficient marginal cost pricing may be reduced by certain modified (hybrid) financing techniques.

At least two additional economic problems occur when marginal cost pricing is used in a society characterized by substantial market imperfections. First, if the government enterprise is operating under increasing returns to scale (decreasing costs), it will incur a loss at the social welfare optimal allocation point where $MC = AR$. Figure 16–2, which essentially reproduces the point C conditions of Figure 16–1, displays this result. Thus, in allocating quantity OQ^2 of this good while charging price OP^2, the government is suffering losses to the extent of the rectangle $wxyz$. The losses are $OC^2\text{-}OP^2$ per unit of output. Since the user price does *not* cover the cost of producing output OQ^2, the difference could be met through tax revenues (or debt).

Under certain conditions, mixed financing utilizing both user prices and general tax revenues would constitute the most rational alternative for financing quasi-public goods. Under other circumstances, it may provide negative allocation and distribution distortions. The use of mixed financing is rational if the good possesses substantial external economies which benefit the society as a whole and which should not be paid for by individual users. Tax funds thus finance the community benefits while user prices finance the private or individual benefits. Moreover, the use of general fund financing to cover the loss rectangle in Figure 16–2 is

FIGURE 16–2

LOSSES AT OPTIMAL ALLOCATION POINT UNDER
DECREASING COST CONDITIONS OF PRODUCTION

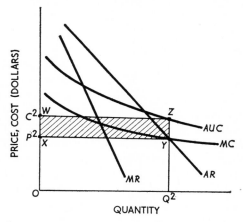

rational if it is collectively determined by the community that fiscal means of this sort should be used to redistribute real income by increasing the allocation of the quasi-public good in question. The combined use of general fund financing and user pricing to finance university education in the United States seems to fit both of the above rationality points, since the benefits of education are both social and private. In addition, improving the education of the poor is an effective means of improving their long-term real income position.

On the other hand, the absence of sufficient external economies to justify tax (or debt) subsidization of the loss rectangle, or the absence of a sufficient community-approved redistribution objective, would make the mixed financing technique irrational. This would be true because private users would derive most or all of the benefits from the consumption of the good and few, if any, social benefits would exist. Yet, general tax funds collected from the society as a whole would subsidize part of the cost of the private consumption. The result is a redistribution of income in favor of the private consumers of the quasi-public good.

Another related problem present in the decreasing cost case is the fact that "subsidized output" at the optimal social allocation point distorts long-run investment planning. There is no profit test to indicate the proper long-run allocation of resources toward the production of the good. In other words, price is not rationing resources among alternative uses in an adequate manner because the price does not cover full costs. A partial solution to this problem is offered by the multipart or peak-load pricing approach. This approach is a hybrid between marginal cost pricing and average cost pricing. All costs are covered by price. Yet, the price schedule is divided into at least two parts: one part for the opportunity to acquire the commodity and the other for the actual quantities demanded. A flat price may thus be charged for the standby opportunity to use a quasi-public good and an incremental price can be charged for each specific usage to cover short-run marginal costs as well as to suggest long-run investment needs. Such multipart pricing techniques are uniquely applicable to industries which produce nonstorable commodities such as electricity and transit services which have uneven demands for their products over a relevant period of time. It is here, in particular, that multipart pricing takes on the name "peak-load pricing."

Peak-load pricing suggests that prices charged at periods of maximum or peak use of capacity should be higher than those charged at off-peak hours. The reasoning behind this approach is that higher prices will more effectively ration short-run use of the capacity at peak-load periods of demand and, at the same time, will help to determine future capacity requirements as well as to help cover the costs of these requirements. Both short-run rationing and long-run investment criteria are thus served by this technique. It would appear that such a pricing approach increases economic rationality as long as the good does not possess substantial external economies which require that output be greater than that provided under conditions when full costs are covered, or as long as a distribution objective is not violated. Though such an approach involves differential prices, this does not necessarily mean that price discrimination exists since the differential prices may be proportional to differences in marginal costs. If so, true price discrimination, which consists of charging different purchasers different prices for the same economic good when such price differentials are not justified by cost differences, is not present.

The following example, related to Figures 16–3a and 16–3b, demonstrates the peak-load pricing approach. Consider the case of a government-owned electric utility. Assume that the peak demand is "firm," that

is, it will not change as the multiprices under consideration are introduced. The marginal cost in off-peak periods of electricity consumption is
merely the cost of the energy itself. On the other hand, the marginal cost
in peak periods is the sum of the energy cost and the cost of capacity.
Suppose that the demand is divided into two equal parts. Thus, one half
of the day represents peak demand for electricity and the other half of
the day represents off-peak demand.

The long-run solution to the problem is demonstrated in Figures
16–3a and 16–3b. There is no need to increase capacity to meet the
energy cost in the off-peak period. The marginal energy cost is repre-

FIGURE 16–3

PRICING UNDER FIRM PEAK CONDITIONS

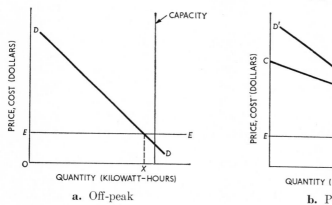

a. Off-peak   **b.** Peak-load

sented by curve EE and the off-peak demand is represented by demand
curve DD in Figure 16–3a. At the intersection of the marginal energy cost
and the off-peak demand curves, the quantity purchased of off-peak
electricity is determined. This quantity is equal to OX on the horizontal
axis.

In Figure 16–3b, it may be observed that the long-run capacity cost
is added to the energy cost for the peak demand situation. This is
economically rational because capacity must be greater to meet the peak
demand as opposed to the off-peak demand for electricity. Hence, line
CC represents the long-term marginal cost for electricity inclusive of
capacity requirements. It is a downward sloping curve in order to characterize a decreasing cost industry such as is frequently associated with
quasi-public goods. Line EE, once again, represents marginal energy
costs. At the intersection of the peak demand curve D^1D^1 and the
long-run marginal cost curve CC (which includes both energy and capacity costs), the quantity purchased of peak demand electricity is determined. This quantity is equal to OX^1 on the horizontal axis.

The long-run equilibrium demonstrated by Figures 16–3a and 16–3b would have been attained through the following adjustments: If the price at peak demand is equal to the sum of the marginal energy cost and the marginal capacity cost and still allocates the entire capacity which is available, optimal capacity exists and there is no reason to change capacity. If this price exceeds the sum of the marginal energy cost and the marginal capacity cost, as under high demand conditions, the results comprise a long-term investment signal that capacity should be expanded. The price in excess of long-run marginal costs, moreover, will help to pay for the expansion of capacity. On the other hand, if the price is less than the sum of the marginal energy and capacity costs, as under low demand conditions, the loss per unit of electricity signals the need for retrenchment in capacity during the long-run time period.

Hence, multipart (peak-load) pricing, under certain conditions, may improve rationality in the use of the commercial principle by government. Yet, it offers only a second-best solution. It must be stressed, once again, that the social welfare optimum of marginal cost pricing serves perfectly as a pricing technique only if all industries are pricing in this manner. This is an unrealistic assumption, however, for the American economy. Nevertheless, marginal cost pricing, and under certain conditions its multipart pricing modification, may still be the best available solution to application of the commercial principle by government for the allocation of quasi-public goods.

Administrative Revenues

Administrative revenues are collected by a unit of government from individuals as part of the performance of general governmental functions. These general governmental functions are primarily regulatory in nature. For example, government must protect persons and property. It must also provide a certain basic framework within which private economic activity will take place. In the performance of these and other general functions, government frequently charges a fee, levies a fine, collects an escheat, or otherwise collects revenue from individuals. The correlation between the payment of an administrative revenue by an individual, and the subsequent service or right acquired by the individual, is usually broad and imprecise. Only in a general sense, therefore, may it be said that a *quid pro quo* relationship exists in the case of administrative revenues.

Fees, licenses, and *permits* are very similar in nature. They all provide administrative revenues to government as part of a regulatory function and all involve the granting of permission by government to the individual to behave in a particular way. A fishing license, for example, allows a person to fish in public waters within the political jurisdiction of the grantor. A barber's license allows the barber to practice a particular trade. Admittedly, permission to behave in a particular manner could be regulated without requiring a monetary payment to government by the individual receiving the privilege. The revenue opportunities for government in requiring payment, though, may be considerable. Collection costs usually are low while the revenue productivity of the administrative charge can be high. Since fees are uniform to all taxpayers, they do not meet well the ability-to-pay principle of tax equity. Moreover, since the *quid pro quo* relationships generally are less than precise, they also usually do not meet the benefits-received principle in a satisfactory manner.

Fines and *forfeitures* clearly involve the performance of a regulatory function by government. Fines are monetary charges levied by a governmental unit as a penalty for a violation of law. Forfeitures, similarly, are penalties. They involve the sacrifice of bail or bond for failure to appear in court, or to complete contracts as prescribed. Except for isolated local government examples (such as "traffic trap" cities), the relative revenue importance of fines and forfeitures to the American public sector is slight.

According to the American legal system, the state level of government possesses the legal right to be the ultimate claimant of property left by deceased persons who have no legal heirs. This legal right of the state to absorb such property is known as an *escheat*. Escheats thus constitute another source of administrative revenues. As with fines and forfeitures, the overall revenue importance of escheats to the public sector is slight.

Special assessments, though usually classified as administrative revenues, are very similar to commercial or user charges. It is not inconsistent, however, to classify them as administrative revenues since they often are closely related to the overall governmental regulatory function of administering community development programs. A special assessment charge for the installation of sewers, street lights, or paved streets as part of the development plan of a community may thus be viewed as a by-product of the general administrative function of government. Special assessment districts at times are set up which are not coterminous with already existing levels of government. In a broad sense, such an assessment district constitutes a separate local unit of government.

Special assessments usually are characterized by the allocation of costs and benefits resulting from the improvement of land. The basis for assessment is usually not in terms of value, but in terms of area or frontage which tends to negatively distort the ability-to-pay principle of tax equity. Considerable procedural variation exists among the various levels and units of government which utilize the special assessment technique for financing the allocation of quasi-public goods.

The American public sector as a whole relies to a minor extent on gambling as a source of administrative revenues. However, one state—New Hampshire—does administer a public lottery. In 1964, the

New Hampshire lottery collected $5.7 million in revenues, a substantial part of which was given to the state's schools. In some nations, such as Australia, the public lottery provides substantial revenues through the selling of "risk."[17] Gambling, however, indirectly provides revenues to many American states which have legalized betting on horse races through the imposition of special pari-mutuel excise taxes on the gains of successful gamblers. The state of Nevada, moreover, receives substantial revenues from the comprehensive legalized gambling operations within that state.

[17] Admittedly, the line which separates the classification of the sale of risk as an administrative revenue instead of as a user price under the application of the commercial principle is a narrow one.

PART IV

Economic Stabilization, Economic Growth,

and the Public Sector

A pure market economy, under the conditions of modern industrial society, does not contain inherent traits which direct the economy toward a noninflationary full-employment equilibrium. Moreover, the conditions of market economic behavior do not automatically assure a satisfactory rate of economic growth. The recognition of these facts in economic theory came slowly. In fact, it was not until the widespread acceptance by economists of Keynesian economic concepts during the 1930's that these important points were appreciated. Subsequently, Western political economies turned toward the deliberate use of monetary and fiscal policy to utilize the inevitable economic impact of government on the private sector, and thus on the economy as a whole, in a manner conducive to the better attainment of full employment, price stability, and a satisfactory rate of economic growth. Formal recognition of the responsibility of the federal government of the United States in this regard came in the form of the Employment Act of 1946.

The ability of governmental budgetary manipulation to promote the macroeconomic goals mentioned above depends upon changes in tax rates, expenditures, or both, in the appropriate direction of change. These effects take the form of the government tax, transfer expenditures, exhaustive expenditures, and balanced budget multipliers. One or more of these fiscal techniques may be applied to help correct deflationary and inflationary gap conditions in the economy. Unfortunately, no good fiscal technique is available for the restraint of monopoly inflation.

Various norms (rules, bench marks) of fiscal policy may be used as reference points for fiscal policy decisions. These include the extreme bench marks of the "annually balanced budget" and "functional finance." In between these two ends of the fiscal norm continuum, hybrid techniques such as the "cyclically balanced budget" and the "high-employment budget" are offered. The best approach for a society seeking to rationalize its public sector impact on aggregate economic activity is that which includes in its "tool kit" (1) both fiscal and monetary policy, (2) both automatic and discretionary stabilizers, and finally (3) a hybrid fiscal norm such as the high-employment budget rule which includes some recognition of both the "control" notion of the annually balanced budget and the acceptance of deliberate budgetary influence as a means of promoting the economic goals of the society. The high-employment fiscal bench mark, when utilized with combined fiscal-monetary policy and the combined automatic-discretionary stabilizers, thus offers a comprehensive and rational approach to governmental fiscal policy.

Public sector budgetary behavior, if budgets are not balanced, will lead to either surplus or deficit results. The latter typically involves the creation of public sector debt to meet the differential between governmental spending and tax collections. Historically, there has probably been no greater area of economic misunderstanding and mythology than that surrounding the effects of central government debt. The creation of government debt, and its retirement at times, can contribute in a significant manner to the achievement of the allocation, distribution, stabilization, and economic growth goals of the society.

Chapter 17

AGGREGATE PERFORMANCE IN A MARKET ECONOMY AND THE NEED FOR FISCAL POLICY

The *great* Enemy of the truth is very often not the lie—deliberate, contrived and dishonest—but the myth—persistent, persuasive and unrealistic. Too often we hold fast to the clichés of our forebears. We subject all facts to a prefabricated set of interpretations. We enjoy the comfort of opinion without the discomfort of thought.

. . . Let us turn to the problem of our fiscal policy. Here the myths are legion and the truth hard to find. . . . These are the problems that we should be talking about—that the political parties and the various groups in our country should be discussing. They cannot be solved by incantations from the forgotten past.[1]

In no part of public finance are economic myths and misconceptions more prevalent than in the basis for macroeconomic fiscal policy. The fact that Americans have been vitally concerned with the stability and growth of the national economy during the last 35 years adds further significance to such fiscal misunderstanding. It is the purpose of this part of the book to review the basic forces (primarily market-directed) which determine both the short-term performance level and the long-term growth rate of the national economy. Then it will be possible to analyze the ability of the public sector to influence these aggregates.

It is inevitable that government exert an important economic influence on the private sector and upon aggregate economic performance in a mixed economic system such as that of the United States. In other words, the public sector cannot act in the budgetary manner of taxing and spending without affecting aggregate production, employment, income, price levels, and economic growth rates. Thus, a fiscal policy exists whether one is desired or not! It is only rational, therefore, to direct this fiscal policy in a deliberate manner toward the achievement of these aggregate economic goals. Of course, if the private sector possesses inherent forces which would automatically attain optimal stabilization and growth results, the case for deliberate government fiscal policy would be considerably weakened. The analysis below, however, demon-

---

[1] Excerpt from an address made by the late President John F. Kennedy at Yale University on June 11, 1962.

strates that the private sector does not possess these traits. The pure market economy does *not* automatically achieve a full-employment equilibrium level of performance nor a satisfactory rate of economic growth. The following section will consider the basic forces which determine aggregate economic behavior in a pure market economy and will demonstrate the distinct possibility that equilibrium performance levels providing either substantial unemployment or substantial inflation can occur. The model, though a simplification of very complex forces, still validly isolates the main determinants of aggregate economic performance.

THE PERFORMANCE OF A PURE MARKET ECONOMY[2]

The Classical Theory of Aggregate Economic Performance— Say's Law

Classical economics, which originated in the late 1700's, offered an optimistic interpretation of the forces which determine the level of aggregate economic performance in a pure market economy. The names of Smith, Say, Ricardo, Mill, Marshall, and others are associated with this school of economics. Classical production and employment theory, in aggregate terms, dominated the thinking of economists concerning aggregate economic activity until the "Keynesian Revolution" of the 1930's. According to classical theory, the pure market economy through the interaction of impersonal market forces will arrive by itself at an aggregate production level which fully employs *all* units of labor who wish to be employed. A pure market economy is thus said to be automatically a full-employment economy, the only deviations from full employment being occasional short periods of adjustment involving fluctuation around the full-employment equilibrium level of aggregate performance.

According to Say's Law, this full-employment level of income and output will exist because "supply creates its own demand." In other words, since the end of all economic activity is assumed to be the pleasure derived from consumption, every resource owner who provides resources for the creation of supply does so from the motivation of increasing his consumption of economic goods. Thus, given flexibility in wages and price levels, the pure market economy will adjust the level of labor employment to the point where involuntary unemployment is absent; that is, aggregate demand equals aggregate supply at full labor employment. In other words, inadequate demand leads to unemployment which causes the *real* wage to fall thus causing a rise in employment.

---

[2] The student may wish to *review* the principles of macroeconomics from a basic *Principles of Economics* textbook before reading this section. The macroeconomic theory presented here will essentially be brief and will assume previous knowledge of macroeconomics by the student.

Obviously, governmental fiscal policy, as it is known today, would *not* be required to promote full employment if the economy automatically directed itself toward the full-employment goal in this manner.

Certain premises essential to aggregate economic performance along classical lines, however, are not present in the contemporary market-directed economies of the Western world. While Say's Law may have been a reasonably adequate explanation of aggregate performance for the preindustrial or early industrial market economies of the late 17th and early 18th centuries, it has become decreasingly applicable to Western nations as they have followed their evolutionary paths toward industrial maturity. This evolutionary industrial development, with its attendant economies of scale, has resulted in substantial price and wage rigidities. Hence, the assumptions of perfect competition in product and resource (factor) markets become less useful and the ability of Say's Law to explain the aggregate performance of mature Western economies is subsequently weakened. A better explanation of pure market economy performance is required. Keynesian analysis meets this test.

The Keynesian Theory of Aggregate Economic Performance

The late British economist John Maynard Keynes is primarily responsible for the development of modern macroeconomic theory.[3] This widely accepted explanation of the basic economic forces which determine economic performance in a market-directed economy concentrates upon three primary determinants of aggregate behavior. These causal forces are Consumption (C), Saving (S), and Investment (I) which operate both as individual forces and in various significant interactions with each other in the determination of aggregate economic performance.

Consumption. In the Keynesian model of the pure market economy, the level of aggregate consumption expenditures is considered to be a function of the level of national income.[4] This functional relationship is known alternately as the "propensity to consume" or the "consumption function." The equation $C = f(Y)$ symbolizes the consumption function relationship. In Figure 17–1, which is plotted from Table 17–1, consumption expenditures (along with saving) are measured on the vertical axis and income is measured on the horizontal axis. However, income is in effect measured along each axis since income by definition is either spent for consumption or not spent for consumption—the latter choice

---

[3] His pioneering work in this regard is *The General Theory of Employment, Interest and Money* (London: Macmillan & Co., 1936).

[4] Technically, national disposable income is a source even closer to actual consumption and saving decisions than is national income. For reason of simplicity in presentation, however, the disposable income concept is *not* used at this point as the basic source of consumption expenditures and of saving.

FIGURE 17-1

CONSUMPTION AND SAVING AS FUNCTIONS OF
INCOME IN THE AGGREGATE ECONOMY

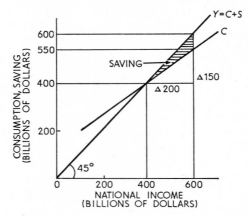

referring to the concept of saving (to be discussed below). Hence, the 45-degree line designated $Y = C + S$ is equidistant from each axis and represents the aggregate amount of income which can be either consumed or saved.

Consumption expenditures normally change in the same direction as income changes. A *positive* functional relationship thus exists between consumption and income. The level of consumption, of course, will also change in response to certain other causal variables, but income is considered to be the primary determinant. The simplified version of the consumption function based on income as the only causal variable is represented by line *C* in Figure 17-1. As income increases from $400 billion to $600 billion, for example, consumption increases by $150 billion from $400 billion to $550 billion. The slope of the consumption function is determined by the *marginal propensity to consume* which refers to the

TABLE 17-1

CONSUMPTION AND SAVING AS FUNCTIONS
OF INCOME IN THE AGGREGATE ECONOMY
(Billions of Dollars)

Y National Income	C Consumption	S Saving
$200	$250	$ − 50
400	400	0
600	550	+50

ratio between a change in the level of income and the resulting change in consumption expenditure. Thus:

$$\text{Marginal Propensity to Consume} = \frac{\text{Change in Consumption}}{\text{Change in Income}}$$

In the above numerical example, the marginal propensity to consume is .75 or 75 percent since:

$$MPC = \frac{\Delta C}{\Delta Y} \text{ and } \frac{\$150 \text{ b.}}{\$200 \text{ b.}} = .75$$

The relationship between the level of consumption and the level of income at any *one* point on the consumption function is known as the *average propensity to consume*. Thus:

$$\text{Average Propensity to Consume} = \frac{\text{Consumption}}{\text{Income}}$$

In the above numerical example, the average propensity to consume at the $600 billion income level is .91% or 91% percent since:

$$APC = \frac{C}{Y} \text{ and } \frac{\$550 \text{ b.}}{\$600 \text{ b.}} = .916$$

The student must be careful not to confuse the instantaneous theoretical nature of the consumption function with empirical studies of consumption-income ratios over time. The basic theoretical consumption function holds as constant other parameters which influence consumption decisions, such as consumer tastes, the introduction of new products, and changes in wealth holdings. It then asks the question: What would aggregate consumption be at various income levels given the constancy of these other forces which influence consumption? Obviously, at any moment of time with these other parameters constant, consumption must rest at some point on the instantaneous short-run consumption function curve.

Duesenberry, in his analysis of the relationship between short-run and long-run consumption functions, concludes that once a consumer achieves a higher income-consumption level, a decrease in income does *not* induce diminished consumption along the same function by which the consumer had reached the higher income-consumption level in the first place.[5] This concept of consumption as a function of "the income to which one is accustomed," however, involves in effect a shift in the consumer tastes parameter which is held constant in the instantaneous short-run consumption function displayed in Figure 17–1.

[5] James S. Duesenberry, *Income, Saving, and the Theory of Consumer Behavior* (Cambridge, Mass.: Harvard University Press, 1952).

Saving. That part of income not spent on consumption is said to be saved. Thus, in Figure 17–1 the shaded area above the consumption line (C) and below the income line ($Y = C + S$) constitutes saving. Saving, like consumption, is a *positive* function of income, that is, saving tends to increase as income increases and to decline as income declines. The *marginal propensity to save* may be defined as the ratio between a change in saving and a change in income while the *average propensity to save* relates saving to income at a given income level. In terms of the example provided in Figure 17–1, the marginal propensity to save is .25 (25 percent) and the average propensity to save at the $600 billion income level is .08⅓ or 8⅓ percent. These results are determined as follows:

$$\text{Marginal Propensity to Save} = \frac{\text{Change in Saving}}{\text{Change in Income}}$$

$$MPS = \frac{\Delta S}{\Delta Y} \text{ and } \frac{\$50 \text{ b.}}{\$200 \text{ b.}} = .25$$

and

$$\text{Average Propensity to Save} = \frac{\text{Saving}}{\text{Income}}$$

$$APS = \frac{S}{Y} \text{ and } \frac{\$50 \text{ b.}}{\$600 \text{ b.}} = .084$$

$$\Delta C + \Delta S = \Delta Y$$
$$\$150\text{b.} + \$50\text{b.} = \$200\text{b.}$$
$$MPC + MPS = 1$$

Investment. The purchase of new capital goods may be motivated in a variety of ways. Modern macroeconomic theory classifies these various motivating forces into two main categories—autonomous and induced investment. *Autonomous investment* is somewhat of a catchall concept. Any motivation for investment *other than* one resulting from a change in the level of (or rate of change in) aggregate economic performance is said to be autonomous. An improvement in technology, for example, may motivate investment spending regardless of the level of or rate of change in national income. The concept of *induced investment,* on the other hand, refers to changes in business spending for capital goods as influenced by changes in aggregate economic performance. Induced investment may thus be described as a functional relationship between investment and the level (or rate of change in) national income.[6] The relationship between induced investment and national income is normally a positive one. Thus, induced investment increases as national income expands and decreases as national income contracts.

The Determination of Aggregate Economic Performance. Having described the individual forces which determine aggregate economic

[6] Induced investment is closely related to the operation of the acceleration principle which is highly significant to economic growth theory.

performance in a market economy (consumption, saving, and investment), it will now be demonstrated how these separately motivated
forces determine the aggregate performance level of the economy
through their various interactions. The following assumptions allow the
analysis to concentrate on those features of the theory which are most
fundamental to its operation: (1) the economy possesses a very small
government sector, that is, one which is large enough *only* to provide
minimal law and order. Thus, taxes and government spending will be
omitted from this simplified version of modern macroeconomic theory;
(2) the economy is a "closed" economy which means that foreign trade is
excluded; (3) all corporation profits are paid out as dividends; and (4)
all investment is autonomous and thus not influenced by changes in the
level of (or rate of change in) national income.

A significant relationship exists between the expected (planned)
sales of economic goods by businesses and the production costs incurred
in producing these goods. In creating *aggregate supply*, the businesses of
a pure market economy incur certain costs in employing the resources
necessary to produce the volume of output which they believe will be
demanded. Moreover, the aggregate supply costs of businesses comprise,
on the receiving end of the flow, the incomes received by consumers. The
consumers use the incomes as the purchasing power sources for their
decisions regarding consumption expenditure and saving. Thus, aggregate supply may be expressed by the equation:

$$Y = C + S$$

The gross incomes received by businesses in the pure market economy are derived from the sale of consumption goods to consumers and
from the sale of investment (capital) goods to other businesses within the
economy. The absence of foreign transactions and of governmental
purchases of economic goods in the closed, pure market economy means
that purchases are made *only* by the domestic private sector and its two
components—consumers and businesses. Thus, *aggregate demand* may
be expressed by the equation:

$$Y = C + I$$

If the expected (planned) sales of consumption and investment
goods are realized, then the equilibrium performance level is directly
attained. If ex ante (expected) sales do not match the ex post realities,
however, a state of disequilibrium exists which will set forces in motion
toward the equilibrium position. Figure 17–2 and Table 17–2 demonstrate this process whereby market forces tend to achieve an equilibrium
level of aggregate economic performance.[7] If expected income (Column 1

[7] The student should be reminded that the macroeconomic model presented
here is a simplified, though valid, description of the basic determinants of aggregate
economic performance in a market economy.

FIGURE 17-2

EQUILIBRIUM NATIONAL INCOME IN A PURE
MARKET ECONOMY

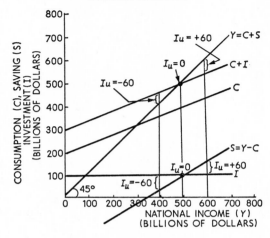

in Table 2), which is based upon the creation by businesses of aggregate supply (Column 5 in Table 2), is less than $500 billion, planned saving is less than planned investment and aggregate supply is less than aggregate demand. This means that businesses will receive more from the sale of consumer and capital goods than they had expected when they created aggregate supply, and an unexpected reduction in business inventories occurs because sales exceed expectations. At an expected income (aggregate supply) level of $400 billion, for example, investment in capital goods by businesses exceeds the planned saving of consumers by $60 billion and an unexpected inventory reduction takes place. Businesses

TABLE 17-2

EQUILIBRIUM NATIONAL INCOME IN A PURE MARKET ECONOMY
(Billions of Dollars)

(1) Y Expected Income	(2) C Planned Consumption	(3) S Planned Saving		(4) I Planned Investment	(5) C + S Aggregate Supply		(6) C + I Aggregate Demand
$ 0	$200	$−200	<	$100	$ 0	<	$300
100	240	−140	<	100	100	<	340
200	280	− 80	<	100	200	<	380
300	320	− 20	<	100	300	<	420
400	360	+ 40	<	100	400	<	460
500	400	+100	=	100	500	=	500
600	440	+160	>	100	600	>	540
700	480	+220	>	100	700	>	580

will thus tend to increase aggregate supply toward the $500 billion equilibrium performance level at which point planned investment and planned saving are equal and no unintended inventory change occurs.

If expected income based on the creation of aggregate supply by businesses is greater than the $500 billion equilibrium level, planned saving is greater than planned investment and aggregate supply is greater than aggregate demand. This means that businesses will receive less from the sale of consumer and capital goods than they had expected when they created aggregate supply and an unplanned expansion in business inventories occurs because sales do not meet the expectations upon which the creation of aggregate supply was based. At an expected income (aggregate supply) level of $600 billion, for example, planned saving exceeds the investment purchases of capital goods by $60 billion and unexpected inventory expansion takes place. Businesses will thus tend to contract aggregate supply toward the $500 billion equilibrium performance level at which point planned saving and planned investment are equal and no unintended inventory change occurs. Hence, the equilibrium level of aggregate economic performance will be at the point (income level) where aggregate supply and aggregate demand are equal.

The *investment multiplier,* which may be defined as the ratio between a change in the level of autonomous investment and the resulting change in the level of national income, bears importantly upon the equilibrium process described above. Figure 17–3, which is based on the lower part of the diagram in Figure 17–2, will be used to display the multiplier process. Consumption, which is common to both aggregate supply ($Y = C + S$) and to aggregate demand ($Y = C + I$), has been excluded from Figure 17–3 so that emphasis may be applied to the critical relationship between saving and investment in the determination of equilibrium.

The multiplier process may be approached from two standpoints: either from the premise of a present state of disequilibrium or from the premise of a shift upward (increase) or downward (decrease) in the autonomous investment function. For example, a movement from the $400 billion national income level to the equilibrium level of $500 billion may be considered as moving from a disequilibrium position to an equilibrium position if I represents the prevailing level of autonomous investment. Planned saving and planned investment are equal and equilibrium is reestablished at the $500 billion income level. The multiplier in this case represents the ratio between *ab* and Y^2Y which, in numerical terms, is the relationship between $60 billion ($100 billion–$40 billion) and $100 billion ($500 billion–$400 billion).

The multiplier may also be viewed from the standpoint of an initial equilibrium position existing at $500 billion and a subsequent move from this equilibrium to a new equilibrium position at a different income level. For example, if autonomous investment increases from *I* to *I*[1] (from $100 billion to $160 billion), national income will increase from $500 billion to $600 billion. This is represented in Figure 17–3 by the ratio between *cd* and *YY*[1]. Since the multiplier may be contractionary as well as expansionary (that is, either negative or positive), a reduction of investment

FIGURE 17–3

THE INVESTMENT MULTIPLIER

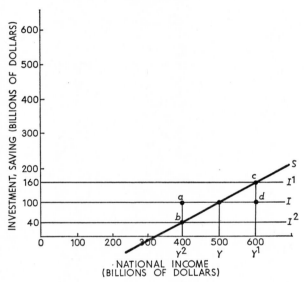

from *I* to *I*[2] will cause national income to decline from $500 billion to $400 billion. The value of the multiplier ratio is determined by the values of the marginal propensities to consume and to save. The multiplier formula, with *K* symbolizing the multiplier, may thus be stated as follows:

$$K = \frac{1}{1 - mpc}$$

or, alternately, as

$$K = \frac{1}{mps}$$

where *mpc* indicates the marginal propensity to consume and *mps* indicates the marginal propensity to save.[8]

In terms of the data in Figure 17–3, the multiplier value is 1.66 (assuming a marginal propensity to save of .60) since a $60 billion increase in autonomous investment leads to a $100 billion increase in national income. From the formula

$$K = \frac{1}{mps} \text{ or } \frac{1}{.60} = 1.66$$

it should be observed that saving is the only leakage from the spending stream in this example of the investment multiplier operating in a closed, pure market economy. Yet, the rather high marginal propensity to save (.60) used in the example results in a multiplier value (1.66) which would be a realistic figure for an open, mixed economy where international and public sector economic transactions provide additional leakages from the spending stream.

Deflationary and Inflationary Gaps

It is very significant that the aggregate economic performance level attained through the process described above does *not* necessarily provide full employment of labor and capital and price stability. There is nothing inherent in the Keynesian model, such as wage and price flexibility, to assure these optimal short-run results. The liquidity trap, moreover, will tend to forestall the ability of changes in the monetary stock to influence aggregate demand through changes in the rate of

[8] Algebraically, the derivation of the investment multiplier may be stated:

$$\Delta I + \Delta C = \Delta Y \quad \text{(true by definition)}$$

dividing through by Y

$$\therefore \frac{\Delta I}{\Delta Y} + \frac{\Delta C}{\Delta Y} = 1$$

$$\therefore \frac{\Delta I}{\Delta Y} = 1 - \frac{\Delta C}{\Delta Y}$$

$$\therefore \frac{\Delta Y}{\Delta I} = \frac{1}{1 - \frac{\Delta C}{\Delta Y}}$$

but $\frac{\Delta Y}{\Delta I} = K$ (multiplier)

and $\frac{\Delta C}{\Delta Y} = mpc$ (marginal propensity to consume)

$$\therefore \text{ multiplier } (K) = \frac{1}{1 - mpc}$$

or, since $mpc + mps = \Delta Y$ or 1

$$\text{multiplier } (K) = \frac{1}{mps}$$

interest.[9] The pure market economy may by coincidence operate at a full-employment noninflationary equilibrium. On the other hand, the economy may attain an undesirable equilibrium level of performance with either substantial labor and capital unemployment or with monetary inflation. The former is known as a *deflationary gap* condition and the latter as an *inflationary gap*. These "less than optimal" results are demonstrated in Figure 17–4 and are described in detail below.

FIGURE 17–4

DEFLATIONARY AND INFLATIONARY GAP CONDITIONS

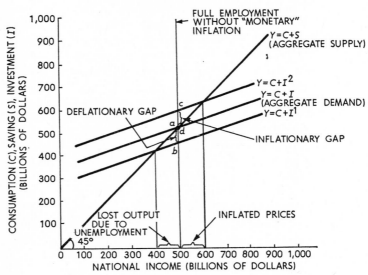

"Optimal" results are attained in the graph at a $500 billion national income level because labor and capital resources are fully employed and monetary inflation does not exist at this performance level. Full employment, of course, must be defined in some acceptable manner. Typically, full employment is said to exist if 4 percent or less of the labor force is involuntarily unemployed and capital capacity in major industries is utilized at approximately 90 percent of capacity. Furthermore, a distinction must be made between monetary (demand) inflation and monopoly (administered price, sellers') inflation. Though monetary inflation does not exist at the $500 billion equilibrium level of performance, monopoly inflation as caused by market imperfections in the product and factor markets may well exist.[10] Thus, if optimal performance is defined to

[9] The student may refer to a *Money and Banking* textbook for a review of the liquidity-preference theory of interest rate determination.

[10] This point will be analyzed further in the next chapter (Chapter 18) with the discussion of the relationship of the Phillips Curve and intergoal nonneutrality to fiscal policy.

include complete price stability, then even the $500 billion level of performance is not optimal when monopoly inflation exists.

Where the intersection of aggregate supply $(Y = C + S)$ and aggregate demand $(Y = C + I)$ sets the performance level at full employment without monetary inflation, as at the $500 billion national income level in Figure 17–4, the society neither suffers from loss output due to unemployment nor from monetary inflation resulting from resource scarcity. Yet, as observed above, this condition would only be accidentally attained under the operational process of a pure market economy. Aggregate demand may be deficient to aggregate supply at full employment $(Y = C + I^1 < Y = C + S)$, thus creating a deflationary gap, or it may exceed aggregate supply at full employment $(Y = C + I^2 > Y = C + S)$, thus creating an inflationary gap situation. *Any* of these three situations may exist. The pure market economy will not automatically tend toward any one of them. The deflationary gap *ab* will cause reduced output by the amount of $100 billion ($500 billion minus $400 billion). The inflationary gap *cd* will lead to inflated output by the amount of $100 billion ($600 billion minus $500 billion). The ratios between *ab* and the "lost output" and between *cd* and the "inflated output" represent the value of the multiplier as discussed in the previous section. Thus, if an *ab* equal to $60 billion causes reduced output of $100 billion, the multiplier value is 1.66.

The Problem of Economic Growth

Not only does the pure market economy fail to assure full employment without monetary inflation, but there is, in addition, no evidence that it will automatically tend to achieve a satisfactory rate of economic growth. The forces which determine economic growth in a market-directed economy are far more complex than those analyzed above for short-run aggregate performance. In addition, they involve significant noneconomic as well as economic variables. No attempt will be made in this book to develop a comprehensive theory of economic growth. Though economic science has contributed many useful theories of economic growth, no single theory is comprehensive enough to be used as a general analytical reference point.[11] Hence, the analysis herein of fiscal

[11] Some of the more important writings which provide insight into the economic growth process are: Roy F. Harrod, "An Essay in Dynamic Theory," *Economic Journal* (March, 1939), pp. 14–33; Evsey Domar, "Expansion and Employment," *American Economic Review* (March, 1947), pp. 34–55; James S. Duesenberry, *Business Cycles and Economic Growth* (New York: McGraw-Hill Book Co., Inc., 1958); Robert M. Solow, "Technical Change and the Aggregate Production Function," *Review of Economics and Statistics* (August, 1957), pp. 312–20, and "Technical Progress, Capital Formation, and Economic Growth," *American Economic Review* (May, 1962), pp. 76–86; William Fellner, *Trends and Cycles in Economic Activity* (New York: Holt, 1956), and John R. Hicks, *A Contribution to the Theory of the Trade Cycle* (Oxford: The Clarendon Press, 1950). The Hicksian Model will be

procedures to assist economic growth will be based on certain widely accepted general aspects of the growth process rather than on a single definitive theory.

There is no question, for example, that both the quantitative expansion of productive resources, particularly capital, as well as the qualitative improvement of these resources are essential to the maintenance of a satisfactory growth rate. In addition, the importance of noneconomic factors such as political stability, particularly in underdeveloped econo-

FIGURE 17–5

LONG SWINGS IN AGGREGATE PRODUCTION, 1860–1961 ANNUAL ESTIMATES
AND NINE-YEAR MOVING AVERAGES

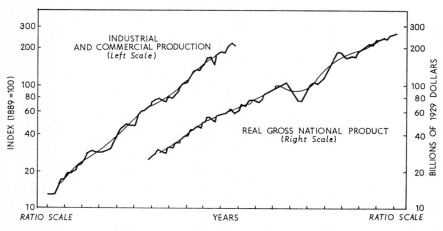

Adapted from Bert G. Hickman, "The Postwar Retardation: Another Long Swing in the Rate of Growth?," *American Economic Review* (May, 1963), Chart I, p. 491.

mies, stands out as a proven fact. There is also no doubt as to the importance of the dual role of investment in the growth process, namely, that investment not only continues its short-run function of utilizing the saving generated at full-employment equilibrium in the economy, but that it also involves the long-run problem of absorbing the incremental output added by net additions to the nation's capital stock.[12] Indeed, if the economy is to grow steadily it must possess a continually rising level of investment in order to keep its aggregate demand abreast of its growing productive capacity.

The fact that the American economy has not always experienced steady growth, nor even satisfactory growth rates, is indicated by Figures

---

summarized in the next chapter because of its relevance to intergoal nonneutrality between the stabilization and economic growth goals and the application of fiscal policy to these goals.

[12] This concept is developed in the Harrod-Domar growth models cited in footnote 11.

FIGURE 17–6

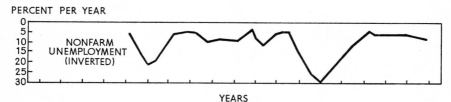

Long Swings in Unemployment
1874–1960

PERCENT PER YEAR

NONFARM
UNEMPLOYMENT
(INVERTED)

YEARS

Adapted from Bert G. Hickman, "The Postwar Retardation: Another Long Swing in the Rate of Growth?," *American Economic Review* (May, 1963), Chart III, p. 495.

17–5 and 17–6 and by Table 17–3. In Figure 17–5, the cyclically interrupted pattern of American economic growth since 1860 is evident. The graph is presented with particular emphasis on the long swing variety of business cycle. Such emphasis is not meant to imply, however, that cycles of shorter duration did not also occur during the period. Figure 17–6 shows the effect of cyclical fluctuations on the employment of nonfarm (industrial) labor. Obviously, growth rates are slowed when involuntary unemployment exists in the economy. Table 17–3 also displays the interrupted pattern of American economic growth with the degree of variation in growth rates during the period 1889–1957 ranging from 4.7 percent between 1948–53 and 4.5 percent between 1889–99 to a very unsatisfactory 0.2 percent between 1929–37. The growth rate for the period (1889–1957) as a whole was 3.5 percent.

TABLE 17–3

Growth of Real Net National Product
1889–1957
(Average Annual Percentage
Rates of Change)

Time Period	Real Net National Product
1889–99	4.5%
1899–1909	4.3
1909–19	3.8
1919–29	3.1
1929–37	0.2
1937–48	4.4
1948–53	4.7
1953–57	2.2
1889–1957	3.5

Source: John W. Kendrick, *Productivity Trends in the United States* (A National Bureau of Economic Research Study) (Princeton, N.J.: Princeton University Press, 1961), Table 6, p. 79. Reprinted by permission of Princeton University Press. Copyright, 1961.

Since there is no inherent process in a market-directed economy to assure either noninflationary full employment or a satisfactory rate of economic growth, a case may thus be built for the deliberate application of governmental economic policy to help achieve these goals. As observed earlier, a fiscal policy exists whether one is desired or not because government cannot act in a budgetary manner without influencing the various economic goals—including short-run stabilization and long-run growth. Hence, the impact of government might just as well be rationalized in terms of deliberate policy. Since the federalistic nature of the American public sector would make an aggregate public sector fiscal policy inclusive of all levels and units of government extremely difficult to coordinate, the primary burden for rational fiscal policy falls to the federal government. It was not until 1946 that Congress formally recognized this fact and passed legislation providing a mandate for federal fiscal (and monetary) policy.

THE EMPLOYMENT ACT OF 1946—A LEGISLATIVE MANDATE FOR FISCAL POLICY

Nature of the Employment Act

The year 1946, the first year of the post–World War II economic era, found the nation's economy operating under severe inflationary gap conditions. The enormous federal spending in support of World War II had exerted tremendous inflationary pressures during the previous four years. Aggregate demand was considerably greater than aggregate supply at full-employment output during the period. Once the war was over, the postponed consumer demand for durable goods such as cars, refrigerators, and houses along with the postponed business demand for peacetime capital goods provided continued inflationary pressures. Once more, this high volume of aggregate demand was made effective by wartime savings. In addition, World War II had allowed the economy to escape a severe decade-long depression, which had begun with a cyclical downturn just prior to the stock market collapse of late 1929. The lingering fears of depression in the minds of senators and congressmen, businessmen, professional economists, and others, along with the then present conditions of inflation, laid the groundwork for the passage of the Employment Act in 1946. The essence of this extremely important legislation reads:

The Congress hereby declares that it is the continuing policy and responsibility of the Federal Government to use all practicable means consistent with its needs and obligations and other essential considerations of national policy, with the assistance and cooperation of industry, agriculture, labor, and State and local governments, to coordinate and utilize all its plans, functions, and resources for the purpose of creating and maintaining, in a manner calculated to foster and promote free competitive enterprise and the general welfare, conditions under which there will be afforded useful employment opportuni-ties, including self-employment, for those able, willing, and seeking work, and to promote maximum employment, production, and purchasing power.[13]

With the passage of such legislation, the central government of the United States joined the governments of other mature Western industrial nations in stipulating a governmental responsibility to promote aggregate economic performance through rational economic policy. Such policy normally takes the form of monetary and fiscal tools. The act clearly authorizes federal government economic activity to favorably influence aggregate economic performance. The federal government, however, is given the mandate to conduct such policy only in cooperation with the considerations of the market sector of the economy as is evident in the part of the above statement which says that the federal government is to act "in a manner calculated to foster and promote free competitive enterprise."

The Employment Act directly specifies the maximum employment goal, but it is somewhat less direct, though by no means unclear, in its mandate for maintaining reasonable price level stability. The latter goal is implicit in the phrase which authorizes efforts to promote "maximum purchasing power" and was also implicit in the congressional debate prior to the passage of the bill. Less precise is the mandate for federal fiscal policy to promote satisfactory rates of economic growth. Increasing emphasis on the growth objective, however, has been present in the fiscal policy of recent years and the interpretation of the Employment Act has clearly been broadened to include the economic growth objective. Simi-larly, it has also been broadened in interpretation in recent years to include the goal of improvement in the nation's balance of international payments.

The Employment Act requires that a report regarding the state of the American economy be submitted to Congress by the executive branch no later than January 20 of each year. The first report under the act was submitted in January of 1947. The *Economic Report of the President* describes such matters as the employment, output, and price level condi-tions and trends of the economy, a review of federal fiscal and monetary policies, and other relevant economic considerations.

The legislation also established a Council of Economic Advisers to assist and advise the President on economic matters. The *Economic Report of the President,* referred to above, is based in part upon analyti-cal work provided by the CEA. The Council of Economic Advisers consists of three members. The act also established the Joint Committee on the Economic Report. This group was first created for the purpose of conducting economic studies pertinent only to the *Economic Report of*

[13] *The Employment Act of 1946,* February 20, 1946, P.L. 304, 79th Cong. 2d sess. (60 Stat. 23).

the President. The analysis conducted by the Committee, however, has been gradually extended over a wide range of economic issues and is no longer solely for the *Economic Report.* Furthermore, the name of the Committee has been subsequently changed to Joint Economic Committee. The JEC consists of eight members each from the Senate and House and is supplemented by a highly competent professional staff. To a large extent, the Joint Economic Committee provides broad economic analysis for the direct benefit of Congress and indirectly for the benefit of academicians, businessmen, and others interested in the performance of the aggregate economy. It does so in a manner analagous to the role performed by the Council of Economic Advisers in its studies which directly benefit the executive branch of the federal government, but which indirectly benefit many other interested parties.

Defining Employment Act Goals

The Stabilization Objective. Effective administration of the Employment Act requires workable definitions of the important aggregate economic goals and, in addition, relies upon the ability to measure these aggregates in an adequate manner. The discussion at this point will classify the full-employment, price stability, and international balance-of-payments goals as subparts of the more comprehensive *stabilization* goal and will consider a satisfactory rate of *economic growth* as the other major aggregate objective. Definitions will be discussed first and measurement approaches considered later in the chapter.

The full-employment goal can be approached, in a strict sense, by defining *full employment* of labor as a situation in which there is a complete absence of involuntary labor unemployment in the economy. Thus, full labor employment could be said to exist when all workers are willing to work at the prevailing wages of their occupation and, in addition, are able to obtain employment. On the other hand, *unemployment* is present if some workers who are willing to work at the prevailing wages of their occupation are unable to find employment after a reasonable time period. In a broader and more practical sense, however, full labor employment could be defined to include a certain minimal amount of involuntary unemployment. An allowance for "frictional unemployment," for example, should be made in any reasonable definition of full employment. A worker is frictionally unemployed if he is out of work due to labor market imperfections such as the time lost in changing occupations, temporary seasonal layoffs, and unemployment resulting from material shortages. Another variety of involuntary unemployment is known as "structural unemployment." This refers to persistent unemployment caused by technological change (including automation), by changes in the composition of product demand, and by the competition provided to domestic products by the importation of foreign economic goods.

In its 1961 report the Commission on Money and Credit suggests that an appropriate target for low-level unemployment as a guide to stabilization policy should consist of a situation where the number of "unfilled vacancies is about the same as the number of unemployed."[14] Under such circumstances, some unemployment exists and there are some unfilled vacancies. Yet, both conditions could be relieved by measures which would improve the functioning of labor markets and which would increase the mobility of workers both geographically and between jobs of different skills, so as to reduce frictional and structural unemployment.[15]

The definition of full labor employment to be used in this book, given the above considerations, is similar to the workable definition used by a majority of policymakers. Full labor employment will be said to exist when 4 percent or less of the labor force is involuntarily unemployed. An allowance thus is made for a modest amount of involuntary labor unemployment resulting from frictional and structural causes. In terms of capital capacity, full employment will be defined along the generally accepted lines of 90 percent utilization.[16]

The term *inflation* refers generally to an increase in a level or index of various relevant prices. Deflation, of course, is the opposite of inflation as price levels decline. Recent decades have witnessed far more reasons to be concerned with rising than with declining prices. The analysis of various types of inflation is importantly related to rational economic policy. There are two basic types of inflation, namely, *monetary* and *monopoly* inflation. The former is identified with inflationary gap conditions (as discussed above). World War II and the immediate postwar era provide an excellent example of monetary inflation whereby aggregate demand as made effective by adequate purchasing power exceeds aggregate supply at full resource employment. Monetary and fiscal policy, especially the former, are reasonably adept at combating this type of inflation. However, monopoly inflation, which derives from market imperfections in product and factor markets, is less ably treated by conventional stabilization policy. Though monopoly inflation is obviously interrelated with the overall relationship between aggregate demand and aggregate supply, particularly as a full-employment equilibrium is approached, empirical evidence and conceptual reasoning indicate that it remains to a large extent independent in its mode of behavior. Oligopoly firms, in particular, have been known to increase prices while operating at considerably less than full capital capacity and while national unemployment rates were above any acceptable minimum.

The most recently added Employment Act goal, though not explic-

---

[14] *Money and Credit* (Report of the Commission on Money and Credit) (Englewood Cliffs, N.J.: Prentice-Hall, 1961), p. 28.

[15] *Ibid.*

[16] It is *not* rational to expect, of course, that all or even most units of the land factor of production (natural resources) be utilized in a given year.

itly stated in the act, is that of attaining a satisfactory equilibrium for the nation in its balance of international payments. Net gold outflow from the American economy to the rest of the world has persisted since the late 1950's. Monetary and fiscal policy have been applied, with some degree of effectiveness, to rectify this situation. It is easy to understand that monetary policy, by affecting interest rates, will influence the flow of American investment dollars into the international economic arena. Fiscal policy, moreover, can influence the nation's balance of international payments through the overall structure and magnitude of federal reve-nue-expenditure patterns in the budget. Though a definition of an ideal balance in international payments involves complex considerations beyond the scope of discussion in this book, it is safe to conclude nonetheless that a persistent gold outflow such as the United States has experienced is undesirable. Thus, deliberate public sector economic policy can be justifiably directed toward improvement of the situation.

The Economic Growth Objective. Economic growth, in a broad sense, has been the subject of economic discussion for many centuries. Adam Smith and the early classical economists were concerned with the long-term development of a market economy. Later, Karl Marx predi-cated his theory of socialism on certain predictions involving long-term economic changes under a capitalistic system. Meanwhile, patterns of economic change in this century, including the industrialization of the Soviet Union and the chronic depressions experienced by mature West-ern market economies during the 1930's, have focused attention on the significant differences which exist between the process of economic growth in nations where industrialization is in early stages of develop-ment as opposed to the growth process in those nations which have already achieved industrial maturity. Thus, for purposes of clarity in discussion, the variant growth processes in immature as opposed to mature economies will be defined as separate categories.

The problems involved in maintaining economic progress in an industrialized economy are primarily, though not exclusively, economic in nature. They often do *not* involve an important interplay between various other facets of what may be termed the culture of the society. On the other hand, the preindustrial or early industrial society can make significant economic advancement *only* through the interdisciplinary efforts of many facets of the society's culture. The underdeveloped society must thus consider sociology, psychology, anthropology, political science, and many other "cultural" tenets along with economics (in the sense of capital accumulation, labor force, and technology) in its efforts to achieve economic progress. Meanwhile, the mature industrial society, though not able to completely ignore interdisciplinary considerations, can concentrate upon those specific economic forces which prevent secular stagnation and which provide a satisfactory rate of economic progress. It can essentially accept the culture of the society as a given or constant because significant social change usually is not prerequisite to important economic decisions in a mature society.

The term *economic growth* may thus be used to refer to the continuing development of an already developed economy while *economic development* may be used to mean initial economic progress in an underdeveloped or nonindustrial nation. The former stresses specific economic problems, such as the maintenance of sufficient aggregate demand to fully utilize growing capital capacity, while the latter involves a broad cultural approach inclusive of both significant economic and noneconomic forces.

The above classification of *economic progress* into growth and development segments, though helpful, cannot be applied on a mutually exclusive basis. In other words, the problems of a nation relevant to economic progress are not necessarily *all* growth nor *all* development problems. A mature industrial nation, for example, may possess regions or localities within its aggregate structure which are relatively underdeveloped. In such instances, noneconomic forces may be required to play an important role in the economic development of these regions. An underdeveloped nation, moreover, may have certain isolated sectors or industries which either have already achieved industrial maturity or which can achieve it without comprehensive social changes. Thus, it is impossible to attain an aggregate distinction between economic growth and economic development which is *precise* enough to place a given nation completely within a single category. The difference between such a precise aggregate classification and the still useful disaggregate distinction between economic growth and economic development should be recognized. The economic progress objective of the United States, though primarily one of economic growth in a mature industrial society, still cannot ignore regional and local underdevelopment problems.

Thus, a national economy (in a sense) grows as a "set of regions." Differential resource endowments designate the economic boundaries between these economic regions. Clearly, if each economic region within a national economy produces according to its comparative advantage, that is, produces those economic goods which it has the best relative efficiencies in producing, the total output of the national economy will be maximized and a higher living standard can be attained. Regional specialization and subsequent trade or exchange thus is beneficial not only to the regions, but also to the entire national economy in that it furthers the attainment of maximum output by the whole economy. Obviously, the same economic principles apply to regional specialization in production and trade *within* nations as apply to national specialization in production and international trade *between* nations. Indeed, rational fiscal policy should reflect these facts.

Measuring Employment Act Goals

The complex nature of the American economy with its closely intertwined private and public sectors requires substantial aggregate economic data for policymaking purposes. Surprisingly, the United States did *not* have a reliable system of aggregate (social) accounting until the 1930's. The system which was introduced at that time, known as National Income and Product Accounting, was primarily initiated through the research efforts of Simon Kuznets and has been formulated under the auspices of the Department of Commerce. More recently developed approaches to social accounting include input-output analysis, flow-of-funds or money-flow accounting, national wealth or balance sheet accounting, and international balance-of-payments accounting. In addition, the Bureau of Labor Statistics of the Department of Labor makes important price-level measurements.

National Income and Product Accounting. These Department of Commerce accounts are built on a premise similar to the income statements used by business enterprises in the sense that they are constructed in a double-entry manner. They emphasize the related flows of income and output in the economy during a particular time period. One calendar year divided into four quarters constitutes the time period. Money is used as the common denominator of value for the aggregates. On the one side, the accounts measure the value of output (product) as it is constituted by the major categories of purchasers of national output. Total American production of new goods and services in a given year is purchased by consumers, businesses, and governments within the nation and by foreign purchasers on an international basis. The output referred to is *final* output, thus eliminating double counting in the various value-added stages of production. In addition, output refers only to currently produced items. Claims against the value of national output are measured on the other side of national income and product accounts. The productive resources which produced the output, indirect business taxes, and capital depreciation allowances are important items on the "claims side" of national income and product accounting.

The Department of Commerce provides four subclassifications which comprise the composite national income and product accounting system. These are: (1) the *personal* income and outlay account which demonstrates the income and expenditure totals for households (consumers); (2) the gross saving and investment account of *business* operations which shows the nation's saving, and the disposition thereof, during the time period involved; (3) the *government* receipts and expenditures account which shows the public sector's resource-allocating activities during the time period; and (4) the foreign account which shows purchases by the United States from foreign nations (imports) and purchases by foreign nations from the United States (exports) during the time period. Thus, a personal sector, a business sector, a government sector, and a foreign sector comprise the comprehensive national income and product accounts which reveal the value of total current production, and claims against this production, for the entire economy during a specified time period.

Among the aggregate concepts derived from these accounts which may be useful for information and policymaking purposes are gross national product, net national product, national income, personal income, and disposable income. *Gross National Product* refers to the money value of all final goods produced by the nation's economy in a certain time period, usually one year. *Net National Product* relates to the money value of all final goods production, as defined above, minus estimated business capital depreciation allowances during the period. *National Income,* which derives from the claims side of the accounts, refers to the factor earnings which accrue to the owners of the resources used to produce national output (gross national product) during the period under consideration. *Personal Income* measures the spending power which individuals and families actually receive as opposed to what they have earned (national income). For example, some earned income such as social security deductions, corporation income taxes, and undistributed corporation profits are not actually received by households. Moreover, some purchasing power is received—transfer payments—though it does not represent current earnings. Finally, *Disposable Income* represents what remains of personal income after various personal taxes such as individual income taxes, personal property taxes, and the like have been paid. The selection of any one of the five aggregate economic indicators cited above will depend, of course, on the purpose in mind.

Thus, it may be observed that the National Income and Product Accounts provide valuable data for policymaking decisions directed toward the major goals of stabilization and economic growth. By measuring aggregate economic performance and its variation over time, the goals of full employment and price stability may be better evaluated. The inclusion of a foreign sector in the accounts, moreover, contributes to the attainment of the international balance of payments goal. Economic growth, in addition, can be evaluated via the comparisons of various economic magnitudes such as real per capita income between different points of time.

In 1966, the Department of Commerce introduced a new computerized model of the American economy as an analytical tool to be used in forecasting. This econometric model utilizes 49 mathematical equations which represent certain important interacting economic variables involved in determining the performance of the economy. The forecasts are provided on a quarterly basis. The model represents the most elaborate, short-run forecasting model yet developed within the federal government.

Input-Output Analysis. While the national income and product accounting approach to aggregate measurement is the most highly developed and most widely used technique, several alternative techniques may be employed to supplement the national income approach. In fact, some of these other techniques are potentially as useful, if not more useful, than national income accounting. Input-output tables, pioneered by Wassily Leontief, use a national income and product accounting premise, but stress interindustry relationships by describing the flow of output between the primary industrial disaggregations in the economy. Input-output analysis, in other words, breaks the economy down into primary producing sectors (industries) and demonstrates how the output of one sector becomes the input of another sector or sectors. Hence, this approach consists of a matrix of transactions between various economic sectors. It may be used either as an endogenous (closed) system or as an exogenous (open) system in the sense of excluding or including *international* economic transactions. In addition, the intersectoral relationships may be studied both from a *national* and from a *regional* point of reference. This measurement technique thus serves the various components of the overall economic stabilization and growth goals.

Flow-of-Funds (Money-Flow) Accounting. The flow-of-funds approach attempts to isolate and measure all monetary and credit (financial) transactions within the economy during a particular period of time. It stresses both the origin and use of money (including credit) in the economy. Ordinarily, the economy is divided into sectors for flow-of-funds accounting. The Federal Reserve System provides the primary use of this variety of social accounting. In effect, flow-of-funds measurements constitute a monetary econometric approach which observes and measures the transactions of every major financial sector of the economy. These transactions are importantly related, of course, to the stabilization and economic growth goals. Though it contributes primarily to monetary policy decisions, flow-of-funds accounting indirectly assists fiscal policy because of the inevitable interrelationship between monetary and fiscal programs.

National Wealth (Balance Sheet) Accounting. This social accounting technique is in only a partial stage of development at the present time. Although the United States has the best accounting system in the world for the measurement of output and income flows, it possesses only fragmentary measurements of the nation's stock of wealth and assets. National wealth accounting attempts to measure both the tangible and intangible assets of the various sectors of the economy including a variety of economic interactions between these sectors such as intersectoral liabilities and equities. In 1962, the Ford Foundation, in response to the wishes of professional and governmental groups, made a financial grant to George Washington University in support of a wealth inventory planning study. The study group was directed to concentrate upon the complex conceptual, statistical, and collection issues which are involved in the compilation of a periodic national inventory of wealth as well as in the construction of a continuing balance sheet and wealth estimates to be used in a supplementary manner with the national income and product accounts. This group reported the results of its study to the Subcommittee on Economic Statistics of the Joint Economic Committee in December, 1964, and hearings were subsequently held during 1965.[17] In addition to its recommendations, the report noted several important policy uses to which national wealth data could be put.[18]

   International Balance-of-Payments Accounting. This approach to social accounting measures the income, product, and financial transactions which occur between the United States and the rest of the world. Thus, it directly serves the balance-of-payments objective. International balance-of-payments accounting is more comprehensive than the foreign sector account of the national income and product accounting system

[17] Report of Subcommittee on Economic Statistics, Joint Economic Committee, Congress of the United States, *Measuring the Nation's Material Wealth* (Washington, D.C.: U.S. Government Printing Office, 1965), p. 2.

[18] These include:

1. Knowledge of the nation's productive capacity and the extent of capacity utilization have important policy implications involving both the rate of economic growth and the reduction of cyclical patterns.

2. Better information on the age distribution of the nation's capital stock will aid in evaluating the progress of technology.

3. Information on the amount and trend in the size and composition of the industrial and economic plant is a prerequisite to reliability of numerous economic projections and indispensable to making still others; for example, the projection of future capital requirements and capital financing needs.

4. Knowledge of the productivity of capital and the degree to which productivity increases over periods of time is fundamental to analyzing trends in costs and prices.

5. In both projection and cyclical analysis, the amount of capital investment in use and needed per worker can only be arrived at if an inventory of productive wealth is available.

6. A national balance sheet as an essential part of the national accounts is prerequisite to improved estimates of potential gross national product at full utilization and in such concepts as the full-employment budget.

7. Aggregative and sectoral measures of national wealth are prerequisite to improved income-distribution data for evaluating a variety of national economic and social policies, such as the mitigation of poverty.

8. An inventory of national wealth based upon systematic objective methodology applied nationwide would be useful in the study of
   (*a*) the efficiency with which public services are being provided,
   (*b*) projection of future capital requirements in the public sector, and
   (*c*) the mitigation of present wide variations in property tax laws and assessments.

since it includes financial transactions as well as measurement of the value of goods and service output and the various claims against this output.

"Current-account" transactions in international balance-of-payments accounting measure the total of goods and services available for consumption by Americans and "capital-account" transactions are concerned with dealings in real property or debt instruments. Both current and capital account transactions are reflected normally by changes in the "cash account." Transactions which increase American cash holdings of foreign currency appear in the current and capital accounts preceded by a plus (+) sign. Those transactions which decrease American cash holdings are preceded in each account by a minus (−) sign. In the cash account itself, however, double-entry book-keeping requires that increases in American cash holdings of foreign currency be preceded by a minus (−) sign while increases in foreign holdings of American currency are preceded by a plus (+) sign. The Department of Commerce collects the data and formulates the balance-of-payments accounts. This social accounting technique is clearly important to the efforts of governmental economic policies to improve the balance of international payments.

Price Level Measurement. The United States does *not* possess an adequate measure of general price level behavior. The three primary price measurement devices in use are the Consumer Price Index (CPI), Wholesale Price Index (WPI), and the GNP-deflator. The *Consumer Price Index* is referred to as a cost-of-living index. This index, which is provided monthly by the Bureau of Labor Statistics of the Department of Labor, serves as a measure of the average change in the prices of goods and services purchased by urban wage earner and clerical worker families as compared to the average level in selected base years. This index is seriously limited in scope, however, since it pertains only to consumer purchases, not to business and government purchases. In addition, it measures only *certain* consumer purchases, namely, those by urban wage earner and clerical worker families. These people comprise just a little more than 50 percent of the total urban population of the nation. The CPI, nonetheless, is the most prominently used indicator of price level behavior for the American economy.

Some 400 items are included in the typical "market basket" of purchases in the CPI. These items are differently weighted in the index as based upon estimates of their relative importance to the average urban wage and clerical worker family. A major review of the market basket of items is undertaken every decade or so. Thus, the CPI was comprehensively revised in 1940, 1953, and 1964. Partial revisions of the index and its market basket composition are made on more frequent occasions.

The most serious weakness of the CPI is not its less than comprehensive character. Instead, it is the inability of the index to adequately account for changes in the *quality* of the 400 economic goods included in the index. The CPI might show stable prices over a five year period, for example, but a 10 percent increase in the quality of the goods consumed during the period would mean that actual deflation had taken place. The purchasing power of the dollar would have increased in this instance, though it would statistically appear that the value of the dollar had not changed. Undue emphasis on the Consumer Price Index for stabilization policy decisions can thus be misleading and lead to undesirable consequences.

The *Wholesale Price Index* is also provided on a monthly basis by the Bureau of Labor Statistics. It is a measure of the average change in the prices of some 2,000 goods and resources at the primary market level (the level at which the goods and resources are first commercially sold in substantial volume) as compared to the average level in selected base years. The WPI is weighted heavily in terms of raw materials and capital goods. Goods and resources sold directly to consumers and to the public sector are excluded from the index. The Bureau of Labor Statistics of the Department of Commerce constructs this index. The WPI suffers from essentially the same problems as the CPI. It is not comprehensive and, importantly, does not allow for quality changes.

A third indicator of price level performance in the American economy is the Implicit Price Deflator for Gross National Product which is known as the *GNP-deflator*. It is provided on a quarterly basis by the Department of Commerce. This is a measure of average changes in the market prices of those goods and services represented in the national income and product accounts, as compared to average levels in selected base years. This is a more comprehensive measurement of national price level performance than are the CPI and WPI. The public sector, for example, is included in this indicator. Yet, the GNP-deflator also fails to adequately consider changes in the quality of the items which it measures. For example, it does not adjust for changes in the productivity of government workers. In this regard, it shares an important weakness with the CPI and WPI. Moreover, an improved indicator of price trends would need to determine whether the price increases are "self-generating" in the sense that they induce abnormal inventory accumulations. In addition, better data are required for the service industries, state and local government economic activities, and in the area of fringe benefits. Indeed, much room lies in the direction of improvement in the ability of the nation to measure the price level trends of the economy.

The Measurement of Economic Growth. The definitions of economic growth and economic development are not easily translated into measurement terms. As classified above, both the economic growth of industrial societies and the economic development of nonindustrial societies involve the attainment of "economic progress." Yet, what is economic progress? How is it measured?

Economic progress, as a term inclusive of both economic growth and economic development, derives from the economic resource base of a society. Yet, economic progress may entail significant noneconomic activities, particularly under conditions of economic development. The social changes in the case of economic development, however, are primarily prerequisites to economic progress. The progress itself derives from the base of economic resources, known as *productive capacity,* which is available to the society.

The productive capacity of an economy thus derives from the land, labor, and capital resources available for the production of economic goods. Yet, the national product or output of the society will be determined not only by the quantity of such resources but also by their quality. In this book, the level of *technology* will be used in a broad sense to refer to the ability of the society through a variety of techniques to improve the quality of its productive resources. Economic growth and development may thus be said to consist of absolute growth in the productive capacity of the economy over a period of time as determined by increases in the quantity and/or quality of productive resources.

Though attractive in many ways, the above definition of economic progress is not completely satisfactory. The expansion of productive capacity over time, for example, does not necessarily mean that the capacity is fully used in producing economic goods. Some of the productive capacity, due to depressions or to natural disasters, may be involuntarily idle during the period in question. Thus, it is not the *potential* production of economic goods, but instead their *actual* production which satisfies human wants. The satisfaction of human wants, of course, is the ultimate objective of all economic activity. Human welfare thus becomes the common denominator of economic progress since it is the primary reason for economic production. Generally speaking, if human welfare has been increased in the society over a period of time, economic progress has occurred.

Welfare, as observed in Part I of the book, is *not* a simple proposition conducive to analysis and measurement. In fact, no precise economic definition of human welfare exists because the allocation of the economic goods which satisfy material wants is subject to the prerequisite of the society's state of distribution. The "proper" distribution of income, wealth, and political voting power in a society is dependent, in turn, upon a noneconomic value judgment. Since distribution is a prerequisite to allocation decisions and to their resulting welfare effects, an aggregate measurement of economic progress such as the growth of aggregate output is not a completely satisfactory indicator. This is true because distribution, by its very nature, is a disaggregate concept. Human welfare from the consumption of economic goods cannot be viewed merely as a total without consideration of the individual composition of that total. Distribution determines such composition. A step in the right direction toward the attainment of the best possible measure of economic progress is found in the conversion of aggregate output (or aggregate income) to *per capita output*. This can be achieved by adjusting the increase in output between two points of time by any population change which may have occurred during the period. If per capita output has increased, there is good indication that economic growth (or development) has taken place.

Increases in per capita output over time, however, may *not* indicate economic progress if significant price level changes have taken place during the period. If per capita output doubles over a 20-year period while the price level also doubles, for example, real per capita output is unchanged and growth seemingly would not have occurred. Thus, real per capita output is superior to any of the other indicators of economic progress which have been discussed to this point.

Real per capita output figures, however, include *both* consumption and capital goods. Since capital goods do not directly satisfy human wants, shifts in the proportions of consumption and capital goods production over time may result in a misleading indicator of changes in human welfare. A strong argument may thus be offered that real per capita consumption is a better indicator of economic progress than is real per capita output. Theoretically, this argument appears valid. A significant portion of consumption goods in a mixed private sector–public sector economy, however, are not subject to convenient measurement. Consumption goods of a pure public or quasi-public nature provided by government, for example, are normally excluded from per capita consumption figures since they are purchased through tax payments rather than from income flows.

Though such asymmetry in the measurement of consumption is theoretically unjustifiable, the difficulty of measuring the consumptive value of governmental activities is recognizable. Hence, the ideal indicator of economic progress—*real per capita consumption* inclusive of consumption goods acquired from both the private and public sectors— cannot be attained in practice. Consequently, real per capita output (or its closely related counterpart, real per capita income) must be selected as the "best available" indicator for the measurement of economic growth and development over time. Ideally, this concept should also consider the state of income distribution preferred by the society. An increase in real per capita output (income), for example, does not necessarily improve the overall welfare of the society if income distribution is *very unequal* and the society's values state a preference for fairly equal income distribution.

The acceptance of real per capita output as the best practical device for measuring economic progress does not mean that alert observers should ignore its imperfections as a measurement device. Some of the more important of these imperfections are summarized below:

1. Expenditures for capital goods, whether by the private sector or by the public sector, are misleading in terms of measuring the increases in the consumption activity which directly provide material welfare to consumers. Yet, these expenditures are included in real per capita output.

2. Real per capita output does not provide a satisfactory means of measuring changes in product quality over time. A 1967 Buick automobile, for example, is generally conceded to be better in quality than a 1947 Buick, but real per capita output figures do not show this.

3. The real per capita output device does not adequately differentiate between changes in the composition of consumer purchases over time. In 1900, wagons and wood stoves were important items of purchase, for example, while in today's market basket they are replaced by such items as automobiles and gas furnaces.

4. Economic goods do not provide *all* human happiness since economics is not a universal jurisdiction comprehending all of mankind's activities. Leisure and other aspects of nonmaterial consumption also provide happiness. A reduced workweek, for example, can indicate an increase in welfare. Yet, it does not show up as economic progress under the real per capita output concept. An aesthetically oriented individual such as a monk, moreover, may derive pleasure from the very act of "not consuming" material economic goods. This, again, would not be included as part of welfare by the real per capita output approach.

5. Real per capita output does not directly consider the pattern of income distribution preferred by the society.

6. Though *disaggregate* concepts for measuring economic progress are theoretically superior to the aggregate concepts of total productive capacity and total output, the *aggregate* concepts hold an advantage in the sense that measurements of the real growth of aggregate resources and output indicate growth in the absolute economic power of the nation. This was important to militaristic societies such as Hitler's Germany and Mussolini's Italy during the 1930's and early 1940's. These societies stressed national power rather than individual welfare in a consumption sense.

In conclusion, it has been observed in this chapter that the public sector will inevitably influence aggregate economic performance in a mixed economy. Since a pure market economy possesses no inherent mechanism to assure optimal employment, price, international payments, and economic growth performances, it is only rational to deliberately structure the economic actions of the public sector in such a manner that they promote the achievement of these goals. Congress recognized such a responsibility for the federal government by passing the Employment Act of 1946. Effective administration of this act requires sound definitions and measurements of the aggregate objectives.

Chapter 18 : TECHNIQUES OF FISCAL POLICY

The inability of a pure market economy, as demonstrated in the previous chapter, to attain automatically the goals of full employment and price stability provides the basis for governmental stabilization policy. Such policy was enacted into law by the Employment Act of 1946 which, in its present interpretation, broadens the responsibility of the federal government in economic matters also to include the promotion of economic growth and the achievement of a satisfactory international payments balance. Governmental economic policy directed toward the Employment Act goals takes the forms of monetary and fiscal policy. As would be expected, the latter will be emphasized in this public finance textbook.

THE MARGINAL PROPENSITY TO TAX

The discussion of fiscal policy techniques requires a more elaborate multiplier concept than the one described in the simplified model of the previous chapter. The earlier treatment was primarily concerned with the functioning of a pure market economy operating in a closed environment devoid of international economic transactions. Yet, a more realistic analysis of the functioning of the American economy requires the introduction of both a government sector and international trade to the model. Importantly, when the aggregate public sector budget and international transactions are added to the analysis, significant new leakages from the spending stream arise. Thus, saving leakages alone do not limit the value of the multiplier, but *tax* and *import* leakages, in addition, must be considered. Saving, tax collections, and importation expenditures *all* take on a functional relationship with the level of income. Although the relevance of the foreign trade leakage, which may be termed the "marginal propensity to import," will not be ignored, it will not be emphasized equally here with the tax leakages because of the need to concentrate upon the latter in a discussion of public finance.

An important relationship thus exists between changes in income and induced changes in tax collections. Even though tax rates do not vary, the tax yield (tax collections, the level of taxes) may be expected to vary as changes occur in income. This relationship may be termed the *marginal propensity to tax* though sometimes it is referred to as the *marginal rate of taxation*. The marginal propensity to tax is represented by the following formula:

$$MPT = \frac{\Delta T}{\Delta Y}$$

where T refers to the tax yield and Y to national income. Thus, similar to the consideration of consumption and saving as functions of income in

FIGURE 18–1

The Marginal Propensity to Tax under Progressive, Proportionate, and Regressive Tax Rate Structures

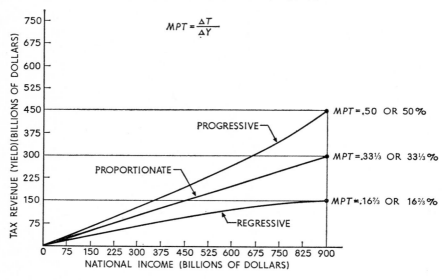

the marginal propensity to consume (save) concept, tax collections are treated as a function of income in the marginal propensity to tax concept. Both the marginal propensity to consume (save) and the marginal propensity to tax represent *positive* functional relationships with income, that is, the dependent variables of consumption, saving, and tax revenues move in the same direction as do changes in the level of income. For purposes of later analysis, however, it is significant to observe that the tax yield is a function of *national income* while consumption, in the consumption function, is more appropriately considered to be a function of *disposable income*.

Figure 18–1 demonstrates the marginal propensity to tax. The linear function represents a particular marginal propensity to tax which has a constant numerical value as national income changes. If a nation collected all of its public sector tax revenues from a *proportionate* income tax, this linear function would accurately represent the behavior of the marginal propensity to tax since both tax collections and national income would increase at the same rate. In the graphical example, the marginal propensity to tax is .33⅓ all along the linear function. If the rate of tax collections increase as the level of national income increases, however, a *progressive* tax rate structure is indicated. In Figure 18–1, the marginal propensity to tax, which is .33⅓ at a national income level of $75 billion, increases to .50 at the $900 billion level. On the other hand, if the percentage relationship of growth in tax revenues to national income declines as the level of national income increases, the tax structure is *regressive*. In the graph, the marginal propensity to tax declines from .33⅓ at a national income level of $75 billion to .16⅔ at the $900 billion level.

As suggested above, the implications for fiscal policy of induced tax collections are considerable. The marginal propensity to tax, of course, would be zero only under the extremely unlikely circumstance that *all* tax collections be derived from a poll tax—a per capita tax not associated with the level of income. Under a comprehensive poll tax system, changes in the level of income would *not* induce changes in the level of tax collections. When income taxes (personal and corporate) are used, however, the marginal propensity to tax takes on a value above zero because "income" becomes the tax base itself and variations in income directly influence the tax yield. Sales taxes also possess a value above zero for the marginal propensity to tax. The relationship between tax collections and income levels, however, is less direct with sales taxes than for income taxes since income, in this instance, is not the tax base itself but is merely the source of purchasing power for acquisition of the economic goods which become the sales tax base when they are purchased.

The fact that the marginal propensity to tax in the American economy possesses a positive value (above zero) means that an additional leakage (other than saving) from the private sector spending stream is present. Hence, it serves as a dampening influence on the value of the multiplier effect resulting from a change in one of the components of aggregate demand such as business investment. The tax system thus becomes a built-in or automatic stabilizer which can help restrain an upward movement in aggregate demand and a possible threat of inflation as well as to cushion a downward movement in the economy.[1] The dampening effect imposed by taxes during an expansion and the cushioning effect provided during a depression would be intensified, of course, under a progressive tax structure whereby tax collections would rise and decline in greater proportions than changes in income.

Relatedly, as the federal income tax reductions of 1964 demonstrated, an initial increase in the size of a budgetary deficit through a tax

---

[1] Automatic stabilizers will be discussed in greater detail in the next chapter.

rate reduction does not necessarily mean that the ultimate deficit will be equal to the amount of the tax reduction. This is true because the increased purchasing power in the private sector made possible by the tax reduction allows national income to increase. A higher national income, of course, yields a greater volume of tax collections. The deficit in the federal administrative budget for the 1962 fiscal year, for example, was $6.4 billion but was reduced following the subsequent federal income and excise tax reductions to $2.3 billion in Fiscal 1966. This occurred, moreover, despite a substantial increase in spending of nearly $20 billion during the four-year period.

The same conclusion could generally be reached for an expansion in the size of a deficit budget brought about through increases in government exhaustive or transfer expenditures. In addition, this analysis suggests that efforts to balance the budget through increases in tax rates may be partly self-defeating since the higher tax rates reduce the level of disposable income and thus cause a lower tax yield. Hence, a deficit budget may be the ultimate result of efforts to achieve a balanced budget through an initial increase in tax rates.

The following algebraic example demonstrates the interaction of the marginal propensities to consume (save) and the marginal propensity to tax and the resulting influence through the multiplier concept on aggregate economic performance. Observe that induced consumption and saving depend upon changes in disposable income which, in turn, does not change at as fast a rate as national income because of the automatic dampening influence of the increasing level of tax collections.

$$K = \text{Multiplier}$$
$$\Delta G = \$10 \text{ billion}$$

$$K = \frac{1}{1 - b + b(d)}$$

$$mpc\ (b) = .80$$

$$K = \frac{1}{1 - .80 + .80(.20)}$$

$$mpt\ (d) = .20$$

$$K = \frac{1}{.20 + .16} = \frac{1}{.36} = 2.77$$

Thus, an increase in business investment expenditures of $10 billion would exert an increase in national income of $10 billion times the multiplier of 2.77. The result would be an ultimate growth in national income of $27.7 billion. The restraining influence of the marginal propensity to tax is obvious since the multiplier value is 5 instead of 2.77 when only the saving leakage is considered. With a multiplier of 5, a $10 billion increase in governmental spending will lead to a $50 billion increase in national income as compared to the much lower figure of $27.7 billion when the tax leakage is also considered. This differential exists because the $10 billion increase in investment expenditure does not represent a $10 billion increase in disposable income when the tax leakage enters the picture. This leakage, plus the saving leakage of one out of every five dollars of income change, reduce the value of the multiplier effect.

THE GOVERNMENT MULTIPLIERS

Fiscal policy techniques are implemented through the budgetary procedures of taxation and expenditure. Thus, changes in either tax rates or government spending, or in both, will exert an impact upon the private sector of the economy and thus influence aggregate economic performance. It is the purpose of fiscal policy to rationalize this influence. The various techniques of fiscal policy which derive from the budgetary procedures of taxation and expenditure take the form of government multipliers. More specifically, the public sector can favorably influence aggregate economic behavior through the deliberate manipulation of the budget, thus creating fiscal forces such as the *tax, transfer expenditures, exhaustive expenditures,* and *balanced budget* multipliers. As observed earlier, the primary burden for deliberate fiscal policy in the United States at the present time is carried by the federal government. Hence, a discussion of the four government multipliers should be considered within the general context of federal budgetary behavior.

The Tax Multiplier

A change in tax rates, and the resulting change in the level of tax collections, creates a multiple change in national income (aggregate economic performance). This phenomenon is known as the *tax multiplier*. A change in tax rates must be distinguished, of course, from the marginal propensity to tax. This difference may be observed in Figure 18–2. In the graph, S refers to saving, T to tax collections, I to business investment, and G to governmental expenditures. A change in tax rates will cause the $S + T$ curve to shift while the marginal propensity to tax merely refers to a movement along the $S + T$ curve since, even with a given set of tax rates in effect, tax collections will continue to vary as a function of the level of income.

In Figure 18–2, the saving, tax collection, investment spending, and governmental expenditure variables are realistically assumed to possess marginal propensities greater than zero, which means, of course, that each magnitude will change as income changes. In addition, each variable is positive in the sense that it moves in the same direction as the change in income. This is represented on the graph by the upward slope of the $S + T$ and $I + G$ functions. Moreover, the graph has netted out consumption from both the aggregate supply ($Y = C + S + T$) and the aggregate demand ($Y = C + I + G$) flows in order to simplify the presentation and allow greater emphasis on the rudiments of the tax multiplier itself. A similar procedure will be followed in the other graphs which follow in this section. Also, for purposes of simplification in presentation, the increase in tax collections is by the same amount at all income levels. Such would be true with the application of a new (or a rate increase in an already existing) lump sum or poll tax.

The initial equilibrium level of aggregate economic performance in Figure 18–2 is at a national income level of $500 billion. This is determined by the intersection at point A of the $S + T$ and $I + G$ curves. If tax rates are increased, with both government transfer and exhaustive expenditures constant, the $S + T$ curve will shift to the left, as from

FIGURE 18–2

THE TAX MULTIPLIER

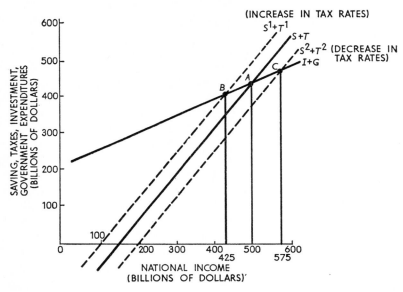

$S + T$ to $S^1 + T^1$, and the new equilibrium performance level will be at point B. Importantly, national income has decreased from $500 billion at point A to $425 billion at point B after tax rates are increased. The increase in tax collections of $25 billion leads to a contraction in national income of $75 billion (from $500 billion to $425 billion) as the result of a tax multiplier with the value of 3.

On the other hand, a reduction in tax rates, with government transfer and exhaustive expenditures constant, will cause the $S + T$ curve to shift to the right, as from $S + T$ to $S^2 + T^2$, and the new equilibrium performance level will be at point C. The reduction in tax rates in this case has led to a new higher national income level at $575 billion. The decline in tax collections equal to $25 billion leads to an expansion in national income of $75 billion (from $500 billion to $575 billion) as the value of the tax multiplier again is 3.

Thus, a variation in tax rates may be either *contractionary* or *expansionary* in its influence on the economy depending upon the direction of the tax rate change. Moreover, the tax multiplier is *negative* in the nature of its relationship between the two principal variables. In other words, changes in aggregate economic performance (national income) move inversely with the direction of changes in tax rates. Thus, an increase in tax rates tends to induce economic contraction and a decrease in tax rates tends to create economic expansion. This is true, of course, because higher tax rates reduce the purchasing power of the private sector and thus reduce aggregate demand, while lower tax rates provide a net increase in private sector purchasing power which leads to a higher level of aggregate demand. Tax changes are similar to government transfer expenditure changes in that each directly affects the volume of private sector purchasing power. In this important sense, a tax may correctly be termed a "negative" transfer payment. Changes in the volume of transfer payments as a fiscal tool are discussed immediately below.

The Transfer Expenditures Multiplier

The spending as well as the tax side of the budget is capable of exerting a multiplier effect. In this regard, government expenditure may be either transfer or exhaustive (resource-absorbing) in nature. A change in the level of transfer payments by government, and the resulting multiple change in national income (aggregate economic performance), is known as the *transfer expenditures multiplier*. This is demonstrated in Figure 18–3. The initial equilibrium level of aggregate economic performance is at a $500 billion level of national income (point A). If transfer expenditures are decreased with tax rates and exhaustive expenditures remaining constant, the S + T curve will shift to the left, as from S + T to $S^1 + T^1$, and the new equilibrium performance level will be at point B which represents a decrease in national income from $500 billion to $425 billion. On the other hand, an increase in transfer expenditures, with tax rates and exhaustive expenditures remaining constant, will cause the S + T curve to shift to the right, as from S + T to $S^2 + T^2$, and national income expands from $500 to $575 billion at point C. The multiplier has a value of 3 if the transfer spending change is $25 billion. Moreover, the transfer expenditures multiplier is *positive* in the direction of its relationship between a change in spending and the resulting multiplier change in aggregate economic performance. In other words, an increase in transfer payments is expansionary and a decrease is contractionary.

An important observation for purposes of subsequent analysis may be made at this point, namely, that both tax and transfer expenditure changes exert their multiplier effects in an "indirect" manner since they

FIGURE 18–3

THE TRANSFER EXPENDITURES MULTIPLIER

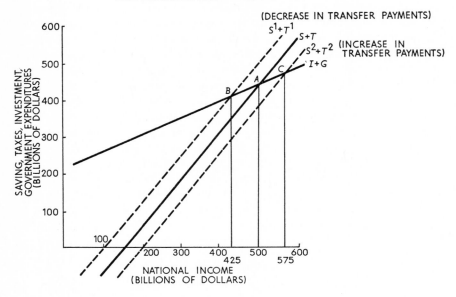

represent the type of governmental budgetary behavior that does not directly absorb resources, but merely changes private sector purchasing power. Subsequent resource-using and saving decisions are then made by the private sector. This is not true of the government exhaustive expenditures multiplier, however, which directly absorbs resources instead of influencing spending indirectly by altering private sector purchasing power.

The Exhaustive Expenditures Multiplier

Federal exhaustive (resource-absorbing) expenditures, which essentially are those enumerated in the administrative budget, may also serve as the basis for fiscal policy. The *exhaustive expenditures multiplier* thus represents a relationship between a change in the level of governmental resource-absorbing expenditures and the resulting multiple change in the level of national income. This multiplier approach is demonstrated in Figure 18–4. A decrease in exhaustive expenditures, with tax rates and transfer expenditures constant, will cause the $I + G$ curve to shift downward, as from $I + G$ to $I^2 + G^2$, and national income will decline from $500 billion to $400 billion at point B because aggregate demand has been "directly" diminished. On the other hand, an increase in exhaustive expenditures will cause the $I + G$ curve to move upward, as from $I + G$ to $I^1 + G^1$, and national income will increase from $500 billion to $600 billion at point *C* because aggregate demand has been directly increased by the incremental exhaustive spending of government. The exhaustive expenditures multiplier, just as the transfer expenditures multiplier, represents a *positive* relationship between the direction of a change in spending and the resulting change in national income since the variables move upward and downward together. In other words, an increase in exhaustive spending exerts an expansionary influence and a decrease in exhaustive spending exerts a contractionary influence on aggregate economic performance.

It is significant that the size of the multiplier effect will be greater in

FIGURE 18–4

THE EXHAUSTIVE EXPENDITURES MULTIPLIER

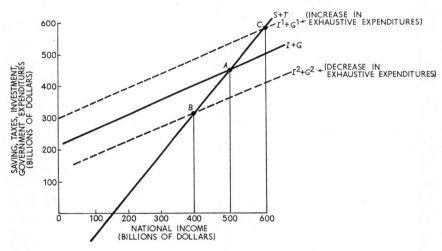

the case of the exhaustive expenditures multiplier than for the tax and transfer expenditures multipliers. This is demonstrated by comparing Figures 18–2, 18–3, and 18–4. These graphs show that a $25 billion increase in tax collections caused by higher tax rates, or a $25 billion decrease in transfer expenditures, will cause national income to decline from $500 billion to $425 billion while a $25 billion decrease in exhaustive expenditures will cause national income to decline from $500 billion to $400 billion. Furthermore, a $25 billion reduction in tax collections caused by a decrease in tax rates, or a $25 billion increase in transfer expenditures, will cause national income to increase from $500 billion to $575 billion, while a $25 billion increase in exhaustive expenditures will cause national income to increase from $500 billion to $600 billion. Why does the exhaustive expenditures multiplier have a greater multiplier value than the tax and transfer expenditures multipliers?

The exhaustive expenditures multiplier has a larger multiplier effect than the tax and transfer expenditures multipliers because a change in government spending involves no change in saving (the marginal propensity to consume of government equals 1) while a change in private sector spending resulting from either a tax or transfer payment change is subject to the marginal propensity to save of the community. An increase of $25 billion in exhaustive governmental expenditures, for example, will directly increase income by this same amount (and output if resource unemployment permits it), and none of the $25 billion is saved. On the other hand, a tax reduction of $25 billion or a transfer expenditure increase of $25 billion will lead to a less than $25 billion increase in consumption because some of the incremental purchasing power will be saved by the private sector. Private sector purchasing power, of course, and *not* resource-absorbing activities, is directly affected by the tax and transfer spending changes. Hence, the amount of additional aggregate demand upon which the ultimate multiplier expansion depends will be less with the decrease in taxes or the increase in transfer payments than it is with the increase in exhaustive expenditures. In other words, the initial round of exhaustive government expenditures is a total direct component of gross national product while the initial round of the tax reduction or transfer spending increment is merely a transfer of purchasing power, some of which will be saved before it enters the spending stream.

The Balanced Budget Multiplier

Each of the government multipliers discussed above emphasizes *either* the tax *or* the spending side of the budget. Furthermore, it was demonstrated that both a tax rate increase and an expenditure reduction are contractionary and that both a tax rate reduction and a spending increase are expansionary in their influence on aggregate economic performance. Thus, it would appear that an increase in taxes matched by an equal increase in spending, and vice versa, would be neutral in its influence on national income. In other words, it would seem that the change in taxes would neutralize the change in spending. Surprisingly, this is *not* the case. The explanation for this significant phenomenon is found in the *balanced budget multiplier* concept which is concerned with the aggregate economic effects that derive from changes in tax collections and in governmental exhaustive expenditures in the same direction and by the same amount. For reasons which will become obvious in the analysis below, the balanced budget multiplier concept is concerned only with exhaustive and not with transfer expenditures.

The classical economists had assumed that a balanced budget change, in the above sense, is neutral. Moreover, even in the early Keynesian era economists ordinarily did not conceptualize that aggregate demand could be significantly influenced by such fiscal action. As often has occurred in the development of economic theory, a new concept is developed simultaneously by several persons working in an independent fashion on the subject. In the early 1940's, the balanced budget multiplier doctrine was promulgated in one form or another by Samuelson, Wallich, and Hansen and Perloff.[2] The Wallich article, in particular, initiated an intense discussion of the balanced budget multiplier concept. Wallich, using a simple arithmetic model, demonstrated that a balanced (proportionate) increase in the tax and expenditure levels of government, though not directly affecting consumption and investment spending in the private sector, would increase aggregate output by the amount of the increase in government expenditures. In other words, the multiplier would have a value of *unity* (one) since national income would increase by the amount of the incremental governmental spending. In 1945, Haavelmo further refined the concept and concluded similarly that a balanced budget change has a direct multiplier effect with the multiplier value equal to one.[3]

The balanced budget multiplier provides the unit multiplier result, however, only under the presence of certain tenuous assumptions.[4] Opposition to the validity of the concept has at times concentrated upon the likelihood that some or all of these assumptions would not hold in the real world. The concept nevertheless contains considerable general validity even though its assumptions may not hold to the precise point of providing an exact unit multiplier. This point will be further clarified later in the discussion. Meanwhile, the example presented in Table 18–1 below will demonstrate the balanced budget multiplier process in operation with all pertinent assumptions holding, thus providing a multiplier result of one. In other words, the change in the size of the balanced budget leads to an equivalent change in the level of national income.

In Table 18–1, the budget is assumed to be balanced in Fiscal Year 1 with both taxes and exhaustive expenditures at the $100 billion level and with equilibrium national income at $500 billion. Then an increase in

---

[2] Paul A. Samuelson, "Full Employment After the War," in *Postwar Economic Problems,* Seymour Harris (ed.) (New York: McGraw–Hill Book Co., Inc., 1943); Alvin H. Hansen and Harvey S. Perloff, *State and Local Finance in the National Economy* (New York: Norton, 1943); Henry C. Wallich, "Income Generating Effects of a Balanced Budget," *Quarterly Journal of Economics* (November, 1944), pp. 78–91.

[3] Trygve Haavelmo, "Multiplier Effects of a Balanced Budget," *Econometrica* (October, 1945), pp. 311–18.

[4] These assumptions include: (1) the requirement that government exhaustive spending be used to acquire goods newly produced by the domestic economy; (2) that the marginal propensities to consume and save of the community not shift during the balanced budget multiplier operation; (3) that the change in the size of the budget not alter the incentives for private investment; (4) that the marginal propensity to consume and save be equal throughout the economy for both those who pay the taxes and those who receive the benefits of government spending, that is, in instances where a differentiation can be made between these two groups; and (5) work-leisure habits must not be altered by the governmental budgetary action.

the size of the balanced budget from $100 billion to $101 billion takes place, with both taxes and expenditure increasing by $1 billion. National income thus increases by the amount of the balanced budget increase, namely, from $500 billion to $501 billion.

TABLE 18–1

BALANCED BUDGET MULTIPLIER EXAMPLE

Fiscal Year	Tax Revenues	Exhaustive Expenditures	National Income
1	$100 billion	$100 billion	$500 billion
2	101	101	501

In this particular example, the marginal propensity to consume equals 90 percent (.90) and the marginal propensity to save equals 10 percent (.10). The investment multiplier thus is 10, as derived from the formula:[5]

$$K = \frac{1}{mps}$$

Significantly, the government spends *all* of the additional $1 billion extracted from the private sector in the form of taxes. If the incremental tax amount had been allowed to remain in the private sector, however, *only* 90 percent of it would have immediately reentered the spending stream as consumption expenditures. Importantly, the fact that the government spends the entire amount of the additional tax collections while the private sector would save 10 percent of the $1 billion incremental tax dollars means that the balanced budget increase in government expenditure is expansionary. This expansion takes place because the $900 million which would have been spent by the private sector is less than the $1 billion spent by the public sector, the $100 million difference providing a *net* increment to aggregate demand and a resulting multiplier effect.

In numercial terms, the multiplier of 10 times the $100 million in differential expenditure between the two sectors yields the $1 billion increase in national income. Thus, a $1 billion increase in government spending, matched by an equivalent increase in tax collections, causes a $1 billion increase in national income. The relationship between the change in government spending, balanced by an equal change in tax collections and the change in national income which it creates, is unity.[6] Oppositely, a decrease in the size of a balanced budget will cause a decline in national income equal to unity.

[5] For simplification in presentation, saving is considered in the example as the only leakage from the spending stream.

[6] The same unity value results regardless of the values of the marginal propensities to consume and save. If the marginal propensity to consume is 80 percent (.80) and the marginal propensity to save is 20 percent (.20), for example, the

The balanced budget multiplier, however, would not operate for transfer as opposed to exhaustive expenditures by government. In other words, if all governmental spending were of a transfer variety, a balanced budget change would be neutral because government would merely be transferring purchasing power from taxpayers to transfer recipients.[7] The balanced budget multiplier would not exist because there would be no net increment to aggregate demand from the public sector resulting from the fact that government has a marginal propensity to consume of 1. Government in this case does not make direct resource-absorbing expenditure decisions. *All* spending decisions are still made by the private sector. Only a transfer of purchasing power has taken place, which results merely in a distributive change in the decision-making power over aggregate demand *within* the private sector, with some of the purchasing power subsequently being saved instead of being spent for consumption.

FISCAL TECHNIQUES FOR ECONOMIC STABILIZATION

The four government multipliers examined above provide the basis for government fiscal policy. Historically, the primary goals of federal fiscal policy have been centered within the stabilization branch of public finance. Specifically, they have been directed toward the attainment of a high level of labor and capital employment and price stability. The former was the primary goal of the 1930's and has intermittently been the main objective since that time (1948, 1954, 1957, and so forth) while the latter has been the primary consideration during wartime (World War II, Korean War, Vietnam War). Other goals, of course, have assumed importance from time to time. This is particularly true in recent years with increased concern for the ability of federal fiscal policy to promote a satisfactory rate of economic growth and an improved balance of international payments. Nevertheless, stabilization in the full-employment and price stability sense remains the primary focal point of federal fiscal policy. Admittedly, the various goals of fiscal policy are interrelated. One goal, however, usually retains priority in any given set of decisions.

Unemployment, as a stabilization problem, is best described in terms of the *deflationary gap* conditions and inflation in terms of the

---

multiplier value is 5. Under this situation, though the government would again spend the entire $1 billion of additional tax collections, the private sector would have withheld $200 million from the spending stream. The $200 million (20 percent) of leakages to private saving times the multiplier of 5, however, also results in a $1 billion increment in national income.

[7] Yet, even in this case, complete neutrality would require the restrictive assumption that the marginal propensities to consume and save between the taxpaying group and the transfer recipients be uniform.

inflationary gap conditions demonstrated in the previous chapter.[8] The latter, of course, is an especially close fit to monetary inflation, but is less indicative of the conditions which lead to monopoly inflation. In Figure 18–5ab, the ability of fiscal policy to alleviate the conditions of involun-

FIGURE 18–5

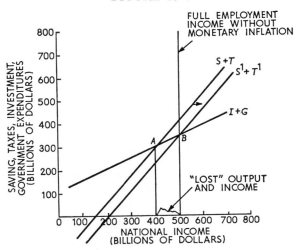

a. Alleviation of a deflationary gap through a reduction in tax rates or through an increase in government transfer expenditures.

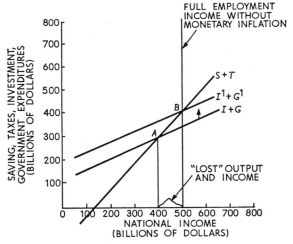

b. Alleviation of a deflationary gap through an increase in government exhaustive expenditures.

[8] For reasons of simplification in presentation, the deflationary gap and inflationary gap graphs used in this section will net consumption (C) out of the spending flows. However, the phenomena described will be identical to those presented in Figure 17–4 of the previous chapter.

FIGURE 18–6

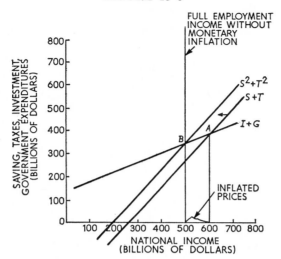

a. Alleviation of an inflationary gap through
an increase in tax rates or through a decrease in
government transfer expenditures

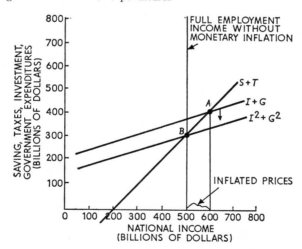

b. Alleviation of an inflationary gap through a
reduction in government exhaustive expenditures

tary labor and capital unemployment is shown. In Figure 18–6ab, the
ability of fiscal policy to combat monetary inflation is demonstrated.

Fiscal Policy Applied to Deflationary Gap Conditions

The excess of aggregate supply $(S + T)$ over aggregate demand
$(I + G)$ at noninflationary full employment characterizes the deflationary gap conditions of Figure 18–5ab. If the national income performance

level of the economy were $500 billion, labor and capital would be fully employed (within reasonable definitions of each term) and the price level would be stable. Under such conditions, federal fiscal policy directed toward stabilization would not be required. The economy, however, is not operating at this full-employment noninflationary level of performance in the graph. Instead, equilibrium is at a $400 billion level of national income which, it will be assumed, provides underfull employment conditions whereby 8 percent of the labor force is involuntarily unemployed and 25 percent of the capital capacity (plant and equipment) of the nation is not being utilized. In this instance, deliberate fiscal policy directed toward the improvement of both labor and capital employment is warranted.

The techniques of fiscal policy for the alleviation of deflationary gap conditions derive primarily from the four government multipliers. The potentially most effective tool would involve use of the exhaustive expenditures multiplier because the government, under this multiplier, has a marginal propensity to consume equal to 1. Thus, in Figure 18–5b an increase in exhaustive expenditures by government would shift the $I + G$ curve upward as in curve $I^1 + G^1$ and, if the increase in spending is sufficiently large—given the limitation imposed by the value of the multiplier as dependent upon the marginal propensities to consume and save of the community and the marginal propensity to tax—a new full-employment equilibrium at the $500 billion level will be attained.

The problem of involuntary labor and capital unemployment can also be attacked via the transfer expenditures multiplier and by the tax multiplier. An increase in transfer payments, for example, will shift the $S + T$ curve to the right as in curve $S^1 + T^1$ (Figure 18–5a) thus expanding the equilibrium level of aggregate economic activity. Alternately, a decrease in tax rates will cause the $S + T$ curve to shift to the right to become $S^1 + T^1$ (see Figure 18–5a) with a similar result of expanded national income. In each case, disposable income within the private sector has been increased. The government transfer expenditures and tax multipliers, however, provide a *smaller* multiplier expansion in national income than the exhaustive expenditures multiplier because the direct change in the former cases is in private sector purchasing power (disposable income) which is subject to a saving leakage. On the other hand, a disadvantage of the exhaustive expenditures multiplier in a market-oriented economy is that it is less conducive to private sector economic activity since the government directly determines the additional resource usage when exhaustive expenditures are increased. To the contrary, however, a tax rate reduction and an increase in transfer payments expands the disposable income of the private sector and thus favors the market in social balance terms. Moreover, an increase in governmental exhaustive spending may undergo a considerable *time lag* before the actual economic impact of the expenditures takes place. In other words, many delays occur between the time when expenditures are appropriated by the legislature and the time when the actual resource-using activity occurs. On the other hand, the tax withholding method of collection allows tax rate changes to be put into effect quickly. This has been demonstrated by the federal income tax rate reductions of 1964 and the stepped-up federal income tax withholding changes of 1966. In summary, though "maximum expansion" will occur through the operation of the exhaustive expenditures multiplier, the tax and transfer expenditures multipliers are more attractive from the motive of favoring the private sector in "social balance" terms, and the tax multiplier is the best of the three in the "timing" of the actual resource absorption.

A final approach to alleviation of deflationary gap conditions utilizes the balanced budget multiplier whereby an increase in tax rates matched by an equal increase in exhaustive governmental expenditures will provide an expansion in national income, the increase in income being equal to the size of the tax-expenditure increase if certain assumptions hold. The relevance of the balanced budget multiplier concept to effective fiscal policy will be further analyzed later in this section.

Fiscal Policy Applied to Inflationary Gap Conditions

The excess of aggregate demand $(I + G)$ over aggregate supply $(S + T)$ at noninflationary full employment characterizes the inflationary gap conditions as displayed in Figure 18–6ab. The $600 billion equilibrium aggregate performance level shown in the graph represents inflated prices to the extent of $100 billion of national income because a $500 billion performance level is sufficient to fully employ labor and capital resources. A case for deliberate fiscal policy directed toward the alleviation of monetary inflation is established.

The tools of fiscal policy for the improvement of inflationary gap conditions also derive primarily from the four government multipliers. Again, the potentially most effective technique involves the use of the exhaustive expenditures multiplier. Hence, in Figure 18–6b a decrease in exhaustive spending by government will cause the $I + G$ curve to shift downward to $I^2 + G^2$, thus decreasing national income through a reduction in inflated prices. A reduction in exhaustive expenditures of adequate size, given the constraint of the relevant leakages from the spending stream, will lower national income back to the optimal noninflationary full-employment equilibrium of $500 billion. In addition, monetary inflation can be alleviated by a decrease in transfer payments (Figure 18–6a) or by an increase in tax rates (Figure 18–6a). In either case, however, the multiplier contraction in national income will be less than that provided by the exhaustive expenditures multiplier since the direct effects are on private sector purchasing power and thus subject to a saving leakage. Finally, a decrease in tax rates matched by an equal decrease in exhaustive spending (the balanced budget multiplier) can also initiate contractionary results to help alleviate inflation.

In addition to providing maximum contraction, the reduction in exhaustive governmental expenditures for the purpose of attaining a contractionary fiscal policy also increases the relative position of private sector resource allocation and thus, unlike its behavior in the expansionary fiscal policy case, favors the market in social balance terms. The achievement of economic contraction through a reduction in exhaustive governmental expenditures, however, is slower to put into effect than would be an increase in taxes. Moreover, an increase in taxes would also lead to a relative expansion in public sector economic activity. A unique form of the tax multiplier, based on changes in the timing of collections rather than a change in tax rates, was enacted by Congress during March of 1966 in the form of *graduated tax withholding schedules*. On the personal income tax, the payroll-withholding rate of a flat 14 percent was changed to a range of rates between 14 and 30 percent depending upon the earnings of an individual. In addition, the rate of payment of corporation income taxes was accelerated by the legislation. Such action, of course, drains purchasing power from the private sector at an earlier time and thus helps to restrain inflationary pressures.

In summary of both the deflationary and inflationary gap situations, the exhaustive expenditures multiplier provides the maximum expansion and contraction as compared to the tax and transfer expenditures multipliers. Regarding social balance, a decrease in tax rates and an increase in transfer spending, especially the former, increases the real allocation of the market sector while higher taxes and a lower level of transfer payments tends to favor the public sector in social balance terms. The tax multiplier holds the "time implementation" advantage over the other two multipliers primarily due to the technique of tax withholding at the source of income.

The Balanced Budget Multiplier and Fiscal Policy

The validity of the balanced budget multiplier concept as a basis for fiscal policy has been challenged on occasion. Baumol and Peston argue, for example, that the balanced budget multiplier concept assumes away those variables which would almost certainly make the value of the multiplier greater or less than unity.[9] It is suggested that the theorem holds in a unity sense *only* under the assumption that the change in tax yield does not alter the marginal propensities to consume and save, as well as the fact that only taxes of the simple poll tax variety would yield this

---

[9] William J. Baumol and Maurice H. Peston, "More on the Multiplier Effects of a Balanced Budget," *American Economic Review* (March, 1955), pp. 140–47.

result because only poll taxes are completely neutral in their influence on consumption behavior. In addition, Baumol and Peston assert that much of the additional spending from the balanced budget increase will not be for newly produced economic goods.[10]

Gurley analyzes the importance of the balanced budget multiplier to full-employment fiscal policy.[11] Reasoning from the premise that a higher level balanced budget is expansionary and a lower level balanced budget is contractionary, he observes that a government effort to stimulate the economy by a deficit, which is followed by a subsequent decrease in both taxes and spending by equal amounts, can have ultimate "contractionary" results. Thus, a decrease in the spending level matched by a decrease in taxes, though a deficit condition continues, can be carried to the point where the level of national income is reduced below what it originally was before the initial deficit was incurred. It thus follows that a government deficit policy could ultimately be either expansionary, contractionary, or neutral *depending upon the level at which it stands*. The opposite of this is also true, namely, that a surplus budget policy may be either contractionary, expansionary, or neutral depending upon its level. Gurley then concludes that only one balanced budget level is consistent with full employment.

The balanced budget multiplier concept thus appears to be a significant dimension of rational fiscal policy. An undue concern with the "precise unity" result, however, endangers the retention of this valuable fiscal concept. The importance of the balanced budget multiplier concept for fiscal purposes does not depend primarily on a proportionate (unity) relationship between a change in balanced budget size and a change in national income, but instead on the *direction* of the relationship, that is, the fact that a larger balanced budget will lead to a higher national income level than a smaller balanced budget.

This phenomenon can then be logically extended to the effects deriving from various budget sizes (levels), whether balanced or unbalanced. The concept thus points out to the policymaker that he must not look to the "simple prescription" of a deficit during depression and a surplus during inflation to solve all problems. Though the deficit or surplus and their respective results are important considerations, it must not be forgotten that the *level* or *size* of the budget—regardless of whether it is a deficit, surplus, or balanced budget—is also extremely important to fiscal decision making. In addition, certain social balance questions are raised by the balanced budget multiplier theorem since, assuming full employment, an expansionary balanced budget change will increase the relative proportion of *public sector* resource allocation in the

---

[10] *Ibid.* pp. 144–47.

[11] John G. Gurley, "Deficits, Surpluses, and National Income," *Southern Economic Journal* (July, 1954), pp. 12–25.

economy and a contractionary balanced budget change will tend to increase the relative proportion of *private sector* production.

FISCAL TECHNIQUES FOR ECONOMIC GROWTH

The lagging growth rate of the American economy during the latter part of the 1950's and the early 1960's brought increased attention to the economic growth goal of public finance. This section of the book will discuss several of the more important tax and expenditure techniques which may be employed by the public sector, especially the federal government, to promote economic growth.[12] First, *tax policies* will be considered in terms of their ability to assist in the achievement of a satisfactory economic growth rate. A tax structure designed to encourage *research and development* efforts, for example, will tend to promote economic growth. The present federal tax law contains certain "loopholes" which encourage patents. Moreover, the ability of businesses to write off research expenditures as costs in the calculation of net profits and taxable income is significant. In addition, special depreciation provisions for research expenditure may be expected to encourage investment in research projects.

The allowance of *accelerated depreciation* for tax purposes can also encourage investment spending and thus promote economic growth. Prior to 1954, the Internal Revenue Code limited taxpayers largely to the use of straight-line depreciation. Under this method, the cost of physical capital is allocated in equal amounts to each year of its economic life (including obsolescence) so that the value of the capital item declines by the same amount each year. Important tax law changes in 1954, however, allowed businesses greater latitude in depreciation accounting which, in turn, undoubtedly contributed to the volume of private investment in the economy. Nevertheless, federal depreciation allowances were still relatively restrictive following the 1954 legislation as compared to those allowed by the central governments of our primary competitors in international trade (Western Europe and Japan). Thus, further liberalizing legislation was passed in 1962 at which time a "guideline life" was established which was applicable to *all* equipment instead of to thousands of *specific* capital items. This not only provided administrative simplification but the guidelines were designed to permit more rapid depreciation write-offs which shortened the average economic lives of the equipment. Certain competitive nations, however, continue to allow much more liberal depreciation than does the United States. Sweden and

---

[12] For an excellent summary of tax and expenditure techniques directed toward the achievement of economic growth, see Paul A. Samuelson, "Fiscal and Financial Policies for Growth," *Proceedings, A Symposium on Economic Growth* (American Bankers Association, 1963), pp. 78–101, especially pp. 90–96.

Germany, for example, allow a large fraction of the value of a capital asset to be written off in the first and second years in order to encourage capital investment. Though the use of accelerated depreciation does not eliminate the eventual tax liability of the business, it does postpone the day of tax payment and amounts to an interest-free loan by the government to the business. Unless the business is already highly liquid in its asset portfolio, the effect of accelerated depreciation should be to make the acquisition of capital goods more attractive.

The *investment credit* against tax liabilities represents an effort by the federal government to promote economic growth by directly subsidizing new investment in capital equipment. The credit, which became part of the Internal Revenue Code in 1962, provides significant nonneutralities though they are definitely positive in terms of the economic growth goal. Generally, net investment over and above those investments undertaken in previous years is allowed a special credit against the tax bill of the investing business. The credit amounts to 7 percent of "qualified investment" except for public utilities, where the amount equals 3 percent. The credit taken in any one year may not be in excess of the first $25,000 of tax liability plus one fourth of any remaining tax liability. Any unused credit first may be carried back to the three preceding tax years and, if not exhausted, it may then be carried forward for as many as five subsequent tax years.

The definition of qualified investment depends both upon the nature of the property and upon its estimated useful life in the hands of the taxpayer. Generally, the credit is allowed on tangible personal property and other depreciable property *excluding* buildings, used as an essential part of manufacturing, production, extraction, transportation, communications, electrical energy production, gas or water transmission, or sewage disposal activities. The property must have a useful life of at least four years before it can become the basis for an investment credit. Qualified investment is limited to 33⅓ percent of the cost of property which has a useful life of more than four years but less than six years. It is limited to 66⅔ percent of the cost of property with a useful life of more than six years but less than eight years. If the property has an estimated useful life of eight years or more, the full cost of the property qualifies as the basis of the investment credit. Qualified investment is limited to $50,000 annually per capital item. In September of 1966, President Johnson asked Congress to enact quickly legislation for the temporary suspension of both the investment credit and accelerated depreciation until January 1, 1968, as a facet of anti-inflationary fiscal policy.

Special treatment for *capital gains* income, as discussed in Chapter 11, comprises another fiscal technique capable of encouraging economic growth. In this instance, the encouragement would apply primarily to "venturesome" investment, though to an extent it would apply to all investments since it allows an individual to pay a lower tax rate on income earned on the purchase and sale of any capital assets held over six months. Asset prices are increased, in effect, by the provision. Moreover, special treatment of capital gains income encourages investment in those industries which tend to reinvest earnings instead of paying them out in dividends. It is hoped that the income will show up in the form of high share values for stock, and thus capital gains when sold, instead of being regular dividend income subject to the higher regular tax rate. Unquestionably, considerable nonneutrality is introduced into investment decisions by the preferential treatment of capital gains under the Internal Revenue Code. It may be surmised, however, that the encouragement of economic growth by such a procedure justifies the classification of this fiscal technique in the positive nonneutrality category.

Various other fiscal tools deriving from the tax side of the budget will now be briefly discussed in terms of their influence upon economic growth. Recent improvements in *income averaging* through the carry-back and carry-forward of profits and losses, for example, have reduced the penalty against risk taking in the economy. In addition, a further *corporation income tax rate reduction* (other than the 1964 legislation), if not the actual elimination of the corporation income tax, would be expected to encourage private investment and thus promote economic growth. Slitor suggests that the corporate income tax rate reductions of 1964 proved to be an important contributor to economic growth.[13]

The goal of economic growth can also be affected by the pattern of public sector *expenditures*. Government, especially the federal government, encourages *research* endeavors through both direct expenditures and subsidization grants. This approach is used in the fields of atomic development, space, and medicine—to mention only a few. The investment of government funds in *education*, in addition, provides a growth in literacy and knowledge which increases economic productivity and ultimately should lead to a higher rate of economic growth.[14] Furthermore, *social overhead investment* in durable capital such as dams, highways, harbors, communications facilities, airports, and other goods with significant traits of publicness provides economic goods which are important to the attainment of economic growth.

Government spending can also be significant as a growth-promotion factor through its ability to increase knowledge and reduce risk in private investment by information promotion programs, government insurance programs, expenditure subsidies, and by joint participation with private enterprise in an industry. In 1965, for example, Congress enacted the

[13] Richard E. Slitor, "The Corporate Tax Cut: What Business Did With the 'Windfall,' " *Challenge* (March–April, 1966), p. 38.

[14] Chapter 21 will consider in greater detail the economic relationship between the public sector and education as an economic (quasi-public) good.

Technical Services Act which provides federal assistance for making scientific information available to private business. This legislation will be particularly beneficial to those industries in which the typical firm is small, that is, too small to do much (if any) of its own research or to be fully apprised of advances in technology. Moreover, several European nations, including France and Sweden, have adopted a policy of combined *business-government planning* whereby business investment plans and government fiscal plans are revealed in advance and then made consistent with each other. A more rational aggregate economic policy is the desired result of such consultation between business and government.

Boulding suggests that an excessive amount of "knowledge industry" efforts are being devoted to the space-military complex, with very little contribution resulting at this time to the civilian economy.[15] He observes that "outside of agriculture and the military . . . American civilian industry is exhibiting a relatively slow rate of technological development" with an increase in labor productivity during the last two decades averaging *not* more than 2.8 percent annually.[16] Thus, a mere increase in the "quantity" of knowledge industry expenditures is not necessarily enough to stimulate a higher rate of economic growth. The proper "quality" allocation is also required.

Finally, an indirect though genuine approach to the promotion of economic growth through governmental fiscal action is to improve the organization of governmental *statistical activities* so that better analysis and policy decisions can be made. The federal government recently undertook a special study for improving economic growth statistics.[17] It has been recommended in this study that action be taken in several areas to improve the organization and coordination of federal statistical collections.[18]

[15] Kenneth E. Boulding, "The Knowledge Boom," *Challenge* (July–August, 1966), p. 7.

[16] *Ibid.*

[17] Joint Economic Committee, Congress of the United States, *Improved Statistics for Economic Growth* (Comments by Government Agencies on Views submitted to the Subcommittee on Economic Statistics) (Washington, D.C.: U.S. Government Printing Office, 1966), comments by Raymond T. Bowman on the recommendations of governmental agencies for improved statistics.

[18] The recommendations include: 1. A national statistical data center should be established. There is a need for greatly improved accessibility to and coordinated use of federal government statistics. Better coordination, for example, is required in the use of computer facilities. The proper filing, collating, and accessibility of data will make possible considerable improvement in the analytical use of existing data for economic growth and other policy purposes.

2. A coordinated system of federal, state, and local government statistics should be established. Part of this problem is to encourage the more detailed and more frequent collection of pertinent statistical data by state and local governments which, as part of the aggregate public sector budget, cannot avoid influencing economic growth through their budgetary actions.

3. A coordinated program of social statistics is required including the growing
(*continued on p. 396*)

In conclusion, it may be observed that numerous tax and expenditure policies of the federal government may be used to favorably influence the rate of economic growth. For the most part, these fiscal techniques attain their results through the creation of distortions (nonneutral effects) in the economy. Fortunately, *rational policy* based upon *economic principles* allows these distortions to provide positive rather than negative effects and the promotion of economic growth becomes the desirable result of such policy.

INTERACTION BETWEEN FISCAL POLICY GOALS

Full Employment versus Inflation

Significant nonneutral effects exist both within and between the various economic goals which the Employment Act seeks to attain through monetary and fiscal policy. The present dilemma (1966–67) between the full-employment and price stability subgoals of the stabilization objective provides an excellent example of intragoal nonneutrality. Figure 18–7 exhibits this problem by means of the so-called Phillips Curve.[19] In this graph, the rate of unemployment in percentage terms is measured on the vertical axis and the annual rate of price increase (inflation) is measured on the horizontal axis. The tradeoff between employment and price stability is apparent. If both inflation and deflation are to be avoided, thus providing price stability, the rate of labor unemployment must rest at 5 percent (point A). On the other hand, if a lower rate of unemployment is desired (say 2 percent), the use of fiscal policy can help to achieve this goal, but not without causing the level of prices

---

need to provide basic data and techniques for appraising the effectiveness of the various social programs.

4. A federal directory of business establishments should be available. The absence of such a master file at the disposal of all official data-gathering agencies creates lack of communication between varied requests for information and places unnecessary burdens on respondents, producers, and users of information.

5. Improved industrial, occupational, and geographic classification is desirable. New products and new occupations, for example, need to be taken into account. Improvements in geographic classifications are required by the recent proliferation of interest in states, counties, and municipalities.

6. Finally, improved coordination based on the national economic accounts and the major models of the behavior of the economy, the educational system, and so on, is desirable. These major economic accounts include the national income and product accounts, the input-output tables, and the flow-of-funds accounts. Improvements could follow such lines as the integration of the national-income-and-product accounts with the flow-of-funds accounts and the extension of the national-income-and-product accounts to include wealth estimates of the value of tangible capital equipment. All of these improvements would tend to make fiscal decision making directed toward the economic growth goal, as well as toward the other fiscal goals, more rational.

[19] See A. W. Phillips, "The Relation Between Unemployment and the Rate of Change of Money Wage Rates in the United Kingdom, 1862–1957," *Economica* (November, 1958), pp. 283–99.

to increase at the rate of 3 percent annually (as at point B). Importantly, the unemployment rate of 4 percent, which is the arbitrarily selected goal of many policymakers in the United States, cannot be achieved without a 1 percent annual rate of price increase (point C). The institutional nature of the economy itself renders the achievement of the combination of a 4 percent unemployment rate and price stability (as at point D) impossible. The considerable monopoly power that exists in both labor and product markets is one of the most important institutional constraints upon the economy in this regard.

FIGURE 18-7

NONNEUTRAL EFFECTS BETWEEN THE GOALS OF FULL
EMPLOYMENT AND PRICE STABILITY

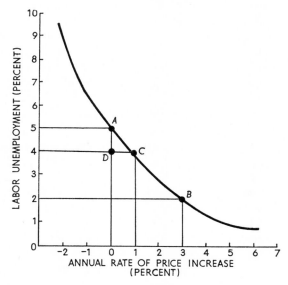

In recent years, the federal government (executive branch) has attempted to use "persuasion" as a means of combating monopoly inflation. This has taken the form of a "wage-price guidelines" policy based on an estimated annual labor productivity increase in the economy of 3.2 percent. It is suggested by the policy that an increase in wages should not exceed the national trend rate of increase in output per man-hour of labor. Moreover, it is suggested that product prices should remain stable in those industries which experience the same productivity growth as the national average, but should rise in those industries with below average productivity growth and should decline in those industries with above average gains in productivity. The guidelines policy, however, carries no direct authority to compel compliance. It merely employs persuasion. Once more, a question of distributive equity is raised since the 3.2 percent maximum is applied to *all* proposed wage increases, even though productivity changes in some industries may be well above that figure.

Unfortunately, no established stabilization policy exists for the purpose of attaining reasonable price stability under conditions of administered price inflation. The federal government, however, has used the indirect techniques of pressure and persuasion from the executive branch on big business and big labor to use restraint in pricing decisions. This can, at best, be only partially effective. The same can be said for the uses in late 1965 of federal government executive influence through the release of government stockpiles to restrain upward price movements in the aluminum and copper industries. Though the Employment Act provides at least an implicit mandate for the federal government to help attain reasonable price stability, monetary and fiscal techniques are admittedly inadequate in combating monopoly (administered price) inflation. Monetary-fiscal techniques, of course, can reduce aggregate demand and thus restrain monopoly inflation, but only at the cost of full employment, as the above analysis has demonstrated. In the long run, however, market concentration with its resultant effects on prices could be favorably influenced by effective government antitrust policy.

Full Employment versus the Allocation, Distribution, and Balance-of-Payments Goals

Next, the analysis will stress the intergoal influence of stabilization policy on the allocation, distribution, and balance of payments objectives of fiscal policy. The effect of stabilization policy on the *allocation* of productive resources, of course, will vary considerably depending upon the type of fiscal policy pursued to attain the stabilization objective. If the stabilization goal of the society is to expand the level of aggregate economic performance, the change can be achieved through a variety of fiscal techniques, some of which impose significant allocation effects. If government spending is increased while taxes are held constant, for example, with the economy operating at full employment, some productive resources are directly removed from the private sector and provided to the public sector. Moreover, even if previously unemployed resources are used by the public sector, a relative expansion of governmental resource allocation still occurs. Furthermore, a change in the allocation of resources within the private sector likely would take place as the recipients of the new government spending change the patterns of their demand for economic goods.

On the other hand, if the increase in national income is approached through a reduction in taxes while government spending remains constant (in a full-employment economy), there would be both an absolute and a relative increase in private sector resource allocation and an absolute and a relative decline in public sector allocation. Once again, there would likely be a change in resource allocation within the private sector as the patterns of effective demand are influenced by the tax reduction. It should thus be concluded that the conceptual area of social balance, as well as specific resource allocation between private and quasi-private goods, can be importantly influenced by the use of fiscal policy to achieve the full-employment goal. Moreover, a specific fiscal technique should not be selected for purely political reasons without regard for the overall consequences of the action since it may create changes in resource allocation between the public and private sectors and within each sector which are undesirable in terms of the collective economic preferences of the community.

Alternative stabilization policies may also directly influence the *distribution* of income and wealth in the society. An increase in government spending, for example, while taxes remain constant may achieve the desired stabilization goal of expanding national income. At the same time, however, income may be redistributed from those who pay the taxes to those who benefit from the incremental government spending. Such redistribution can be either desirable or undesirable depending upon the value judgments of the community regarding the proper state of income distribution. Furthermore, the desired increase in national income may also be achieved through a reduction in taxes while government spending is held constant, but the tax reduction will change the distribution of income in accordance with the income brackets which receive the greatest effects of the tax reduction. The various policies aimed at stabilization thus may exert an important influence upon the distribution of income and wealth in the society. Since a given state of distribution is prerequisite to allocation decisions (see Chapters 4 and 5), fiscal policy which alters distribution will also influence effective demand and allocation.

In addition to exerting important allocation and distribution effects, fiscal policy directed toward stabilization may also have a significant impact on the nation's *balance of international payments*. An adverse payments effect would result, for example, if the rising economic activity resulting from an expansionary fiscal policy increased the level of prices which, in turn, tended to reduce the competitive position of American goods in international markets. Moreover, American goods would become less competitive at a time when higher national income is providing Americans with greater purchasing power to acquire imported foreign goods. Fiscal policies which can improve the balance of international payments include those which stimulate U.S. exports by improving the productivity of labor and capital in American industries and by providing

price stability. In addition, fiscal policies which encourage foreign investment in the United States and discourage American investment in foreign
nations, by making domestic investment more attractive, will tend to
relieve the balance of payments problem.

Government Fiscal Policy and Interrelated Growth-Cycle Objectives

As observed above, most fiscal policy has historically stressed
short-run stabilization objectives. There have been recent exceptions to
this fact, however, in the form of the federal tax reductions of 1964 and
1965 as well as in federal policies regarding accelerated depreciation and
the investment credit. Seemingly, a policy which expands aggregate
short-run performance should also facilitate the long-run economic
growth objective. Extreme caution, however, must be used in formulating
policy on this basis. A short-run policy which stresses growth in consumption and not in investment, for example, will reduce the amount of capital
formation and likely slow down the rate of economic growth over a
period of time. A realistic example of the importance of this fact is offered
by the economic history of the Soviet Union between 1928 (the beginning
of the first Soviet Five-Year Plan for economic development) and the
1960's. By stressing capital formation at the sacrifice of consumption, the
Soviet Union experienced a substantial rate of economic growth during
this period. Though American value judgments might condemn the
extreme sacrifice of consumption imposed upon the Soviet people during
the period, the influence of capital formation on economic development
cannot be denied. Thus, although a positive correlation generally exists
between expansionary stabilization policies and satisfactory economic
growth, many qualifying circumstances must be considered for policymaking purposes.

Alternate types of stabilization policy, of course, exert differential
effects upon the rate of economic growth. These effects depend primarily
upon the manner in which the various fiscal policies influence investment
decisions. An expansionary fiscal policy, for example, can be based upon
budgetary techniques which directly encourage investment, such as
accelerated depreciation and the investment credit. Furthermore, an
increase in government spending for items such as education and health
may be expected to increase significantly the rate of economic growth
because of the high economic returns derived from improving the productive capabilities of the labor factor of production. If the incremental
governmental spending is for national defense rather than for investment
in human capital, however, the rate of economic growth would likely be
less except for that amount of technological change which would be a
product of the "fallout" from the research and development expenditures

of the defense sector. Moreover, if the increase in national income is brought about by a reduction in the corporation income tax, the amount of new investment will tend to increase by a greater amount than it would increase under conditions where the tax reduction takes the form of rate reductions in the lower ranges of the personal income tax.

The interaction between stabilization and growth policy, of course, derives from the basic nature of the relationship between the "trend" and the "cycle." The model of John R. Hicks which relates some of the strategic elements of this relationship will be summarized at this time.[20]

FIGURE 18–8

Hicksian Growth-Cycle Theory and Fiscal Policy Applications

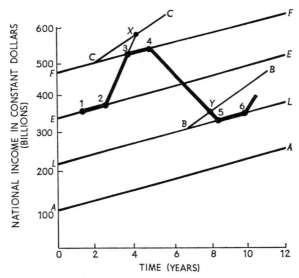

SOURCE: The basic graph, without the fiscal policy applications, is derived from John R. Hicks, *A Contribution to the Theory of the Trade Cycle* (Oxford: The Clarendon Press, 1950), p. 97.

Then the Hicksian model will be used as a basis for the application of fiscal policy with positive nonneutral effects toward the interrelated attainment of *both* the stabilization (anticyclical) and economic growth goals of the society.

Figure 18–8 will now be used to demonstrate the basic tenets of the Hicksian model, and later for the application of fiscal policy to the interrelated stabilization and growth goals. Output (real income) is measured on the vertical axis and time is measured on the horizontal axis. Investment is divided into the traditional autonomous and induced cate-

[20] John R. Hicks, *A Contribution to the Theory of the Trade Cycle* (Oxford: The Clarendon Press, 1950).

gories. It is assumed that autonomous investment will grow at a constant percentage rate along line *AA* due to long-run trend factors such as improvements in technology and population growth. This constant growth in autonomous investment, working through the multiplier process, provides an equilibrium level of national income growth along line *LL*. Growth of national income along *LL*, however, will lead to induced investment resulting from expanding output (real income) and will set the acceleration principle into motion. The combination of the multiplier and the accelerator, which may be referred to as the "supermultiplier," determines a higher equilibrium growth path for national income along line *EE*. The highest line on the graph, line *FF*, represents the ceiling rate of national income growth as set by the productive capacity of the economy. In other words, line *FF* represents the equilibrium path of the full-employment growth of national income. This ceiling rate of growth is assumed to be the same rate as the growth of autonomous investment since both depend upon improvements in technology and upon population growth.

At points 1 and 2, national income grows at the rate set by the interaction of the multiplier and accelerator. An outside disturbance such as a "sudden burst" in autonomous investment then causes the rate of national income growth to depart in an upward direction from growth path *EE*. If only the multiplier were involved, the upward movement would not be "explosive" and national income would soon return to the growth path *EE*. The accelerator working with the multiplier, however, will provide explosive growth which will terminate only when the full-employment growth path *FF* is reached at point 3. The scarcity of productive resources will cause the accelerator to lose its explosive character and, at best, the growth in national income can only continue in the pattern along line *FF* as determined by autonomous investment alone with its multiplier effect.

National income can grow along line *FF*, however, as between points 3 and 4, for only a limited period of time because the equilibrium growth path becomes *LL*, not *EE* or *FF*, when only autonomous investment (through the multiplier) is exerting an expansionary influence. National income thus turns downward, which explains the "upper turning point" of the cycle. The downward movement in national income between points 4 and 5 will be more gradual than the upward movement between points 2 and 3 had been since only the multiplier is at work in the downswing, *not* both the multiplier and accelerator as is true during the upswing. Eventually, the downswing will end at a "lower turning point" and a new upswing will begin as an increase in replacement demand resulting from the physical depreciation of capital goods occurs. Thus, new acceleration activity becomes integrated with the expansionary multiplier and a new surge of explosive growth begins. The turning point upward, which begins a new cycle, occurs at point 6 along growth path *LL*. The downswing had not carried national income below line *LL* where the growth path of national income reflects the continuous expansion created by the multiplier effects of the rate of growth in autonomous investment.

In summary, a full-employment ceiling caused by productive capacity limitations sets the upper turning point of the business cycle, according to Hicks, while the lower turning point is set by autonomous investment working through the investment multiplier. Business cycle fluctuations will occur between these maximum and minimum growth paths. The fact that both the full-employment trend line (line *FF*) and the slump trend line (line *LL*) slope upward, reflecting economic growth, is assured by the continued rate of growth in autonomous investment (line *AA*). Thus, Hicks skillfully integrates the secular trend and the cycle into a meaningful theory. Both the upswing (boom) and the downswing (bust) of the business cycle, moreover, are shown as inevitable results of the operation of a dynamic market economy through the interacting operation of the multiplier and the accelerator.

Next, the ability of federal fiscal policy to directly influence growth-cycle patterns is also exhibited in Figure 18–8. Certain fiscal policy alternatives which are capable of either reducing cyclical instability or promoting economic growth, or both, are adapted to the Hick's model in this graph. Line *CC* indicates how fiscal policy may increase the resource ceiling over time and thus delay or avoid the cyclical downturn. The resource ceiling of the economy can be expanded by those fiscal policies which increase the *quantity* and/or *quality* of productive resources. In this regard, "capital formation"—the net additions of private and social capital to the nation's capital stock—is of particular importance. Hence, the cyclical downturn need not occur at point 4. Instead, the appropriate "resource-expanding" fiscal policy can cause it to occur at a higher point such as point *X*, as shown on the higher growth line *CC*.

A second fiscal policy alternative would be to stop the downward swing between points 4 and 5, somewhere above point 5. At point 5, it should be remembered, the influence of the multiplier as derived from the rate of growth in autonomous investment sets the pattern for the eventual cyclical upturn. Fiscal policy may set a higher minimum trough and eventual upturn point for the cycle. Thus, an increase in the level of private investment, or in its rate of growth, resulting from such fiscal devices as *accelerated depreciation* and the *investment credit*, can cause national income to follow line *BB* instead of continuing between points 5 and 6. Line *BB*, of course, constitutes a higher cyclical trough than line *LL*. The eventual upturn thus may occur at point *Y* instead of at point 6.

Other fiscal alternatives such as an increase in tax rates, a reduction in transfer and/or exhaustive expenditures, or both, or a balanced reduction in budget size could be applied between points 3 and 4 to prevent possible monetary inflation. Moreover, a reduction in tax rates, an increase in spending, or a higher overall budget level can be applied at point 4 to "prevent" the downturn, or somewhere below point 4 to "cushion" the downturn. The latter policy would result in the operation of a government multiplier capable of reducing the depth of the cyclical downturn without, as in the accelerated depreciation-investment credit approach, directly increasing private autonomous investment. Hence, this should be classified as a separate fiscal approach directed toward the same ultimate goal of cushioning the downturn by raising the eventual trough level of the cycle.

Fiscal Policy and Regional Economic Activity

The *composition* of governmental budgetary activity will inevitably influence both short-run regional economic performance and long-run regional economic growth. Some regions and the states which comprise them, for example, are net importers of federal budgetary benefits both of an expenditure and tax subsidy variety. These two aspects of budgeting, of course, need to be symmetrically considered for purposes of attaining a complete and rational analysis. National defense expenditures provide a good example of how some regions and states benefit more from certain types of federal spending than do others. National fiscal policy, it should be observed, may be frustrated also by the choice between attainment of the distribution goal of equity, in the sense of achieving a pattern of balanced growth between the various economic regions within a nation, and the national growth objective. In other words, the distributive goal of making real per capita income and living standards *more equal* between regions may lessen the rate of national economic growth. This could easily occur because specialized economic production based upon the economic principle of comparative advantage, and the subsequent exchange of goods produced under specialization, would tend to create substantial per capita income differences between the various regions of a society at a time when it is attaining maximum aggregate output as a result of its regional specialization.

The United States, of course, has never completely followed a laissez-faire policy for resource allocation among economic regions. Historically, federal policies toward land disposal, tariffs, the development of agricultural technology, the development of transportation sectors, and the like have had significant influence upon the patterns of regional economic development as well as national economic development. Federal policies continue to influence regional economic growth though some transitional changes in the type of policy have occurred. Technological change and population growth, for example, have added emphasis to policies of natural resource conservation, the development of recreational areas, public power projects (such as TVA), interstate highway development, and the support of housing. However, Borts and Stein comment that regional economic policies of the federal government have *not* historically been formulated in terms of "an over-all view of an efficient free market economy."[21] Yet, the federal government is more likely to increase rather than decrease its future regional economic policies and influence. This has been indicated in recent years by the passage of the Area Redevelopment Act and the Economic Development Act, the latter an important new item of legislation which, it is predicted, will sharply increase the magnitude of federal regional development programs.[22] Encouragingly, Borts and Stein observe that, in terms of efficiency, the interregional and interindustrial growth pattern of the United States appears now to be moving toward an intertemporal competitive equilibrium and thus in the direction of intertemporal efficiency.[23]

TECHNIQUES OF DEFICIT FINANCING AND SURPLUS DISPOSAL

The Deficit Budget

The use of tax and spending (both transfer and exhaustive) changes to promote economic goals, as discussed throughout this chapter, will frequently result in either a deficit or a surplus budget. There are various means, moreover, by which the federal government may finance a deficit budget (when expenditures have exceeded tax collections) and dispose of a surplus (when tax collections have exceeded expenditures). The particular deficit financing and surplus disposal techniques selected, however, may exert substantially different *secondary effects* on aggregate economic activity. A deficit budget resulting from lower tax rates and/or higher government spending, or both, tends to be expansionary and a surplus budget resulting from higher tax rates and reduced government spending tends to be contractionary. The expansionary and contractionary results involve the multiplier effect which the public sector exerts on the private sector when government provides *either* a "net increment" in private sector purchasing power through a deficit budget *or* a "net decrement" in private sector purchasing power through a surplus budget. Yet, once these *direct* multiplier effects are set in motion, the particular means of financing a deficit or disposing of a surplus take on considerable importance because of their ability to exert *secondary* economic effects.

[21] George H. Borts and Jerome L. Stein, *Economic Growth in a Free Market* (New York: Columbia University Press, 1964), p. 189.

[22] This new legislation is discussed in greater detail in Chapter 22.

[23] Borts and Stein, *op. cit.*, p. 214.

The present discussion will consider five alternative methods of financing a federal deficit budget. These are:

1. The Treasury Department sells securities to the private sector (excluding commercial banks and the Federal Reserve System).
2. The Treasury Department sells securities to commercial banks at a time when they do *not* have excess loanable reserves.
3. The Treasury Department sells securities to commercial banks at a time when they do possess substantial excess reserves.
4. The Treasury Department sells securities to the nation's central bank—the Federal Reserve System.
5. The government creates or prints *fiat* money.

The least expansionary means of financing a federal deficit is listed first above and, as the numbering approaches five, the means of financing the deficit become increasingly expansionary. A sale of treasury securities (debt instruments) to private individuals and businesses in the market sector of the economy equal in volume to the amount of the deficit, for example, would withdraw purchasing power from the private sector equal to the amount introduced into the private sector by the deficit budget itself. This indeed must be classified as a restrictive means of financing a deficit budget since the secondary effects of the financing technique selected neutralize the primary effects of the initial multiplier.

Another highly restrictive means of financing a deficit budget occurs when the Treasury Department sells securities to the commercial banking system at a time when the banks do *not* possess excess loanable reserves. Under such conditions, commercial banks would necessarily restrict their loans to the private sector and/or to state and local levels of government in order to finance the purchase of the securities. This would cause a reduction in aggregate demand which would tend to neutralize or offset the primary expansionary effects of the initial multiplier.

On the other hand, if treasury securities equal to the amount of the deficit are sold to the commercial banking system at a time when the banks possess substantial excess reserves, the initial multiplier expansion need not be severely neutralized, if neutralized at all, by restrictive secondary effects because the banks can purchase the securities from their excess reserves without reducing their volume of loans to the private sector and to state-local government. Moreover, an expansion of the money supply, as the excess reserves are put to work through the operation of a fractional reserve banking system, will allow the greater magnitude of economic activity made possible by the expansionary multiplier to take place. The expanding money supply will reinforce, not neutralize or offset, the multiplier-caused expansion.

An additional expansionary means of financing a deficit budget is to sell treasury securities to the Federal Reserve System. This process involves the concept of *debt monetization*. The effect in this case is at least as expansionary as that of the sale of securities to commercial banks at a time when they have substantial excess reserves. The following paragraph provides a description of the "debt monetization process" derived from the sale of treasury securities to the Federal Reserve System.

The Treasury Department sells government securities (debt instruments) to the Federal Reserve banks. The Federal Reserve banks then create new treasury deposit accounts, or expand present Treasury deposit accounts, at the banks. These deposit accounts are liabilities to the Federal Reserve System, but the securities purchased by the Federal Reserve System are classified as assets. The government then spends the funds for purchasing economic goods and productive resources from the private sector. Subsequently, checks are drawn by the Treasury Department on its deposit accounts in the Federal Reserve System as the money is spent for government acquisitions. Individuals and business firms in the private sector who sell productive resources and economic goods to the federal government receive these checks as payments. Ordinarily, the checks will be deposited in the commercial banking system and the commercial banks, upon receiving the checks as deposits, will credit the deposit accounts of the private individuals and business firms. The commercial banks, in turn, send the checks to the Federal Reserve banks and the commercial bank reserve accounts within the Federal Reserve System are subsequently increased by the full amount of the checks. The commercial banking system thus possesses new excess reserves over and above the reserve amount required legally behind the new demand deposits. This monetary expansion (debt monetization) will reinforce the expansionary influence of the original multiplier.

The federal government, of course, need not resort to ordinary debt creation to finance a deficit budget. It could simply print *fiat* money equal to the amount of the excess of government spending over tax collections. Historically, such unrestricted monetary creation by government has caused considerable consternation and fear of governmental waste and hyperinflation. Such results, however, need not occur in a well-controlled, monetary exchange economy which answers to the dictates of the people through a democratic political process. This technique of financing a deficit, which is a unique form of debt creation, is also extremely expansionary and in no way neutralizes the primary multiplier expansion through the imposition of offsetting secondary effects.

The Surplus Budget

When the federal government collects more in taxes than it spends, the resulting surplus may be utilized in a variety of ways. An increase in tax rates and/or a reduction in government spending may lead to a surplus budget. Depending upon the particular surplus disposal technique selected, the contractionary effect of the surplus budget working through a negative multiplier may be either reinforced or neutralized. If

TABLE 18–2—ALLOCATION AND DISTRIBUTION EFFECTS OF ALTERNATIVE SURPLUS DISPOSAL TECHNIQUES

Six Alternatives	Federal Tax Effect	Overall Tax Burden Effect	Effectiveness of Plan From a State and Local Standpoint	Intergovernmental Relations Effect
COMPENSATORY FISCAL APPROACH—cut federal income tax or reduce the national debt or both depending on economic conditions.	Federal income taxpayers could expect further reductions in tax liability.	The overall federal-state-local tax system would be less progressive because the nation would be required to place increasing reliance on proportional and regressive state and local taxes to finance rising domestic needs.	Least efficient because direct benefits accrue to individual federal income taxpayers—indirect benefit to the extent that a compensatory fiscal policy promotes greater economic activity and expands the state and local tax base. Can affect willingness to raise state and local taxes either way.	Federal role somewhat diminished by the relinquishment of effective control of part of its fiscal resources and state and local government roles commensurately enhanced.
TAX CREDIT OPTION APPROACH—provide federal income taxpayers a more generous write-off of their state and local taxes with an option plan permitting them either to itemize their state and local tax payments (as they can do now) or receive a tax credit for state and local tax payments in excess of ___% of their net income.	Persons in the low and middle tax brackets carrying above average state and local tax loads would receive the most benefit. Persons in the high tax brackets now enjoy a liberal write-off privilege through itemization.	The overall effect slightly more progressive because (a) low and middle income tax bracket taxpayers receive larger write-offs and (b) state and local governments would be encouraged to place more reliance on income taxes in order to maximize tax credit possibilities.	More efficient than outright tax cut only to extent that tax credit's overcome resistance to higher state and local tax rates. Much less efficient than sharing or grant approaches because direct aid is to taxpayers rather than to governments.	Federal role somewhat diminished—state and local governments somewhat enhanced because a more liberal write-off of state and local taxes could help to overcome resistance to higher state and local taxes.
TAX SHARING APPROACH—distribute to the states a designated percentage of the federal tax revenue on the basis of collection.	None.	No marked change in the tax incidence picture unless federal dollars actually replace state and local revenue sources. In that case, there is a slight progressive effect.	An efficient aid mechanism because states are left free to allocate the funds among competing needs. Local governments' benefit dependent on how they share in the funds.	Federal role diminished; states' role enhanced because these governments determine how funds would be spent.
UNCONDITIONAL GRANT APPROACH—through a permanent trust fund, distribute among the states for general government purposes, on a per capita basis, an amount equal to 1% or 2% of the federal income tax base (proposal of President's Task Force on Intergovernmental Fiscal Co-operation).	None.	No marked change in the tax incidence picture unless federal dollars actually replace state and local revenue sources. In that case, there is a slight progressive effect.	An efficient aid mechanism because states are left free to allocate the funds among competing needs. Local governments' benefit dependent on how they share in the funds.	Federal role diminished; states' role enhanced because these governments determine how funds would be spent.
CONDITIONAL GRANT APPROACH—expand present type of conditional grant-in-aid programs to finance specific functions.	None.	No marked change in the tax incidence picture unless need for state and local matching funds requires increases in regressive type taxes.	A fairly efficient aid mechanism. Both state and local governments are directly benefited but because of their specific expenditure focus, conditional grants tend to distort allocation of funds among programs.	Federal role definitely enhanced in relation to state and local governments.
DIRECT FEDERAL EXPENDITURE APPROACH—step up direct federal expenditure for such programs as river and harbor construction projects; or launch new programs to deal with domestic problems of an interstate character, such as air pollution and mass transportation.	None.	No marked change in the tax incidence picture. Distribution of benefits for construction-type project likely to be less favorable to low-income groups than expenditures on social purposes.	An indirect aid to the extent that direct federal activity relieves state and local governments of the responsibility for financing the program. Far less effective than tax sharing or grant approaches.	Federal role definitely enhanced in relation to state and local governments.

SOURCE: Advisory Commission on Intergovernmental Relations.

maximum economic contraction is desired, the surplus funds should be held idle and not allowed to reenter the private sector. Under such conditions, no neutralization to the negative multiplier occurs since a net decrease in private sector purchasing power has taken place. On the other hand, if some degree of neutralization is desired the surplus can be (1) distributed among groups who will spend most of it immediately, which would yield a substantial offset to the contractionary effects of the surplus, or (2) the surplus can be used to retire already existing government debt. In the latter case, depending upon who holds the debt that is to be retired, varying degrees of partial neutralization will result.

The disposal of a surplus, in addition to influencing the degree of multiplier-caused contraction, may also exert significant allocation and distribution effects depending upon the pattern of surplus disposal which is selected. The allocation effects consist of resource pattern changes both *between* the public and private sectors and *within* each sector. Table 18–2 summarizes some of the more significant allocation and distribution results which derive from alternate procedures of disposing of a federal surplus.

Thus, it is observed that not only do unbalanced budgets provide primary multiplier effects through tax rate and spending changes, but also that important secondary economic effects may result depending upon the particular technique used to finance a deficit or to dispose of a surplus. The specific technique selected, however, will necessarily depend upon policy objectives and upon the overall conditions of the economy. The huge federal deficits of World War II were inevitable, for example, and the proper fiscal policy under these conditions—a surplus budget—could not be used despite the inflationary gap conditions which prevailed. The next best approach was to finance the deficit in the most restrictive way possible in terms of secondary effects. Consequently, an enormous effort was made to sell war bonds to the private sector of the economy as well as to the banking system, while at the same time monetary policy attempted generally to restrict private credit. It is seen in this example that fiscal and monetary policy cannot be totally divorced from each other. Instead, they require coordination to achieve mutual economic objectives. It is perhaps noteworthy, in terms of improved future policy, to observe that the institutional arrangement for monetary policy working through the "quasi-independent" Federal Reserve System is considerably different from the institutional arrangement for fiscal policy which works "slowly" through the government budget as requested by the executive branch of government but as implemented through the legislative actions of Congress. The relationship between fiscal policy and monetary policy will be explored further in the following chapter, which analyzes the various fiscal policy norms or bench marks and their monetary policy alternatives.

Chapter 19

FISCAL POLICY NORMS

It is customary to relate the techniques of fiscal policy discussed in the previous chapter to specific fiscal norms (guidelines, bench marks) when policy decisions are made. The array of possible fiscal policy norms extends over a wide range between the two extremes of a continuum. Figure 19–1 displays such a continuum, including the

FIGURE 19–1

CONTINUUM OF VARIOUS FISCAL POLICY NORMS

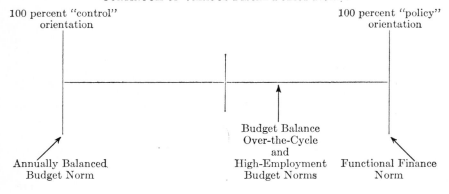

approximate relative positions of certain important fiscal norms. On one end, for example, is the *annually balanced budget* norm while the *functional finance* bench mark is at the other extreme. Various intermediate positions include the general concept of the *cyclically balanced budget* and the *high-employment budget* rule.[1] For reasons to be discussed

---

[1] The discussion of fiscal policy norms in this chapter necessarily includes frequent reference to *government debt* since each of the important norms bears at least indirect implications for public sector debt. Government debt creation, for example, is a necessary corollary to a discussion of the annually balanced budget rule because the failure to maintain budget balance by allowing expenditures to exceed tax collections creates a condition of deficit spending which is likely to be financed through debt creation. However, since government debt is the subject of Chapter 20, it will be discussed in this chapter only to the extent necessary for a proper evaluation of the various fiscal policy norms.

below, these two intermediate norms are *not* placed in the exact middle of the continuum.

The Annually Balanced Budget Fiscal Norm

Since the early days of the sovereign history of the United States, a strong perference has existed for an annually balanced federal government budget. In fact, the philosophy favoring an annually balanced budget has also been extended to the public sector as a whole as is indicated by the various restrictions on unbalanced budgets as well as the various spending limitations imposed by state government constitutions on the fiscal operations of state and local governments. The belief that an annually balanced budget is desirable per se is apparently based upon the cultural notion that government budgetary behavior should be "thrifty" since a balanced budget supposedly indicates fiscal responsibility and efficiency for government just as it does for the household and business segments of the private sector. Yet, households and businesses are increasingly carrying debt and apparently are doing so with a wide degree of safety. Hence, the long-established feeling that only a balanced budget is efficient applies, it would seem, on a declining basis to the private sector. Moreover, the analogy between private and public debt is highly tenuous.[2]

The annually balanced budget principle was developed by the classical economists (with a few dissenters) and has been perpetuated for well over a century as a guideline for governmental fiscal behavior. Government debt had not existed on a wide-scale basis until the establishment of the monetary-exchange type of economy under capitalism. To be sure, some debt creation had occurred during feudalism, but this practice was not extensive. The development of public debt and credit on a widespread basis first occurred during the 18th century. David Hume, Adam Smith, and others expressed strong opposition to unbalanced (deficit) government budgets at this time. Certain moderate positions were to be found, however, including those of Thomas Malthus in England and the first Secretary of the Treasury, Alexander Hamilton, in the United States.

The classical case for the annually balanced budget was based upon the following arguments: (1) private sector economic development is retarded by the sale of government debt to the private sector since fewer capital funds are then available for the acquisition of private capital goods, (2) government deficit spending allows a relative expansion of the public sector as opposed to the private sector, in social balance terms, and (3) deficit spending necessarily leads to inflation.

Adam Smith defended the annually balanced budget as part of his

---

[2] This point will be described in the following chapter on the subject of *Public Sector Debt.*

basic opposition to central government debt.[3] The Smith position on debt, though partly economic, also displays considerable political interpretation as a result of his strong antimercantilist feelings. Smith believed that government was fundamentally wasteful in terms of its financial operations. He felt that the money capital needed by the private sector for economic development would be diverted unnecessarily from the private to the public sector if debt creation were allowed. Thus, an insufficient growth in capital goods would take place which, in turn, would retard economic development. He also believed that the financing of wars through borrowing rather than through taxation encouraged the government to wage needless wars. Smith was not particularly concerned with the burden of an *existing* debt, but with the burdens created *at the time the debt was created,* though the burden of existing debt still bore some importance in his evaluation.

Other classical economists such as Say, Ricardo, and Mill opposed government deficit spending to varying degrees and thus, at least implicitly, approved the annually balanced budget concept. Malthus, however, did not believe the national debt to be evil per se. He observed that the individuals who receive interest earnings from public debt spend such earnings, at least in part, for economic goods. Hence, debt contributes to the demand for economic goods. Malthus, at certain other places in his writings, takes a stronger position against government debt, but he never completely condemns it. Mill also took a less firm position against deficit spending than did many other classical economists and noted that government borrowing does not always lead to undesirable results. Following Mill, the classical economists paid less attention to the public debt issue. In fact, Alfred Marshall's *Principles* ignores the subject. Late in the 19th century, Bastable observed that one characteristic of a mature economic society is the ability to create public debt. Thus, considerable moderation of the "anti-debt" and "pro-balanced budget" position occurred between the early days of classical economics and the early 20th century. Yet, significant opposition in economics to the annually balanced budget principle did not arrive until the era of Keynesian economics in the 1930's.

Franklin D. Roosevelt was elected President during the Great Depression in 1932 on a political platform which included an annually balanced budget plank. The effects of Keynesian economic analysis were beginning to be felt in the political and economic circles of the Western world, however, by the beginning of Roosevelt's second term of office in 1937 and the first deliberate uses of fiscal policy to promote the economic stabilization objective had come into being. Since the advent of modern

---

[3] For an excellent discussion of the classical and neoclassical position on government debt, see Jesse Burkhead, "The Balanced Budget," *Quarterly Journal of Economics* (May, 1954), pp. 191–216.

aggregative economics, most economists have accepted the legitimacy of the use of the federal government budget to promote economic stabilization and growth objectives. Politicians, however, have accepted such legitimacy to a lesser extent. Nevertheless, a pronounced trend toward greater political acceptance of these fiscal tools has occurred during recent decades. This is indicated by the late President Kennedy's request to Congress in 1963 for tax reductions to achieve the macroeconomic goals of full employment and satisfactory economic growth. This suggestion reached fruition under President Johnson in the form of the income tax (personal and corporate) reductions of 1964 and the excise tax reductions of 1965.

The annually balanced budget fiscal rule seems seriously deficient and unnecessarily restrictive in a rational, mid-20th century, mature, democratic political economy. The fact that it represents an unacceptable extreme on a continuum of fiscal bench marks, however, does not suggest that it possesses no merit whatsoever. In a society which states a preference for the market allocation of resources, the notion that the annually balanced budget norm exerts control over excesses by government and thus over the relative expansion of the public sector contains some merit. Thus, some of the compromise bench marks discussed below retain certain aspects of the control function of the annually balanced budget, though such acceptance remains secondary to the acceptance of deliberate budget manipulation as a fiscal tool. Finally, even if the annually balanced budget were a totally acceptable fiscal norm, certain institutional impediments exist which would tend to prevent its realization. For example, the lobbying influence of pressure groups which are encouraged by the American political structure leads to a bias in favor of deficit budgets. This occurs because lobbies attempt to improve the economic status of those whom they represent by either increasing the receipt of government expenditures or decreasing the tax payments of their constituents, or both. Obviously, higher governmental spending and lower taxes add up to a movement toward, if not the actual realization of, a deficit budget. The individual pressure groups may separately decry deficit spending, but their collective actions frequently add up to this result.

Functional Finance

The complete antithesis to the annually balanced budget norm is the functional finance fiscal rule. While the balanced budget norm stresses the importance of control and regulation over governmental fiscal activities, the functional finance norm advocates that the government budget be used to promote macroeconomic objectives without regard to balance. Thus, it is less concerned than the annually balanced budget with allocation and distribution goals and more concerned with aggregate economic performance and growth objectives.

The functional finance concept was developed rather early in the Keynesian era and is built upon Keynesian economic theory. The early statements of the principle primarily considered stabilization, with emphasis on the relief of unemployment as it existed during the 1930's, and did not stress economic growth as such. Emphasis on economic growth, however, has appeared during the latter part of the 1950's and the early 1960's. The most famous statement of the functional finance norm was provided by Abba Lerner in 1943.[4] Lerner observed that the war years (just prior to 1943) had proven the ability of government fiscal action to maintain full employment. The chronic depression conditions that preceded World War II had been relieved as defense-supported aggregate demand expanded. Yet, Lerner asserted that many well-intentioned individuals who recognize that deficit spending actually works still oppose it because of a less than complete understanding of its operation and because of a misinformed fear regarding its consequences.

Lerner argued that the essential idea of government economic policy—which involves governmental spending, taxing, borrowing, the repayment of loans, the issue of new money, and the withdrawal of money from circulation—should be undertaken with the effects of these actions on the national economy in mind. Attachment to any established fiscal doctrine such as the annually balanced budget rule should not receive priority consideration. "The principle of judging fiscal measures by the way they work or function in the economy we may call *Functional Finance*."[5]

The *first* law (governmental responsibility) of functional finance, according to Lerner, is that the government budget should be directed toward the achievement of full employment and stable prices. It should *not* concern itself with whether tax receipts and governmental expenditures are balanced or unbalanced. In other words, tax collections need not equal the level of government spending, as advocated by the annually balanced budget norm, and taxes need to be imposed only to prevent inflation. The *second* law of functional finance states that the government should incur debt by borrowing money from the private sector *only* if it is desirable that the private sector have less money to spend and more government bonds to hold. This would be a desirable goal if, in the absence of debt, the rate of interest were too low, thus inducing an inflationary excess of private investment. *Third*, functional finance would prescribe that any excess of money outlays over money revenues to government which cannot be met out of private money hoards for the purchase of the government debt should be met by the printing of new money. Conversely, any excess of revenues over outlays can be either

[4] Abba P. Lerner, "Functional Finance and the Federal Debt," *Social Research* (February, 1943), pp. 38–51.

[5] *Ibid.*, p. 39.

destroyed or used to replenish private sector money hoards. In effect, the printing, hoarding, or destruction of money should be conducted as required for the achievement of full employment and price stability.

Lerner observed that functional finance is not related to any particular type of political-economic system but instead only to the existence of a mature money exchange economy. Hence, the functional finance approach may be summarized as follows:

Functional Finance is not especially related to democracy or to private enterprise. It is applicable to a communist society just as well as to a fascist society or a democratic society. It is applicable to any society in which money is used as an important element in the economic mechanism. It consists of the simple principle of giving up our preconceptions of what is proper or sound or traditional, of what "is done," and instead considering the *functions* performed in the economy by government taxing and spending and borrowing and lending. It means using these instruments simply as instruments, and not as magic charms that will cause mysterious hurt if they are manipulated by the wrong people or without due reverence for tradition. Like any other mechanism, Functional Finance will work no matter who pulls the levers. Its relationship to democracy and free enterprise consists simply in the fact that if the people who believe in these things will not use Functional Finance, they will stand no chance in the long run against others who will.[6]

A Comparison of the Annually Balanced Budget and Functional Finance Norms

Though the functional finance fiscal norm is extreme in its complete noncommitment to budgetary "control," thus placing social balance and other allocation considerations in a secondary position, it contributes importantly to the recognition of the fact that government budgetary action is capable of promoting macroeconomic goals in a market-oriented economy. Hence, just as control generally must be recognized as a desirable element of the annually balanced budget rule, so must the ability of fiscal policy to "improve" employment, price level, economic growth, and balance-of-payments conditions be recognized as an advantage of the functional finance norm. A rational fiscal norm, of course, should contain some reference to both control and macroeconomic objectives. Nevertheless, the control objective—as long as some self-imposed constraint is present—seems secondary in importance to the fact that governmental budgetary actions can be deliberately used to improve aggregate economic performance.

The annually balanced budget norm would appear to serve the allocation objective in a very adequate manner by revealing the opportunity costs involved in the employment of resources between the public

[6] *Ibid.*, pp. 50–51.

and private sectors. In other words, the benefit principle of taxation would be applied in a balanced sense. The nature of public and quasi-public goods (as described in Part I of the book), however, suggests that various features of these goods, such as indivisibilities, would cause the annually balanced budget rule to depart in practice from its apparent theoretical excellence under the benefit principle. In other words, the annually balanced budget norm would not serve the allocation objective in a perfect manner even if this objective were to receive the full stress of policy with the other goals of public finance being ignored. This is true because the balanced budget rule does not provide, in practice, a perfect *quid pro quo* relationship between tax and expenditure decisions and thus does not determine that resource division point between the public and private sectors which best serves the preference patterns of the community. Thus, whether the budget is balanced or unbalanced is irrelevant to the determination of efficient resource allocation between the two sectors of the economy.

Furthermore, undue emphasis on the allocation goal can seriously impede the attainment of the stabilization and economic growth goals. The annually balanced budget rule, for example, requires a reduction in government spending and/or an increase in tax rates when the level of national income decreases and vice versa when the level of income rises. Such policy provides a tendency toward a surplus budget during an economic downturn and toward a deficit budget during an economic expansion. These results obviously clash with rational stabilization policy since they introduce a positive multiplier during prosperity and a negative multiplier during recession, which reinforces rather than offsets the cyclical conditions.

Thus, no fiscal norm can be expected to attain perfectly all fiscal goals.[7] Instead, it is a give-and-take arrangement. The complete attainment of the stabilization goal, for example, would likely cause less than optimal attainment of the allocation objective, and vice versa, as discussed above. Musgrave observes that "at the normative level, no conflict exists between the allocation and stabilization functions of budget policy" since the allocation budget is planned ideally to meet individual preferences on the basis of a full-employment income.[8] "Fiscal politics," however, can create a conflict between the allocation and stabilization objectives.[9] If a deficit budget is called for by the stabilization objective, for example, in order to promote the expansion of employment and income, some people may erroneously conclude that the extension of

---

[7] This discussion is related to the "interacting fiscal policy goals" discussion of the previous chapter.

[8] Richard A. Musgrave, *The Theory of Public Finance* (New York: McGraw–Hill Book Co., Inc., 1959), p. 522.

[9] *Ibid.*

additional public (and quasi-public) goods is virtually costless which, in turn, can lead to an overallocation of public (and quasi-public) goods and resulting allocation (social balance) distortion. Taxes thus would not be serving their function as an index of opportunity cost.[10] Oppositely, if a surplus budget is required for stabilization purposes to combat monetary inflation, some of the population may erroneously conclude that public economic goods are more costly (in terms of resource usage) than they actually are—the result being that the supply of public and quasi-public goods will be less than called for by community preferences in reference to the allocation goal. Thus, budget policy directed toward the stabilization objective may significantly distort the allocation objective. Indeed, fiscal norms alone cannot provide comprehensive guidelines to decision making between interrelated goals.

An adequate fiscal norm should thus attempt to meet all fiscal objectives in an attainable second-best manner. It should not totally ignore one goal for the attainment of another unless the preferences of the community clearly dictate such action. Relatedly, a sound fiscal norm should contain some recognition of both the control and functional finance approaches. Yet, no norm is comprehensive in its ability to provide precise guidelines to fiscal decisions on interrelated goals such as stabilization and allocation.

The remaining fiscal rules (to be discussed below) represent compromise positions between the annually balanced budget and the functional finance extremes. Each "intermediate" norm recognizes both the importance of budgetary control for allocation purposes and the ability of governmental budgetary behavior to improve aggregate economic performance through rational fiscal policy, though emphasis is placed on the latter objective in each case. Yet, these rules, just as the "extreme" rules, also fail to provide precise guidelines to fiscal policy directed toward the complete attainment of both control and aggregate performance objectives and toward the various interrelated societal goals in the allocation, distribution, stabilization, and economic growth branches of public finance.

The "Cyclically Balanced Budget" Fiscal Norm

This intermediate approach to fiscal rationality advocates budget balance over the course of a complete business cycle rather than in a particular fiscal or calendar year period. Thus, tax receipts and expenditures would be equal over the course of the cycle—whether measured from "peak-to-peak" or from "trough-to-trough." Figure 19–2 displays the cyclically balanced budget fiscal rule. The policy prescription under this norm calls for the central government to apply a surplus budget at the

[10] *Ibid.*

time of a cyclical peak or prosperity in order to restrain the pressures of
monetary inflation and to establish a deficit budget under conditions of
cyclical depression. Ideally, the surpluses and deficits would offset each
other in equal magnitude over the period of the cycle, thus providing
budget balance over the cycle rather than for an annual fiscal or calendar
year. It is argued that both the aggregate performance and control goals
would be well served by this compromise rule, though some allocation
distortion still would continue to exist.

FIGURE 19-2

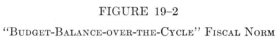

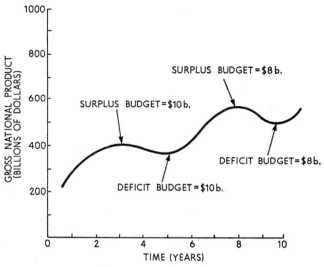

Many practical difficulties, however, arise in the application of the
cyclically balanced budget norm. These obstacles include, first, the unlikelihood that a given cycle will be symmetrical in the sense that the
size of the surplus necessary to restrain monetary inflation will be equal to
the size of the deficit necessary to reverse a downturn and stimulate expansion. Only by great coincidence would an exact cyclical balance occur.
There is no built-in mechanism to assure a symmetrical cycle. In addition,
the peak of a cycle need not be inflationary. In fact, the peak may not
even provide full-employment output, in which case a surplus budget
would constitute extremely irrational stabilization policy.

A further drawback of the cyclically balanced budget norm rests on
the institutional fact that in a democratic political structure, such as that
of the United States, lobby groups exert considerable influence over
legislation. As a result, there exists a built-in bias in favor of deficit and
opposed to surplus budgets. Thus, even if the cycle were symmetrical, the

institutional impediment to surplus budgets would make it very difficult to precisely apply the norm. In general terms, however, the cyclically balanced budget bench mark contains some merit in that it accepts the best element of functional finance, namely, the recognition that deliberate fiscal policy can favorably affect macroeconomic objectives and yet still retain some consideration of budgetary control in reference to the allocation goal.

The High-Employment Budget Fiscal Norm

The compromise fiscal norm represented by the cyclically balanced budget has received only modest general acceptance. A much more specific and more widely accepted approach exists in the form of the *high-employment budget* fiscal bench mark which is also known as the *full-employment balanced budget* (or slight surplus) fiscal rule. Primary initial support for this fiscal norm came from the Committee for Economic Development in 1947.[11] The CED proposal, which was conceptually structured in terms of the consolidated-cash budget, recommended that tax rates be set to not only balance the budget but also to provide a surplus budget for debt retirement at an agreed high-employment and national income level. Once these rates are set, they should be left alone unless there is some major change in national policy or condition of national life.

The above norm thus does not require "specific balance" at full employment and stable prices, but willingly accepts a "modest surplus" for debt retirement purposes. Ideally, the CED advocated a full-employment budget surplus of approximately $3 billion (in 1947) at a time when approximately 96 percent or more of the labor force was employed. Most unemployment is of the "between-jobs" variety when the acceptable unemployment rate is set at 4 percent.

The high-employment balanced budget rule is based upon the use of *automatic stabilizers* and thus avoids discretionary changes in tax rates except under conditions of major national emergency.[12] In this regard, the high-employment budget norm is significantly different from the cyclically balanced budget rule, which allows full use of discretionary actions to balance the budget. Since the major components of the federal tax base are closely related to the level of national income, tax collections tend to rise and fall in positive relationship to changes in the level of national income. This occurs automatically and does not depend upon discretionary changes in tax rates. Thus, rising national income will be accompa-

---

[11] Committee for Economic Development, *Taxes and the Budget: A Program for Prosperity In a Free Society*, New York, November, 1947.

[12] It is strongly argued by some economists that automatic stabilizers are a misnomer and that only discretionary action can be a basic stabilizer. This point will be considered in the discussion which follows.

nied by increasing income tax, payroll tax, and excise tax collections and by a declining volume of unemployment compensation payments. Conversely, declining national income will be accompanied by declining income tax, payroll tax, and excise tax collections and by an increased volume of unemployment compensation payments. In either case, built-in elements in the budget work in a rational anticyclical manner because aggregate demand is "restrained" during expansion and "reinforced" during a state of contraction in the economy.

The stabilizing budget principle of the CED emphasizes automatic tax and expenditure responses because, it is argued, such devices do not depend heavily upon an "impossible accuracy" in forecasting economic fluctuations. Moreover, it is argued that automatic stabilizers do not require an "impossible speed" in making tax and expenditure decisions in the legislature and then implementing them into meaningful fiscal action through the executive branch. The CED enumerates three exceptions to its nondiscretionary approach, that is, three conditions requiring discretionary fiscal actions. These are:[13]

1. When a growing population and increasing productivity cause national income and full employment gradually to increase. The discretionary readjustments of tax rates as made necessary by long-term growth in the tax base would need to be made, however, only at reasonable intervals, say, five years apart.
2. Occasionally, an urgent need may arise, such as in a war, for extraordinary types of expenditure, large in amount but temporary in nature. Often, it would be undesirable under such circumstances to raise tax rates sharply in order to finance the expenditures on a current basis and then reduce tax rates sharply when the expenditure ceases. Under such circumstances, the expenditures can be met through incremental taxes collected over a period of time longer than one year instead of marginally balancing the additional tax collections and expenditures in a single fiscal year.
3. If the recommendations of the CED are combined with appropriate measures in other fields, it is believed that economic fluctuations can be confined to "moderate departures" from a high performance level. Yet, in the case of severe depression or major inflation, discretionary fiscal action should be undertaken. Under such extreme emergencies, the best approach apparently is to change tax rates.

Heller doubts that a genuinely automatic fiscal mechanism can exist because any such mechanism would require that its very establishment, continuance, modification, and abolishment be accomplished through "discretionary decisions."[14] Under the CED proposal, human discretion *is*

---

[13] Committee for Economic Development, *op. cit.*

[14] Walter W. Heller, "CED's Stabilizing Budget Policy After 10 Years," *American Economic Review* (September, 1957), pp. 634–51.

allowed to determine when a recession is sufficiently moderate to ignore deliberate tax rate or expenditure changes as well as when a recession or inflation is severe enough to merit deliberate budgetary action. While a case can be established for the use of automatic stabilizers as part of a comprehensive set of fiscal tools, it would be foolish to conclude that "non-automatic policy is uncertainly managed by fallible men while an automatic fiscal policy is divinely guided by infallible rules."[15]

In addition, the CED position on the inadequacy of *economic forecasting* may be questioned. The operation of a completely automatic stabilization policy would still involve a considerable number of both explicit and implicit economic assumptions and forecasts. Revenues and expenditures under existing programs must be calculated in terms of full-employment output and income, for example, and this requires assumptions regarding such relevant considerations as price levels, labor force, and productivity. Furthermore, it is highly probable that better data are available for economic forecasting now than were available at the time of the initial CED proposal in 1947, which tends to reduce the strength of the CED argument based on forecasting difficulty.

Musgrave, in discussing the high-employment budget norm, observes that the rule helps to provide a certain "disciplinary" effect by requiring that any new expenditure program be met by an increase in tax rates sufficient to provide an *equal amount* of increased tax yield at a full-employment level of income and output.[16] The allocation (disciplinary) effect, in this case, results in public and quasi-public goods being somewhat underpriced in recessions and somewhat overpriced in prosperities (as observed above), but the differential with true cost is considerably less than in the cases of an outright deficit or surplus budget with no long-term balance concept attached. Hence, the discipline objective of preserving allocation (social balance) efficiency is served reasonably well by this approach. The stabilization and economic growth objectives, however, are served much less adequately. Automatic stabilization efforts, for example, do not assure that full-employment income and output will be maintained or even reached.[17] Thus, in the event of a long-term depression, the automatic stabilizers may provide a peak aggregate performance level for the economy which is below a full-employment level. Oppositely, the secular upward tendency may well yield inflationary results from the use of automatic stabilizers. The full-employment objective can be improved, however, by amending the rule to stipulate that tax rates should be set so as to provide whatever deficit or surplus is necessary, on the average, to secure full-employment income

[15] Heller, *op.cit.*, p. 640.
[16] Musgrave, *op. cit.*, p. 523.
[17] *Ibid.*, p. 524.

and output. Yet, even in this instance, the cyclical fluctuations may still be considerable when *only* automatic stabilization devices are used.[18]

Musgrave then considers the possibility of permitting a deficit or surplus for the *total budget,* but requiring a *marginal balance* for a change in expenditures.[19] The allocation efficiency objective would be served rather adequately by this form of the rule, but the performance on stabilization grounds once again is inadequate. This fact is demonstrated by the following example: suppose that an underfull-employment equilibrium has been offset and that full employment has been restored through a deficit budget policy resulting from lower tax rates and/or a higher level of governmental expenditures. Then, suppose that the community wishes to increase its level of consumption of public (and quasi-public) goods. If demand is to be held constant, as is required for the maintenance of full employment, the required change in tax yield must exceed the change in public spending. Thus, public and quasi-public goods are overpriced. Yet, if this is avoided through the use of strict marginal balance, the stabilization goal is inadequately served. Long-term growth policy, however, likely would not be as seriously affected by the marginally balanced budget approach.

It is concluded that the marginally balanced budget will do no better than the totally balanced budget in meeting the objective of reducing fluctuations and that the main superiority of the marginally balanced budget is the fact that it may help to adjust the *level* of aggregate demand around which cyclical fluctuations occur.[20] Apparently, the optimal approach to improving allocation efficiency is to *improve the decision-making process* whereby the community determines its relative preferences between the various public finance goals and, more specifically, between its relative emphasis on public versus private sector resource allocation. Then, the unbalanced budget approach can be more freely used to pursue the macroeconomic goals of stabilization and economic growth.

The Full-Employment Budget Surplus Concept as an Explanation of Slow Economic Growth

The norm which seeks a balanced budget or modest surplus at full employment through the operation of automatic stabilizers has been used as a basis for explaining the fiscal stagnation (slow economic growth) of the American economy between the mid-1950's and the early 1960's. This retarded growth rate alarmed many policymakers, economists, business-

[18] *Ibid.*
[19] *Ibid.*
[20] *Ibid.*

men, and others interested in the performance of the economy and an explanation was sought. Some experts suggested that the answer lay in the fact that the automatic stabilizers, which are based upon *constant* tax rates, would collect too great an excess of taxes over expenditures if the economy were performing at an acceptably defined full-employment level (no more than 4 percent of the labor force unemployed). Beginning in 1961, the Kennedy Council of Economic Advisors supported this explanation. The CEA suggested that budget surpluses occur "too early" in an economic expansion thus preventing the achievement of full employment.

The *Annual Report* of the Council of Economic Advisors in 1962 divided the "full-employment surplus" discussion into three components, namely, the "GNP Gap," the national-income-accounts-budget, and the full-employment budget surplus concept itself.[21] The GNP Gap is the difference between *actual* and *potential* gross national product. Potential GNP refers to the volume of economic goods which the nation's economy can produce at reasonably stable prices using the best available technologies, least cost combinations of inputs, and rates of utilization of both capital and labor consistent with the prevailing full-employment norms or bench marks of the economy.[22] Actual and potential GNP, of course, are synonymous if the full-employment goal has been attained. The gap itself suggests that resources are being underutilized and that fiscal stagnation is present. Estimates of potential GNP over a period of time, of course, should include estimated changes in the quantity and quality of productive resources.

The national-income-accounts-budget (see Chapter 6) provides the basic analytical framework for the full-employment budget surplus explanation of fiscal stagnation. Importantly, the national-income-accounts-budget represents actual resource-absorbing activities by the federal component of the public sector, an important trait not equally present in the administrative and consolidated-cash budgets. Since national output *directly* results from resource utilization, it is only rational that the national-income-accounts-budget serve as the basis of the present analysis. The *full-employment budget surplus* thus may be defined as that federal budget surplus, in terms of the national-income-accounts-budget, that would be generated by an established budgetary program if the economy were operating at full employment (no more than 4 percent of the labor force involuntarily unemployed) and stable prices throughout an entire fiscal year. The full-employment budget surplus, in other words,

[21] Council of Economic Advisers, *Annual Report—1962*, chap. 5–7.
[22] For a good discussion of the full-employment budget surplus concept, see Michael E. Levy, *Fiscal Policy, Cycles and Growth* (New York: National Industrial Conference Board, 1963).

represents the volume of *government saving* that would be generated if full employment and stable prices were maintained throughout the fiscal year.

Figure 19–3 demonstrates the relationship between the unemployment rate and the GNP Gap measured as a percent of potential full-employment GNP for the years 1955–65. Figure 19–4, on the other hand, distinguishes automatic from discretionary fiscal policy and demon-

FIGURE 19–3

GROSS NATIONAL PRODUCT, ACTUAL AND POTENTIAL, AND UNEMPLOYMENT RATE

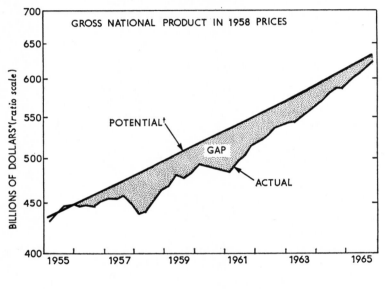

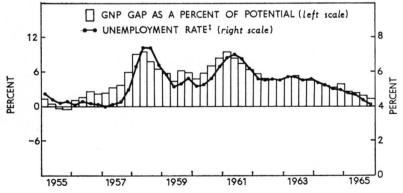

* Seasonally adjusted annual rates.
† Trend line of 3½% through middle in 1955 to 1962 IV; trend line of 3¼% thereafter.
‡ Unemployment as percent of civilian labor force; seasonally adjusted.
SOURCE: *Economic Report of President, 1966*, p. 41.

strates, in addition, how alternative automatic stabilization policies, depending upon the pattern of tax rates and expenditures, will cause the size of the full-employment budget surplus to vary with resulting differential effects on the level of aggregate economic performance.

The full-employment budget surplus concept is, of course, based upon the operation of automatic or nondiscretionary tax rates and expenditure patterns. Whenever discretionary changes in taxes and

FIGURE 19-4

The Full-Employment Budget Surplus
(in National-Income-Accounts-Budget Terms)

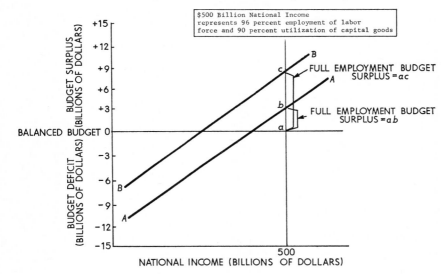

expenditures are made in the budgetary items which operate as automatic stabilizers, however, different economic results tend to occur. Thus, a stabilizer is "automatic" only so long as its pattern is not changed by discretionary budgetary actions. In Figure 19-4, for example, either line *AA* or line *BB* represents by itself a given set of tax rates and expenditures for the automatic stabilizers. Hence, as national income changes along the horizontal axis, the budget relationship between the automatic tax and expenditure stabilizers moves from a deficit toward a surplus budget position. Discretionary changes applied to the automatic stabilizers, however, can shift the budgetary behavior of the automatic stabilizers from line *AA* to line *BB* by increasing tax rates and/or decreasing expenditures or from line *BB* to line *AA* by decreasing tax rates and/or increasing expenditures. The full-employment budget surplus explanation of fiscal stagnation now becomes evident since the more restrictive budgetary structure represented by line *BB*, as compared to line *AA*, provides the budget surplus *ac* at the full-employment income of $500 billion which is greater than the full-employment budget surplus *ab* resulting from the more liberal budgetary structure. The greater potential surplus *ac*, of course, makes it more difficult for the economy actually to attain the full-employment income and output level of $500 billion.

In general terms, the full-employment budget surplus concept can be valuable in directing discretionary fiscal policy per se as well as for directing the time-to-time discretionary changes which set the pattern of performance for the automatic stabilizers. There is little doubt that the concept played an important role in the accomplishment of the income tax reductions of 1964 and the excise tax reductions of 1965, both of which contributed heavily toward the improvement of the performance level and growth rate of the American economy. In fact, the full-employment American economy at the conclusion of the 1966 fiscal year (June 30, 1966) provided a federal administrative budget deficit of $2.3 billion. This represented $104.6 billion in revenues and $106.9 billion in expenditures. The "potential" full-employment surplus had been converted to an "actual" deficit by tax rate reductions and, very importantly, the economy was fully employing its resources.

Although the fiscal stagnation concept discussed above is stated in terms of the administrative budget, policy decisions should also consider the relevance of the consolidated-cash budget. For example, the fact that rising social security tax rates are predicted to provide a surplus over social security outpayments of some $16 billion during the latter half of the 1960's could be, in itself, an important "fiscal drag" consideration.

A Further Discussion of Automatic Fiscal Stabilizers

As discussed above, fiscal stabilizers may be built into the budgetary structure as automatic responses or they may consist of separate and deliberate budgetary changes. The former are known as *automatic stabilizers* and the latter as *discretionary stabilizers*. Lewis, in his comprehensive study of federal fiscal policy in the postwar era, concludes that automatic stabilizers limited both the duration and the severity of post–World War II economic contractions.[23] Automatic fiscal stabilizers may be classified into those which *directly* affect disposable income and those which *indirectly* affect it.[24] Direct built-in stabilizers have become relatively more important in recent times than those which exert indirect influence. The direct automatic stabilizers in the federal consolidated-cash budget include the personal income tax, employment taxes, and unemployment compensation payments. Moreover, the payroll tax rate increase which became effective on January 1, 1966, enlarges the impor-

[23] Wilfred Lewis, Jr., *Federal Fiscal Policy in the Postwar Recessions* (Washington, D.C.: Brookings Institution, 1962).

[24] *Ibid.*, pp. 16–17.

tance of employment taxes as an automatic stabilizer. Although the indirect automatic stabilizers—the corporation income tax and the various excise taxes—account for sizable portions of any change in a federal surplus or deficit, they tend to be rather ineffective in minor recessions because they add substantially less to private spending than they subtract from federal budget receipts.[25] Recent policy changes (1966), it should be noted, have made the federal corporation income tax more direct as an automatic stabilizer by means of an accelerated (more current) payment procedure.

The corporation income tax is the largest automatic stabilizer in terms of dollar impact on the federal budget. In percentage terms, corporate income tax receipts decrease significantly more in recession than does GNP, and the volatility of the tax accounts for at least one half of the automatic decrease in federal tax receipts during the postwar recessions.[26] The volatility of the corporation income tax yield results from changes in the level of corporate profits over the cycle and *not* from a high rate of tax rate progressivity. Though the corporation income tax is reasonably important as an automatic stabilizer because the volume of its collections decrease in recession, thus pushing the federal budget toward a deficit, and increase during prosperity, thus reducing the danger of monetary inflation, it is not as important an automatic stabilizer as the personal income tax since its effect (as observed above) on disposable income is less direct and less complete.

The personal income tax, payroll taxes, and unemployment compensation payments serve as the primary built-in fiscal stabilizers. In fact, approximately 40 percent of administrative budget receipts are accounted for by the personal income tax. The personal income tax, in addition, possesses the advantage that it provides prompt response of individual tax liabilities to changes in aggregate economic activity. This result is essentially implemented through the withholding means of payment. The progressive rate structure of the tax, moreover, increases its dampening effects against monetary inflation and its cushioning effects against economic downturns. This can be made even more effective with a progressive withholding system such as now exists.

Employment tax collections increase and unemployment compensation payments decline as labor employment expands toward full employment, thus creating restraint against monetary inflation. Oppositely, employment tax collections decline and unemployment compensation payments increase as a greater number of workers are involuntarily unemployed, which provides a cushioning effect against recession. Hence, payroll taxes serve as an important automatic stabilizer on the

[25] *Ibid.*, p. 17.
[26] *Ibid.*, p. 31.

revenue side of the budget while unemployment compensation payments to the involuntarily unemployed constitute the most important built-in stabilizer on the expenditure side of the federal budget. At the very time when payroll tax collections are declining due to unemployment, transfer expenditures in the form of unemployment compensation are increasing, with a resulting increase in private sector purchasing power. The net increase in purchasing power, in turn, exerts an expansionary multiplier effect.

Federal excise taxes also demonstrate sensitivity to cyclical changes in aggregate economic performance. The direction of the volume of excise tax collections varies directly with changes in aggregate economic activity, that is, federal excise tax collections increase as national income increases since higher disposable income provides greater purchases of those economic goods subject to excise taxes. Meanwhile, the declining purchasing power during a recession reduces the volume of expenditures for the taxed items and the volume of federal excise tax collections declines.

A recent study by Eilbott lends strong support to the anticyclical effectiveness of automatic fiscal stabilizers.[27] The study estimates, on the basis of a multiplier model, the percentage by which the stabilizers reduced the potential change in income in each of the three expansions and recessions during the period 1948–60. The analysis which stresses the anticyclical and not the growth impact of the stabilizers selects personal and corporation income taxes, federal excise taxes, OASDI payroll taxes, and OASDI benefit payments as the basic automatic fiscal stabilizers. Depending upon the assumed values of the marginal propensity to consume out of disposable income and the marginal propensity to invest out of retained corporate earnings, the model indicates that the above fiscal stabilizers prevented an average of from 36 to 52 percent of the income declines which would have taken place in their absence.[28] On the other hand, the model indicates that the automatic fiscal stabilizers would have reduced the potential income increases during the three expansions by an average of from 25 to 42 percent depending upon the propensity assumptions.[29]

In conclusion, there appears to be no doubt that the automatic fiscal stabilizers have provided favorable stabilization and economic growth results since 1945. It should be observed, however, that fiscal stabilizers (both automatic and discretionary) are not the only stabilization forces at work during recessions.[30] Corporate saving, for example, absorbs part

[27] Peter Eilbott, "The Effectiveness of Automatic Stabilizers," *American Economic Review* (June, 1966), pp. 450–65.

[28] *Ibid.*, p. 458.

[29] *Ibid.*, p. 460.

[30] See the discussion in Lewis, *op. cit.*, p. 90.

of the income decline and thus cushions the fall or decline of personal income. In addition, residential construction tends to provide a significant semiautomatic stimulus to the economy in periods of recovery though its timing is far from perfect. Furthermore, capital outlays by state and local units of government tend to provide a stabilizing response to easy credit conditions in recession years. They are less volatile in this regard, however, than is residential construction. Finally, the reader should *not* conclude that federal, state, and local government budgetary devices, as well as the private sector stabilization forces, provide a complete explanation of the relative economic stability of the postwar era. Importantly, the efforts of monetary policy have also been significant, especially since the Treasury–Federal Reserve System "Accord of 1951."[31]

MONETARY POLICY AS A NORM FOR RATIONAL ECONOMIC POLICY

An interesting stabilization policy approach presented by Friedman in 1948 suggests bold changes in the monetary system of the nation. The approach, in addition, contains significant fiscal implications.[32] The Friedman proposal, which is based upon the value judgment preference for competitive market-type economic behavior in the allocation of resources, involves the following rules:

1. A reform of the money and banking system so as to eliminate both the private creation and destruction of money by commercial banks as well as discretionary control over the quantity of money exerted by the Federal Reserve System. The former could be attained, it was suggested, by adopting a 100 percent reserve requirement for commercial banks while the latter could be accomplished by the same approach plus the elimination of existing central bank authority to engage in open-market operations, the setting of stock margins, and the use of consumer credit controls (as during World War II). The remaining obligations of the private banking system would thus consist of the provision of depository facilities, check clearing, and the like while the central bank would exist primarily for the purpose of creating money to meet governmental fiscal deficits or retiring money when the government shows a surplus.

2. A policy should be established to determine the level of exhaustive government spending on economic goods and resources—excluding transfer expenditures—totally on the basis of the community's preferences for public goods. No discretionary expenditure changes should be undertaken, according

---

[31] During the 1940's and early 1950's, the Federal Reserve System preferred high interest rates to combat inflation while the Treasury Department desired low interest rates in order to reduce the cost of financing the debt. Until March, 1951, the Treasury prevailed and stabilization policy was subsequently frustrated.

[32] Milton Friedman, "A Monetary and Fiscal Framework for Economic Stability," *American Economic Review* (June, 1948), pp. 245–64.

to Friedman, for anticyclical reasons, but only when preferences for public goods by the community change over time. Such changes would be gradual.

3. A predetermined program of transfer expenditures, consisting of a statement of the conditions and terms under which relief and assistance and other transfer expenditures will be provided, should be established. This program should be changed only when the community indicates that a change in the distribution of income is desirable and that it should be accomplished through this approach. The transfer expenditures would not be changed for stabilization purposes. Absolute outlays and tax collections will, of course, vary automatically over the cycle, but discretionary changes would not be undertaken.

4. A progressive tax rate structure placing primary reliance on the personal income tax should be used. This tax structure should not be varied in response to cyclical fluctuations though actual receipts will vary. Again, changes in the tax structure, just as changes in the expenditure structure of the budget, should reflect the community's preferences for either changes in the level of public goods, in an allocation sense, or for transfer expenditure changes to serve a distribution goal. The increased public expenditures should be accompanied by increased taxes. Calculations of both the cost of additional public goods or transfer payments and the yield of additional taxes should be made at a hypothetical (ideal) level of income rather than at the actual level of income. Thus, the government would keep two budgets, namely, a stabilization budget in which all figures refer to an ideal national income level and the actual budget. The principle of balancing expenditures and receipts at a *hypothetical* income level would be substituted for the principle of balancing *actual* outlays and receipts. In this sense, the Friedman proposal is similar to the CED approach discussed above.[33]

It is obvious that the above proposal places heavy emphasis on automatic as opposed to discretionary economic policy. Moreover, it incorporates monetary policy into macroeconomic policy. Under the proposal, government spending would be financed by *either* tax revenues *or* by the creation of money (the issuance of noninterest-bearing securities). Thus, government debt creation in the form of the sale of securities is avoided under the proposal. Deficits or surpluses in the government budget, as a result, reflect dollar changes in the quantity of money and oppositely the quantity of money will change only as a result of deficit or surplus budgets. A deficit budget thus means an increase and a surplus budget means a decrease in the stock of money. Importantly, the deficits or surpluses themselves are the "automatic consequences" of changes in the level of aggregate economic performance. An essential element of the proposal is that the level and composition of fiscal activities undertaken by government is to be determined on allocation grounds and not for the achievement of the stabilization goal.

Friedman admits that rigidities in prices could impede the attain-

[33] *Ibid.,* pp. 247–50.

ment of the cyclical objectives of his proposal.[34] Yet, given the general environment of price flexibility for both products and productive resources and a minimum of lags in other significant responses, he believes that the monetary-fiscal system resulting from his proposal would be capable of moving the economy toward a full-employment equilibrium. In accomplishing this, it is argued that the system would provide a stable framework which eliminates uncertainty and the undesirable political implications which may result from discretionary stabilization action by governmental authorities. In addition, it is claimed that the system would provide a minimal reliance on the uncertain and untested knowledge which tends to make discretionary actions inadequate.

Writing in 1960, Friedman reviewed this earlier proposal (1948) linking changes in the money supply to the state of the budget as a stabilization approach.[35] At the later date, though, he continues to believe that his earlier proposal would work well in providing a stable monetary background which would render major fluctuations virtually impossible and which would not reinforce, but possibly alleviate, minor fluctuations.[36] He suggests, however, that the original proposal was more sophisticated and complex than was necessary and that a much simpler rule would have two important advantages: *first,* its simplicity would facilitate public understanding and backing and, *second,* it would largely separate the monetary problem from the fiscal problem in terms of the stabilization goal, and thus would require less far-reaching reform.[37]

The simpler rule would provide for a constant rate of growth in the stock of money.[38] The stock of money is defined as inclusive of currency outside of commercial banks plus all deposits in commercial banks. Under the plan, the Federal Reserve System would see to it that the total stock of money (as defined above) increases monthly, and if possible daily, at an annual rate of x percent where x is some number between 3 and 5. For fiscal policy, Friedman continues to suggest (as in 1948) that the appropriate counterpart to the monetary rule would be to plan expenditure programs entirely in terms of what the community wishes to achieve through governmental allocation and without regard to the problems of economic stability. Moreover, tax rates would be planned for the purpose of providing sufficient revenues to cover planned expenditures on the average of one year with another—again without regard to yearly

---

[34] *Ibid.,* p. 263.

[35] Milton Friedman, *A Program for Monetary Stability* (New York: Fordham University Press, 1960).

[36] *Ibid.,* p. 90.

[37] *Ibid.,* pp. 89–90.

[38] For additional discussion of the proposal, see Milton Friedman, *Capitalism and Freedom* (Chicago: University of Chicago Press, 1962), p. 54.

changes in economic stability. In addition, erratic changes in either governmental spending or taxation should be minimized, though some substantial changes may be unavoidable due to the international situation or similar causes.[39]

Shaw also supports the case for an automatic monetary pilot.[40] He observes that the nation takes pride in its built-in fiscal stabilizers and that it is not a radical proposal to suggest that monetary control should also be added to the list of self-activating countermeasures against disturbances in the aggregate performance and economic growth processes. The proposed action is defended further on the basis that (1) discretionary control of the money supply has not performed well and (2) stable growth in money would contribute to efficiency in other economic dimensions such as an improved payments mechanism.[41] In addition, it is claimed that stable growth in the money supply would reduce one important hazard of both private and governmental economic planning, namely, uncertainty concerning the value of the dollar over time as used to measure potential costs and revenues.

Samuelson takes strong opposition to the above automatic monetary rule proposals.[42] He observes that, in principle, the choice has *never* been one between discretionary and nondiscretionary action since, when men set up a definitive mechanism which is to run indefinitely by itself, an act of discretion of considerable magnitude has already been made. The *single* act of discretion which sets up an automatic stabilizer, in this case an automatic monetary pilot ". . . transcends both in its arrogance and its capacity for potential harm any repeated acts of foolish discretion that can be imagined."[43] Thus, since all stabilization action must be discretionary action, the *relevant choices* are those made between the "good" and "bad" effects of the various forms of discretionary action. In addition, for an automatic monetary pilot to work effectively, the quantity theory of money—with its invariant causal relationship between money income and spending and the supply of money—must fully operate. Samuelson argues that little evidence exists in this regard.[44]

THE NEED FOR COMPREHENSIVE AND FLEXIBLE ECONOMIC POLICY

The most effective and rational economic policy approach for the attainment of the macroeconomic objectives of stabilization and growth,

[39] *Ibid.*, p. 79.

[40] Edward S. Shaw, "The Case for an Automatic Monetary Pilot," a paper presented to the American Assembly during 1958.

[41] *Ibid.*

[42] From testimony presented by Paul A. Samuelson to the Canadian Royal Commission on Banking and Finance in 1962.

[43] *Ibid.*

[44] *Ibid.*

as well as for achieving the microeconomic goals of allocation and distribution, is that which incorporates an "eclectic" combination of the best
elements of the various specific norms and types of economic policy.[45]
Thus, elements of both the annually balanced budget and functional
finance norms must be included in such an approach with the result that
one of the intermediate norms is to be preferred. In addition, the combination of both discretionary and automatic economic stabilizers along
with the coordinated use of both fiscal and monetary policy is desirable.
The discussion below will demonstrate the contributions to economic
rationality which are made by such a comprehensive and flexible policy
approach.

One extreme position on the continuum of fiscal bench mark possibilities—the annually balanced budget rule—contributes something of
general importance to the eclectic norm in the form of the concept of
budgetary "control" or "discipline." This is particularly important to a
society which voices a preference for market allocation of resources. An
overemphasis on the discipline function of the budget, however, may
lead to severe sacrifices in terms of the other legitimate public finance
goals, especially those of economic stabilization and growth. Since
governmental budgetary actions cannot avoid influencing the macroeconomic variables of stabilization and growth, the functional finance extreme
on the continuum contains the considerable merit of "rationalizing" the
inevitable ability of the budget to influence macroeconomic performance.
Moreover, the overemphasis on allocation which the annually balanced
budget rule provides leads to several fundamental inconsistencies.

First, as developed in Part I of the book, it should be remembered
that conditions such as product indivisibility, externalities, and decreasing-cost conditions of production suggest that rather substantial quantities of public and quasi-public goods must be either produced or significantly influenced in their production by the public sector if an optimal
social balance consistent with the value judgments of the American
people is to be approached. This may well be impossible to accomplish,
however, with an annually balanced budget. Moreover, the annually
balanced budget rule is based on an irrational fear of government debt
(especially federal debt). This fear, however, is not consistent with the
nature of the present conditions of federal debt in the United States.[46]
The federal debt has been a declining proportion of gross national
product during recent decades, for example, and is internally held to a
very large degree. Furthermore, it has been demonstrated in an earlier
chapter (Chapter 17) that the American economy like any market-
oriented economy does not automatically arrive at a noninflationary
full-employment equilibrium. Thus, it is possible for an underfull-

---

[45] The macroeconomic goals, of course, are emphasized in this section of the
book.

[46] The next chapter will elaborate on this point.

employment equilibrium of aggregate economic performance to be so severe that the reduced total product will lower the living standard of the society. This would be true if the underfull-employment equilibrium leads to an absolute reduction in the outputs of both public and private goods so that per capita output declines. In this instance, emphasis on the distribution of income and wealth and/or on allocation would be irrational in terms of the ultimate results.

The best elements of the functional finance and annually balanced budget norms should thus be combined to form an acceptable intermediate norm. An effort is made in this regard by the cyclically balanced budget bench mark. This rule recognizes the control (discipline) function of the budget while at the same time acknowledging the ability of the budget to promote macroeconomic goals. Nevertheless, it is not a refined approach and is subject to the rather severe limitations discussed earlier in the chapter. A superior hybrid approach is represented by the high-employment budget rule which, though it overemphasizes the relative importance of automatic stabilizers, importantly stresses the obvious need to rationalize the impact of the public sector on aggregate economic performance. Moreover, it is not subject to the inherent weaknesses of the cyclically balanced budget approach such as the unlikelihood of matching upswing and downswing phases of the business cycle with resulting matching surpluses and deficits over the period of a cycle. By contrast, the high-employment budget possesses a workable ability to achieve budget balance at a time when near-optimal employment and price level conditions are present in the economy.[47]

The high-employment budget approach, in the form proposed by the Committee for Economic Development, suggests that automatic rather than discretionary fiscal stabilizers be used to achieve stabilization objectives. Automatic stabilization efforts alone, however, though extremely valuable, do not constitute a complete fiscal policy approach. There is no reason why, given the recent improvements in data collection and in forecasting and the evident success of the discretionary tax reductions of 1964 and 1965, discretionary fiscal efforts should not be used in an intelligent and rational manner along with the automatic stabilizers. Moreover, the apparent validity of the fiscal drag explanation of retarded growth rates in the economy during the late 1950's and early 1960's suggests a further modification in the CED approach, namely, the selection of *budget balance* at full employment instead of a *modest surplus* as an objective.

Perhaps one significant institutional contribution can be made in the near future to improve the effectiveness of the discretionary stabilizers. This consists of the proposal made by the late President Kennedy that

---

[47] Near-optimal instead of optimal conditions are attainable. See the relevant discussion in the previous chapter concerning the full-employment inflation paradox.

Congress give authority to the President, within limits prescribed by Congress, to alter tax rates for the purpose of countercyclical fiscal policy. This would greatly improve the timing of discretionary fiscal action since the policy could be made effective without involvement in the time-consuming legislative process for each separate tax change. Furthermore, the tax effects could be quickly implemented through the withholding technique of tax collection. Opponents of this proposal argue that it would upset the fiscal "balance of power" between the legislative and executive branches of the federal government.

Finally, a comprehensive and rational economic policy approach should include the coordinated use of both fiscal and monetary tools. The inevitable interaction between fiscal and monetary policy, whether rationalized or not, is demonstrated by the *IS-LM* model which describes the process whereby equilibrium conditions are simultaneously reached in both the money and product markets.[48] In Figure 19–5ab, the rate of interest is measured on the vertical axis and national income is measured on the horizontal axis. The *IS* curve displays a series of points at which investment and saving are equal at various interest rate and income levels. The *LM* curve, on the other hand, represents a series of points at which the demand for and supply of money are equal at various interest rate and income levels. In each graph, at the intersection of the two

FIGURE 19–5

Fiscal Policy and Monetary Policy as Demonstrated by the *IS-LM* Model

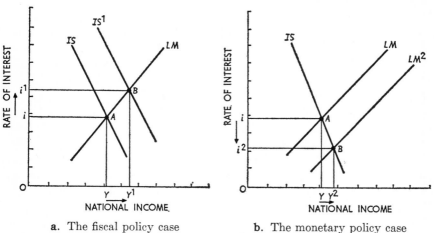

a. The fiscal policy case   b. The monetary policy case

[48] For a more detailed discussion of the determination of simultaneous equilibrium conditions in both the money and product markets see Thomas F. Dernberg and Duncan M. McDougall, *Macro-Economics* (New York: McGraw–Hill Book Co., Inc. 1963), chap. 9; and Norman F. Keiser, *Macroeconomics, Fiscal Policy, and Economic Growth* (New York: Wiley, 1964), chap. 7.

curves (*IS, LM*) at point *A*, the rate of interest (*i*) in the money market and the level of national income (*Y*) in the product market are determined.

Figure 19–5a shows that monetary neutrality does not necessarily result when fiscal policy is applied.[49] The *IS* curve may be shifted to either the right or to the left from its original equilibrium position through *governmental budgetary policy*.[50] The example shown considers only an expansionary fiscal policy which can be brought about by such budgetary policies as a decrease in tax rates and/or an increase in governmental spending, or by an increase in budget size. The resulting government multiplier causes the *IS* curve to shift from its initial equilibrium with *LM* at national income level (*Y*) and interest rate level (*i*) and a new equilibrium is established (Point *B*) at the higher income level (*Y¹*) and, very importantly, at the higher interest rate level (*i¹*). Monetary neutrality thus is *not* maintained and the interest rate increase may offset some or all of the potential national income growth deriving from the expansionary fiscal policy.

In contrast to Figure 19–5a, which displays the interest rate results of fiscal policy, Figure 19–5b demonstrates the results of monetary policy. In this instance the *LM* curve shifts to the right, indicating an increase in the stock of money. National income is thus expanded from (*Y*) to (*Y²*) through monetary policy and, quite significantly, the interest rate decreases from (*i*) to (*i²*). Hence, it is argued that monetary policy is superior to fiscal policy when expansion is desired because it does not create the neutralizing influence of higher interest rates which occurs in the fiscal policy case (Figure 19–5a).

No direct conclusion, however, can be made with regard to whether monetary or fiscal policy is a superior tool for aggregate economic expansion. Each case will differ depending upon many relevant variables such as private sector incentives and the elasticity of the *IS* and *LM* curves. Moreover, it must be acknowledged that fiscal policy holds an advantage over monetary policy in the sense that exhaustive governmental expenditures directly compel resource absorption and thus directly expand aggregate demand while lower interest rates merely make additional consumption and investment spending possible. Importantly, monetary policy does not lead necessarily to an expansion in aggregate demand by lowering interest rates, as was demonstrated during the depression of the 1930's in the United States.

---

[49] The presentation here will be kept in simple form. However, it should be observed that the *elasticity* of the *IS* and *LM* curves can have important bearing upon policy decisions. Nevertheless, space does not permit an elaborate discussion of the various elasticity implications in this book.

[50] Changes in the level of autonomous private investment can also cause the *IS* curve to shift.

The *IS-LM* model makes an additional contribution to rational fiscal policy since the discussion to this point in the book has concentrated upon multipliers which implicitly assumed monetary neutrality. In other words, changes in the level of private (autonomous) investment and in governmental budgetary behavior regarding taxes and expenditures were assumed *not* to influence the rate of interest. Yet, such influence is possible and an expansionary fiscal policy could be partly or totally neutralized, though complete neutralization is very unlikely, by an increase in the rate of interest. In the absence of an interest rate change, of course, the full multiplier effect on aggregate economic activity will take place.

The need for a coordinated fiscal and monetary approach is also indicated by the various stabilization policy *lags*. The "recognition lag," which relates to the detection of undesirable unemployment and inflationary trends, depends upon the quality of data and the analytical quality of its interpretation for forecasting. Since both fiscal and monetary policy equally face the economic forecasting problem, no preference between fiscal and monetary policy may be detected on this point. However, when we consider the "administrative lag," which refers to the time taken to make policy decisions after the need for action is detected, discretionary monetary policy carries the advantage over discretionary fiscal policy with its ability to make decisions more quickly due to the semi-autonomous nature of the Federal Reserve System. Yet, fiscal policy holds the advantage when the "operation lag" is considered, that is, in terms of the length of time between policy decisions and their actual impact on the economy. This is true because fiscal policy deals directly with resource usage and income flows while monetary policy affects these flows through the indirect manner of influencing the structure of liquidity and assets in the economy. In the latter case, the operational impact on the economy tends to occur over a longer period of time.

In conclusion, the desirability of a *comprehensive and flexible economic policy* directed toward the attainment of the macroeconomic goals of full employment, price stability, satisfactory economic growth, and a sound balance of international payments is apparent. Hence, the appropriate efforts of both monetary and fiscal tools, discretionary as well as automatic, should be cooperatively employed to promote these objectives. Moreover, a further requirement consists of a hybrid fiscal norm inclusive of some recognition of both the importance of control for allocation efficiency purposes and also of the need to rationalize budgetary procedure so that the inevitable impact of fiscal behavior on aggregate performance will be a desirable one.

The *high-employment budget* rule best meets the above criteria. Hence, tax rates and spending programs should be set in such a manner that a reasonably defined level of full employment, with minimal monetary inflation, would be automatically achieved when the budget is balanced.[51] Moreover, discretionary fiscal actions which change the tax and expenditure parameters of the budget should also be utilized as required. In addition, the high-employment budget rule, inclusive of both automatic and discretionary techniques, should be implemented in coordination with the goals and techniques of monetary policy. It would seem that a rational, democratic political economy should be capable of promoting, to a reasonable degree of attainment, the various macroeconomic goals of the society in terms of employment, prices, economic growth, and the balance-of-payments conditions—not to mention the important microeconomic objectives of allocation and distribution.

[51] As observed previously, a commonly accepted definition of *full employment* is when 4 percent or less of the labor force is involuntarily unemployed and at least 90 percent of the capital capacity of manufacturing industries is being utilized.

Chapter 20 PUBLIC SECTOR DEBT

Public sector debt is interrelated to the basic governmental fiscal flows of taxation and spending. If the volume of spending exceeds the volume of taxation, a deficit budget exists. The deficit budget provides the fundamental precondition for debt creation, but it is not synonymous with debt creation. Instead, the creation of debt involves a financial arrangement which is separate from, though related to, the fiscal flows of spending and taxing. This separation is evident from the fact that a deficit budget need not involve direct debt creation in the sense of interest-bearing securities since it may be financed by alternate means such as the printing of money.[1] If government spending is not covered by tax revenues, some means must be found to finance the deficit, and borrowing is merely one of the available techniques. Debt, once having been created, requires both interest payments to maintain the debt and refinancing operations if the debt is to be continued beyond the maturities of the present securities.

HISTORY OF PUBLIC SECTOR DEBT IN THE UNITED STATES

Federal Government Debt

The first federal government debt arose out of the assumption of the state government debts which had been incurred in winning the Revolutionary War. Hamilton generally favored, while Jefferson opposed, assumption of the state debts. The view of the former prevailed and the gross federal debt reached a peak of $84 million in 1795. The next debt peak was reached in 1803 at a level of $86 million. The federal debt then declined, reaching a low point in 1811, and rose once again during the War of 1812. A peak of $127 million occurred in 1815. Following this, the general trend was downward with the debt reaching a level of less than $100,000 in 1834. During the next 17 years, the trend was upward with a peak of $68 million in 1851. By 1865, the last year of the Civil War, the

---

[1] A continuum of alternative financing techniques exists ranging from the meeting of all expenditures with taxes *at one extreme, through* the financing of deficits by borrowing or money issuance, to *the other extreme* of repudiating (never paying back) a debt externally held by other nations.

federal debt was in excess of $2 billion. Then, a general decline in federal debt began and by 1888 the debt was less than $1 billion. It next reached the billion-dollar range during the Spanish-American War period, but dropped below $1 billion and remained below until World War I pushed it to over $25 billion in 1919. The decade of the 1920's witnessed debt retirement, the total federal debt dropping to below $17 billion in 1929. It increased again during the 1930's due to antidepression spending and was $43 billion by 1940. World War II caused the federal debt to skyrocket to $269 billion in 1946. Since that time, bolstered by Korean War, cold war, and Vietnam War defense expenditures, the federal debt has followed a gradual upward trend. It stood at $321 billion in 1966.

State Government Debt

During the 19th century, combined state-local debt at times exceeded federal debt. Moreover, local debt frequently exceeded state government debt. In fact, during certain years, such as 1860, local debt was much greater than federal government debt. State debt, which totaled only $25 million in 1829, ascended to $170 million in 1839, to $185 million in 1849, and to $251 million in 1859. During the next 10 years, state debt grew by more than $100 million and reached a level of $357 million in 1869. Despite a rapidly growing population, the trend in state government debt was downward during the next two decades and by 1889 it had dropped to a level of $208 million. During the early 20th century, the downward trend was reversed and by the early 1920's state debt exceeded $1 billion for the first time. From 1930 to post–World War II, state debt stayed generally within the $2–$3 billion range. Then, it began to increase rapidly following World War II and by the mid-1960's was approximately $25 billion.

Local Government Debt

Local government debt, which in 1839 was only about one seventh the level of state debt, grew rapidly during the next three decades and was substantially greater than state debt by 1869. At that time, state debt was $357 million while local debt totaled $523 million. The gap between local and state debt widened during the decade of the 1870's and by 1879 local debt was $805 million while state debt was only $222 million. This trend continued during the next few decades. In 1902, local debt of $1.9 billion greatly exceeded the state debt of $270 million. As the 20th century progressed, local debt continued to exceed state debt, but by a gradually narrowing ratio. The absolute growth of local debt has been substantial during the 20th century. It has expanded from $1.9 billion in 1902, to $4 billion in 1913, to $9 billion in 1922, to nearly $13 billion in 1927, to nearly $17 billion in 1940, to over $20 billion in the early 1950's, and to the vicinity of $70 billion by the mid-1960's. The tremendous absolute growth of local debt since 1950 should be noted with significance.

Intergovernmental Debt Data and Trends

In Table 20–1, 20th-century debt trends are presented on an intergovernmental basis. For selected years, absolute debt as well as per capita debt are presented for each level of government. Then, the percentage distribution of debt between the federal, state, and local components of the public sector is provided. The table clearly demonstrates the enormous growth of public sector debt, in absolute dollar terms, for all levels of government during this century. Interestingly, the

TABLE 20–1

Gross Debt,* Per Capita Debt, and Percentage Distribution of Debt for Federal, State, and Local Government, Selected Years, 1902–1964

| Year | Absolute Amount of Debt (Millions) | | | Per Capita Debt | | | Percentage Distribution of Debt | | |
	Federal Debt	State Debt	Local Debt	Federal Debt	State Debt	Local Debt	Federal Debt	State Debt	Local Debt
1902.....	$ 1,178	$ 230	$ 1,877	$ 15	$ 3	$ 24	35.9%	7.0%	57.1%
1913.....	1,193	379	4,035	13	4	42	21.3	6.7	72.0
1922.....	22,963	1,131	8,978	209	10	82	69.4	3.5	27.1
1932.....	19,487	2,832	16,373	156	23	131	50.4	7.3	42.3
1940.....	42,968	3,590	16,693	326	27	127	67.9	5.7	26.4
1946.....	269,422	2,353	13,564	1,924	17	97	94.4	0.8	4.8
1950.....	257,357	5,285	18,830	1,702	35	125	91.4	1.9	6.7
1955.....	274,374	11,198	33,069	1,670	68	201	86.1	3.5	10.4
1960.....	286,331	18,543	51,412	1,591	103	286	80.4	5.2	14.4
1962.....	298,201	22,023	58,779	1,604	118	319	78.6	5.8	15.6
1964.....	311,713	25,000	68,400	1,629	131	357	76.9	6.2	16.9

* Gross debt includes both "interest-bearing" and "noninterest-bearing" debt.

Source: Department of Commerce, Treasury Department. Adapted from Tables 10 and 11, pages 25–26, *Facts and Figures on Government Finance, 1964–65*, (New York: Tax Foundation, 1965).

fact that federal debt has been increasing much more slowly than state and local debt since World War II is often overlooked. While federal debt in 1964 was only 116 percent of what it was in 1946, state debt was 1,042 percent and local debt was 503 percent of 1946 levels.

Though the per capita government debt burden has risen during this century, it has not risen at the same rate as absolute government debt because of population growth during the century. Public sector per capita debt (the sum of columns 5, 6, and 7), for example, was $42 in 1902; and $2,117 per person in 1964—an increase of 5,040 percent. During the same period, however, public sector debt in absolute terms (the sum of columns 2, 3, and 4) increased from $3,285 billion to

$405,113 billion—a much higher growth rate of 12,313 percent. Moreover, though the figures are not shown in Table 20-1, the ability to carry the greater debt burden per capita has increased enormously during the century as the nation's productive power and wealth have grown on a per capita basis. Furthermore, it may be observed that the government debt per capita of $2,117 in 1964 is little more than it was at the close of World War II, as indicated by the 1946 figure of $2,038 (the sum of columns 5, 6, and 7) per person.

Table 20-1 reveals some additional significant debt trends. Intergovernmental trends are particularly discernible in the data showing changes in the percentage distribution of public sector debt between the three levels of American government. A cursory glance at this part of the table, comparing 1902 and 1964, shows that federal debt has more than doubled as a percentage of total public sector debt. During the same 62-year period, the relative importance of local debt has decreased sharply to a ratio of less than one third what it was at the beginning of the century. State debt declined more modestly during the same period. Thus, while combined state-local debt was 64.1 percent of total government debt in 1902, it was only 23.1 percent of the public sector debt in 1964. The present state-local share, however, is several times greater than the 5.6 percent state-local distribution in 1946 and the 8.6 percent distribution in 1950. In other words, since the close of World War II there has been a downward trend in federal debt as a percentage of total public sector debt and an upward trend in state and local government debt, considered both together and separately for each of the two levels. At the present time, no sign of reversal in this trend is indicated.

The primary cause of growth in federal government debt has been national defense and war. This is evident from Table 20-1. The large increases in federal debt from 1913 to 1922 and again between 1940 and 1946 reflect World War I and World War II expenditures, respectively. Also, much of the gradual post–World War II growth in federal debt is attributable to defense-related activities. On the other hand, growing population and the derived demand for education, roads, and so forth, represent the major source of growth in state and local government debt.[2]

ANALYSIS OF PUBLIC SECTOR DEBT IN THE UNITED STATES

Debt Misconceptions

Probably no economic concept is subjected to as much misunderstanding regarding its true nature as government debt. There are many sources of such confusion. One of the most important of these sources is the false parallel often drawn between government debt and private

[2] The functional causes of growth in government debt are discussed in Chapters 7 and 8.

debt.[3] Important dissimilarities exist between public sector and private sector debt. These differences reach their greatest extreme when federal government debt is compared to private consumer debt.

Another area of debt misconception is the confusion between the fiscal flows of taxing and spending and the separate, though related, phenomenon of government debt. As suggested earlier in this chapter, taxing and spending involve the nucleus of the fiscal or budgetary process. On the other hand, debt is merely one of several alternative financial means of meeting a particular budgetary situation, namely, a deficit budget caused by the excess of government spending over tax receipts. Both the fiscal flows of taxation and spending as well as debt creation and retirement may exert effects upon the public finance objectives of allocation, distribution, stabilization, and economic growth. Yet, it is important not to ignore the critical fact that fiscal flows on the one hand, and debt on the other, may exert such influences in somewhat different ways because they are essentially different phenomena.

A third source of confusion regarding public sector debt is the attempt by some people to solve the social balance issue by means of a debt-oriented analogy. Government debt, whether large or small or nonexistent, provides no *direct* implication about the proper size of the public sector relative to the size of the private sector. Conceivably, government could allocate 90 or even 100 percent of society's resources and possess no interest-bearing debt. On the other hand, the public sector could allocate only a small percentage of total productive resources, yet incur a sizable debt. In the latter case, however, the creation of debt by the public sector may exert *indirect*, though important, influence upon the allocation, distribution, stabilization, and growth branches of public finance. These effects will be discussed later in the chapter.

Internal versus External Debt

The need to distinguish between public and private debt, as discussed above, leads also to a necessary distinction between internally and externally held debt. *Internal debt* may be defined as a situation where the borrowing unit acquires the money from itself (lends to itself). *External debt* is a condition where the borrowing unit acquires money from some lending unit or units other than itself. The borrowing unit may be a unit of government, a business, or a consumer. Political jurisdiction essentially determines the "internal borrowing limit" of government debt while market conditions determine the internal borrowing limit of private debt. Government borrowing may be termed "public borrowing" while business and consumer borrowing may be termed "private borrowing."

---

[3] *Public* and *private* debt, of course, are similar in the "generic" sense that each involves a creditor-debtor relationship with corresponding debt instruments such as securities and promissory notes.

The only possible case of "purely internal debt" within a nation exists under the category of public borrowing and then only for a sovereign national unit of government. However, this is a sufficient, but not a necessary, condition of purely internal debt. In other words, only a national (central) government debt can be purely internal. However, even it need not be an internal debt. Our entire federal debt, or part thereof, could be owed to foreigners. In fact, a small part of it is owed to foreigners. Yet, if the gross federal debt of the United States were financed totally by the sale of securities to *American* governmental agencies, financial institutions, businesses, and individuals, the debt would be a pure internal debt. No claims against the borrowing unit would arise from outside the borrowing unit. The United States as a sovereign nation, and composed of the people of the nation, would be "borrowing money from itself." The lenders are part of the borrowing unit. There is no outside or external claim against American productive resources nor against the income and output which these resources can create. In reality, as noted above, most federal debt in the United States is held internally. By legislation, the nation could have easily forbidden the sale of *any* debt outside the political boundaries of the United States. Hence, the debt could have been 100 percent internal.

Since only the federal government possesses the power to issue money, it holds a unique ability to maintain or repay debt. State and local government do not possess the power of money issuance. They do, however, share with the federal government the power to compel taxation for purposes of maintaining or repaying debt. In addition, all three levels of government tend to acquire offsetting productive assets when they incur debt. Hence, the public sector holds important fiscal advantages as compared to private borrowing. The private sector cannot issue money or collect taxes. Moreover, private borrowing of a consumptive sort does not ordinarily result in offsetting assets of a real productive (income-producing) nature. Thus, public borrowing, particularly that of the federal government, tends to create debts which are not only more internal in nature than those resulting from private borrowing, but which also are easier to carry since additional financing devices and offsetting productive assets are more readily available. Table 20–2 summarizes the above points.

Real versus Financial Debt Burdens and Symmetrical versus Asymmetrical Debt Distribution

Further discussion is desirable at this time regarding the distinction between real and financial debt burdens and, in addition, the distinction between symmetrical and asymmetrical debt distribution. The burden of debt may be considered *real* when the direct use of productive resources is involved, resulting in a reduced amount of consumer and/or capital

TABLE 20–2

Continuum of Internal and External Debt Categories and Offsets
to Debt Burdens

Categories of Borrowing

Pure Internal Debt	PUBLIC BORROWING		PRIVATE BORROWING		Pure External Debt
	Federal Government Borrowing	State and Local Government Borrowing	Business Borrowing	Consumer Borrowing	
	1. Money issuance power 2. Tax power 3. Many expenditures provide offsetting productive assets.		1. No money issuance power 2. No tax power 3. Expenditures may be for consumptive goods.		

←———— Increasing Offsets to Debt Burdens ————

goods. On the other hand, the burden may be considered *financial* when
it involves the direct transfer of money payments rather than resource
usage. Furthermore, both real and financial aspects of debt are concerned
with the distinction between symmetrical and asymmetrical debt distribution.

A debt burden is *symmetrical* when the debt instruments are held
equally by the various spending units of the population who likewise pay
equal amounts of taxes to finance the debt. The symmetry in this instance
involves the debt burden in a "financial" sense. The symmetrical distribution of the debt burden takes on a "real" burden connotation, however,
when the actual economic goods provided through debt creation are
considered. Thus, if the economic goods financed with debt creation are
divided among the population in proportion to the payment of taxes to
finance the debt, symmetry exists in a real burden sense. An *asymmetrical*
debt burden, on the other hand, is one characterized either by disproportionate distribution of the securities and tax payments, in financial
burden terms, or by a lack of proportionality between the consumption of
debt-financed economic goods and the payment of taxes to finance the
debt which paid for these goods, in the real burden sense.

The direct real burden of World War II was in the resources used
by the generation which fought the war.[4] These include lost lives, injuries, and sacrificed consumption. Thus, direct real resource absorption
involves a sacrifice by the current generation which experiences the

---

[4] Under certain circumstances, however, real debt burdens may be transferred
indirectly to future generations. This will be explained in detail later in the chapter
under the discussion of intergeneration transfers of debt burdens.

sacrificed "real alternatives" of consumption. Only by *indirect* effects, such as reduced savings and capital formation, can the real burden be transferred to future generations.[5] Furthermore, if the debt is a pure internal debt, no external claims from other nations against society's resources exist for either the present or future generations. In addition, if the benefits of the debt-financed *expenditures* are proportionately (symmetrically) distributed among the population in relationship to the tax payments necessary to finance the debt, no "transfer effects" of real resources exist within the present generation and no real burden may be transferred through inheritance to future generations. If the real benefits are disproportionately (asymmetrically) distributed among the population, however, transfer effects of a redistributive sort (in terms of real resources) do occur within the present generation and these may be transferred by inheritance to future generations.

The financial burden of a pure internal debt may be borne either by the present or by future generations. If the interest on the debt is paid and the debt is then retired by the generation which incurs the debt, and if the debt is proportionately (symmetrically) held and taxes are proportionately (symmetrically) collected, the financial burden stays within the present generation and no transfer effects of a financial nature occur. On the other hand, if the debt is maintained or repaid by future generations (at least in part), then some of the financial burden may be transferred to the future generations. Furthermore, if the debt is held and tax-financed in an asymmetrical manner, transfer effects of a redistributive sort occur as income and wealth are redistributed. This redistribution may take place either within the present generation or between generations, or both. Some of the distinctions between real and financial burdens and between symmetrical and asymmetrical debt are indicated in the following example:

Suppose that the present federal debt is $300 billion. Suppose also that the securities held against this debt are divided equally among some 100 million family (or unmarried adult) spending units in the United States. Thus, every spending unit would possess $3,000 in Treasury securities. If the annual interest paid on the securities is 4 percent, each spending unit will receive $120 ($3,000 × .04) in annual interest payments. The federal government could tax every spending unit $120 and then turn around and pay each spending unit $120 in interest. Since the debt is internal, no real resource burden is imposed upon the society as a whole from outside the society. There is no external drain on the society's productive resources and the wealth and income which they can create. Since the debt is held and tax-financed in a symmetrical manner, no transfer effects of the financial burden variety occur. The only possible

---

[5] See footnote 4.

redistributive effects would result from a disproportionate receipt of the public goods provided with the debt-created funds. Of course, if the goods financed with the expenditures are pure public goods such as national defense, no redistributive effect in a real resource sense occurs since pure public goods are "consumed equally by all."

In contrast to the above example, it should be observed that unequal (asymmetrical) holdings of the securities by the various spending units, or unequal tax collections from the various spending units, or unequal receipt of the economic goods provided through the debt-created funds would cause transfer effects among the bondholders and taxpayers. Some spending units would enjoy redistributive gains while others would suffer redistributive losses. The redistribution resulting from an asymmetrical debt will, in turn, exert influence upon the other public finance goals of allocation, stabilization, and economic growth.

INTERGENERATION TRANSFER OF DEBT BURDENS

The classical economic viewpoint regarding the intergeneration transfer of debt burdens, which was later adapted to Keynesian economic theory, has been challenged in recent years by Buchanan, Bowen, Davis, Kopf, Musgrave, Modigliani, and others.[6] The orthodox position holds that a debt burden may be shifted to future generations *only* if the present generation reduces its rate of saving as a result of the debt-creation activity. This argument, which descends from Ricardo, was stated brilliantly by Pigou and later adapted to Keynesian terms by economists such as Lerner and Samuelson.[7]

The traditional argument thus suggests that the present generation bears the real burden of debt, except in the following case: Reduced savings by the present debt-creating generation causes future generations to inherit a smaller amount of real productive capital (that is, plant and equipment) with consequent reduced income and consumption by the future generations. Present saving will more likely be reduced when debt instead of tax financing is used because tax obligations are seen *clearly* by

[6] James M. Buchanan, *Public Principles of Public Debt* (Homewood, Ill.: Richard D. Irwin, Inc., 1958); William G. Bowen, Richard C. Davis, and David H. Kopf, "The Public Debt: A Burden on Future Generations?" *American Economic Review* (September, 1960), pp. 701–6; Richard A. Musgrave, *The Theory of Public Finance* (New York: McGraw-Hill Book Co., Inc., 1959), chap. 23; Franco Modigliani, "Long-Run Implications of Alternative Fiscal Policies and the Burden of the National Debt," *Economic Journal* (December, 1961), pp. 730–55.

[7] Abba P. Lerner, "The Burden of the National Debt," in *Income, Employment and Public Policy* (New York: Norton, 1948), pp. 255–75; Abba P. Lerner, review of James A. Buchanan's book *Public Principles of Public Debt* in the *Journal of Political Economy* (April, 1959), pp. 203–6; Abba P. Lerner, "The Burden of Debt," *Review of Economics and Statistics* (May, 1961), pp. 139–41; Paul A. Samuelson, *Economics* (New York: McGraw-Hill Book Co., Inc., 1964), chap. 18.

the present generation while debt obligations involve future rather than present tax payments (as the debt is financed and repaid) which are *less certain* in the eyes of the present generation taxpayer. Hence, it is likely that purchasers of bonds will pay for them more out of saving than consumption when debt financing is used because they consider their net wealth position better under loan finance than under tax finance. As a result, the reduced level of saving causes less real capital to be inherited by future generations, and a real burden in the form of reduced income and consumption is passed through this "indirect" means to future generations.

Much of the current controversy over the intergeneration transfer of debt burdens centers upon semantics, special assumptions, and the need to distinguish between direct and indirect burdens and effects. This should be kept in mind by the reader as the various arguments challenging the orthodox viewpoint are described below. After the individual arguments are presented, a synthesis and summary of the current state of public debt theory will be provided.

James M. Buchanan supplied the opening volley against the traditional position in 1958 in his book *Public Principles of Public Debt.*[8] Buchanan denies that the present generation bears the burden of public debt since those individuals who purchase the government securities do so on a "voluntary" basis. These individuals acquire present assets in lieu of present consumption—with future earnings from and repayment of these assets in mind. In other words, they do not realize a *present burden* because they are merely postponing present consumption to the future when they redeem their securities. Meanwhile, these individuals will also earn interest compensation on their bonds.

Since the government securities are purchased "voluntarily," those in the present generation who purchase them do not consider themselves to be undergoing a sacrifice whereas those in future generations who pay the interest and redeem the bonds do experience a sacrifice through "compulsory" tax payments. It is contended that the taxes are a real net burden and not merely a transfer or redistribution burden because they would not have been collected from the future generations if the present generation had met its expenditures through taxation—while the bondholders would have received income in any case from whatever assets in which they would have invested their savings.

In evaluating the Buchanan argument on intergeneration debt shifting, it should be observed that the argument rests upon a voluntary or individualistic theory of the state since it uses freedom of choice as the primary bench mark for determining debt burden, or lack thereof, instead of using real costs in resource terms as the bench mark. Moreover,

---

[8] Buchanan, *op. cit.*

the Buchanan approach concentrates upon the disaggregation of burden among individuals instead of the aggregate or total debt burden of the society.

Another volley was directed toward the orthodox debt position by William G. Bowen, Richard G. Davis, and David H. Kopf.[9] Bowen-Davis-Kopf attack the traditional viewpoint by positing an extreme case where it is assumed that the bonds are purchased from funds taken out of consumption, not out of saving—the locus where the only intergeneration burden transfer can occur under the orthodox argument. If an intergeneration burden transfer can occur when saving is not reduced, an effective challenge will have been presented to the orthodox position. As Carl S. Shoup demonstrates, however, the Bowen-Davis-Kopf argument does not disprove the traditional analysis.[10] Indeed, the generation initiating the debt *does* pass a reduced amount of real productive capital to the next generation, that is, the future generation *does not inherit* the same amount of capital stock that it would have inherited had the debt not been incurred. However, the *future generation* would manage to attain the same amount of capital stock that it would have possessed without the debt financing of the *present generation only* because it reduces its own consumption, *not* because it inherits the same (higher) amount of capital goods. Hence, the orthodox position that future generations can be burdened only if they inherit a smaller amount of real productive capital remains intact.

Richard A. Musgrave argues that loan (debt) finance *necessarily* spreads the burden among different generations while tax finance causes the present generation to bear the burden.[11] The Musgrave approach is based upon the benefit principle of equity as applied to the financing of durable capital items which will last through several generations of taxpayers. The following example is provided by Musgrave:

. . . consider a project whose services become available in equal installments over three periods. Also, suppose that the life (or residency) span of each generation covers three periods, and that the population is stable. Finally, assume that loans advanced by any one generation must be repaid within its life span. In each period the benefits accrue to three generations, including generations 1, 2, 3 in the first period; 2, 3, 4 in the second; and 3, 4, 5 in the third period. To contribute their proper share, generations 1 and 5 should pay ⅑ of the cost; generations 2 and 4 should each pay ⅔; and generation 3 should pay ⅗. Let us now suppose that the total cost is $100, and that it is to be allocated accordingly. To simplify matters, we will disregard the allocation of interest cost.

---

[9] Bowen, Davis, Kopf, *op. cit.*

[10] Carl S. Shoup, "Debt Financing and Future Generations," *Economic Journal* (December, 1962), pp. 889–92.

[11] Musgrave, *op. cit.*, chap. 23.

The entire outlay of $100 must be raised and spent in the first period. Of this, $33.3 is obtained by taxation, divided equally between generations 1, 2, and 3. The remainder is obtained by loans from generations 2 and 3. There can be no loans from generation 1 owing to our rule that each generation must be repaid during its life span. In the second period, tax revenue is again $33.3, contributed now by generations 2, 3, and 4; the debt held by generation 2 is retired in full, and loans of $16.6 are advanced by generation 4 to retire part of the debt held by generation 3. In the third period, the tax revenue of $33.3 is contributed by generations 3, 4, and 5. It is used to retire the remainder of the debt held by generations 3 and 4. In retrospect, the total cost has been divided between the five generations in accordance with benefits received. Loan finance in this case not only provided credit to taxpayers but resulted in a bona fide division of the cost between generations—a result impossible to secure through tax finance.[12]

In order for the Musgrave case to serve as a valid challenge to the orthodox debt position, the consumption-saving reaction of generation 1 to loan financing must be irrelevant because such reaction is the only means through which intergeneration burden transfer may occur under the traditional analysis. However, the irrelevancy of the consumption-saving reaction of generation 1 is accomplished in the Musgrave analysis only upon the basis of a somewhat unrealistic (and implicit rather than explicit) assumption that "inheritance does not take place." Hence, the Musgrave approach is not acceptable as an effective confrontation to the orthodox position.

Franco Modigliani suggests that intergeneration burden analysis should concentrate upon *stock* as well as *flow* variables and *long-run* as well as *impact* effects.[13] Modigliani contends that a debt-financed government expenditure *must* place a gross burden on future generations through a reduction in the stock of private capital, which tends to reduce future income and the future flow of economic goods. The traditional approach had contended merely that debt financing *may* place a burden on future generations by reducing the supply of capital. The Modigliani argument, which is presented in a Keynesian macroeconomic framework, is asserted to hold (but to different degrees) for both full-employment and less than full-employment conditions.

According to Modigliani, though a full-employment economy cannot increase governmental expenditures without reducing private capital (investment) spending, debt financing reduces investment spending by a greater amount than does tax financing. This occurs because government borrowing obtains funds which mostly come out of savings while taxes bear more heavily upon consumption. This is true, according to Modigliani, because debt financing—which does not lower the net

[12] *Ibid.*, p. 563.
[13] Modigliani, *op. cit.*, p. 731.

worth of an individual—does not induce the individual to reduce his level of consumption. On the other hand, the payment of taxes lowers the net worth of an individual and, consequently, induces him to lower his level of consumption. Hence, the higher volume of consumption which occurs under debt financing as opposed to tax financing means a lower level of saving and investment in a full-employment economy. Thus, with a reduced amount of capital stock passed on to future generations, the future flows of income and economic goods will be less than they would have been if the present generation had used tax financing.

As Mishan points out, a basic weakness in the Modigliani approach, as well as in the related approaches of the whole group of dissenters referred to by Mishan as "burden mongers," is the failure to consider that the gross burden may be offset by secondary effects in the form of the future returns derived from the present public expenditures.[14] The failure of intergovernmental debt burden analysis to consider as important the aggregate of both public and private sector investment and their returns is a serious defect which may mislead the general public and government policymakers.[15] This matter may be looked upon as the failure of inter-generation debt burden discussants to distinguish adequately between "primary" and "secondary" burdens and, indeed, to define debt "burden" as distinct from debt "effect."

Earlier in this chapter, real burden was distinguished from financial burden. The former was said to relate to the sacrifice of productive resources in the provision of consumer and capital goods (both private and public capital) and the latter was said to refer to the monetary arrangement whereby government debt is maintained (interest payments) and repaid through tax revenues. The financial burden often involves transfer or redistribution effects. Significantly, many effects of debt financing, as contrasted to tax financing, bear upon the nature of the real and financial burdens of debt. For example, changes in consumption-saving patterns, capital formation, inheritance patterns, net worth positions, the types of governmental expenditures which are financed with the debt, and the like, essentially are effects which help through market adjustments to determine the ultimate real and financial burdens.

Closely related to the desirability of some distinction (though rough) between the terms "burden" and "effect" is the need to distinguish "primary" from "secondary" results. Essentially, primary results refer to *burdens*—real and financial—and secondary results refer to the *effects* of debt financing which will influence the nature of the burdens. Although the literature on debt does not make this precise distinction, the terms

---

[14] E. J. Mishan, "How to Make a Burden of the Public Debt," *Journal of Political Economy* (December, 1963), pp. 537–42.

[15] *Ibid.*, pp. 540–42.

"primary burden" and "secondary effect" will be accepted here for the reasons stated above.

In conclusion, it should be observed that the Classical-Keynesian (orthodox) debt position regarding intergeneration transfers has withstood the attacks made on it by the so-called "burden mongers." The Buchanan, Bowen-Davis-Kopf, Musgrave, and Modigliani arguments essentially consist of special cases involving highly specialized assumptions and definitions. Buchanan, for example, stresses freedom of choice for the individual and, in so doing, tends to define burden as an individual burden instead of an aggregate societal burden. The Bowen-Davis-Kopf and Musgrave approaches involve special, somewhat unrealistic assumptions regarding inheritance. Modigliani underemphasizes (as do some of the others) the importance of secondary effects and their ability to influence debt burdens.

All of the dissenting arguments mentioned above are logically consistent. However, they are not comprehensive enough nor realistic enough in terms of their assumptions to repudiate the traditional analysis. In retrospect, the present generation *does* bear the direct real resource burden of debt-financed expenditures, though the financial burden may be passed partially to future generations through redistribution effects. Secondary effects, however, *may* allow some indirect transference of the real burden through reduced capital stock, inefficient government investment, and the like. However, it is unlikely that any significant *net real burden* will be transferred in this case because many government expenditures are for public and quasi-public goods which contain considerable external economies, some of which may be expected to accrue to future generations. The failure to use a comprehensive approach to intergeneration debt equity, that is, the failure to consider fully the important secondary effects including the social returns from public and quasi-public goods, has been the major weakness in contemporary debt analysis. The dissenters to the orthodox approach, though forcing the orthodoxy to state its position more precisely, have not themselves contributed a comprehensive approach. Moreover, Mishan's concern over the implications of this upon policymakers perhaps should not be taken lightly.[16]

FEDERAL DEBT AND INTEREST PAYMENTS IN RELATION TO NATIONAL ECONOMIC AGGREGATES

The ability to carry private debt is determined largely by the wealth and earning power of the consumer or business debtor. These considerations are less crucial, however, to a sovereign national government

[16] *Ibid.*, p. 542.

possessing the fiscal powers of taxation and money issuance. Nevertheless, the resource base of a nation and the aggregate level of national economic performance deriving from that base do reflect something about the ability of a nation to carry debt. Clearly, a nation with 200 million people can make interest payments and refinance a $300 billion national debt more safely if its productive resources allow it to produce a national output of $600 billion as opposed, say, to one of $100 billion. It should be kept in mind, however, that the safety of carrying federal debt will depend much more upon such considerations as whether the debt is internally or externally held and the way that the debt is managed than it will upon the ratio of the debt to aggregate economic performance. Yet the latter does bear some significance.

Table 20–3 displays the historical relationship of gross federal debt

TABLE 20–3

Gross Federal Debt* as a Percentage of National Income,
Selected Years, 1799–1966
(Data Rounded Off)

Year	Gross Federal Debt (Billions)	National Income (Billions)	Federal Debt as a Percentage of National Income
1799	$ 0.08	$ 0.7	11%
1869	2.2	6.8	32
1920	24.1	79.1	30
1929	16.6	87.4	19
1932	19.2	39.6	48
1941	48.4	103.9	47
1946	268.1	180.3	149
1950	255.2	239.0	107
1960	286.3	414.5	69
1966 (March)	321.5	587.7	55

* Includes both interest-bearing and noninterest-bearing debt.

Source: U.S. Treasury Department; U.S. Department of Commerce; adapted from Paul Studenski and Herman E. Krooss, *Financial History of the United States* (New York: McGraw-Hill Book Co., Inc., 1963), Table 1 and Appendix.

to national income. Early in American history (1799), the federal debt was only 11 percent of national income; it increased to 32 percent by 1869, however, mostly because of the Civil War. The ratio did not change appreciably by 1920, following World War I, at which time the federal debt was 30 percent of national income. Debt repayment during the 1920's, and a rising national income, caused the percentage to drop to 19 percent at the end of the decade in 1929. Then, the astounding drop in national income, production, and employment during the Great Depression (national income dropped from $87.8 billion in 1929 to $40.2 billion in 1933) caused the federal debt to skyrocket to 48 percent of national income in 1932. The partial economic recovery achieved under Franklin D. Roosevelt's New Deal administration during the remainder of the decade resulted in a federal debt percentage at 47 percent of national income in 1941. Then, following the tremendous wartime spending of World War II, the federal debt zoomed to 149 percent of national income by 1946.

Since 1946, the trend of the federal debt in relation to national income has been a declining percentage. From the 1946 ratio of 149 percent of national income, the federal debt ratio has steadily declined to 107 percent of national income in 1950, to 69 percent in 1960, and still further to 55 percent in 1966 as the nation was riding a full-employment

TABLE 20–4

NET FEDERAL DEBT AS A PERCENTAGE OF GROSS NATIONAL PRODUCT,
SELECTED YEARS, 1902–1966
(Data Rounded Off)

Year	Net Federal Debt (Billions)	Gross National Product (Billions)	Net Federal Debt as a Percentage of GNP
1902	$ 1.2	$ 24.2*	5.0%
1913	1.2	40.3*	3.0
1922	22.5	74.0	30.4
1927	17.8	96.3	18.4
1932	18.9	58.0	32.6
1936	31.8	82.5	38.6
1940	36.2	99.7	36.3
1944	182.1	210.1	86.7
1946	240.3	208.5	115.3
1950	219.5	284.8	77.1
1955	223.8	398.0	56.2
1960	235.3	503.8	46.7
1966 (Mar.)	259.8	713.9†	36.4

* Estimates based upon Kuznets' data.
† Estimated GNP.

SOURCE: *Historical Statistics of the United States—Colonial Times to 1957*, Department of Commerce, p. 724; and Board of Governors of the Federal Reserve System, *Federal Reserve Bulletin* (Washington, D.C., May, 1966), p. 696.

prosperity. Indeed, the debt does not appear to be an increasing burden for the American people.

Table 20–4 relates net federal debt to gross national product for selected years during the 20th century. "Net" federal debt refers to that debt which is held "outside" of the federal government, including debt held by the Federal Reserve System. In other words, the difference between "gross" federal debt and "net" federal debt relates to the debt held by federal agencies and by federal trust funds, which are included in the former concept and excluded from the latter concept. The general trends noted in the previous paragraphs, as indicated by Table 20–3 which relates gross federal debt to national income, are verified again in Table 20–4. For example, the effects of war, of the income decline of the Great Depression, and the declining ratio of federal debt to national economic performance data since 1946 are evident in the table.

In Table 20–5 it may be observed that the federal government's

TABLE 20–5

FEDERAL INTEREST PAYMENTS AS A PERCENTAGE OF GROSS NATIONAL PRODUCT, SELECTED YEARS, 1930–66

Year	Federal Interests Payments (Billions)	Gross National Product (Billions)	Federal Interest Payments as a Percentage of GNP
1930	$ 0.7	$ 90.4	0.8%
1940	1.1	99.7	1.1
1946	4.8	208.5	2.3
1950	5.8	284.8	2.0
1960	9.3	503.8	1.8
1964	10.8	628.7	1.7
1966*	12.1	713.9	1.7

* Estimated figures for 1966.

SOURCE: Bureau of the Budget; U.S. Treasury Department; U.S. Department of Commerce and *Economic Report of the President*, 1966, pp. 213, 217.

interest payments on its debt have ranged from a high of 2.3 percent to a low of 1.7 percent of gross national product for the years shown since the end of World War II. Indeed, these ratios indicate no alarming trend concerning the ability of the federal government, and the productive resource base of the nation, to carry the federal debt. In fact, the trend is an improving one because the ratio of 1.7 percent was realized in 1966 as opposed to the highest figure of 2.3 percent being reached 20 years earlier in 1946. However, the post–World War II ratios are higher than those for the decade preceding the war. Federal interest payments rose from less than 1 percent of gross national product at the beginning of the Great Depression in 1930 to 1.1 percent in 1940, and then to 2.3 percent in 1946. The growth between 1930 and 1940 is due primarily to antidepression spending and that between 1940 and 1946 to World War II. The fact that the growth in interest payments in relation to gross national product is modest between 1940 and 1946, while the growth in federal debt was considerable, is explained by the rapid growth in GNP during the war as the economy's productive resources became fully employed for the first time in more than a decade.

DOES PUBLIC DEBT EVENTUALLY HAVE TO BE REPAID?

This highly relevant question is related closely to the above discussion. The answer generally is "no," especially if the debt is an internal debt of the central government. Indeed, the public sector, like businesses and individuals, must honor and repay *specific* obligations at maturity. However, just as businesses under proper conditions can refinance and thus maintain or raise their total outstanding debt so also can units of government refinance and continue to carry or expand debt. In fact, a sovereign national government such as the federal government can carry and expand debt much more safely than can either private business or state-local government. This is true because the federal government alone possesses the important financial power of issuing money. The power of the federal government (and the public sector) to tax, moreover, gives it a considerable debt-carrying advantage over business, including highly successful corporate giants such as the American Telephone and Telegraph Co. (A.T. & T.).

Though A.T. & T.'s total debt outstanding has increased approximately 800 percent during the last three decades, no one is suggesting that the company is threatened with bankruptcy and that its debt should be repaid. The company has much greater earning power today than it did 30 years ago because it possesses a much larger stock of more technically efficient capital. In addition, A.T. & T.'s markets are more lucrative in terms of potential demand due to (1) the high level of aggregate economic activity in the nation at the present time and (2) population growth. Yet, the debt of A.T. & T. is an external debt—it is owed to lenders outside of the company. Consequently, if A.T. & T. need not retire its debt to prevent bankruptcy—and indeed it need not—why should the federal government retire its debt, particularly when it is an internal rather than an external debt and when the nation's economic ability to carry it in the form of productive resources and income-creating power is expanding more rapidly than the debt itself?

STATISTICAL COMPARISON OF PRIVATE DEBT AND PUBLIC DEBT

Table 20–6 reflects, in absolute terms, the growth of debt in the United States between 1930 and 1965. It may be noted with interest that total debt at the end of the depression of the 1930's actually stood at a lower level than it had at the beginning of the Great Depression. This was caused by a decline in both the corporate and noncorporate individual components of private debt during the period. Then an enormous rise in debt occurred during the first half of the 1940's due to World War II,

TABLE 20–6

Public and Private Debt in the United States,
Selected Years, 1930–65
(Billions of Dollars)

Year	Federal Gross Debt	State and Local Debt	Total Public Debt	Corporate Debt	Individuals and Noncorporate Debt	Total Private Debt	Total U.S. Debt
1930	$ 16.2	$18.5	$ 34.7	$107.4	$ 71.1	$178.5	$ 213.2
1935	28.7	19.3	48.0	89.8	49.3	139.1	187.1
1940	43.0	20.2	63.2	88.9	53.0	141.9	205.1
1945	258.7	16.6	275.3	97.5	54.7	152.2	427.5
1950	257.4	24.2	281.6	167.1	108.9	276.0	557.6
1960	286.3	67.1	353.4	361.7	286.7	648.4	1,001.8
1965	321.4	98.7	420.1	533.0	459.8	992.8	1,412.9

Source: *Statistical Abstract of the United States for 1965* (Washington, D.C.: U.S. Government Printing Office, 1965), pp. 407–8; U.S. Department of Commerce, *Survey of Current Business*, No. 5, Vol. 46 (May, 1966), p. 12; *Federal Reserve Bulletin*, January, 1966.

almost all of the increase coming in the form of public debt owed by the federal component of the public sector. Since World War II, debt in the United States has continued to grow rapidly, but most of the debt growth during this recent era has been in the form of private debt and state-local debt. By 1965, total United States debt (both public and private) stood at a figure in excess of $1.4 trillion.

The years since World War II have witnessed some astonishing trends in the composition of total debt in the United States between the public and private sectors. Furthermore, significant changes have occurred within each component. Table 20–7 presents the relevant data in percentage terms. While public sector debt represented 64 percent of total debt in 1945, it declined sharply to 50 percent in 1950 and to only 30 percent of total debt in 1965. Public debt thus declined in a short space of 20 years from approximately ⅔ to approximately ⅓ of total United States debt. At the same time, private debt was increasing from 36 percent of the total in 1945 to 50 percent in 1950 and to 70 percent of total debt in 1965.

A trend even more surprising than the strong trend toward relatively greater private debt is revealed in a disaggregation of the public sector for these years. While federal debt was 60 percent of total debt and 94 percent of public sector debt in 1945, it constituted only 23 percent of total debt and 77 percent of public debt in 1965. In the meantime, state and local government debt was rising from 4 percent of total debt to 7 percent of total debt between 1945 and 1965 and from 6 percent to 23 percent of public sector debt during the same period. The

TABLE 20–7

PERCENTAGE DISTRIBUTION OF TOTAL UNITED STATES
DEBT BETWEEN PUBLIC AND PRIVATE DEBT AND
BETWEEN IMPORTANT SUBCATEGORIES OF EACH
(Percent of Total U.S. Debt)

Year	Federal Gross Debt	State and Local Debt	Total Public Debt	Corpo- rate Debt	Individ- ual and Noncor- porate Business Debt	Total Private Debt	Total U.S. Debt
1945	60%	4%	64%	23%	13%	36%	100%
1950	46%	4%	50%	30%	20%	50%	100%
1965	23%	7%	30%	38%	32%	70%	100%

SOURCE: Computations based on data presented in Table 20–6.

strong relative and absolute growth of private debt since World War II is explained by rapid growth both in corporate debt and in noncorporate individual debt. Corporate debt, for example, was 23 percent of total debt in 1945 but was 38 percent of total debt in the nation during 1965. Individual and noncorporate business debt rose from 13 percent to 32 percent of total debt during the same time period.

The significant growth in private debt relative to public debt since World War II, and the sharply declining relative importance of federal government debt during this period, raises a question regarding present debt misconceptions and "mythology" in the United States. Why is the absolute growth in federal debt stressed as being "dangerous" by so many people while the much more rapidly growing private debt and state-local debt are virtually ignored?[17] The answer lies apparently in the failure of many people to acquaint themselves with the facts.

COMPOSITION AND INSTITUTIONAL USES OF THE FEDERAL DEBT

In order to evaluate the influence of the federal debt upon the economy, it is important to consider the composition of the debt with respect to ownership categories. In other words, who holds the federal debt? Table 20–8 provides the basic data. First, it may be noted that only 5 percent of the debt is owed to foreign investors. Thus, 95 percent of the federal debt is internal debt and only 5 percent is external debt. This fact is highly relevant to the earlier discussion concerning the ability of a

---

[17] The author does not wish to suggest that large private debt and large state-local debt are either desirable or undesirable per se.

TABLE 20-8

Ownership Composition of Federal Debt, March, 1966
(Figures Rounded Off)

	Total Gross Debt	U.S. Gov't. Agencies & Trust Funds (Federal-Held Debt)	Federal Securities Held by — NET DEBT									Total Debt Held Outside Fed. Gov't.
			Federal Reserve Banks	Commercial Banks	Mutual Savings Banks	Insurance Companies	Other Corporations	State and Local Gov'ts	Individuals	Foreign Investors	Misc.	
Absolute value in billions of dollars........	$321.4	$61.7	$40.7	$56.9	$5.5	$10.2	$16.6	$24.5	$73.6	$16.1	$15.6	$259.7
Percent of total federal debt...	100%	19.2%	12.6%	17.7%	1.7%	3.2%	5.2%	7.6%	22.9%	5%	4.9%	80.8%

Source: Computed from data in the *Federal Reserve Bulletin*, May, 1966, p. 696.

nation to carry a large central government debt. Clearly, the fact that most of the federal debt in the United States is held internally does much to validate the ability of the nation to carry a large central government debt since a relatively small real resource transfer to foreigners is involved.

An institutional breakdown of the composition of the federal debt, moreover, reveals that more than 31 percent of the debt is held within the federal government if the Federal Reserve System is classified as federal government. Furthermore, even if the usual definition of net debt is employed, the percentage of federal debt held by the federal government is still a substantial 19.2 percent. Of the federal gross debt of $321.4 billion (March, 1966), $61.7 billion or 19.2 percent thus is held by U.S. government agencies and trust funds such as the social security and interstate highway trust funds. The remaining 80.8 percent of the debt, other than that part held by the Federal Reserve System, is held by institutional investors, both public and private, outside the federal government of the United States.

Many important uses are rendered by the federal debt to the federal government. Treasury securities, for example, serve as an ideal investment source for federal trust funds. They allow no "conflict of interest" such as would inevitably occur if the federal trust funds were forced to purchase the securities sold by private businesses. In addition, they are safe, relatively stable in value, and easily convertible to cash (highly liquid) except in the rare instances of a general liquidity crisis. Moreover, these securities serve the federal government importantly in their usage by the Federal Reserve System—the nation's central bank. Under present legislation, Federal Reserve Notes, the nation's principal currency, may be backed by Treasury securities up to a maximum limit of 75 percent of their value. Thus, if the Federal Reserve currency outstanding totals $28 billion, as much as $21 billion of the currency can be backed by Treasury securities. Treasury securities, in addition, are used by the Federal Reserve System as the vehicle for conducting open-market operations, the primary technique used to affect the volume of money and credit in the economy. By buying and selling Treasury securities on the open market, the Federal Reserve System can affect purchasing power and interest rate levels in the economy in a manner consistent with the *Employment Act* objectives of full employment and stable prices. Since the federal debt became large during World War II, open-market operations have emerged as the most important monetary policy tool of the Federal Reserve System.

Individual investors and commercial banks head the institutional list of federal debt holders outside the federal government. As observed above in Table 20–8, 80.8 percent of the federal debt valued at $259.7 billion (the net federal debt) is held outside the federal government.

Individual investors hold nearly 23 percent of the gross federal debt and commercial banks hold almost 18 percent. As may be noted in the table, lesser amounts, in order of value, are held by such institutional categories as the Federal Reserve System, state and local governments, business corporations (other than financial institutions), foreign investors, miscellaneous investors, insurance companies, and mutual savings banks. Treasury securities serve the private sector as ideal investment assets, particularly for financial institutions because of their tendency to be relatively stable in value, low in risk, and highly liquid.[18] Clearly, if the federal debt did not exist in something approaching its present size, many investors, both private and public, would have to undergo a painful transition to the acquisition of other suitable assets for investment. In fact, in many instances it appears that equally suitable assets would not be available.

FEDERAL DEBT, DEBT MANAGEMENT, AND AGGREGATE ECONOMIC EFFECTS

The assertion is often made that the creation of debt by the central government is inflationary per se. Although this is not a necessary consequence, under certain conditions the full effect of the issuance of the securities may tend to produce price changes. It should be pointed out, however, that alternative arrangements such as printing money are more likely to produce price increases since, under full-employment conditions, the resources required can be released only through increased prices reducing demand for resources in some sector of the economy other than the one where the government seeks to spend its new money. The conditions required for price inflation to occur in the debt-creation case are more complex. There are two general cases against which the alleged inflationary effects of debt creation must be examined—the case in which there is unemployment and the case in which full employment (or a reasonably close approximation) exists.

In the case of *unemployment*, the issuance of new debt by the government generally will not produce inflation. However, the issuance of the new securities will tend to produce interest rate changes which, given highly elastic supply elasticities in a number of important industries, could cause the general level of prices to rise. The price rise, however, would be slight and the probability of the requisite conditions existing is slight. When the proceeds of the debt creation are spent, however, there are likely to be price changes, though a major portion of the adjustment will be in the direction of increased output and increased employment. In the case of approximate *full employment*, the issuance of the debt instruments will tend to cause a rise in interest rates and,

---

[18] Their liquidity falters, of course, in the event of a liquidity crisis.

unless the decrease in spending is equal to the increase in expenditure from the proceeds of the loan, the likely result will be a general price increase. Even in the full-employment case, however, it should be noted that price inflation does not necessarily follow as a consequence of debt creation.

The existence of debt could be inflationary through a redistribution effect, under full-employment conditions, if the government obtains the funds for debt service by taxing those with a lower marginal propensity to consume than those who receive the interest payments.[19] This redistribution effect, however, is unlikely to serve in practice as a substantial cause of inflation particularly since the evidence presented earlier on ownership of the debt suggests that relatively high income (and hence relatively lower marginal propensity to consume) units are the recipients of the debt interest payments. A complete answer to this question demands an empirical investigation which requires knowledge of the wealth status of interest-receiving units as well as a knowledge of the structure of the tax system. In any event, it is extremely unlikely that this effect is of any great consequence in the United States.

Depending upon the manner in which Treasury securities are sold to meet a newly created debt, the *expansionary effects* on the economy of an increase in aggregate demand resulting from the deficit may be considerably *dampened* or *reinforced*.[20] The expansionary effects of a deficit are exerted primarily through the multiplier effect, though these expansionary forces may be bolstered further by the monetary expansion possible through a fractional reserve banking system. The means of selling the Treasury securities which will dampen the expansionary forces to the greatest extent is to sell them to the general public, that is, to individual and business investors. Thus, if a $5 billion deficit is financed by the sale of $5 billion in securities to the general public, considerable neutralization of the expansionary multiplier effects of the deficit would take place as purchasing power is withdrawn from the economy.

Another dampening means of selling the securities is to sell them to commercial banks at a time when the banking system does not possess excess reserves. In this event, a $5 billion deficit would be financed by the sale of $5 billion in securities to commercial banks which would have to contract loans to the private sector in order to purchase the securities. Once again, considerable neutralization of the expansionary effects of the deficit budget would occur. However, since wealth increases by the amount of additional securities in bank portfolios, some increases in

---

[19] Even if full employment does not exist, given appropriate elasticities of supply in the industries in which the two groups spend their incomes, inflation could occur.

[20] This phenomenon is discussed in greater detail in Chapter 18.

spending could result which would work against complete neutralization.[21]

If the securities to finance a deficit are sold to commercial banks
when they possess sufficient excess reserves to purchase the securities
without contracting loans to the private sector, the expansionary multiplier effects of the deficit budget would *not* be neutralized by contraction
of purchasing power in the private sector. Another expansionary means of
selling the securities is to sell them to the Federal Reserve System. These
techniques not only allow full multiplier expansion to take place but, in
addition, they reinforce the multiplier expansion by the expansion of the
money supply through the facilities of a fractional reserve banking
system.

Management of the federal debt is frequently at "policy odds" with
the monetary policy of the Federal Reserve System. An important objective in the Treasury Department's management of the federal debt is to
finance and refinance it at the *lowest possible interest rates*. On the other
hand, the economic stabilization objective of Federal Reserve monetary
policy dictates *high interest rates* in times of monetary inflation.[22] The
conflict was resolved in favor of low Treasury interest costs from the end
of World War II until March of 1951. Since that time the Federal Reserve
System has had greater, but not complete, discretion in conducting its
monetary policy along proper stabilization lines.

Ideally, the Treasury would like to sell long-term securities at
cyclical troughs or depressions, when interest rates are low, and it would
like to sell short-term securities at peak periods of the cycle, when
interest rates are high, in order to minimize interest costs over a period of
time.[23] This conflicts once again with Federal Reserve monetary policy
because extensive Treasury borrowing during a depression would make
money capital more scarce, thus raising interest rates and making private
investment—which lags during a depression—even less attractive. In a
period of monetary inflation, moreover, the Treasury prefers to minimize
long-term borrowing because of high interest rates. Yet, proper stabilization policy would require the Treasury to do considerable long-term
borrowing in order to reduce the capital funds available to the private
sector and thus reduce aggregate demand. Often, this dilemma has been
resolved in favor of low interest costs to the Treasury rather than optimal
stabilization policy.

A recent development in debt management policy which has
assisted the Treasury in its ever-present problem of debt refinancing is
the technique of "advance refunding." By this approach, security holders

[21] Spending tends to be related in a positive manner to increases in wealth.

[22] Monetary policy tends to be less effective against monopoly inflation.

[23] Treasury security offerings vary in maturities from 91-day bills, to one-year
certificates, to two-five-year notes, to long-term bonds with durations up to 35 years.

are given the opportunity to exchange their present securities under favorable terms for new securities several years before the present securities mature. This helps to reduce the likelihood of shifts from Treasury securities to other assets at the time when the Treasury securities become due. In recent years, this has assisted in lengthening the average maturity of the federal debt.

PART V

The Public Sector and Specific Economic

Issues

This final part of the book considers several of the more important economic and social issues facing the American people which can be importantly influenced by governmental fiscal policy. These include the elimination of poverty, particularly as it may be reduced through the improvement of educational facilities and opportunities. A society with the overall affluence of American society cannot justify, in economic terms or otherwise, the "pockets of poverty" which still exist in the nation. In addition, the growing trend toward urban living for the American people, along with the overlapping jurisdictions of local governments deriving from the federalistic nature of the American political structure, has created vast and serious problems for American cities and suburban areas. The recent enactment by Congress of legislation setting up a cabinet-level Department of Housing and Urban Development gives recognition to this important issue. Moreover, regional economic performance poses certain significant economic problems.

Finally, the American economy has been faced with the need to divert considerable resources for national survival during the last 25 years. The economic impact of such defense efforts has been considerable. The economic effects of such spending have been mixed between both beneficial and harmful results. Undoubtedly, certain research and development results have been favorable. Yet, the resources devoted to national security could have been allocated, in the absence of need for national survival considerations, to the provision of the many important public and private goods which the society still requires. These include the improved ability to meet both health and educational needs. On the positive side of defense activity, however, has been the successful introduction of an efficient cost-benefit approach into decision-making within the Department of Defense. These efforts now are also being introduced into the civilian agencies of the federal government.

Chapter 21

EDUCATION AND THE
ELIMINATION OF POVERTY

THE CURRENT STATUS OF INCOME AND WEALTH
DISTRIBUTION IN THE UNITED STATES

The living standard of a society is determined, in part, by its patterns of income and wealth distribution. Average figures of income and wealth, of course, are grossly misleading. A nation may enjoy a very high per capita income for its residents. Yet, the distribution of its income may be quite unequal. Although the average would indicate a prosperous nation, the fact is that the living standards of many residents can be low.

Virtually every nation in the world is confronted with a problem of poverty. This statement includes the so-called affluent industrial nations of Western Europe and the United States. Poverty in a mature industrial nation stems largely from the status of income and wealth *distribution* in that nation. On the other hand, poverty in an underdeveloped nation derives largely from the need for *economic growth*. The public sector of a nation, through its fiscal process of taxation and expenditure, may influence both the distribution of income and wealth and the rate of economic growth. Hence, the elimination of poverty—whether it be in a mature or in an underdeveloped nation—can be approached through governmental budgetary policy. The emphasis in this chapter will be on poverty as a problem in distribution, with particular stress on the ability of education to change the real distribution of income and thus eliminate poverty.

Income Distribution in the United States

Recent decades have witnessed a gradual movement toward greater equality in the distribution of income among Americans. This is evident from Table 21–1 which displays the share of money income received by each one-fifth (quintile) of total spending units as well as by the top 5 percent of spending units for the years 1950, 1956, and 1962. The "spending units" are defined as all persons living in the same dwelling and belonging to the same family who pool their incomes to meet their major expenses. In this context, a spending unit may consist of a single

TABLE 21-1

DISTRIBUTION OF FAMILY PERSONAL INCOME AMONG QUINTILES AND
AMONG TOP 5 PERCENT OF CONSUMER UNITS[1] FOR 1950, 1956, AND 1962

Consumer Spending Units Ranked from Lowest to Highest Income	Percentage of Total Income during Selected Years		
	1950	1956	1962
Lowest quintile....................	4.8	5.0	4.6
Second quintile....................	10.9	11.3	10.9
Third quintile....................	16.1	16.5	16.3
Fourth quintile....................	22.1	22.3	22.7
Highest quintile....................	46.1	44.9	45.5
Total....................	100.0	100.0	100.0
Top 5 percent....................	21.4	20.1	19.6

[1] Consumer Units are ranked by size of family personal income.
SOURCE: 1962 data are from "Size Distribution of Income in 1963," by Jeannett M.
Fitzwilliams, *Survey of Current Business* (April 1964), Table 10, p. 8; 1950 and 1956 data are
from "Size Distribution of Personal Income," by Selma F. Goldsmith, *Survey of Current Business*
(April 1958), Table 3, p. 13 and Table 10, p. 17.

person as well as a number of persons. It may be observed that the
percent of total money income received by the highest quintile decreased
slightly between 1950 and 1962 while the combined percentage received
by the fourth, third, and second quintiles (the middle quintiles) tended
to increase during the period. The proportion of total money income

FIGURE 21-1

LORENZ CURVE OF MONEY INCOME RECEIVED BY EACH
QUINTILE OF ALL SPENDING UNITS, 1962, AND THE ABILITY
OF BUDGETARY POLICY TO CHANGE THE DISTRIBUTION

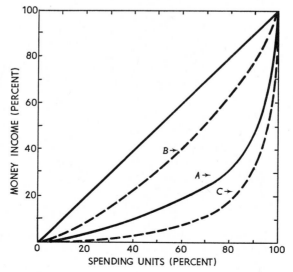

SOURCE: Based on data from Table 21-1.

accruing to the lowest twenty percent of income receivers declined slightly during these years. The absolute extent of poverty is suggested by the fact (not shown in the table) that 29 percent of consumer spending units earned less than $4,000 during 1963.

Figure 21-1, which is based on the data contained in Table 21-1, graphically demonstrates the degree of inequality in the distribution of income which existed among spending units in 1962. Hypothetical income distribution lines *B* and *C* indicate the ability of governmental budgetary procedure to either increase the degree of equality (line *B*), or to increase the degree of inequality (line *C*), as compared to the initial 1962 distribution (line *A*).

Wealth Distribution in the United States

More than 30 percent of the assets and equities held in the personal sector of the economy in 1953 were held by the top wealth holders, who constituted only 1.6 percent of the adult population during that year.[1]

TABLE 21-2

SHARE OF PERSONAL SECTOR WEALTH (EQUITY) HELD BY TOP WEALTH-HOLDERS, SELECTED YEARS, 1922-56

Year	Top 1% of Adults	Top 0.5% of All Persons
1922	31.6	29.8
1929	36.3	32.4
1933	28.3	25.2
1939	30.6	28.0
1945	23.3	20.9
1949	20.8	19.3
1953	24.2	22.7
1956	26.0	25.0

SOURCE: Robert J. Lampman, *The Share of Top Wealth-Holders in National Wealth—1922–56* (Princeton, N.J.: Princeton University Press, 1962), Table 6 (A National Bureau of Economic Research Study), p. 24. Reprinted by permission of Princeton University Press. Copyright, 1962.

The top group owned approximately 80 percent of the corporate stock, virtually all of the state and local government securities, and between 10 and 33 percent of each other type of property owned in the personal sector.[2] However, the degree of inequality in wealth distribution apparently is declining, as is suggested by the data shown in Table 21-2 and

[1] Robert J. Lampman, *The Share of Top Wealth-Holders in National Wealth—1922–56* (A National Bureau of Economic Research Study) (Princeton, N.J.: Princeton University Press, 1962), p. 23. The wealth data presented in this chapter, though not recent, are the most recent available. This fact helps to point out the need for a better social accounting system for wealth measurements in the United States as discussed in Chapter 17.

[2] *Ibid.*, p. 23.

in Figure 21–2. According to these data, the top 1 percent of the adult population, who held 31.6 percent of the personal sector wealth (equity) in 1922, held 26 percent in 1956. Moreover, the top 0.5 percent of all persons, who held 29.8 percent of the personal sector wealth in 1922, saw their proportion decrease to 25 percent in 1956. Despite the gradual trend toward reduced wealth concentration in the United States, considerable inequality in wealth holding remains. In 1960, for example, it was estimated that 24 percent of the spending units (families and unattached adults) in the United States owned no liquid assets.[3] In addition, 27

FIGURE 21–2

SHARE OF PERSONAL SECTOR WEALTH (EQUITY)
HELD BY TOP WEALTH-HOLDERS, SELECTED
YEARS, 1922–56

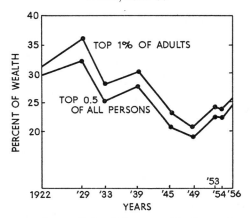

SOURCE: Robert J. Lampman, *The Share of Top Wealth-Holders in National Wealth—1922–56* (A National Bureau of Economic Research Study) (Princeton, N.J.: Princeton University Press, 1962), p. 25.

percent of the spending units held liquid assets valued between $1 and $500 and nearly two thirds of the spending units held either no liquid assets, or liquid assets valued at less than $1,000.[4]

A comparison of income and wealth distribution in the United States is provided in Table 21–3 and in Figure 21–3.[5] The Lorenz curves indicate that the degree of wealth inequality is greater than the inequality in the distribution of income. The highest 11 percent of spending units

[3] Gabriel Kolko, *Wealth and Power in America* (New York: Praeger, 1962), pp. 46–51.

[4] *Ibid.*

[5] Again, the wealth data presented at this point are not recent because of the nonavailability of recent data. The income data which are presented are for a year close to the year of the wealth data in order to provide consistency.

ranked by net worth, for example, held 60 percent of the net worth while the highest 9 percent of spending units ranked by income earned only 28 percent of total money income before taxes.

The reverse extreme from poverty, of course, could be cited as the number of millionaires in the population of the nation. This number appears to be growing rapidly. In 1948, for example, some 13,000 millionaires (families or adult individuals with wealth in excess of $1 million) could be counted, but this figure skyrocketed to a total of 90,000 by the mid-1960's. Approximately two thirds of the total assets of the millionaire group is held in the form of corporation stock with tax-exempt bonds comprising the next largest segment (8.5 percent) of the total.

A critical need exists for the development of a more elaborate procedure for the collection of wealth data in the United States. Lampman describes this need:

Estimates of the national wealth and of claims on it by sectors and within sectors will add meaning and lend symmetry to the other systems of accounting now in use, namely, national income and product, balance of payments, flow of funds, and input-output systems. Such estimates will be valuable in answering numerous questions that are of interest to economic theory and practice. They will contribute to deeper understanding of how our economic system functions and changes over time and hence to more accurate appraisal of policy recommendations.[6]

TABLE 21–3

COMPARISON OF DISTRIBUTION OF MONEY INCOME AND NET WORTH AMONG SPENDING UNITS, 1952–53

Percent of Spending Units Ranked by Income	Percent of Money Income in 1952 before Taxes
Lowest 11	1
14	5
16	10
18	15
15	16
17	25
Highest 9	28
100	100

Percent of Spending Units Ranked by Net Worth	Percent of Net Worth in 1953
Lowest 31	1
23	5
35	34
11	60
100	100

SOURCE: Robert J. Lampman, *The Share of Top Wealth-Holders in National Wealth—1922–56* (A National Bureau of Economic Research Study) (Princeton, N.J.: Princeton University Press, 1962), Table 109, p. 231. Reprinted by permission of Princeton University Press. Copyright, 1962.

Poverty in the United States

As noted earlier, poverty in the United States derives largely from the structure of income and wealth distribution in the nation rather than from any historic inability to experience satisfactory economic growth. If poverty is defined for the American environment as the earning of a family income of $3,000 or less before taxes, 9.3 million of America's 47

---

[6] Robert J. Lampman, Joint Economic Committee Hearings, *Measuring the Nation's Wealth,* June 1, 2, and 3, 1965, p. 37.

FIGURE 21-3

LORENZ CURVES OF TOTAL MONEY INCOME
AND NET WORTH AMONG SPENDING UNITS
RANKED BY INCOME AND NET WORTH, 1952–53

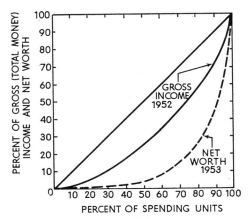

SOURCE: Robert J. Lampman, *The Share of Top Wealth-Holders in National Wealth—1922–56* (A National Bureau of Economic Research Study) (Princeton, N.J.: Princeton University Press, 1962), p. 232. Reprinted by permission of Princeton University Press. Copyright, 1962.

million families during 1962 would be classified as poor.[7] These families were composed of approximately 30 million people. Moreover, 11 million of the 30 million people were children—approximately one sixth of the youth of the nation. In addition, more than one half of the 9.3 million families, comprising 17 million persons, earned incomes below $2,000. Furthermore, approximately 5 million adult individuals not engaged in family living earned incomes of less than $1,500. Thus, it may be estimated that around 35 million Americans were living in poverty during 1962. Some 10 million of these 35 million people lived in cities with 2,500 or less population and 5 million lived on farms. The rural poverty groups primarily consisted of: (1) Negroes, (2) whites living in Appalachia, (3) Spanish-American people living in the Southwest, and (4) the American Indian.[8]

A further breakdown of the composition of poverty in the United States is provided in Table 21–4. The data in this table indicate that a greater propensity for poverty exists when: (1) the head of the house-

[7] Most data in this paragraph are selected from the *Economic Report of the President—1964*, and the *Annual Report of the Council of Economic Advisors—1964*.

[8] The definition of poverty used in this paragraph is that provided by the President's Council of Economic Advisors. An excellent discussion of poverty and its measurement appears in the forthcoming publication, "Poverty: Existing and Possible Income Measures," by Yung-Ping Chen, Department of Economics, University of California at Los Angeles.

TABLE 21-4

FAMILY CIRCUMSTANCES—AVERAGE OCCURRENCE IN
UNITED STATES AND OCCURRENCE UNDER
CONDITIONS OF POVERTY

Type of Family	Among All Families (% Occurrence in U.S.)	Among Poverty Families (% Classified in Poverty)
Head of household over 65	14%	34%
8 years or less of education	35	61
Fatherless homes	10	25
Head of household unemployed	18	44
Nonwhite	10	22
Rural	29	46

SOURCE: *The Economic Report of the President—1964*

hold is over 65, (2) the head of the household has had eight years or less of education, (3) the father is absent, (4) the head of the household is unemployed, that is, he is not classified in the labor force, (5) the family is a nonwhite family, and (6) the family lives in a rural area. Individuals caught in such circumstances often find themselves in a vicious cycle whereby "poverty begets poverty." Historical statistics suggest a high probability that the children of the poor will remain poor.

Under conditions of poverty, such diverse circumstances exist as a higher than average risk of illness accompanied by a lower financial ability to obtain medical care, lack of geographical and occupational mobility, limited access to education, training, and information, and inadequate housing. Regarding the latter, the Census data of 1960 show that approximately 9.3 million housing units in the United States were seriously deficient at that time. This constituted approximately one sixth of all housing. In metropolitan areas, 7.5 percent of all owner-occupied housing and 21 percent of all renter-occupied housing were classified as unsound. Once more, inadequate housing percentages were even higher for poverty families earning under $3,000 annually. For these people, 34 percent of owner-occupied residences and 60 percent of renter-occupied residences were unsound. Moreover, 4 out of 5 families earning less than $2,000 annual income lived under deficient housing conditions. Furthermore, less than 1 percent of the new houses being constructed are being built for purchasers with annual incomes under $4,000. Yet, the vicious cycle of poverty is not inevitable. To the contrary, appropriate budgetary policy by the public sector is capable of greatly reducing or eliminating poverty in the United States. Indeed, the nation possesses the productive resources necessary to reach this goal.

Poverty in the World

Poverty, of course, is more generally a world problem than it is a specific national problem for the United States. In other words, real per capita income is considerably higher for the United States than it is for most nations of the world. The staggering facts of world poverty tell us that 2 billion people—two thirds of the world's population—do not have enough food. Advanced communications and transportation networks, however, make it impossible for the United States to isolate itself from conditions elsewhere in the world. Involvement of the United States in wars—both "hot" and "cold"—along with the extensive international economic aid programs of recent decades verify this inability to achieve national isolation.

It has been suggested, at times, that the best international economic approach for the United States would be to assist in the elimination of world poverty. The Department of Agriculture estimates, for example, that the food deficit of the non-Communist nations of the world could be eliminated if American farmers would: (1) increase milk output by one half, (2) increase wheat and vegetable oil production by one third, (3) increase soybean production by one quarter. Moreover, it appears that American farmers could meet this challenge given the removal of production controls and the clearing of international economic impediments. In other words, the production capabilities are present—only the breakdown of international politics and economics seems to be the barrier. Such a "Food for Peace" program, however, would need to encourage the recipient nation to work toward the long-run development of its own agricultural sector.

EDUCATION AS AN ECONOMIC GOOD

Education may serve as a primary means of eliminating or reducing poverty. Yet, education serves many additional economic functions. In fact, the entire array of broad economic goals—allocation efficiency, distribution equity, aggregate economic stability, and satisfactory economic growth—may be influenced in a significant manner by the quantity and quality of a society's education and by the distribution of educational opportunities among the population. It is thus critically important to further investigate the nature of education as an economic good.

In the terminology of this book, education may be classified as a quasi-public good. Substantial social or community benefits derive from education, though many of the external economies are of the nonmarket variety which cannot be quantified or priced. Many benefits of education, however, accrue directly to the individual and rough estimates of the monetary value of some of these private benefits can be obtained. The dual provision of both social and private benefits by education warrants its classification as a quasi-public good. This classification may be supported by such other characteristics as the economies of scale which tend to occur in the production of education.

Social and Individual Benefits from Education

A modern society, which allows the citizen by virtue of his citizenship to participate in and derive benefit from the fruits of the society, receives considerable support from a good educational system. The term "modern," of course, does not refer simply to a defined set of economic conditions present in the society such as advanced technology or a high degree of interdependence between and among producers (both private and government) and consumers. On the contrary, the term is much broader in scope since it refers to a particular social, political, and economic organization of society. Modern societies, for example, are characterized by universalism (equality before the law), a propensity to accept change, orientation toward performance of a role rather than the creation of it, substantial differentiation, specialization in production, a scientific viewpoint, and a common concept of sovereignty, social values, and justice among its citizens. Significantly, it is through education itself, and through the development of a system for the production and distribution of knowledge, that the above characteristics and attitudes are adopted on a societywide basis. In addition to its contribution to the necessary social cohesion in a modern society, education may also serve the important goal of developing the nation's human capital in the technical sense necessary to increase productivity and to promote economic growth.

Household demand for education is based upon both the value of the educational service to the pupil or his family (internal benefits) and the value that other unrelated individuals receive from the education (external benefits). The benefits which accrue to the individual include better employment opportunities, higher lifetime earnings, certain nonmarket benefits, and family-related benefits. Children derive benefit from being raised in an educated environment. In many instances, children of the poor and illiterate are one or two years retarded because the parents lack the facility to provide satisfactory preschool training to their children. This lack of training becomes a social cost when the children enter school since it requires the provision of special educational facilities.

Besides the various market-oriented returns which the individual derives from education, significant nonmarket returns also may accrue to a person. The individual may acquire the ability to perform certain tasks for himself rather than purchase the services of another person. The nonmarket benefits, moreover, may take the form of enhanced social status resulting from the completion of one's education, particularly higher education. Undoubtedly, "conspicuous consumption" is capable of increasing the utility (satisfaction) of some people. In addition, the individual may be able to find greater personal satisfaction in the use of leisure time if he has been educated. This is of special significance in light of the current trend toward more leisure time.

In addition to the individual satisfaction which results from literacy, the society as a whole gains because a political democracy cannot operate effectively without a literate population. Moreover, the simplest of transactions may be restricted without the ability to communicate and to understand communication. In the market, communications provides knowledge of new products, prices, and of employment opportunities to the individual. In the political system, communications contributes to the operation of plebiscitarian principles, social and political stability, the achievement of democratic aims, educated neighbors, educated civic workers, and a coordinated effort in times of war.

Education and the Stabilization-Growth Goals

Improvement in the quantity and quality of the labor factor of production enhances both the stabilization and growth goals of public finance. In the former case, individuals will have better technical skills in an industrial society and should thus find it easier to gain employment. As a result, structural unemployment would be reduced and aggregate demand will expand as these workers possess additional purchasing power. The total output of the society should increase as the quality of the labor force increases. In other words, greater efficiency from productive inputs should expand the aggregate economic product of the society.

Likewise, education will contribute toward a higher rate of economic growth. In this regard, a study by Schultz indicates that although the ratio of physical to human capital in American production has remained constant over the past half century, the society has grown enormously.[9] Denison, moreover, attributes 23 percent of the growth in total real national income and 42 percent of the growth in per capita real income during the period 1929–59 to higher educational attainments.[10] This resulted from increases in productivity, greater adaptability to change, and the "freeing" of productive resources.

Despite the difficulties involved in making such comparisons, an examination of the average per capita income of a nation and its educa-

[9] Theodore W. Schultz, "Capital Formation by Education," *Journal of Political Economy* (December, 1960), pp. 571–83.

[10] Edward F. Denison, *The Sources of Economic Growth in the United States and the Alternatives Before Us* (New York: Committee for Economic Development, 1962), pp. 67–79.

tional attainment suggests that education is a functional precursor of economic development (see Table 21–5). Nations such as Brazil, which are rich in natural resources but low in educational attainment, have only a fraction of the per capita income of nations with high educational attainment. Furthermore, nations which are poor in natural resources but which have attained high educational attainment (Denmark, Switzerland) are able to provide high living standards to their citizens.

The benefits associated with economic growth occur over an extended period of time as well as in the short run. Most of the gains, however, accrue to future generations rather than to the present one. Yet, future generations exert no preference on the present use of productive resources. Market-determined outlays for education will, therefore, not reflect the value of education to future generations.[11] Thus, total reliance

TABLE 21–5

NATURAL RESOURCES, EDUCATIONAL ATTAINMENT, AND PER CAPITA INCOME, SELECTED COUNTRIES

Country	Natural Resources	Educational Attainment	Per Capita Income (1952– 54 Average)
Brazil...............	Many	Low	$ 230
Denmark.............	Few	High	750
Switzerland...........	Few	High	1,010
United States..........	Many	High	1,870

SOURCE: Adapted from John K. Norton, *Changing Demands on Education and their Fiscal Implications* (Washington, D.C.: National Committee for Support of Public Schools, 1963), Table I, p. 39.

on market-type determination of the supply of education may result in a serious underinvestment in education.

Education and the Allocation-Distribution Goals

An underallocation of resources to education may also result from the following conditions:

1. Education possesses substantial externalities, mostly of a benefit nature, which are indivisible and which thus escape the pricing mechanism.
2. Imperfections in the political process may cause the public sector (which provides most education in the United States) to underinvest in the production of education because of the inability to interpret community preferences properly.
3. The public itself may not fully appreciate the individual and social benefits which derive from an educated population.

[11] See Jerry Miner, *Social and Economic Factors in Spending for Public Education* (Syracuse, N.Y.: Syracuse University Press, 1963), p. 29.

The planning, financing, and production of public education in the United States takes place primarily at the state and local levels of government. State governments are essentially concerned with higher education (college education) while the brunt of responsibility for the provision of elementary and high school education is borne by local units of government. The latter involves considerable decentralization in the production of public school education since approximately 50,000 units of local government (primarily school districts) share in the aggregate decisions regarding the supply, quality, and distribution of the public elementary and high school education received by American children.

Not only is the allocation of resources toward an optimal or near-optimal supply of education important both to the individual who is educated and to the nation as a whole (as discussed above), but it is also important to the local community which produces public school education. Because of the high degree of interdependence in American society, the quantity and quality of education produced by one community will exert external effects on other communities. A given community produces certain educational effects which it "exports" to other communities. The nonoptimal allocation of resources which may result from such spillover effects, as well as from the other factors mentioned above, justifies an investigation of the allocative characteristics of education. In addition, distribution is also a relevant consideration both because of its nature as a prerequisite to allocation decisions and also because, insofar as the benefit principle of tax equity is applied to education, the costs of education should be borne by those who receive the benefits.

It is important to distinguish between the allocative and distributive issues. A discussion of allocation efficiency stresses the maximization of real income (welfare), given the constraints of available inputs, the level of technology, and the distributions of income, wealth, and political voting which make consumer preferences "effective." (See Part I of the book.) By contrast, distribution efficiency concentrates on achieving that initial (ex ante) wealth and voting power distribution which the society prefers and which is a prerequisite to actual allocation.

Weisbrod has conducted an excellent analysis of the allocation problem and the external benefits of public education.[12] Before attempting to quantify the external effects of public education, he discusses the nature of the total benefits which accrue from education. He views the *individual student* as receiving:[13] (1) a direct financial return in terms of the incremental earnings which usually accompany additional education; (2) a financial option consisting of the opportunity to obtain still further

[12] See Burton A. Weisbrod, *External Benefits of Public Education* (Princeton, N.J.: Industrial Relations Section, Department of Economics, Princeton University, 1964).

[13] *Ibid.*, pp. 15–27.

education; (3) a hedging option consisting of the increased ability to adjust to changing job opportunities caused by such phenomena as automation and changing consumer preferences; and (4) certain nonmarket returns to the individual such as the individual advantages of literacy.

Regarding the social or external benefits of education, Weisbrod separates the persons receiving such benefits into three categories:[14] (1) residence-related beneficiaries, that is, those who benefit by virtue of some relationship between their place of residence and that of the person who is educated; (2) employment-related beneficiaries, that is, those who benefit by virtue of some employment relationship with the person receiving the education; and (3) the society as a whole. These external benefits of education occur at various times and in various places. The benefits do not necessarily accrue to the people who financially support the production of the education, nor do they necessarily reside in the community where it is produced. More specifically, the process of migration provides *spatial shifting* of some of the external effects of education. The phenomenon of migration and spatial shifting is highly relevant to the questions of allocative and distributive efficiency in education.

There are various means whereby a community may financially benefit from satisfactory education. Since education tends to increase labor productivity and income, for example, it will also tend to increase aggregate community income as long as the educational capital (those educated) remains in the community. Moreover, even if the only incomes which increase are those of the educated people, the rest of the community may indirectly benefit from the additional governmental services which can be financed from the higher taxes paid by the educated people. In addition, the redistribution motive may be present in the sense that improved allocation of education at the present time may reduce the future need for redistributive transfer or welfare payments to combat poverty. Furthermore, if the productivity and income of some persons in the community are raised by education, there may be secondary effects on the level of income and employment of others in the community.

Weisbrod conducted an empirical study of Clayton, Missouri, a suburb of St. Louis, to supplement his analysis.[15] Estimates are provided for: (1) the educational capital produced by the public school system of Clayton; (2) the portion of that capital which may be expected to remain in Clayton; and (3) the amount of educational capital which may be expected to move into Clayton from other communities. The study reveals a net migration loss of educational capital for the community under consideration. An estimate of returns to the rest of the Clayton community, in the form of incremental tax revenue resulting from the investment in

[14] *Ibid.*, pp. 28–39.
[15] *Ibid.*

education, also is provided. The conclusion is reached that part of the financial return which a student obtains from his education was returned to the community through taxation, but that most of it accrued to fiscal units other than the Clayton School District. With respect to external financial burdens and the Clayton case, the higher educational level of the community (13.3 years as compared to 10 years for the United States) is reflected in the lower unemployment tax on employers. In addition, the community may receive beneficial nonmarket results because of the direct relationship between the level of educational attainment and the degree of political participation.

The study concludes that education is considered, in the political process, as an investment based upon the expectation of returns.[16] Thus, in areas where a substantial outmigration occurs, the level of per capita educational expenditures tends to be lower than otherwise. In addition, the spillover effects tend to shift the financing of education increasingly from the local to the state level of government. The principal conclusions are that education does indeed benefit communities other than the ones producing the education and that no compulsion exists for the educational benefits consumed and provided by any particular community to be equal. The allocation of resources toward education thus tends to be suboptimal. Weisbrod considers two remedies:[17] (1) the widening of the political decision-making unit so as to internalize more of the benefits of education or (2) the adoption by all states of educational standards which are high enough to bring educational attainment and quality throughout the nation closer to those of the best state. He prefers the first solution.

Education and Poverty

As observed earlier in this chapter, education as an economic good is capable of significantly influencing the broad goals of public finance— efficient allocation, distribution, stabilization and economic growth. Specifically, education also an contribute to the elimination of poverty in a society rich enough in resources to accomplish this task.

While the reduction of poverty may be approached in the short run via government transfer payments of a redistributive variety, the educational approach to combat poverty involves an allocative technique. If the education of the poor were increased in quantity and quality, for example, the incomes of the poor would likely increase during subsequent years. The unemployment of an individual tends to drop significantly as the quantity of his education increases. The allocation of additional productive resources to education in the short run will thus contribute to

---

[16] *Ibid.*
[17] *Ibid.,* chap. 10.

the elimination of poverty in the long run. By this approach, the real (ex post) distribution of income as well as a minimally acceptable living standard for all can be reached through the allocation of more resources to education.

Although the allocation of additional resources to the education of the poor stands as the primary allocative technique for the elimination of poverty, improved allocation of certain other goods may also render significant contributions in the battle against poverty. For example, improved health services for the poor are in critical need.[18] In addition, the improvement of housing facilities through more efficient resource allocation would be helpful. Furthermore, the elimination of job discrimination against racial and religious minorities would help to eliminate poverty in the United States.[19]

Rayack, in discussing discrimination and the occupational progress of Negroes, concludes that the progress made by Negroes since the beginning of World War II in securing better occupational opportunities was largely the result of the acute labor shortage during the first part of this period rather than of a significant reduction in discrimination.[20] The shortage of labor between 1940–48 opened up a wider range of job opportunities for Negroes. The disappearance of severe labor shortages after 1948 considerably reduced the occupational advancement of Negroes relative to whites and, in fact, has contributed to a slight decline in the relative position of Negroes since 1950.[21]

Job and educational discrimination is costly, in economic terms, to the nation. The Council of Economic Advisors stated during 1965 that "if Negroes also had the same educational attainment as white workers, and earned the same pay, and experienced the same unemployment as whites, their personal income . . . and that of the Nation . . . would be $20.6 billion higher."[22]

Job discrimination is closely related to the need for better education of the poor. In 1961, approximately 400,000 high school graduates who finished in the upper half of their classes were unable to attend college because of financial reasons. The United States has left uneducated a remarkable number of its citizens. According to the U.S. Census, 2.58 million persons were classified in 1959 as illiterate (unable to read or

[18] It has been suggested at times that "medical care for the needy" be made part of the social security system as was done during 1965 for the aged.

[19] Since health services are discussed in detail in Chapter 16, and housing facilities are discussed in detail in Chapter 22, these subjects will not be emphasized here. However, additional comments will be made at this point regarding the correlation between job discrimination and poverty.

[20] Elton Rayack, "Discrimination and the Occupational Progress of Negroes," *Review of Economics and Statistics* (May, 1961), pp. 209–14.

[21] *Ibid.*

[22] *Report,* Council of Economic Advisors, March 26, 1965.

write) and another 8.3 million over age 25 were classified as "functionally illiterate" (completed less than five years of schooling and generally were lacking in the ability to make effective use of reading and writing). Thus, about 5 percent of the American people, for all practical purposes, are illiterate and unable to participate fully in the political and economic functioning of the society. Significantly, the Negro rate of illiteracy (complete or functional) is four times greater than that of white Americans.[23] This fact is of special importance to the Negro in his efforts to eliminate voting, job, and social discrimination.

For the Negro and other minority groups, education is a means of gaining equality of opportunity and for terminating the segregationist attitudes of those who discriminate. Yet, the lack of "educational opportunity" is responsible only in part for the high rate of illiteracy. In many cases, the cause stems from the nonenforcement of school attendance laws, the shortage of remedial reading classes, the lack of special provisions for minority groups, and oversize classes.[24] Welfare measures which alleviate poverty on a temporary basis are not a sufficient solution to the problem. Any rational long-run program must attack the basic causes of poverty and thus concentrate upon improved education, health services, housing, and reduced discrimination for the poor and minority groups.

Education as an Investment

Since 1900, occupational trends have been toward a relative decline in farm and unskilled laborers and toward increasing employment in

TABLE 21-6

Trends in the Occupational Distribution of Workers and Estimates for 1975, by Selected Year and by Percentage of Total Labor Force
(Percent of Total Labor Force)

Year	Professional and Technical	Farm	Unskilled Industrial Labor
1900	4.4	37.5	12.5
1920	5.4	27.0	11.6
1940	7.5	17.4	9.4
1950	8.6	11.8	6.6
1960	11.2	8.1	5.5
1975 (est.)	14.0	5.3	4.4

Source: Adapted from John K. Norton, *Changing Demands on Education and Their Fiscal Implications* (Washington, D.C.: National Committee for the Support of Public Schools, 1963), Fig. 1, p. 5.

[23] John K. Norton, *Changing Demands on Education and their Fiscal Implications* (Washington, D.C., National Committee for Support of Public Schools, 1963), p. 46.

[24] *Ibid.*, p. 47.

professional and technical occupations (See Table 21–6). In the period 1955–65, the number of persons employed as professional and technical workers increased by 43.1 percent.[25] This occupational group also has the highest educational attainment of all the major groups. In 1960, 90 percent of the men age 25 or older in this group had at least graduated from high school and nearly 60 percent of them had four or more years of college. A special committee on higher education in New York State estimates that, during the period 1960–75, between 1 and 1.5 million of the nearly 2.1 million projected new job openings in the state will require college-trained individuals.[26] The growing demand for college graduates, moreover, appears to be increasing at a more rapid rate than the increasing supply of such people.

As the level of education increases, so does the potential financial return to an individual from his job. This is evident from the data shown in Table 21–7. Becker, in comparing the difference in earnings by white

TABLE 21–7

AVERAGE INCOME (1958) OF MALES 25 YEARS OLD, BY EDUCATION AND
ESTIMATED EARNINGS, AGE 18 TO DEATH

Quantity of Education	Average Earnings ($)	Lifetime Earnings ($)
Less than 8 years	$2,551	$129,764
8 years	3,769	181,695
High school, 1 to 3 years	4,618	211,193
High school, 4 years	5,567	257,557
College, 1 to 3 years	6,966	315,504
College, 4 or more years	9,206	435,242

SOURCE: Adapted from Herman P. Miller, "Annual and Lifetime Income in Relation to Education," *American Economic Review*, Vol. 50, No. 5 (December, 1960), Table 1 on page 966 and Table 11 on page 981.

urban males with four or more years of college, suggests that the return of an investment in higher education is comparable to the return of an investment in business.[27] In 1940, the return was estimated to be 12.5 percent and in 1950, 10 percent. Additional refinement of these estimates, in order to base them on the "total cost" rather than on the "individual cost" of acquiring a college education, indicates that the

[25] Charles A. Myers, "Labor Force Projections and Problems of Unemployment," in *Studies in Unemployment* (Special Committee on Unemployment Problems, U.S. Senate, 86th Cong.) (Washington, D.C.: U.S. Government Printing Office), p. 60.

[26] Committee on Higher Education, New York State, *Meeting the Increased Demand for Higher Education in New York State*, (Albany, N.Y.: November, 1960), p. 11.

[27] Gary S. Becker, "Underinvestment in College Education?" in Edmund S. Phelps (ed.), *The Goal of Economic Growth* (New York: Norton, 1962), pp. 121–28.

return on educational investment before taxes was 9 percent in both 1940 and 1950.[28]

Governmental Programs and Policies toward Education

Government involvement in American education is not a recent phenomenon. Educational laws passed by the colonies date back as far as the mid-17th century. It was not until the late 19th century, however, that government began to take a major interest in the production of education. During the past 50 years, in absolute terms, annual expenditures on education have risen from $238 million to $18 billion. The increase, however, is not as impressive as it appears. Much of the growth in expenditures has been neutralized by inflated prices, population growth, lengthening of the school year, and changes in the minimum level of educational quality. If adjustment is made for these factors, the expenditures in constant dollars on the basis of daily per-pupil attendance have changed very little during the past half century.[29] In fact, the elasticity of demand for educational services during this period has been no greater than unity, that is, no more than proportional to increases in national income. This allocation pattern may soon change, however, since it is estimated that the number of college students will be 9 million by 1975—nearly three times the number enrolled in college in 1960.

The state level of government is theoretically responsible for equating the burden of financial support of education with the benefits received from education and, on this basis, for distributing the burden properly throughout the various communities in the state. The federal government, moreover, has a responsibility to insure that the states and communities are compensated for the benefits that accrue outside their jurisdictions and for the redistribution of funds into low-attainment areas. The latter may be referred to as "horizontal equity" in educational opportunities. In other words, equals should be treated equally within the United States in terms of their educational opportunities.

Practically, there has been little advancement in the fiscal structure of support for education—except those changes brought about by depression or war. Even *sputnik* introduced only moderate changes in the structure, these changes including such legislation as the National Defense Education Act of 1958. The state will provide funds to the community only on the basis of (1) average daily attendance or (2) in cases where the local community is unable through reasonable tax practices to meet minimum state educational requirements. The role of the federal government in public school education has been quite modest over the years. It has been somewhat more instrumental, however, in supporting higher education, particularly at the research level. In fact,

[28] *Ibid.*, p. 115.
[29] Norton, *op. cit.*, pp. 83–85.

the public sector (primarily the federal component) provided some $13 billion or 65 percent of the nation's Research and Development (R and D) funds during 1965.[30] This government-financed research, of course, does not all directly benefit higher education, though substantial portions of the total amount go for this purpose. There is, in addition, some spillover of government research benefits into "adjacent" civilian industries, with a particularly high social payoff deriving from government-financed research in the field of health.[31] Moreover, the historically modest federal role in supporting education appears to be undergoing a transition. For example, federal spending for education, including aid to local schools, has increased from $1.1 billion in 1946 and $2.2 billion in 1956 to a sizable $8.7 billion in 1966.

Table 21–8 displays the changing pattern of public education

TABLE 21–8

GOVERNMENT FINANCIAL SUPPORT FOR PUBLIC EDUCATION,
BY LEVEL OF GOVERNMENT, SELECTED YEARS, 1920–65
(Percent of Total Educational Expenditure)

School Year	Federal	State	Local
1920	.3	16.5	83.2
1930	.4	16.9	82.7
1940	1.8	30.3	67.9
1950	2.8	39.8	57.4
1960	4.4	39.1	56.5
1965	6.8	36.3	56.9

SOURCE: Computed from *Government Finances*, Department of Commerce, Bureau of the Census, 1965, and *Historical Statistics*, Bureau of the Census.

support by the various levels of government between 1920 and 1960. While local government remains the primary allocator of public educational services, the relative roles of the state and federal levels of government have increased during the period. This is especially true regarding the state level of government though recent indications are that federal aid to education may be on the threshold of a major breakthrough.

It would seem that future policy should continue to provide elementary and high school education on a "free" public school basis without tuition charges in order to derive the social benefits of a literate and educated population. Furthermore, it would appear rational to continue to price that part of the benefits of higher education which truly takes on investment aspects for the individual. The remainder of the

[30] Richard E. Slitor, "The Tax Treatment of Research and Innovative Investment," in Papers and Proceedings of the American Economic Association, *American Economic Review* (May, 1966), p. 222.

[31] *Ibid.*, p. 223.

benefits, because of the externalities derived by the public from an educated population, should be financed through general taxation. The education, in turn, could be either produced by government or produced by the private sector and subsidized by government. Importantly, future educational policy must also seek to improve the distribution of educational opportunities among the population.

THE ECONOMIC OPPORTUNITY ACT OF 1964

A significant specific effort by the federal government to eliminate poverty in the United States was enacted by Congress in the form of the Economic Opportunity Act of 1964. This act, which includes provisions to improve the educational opportunities of the poor, contains several other important facets. Generally, the "War on Poverty" program which derives from this legislation falls into seven categories.

First, (Title I of the Legislation), a Job Corps was established whose purpose is to enroll persons between the ages of 16 and 21 who are out of school, unemployed, or in "dead-end" jobs. Those enrolled are given the opportunity to receive general education, vocational training, useful work, and physical conditioning. In addition, federal assistance will be provided to programs established by state and local governments and by private agencies for this same age group as long as the programs meet federal standards. This approach emphasizes programs which encourage potential dropouts to remain in school and actual dropouts to return to school. In addition, Title I of the Act establishes a work-study program to assist youths from low-income families. This facet of the program applies both to students and to potential students. It is administered by institutions of higher learning.

Title II provides for urban and rural community action programs. Federal grants are made to public and nonprofit agencies (in qualifying communities) for aid programs developed at local (urban and rural) levels to combat poverty. These programs relate to such problems as youth unemployment, deficient education, slum conditions, and ill-health. Federal aid is also provided in the form of grants to local educational programs for deprived adults. In addition, this title of the act establishes information centers.

Title III allows for special projects to combat poverty in rural areas. These projects include loans to low-income families in agriculture to help them acquire land, improve their holdings, reduce debt, or participate in cooperatives. Furthermore, a provision to assist migrant workers through loans to interested agencies is included in the law. Title IV relates to employment and investment incentives and establishes a system of loans to assist small business firms and to help them become established. Such loans cannot exceed the amount of $25,000. Title V provides work experience programs which focus upon experimental demonstration or pilot projects to help adults get off relief rolls and to obtain employment.

Title VI of the Economic Opportunity Act of 1964 sets up the administration and coordination of the legislation. The Office of Economic Opportunity is established by this section. This agency is known as VISTA. Its director is authorized to enlist volunteers for the War on Poverty. In addition, the Economic Opportunity Council was established to provide more effective coordination between the various facets of the War on Poverty program. The membership of the Council is comprised of the Director of the Office of Economic Opportunity, as chairman, the Secretaries of Defense, Interior, Agriculture, Commerce, Labor, Health-Education-Welfare, the Attorney General, the Housing and Home Finance Administrator, the Small Business Administrator, the Chairman of the Council of Economic Advisors, the Director of Selective Service, and other agency heads who may be designated by the President. Title VII of the act stipulates that assistance under the act (up to certain amounts) should not limit the right of individuals to receive unemployment compensation or public assistance. At this writing, the Economic Opportunity Act had not been under way long enough for scientific evaluation.

THE "NEGATIVE INCOME TAX" AND THE ELIMINATION OF POVERTY

In 1966 active interest could be detected at the federal level of government and in academic circles for the use of a "government-guaranteed" income technique to alleviate poverty. Surprisingly, the genesis of the idea in this country is not new. In 1933, for example, Francis Townsend, a California physician, received national publicity (and criticism) for his suggestion that the public sector pay $200 per month to all aged persons. In addition, a certain resemblance to the current plan took the form in 1948 of the proposed "Brannan Plan" of outright payments to farmers for the difference between the free market price of certain perishable commodities and an established parity price. Furthermore, Friedman in 1962 recommended the adoption of a negative income tax to replace federal welfare programs.[32]

The current version of government-guaranteed income takes the form of a *negative income tax* for the poor. Just as its name suggests, a negative income tax is an "income tax in reverse." While a positive income tax collects revenues from individuals who have taxable incomes in excess of certain allowable deductions, exemptions, and credits, the negative income tax requires that the government make payments to

[32] Milton Friedman, *Capitalism and Freedom* (Chicago: University of Chicago Press, 1962), pp. 191–95.

individuals who have incomes below some specified poverty level. Instead of yielding revenue through taxation, the plan thus has the government subsidizing people with low incomes.

The negative income tax could either be used as a replacement for various federal welfare and educational programs (as suggested by Friedman) or as a supplement to such programs. The subsidy, moreover, could be either 100 percent or some fraction thereof. If the income level of the taxpayer (spending unit) is $1,500, for example, while the minimum poverty level income is set at $3,000, a 100 percent subsidy would require an outright negative income tax payment to the taxpayer of $1,500. If the percentage payment is set at 50 percent, however, the payment would amount to one half of the deficit income or $750. It is estimated that the goal of a minimum income level of $3,000 for all spending units in the United States would require approximately $12 billion annually in negative income tax payments under present conditions. Moreover, a goal of $4,000 as the minimum income level would require approximately $25 billion in payments while the figure would climb to $40 billion if the objective were $5,000.

Chapter 22

URBAN AND REGIONAL ECONOMIC PROBLEMS

URBAN ECONOMIC PROBLEMS

Growth of Urban Areas

There has been no more significant trend in American history than the evolutionary movement whereby the nation has been transformed from a basically rural to a basically urban society. In 1790, only 5 percent of the American population resided in urban areas. With the urban growth trend becoming very pronounced after 1880, this percentage increased to 40 percent by 1900. In 1920, for the first time, more Americans lived in the city than in rural areas. The transition toward urban living has continued since that date and is expected to continue well into the future. In 1965, approximately two out of every three Americans resided in cities. This figure grows to 90 percent if those people living in communities with less than 2,500 inhabitants, and in unincorporated suburban areas, are included.

The growth of urban areas in the United States, for the most part, has been a function of industrialization. More specifically, the growth has been a product of innovation and technological advancements in the fields of manufacturing, commerce, transportation, and agriculture. Industrialization introduces specialization in production which, in turn, is accompanied necessarily by a high degree of interdependence between the various economic units in both the public and private sectors of the economy. For example, the concentration of productive resources such as a pool of skilled labor in a particular geographical area permits lower cost production of economic goods. Furthermore, the interdependence between money markets and the production of and the demand for economic goods encourages geographical economic concentration. In addition, technological improvements in transportation and in sources of power have given both impetus and feasibility to industrialization and urban concentration. The growth of cities, moreover, has been supported by the population decline in rural areas made possible by the income-inelastic demand for most farm products and the fact that improving technology allows much greater farm output per unit of labor input.

The social, political, and economic complexities of urbanization are substantial. Indeed, the economic blessings resulting from industrialization, and from the urbanization which it sponsors, are neutralized, to an extent, by some of the problems which result from industrialization and urbanization. These problems are not insoluble. The failure to meet them adequately in recent decades, however, has been alarming.

Definitions of Local Government

The Bureau of the Census classifies local governments into several categories: (1) standard metropolitan statistical areas, (2) counties, (3) municipalities, (4) townships, and (5) special districts. The multiplicity of local government decision-making units on fiscal matters is evident. The Census of Governments for 1962, for example, reports that 212 standard metropolitan statistical areas existed in the United States during that year. These metropolitan areas encompassed a multitude of local government units, namely 310 separate counties, 4,142 municipalities, 2,575 townships, and 5,411 special districts such as those for sewage disposal, water supply, road and street improvement, and fire protection. In addition, the local government level in the United States encompassed more than 6,000 independent school districts and 35 dependent school systems in 1962. According to Burkhead: "This is grass-roots government with a vengeance: it is one of the oddities of American democracy that little government finds such generous representation in the standard metropolitan areas."[1] Indeed, many of the significant contemporary fiscal problems of urban areas derive from the decentralized nature of local government structure in the urban areas of the United States.

Sacks introduces a "spatial" or "locational" approach for defining urban areas.[2] Spatial considerations are used to establish the position of a given community within a total urban area regarding its placement as either a central city, an inner core, or an outer ring community. Locational considerations emphasize the effects of proximity and contiguity on expenditure decisions. An urban area is defined on the basis of the full valuation of real property per square mile. This not only delimits the urban community but also adds a quantitative dimension for empirical purposes. The study applies this urban area definition to empirical evidence for New York State and for Cleveland.

It is concluded by Sacks that:[3] (1) expenditures for *police protection* per square mile decline in all directions as one moves outward from the central core area, regardless of the expenditure both per capita and

[1] Jesse Burkhead, *Public School Finance* (Syracuse, N.Y.: Syracuse University Press, 1964), p. 133.

[2] Seymour Sacks, "Spatial and Locational Aspects of Local Government Expenditures," in *Public Expenditure Decisions in the Urban Community,* ed. by Howard G. Schaller (Washington, D.C.: Resources for the Future, 1963), pp. 180–98.

[3] *Ibid.,* pp. 188–97.

per $1,000 of equalized valuation. In Cleveland, these expenditures ranged from $145,000 per square mile in the core area to $2,000 per square mile in the periphery; (2) the same pattern emerges for *fire protection* expenditures, that is, a direct correlation exists between property value per square mile and the cost of providing fire protection; and (3) the spatial pattern that emerges in analyzing police and fire expenditures also appears, when *all municipal expenditures* are considered. Total municipal expenditures per square mile are highest in the central city even without the inclusion of welfare expenditures. The regression coefficient indicates that for every $1 million of incremental valuation per square mile, there are additional municipal expenditures of $6,711 per square mile.

The Nature of Urban Economic Problems and Possible Solutions

The concentration of people in cities is not the sole dimension of the complex socio-political-economic problems of an urban-industrial society. Equally important is the shift of population and industry away from the heart of the city into the suburbs. New and complex problems arise with this latter dimension of urban living. Some 60 percent of the American population presently resides in metropolitan areas, and it is estimated that the percentage will grow to nearly 64 percent by 1975.[4] More importantly, only one half of this population lives in the central city, the remainder living in the surrounding area. It is projected that the suburban population of metropolitan areas will continue to experience both absolute and relative growth, with more than 57 percent of the population of metropolitan areas residing outside the central cities by 1975.[5]

Thus, a central city must provide governmental services for a population greater than what resides within its political boundaries while the suburban political jurisdictions are faced with the pressing needs of a growing area including such requirements as new schools, water systems, sewage disposal systems, streets, fire protection, and police protection. Each new house in the suburbs requires, on the average, some $3,000 of incremental governmental services. Meanwhile, the movement of people and industry from the central city to the suburbs tends to decrease the property and income tax bases of the central city while the suburban governments often are inadequate for the performance of the complex functions required of them. The tax burden on those remaining in the central city, moreover, will probably increase as the tax base declines, thus stimulating an additional exodus to the suburbs. Moreover, since many people who live in the suburbs work in the central city, an extreme demand for transportation facilities, particularly roads for highway transportation, faces the central city.

[4] Estimate made by the Committee for Economic Development.

[5] Estimate made by the Committee for Economic Development.

It is evident that substantial externalities—both benefits and costs—exist among the multitude of political jurisdictions comprising urban areas in the United States. Yet, the decentralization of decision making causes a divergence between the revenue sources and the expenditure decisions of these various political jurisdictions. This divergence exists despite the fact that the problems to be solved and the governmental economic goods to be provided are common to the entire urban area because of externalities. There is an inability to pool financial resources and to coordinate decision making to meet the problems which face the entire urban complex. The discussion below, which at times refers to certain professional analyses of urban economic problems, will elaborate upon the basic nature of urban economic problems and then discuss possible solutions to these problems. Though the discussion will be primarily economic in nature, it is inevitable that it sometimes consider the noneconomic aspects of urban problems.

It seems incongruous that urban governments operate under crisis conditions when a disproportionately large proportion of the nation's wealth is concentrated in these areas. Margolis asks: What are the sources of these crises? Are they becoming more critical?[6] He observes that the basic core of metropolitan financial problems lies in "spatial differentiation." Differentiation and specialization in economic functions make increasing efficiency possible, but they also give rise to costs of organization. The possible chaos which might arise because of "functional differentiation" can be overcome by the organization of markets. Likewise, spatial differentiation requires organization, but the role of the market as a spatial organizing force is quite different. Spatial differentiation, in this context, refers to the fact that every activity must occupy a unique site within the city. In this instance, the market is of minor significance and governments must perform the vital organizing role. Yet, can government establish a framework for economic and social activity within the city? Does the structure of local government—its limited territorial jurisdiction, functional specialization, and restricted fiscal tools—inhibit it as an efficient organizer?

Margolis observes that locational sites within cities are highly substitutable.[7] Continuous spatial shifting of residential and commercial activities thus occurs, with this shifting causing conflicts of interest among individuals since taxes are not assessed in proportion to the benefits received. The larger the number of government units in a metropolitan area, the greater the frustration of local governments from the vetoes of those whose gains do not compensate for their losses. Hence, the fiscal

[6] Julius Margolis, "Metropolitan Finance Problems: Territories, Functions, and Growth," National Bureau of Economic Research, in *Public Finances: Needs, Sources, and Utilization* (Princeton, N.J.: Princeton University Press, 1961), pp. 229–93.

[7] *Ibid.*, p. 233.

crisis worsens, not because of overall inadequacy in revenue sources, but because of the inability to organize. Indeed, the propensity for self-interest to frustrate political decision making is reinforced by the functional and territorial balkanization of the metropolitan areas. Margolis suggests the adoption of more general multipurpose budgets as a possible solution to this problem.

McKean also is concerned with the influence of self-interest on public sector decision making.[8] According to McKean, it must be recognized that serious discrepancies exist between the interests of the individual voter, employee, or government official and the interests of the whole group. There are important divergences between the costs and gains felt by each *individual* alone and the *total* economic effects which cost-benefit analysis seeks to measure. Such interdependent effects are called externalities in the private sector, but an analogous phenomenon is present in the public sector. In fact, it is probably even more difficult in the case of public sector externalities to bring self-interest into line with community interest. Government decision makers often will make decisions which look good to their voting constituents even though they may be harmful to others. Furthermore, government decision makers often will *not* take steps which look bad from their standpoint even though such actions might confer significant gains on others.

Recognizing that emphasis on conflicting political pressures is nothing new, McKean believes that emphasis also should be placed on the facts that:[9] (1) such pressures derive mainly from the cost-gain patterns which confront each decision maker; (2) that self-interest is a powerful force; and (3) that social organization should attempt to harness rather than to override self-interest. In terms of policy, he suggests that:[10] (1) marginal modifications of cities within present urban political frameworks be undertaken and (2) changes be adopted in political frameworks in order to improve bargaining processes. The *former* approach would require that the urban planner lower the level of his objectives. Cost-benefit analysis would be used to compare the marginal modifications of municipal policies which consist of "modest plans" possessing reasonable chances of acceptance under present political arrangements. The *latter* approach would seek better ways of manipulating the cost-reward patterns which confront the various participants. Thus, federal subsidies, stronger manager-council government, and greater use of tax and compensation provisions would be undertaken in order to bring individual and community interests closer together. However, additional

[8] Roland N. McKean, "Costs and Benefits from Different Viewpoints," in *Public Expenditure Decisions . . . op. cit.,* pp. 147–62.

[9] *Ibid.,* p. 154.

[10] *Ibid.,* pp. 159–62.

knowledge of cost-gain patterns, from the viewpoints of the various groups, is required for this approach to be successful.

Lichfield and Margolis demonstrate how cost-benefit analysis can and should be used to improve the decision-making process of urban government.[11] The elements of the decison-making model, within which cost-benefit analysis would be used, are few in number. These elements, however, are difficult to formulate for quantitative analysis. They involve: goal formulation, constraint identification, target specification, criteria, and final cost-benefit analysis of alternatives.

The formal theoretical model of cost-benefit analysis for urban government consists of the following procedure.[12] Each department specifies its assumed goals, constraints, and criteria. The production function contains alternate ways to achieve the agency's objectives as well as an evaluation of the consequences and the payoffs in extending the agency's services along different lines. The various departments then submit their programs to the policymakers. The policymakers review the programs and return them to the departments for reformulation within an amended framework. The amended framework incorporates the definite goals, constraints, and criteria.

A lower level, nonwelfare-maximizing model consists of the following procedure:[13] Prior to a request for new funds, each agency provides an analysis of the current operations of its programs. From the appraisal of these results, the agency takes four constructive steps: (1) the agency prepares indices of expenditure per unit of service or output, (2) it uses the indices of expenditure as a basis of preparing performance budgets, (3) in the revenue budget, it considers the reallocation of variable costs among particular related services with "payoffs" (benefits) in mind, and (4) in the capital budget, it can compare the benefits to be obtained from the marginal transfers of investment funds among the various governmental services within the departmental budget constraint.

Baumol discusses the interdependence between public sector and private sector decisions regarding urban economic matters.[14] The analysis concentrates upon: (1) the advantages accruing to the private sector from the substitution of public for private urban services, (2) the influence of changing conditions in the private sector on the provision of public services, and (3) the different results which accrue from alternative methods of governmental participation in the provison of urban services.

[11] Nathaniel Lichfield and Julius Margolis, "Benefit-Cost Analysis as a Tool in Urban Government Decision Making," in *Public Expenditure Decisions* . . . *op. cit.* pp. 118–46.

[12] *Ibid.*, p. 125.

[13] *Ibid.*, p. 126.

[14] William J. Baumol, "Urban Services: Interactions of Public and Private Decisions," in *Public Expenditure Decisions* . . . *op. cit.*, pp. 1–18.

Concerning the first point, government allocation can prevent or ameliorate undesirable agreements or arrangements. For example, poverty and the inequality of opportunity resulting from severe disparities in the distribution of wealth and income can be influenced by government. This is a particularly important reason for the provision of urban services such as free public education, slum clearance, police activities, street lighting, public parks, and the prevention of air pollution.

Concerning changing conditions in the private sector as a stimulant to public sector economic activity, it can be observed that growing wealth and productivity create higher incomes which, in turn, produce a growing demand for both privately and publicly produced economic goods. A growing urban population, moreover, tends to produce diseconomies of scale in a large number of the service supply operations provided by urban governments, particularly transportation, and substantial external effects result. In addition, technological change creates externalities, particularly those of a diseconomy variety. Furthermore, changes necessitating governmental action include the movement of population to the suburbs and urban blight. Baumol thus concludes that:[15] (1) these trends (in points number one and two) require increases in governmental economic activity; (2) the government intervention must be tailored carefully in a manner designed to restore public sovereignty, not to further frustrate it; and (3) the solution to these problems may require radical measures.

Finally, once it has been decided that some additional urban services are to be provided by government, the question turns to the most effective means of supplying the services. According to Baumol, the principles by which the proper allocative method should be selected are:[16] (1) technical efficiency, that is, using the means which accomplish the objective with the smallest use of resources; (2) the consideration of secondary effects on the private sector; (3) psychic effects on the people of the area; and (4) equity considerations in the sense of the community's concept of distributive justice.

As observed in Chapter 16, two broad financing categories exist for the allocation of economic goods by government, namely, *general* taxes levied without close attention to the manner in which the taxpayer benefits from public services or to the costs of rendering the services, and *specific* taxes, fees, or prices which attempt to reflect such benefits and costs. Vickrey considers the possibility that increased efforts to correlate charges with benefits and costs may increase the efficiency with which public services are utilized, may prevent waste, and generally may

[15] *Ibid.*, pp. 14–15.
[16] *Ibid.*, pp. 15–18.

improve the patterns along which the mushrooming metropolises grow.[17] Several principles or criteria are suggested to help determine whether a municipal service should be financed by a specific charge. These are:[18] (1) the relative distributional impact of the charge versus that of the general tax which it would displace; (2) the extent to which the proposed charge can be related to the benefits derived from the service; and (3) consideration of allocative efficiency such as the possibility of extending the concept of marginal cost pricing into the realm of municipal services. The criteria are thus applied to specific governmental services, some of which are more conducive to the pricing technique than others.

A summary of these specific applications follows:[19]

1. *Fire Protection.* From the benefit point of view, the proper way to charge would be on the basis of assessed valuation of property. From the cost point of view, however, the best way to charge would be on the basis of area as characterized by such factors as extent of land occupancy and zoning features.

2. *Transportation Facilities.* All costs of streets would be assigned to vehicular traffic and tolls would vary with the time of day.

3. *Water Supply.* A charge could be made on the basis of use with rates varying according to the cost of the water.

4. *Police and Custodial Services.* It is difficult to find a suitable benefit criterion for this type of service which is not extremely regressive in its distributional effects.

5. *Recreational Facilities.* It is difficult to isolate a marginal cost of recreational services which is rational in nature.

6. *Education.* A sensible approach here would be to turn a portion of federal income tax receipts over to the state in which the taxpayer receives his education. This would compensate for exports of educational capital.

7. *Health and Hospital Services.* This problem is so diverse that about all that can be done is to list the area as one in which there is a possibility of some financing by fees.

8. *Public Utility Services.* Rates can be charged on a marginal cost basis with a supplemental charge in the form of a "front-footage tax" to cover the basic cost of the distribution system.

Certain broad approaches may be selected to assist in the solution of urban problems. Since several of these policies were discussed in detail at other appropriate locations in this book, however, they will be

---

[17] William S. Vickrey, "General and Specific Financing of Urban Services," in *Public Expenditure Decisions . . . op. cit.,* pp. 62–90.

[18] *Ibid.,* pp. 62–64.

[19] *Ibid.,* pp. 64–86.

mentioned only in summary fashion at this point.[20] Local government revenue problems may be attacked through such approaches as the separation of tax sources, shared taxes, and additional grants-in-aid. Other approaches to urban fiscal problems include the proposals aimed at greater centralization of local government functions and the use of special subsidies to attract industry.

The *separation of tax sources* device would assign certain taxes to the exclusive use of local government. Under the *shared tax* scheme, the state determines the form and rates of taxes and then divides the yield with local government. *Tax credits* help to introduce uniformity in the tax structures of various units of government at different levels. By this technique, one unit of government permits a credit or allowance for taxes paid by taxpayers to another unit of government. While *grants-in-aid* have been in long-term usage in this nation, their importance has been increasing in recent decades. For example, there has been increasing support of educational production at the local level of government in the form of grants-in-aid from state governments and to a lesser extent, but to a growing degree of importance, from the federal government. The proposed Heller Plan, moreover, would provide for *unconditional grants-in-aid* from the federal government directly to state governments, but indirectly (in part) to local governments. This procedure would assist urban areas in their financing problems. Another technique used to assist urban areas, particularly in attracting industry, is the granting of special tax and other *subsidies to business*. This technique is discussed elsewhere in the book and has been judged a "questionable practice" because of the significant allocation and distribution distortions, primarily negative in nature, which it introduces.

Urban Transportation Problems. Among the most critical *specific* problem areas concerning urban living are those involving transportation and the need for urban renewal. These two outstanding urban economic issues will be analyzed in some detail in this chapter. First, the problem of transportation will be considered.[21] The patterns of urban life and the structure of urban communities are significantly influenced by the historical development and present nature of transportation in the community. Variations among urban communities in such matters as population density, growth rates, income levels, and the geographic nature of land help determine the nature of the demand for urban transportation. A close economic interrelationship exists, moreover, between the alternative

[20] For example, the arguments concerning governmental centralization at the local government level are discussed in Chapters 8 and 9.

[21] See Lyle C. Fitch and Associates, *Urban Transportation and Public Policy* (San Francisco: Chandler, 1964), for an excellent survey of urban transportation problems and solutions. Much of the discussion immediately below is based upon this source.

modes of urban transportation. The price and quality of public transportation facilities, for example, will affect the demand for highway usage. Furthermore, the extent of automobile traffic congestion will influence the demand for public transportation as well as the efficiency of surface public transportation.

A critical element of present urban transportation problems is the failure of the public sector, whose decision making on these matters is divided among numerous political jurisdictions, to provide an area-wide or regional approach to urban transportation needs. There is a severe need, moreover, for greater equality in the degree of governmental subsidization and support of the alternative modes of urban transportation. Private research and development expenditures on automobiles are much greater than those for public transportation. Present systems of financing tend to distort both investment and consumer decisions. The former decisions are distorted, for example, by the fact that federal and state aid is provided for the construction of highways, but *not* equally provided for the support of public transit facilities. The cost of providing road space for automotive use in large, high-density urban areas may substantially exceed the revenues collected from motor fuel taxes and other user charges. In addition, motor vehicles cause social costs in the form of air pollution and the time lost from traffic congestion. Meanwhile, public land transportation is much more efficient in land use than is the private automobile: "Depending on assumptions concerning loading, auto movement at 20 miles per hour requires from 6 to 45 times as much road space per person as does a transit bus, and from 10 to 90 times as much as does a multiple-unit rail car."[22] Such efficiency and subsequent cost differences reveal their economic significance in a particular manner at peak-load periods of traffic.

Any program directed toward the solution of urban transportation problems should encompass area-wide planning rather than decentralized decision making among a multitide of political jurisdictions. Urban transportation problems, moreover, can be solved in the long run only if economic rationality is applied to the issues. Social and private costs must be considered for each alternative mode of urban transportation and the existence of externalities between modes is also a highly relevant consideration. Furthermore, if a given mode of transportation cannot meet all costs (both social and private) on a pricing basis, the degree of governmental subsidization should be approximately equal among the various transportation modes. Otherwise, investment and consumption distortions will result. The degree of automotive subsidization thus should be reduced and that for public transportation facilities increased. It would appear that, since the entire society, not the urban area alone, derives

[22] *Ibid.*, pp. 2–3, 14.

significant externalities from efficient transportation, the federal government should bear part of the responsibility for improved urban transportation. Fitch suggests four possible alternative forms of federal assistance for the improvement of urban transportation:[23]

1. *Grants for costs of capital improvement not met by revenues with matching contributions from local government sources.* This alternative would be the most effective form of assistance, but it would place the greatest financial burden upon the federal government.

2. *Matching grants for net-debt service requirements on public agency obligations issued to finance public transportation facilities.* This alternative would require considerably less federal financing and would be nearly as effective as the outright grant program. This is the most desirable of the four alternatives.

3. *Loans to state or local public agencies at the cost of federal borrowing.* Loans at rates less than the cost to the federal government are undesirable since they constitute a subsidy which can be made with greater efficiency on a direct basis. The subsidy, moreover, would raise objections from private financial interests.

4. *Grants for long life improvements in rights-of-way and structures and loans for rolling stock.* This combination would be more effective than a pure loan program and would avoid some of the objections to grants for the purpose of acquiring rolling stock.

The critical importance of transportation and its problems to American society is indicated by the enactment of legislation during 1966 for the establishment of a new cabinet-level Department of Transportation.

Housing and Urban Renewal Problems. Most metropolitan areas have sections where slum living conditions persist. Basically, the existence of slums is a mere exhibit of the existence of a poverty concentration. Ultimately, the permanent elimination of slums can be realized only when the income and wealth levels of *all* spending units have been raised to some acceptable minimum, thus eliminating poverty. Nevertheless, short-run policies for the eradication of slums, primarily in the form of urban renewal programs, are undertaken with some success by the public sector. The urban renewal approach received the impetus of federal government support through Title I of the Housing Act of 1949. Its results, though mixed, have generally been beneficial.

The legislation in 1949 instituted a program of federal financial assistance for urban communities endeavoring to eliminate slums.[24] The legislation envisaged federal aid as a device to facilitate and encourage the redevelopment and rehabilitation of blighted slum areas, though experience between 1949 and 1954 subsequently revealed that the clear-

[23] *Ibid.,* p. 8.

[24] For an excellent discussion of the Federal Urban Renewal Program, see Robert K. Brown, *Real Estate Economics* (Boston: Houghton Mifflin, 1965), chap. 20.

ing of residential slums was only *one* aspect of the comprehensive urban renewal problem. At the present time, the concept of urban renewal encompasses the entire problem of city development. It attempts to meet the need for orderly urban development from three points of view:[25] (1) *total clearance,* which is concerned with the demolition and clearing of slum areas where the physical facilities are without appreciable salvage value, (2) *rehabilitation,* which is concerned with the redevelopment of slum areas that can be restored in an economically rational manner, and (3) *conservation,* which concerns long-range plans for the maintenance of the physical condition of urban housing above slum levels.

The federal urban renewal program does *not* replace private enterprise. Instead, it is initiated by the actions of a local community itself through the cooperative planning of local government and business officials. An urban renewal program cannot attain its goals without the overwhelming cooperation of various elements of the community. The federal financial assistance merely consists of supplementary assistance to the local communities whose own financial resources may be inadequate to accomplish the task on a singular basis. The following steps would be typical for a community endeavoring to initiate an urban renewal program with federal assistance:[26]

1. Recognize the need for an urban redevelopment program.
2. Take positive steps toward accomplishing the objective and formulate a workable program.
3. Apply for federal assistance.
4. Commit the community to institute adequate housing, health, and safety codes which will be enforced in an effective manner.
5. Make a detailed analysis of the blighted areas to determine the specific treatment required.
6. Set up an adequate administrative structure to direct the program.
7. Be certain of the adequacy of the financial sources available to the local government for the conduct of the program.
8. Assume that adequate housing is made available for those displaced under the program.
9. Have strong support for the program from the community.
10. With the approval by the federal government of the program, the undertaking then becomes a "joint undertaking" of the federal government and the local community.

The federal government through the Urban Renewal Administration will lend money to cities for various facets of the program. Loans can be obtained in early stages of the proposed program, for example, to determine the feasibility of an urban renewal project. If feasible, additional loans can be acquired to formulate a renewal plan. The local

[25] *Ibid.,* p. 324.
[26] *Ibid.,* pp. 325–26.

community can then obtain a loan for the acquisition of land through purchase from its owners. Finally, the federal government will pay, by means of a grant to the local government, two thirds of the difference between the total acquisition cost and the total community receipts realized upon sale of the cleared tracts to public and/or private developers. In this context, the *total* acquisition cost includes the cost of purchasing, clearing, and preparing the land for subsequent development.

Davis and Whinston provide a detailed study of the economic problems of urban renewal.[27] They examine the assumptions upon which urban renewal is based, namely, that the market has not functioned properly in regard to urban property and that governmental action can improve the situation. The tools of welfare economics are used to examine these assumptions. The first conclusion reached, based upon a game theory matrix, is that the cause of urban blight is the existence of externalities in the utility functions for urban property, that is, both satisfaction and the return on investment from urban property depend not only on the property itself but also upon the characteristics of nearby property. It thus becomes more desirable or profitable at times for an individual to allow his property to deteriorate rather than to maintain it in satisfactory repair.

Accepting the validity of the above analysis, it is clear that situations may exist where individually rational action will not allow for socially desirable investment in the redevelopment of urban property.[28] Blight is thus defined as existing whenever: (1) strictly individual action does not result in redevelopment, (2) the coordination of decision making via some technique would result in redevelopment, and (3) the sum of benefits from renewal could be greater than the sum of urban renewal costs. It thus becomes a problem of social policy to develop methods whereby blighted areas can be reorganized and positive action can be taken to facilitate urban renewal. In terms of policy, the problem is to discover the institutional arrangement by which redevelopment can be carried out with a reduction in the misallocation of resources.

Davis and Whinston propose two courses of action, namely, "preventive" action and "reconstructive" action.[29] The approach to *prevent* urban blight attempts to establish methods for coordinating spending decisions concerning repair and upkeep so that the individually and socially desirable choices are equated. This can be accomplished through such devices as the use of a special building code which specifies

[27] Otto A. Davis and Andrew B. Whinston, "Economic Problems in Urban Renewal," in *Private Wants and Public Needs,* edited by Edmund Phelps (rev. ed.; New York: Norton, 1965).

[28] *Ibid.,* p. 146.

[29] *Ibid.,* pp. 148–53.

minimum levels of repair and upkeep. It can provide a rough approximation of optimal levels of coordination.

The *reconstructive* approach essentially follows the broad outline of the present federal urban renewal program. It involves the city's purchasing the blighted areas, demolishing the structures, and then selling the lots to entrepreneurs who have agreed in advance to construct certain approved types of buildings. This eliminates or reduces negative externalities and helps to equate the private and social products. In this instance, the criterion used to indicate whether or not a project should be undertaken is that which asks whether the revenues derived from the project exceed the costs. This is a rational approach since, in the absence of externalities, the social benefit–social cost concept reduces in effect to revenues and costs. The latter (reconstructive) approach is unnecessary, of course, if the former (preventive) approach is successful.

The Department of Housing and Urban Development. A recent effort to combat urban economic problems occurred in the passage by Congress of legislation creating a separate cabinet department to be known as the Department of Housing and Urban Development (HUD). The first attempt to establish such a department was made by President Kennedy, but the idea did not reach fruition until September 9, 1965, when President Johnson signed it into law. The new department helps to meet the need for a clearinghouse and research center for urban affairs. Previously, the primary agency concerned with urban affairs was the Housing and Home Finance Agency. This agency, however, is concerned primarily with housing and urban renewal and cannot function as a clearinghouse for the complex variety of urban problems.

The Department of Housing and Urban Development will function in four major areas, namely, urban renewal, finance, metropolitan planning, and general operations. *Urban renewal* includes aid to small business, site clearance grants, public housing, and the like. The *finance* category encompasses such activities as FHA (Federal Housing Administration), mortgage insurance for new and used single-family dwellings, multifamily and co-op housing, and college dormitories as well as the operation of the Federal National Mortgage Association which stabilizes the secondary mortgage market. In *metropolitan planning*, the new department will be concerned with assisting area-wide planning through "701 Computer Grants," and will provide water and sewer grants (50 percent federal financing) as well as partial federal financing (50 percent) of land acquired for parks and for community centers and health stations (67 percent). Finally, the *general operations* segment of HUD includes housing research programs to seek new ways to finance rehabilitation and relocation programs, manpower training, and the improvement of local building codes, zoning, and taxation methods.

The critical importance of urban areas and their problems is brought to light by the statement of President Johnson at the time the bill creating the new department was signed.

Between now and the end of the century urban population and urban area will double. . . . In the next 35 years we must literally build a second America —putting in place as many houses, schools, apartments, parks and offices as we have built through all the time since the Pilgrims arrived on these shores.[30]

Indeed, the nation, in order to plan its future in a rational manner, must be aware of the high urban growth trend and the problems which it creates. The Department of Housing and Urban Development seems to be an appropriate addition as the 11th cabinet-level department of the federal government.

REGIONAL ECONOMIC PROBLEMS

Many of the critical economic issues of the present time cannot be isolated within the environment of a particular community or state but instead are regional in nature. To an extent, the historic development of the American economy required a regional approach. This is verified by such a governmental policy as the Gallatin Plan, which provided the Cumberland Road. This program assisted greatly in the early development of the Appalachian area and the Mid-South states as well as parts of the Midwest. The Erie Canal, moreover, sponsored by New York State provided the basis for the development of the Upper Great Lakes region as well as that for the commercial importance of New York City. Other notable historical examples of regional development programs include the land-grant subsidies to the Western railroads following the Civil War and the Tennessee Valley Authority (TVA) program of the 1930's. Regional issues, however, are at least as important today as they were in earlier American history.

Recent years have witnessed significant federal legislation directed toward regional economic development. The present pattern of legislation began during the 1950's. The new concept was sponsored by several state governors and was introduced in the form of a bill by Senator Paul Douglas (Illinois) in 1955. The Douglas bill proposed aid to areas suffering from chronic unemployment. It included aid for the development of new industry or the expansion of present industries, assistance for the training of unemployed workers, and accelerated tax amortization provisions. The initial bill was unsuccessful in Congress, but Douglas introduced a similar bill in 1957. This bill, after merger with another bill which changed the Douglas bill only slightly, was passed by Congress but failed to become law when President Eisenhower applied the pocket veto to it. Subsequent attempts for passage of a regional development

[30] President Lyndon B. Johnson, September 9, 1965.

program were unsuccessful until 1961, at which time, with the backing of President Kennedy, another Douglas-introduced bill, known as the Area Redevelopment Act, became law.

The legislation of 1961 established the Area Redevelopment Administration (ARA) within the Department of Commerce. The objective of the new law was to encourage the development of long-term employment opportunities by encouraging industries to expand into urban and rural areas which have been plagued by chronic unemployment. Specifically, the ARA was: (1) to provide communities with technical assistance grants and to assist in planning for industrial expansion; (2) to provide loans under certain conditions when private credit is not available; (3) to provide loans and grants for modern public facilities in order to attract new industries; and (4) to provide funds for the training and retraining of the labor force.[31]

Meanwhile, after a two-year study by the President's special Appalachian Regional Commission, Congress in 1965 enacted the Appalachia Regional Development Act. A partnership arrangement between the federal and state levels of government is provided by this legislation. Proposed programs can be vetoed by a state government if they are deemed unsatisfactory. The federal government will provide 80 percent of the funds. This program stresses road construction, but it includes also expenditures for hospital construction, hospital maintenance, construction of vocational schools, development of timber stands, construction of sewage-treatment systems, reclamation of strip-mined lands, and the operational expenses of administration. However, 80 percent of the $840 million appropriation for the first year of the program is directed toward road construction. Caudill, a recognized expert on the problems of Appalachia, believes that the federal program for Appalachia is based more on relief provisions than on policies directed toward the basic conditions which created the Appalachian problem.[32] These basic problems include the regressive tax structure and the export of the proceeds of Appalachia's mineral wealth to other parts of the nation.[33]

During 1965, political logrolling was prominent in the passage of regional development legislation. It is apparent that supporters of the Appalachia legislation supported, in turn, the highly significant but little publicized Economic Development Act of 1965 (EDA).[34] This legislation continues in force, with renewed strength and under a new name, the controversial Area Redevelopment Administration discussed above. ARA

---

[31] For an excellent discussion of the act, see Conley H. Dillon, "Area Redevelopment Act—What Has It Accomplished?" *Challenge* (April, 1963), pp. 21–24.

[32] Harry M. Caudill, "Misdeal in Appalachia," *Atlantic* (June, 1965), p. 44.

[33] *Ibid.*

[34] For an excellent discussion of the Economic Development Act, see Don Oberdorfer, "The Proliferating Appalachias," *Reporter* (September 9, 1965), pp. 22–27.

was scheduled to terminate on June 30, 1965. Title V of the Economic Development Act provides the most significant intensification of federal regional development efforts. It provides a political and legal framework whereby other economic regions of the nation (besides Appalachia) may adopt substantial regional development programs. The act, moreover, authorizes an initial annual expenditure of $660 million to support the program. Furthermore, it is predicted by experts that expenditures could easily reach $3 billion during the next five years, an amount about the size of present foreign aid expenditures.[35]

The proposed new economic development regions will receive initial funds amounting to $15 million, which will be used to organize study groups for the formulation of the various regional programs of federal grants and loans. Specifically, Title V of EDA authorizes the Secretary of Commerce to create economic development regions, with the approval of the involved states, in those instances where the region has lagged behind the nation as a whole in economic development. Each region will have a federal-state commission, with a federal co-chairman appointed by the President. Current efforts are being made to adopt regional economic development plans for the Ozark Mountain region inclusive of parts of Arkansas, Oklahoma, and Missouri; the Mesabi Range area of upper Minnesota, Wisconsin, and Michigan; New England; the Great Plains area involving North Dakota, South Dakota, Wyoming, and Montana, and the Four Corners area consisting of parts of Colorado, New Mexico, Arizona, and Utah. The principal challenges to the worthiness of the Economic Development Act will center around its ability to avoid irrational pork-barreling and to contribute positively toward the formulation of economically rational regional development programs.

---

[35] *Ibid.*, p. 23.

Chapter 23 | DEFENSE ECONOMICS

NATIONAL DEFENSE AND THE NATIONAL ECONOMY

Federal government expenditures for national defense have exerted a significant impact upon the American economy during the past 25 years. This period of expanded defense importance began in 1941 with the military buildup prior to the entrance of the United States into World War II. The effects of World War II defense spending on the American economy were pronounced. For more than a decade prior to 1941, the national economy had limped along under conditions of chronic depression. To be sure, the degrees of depression varied during the period. At no time between November of 1929 and World War II, however, did the economy operate under conditions where aggregate demand (private sector plus public sector spending) was sufficient to fully employ the nation's labor and capital resources. In 1933, before President Franklin D. Roosevelt's New Deal antidepression policies had partially alleviated the depression conditions, 12.8 million people were unemployed. This number constituted nearly 25 percent of the civilian labor force. Full employment, however, returned with World War II and the nation has not experienced deep and prolonged depression conditions since that time. The question may be asked whether the continued post–World War II importance of defense spending is a primary cause of America's continued prosperity.

The Secular Stagnation Hypothesis

The above question will be approached through the analytical structure of the *secular stagnation hypothesis*. During the depression years of the 1930's, significant advances were made in the development and refinement of aggregate economic theory. Led by the late British economist John Maynard Keynes, macroeconomic theory was improved to the point where it could provide a highly rational framework for understanding the operation of market-oriented economies.[1] Among the

[1] See John Maynard Keynes, *The General Theory of Employment, Interest, and Money* (New York: Harcourt, Brace, 1935). See also the discussion of macroeconomic theory in Chapter 17.

506

various hypotheses offered as explanations for the prolonged depression in the United States and for the similar economic downturns in the market-oriented economies of Western Europe, the secular stagnation hypothesis, which was based upon a Keynesian framework, stood out as the most feasible. This hypothesis is associated primarily with Alvin Hansen, the renowned Harvard University economist.[2] Though contro-

FIGURE 23-1

AN ECONOMY IN "SECULAR STAGNATION"*

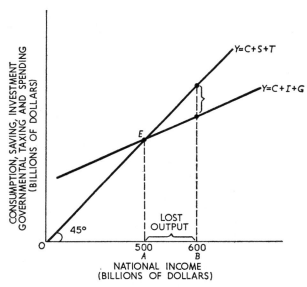

* The deflationary gap condition of production persists on a chronic or long-term basis.

versial in a politico-economic sense, the secular stagnation explanation received considerable support from both academicians and laymen.

In technical economic terms, secular stagnation may be described as consisting of a chronic deflationary gap condition. Figure 23-1 displays this phenomenon, with the appended statement that the conditions of underfull-employment equilibrium persist for a secular or long-term period of time. In the graph, let aggregate output *OB* ($600 b.), measured in national income terms, equal the output necessary to fully employ the nation's labor and capital resources. Aggregate public and private sector demand, however, is insufficient for full-employment production and the economy produces the reduced output *OA* ($500 b.).

[2] Alvin H. Hansen, *Fiscal Policy and Business Cycles* (New York: Norton, 1941), pp. 38–46.

Potential output *AB* ($100 b.) is lost because of unutilized productive resources. Conditions such as this prevailed in the American economy during the entire decade of the 1930's and in Western Europe during the early part of the same decade. In the latter case, defense spending prior to World War II began at an earlier point of time than it did in the United States.

The secular stagnation hypothesis suggested that chronic deflationary gaps are *normal* for mature capitalistic industrial nations. As applied to the United States, it was reasoned that America's industrial growth to a point of economic maturity by the 1930's had been stimulated historically by three major sources of investment demand. These were: (1) the existence of a *frontier* of undeveloped land during most of American history, (2) rapidly increasing *population,* both from immigration and from domestic birth rate causes, and (3) continually improving *technology.* By the 1930's, however, two of the three investment demand sources had been reduced in their effectiveness. America no longer had a frontier of free land to stimulate private investment. The long-term expansion of population at an increasing rate of growth, moreover, had slowed down by the 1930's to become a moderate population expansion at decreasing rates of growth. The only one of the three primary investment demand sources which remained as a stimulant was technological innovation. The hypothesis thus concluded that the tremendous amount of saving (including taxes) which America's mature industrial economy would generate at full employment could not be met with private investment demand plus the then prevailing level of public sector demand. Consequently, the economy settled at an underfull-employment equilibrium on a chronic basis.

Defense Spending and Prosperity

The time correlation between the termination of secular depression in the United States and substantially expanded long-term defense spending poses the interesting question raised earlier in this chapter. Is there a functional cause-and-effect relationship between the increased federal government defense spending of the last 25 years and the ability of the national economy to avoid prolonged depression during this period? In technical terms, has long-term prosperity—or near-prosperity—been attained *only* because aggregate demand has been sufficiently increased by defense spending to help absorb all of the enormous amount of savings which the American economy creates at full employment output? Unfortunately, no definitive answer to this question based on sound empirical analysis can be provided. Yet, it appears likely that military outlays have been a substantial stimulant to aggregate economic activity during the last 25 years. The only segment of this time period when such expenditures decreased sharply in relative importance was during the interim period between the end of World War II (1945) and the beginning of the cold war (1948). The private component of aggregate demand, however, remained abnormally high during these three years because of the postponed private consumption and investment demands of the war years which were then being met.

Table 23–1, which relates federal defense expenditures to gross

TABLE 23–1

Defense-Related Expenditures,* in Absolute Terms and as a Percentage of Gross National Product, Selected Fiscal Years, 1902–66

Year	Defense-Related Expenditures (Billions of Dollars, Current)	Defense-Related Expenditures as a Percentage of Gross National Product
1902	$ 0.3	1.6%
1913	0.5	1.2
1922	2.4	3.2
1927	2.0	2.1
1932	2.2	3.8
1934	1.6	2.4
1936	3.0	3.7
1938	2.1	2.4
1940	2.5	2.5
1942	27.7	17.4
1944	87.9	41.6
1946	57.0	27.0
1948	26.3	10.1
1950	28.3	10.0
1952	56.5	16.3
1954	57.5	15.8
1956	51.8	12.4
1958	56.2	12.6
1960	59.0	11.6
1962	65.2	11.7
1965	71.4	10.6
1966	77.7	10.9

* Defense-related expenditures include spending for major national security, war-related interest on the debt, veterans affairs, international relations, and the space program.
Source: Bureau of the Budget and Department of Commerce.

national product for selected years of the 20th century, demonstrates the secular increase in the importance of defense activities to the national economy during the last 25 years.[3] Indeed, it cannot be doubted that such expenditures have been important to aggregate economic activity during this time. Nevertheless, it cannot be stated with certitude that defense spending has been the *primary* contributant to the nation's continued economic prosperity.

[3] See Chapter 7 for further historical data concerning defense-related spending.

DISARMAMENT AND THE NATIONAL ECONOMY

The intense interest shown toward the subject of disarmament in recent years is strong testimony to the widespread impression that defense spending has contributed greatly toward the economic prosperity of recent decades. During the mid-1960's, however, a trend toward decreased relative importance for defense (despite the war in Vietnam) appeared to be under way. In September of 1965, a special Presidential Committee on the Economic Impact of Defense and Disarmament, headed by Chairman Gardner Ackley of the Council of Economic Advisers, recommended that defense contractors, the federal government, and local communities initiate preparations for the declining relative role of defense in the national economy. Defense spending (narrowly defined) which had been around 10 percent of gross national product between 1955 and 1963 decreased to 8.4 percent of GNP in 1965.

If defense expenditures were to remain at their 1965 levels through the next five years, the federal government will face a series of major fiscal policy decisions. During this time, the growing economy will provide a sharp increase in federal income tax collections and, according to the Committee, despite built-in increases in the outlays for existing programs, the federal government will have an additional $25 to $30 billion in surplus revenues.[4] The alternative uses of the incremental federal revenues include the options of (1) passing all of the additional revenues along to the private sector in the form of tax cuts, (2) the transference of the entire amount into either new federal programs or into the significant expansion of existing programs, and (3) an expanded program of federal grants-in-aid to state and local units of government, which is essentially the Heller Plan as discussed in Chapter 9.

The impact of *disarmament* on the nation would be many times greater than that of the *defense slowdown* discussed above. In fact, complete multilateral disarmament by all nations would exert a profound influence on the world economy as a whole. The "world war industry" constitutes a total sum of productive resources devoted to the international preparation for war, or its actual conduct, valued between $100 and $120 billion annually—an amount equal to the total income of the poorer half of mankind.[5]

Any rational approach to disarmament requires an understanding of

[4] Soon after the Presidential Task Force made its report, intensification of the war in Vietnam seemed to nullify for the present time the fiscal worries expressed in the report. However, they still remain relevant for some future period when defense efforts may be reduced.

[5] Kenneth Boulding, "The World War Industry as an Economic Problem," in *Disarmament and the Economy*, ed. by Kenneth Boulding and Emile Benoit (New York: Harper and Row, 1963), pp. 3–27.

the economic nature of international military conflict. An enlightening discussion relevant to this point is provided by Boulding.[6] According to Boulding, if one thinks of the division of the world war industry into firms, then the armed forces of each nation constitute a firm. The name "milorg" (short for military organization) is attached to these firms. Milorgs are similar to private firms in many ways, but they do not buy all their labor inputs in a free market. Instead, they usually employ conscript labor. In addition, the milorg is nonprofit in orientation and obtains its revenues from taxation or money creation rather than from the sale of its product on the market. The product provided by the milorg, national security, is a service which is psychological in nature.

The primary demand for the product of the milorg is produced by the existence of another and competing milorg. Milorgs compete only against one another. According to Boulding:

this . . . is the source of the real distinction between the world war industry and commercial industry. War industry produces its own demand. The only justification for the existence of a milorg is the existence of another milorg in some other place. This is not true of any other social organization. It is a unique property of the milorg and of the war industry.[7]

Considerable interdependence exists between milorgs. The action of one milorg, for example, will be perceived and will produce reactions in other milorgs. The situation is somewhat analogous to oligopolistic interaction in private markets. Rationality principles can be applied as a guide to the resolution of these conflicts.

Further insight into the "economics of disarmament" is provided by Benoit.[8] He employs a model based upon the multilateral disarmament concept which involves general and complete disarmament under a supranational authority endowed with preponderant powers.[9] After various assumptions are made, the politico-military disarmament model is translated into an economic model by estimating the changes in expenditures involved at each stage of disarmament and in each category of action. The result is a projected reduction in U.S. defense expenditures of about $46 billion (in 1960 dollars), of which approximately $17 billion would occur in the first three years. If allowance is made for the offsets provided by the U.S. contribution to the international disarmament organization and for the planned expansion in civilian and in atomic energy programs, the *net* decline would not be more than $32 billion in

[6] *Ibid.*, pp. 7–11.

[7] *Ibid.*, p. 10.

[8] Emile Benoit, "The Disarmament Model," in *Disarmament and the Economy, op. cit.*, pp. 28–49.

[9] Other than being multilateral, disarmament may be bilateral, involving two nations, or unilateral, involving only one nation.

all, and not more than $5 billion a year even during the critical three-year introductory period of maximum impact.

Using a Leontief input-output model, Benoit calculates the estimated effect of disarmament upon employment.[10] The result is a projected decline of about 6.25 million workers in total employment dependent upon defense. This total includes approximately 2.5 million from the armed forces, nearly 1 million from the civilian employees of federal defense agencies, and more than 2.8 million from private defense industry. Moreover, substantial numbers of workers in trade, services, transportation, and other industries would be affected even though they are not directly engaged in the production of national security. It must be remembered, however, that the decline in defense employment is not the same total as the increase in unemployment since the changes in other demands will bear importantly upon the latter figure.

The magnitude of the redeployment problem is estimated at 8 percent of the labor force. Concerning specific industries, it is estimated that redeployment burdens will be high in only a few industries. Thus, in aircraft and ordnance, nine out of every ten workers would be affected by disarmament; in ships and boats, one out of two workers; in radio communications, one out of three workers; and so on. These figures, however, relate to the total impact on the respective industries. The impact during the first three years would be less severe.

Nelson discusses the impact of disarmament on research and development activities.[11] Approximately 15 percent of defense expenditures are for research and development. Moreover, between 50 and 60 percent of the total research and development expenditures in the nation are financed by defense agencies. Thus, it is obvious that disarmament would have a substantial impact on the size and allocation of the nation's research and development efforts. The impact would not only create a problem of adjustment and frictional unemployment, but it may also retard the rate of technological growth if the research and development cutback is too great. Assuming a 50 percent cutback in defense spending spread over a number of years, Nelson estimates that a $3.2 billion reduction in total research and development outlay would occur—an amount equal to approximately 23 percent of the total research and development expenditures of the nation.[12] An increase in nondefense final demand, however, would tend to offset this result though it may not be expected to neutralize it entirely.

Financial patterns also may be influenced by disarmament. Kavesh and Mackey study the effect of disarmament on the pattern of ownership

[10] Benoit, *op. cit.*

[11] Richard R. Nelson, "Impact of Disarmament on Research and Development," in *Disarmament and the Economy, op. cit.*, pp. 112–28.

[12] *Ibid.*, pp. 116–17.

of securities.[13] Their analysis, in exploring the financial implications of alternative fiscal policies made necessary by disarmament, emphasizes the "tax cut" and "debt cut" models. Under the *tax cut model,* defense outlays will be precisely offset by reductions in federal taxes with no changes in the level of federal debt and no increment in federal expenditures. Under the *debt cut model,* defense outlays will be precisely offset by a reduction in federal debt with no reductions in federal taxes and no increment in federal expenditures.

The predicted results from the tax cut model are:[14] (1) a substantial increase in the volume of investable funds, (2) declining rates of interest, (3) a bull stock market, (4) increased investment and consumption, and (5) a large expansion of primary securities. The predicted results from the debt cut model are:[15] (1) an increase in savings, (2) declining rates of interest, (3) decreased dependence by business on the capital market, and (4) a smaller increase in primary securities than in any of the other fiscal policy models examined. In addition to the absolute magnitude of primary securities, another difference between the two models would be the effect on the types of existing securities. For example, a much larger amount of corporate stock outstanding would appear under the tax adjustment model and a much smaller amount of federal debt would appear under the debt cut model.

Besides the specific problems of adjustment to disarmament such as the impact of disarmament on research and development and on financial structure as discussed above, the *overall effects* of disarmament on the economy should be analyzed. According to Benoit, this overall adjustment problem falls into two major segments:[16] *First,* there exists a problem of maintaining adequate aggregate demand for the new goods and services produced with the rechanneled defense resources. This essentially is the domain of fiscal and monetary policies. *Second,* there exists a structural problem of overcoming various obstacles to a prompt and smooth transfer of the displaced resources into the new uses.

Using an econometric approach, it is concluded that disarmament, with no offsets, would produce a decline in gross national product of between $37 and $48 billion and a decline in employment of between 4.1 and 5.3 million workers. If the disarmament were coupled with a balanced budget through a tax cut, the change would be a decline of $12.3 billion in GNP and of 2.9 million in employment. For a balanced budget with a partial tax cut and new government programs, GNP would

---

[13] Robert Kavesh and Judith Mackey, "Impact of Disarmament on the Financial Structure of the U.S.," in *Disarmament and the Economy, op. cit.,* pp. 157–72.

[14] *Ibid.,* pp. 160–62.

[15] *Ibid.,* pp. 162–65.

[16] Emile Benoit, "Economic Adjustments to Disarmament," in *Disarmament and the Economy, op. cit.,* pp. 275–76.

decline by $8.4 billion and employment would decline by 2 million persons. For a split between a tax cut, new government programs, and debt retirement—with a surplus budget of $6.8 billion—there would be a reduction of between $14.8 and $19.2 billion in GNP and a decline in employment of between 2 and 2.6 million persons. If there is a tax cut of $43 billion, with a budget deficit of $6.8 billion, GNP will not change, but employment will decrease by 2 million. If the tax cut were $69.3 billion and the budget deficit $23.3 billion, GNP would increase by $29.6 billion and employment would not change. Finally, with both a tax cut and new government programs, and a deficit budget of $3.1 billion, GNP would increase by $.4 billion and employment would decline by .8 million workers.

As a solution, Benoit suggests the "balanced-offsets fiscal policy," which would achieve some desirable results for both production and employment, with the benefits being divided between individuals and the community. Thus, the disarmament adjustment problem may be viewed not to be essentially a problem of "finding a place to park the released resources and keep them from becoming a nuisance" but instead as an opportunity which comes once in a lifetime "to apply some highly valuable although specialized resources to carefully selected alternative uses in which they could contribute more effectively to the highest priority needs of mankind."[17] Along these lines, the reallocation of defense resources could be used to raise low incomes, improve housing, support urban renewal and urban transportation, develop natural resources in a national manner, support education, improve medical services, and increase research and development.

EFFICIENCY IN THE DEFENSE BUDGET

Since defense spending has been such a prominent part of federal fiscal activities during the past 25 years, it is important that efficiency—both in a technical input-output sense and in an allocative sense—be sought in defense budget decision making. Considerable attention has been paid during recent years to this subject. These efforts to introduce rationality into defense decision making have experienced substantial success.[18] The story begins in the immediate post–World War II period when economists and military officers were pursuing their own separate courses. The story ends with the contemporary situation in which many economists make a significant contribution to the selection among alterna-

[17] *Ibid.*, p. 300.

[18] For an excellent summary of the history of the use of economic analysis in the Department of Defense, see Stephen Enke, "Using Costs to Select Weapons," *Papers and Proceedings of the American Economic Association*, May, 1965, pp. 416–26.

tive weapon systems, costing alternative future force structures, and other efficiency decisions.

In the late 1940's, specialists were at work at the Rand Corporation to determine the best strategic bomber for development and next generation use by the Air Force. Each specialist, however, emphasized his own area and there was no agreement upon what should be minimized to accomplish the strategic objective. Eventually, an economist suggested that dollars, which represent a common denominator of resource inputs, should be minimized. In this manner, cost effectiveness which later became the basis of "McNamara-Hitch program packaging" was integrated into defense decision making.[19] In subsequent years, additional economists were brought into the military choice program and the concept of opportunity cost, as applied to military problems, was further developed.

The application of the principles of variable proportions and opportunity cost to military decision making was of particular importance. Previously, in the case of developing a strategic bombing capacity, those concerned with bombers had treated bombs as a free good while those concerned with bombs had treated bombers as a free good.[20] Now a more sophisticated method was employed. If the targets destroyed are considered the output, the two main inputs were clearly fissionable materials and delivery vehicles. Once the problem had been framed in these terms, it was a simple matter to establish the rate of substitution between one marginal bomber and a marginal kilogram of fissionable material. In addition, once the cost of acquiring and keeping a bomber was known, the use value of fissionable material was obviously the delivery cost which it saved. In the 1950's, the marginal use value of fissionable materials appeared to be several times larger than the Atomic Energy Commission's marginal cost of production. This suggested that the Oak Ridge gaseous diffusion plant should be operated more intensively. Such analysis was also applied to the substitution values between two uses—strategic v. tactical bomber systems. An estimate was made of the marginal values in dollars of x kilograms of fissionable materials as a substitute for strategic bombers and as a substitute for tactical bombers. The conclusion was reached that the nuclear stockpile needed to be reallocated, in part, with some new weapons being reserved for tactical air missions in NATO (North Atlantic Treaty Alliance).[21]

In 1961, the Department of Defense officially adopted costing meth-

[19] The McNamara-Hitch approach will be explained in greater detail below.

[20] A free good is one which provides utility (satisfaction), although its production is *not* contingent upon the problem of resource scarcity.

[21] There was difficulty in costing alternative and hypothetical delivery systems in the above analysis. The Air Force did not maintain cost data in such a form that a bomber wing could be costed. Thus, only approximations could be made.

ods and analytical practices similar to those which had evolved in the Rand Project. This was largely the accomplishment of Charles J. Hitch, an economist who became Comptroller of the Department of Defense under Secretary of Defense Robert McNamara. The successful application of such cost-effectiveness budgeting in the Department of Defense has led to the requirement that the *civilian agencies* of the federal government put it into use by the 1968 fiscal year.

The military establishment is costed by program elements. There are several advantages to this approach. First, two elements which possess roughly the same kind of output can be compared for cost effectiveness, and one element or system may then show a distinct superiority in output per million dollars of resource input. Furthermore, economies of scale may dictate the selection of one system and the rejection of an alternative system, even though the short-run cost effectiveness is identical for each system. More importantly, a program package can be formed in those instances where different and complementary program elements have measurable outputs which relate to the same national objective (such as defense of the United States from air attack).

Despite the overall advantages of these methods, limitations exist since: (1) extreme differences may exist in the nature of weapon systems, (2) some systems are multipurpose, with more than one military output, and (3) some program elements have no obviously measurable output. It is possible, nevertheless, to classify most military costs by program elements, thus increasing the efficiency of decision making in the Department of Defense.

Enke suggests certain refinements in the art of defense economics:[22] (1) The use of a *rate of discount:* alternative systems can have very different service lives. Sometimes, one of two competing (alternative) systems involves much higher initial costs, but much lower operating costs. In such instances, a rate of discount is needed in order to obtain comparable present values, (2) *Better dynamic costing:* the discounted salvage values of assets bequeathed eventually by the first generation system should be deducted from that system's cost, (3) *Budget reactions of enemy planners:* when major weapon systems which can seriously alter the balance of power between the United States and potential enemy nations are being considered, it is necessary to consider the reactions of such enemies. This is analogous to oligopoly-type interdependence in the private sector of the economy.

Writing in 1961, Enthoven and Rowen describe two points of view on the shortcomings of defense organization and make suggestions regarding what should be done about it.[23] *One* of these viewpoints,

---

[22] Enke, *op. cit.*, pp. 425–26.

termed the "Eisenhower viewpoint," criticizes the fact that different services are defined by different modes of transportation rather than by missions or purposes which are relevant to the strategic problem of the day. According to this explanation, the situation has prevented the development of unified strategic planning to accomplish broad military objectives and has encouraged wasteful and harmful interservice rivalry. This rivalry supposedly has diverted attention from important problems and has led to an undesirable amount of duplication. The *second* point of view holds that the fundamental defects in defense organization rest largely in the inadequacies of the mechanism for choice among alternatives. Enthoven and Rowen are sympathetic to the latter explanation and conclude that amalgamation of the services would not eliminate these inadequacies. Moreover, interservice rivalry may provide certain "values of competition."[24]

It is suggested that defense organization can be improved by the following steps:[25] (1) one basic conceptual framework brought to bear on the problem should be centered around the notion of a "constrained maximum," that is, at any point of time a given set of resources must be allocated. The limited resources should be used to maximize a relevant set of output measures or military worth; (2) an important step for improvement is to identify output independently of inputs so that different weapon systems can be considered for the various objectives; (3) programming and budgeting should be made to correspond to output categories; and (4) a partial separation between the questions of budget level and allocation should be found so that the extent to which one year's allocation can be used as an instrument to increase the subsequent year's budget can be reduced. This separation, moreover, would allow the problem of efficient allocation within a given budget to be faced in a direct manner.

As observed above, Charles J. Hitch, as Comptroller for the Department of Defense, has played an important role in improving the economic efficiency of national defense operations. The issue of efficiency in defense economics was discussed brilliantly by Hitch, along with Roland N. McKean, in a book published in 1960.[26] Their study suggests that the essence of economic choice in military planning involves a comparison of all the relevant alternatives from the point of view of the objectives which

[23] Alain Enthoven and Henry Rowen, "Defense Planning and Organization," in *Public Finances: Needs, Sources, and Utilization*, National Bureau of Economic Research (Princeton, N.J.: Princeton University Press, 1961), pp. 365–420.

[24] *Ibid.*, p. 368.

[25] *Ibid.*, pp. 408–13.

[26] Charles J. Hitch and Roland N. McKean, *The Economics of Defense in the Nuclear Age* (Cambridge, Mass.: Harvard University Press, 1960).

each can accomplish and the cost which each involves, and then the selection of the best alternative through the use of appropriate economic criteria.[27] The essential elements involved are: (1) an objective or objectives; (2) alternative means for accomplishing the objective or objectives; (3) the costs (resources used) of the alternative means; (4) a model or models for analysis; and (5) a criterion by which one alternative means may be selected from among the group.

The Hitch-McKean analysis shows that, in principle, this criterion is obvious—the optimal system is the one which yields the greatest excess of positive values (objectives) over negative values (resources used up or costs).[28] Yet, this is seldom practical in military problems. Objectives and costs usually do not have a common measure. There is no generally acceptable way, for example, to subtract dollars spent or aircraft lost from enemy targets destroyed. The criterion used, therefore, must be an approximation to the optimal criterion. That is, it must be a "suboptimization" criterion. It must be emphasized that economic choice is a way of looking at problems and does not necessarily depend upon the use of any analytical aids or computational devices. The suboptimal approach can be attainable and useful.

Recognition of the importance of relating the major outputs of defense activity more closely to resource inputs has led the Department of Defense to adopt a formal programming system based upon many characteristics derived from the experiences of military cost analysis.[29] The primary components of the programming system are a five-year force structure estimate for the Department of Defense and financial programs expressed in terms of such an objective as "strategic retaliatory forces." The programming approach, moreover, includes systematic reviews of possible changes in relevant variables. This programming system is viewed by the top management of the Department of Defense as the essential link between military planning and budgeting.[30]

PROCUREMENT EFFICIENCY

A recent report (July, 1965) by the Subcommittee on Federal Procurement and Regulation of the Joint Economic Committee of Congress discusses the efforts to increase the efficiency of federal

---

[27] *Ibid.*

[28] *Ibid.*

[29] For a relevant discussion, see Robert N. Grosse and Arnold Proschan, "Military Cost Analysis," *Papers and Proceedings of the American Economic Association* (May, 1965), pp. 427–33.

[30] *Ibid.*

procurement procedures.[31] Efficiency in this sense is important since billions of dollars of procurement are involved. In Fiscal 1965, the federal government purchased nearly $49 billion in contractual services and supplies and an additional $29.4 billion in capital assets.[32] Thus, a total of $78.4 billion of procurement activities was undertaken by the federal government during the year. Procurement is one of the major functions of the federal government, but unfortunately it has historically been one of the most wasteful.

The Department of Defense alone issues approximately 10 million contract actions annually. This department has made considerable improvement in recent years in the efficiency of its procurement procedures. It is estimated that the cost reduction program of the Department of Defense will reflect $4.1 billion in savings in the Fiscal 1966 budget and the goal for Fiscal 1968 is savings of $4.8 billion.[33] At the encouragement of the Procurement and Regulation Subcommittee, moreover, the Department of Defense and the General Services Administration, with the participation of the Bureau of the Budget, have entered into a cooperative agreement for the development of a *national supply system* to improve procurement efficiency.

Other evidence of efforts to improve the rationality of federal resource procedure include the Department of Defense's efficiency efforts in disposing of surplus resources. From January 20, 1961, through December 31, 1964, nearly 150,000 unnecessary jobs were eliminated and nearly 1.5 million acres of land were released, with a total annual savings of more than $1 billion.[34] The Department of Defense has also made progress in recent years by practicing competitive advertised bidding for procurement items. During the first eight months of Fiscal 1965, 18.6 percent of the department's contracts were awarded through advertised competitive bidding as compared with 11.9 percent in 1961 and 14.8 percent during 1964.[35]

---

[31] *Economic Impact of Federal Procurement,* Report of the Subcommittee on Federal Procurement and Regulation of the Joint Economic Committee, Congress of the United States, July, 1965.

[32] *Ibid.,* pp. 1–2.

[33] *Ibid.,* p. 2.

[34] *Ibid.,* p. 6.

[35] *Ibid.,* p. 11.

INDEX

INDEX

This book has been set in 10 and 9 point Caledonia, leaded two points. Part numbers, part titles, and chapter numbers are in 18 point Futura Medium italics; chapter titles are in 18 point Futura Medium. The size of the type page is 27 by 45½ picas.